murach's
JavaScript
and jQuery

3RD EDITION

Mary Delamater

Zak Ruvalcaba

BEGINNER TO PRO

murach's
JavaScript
and jQuery

3RD EDITION

Mary Delamater

Zak Ruvalcaba

MIKE MURACH & ASSOCIATES, INC.

4340 N. Knoll Ave. • Fresno, CA 93722
www.murach.com • murachbooks@murach.com

Editorial team

Authors: Mary Delamater
                  Zak Ruvalcaba

Editor: Anne Boehm

Production: Maria Spera

Books for web developers

Murach's HTML5 and CSS3 (4th Edition)
Murach's JavaScript (2nd Edition)
Murach's PHP and MySQL (3rd Edition)
Murach's Java Servlets and JSP (3rd Edition)
Murach's ASP.NET 4.6 Web Programming with C# 2015
Murach's ASP.NET Web Programming with VB

Books on core Python, Java, C#, and VB

Murach's Python Programming
Murach's Beginning Java with NetBeans
Murach's Beginning Java with Eclipse
Murach's Java Programming (5th Edition)
Murach's C# 2015
Murach's Visual Basic 2015

Books for database programmers

Murach's MySQL (2nd Edition)
Murach's Oracle SQL and PL/SQL (2nd Edition)
Murach's SQL Server 2016 for Developers

For more on Murach books, please visit us at www.murach.com

10 9 8 7 6 5 4 3 2
ISBN: 978-1-943872-05-3

Contents

Expanded contents

Chapter 3   The essential JavaScript statements

Chapter 4   How to work with JavaScript objects, functions, and events

Chapter 5   How to test and debug a JavaScript application

Section 2 jQuery essentials

Section 3 Advanced JavaScript skills

Chapter 18   How to create and use closures, IIFEs, the module pattern, and plugins

Introduction

Today, JavaScript is used on most of the pages of a modern website, from small individual sites to the largest commercial sites. And wherever JavaScript is used, you'll also find jQuery. That's because jQuery is a JavaScript library that makes it easier to develop JavaScript applications. And that's why every web developer should know how to use both JavaScript and jQuery, right along with HTML5 and CSS3.

Now, this one book presents all of the JavaScript and jQuery skills that every web developer should have. This book works if you're a web designer who's coming from an HTML and CSS background and has no programming experience. But it also works if you're a server-side programmer who has experience with a language like Java, C#, PHP, or Python. Either way, you'll end up with a solid set of the JavaScript and jQuery skills that you'll need on the job.

What this book does

This book is divided into three sections, and each takes you to a new level of expertise:

- Section 1 presents a seven-chapter course in JavaScript that gets you off to a great start. This section works for programming novices as well as experienced programmers because it lets you set your own pace. If you're a beginner, you'll move slowly and do all the exercises. If you have some experience, you'll move more quickly as you focus on the differences between JavaScript and the other languages that you've used. When you finish this section, you'll have a solid set of JavaScript skills, especially the skills that help you get the most from jQuery.

- After you learn the JavaScript essentials, the five chapters in section 2 present the jQuery skills that every web developer should have. The first chapter in this section presents the core jQuery skills, and the next three chapters focus on effects and animations, forms and data validation, jQuery plugins, and jQuery UI widgets. Then, the last chapter in this section shows you how to use jQuery for Ajax and JSON so you can get data from a web server and add it to a web page without reloading the entire page.

- After you finish sections 1 and 2, you'll have the JavaScript and jQuery skills that every web developer should have. Then, the six chapters in section 3 will take your JavaScript skills to the next level. Here, you'll learn how to work with numbers, strings, and dates...how to handle exceptions and use regular expressions...when and how to use browser objects, cookies, web storage, and arrays...and how to create and use your own objects. Then, the last chapter presents expert level skills like how to use closures, the module pattern, and IIFEs as you create your own jQuery plugins.

- What's especially interesting about section 3 is that all of the examples show you how to use the JavaScript skills that you're learning in conjunction with your jQuery skills. Because that's the way applications are coded in the real world, this is clearly the best way to learn advanced JavaScript skills. And yet, we haven't seen another book that combines JavaScript and jQuery in this way.

Why you'll learn faster and better with this book

Like all our books, this one has features that you won't find in competing books. That's why we believe you'll learn faster and better with our book than with any other. Here are a few of those features.

- This book is designed to teach you the skills you're going to need on the job without wasting your time on skills that you aren't likely to need. That sounds simple, but most JavaScript books either overwhelm you with information that you'll never need or trivialize the subject by avoiding all of the complications. For instance, this book shows you the basics of DOM scripting with JavaScript, but then it shows you how to use jQuery for DOM scripting because that's the best way to develop JavaScript applications today.

- If you page through this book, you'll see that all of the information is presented in "paired pages," with the essential syntax, guidelines, and examples on the right page and the perspective and extra explanation on the left page. This helps you learn faster by reading less...and this is the ideal reference format when you need to refresh your memory about how to do something.

- To show you how JavaScript and jQuery work, this book presents 50 complete JavaScript and jQuery applications that range from the simple to the complex. Even better, from section 2 on, both JavaScript and jQuery are used in every application because that's the best way to develop JavaScript applications. We believe that studying the code for complete applications is critical to the learning process...and yet you won't find programs like ours in other JavaScript and jQuery books.

- Of course, this book also presents dozens of short examples, so it's easy to find an example that shows you how to do what you want to do. Even better, our paired pages make it much easier to find the examples that you're looking for than it is with traditional books in which the examples are embedded in the text.

- Like all our books, this one has exercises at the end of each chapter that give you hands-on experience by letting you practice what you've learned. These exercises also encourage you to experiment and to apply what you've learned in new ways...just as you'll have to do on the job.

What software you need

To develop JavaScript applications, you can use any text editor. However, a text editor that includes syntax coloring and auto-completion will help you develop applications more quickly and with fewer errors. That's why we recommend Aptana Studio 3 for both Windows and Mac OS users. Although Aptana is free, it provides many powerful features.

Then, to test a web page, we recommend that you do your primary testing with Google's Chrome browser. As you will see, Chrome's developer tools have excellent features for testing and debugging your JavaScript applications.

If you decide to use Aptana, chapter 1 presents a short tutorial that will get you started right. And to help you install Aptana and Chrome, appendix A provides the website addresses and procedures that you need for both Windows and Mac systems.

How our downloadable files can help you learn

If you go to our website at www.murach.com, you can download all of the files that you need for getting the most from this book. This includes the files for:

- all of the applications in this book
- the starting points for the chapter exercises
- the solutions to the exercises

These files let you test, review, and copy the code. If you have any problems with the exercises, the solutions are there to help you over the learning blocks, an essential part of the learning process. And in some cases, the solutions will show you a more elegant way to handle a problem, even when you've come up with a solution that works. Here again, appendix A shows you how to download and install these files.

Support materials for instructors and trainers

If you're a college instructor or corporate trainer who would like to use this book as a course text, we offer a full set of the support materials you need for a turnkey course. That includes:

- instructional objectives that help your students focus on the skills that they need to develop
- test banks that let you measure how well your students have mastered those skills
- extra exercises that let your students prove how well they have mastered those skills
- a complete set of PowerPoint slides that you can use to review and reinforce the content of the book

Instructors tell us that this is everything they need for a course without all the busywork that they get from other publishers.

To learn more about our instructor's materials, please go to our website at www.murachforinstructors.com if you're an instructor. Or if you're a trainer, please go to www.murach.com and click on the *Courseware for Trainers* link, or contact Kelly at 1-800-221-5528 or kelly@murach.com.

Please remember, though, that the primary component for a successful JavaScript and jQuery course is this book. Because your students will learn faster and more thoroughly when they use our book, they will have better questions and be more prepared when they come to class. Because our guided exercises start from partial applications, your students will get more practice with new skills in lab. And because our paired pages are so good for reference, your students will be able to review for tests and do their projects more efficiently.

Companion books

Besides JavaScript and jQuery, the best web developers also master HTML5 and CSS3. To that end, you'll find that *Murach's HTML5 and CSS3* is the perfect companion to this JavaScript and jQuery book. With both books at your side, you'll be able to develop web pages that use HTML5, CSS3, JavaScript, and jQuery the way the best professionals use them.

We also offer books on server-side programming in languages like Java, C#, PHP, and Python. To find out more about our new books and latest editions, please go to our website at www.murach.com. There, you'll find the details for all of our books, including complete tables of contents.

Please let us know how this book works for you

From the start of this project, we had three primary goals. First, we wanted to present all of the JavaScript and jQuery skills that every web developer should have in a single book. Second, we wanted to do that in a way that works for web designers with no programming background as well as experienced programmers. Third, we wanted to make this the best on-the-job reference you've ever used.

Now, we think we've succeeded. We thank you for buying this book. We wish you all the best with your JavaScript and jQuery programming. And if you have any comments, we would appreciate hearing from you.

Mary Delamater, Author
maryd@techknowsolve.com

Mike Murach
Publisher

Section 1

JavaScript essentials

This section presents the essential JavaScript skills. This subset of skills will get you off to a fast start with JavaScript. And this subset of JavaScript skills is the least you need to know for using jQuery effectively.

Chapter 1 in this section presents the concepts and terms that you need for developing JavaScript applications. It also shows you how to use the Aptana IDE, which is one of the many IDEs that are available for developing JavaScript applications.

Then, chapter 2 presents a starting subset of the JavaScript language. Chapters 3 and 4 complete that subset. Chapter 5 shows you how to test and debug your JavaScript applications. Chapter 6 shows you how to use that subset for DOM scripting, the predominant use of JavaScript. And chapter 7 shows you how to work with images and timers.

At that point, you'll be well on your way to developing JavaScript applications at a professional level. Then, you can dive right into jQuery by moving on to section 2.

1

Introduction to web development

This chapter presents the background concepts, terms, and skills that you need for developing JavaScript applications. That includes a quick review of the HTML and CSS skills that you need. That also includes a quick tutorial on how to use Aptana Studio 3, which is the IDE that we used to develop the JavaScript applications for this book.

If you have some web development experience, you should be able to go through this chapter quickly by skimming the topics that you already know. But if you're new to web development, you should take the time to master the concepts and terms of this chapter.

How a web application works

A web application consists of many components that work together as they bring the application to your computer or mobile device. Before you can start developing JavaScript applications, you should have a basic understanding of how these components work together.

The components of a web application

The diagram in figure 1-1 shows that web applications consist of *clients* and a *web server.* The clients are the computers, tablets, and mobile devices that use the web applications. They access the web pages through *web browsers.* The web server holds the files that make up a web application.

A *network* is a system that allows clients and servers to communicate. The *Internet* is a large network that consists of many smaller networks. In a diagram like the one in this figure, the "cloud" represents the network or Internet that connects the clients and servers.

In general, you don't need to know how the cloud works. But you should have a general idea of what's going on.

To start, networks can be categorized by size. A *local area network* (*LAN*) is a small network of computers that are near each other and can communicate with each other over short distances. Computers in a LAN are typically in the same building or adjacent buildings. This type of network is often called an *intranet*, and it can be used to run web applications for use by employees only.

In contrast, a *wide area network* (*WAN*) consists of multiple LANs that have been connected. To pass information from one client to another, a router determines which network is closest to the destination and sends the information over that network. A WAN can be owned privately by one company or it can be shared by multiple companies.

An *Internet service provider* (*ISP*) is a company that owns a WAN that is connected to the Internet. An ISP leases access to its network to companies that need to be connected to the Internet.

The components of a web application

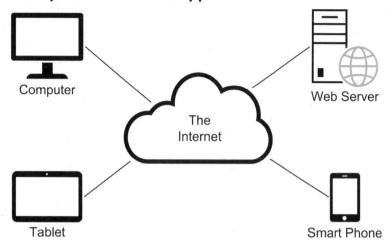

Description

- A web application consists of clients, a web server, and a network.
- The *clients* use programs known as *web browsers* to request web pages from the web server. Today, the clients can be computers, smart phones like the iPhone, or tablets like the iPad.
- The *web server* returns the pages that are requested to the browser.
- A *network* connects the clients to the web server.
- An *intranet* is a *local area network* (or *LAN*) that connects computers that are near each other, usually within the same building.
- The *Internet* is a network that consists of many *wide area networks* (*WANs*), and each of those consists of two or more LANs. Today, the Internet is often referred to as "the Cloud", which implies that you really don't have to understand how it works.
- An *Internet service provider* (*ISP*) owns a WAN that is connected to the Internet.

Figure 1-1   The components of a web application

How static web pages are processed

A *static web page* like the one in figure 1-2 is a web page that doesn't change each time it is requested. This type of web page is sent directly from the web server to the web browser when the browser requests it. You can spot static pages in a web browser by looking at the extension in the address bar. If the extension is .htm or .html, the page is probably a static web page.

The diagram in this figure shows how a web server processes a request for a static web page. This process begins when a client requests a web page in a web browser. To do that, the user can either type the address of the page into the browser's address bar or click a link in the current page that specifies the next page to load.

In either case, the web browser builds a request for the web page and sends it to the web server. This request, known as an *HTTP request*, is formatted using the *HyperText Transfer Protocol* (HTTP), which lets the web server know which file is being requested.

When the web server receives the HTTP request, it retrieves the requested file from the disk drive. This file contains the *HTML* (*HyperText Markup Language*) for the requested page. Then, the web server sends the file back to the browser as part of an *HTTP response*.

When the browser receives the HTTP response, it *renders* (translates) the HTML into a web page that is displayed in the browser. Then, the user can view the content. If the user requests another page, either by clicking a link or typing another web address into the browser's address bar, the process begins again.

A static web page at http://www.modulemedia.com/ourwork/index.html

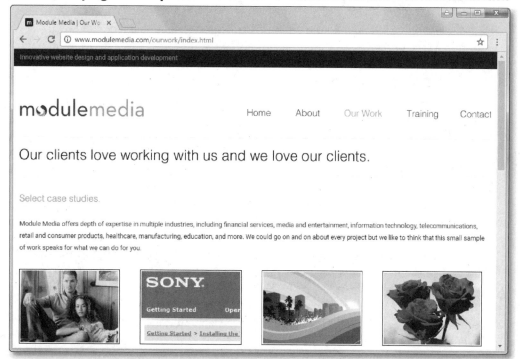

How a web server processes a static web page

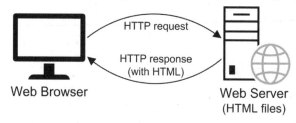

Web Browser   Web Server
                               (HTML files)

Description

- *Hypertext Markup Language* (*HTML*) is the language used to define the content for the web pages of an application.

- A *static web page* is an HTML document that's stored on the web server and doesn't change. The filenames for static web pages have .htm or .html extensions.

- When the user requests a static web page, the browser sends an *HTTP request* to the web server that includes the name of the file that's being requested.

- When the web server receives the request, it retrieves the HTML for the web page and sends it back to the browser as part of an *HTTP response*.

- When the browser receives the HTTP response, it *renders* the HTML into a web page that is displayed in the browser.

Figure 1-2   How static web pages are processed

How dynamic web pages are processed

A *dynamic web page* like the one in figure 1-3 is a page that's created by a program or script on the web server each time it is requested. This program or script is executed by an *application server* based on the data that's sent along with the HTTP request. In this example, the HTTP request identified the book that's shown. Then, the program or script retrieved the image and data for that book from a *database server*.

The diagram in this figure shows how a web server processes a dynamic web page. The process begins when the user requests a page in a web browser. To do that, the user can either type the URL of the page into the browser's address bar, click a link that specifies the dynamic page to load, or click a button that submits a form containing the data the dynamic page should process.

In each case, the web browser builds an HTTP request and sends it to the web server. This request includes whatever data the application needs for processing the request. If, for example, the user has entered data into a form, that data will be included in the HTTP request.

When the web server receives the HTTP request, the server examines the file extension of the requested web page to identify the application server that should process the request. The web server then forwards the request to the application server that processes that type of web page.

Next, the application server retrieves the appropriate program or script from the hard drive. It also loads any form data that the user submitted. Then, it executes the script. As the script executes, it generates the HTML for the web page. If necessary, the script will request data from a database server and use that data as part of the web page it is generating. The processing that's done on the application server can be referred to as *server-side processing*.

When the script is finished, the application server sends the dynamically generated HTML back to the web server. Then, the web server sends the HTML back to the browser in an HTTP response.

When the web browser receives the HTTP response, it renders the HTML and displays the web page. Note, however, that the web browser has no way to tell whether the HTML in the HTTP response was for a static page or a dynamic page. It just renders the HTML.

When the page is displayed, the user can view the content. Then, when the user requests another page, the process begins again. The process that begins with the user requesting a web page and ends with the server sending a response back to the client is called a *round trip*.

A dynamic web page at amazon.com

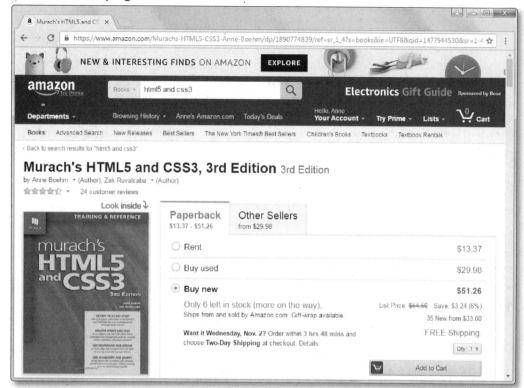

How a web server processes a dynamic web page

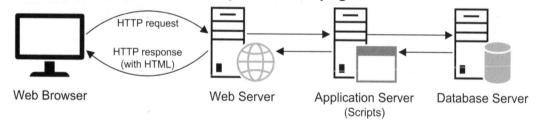

Web Browser   Web Server   Application Server   Database Server
                                          (Scripts)

Description

- A *dynamic web page* is a web page that's generated by a program or script that is running on a server.

- When a web server receives a request for a dynamic web page, it looks up the extension of the requested file to find out which *application server* should process the request.

- When the application server receives a request, it runs the specified script. Often, this script uses the data that it gets from the web browser to get the appropriate data from a *database server*. This script can also store the data that it receives in the database.

- When the application server finishes processing the data, it generates the HTML for a web page and returns it to the web server. Then, the web server returns the HTML to the web browser as part of an HTTP response.

Figure 1-3   How dynamic web pages are processed

How JavaScript is used for client-side processing

In contrast to the server-side processing that's done for dynamic web pages, *JavaScript* is a *scripting language* that provides for *client-side processing*. In the web page in figure 1-4, for example, JavaScript is used to change the images that are shown without using server-side processing.

To make this work, all of the required images are loaded into the browser's cache when the page is requested. Then, if the user clicks on one of the color swatches below a shirt, the shirt image is changed to the one with the right color. This is called an *image swap*. Similarly, if the user moves the mouse over a shirt, the image showing the front of the shirt is replaced with an image showing the back of the shirt. This is called an *image rollover*.

The diagram in this figure shows how JavaScript processing works. When a browser requests a web page, both the HTML and the related JavaScript are returned to the browser by the web server. Then, the JavaScript code is executed in the web browser by the browser's *JavaScript engine*. This takes some of the processing burden off the server and makes the application run faster. Often, JavaScript is used in conjunction with dynamic web pages, but it is also commonly used with static web pages.

Besides image swaps and rollovers, there are many other uses for JavaScript. For instance, another common use is to validate the data that the user enters into an HTML form before it is sent to the server for processing. This is called *data validation*, and that saves unnecessary trips to the server. Other common uses of JavaScript are to run slide shows and carousels and to provide information in tabs or accordions.

Over time, programmers have developed JavaScript libraries that contain code that makes it easier to do these and other common functions. The most popular of these libraries is *jQuery*, which you'll learn about in section 2 of this book.

A web page with image swaps and rollovers

How JavaScript fits into this architecture

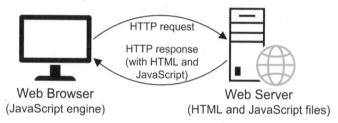

Three of the many uses of JavaScript and jQuery

- Data validation
- Image swaps and rollovers
- Slide shows

Description

- *JavaScript* is a *scripting language* that is run by the *JavaScript engine* of a web browser and controls the operation of the browser.
- When the browser requests an HTML page that contains JavaScript or a link to a JavaScript file, both the HTML and the JavaScript are loaded into the browser.
- Because JavaScript runs on the client, not the server, its functions don't require a trip back to the server. This helps an application run more efficiently.
- *jQuery* is a JavaScript library that makes it easier to do many of the common functions that JavaScript is used for.

Figure 1-4   How JavaScript is used for client-side processing

What you need to know about the ECMAScript specification

JavaScript was invented by NetScape in 1995 and released as part of the Netscape Navigator web browser in early 1996. In response, Microsoft developed a similar language called JScript and released it as part of the Internet Explorer web browser in late 1996.

Since there were differences between the two scripting languages, Netscape gave JavaScript to the *European Computer Manufacturers Association (ECMA)* to develop a standard. The standard is called the *ECMAScript specification,* and the first version was released in June 1997. Since then, several versions have been released, as shown in the table in figure 1-5.

In June 2015 the sixth version of the ECMAScript, or ES, specification was released. At the same time, the committee in charge of the specification changed how it would release new versions going forward. Instead of having a set specification that they would release when all the features were completed, they moved to yearly releases of features that had been approved to that point. Thus, the version released in 2015 was officially named ECMAScript 2015, though you'll often see it referred to as ES6. After that, ECMAScript 2016, or ES7, was released in June 2016.

ES5, ES2015, and ES2016 added several important features to JavaScript, as described in this figure. The features of ES5 are fully supported by all modern browsers. However, a few of these features won't work in older browsers like Internet Explorer 7, 8, and 9 (which can be referred to as IE7, IE8, and IE9).

Because they're newer, the features of ES2015 and ES2016 aren't as fully supported by modern browsers, although they'll become more supported with time. Also, like ES5, the features of ES2015 and ES2016 won't work in older browsers.

If you want your web pages to support older browsers, then, you'll need to choose the features you use carefully. Alternatively, you can add workarounds to your code that will make many of the features work in older browsers that don't support them. These workarounds will also help you use some of the features of ES2015 and ES2016 in modern browsers that don't support them. You'll learn more about that in figure 1-17.

To see which browsers support which features, you can use the URL in this figure. Note that even though the page at this URL is for ES6/2015, this page contains links that display other pages with information about the features that are supported by ES5 and ES2016.

The versions and release dates of the ECMAScript specification

Version	Release date
1	June 1997
2	June 1998
3	December 1999
4	Abandoned (never released)
5	December 2009
5.1	June 2011
2015	June 2015
2016	June 2016

Some of the important additions in the most recent specifications

ECMAScript 5 (ES5)

- Allows you to run in strict mode.
- Adds several methods that make it easier to work with arrays.
- Adds a safer way to create an object and more control over an object's properties.
- Adds a built-in way to work with JavaScript Object Notation (JSON).

ECMAScript 2015 (ES6)

- Adds Promises, which is a simpler syntax for callback functions.
- Adds several syntactic improvements that make code easier to read and understand.
- Adds block scope and easier ways to work with classes.
- Adds several built-in methods for working with strings, numbers, objects, and arrays.

ECMAScript 2016 (ES7)

- Adds a simpler syntax for computation with powers.
- Adds an array method to check if an array includes a specified element.

The URL for a browser compatibility table

`http://kangax.github.io/compat-table/es6/`

Description

- Netscape invented JavaScript in 1995, and turned it over to the *European Computer Manufacturers Association (ECMA)* for standardization in 1996. The *ECMAScript specification* details the standards that scripting languages like JavaScript should meet.

- All of the ES5 features are supported by all modern browsers. The features of ES2015 and ES2016, though, are less consistently supported. You can use the table at the URL listed above to see which features are supported in which browsers.

- Later in this chapter, you'll learn how to provide for cross-browser compatibility so your web pages will work with as many browsers as possible.

Figure 1-5   What you need to know about the ECMAScript specification

The components
of a JavaScript application

When you develop a JavaScript application, you use HTML to define the content and structure of the page. You use CSS to format that content. And you use JavaScript to do the client-side processing. This is illustrated by the Email List application that is presented in the next three figures.

Figure 1-6 starts with the user interface for the application. It asks the user to make three entries and then click on the Join our List button. The asterisks to the right of the text boxes for the entries indicate that these entries are required.

When the user clicks on the button, JavaScript checks the entries to make sure they're valid. If they are, the entries are sent to the web server for server-side processing. If they aren't, messages are displayed so the user can correct the entries. This is a common type of JavaScript application called *data validation* that saves a trip to the server when the entries are invalid.

You might have noticed that the user interface in this figure isn't much to look at. This is what a plain HTML document with no formatting looks like. In the next figure, though, you'll see how applying some CSS can improve its appearance.

The HTML

HyperText Markup Language (*HTML*) is used to define the content and structure of a web page. In figure 1-6, you can see the HTML for the Email List application. In general, this book assumes that you are already familiar with HTML, but here are a few highlights.

First, note that this document starts with a DOCTYPE declaration. This declaration is the one you'll use with HTML5, and you must code it exactly as it's shown here. If you aren't already using HTML5, you can see that this declaration is much simpler than the declaration for earlier versions of HTML. In this book, all of the applications use HTML5.

Second, in the head section of the HTML document, you can see a meta element that specifies that UTF-8 is the character encoding that's used for the page. Then, there is an HTML comment indicating that any link, style, and script elements go here in the head element. In the next figure, you'll see a link element that specifies the CSS file that should be used to format this HTML. And in the figure after that, you'll see a script element that specifies the JavaScript file that should be used to process the user's entries.

Third, in the body section, you can see the use of a main element. That is one of the HTML5 elements that we'll be using throughout this book. Within this element, you can see the use of h1, form, label, input, and span elements.

In this book, as you've just seen, we refer to *HTML elements* like the <link>, <script>, <main>, and <h1> elements as the link, script, main, and h1 elements. However, to prevent confusion when referring to one-letter elements like p and a elements, we enclose the letters in brackets, as in the <p> element or the <a> element.

The HTML file in a browser with no CSS applied to it

The code for the HTML file named index.html

```html
<!DOCTYPE html>
<html>
<head>
    <meta charset="UTF-8">
    <title>Join Email List</title>
    <!-- link, style, and script elements go here -->
</head>
<body>
    <main>
        <h1>Please join our email list</h1>
        <form id="email_form" name="email_form"
            action="join.html" method="get">
            <label for="email_address1">Email Address:</label>
            <input type="text" id="email_address1" name="email_address1">
            <span id="email_address1_error">*</span><br>

            <label for="email_address2">Re-enter Email Address:</label>
            <input type="text" id="email_address2" name="email_address2">
            <span id="email_address2_error">*</span><br>

            <label for="first_name">First Name</label>
            <input type="text" id="first_name" name="first_name">
            <span id="first_name_error">*</span><br>

            <label> </label>
            <input type="button" id="join_list" value="Join our List">
        </form>
    </main>
</body>
</html>
```

Description

- *HTML (HyperText Markup Language)* is used to define the structure and content of a web page.

- To add CSS and JavaScript files to a web page, you code link and script elements in the head element. To embed CSS and JavaScript in a page, you code style and script elements.

Figure 1-6   The HTML for the web page

In practice, you'll often hear *elements* called *tags* so you can think of them as synonyms. In this book, we occasionally use the term *tag*, especially when referring to an opening tag like <h1> or a closing tag like </h1>.

The CSS

In the early days of web development, HTML documents were coded so the HTML not only defined the content and structure of the web page but also the formatting of that content. However, this mix of structural and formatting elements made it hard to edit, maintain, and reformat the web pages.

Today, *Cascading Style Sheets* (*CSS*) let you separate the formatting from the content and structure of a web page. As a result, the formatting that was once done with HTML should now be done with CSS.

In figure 1-7, then, you can see the link element that links the external CSS file to the HTML. As you saw in figure 1-6, this link element goes in the HTML head element. You can also see how this CSS has changed the appearance of the page in the browser.

After that, you can see the CSS that's used to format the HTML in the last figure. Here again, this book assumes that you are already familiar with CSS, but here is a quick description of what this CSS is doing.

In the style rule for the body element, the font-family property sets the font for the entire document, the margin property centers the body in the browser window, the width property sets the width of the body to 670 pixels, the border property puts a blue border around the body, and the padding property puts space between the contents and the right, left, and bottom borders. This is typical CSS for the applications in the book, just to make them look better.

Similarly, the style rules for the h1, label, and input elements are intended to make these elements look better. For instance, the style rule for the h1 element sets the font color to blue. And the style rule for the labels floats them left so the text boxes will be to their right. This style rule also sets the width of the labels to 11ems, and it aligns the text for the labels on the right.

Then, the style rule for the input elements sets the left margin so there's space between the labels and the text boxes. It also sets the bottom margin so there's space after each label and text box.

Last, the style rule for the span elements sets the text color to red. When the HTML page is first loaded, these span elements only contain asterisks (*) to indicate that these entries are required. But the JavaScript changes those asterisks to error messages if the related entries are invalid, and it removes the asterisks if the related entries are valid.

The web page in a browser after CSS has been applied to it

The link element in the HTML head element that applies the CSS file

```
<link rel="stylesheet" href="email_list.css">
```

The code for the CSS file named email_list.css

```css
body {
    font-family: Arial, Helvetica, sans-serif;
    background-color: white;
    margin: 0 auto;
    width: 670px;
    border: 3px solid blue;
    padding: 0 2em 1em;
}
h1 {
    color: blue;
}
label {
    float: left;
    width: 11em;
    text-align: right;
}
input {
    margin-left: 1em;
    margin-bottom: .5em;
}
span {
    color: red;
}
```

Description

- *Cascading Style Sheets* (*CSS*) are used to control how web pages are displayed by specifying the fonts, colors, borders, spacing, and layout of the pages.

Figure 1-7   The CSS for the web page

The JavaScript

Figure 1-8 shows how this application looks in a browser if the JavaScript finds any invalid data after the user clicks the Join our List button. Here, you can see that error messages are displayed to the right of the user entries for the second and third text boxes. In other words, the JavaScript has actually changed the contents of the span elements.

When JavaScript changes the HTML for a page, it is called *DOM scripting*. That's because the JavaScript is actually changing the *Document Object Model* (or *DOM*) that's generated by the browser when the page is loaded. This DOM represents all of the elements and attributes that are coded in the HTML. Then, when JavaScript changes any aspect of the DOM, the change is immediately made to the browser display too.

After the browser display, this figure shows the script element that links the external JavaScript file to the HTML. This element is typically coded in the HTML head element.

Then, this figure shows the JavaScript for this application. Since you are going to learn how all of this code works in the next six chapters, you may want to skip over this code right now. But if you have any programming experience, it may be worth taking a quick look at it. In that case, here are a few highlights.

To start, this code consists of three functions: a $ function, a joinList() function that is executed when the user clicks on the button, and a function that is run after the DOM has been loaded into the browser. Then, in the joinList() function, you can see four if-else statements that provide most of the logic for this application.

Here, you can see that the if-else structures are similar to those in any modern programming language like Java, C#, or PHP. You can also see that declaring a variable (var) and assigning a variable is done in a way that's similar to the way that it's done in other programming languages.

What's different about JavaScript is that it provides methods and properties that let you modify the DOM. For instance, the $ function uses the getElementById() method to get the object with the id that's passed to the function. Then, the first statement in the joinList() function uses the $ function to get the object that represents the first text box in the HTML. This statement also uses the value property to get the value that the user entered into that text box.

Later, the first if statement checks whether that value is an empty string (`""`), which means the user didn't make an entry. If it is, the JavaScript replaces the `*` in the span element for that text box with an error message. To do that, it uses this code:

```
$("email_address1_error").firstChild.nodeValue =
    "This field is required.";
```

Although this code may look daunting right now, you'll see that it's all quite manageable. You'll also come to realize that DOM scripting is where JavaScript get its power.

The web page in a browser with JavaScript used for data validation

The script element in the HTML head element that adds the JavaScript file

```
<script src="email_list.js"></script>
```

The code for the JavaScript file named email_list.js

```
var $ = function(id) {
    return document.getElementById(id);
};
var joinList = function() {
    var emailAddress1 = $("email_address1").value;
    var emailAddress2 = $("email_address2").value;
    var isValid = true;

    if (emailAddress1 == "") {
        $("email_address1_error").firstChild.nodeValue =
            "This field is required.";
        isValid = false;
    } else { $("email_address1_error").firstChild.nodeValue = ""; }

    if (emailAddress1 != emailAddress2) {
        $("email_address2_error").firstChild.nodeValue =
            "This entry must equal first entry.";
        isValid = false;
    } else { $("email_address2_error").firstChild.nodeValue = ""; }

    if ($("first_name").value == "") {
        $("first_name_error").firstChild.nodeValue =
            "This field is required.";
        isValid = false;
    } else { $("first_name_error").firstChild.nodeValue = ""; }

    if (isValid) {
        // submit the form if all entries are valid
        $("email_form").submit(); }
};
window.onload = function() {
    $("join_list").onclick = joinList;
    $("email_address1").focus();
};
```

Figure 1-8   The JavaScript for the web page

The HTML skills that you need for this book

Although this book assumes that you are already familiar with HTML, the next three topics present a quick review of the HTML skills that you're going to need for this book. If you don't already have these skills and you can't pick them up from the topics that follow, we recommend that you use *Murach's HTML5 and CSS3* as a reference while you're learning JavaScript.

How to use the HTML5 semantic elements

All of the applications in this book use the *HTML5 semantic elements* whenever they're appropriate. If you aren't already using them or at least familiar with them, figure 1-9 summarizes what you need to know.

In particular, the applications in this book use the main, section, aside, and nav elements. That makes it easier to apply CSS to these elements because you don't have to code id attributes that are used by the CSS. Instead, you can apply the CSS to the elements themselves.

Be aware, however, that older browsers like IE7 and IE8 won't recognize the HTML5 semantic elements, which means that you won't be able to use CSS to apply formatting to them. So, if you want your HTML5 and CSS to work in older browsers, you need to provide a workaround. You'll learn how to do that in figure 1-17.

The primary HTML5 semantic elements

Element	Contents
header	The header for a page.
main	The main content of a page. Can only appear once per page, and cannot be the child of an article, aside, footer, header, or nav element.
section	A generic section of a document that doesn't indicate the type of content.
article	A composition like an article in the paper.
aside	A portion of a page like a sidebar that is related to the content that's near it.
nav	A portion of a page that contains links to other pages or placeholders.
figure	An image, table, or other component that's treated as a figure.
footer	The footer for a page.

A page that's structured with header, main, and footer elements

```
<body>
    <header>
        <h1>San Joaquin Valley Town Hall</h1>
    </header>
    <main>
        <p>Welcome to San Joaquin Valley Town Hall. We have some
            fascinating speakers for you this season!</p>
    </main>
    <footer>
        <p>&copy; San Joaquin Valley Town Hall.</p>
    </footer>
</body>
```

The page displayed in a web browser

San Joaquin Valley Town Hall

Welcome to San Joaquin Valley Town Hall. We have some fascinating speakers for you this season!

© San Joaquin Valley Town Hall.

Description

- HTML5 provides *semantic elements* that you should use to structure the contents of a web page. Using these elements can be referred to as *HTML5 semantics*.
- All of the HTML5 elements are supported by the modern browsers. They will also work in older browsers if you provide for cross-browser compatibility as shown in figure 1-17.
- This book also uses standard HTML elements like h1 and h2 elements for headings, img elements for images, <a> elements for links, and <p> elements for paragraphs.

Figure 1-9   How to use the HTML5 semantic elements

How to use the div and span elements

If you've been using HTML for a while, you are certainly familiar with the div element. It has traditionally been used to divide an HTML document into divisions that are identified by id attributes. Then, CSS can use the ids to apply formatting to the divisions.

But now that HTML5 is available, div elements shouldn't be used to structure a document. Instead, they should only be used when the HTML5 semantic elements aren't appropriate.

Note, however, that div elements are often used in JavaScript applications. If, for example, a section element contains three h2 elements with each followed by a div element, JavaScript can be used to display or hide a div element whenever the heading that precedes it is clicked. This structure is illustrated by the first example in figure 1-10, and you'll see how this works in chapter 6.

Similarly, span elements have historically been used to identify portions of text that can be formatted by CSS. By today's standards, though, it's better to use elements that indicate the contents of the elements, like the cite, code, and <q> elements.

But here again, span elements are often used in JavaScript applications, as shown by the second example in this figure. In fact, you've just seen this in the Email List application. In that application, JavaScript puts the error messages in the appropriate span elements.

The div and span elements

Element	Description
div	A block element that provides a container for other elements.
span	An inline element that lets you identify text that can be formatted with CSS.

Div elements in the HTML for a JavaScript application

```
<section id="faqs">
    <h1>jQuery FAQs</h1>
    <h2>What is JavaScript?</h2>
    <div>
        // contents
    </div>
    <h2>What is jQuery?</h2>
    <div>
        // contents
    </div>
    <h2>Why is jQuery becoming so popular?</h2>
    <div>
        // contents
    </div>
</section>
```

Span elements in the HTML for a JavaScript application

```
<label for="email_address1">Email Address:</label>
<input type="text" id="email_address1" name="email_address1">
<span id="email_address1_error">*</span><br>

<label for="email_address2">Re-enter Email Address:</label>
<input type="text" id="email_address2" name="email_address2">
<span id="email_address2_error">*</span><br>

<label for="first_name">First Name</label>
<input type="text" id="first_name" name="first_name">
<span id="first_name_error">*</span>
```

Description

- Before HTML5, div elements were used to define the structure within the body of a document. The ids for these div elements were then used by the CSS to apply formatting to the elements.

- Today, the HTML5 semantic elements should be used to make the structure of a page more apparent. However, you will still use div elements to define blocks of code that are used in JavaScript applications.

- Before HTML5, span elements were often used to identify portions of text that you could apply formatting to.

- Today, a better practice is to use specific elements to identify content. However, you will still use span elements for some JavaScript applications, like the Email List application in figures 1-6 through 1-8.

Figure 1-10   How to use the div and span elements

How to use the basic HTML attributes

Figure 1-11 presents the HTML *attributes* that are commonly used in JavaScript applications. You should already be familiar with the *id attribute* that identifies one HTML element and with *class attributes* that can be applied to more than one HTML element. You should also be familiar with the *for attribute* that relates a label to an input element and with the *title attribute* that can be used to provide a tooltip for an element.

When you use JavaScript, you will commonly use the *name attribute* so the server-side code can access the data that is submitted to it. You will sometimes add or remove class attributes to change the formatting of elements. And you will sometimes use title attributes to provide text that's related to elements.

In practice, you usually use the same value for the id and name attributes of an element. For instance, the example in this figure uses "email" as the value of both the id and name attributes for the text box. That makes it easier to remember the attribute values.

The basic HTML attributes

Attribute	Description
id	Specifies a unique identifier for an element that can be referred to by CSS.
class	Specifies one or more class names that can be referred to by CSS, and the same name can be used for more than one element. To code more than one class name, separate the class names with spaces.
name	Specifies a unique name for an element that is commonly used by the server-side code and can also be used by the JavaScript code.
for	In a label element, this attribute specifies the id of the control that it applies to.
title	Specifies additional information about an element. For some elements, the title appears in a tooltip when the user hovers the mouse over the element.

HTML that uses these attributes

```
<body>
    <h1>San Joaquin Valley Town Hall</h1>
    <h2 class="first_h2">Welcome to San Joaquin Valley Town Hall.</h2>
    <p>Please enter your e-mail address to subscribe to our
        newsletter.</p>
    <form id="email_form" name="email_form"
          action="join.html" method="get">
        <label for="email">E-Mail: </label>
        <input type="text" id="email" name="email"
               title="Enter e-mail address here.">
        <input type="button" value="Subscribe">
    </form>
</body>
```

The HTML in a web browser with a tooltip displayed for the text box

Description

- An *attribute* consists of an attribute name, an equals sign, and the value of the attribute enclosed in either single or double quotation marks.
- The *id* and *class attributes* are commonly used to apply CSS formatting,
- The *name attribute* is commonly used by the server-side code to access the data that is sent to it, but this attribute can also be used by the JavaScript code.
- The *for attribute* in a label element is used to identify the control that it applies to.

Figure 1-11.   How to use the basic HTML attributes

The CSS skills that you need for this book

Although this book assumes that you are already familiar with CSS, the next three topics present a quick review of the CSS skills that you're going to need for this book. If you don't already have these skills and you can't pick them up from the topics that follow, we recommend that you use *Murach's HTML5 and CSS3* as a reference while you're learning JavaScript.

How to provide the CSS styles for an HTML page

Figure 1-12 shows two ways that you can include CSS styles for an HTML document. First, you can code a link element in the head section of an HTML document that specifies a file that contains the CSS for the page. This is referred to as an *external style sheet*, and this is the method that's used for most of the applications in this book.

Second, you can code a style element in the head section that contains the CSS for the page. This can be referred to as *embedded styles*. In general, it's better to use external style sheets because that makes it easier to use them for more than one page. However, embedded styles can be easier to use for simple applications like the ones in this book because you don't need to create an extra file.

In some cases, you may want to use two or more external style sheets for a single page. You may even want to use both external style sheets and embedded styles for a page. In these cases, the styles are applied from the first external style sheet to the last one and then the embedded styles are applied.

Two ways to provide styles

Use an external style sheet by coding a link element in the head section

```
<link rel="stylesheet" href="styles/main.css">
```

Embed the styles in the head section

```
<style>
    body {
        font-family: Arial, Helvetica, sans-serif;
        font-size: 87.5%; }
    h1 { font-size: 250%; }
</style>
```

The sequence in which styles are applied

- Styles from an external style sheet
- Embedded styles

A head element that includes two external style sheets

```
<head>
    <title>San Joaquin Valley Town Hall</title>
    <link rel="stylesheet" href="../styles/main.css">
    <link rel="stylesheet" href="../styles/speaker.css">
</head>
```

The sequence in which styles are applied

- From the first external style sheet to the last

Description

- When you use *external style sheets*, you separate content (HTML) from formatting (CSS). That makes it easy to use the same styles for two or more pages.

- If you use *embedded styles*, you have to copy the styles to other documents before you can use them in those documents.

- If more than one rule for the same property is applied to the same element, the last rule overrides the earlier rules.

- When you specify a relative URL for an external CSS file, the URL is relative to the current file.

Figure 1-12   How to provide the CSS styles for an HTML page

How to code the basic CSS selectors

Figure 1-13 shows how to code the basic *CSS selectors* for applying styles to HTML elements. To start, this figure shows the body of an HTML document that contains a main and a footer element. Here, the two <p> elements in the main element have class attributes with the value "blue". Also, the <p> element in the footer has an id attribute with the value "copyright" and a class attribute with two values: "blue" and "right". This means that this element is assigned to two classes.

The four style rules in the first group of examples are *type selectors*. To code a type selector, you just code the name of the element. As a result, the first style rule in this group selects the body element. The second style rule selects the main element. The third style rule selects the h1 element. And the fourth style rule selects all <p> elements.

In these examples, the first style rule changes the font for the body, and all of the elements within the body inherit this change. This style rule also sets the width of the body and centers it in the browser. Then, the second style rule puts a border around the main element and puts some padding inside the border. It also makes the main element a block element. This is necessary for IE because IE doesn't treat the main element as a block element.

The third style rule that uses a type selector sets the margins for the heading. In this case, all the margins are set to zero except for the bottom margin. Last, the style rule for the paragraphs sets the margins for the top, bottom, and left side of the paragraphs. That's why the paragraphs in the main element are indented.

The style rule in the second group of examples uses an *id selector* to select an element by its id. To do that, the selector is a pound sign (#) followed by the id value that uniquely identifies an element. As a result, this style rule selects the <p> element that has an id of "copyright". Then, its one property declaration sets the font-size for the paragraph to 90% of the default font size.

The two style rules in the last group of examples use *class selectors* to select HTML elements by class. To do that, the selector is a period (.) followed by the class name. As a result, the first style rule selects all elements that have been assigned to the "blue" class, which are all three <p> elements. The second style rule selects any elements that have been assigned to the "right" class. That is the paragraph in the footer. Then, the first style rule sets the color of the font to blue and the second style rule aligns the paragraph on the right.

One of the key points here is that a class attribute can have the same value for more than one element on a page. Then, if you code a selector for that class, it will be used to format all the elements in that class. In contrast, since the id for an element must be unique, an id selector can only be used to format a single element.

As you probably know, there are several other selectors that you can use with CSS. But the ones in this figure will get you started. Then, whenever an application in this book requires other selectors, the selectors will be explained in detail.

HTML that can be selected by element type, id, or class

```
<body>
    <main>
        <h1>The Speaker Lineup</h1>
        <p class="blue">October 19: Jeffrey Toobin</p>
        <p class="blue">November 16: Andrew Ross Sorkin</p>
    </main>
    <footer>
        <p id="copyright" class="blue right">Copyright SJV Town Hall</p>
    </footer>
</body>
```

CSS style rules that select by element type, id, and class

Three elements by type

```
body {
    font-family: Arial, Helvetica, sans-serif;
    width: 400px;
    margin: 1em auto; }
main {
    display: block;
    padding: 1em;
    border: 2px solid black; }
h1 { margin: 0 0 .25em; }
p { margin: .25em 0 .25em 3em; }
```

One element by ID

```
#copyright { font-size: 90%; }
```

Two elements by class

```
.blue { color: blue; }
.right { text-align: right; }
```

The elements displayed in a browser

Description

- You code a selector for all elements of a specific type by naming the element. This is referred to as a *type selector*.
- You code a selector for an element with an id attribute by coding a pound sign (#) followed by the id value. This is known as an *id selector*.
- You code a selector for an element with a class attribute by coding a period followed by the class name. Then, the style rule applies to all elements with that class name. This is known as a *class selector*.

Figure 1-13   How to code the basic CSS selectors

How to code CSS style rules

Figure 1-14 presents the CSS for the Email List application that was presented earlier in this chapter. This is typical of the CSS for the applications in this book. Since the focus of this book is on JavaScript, not CSS, the CSS for the book applications is usually limited. For instance, the CSS in this example doesn't require id or class selectors.

Just to make sure we're using the same terminology, this CSS contains five *style rules*. Each style rule consists of a selector, a set of braces { }, and one or more *property declarations* within the braces. Also, each property declaration consists of a *property name*, a colon, the value or values for the rule, and an ending semicolon.

For instance, the first style rule is for the body element. It consists of six property declarations that set the font, background color, margins, width, border, and padding for the body. Here, the declaration for the margin property sets the top and bottom margins to zero and the right and left margins to "auto", which means the body will be centered in the browser window. And the declaration for the padding property sets the padding around the contents to 2 ems on the right and left and 1 em on the bottom. (An *em* is a typesetting term that is approximately equal to the width of a capital letter M.)

The second style rule is for the h1 element, and its one property declaration sets the color of the font to blue. Then, the third style rule is for the label elements, and the fourth style rule is for the input elements. The third style rule floats the labels to the left of the input elements, sets the labels to a width of 11 ems, and aligns the text in the labels on the right. The fourth style rule sets the left margin of the input elements to 1 em so there's separation between the labels and text boxes, and it sets the bottom margin to .5 em so there's some vertical spacing between the rows of labels and input elements.

The last style rule is for the span elements that follow the input elements. It just sets the color of the text in these elements to red because these elements will display the error messages for the application.

Beyond this brief introduction to CSS, this book will explain any of the CSS that is relevant to the JavaScript for an application. So for now, if you understand the style rules in this figure, you're ready to continue.

The CSS file for a typical application in this book

```
body {
    font-family: Arial, Helvetica, sans-serif;
    background-color: white;
    margin: 0 auto;
    width: 670px;
    border: 3px solid blue;
    padding: 0 2em 1em;
}
h1 {
    color: blue;
}
label {
    float: left;
    width: 11em;
    text-align: right;
}
input {
    margin-left: 1em;
    margin-bottom: .5em;
}
span {
    color: red;
}
```

Description

- Because the focus of this book is JavaScript, not CSS, the CSS that's used in this book is usually simple. We just apply enough CSS to make each application look okay and work correctly.

- In fact, for most of the applications in this book, you won't have to understand the CSS so it won't even be shown. Whenever the CSS is critical to the understanding of the JavaScript application, though, it will be explained in detail.

- At the least, you should know that the CSS for an HTML document consists of one or more *style rules*. Each of these style rules starts with the selector for the style rule followed by a set of braces { }. Within the braces are one or more property declarations.

- You should also know that each CSS *property declaration* consists of a *property name*, a colon, the value or values for the property, and a semicolon.

Figure 1-14   How to code CSS style rules

How to test a JavaScript application

Next, you'll learn how to test a JavaScript application. To do that, you run the HTML for the web page that uses the JavaScript.

How to run a JavaScript application

When you develop a JavaScript application, you're usually working on your own computer or your company's server. Then, to run the application, you use one of the four methods shown in figure 1-15. Of the four, it's easiest to run the HTML page from the IDE that you're using to develop the HTML, CSS, and JavaScript files. You'll learn more about that in a moment.

Otherwise, you can open the HTML file from your browser. To do that, you can press Ctrl+O to start the Open command. Or, you can find the file using the file explorer for your system and double-click on it. If you're using Windows, for example, you can find the file using Windows Explorer (Windows 7 or earlier) or File Explorer (Windows 8 or later). That will open the page in your system's default browser. Of course, you can also run a new page by clicking on the link to it in the current page.

After an application has been uploaded to an Internet web server, you can use the second set of methods in this figure to run the application. The first way is to enter a *Uniform Resource Locator* (*URL*) into the address bar of your browser. The second way is to click on a link in one web page that requests another page.

As the diagram in this figure shows, the URL for an Internet page consists of four components. In most cases, the *protocol* is HTTP. If you omit the protocol, the browser uses HTTP as the default.

The second component is the *domain name* that identifies the web server that the HTTP request will be sent to. The web browser uses this name to look up the address of the web server for the domain. Although you can't omit the domain name, you can often omit the "www." from the domain name.

The third component is the *path* where the file resides on the server. The path lists the folders that contain the file. Forward slashes are used to separate the names in the path and to represent the server's top-level folder at the start of the path. In this example, the path is "/ourwork/".

The last component is the name of the file. In this example, the file is named index.html. If you omit the filename, the web server will search for a default document in the path. Depending on the web server, this file will usually be named index.html, default.htm, or some variation of the two.

The web page at c:/javascript/book_apps/ch01/email_list/index.html

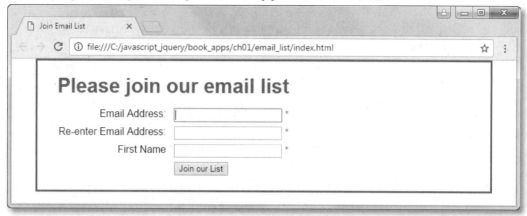

Four ways to run an HTML page that's on your own server or computer

• From your browser, use the Ctrl+O shortcut key combination to start the Open command. Then, browse to the HTML file and double-click on it.

• Use the file explorer on your system to find the HTML file, and double-click on it.

• Use the features of your text editor or IDE.

• Click on a link in the current web page to load the next web page.

Two ways to run an HTML page that's on the Internet

• Enter the URL of the web page into the browser's address bar.

• Click on a link in the current web page to load the next web page.

The components of an HTTP URL on the Internet

What happens if you omit parts of a URL

• If you omit the protocol, the default of http:// will be used.

• If you omit the filename, the default document name for the web server will be used. This is typically index.html, default.htm, or some variation.

Description

• When you are developing JavaScript applications, you usually store them on your own computer instead of the Internet. So when you test the applications, you run them from your own computer.

• Later, after the applications are deployed to your Internet web server, you can run the applications from the Internet.

Figure 1-15 How to run a JavaScript application

How to find errors in your code

As you test even the simplest of applications, you're likely to have errors in your code. When that happens, the JavaScript may not run at all, or it may run for a short while and then stop. That's why figure 1-16 shows you how to find the errors in your code.

As this figure shows, if a JavaScript application doesn't run or stops running, you start by opening the *developer tools*. Although there are several ways to do that, you'll use the F12 key most of the time. That's why the developer tools for Chrome and other browsers are often referred to as the *F12 tools*.

Next, you open the Console panel of the developer tools to see if there's an error message. In this figure, the console shows a message for an error that occurred when the user started the Email List application, clicked on the Join our List button, and nothing happened.

Then, if you click on the link to the right of the error message, the JavaScript source code is displayed with the statement that caused the error highlighted. In this case, the problem is that "email_address" should be "email_address2" since that's the id of the second text box in the HTML.

In chapter 5, you'll learn more about testing and debugging, but this technique will be all that you need until your applications get more complicated.

Chrome with an open Console panel that shows an error

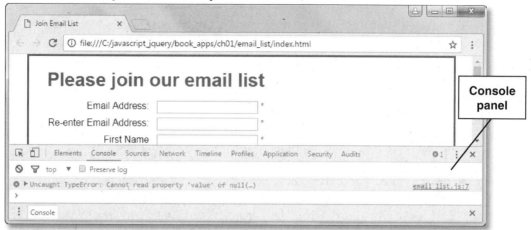

The Sources panel after the link in the Console panel has been clicked

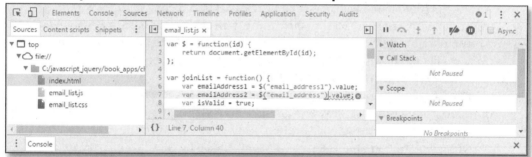

How to open or close Chrome's developer tools

- To open the developer tools, press F12 or Ctrl+Shift+I. Or, click on the Menu button in the upper right corner of the browser, and select More Tools→Developer Tools.

- To close the developer tools, click on the X in the upper right corner of the tools panel or press F12.

How to find the JavaScript statement that caused the error

- Open the Console panel by clicking on the Console tab. You should see an error message like the one above along with the line of code that caused the error.

- Click on the link to the right of the error message that indicates the line of code. That will open the Sources panel with the portion of JavaScript code that contains the statement displayed and the statement highlighted.

Description

- Chrome's *developer tools* provide some excellent debugging features, like identifying the JavaScript statement that caused an error.

- Because you usually start the developer tools by pressing the F12 key, these tools are often referred to as the *F12 tools*.

Figure 1-16   How to find errors in your code

How to provide cross-browser compatibility

If you want your website to be used by as many visitors as possible, you need to make sure that your web pages are compatible with as many browsers as possible. That's known as *cross-browser compatibility*. That means you should test your applications on as many browsers as possible, including the six browsers in the table in figure 1-17. This table shows the variance in the levels of HTML5 compatibility for these browsers. (A perfect score is 555.)

Today, all modern browsers support the HTML5 semantic elements as well as ECMAScript 5, so you shouldn't have any problems with those browsers. It's the older browsers that you may need to be concerned about, especially versions of Internet Explorer before IE9. These browsers represent a small portion of the market, though. In addition, while Chrome supports most of the features of ES2015+, not all of the other modern browsers do. That's why this figure presents workarounds for making your applications work with most browsers.

The first workaround is called the *JavaScript shiv*. This shiv loads a JavaScript file into the web page that provides HTML5 compatibility with older browsers. You can get this shiv from a web server that hosts open-source software, called a *CDN* (*Content Delivery Network*). This is illustrated by the first example in this figure. To use a file from a CDN, you code its URL on the src attribute of a script tag in the head element for a page.

The second workaround is the normalize.css style sheet that will fix minor differences in the current browsers. To use this style sheet, you download it and then include it as the first style sheet for all of your web pages.

The third workaround is a series of shim and sham files that provide for ECMAScript compatibility. These are JavaScript files that make some of the ES5, ES2015, and ES2016 features work with browsers that only support ES3. To implement this workaround, you code the URLs for the CDNs shown in this figure within script tags in the head element. (Unlike the other URLs, the last one causes the most current shim file for ES2016 to be included.) It's recommended that you always include the ES5 shim file when you use the ES6 shim file.

Note that the sham files contain ECMAScript features that can't be implemented with ES3. Although these files keep your application from throwing errors when you use the unsupported features, that may not be what you want. Also, a sham file depends on its shim file, so it must be coded after the shim file.

The fourth workaround is to use a *transpiler*, which translates ES2015+ code to its ES5 equivalent. You might want to use a transpiler because the ES6 shim doesn't make the new syntax added in ES2015 available. A popular transpiler is Babel, which also has a live transpiler page that lets you see translated code. Note that because most transpilers translate to ES5, you'll still need to use the ES5 shim if you want to support older browsers that use ES3.

While you're learning, you won't need to test your web pages on old browsers. That's why none of these workarounds is used by any of the applications in this book.

By the way, IE11 still doesn't support the HTML5 main element, but you can use the JavaScript shiv or the normalize.css style sheet to fix this problem. Note, however, that Microsoft Edge does support the main element.

The current browsers and their HTML5 ratings (www.html5test.com)

Browser	Release	HTML5 Test Rating
Google Chrome	52	492
Opera	37	489
Mozilla Firefox	48	461
Apple Safari	9.1	370
Internet Explorer	11	312
Microsoft Edge	14	460

The CDN for the JavaScript shiv for HTML5 compatibility

```
http://cdnjs.cloudflare.com/ajax/libs/html5shiv/3.7.3/html5shiv.js
```

The URL for downloading the normalize.css style sheet

http://necolas.github.io/normalize.css/

What the normalize.css style sheet does

- Normalize.css is a style sheet that makes adjustments to browser defaults so all browsers render HTML elements the same way.

The CDNs for the ECMAScript compatibility shims and shams

```
https://cdnjs.cloudflare.com/ajax/libs/es5-shim/4.5.7/es5-shim.min.js
https://cdnjs.cloudflare.com/ajax/libs/es5-shim/4.5.7/es5-sham.min.js
https://cdnjs.cloudflare.com/ajax/libs/es6-shim/0.34.2/es6-shim.min.js
https://cdnjs.cloudflare.com/ajax/libs/es6-shim/0.34.2/es6-sham.min.js
https://wzrd.in/standalone/es7-shim@latest
```

The difference between the shim and sham files

- The shim.js files contain features that will run properly in older browsers. A shim.js file can run without its associated sham.js file.
- The sham.js files contain features that can't be implemented in older browsers. A sham.js file requires and must come after its associated shim.js file.

The URLs for the Babel transpiler website and its live transpiler page

https://babeljs.io/   https://babeljs.io/repl

Description

- To provide *cross-browser compatibility* for HTML5 and CSS3, you can use the *JavaScript shiv* and the *normalize.css style sheet*.
- To make sure the ECMAScript features work on older browsers, you can use the shim.js and sham.js files shown above. However, the shim files for ES2015+ only work for the features that are additions to existing objects. To use the new syntax features, you'll need to use a *transpiler*, which translates the ES2015+ code to ES5 code.

Figure 1-17   How to provide cross-browser compatibility

How to use Aptana to develop JavaScript applications

Because HTML, CSS, and JavaScript are just text, you can use any text editor to create the files for a JavaScript application. However, a better editor or an *Integrated Development Environment* (*IDE*) can speed development time and reduce coding errors. For this book, we used Aptana Studio 3. It is a free IDE that runs on Windows, Mac OS, and Linux, and it can greatly improve your productivity.

In the appendix for this book, you can learn how to install Aptana. You can also learn how to use Aptana for the common development functions in the topics that follow. If you prefer to use another editor, you can skip these topics. But even then, you may want to browse these topics because they will give you a good idea of what an IDE should be able to do. They may also encourage you to give Aptana a try.

How to create or import a project

In Aptana, a *project* consists of the folders and files for a complete web application. Once you create a project, it's easier to work with its folders and files, to create new files for the project, and so forth.

To create a project, you use the first command in figure 1-18 and complete the dialog boxes. The result is a named project that starts with the top-level folder for the application. Then, you can easily access the folders and files for the application by using the App Explorer window that's shown in the next figure.

To make it easier to work with the applications for this book, we recommend that you import them into one Aptana project that includes all of the book applications. To do that, you can use the second procedure in this figure. The dialog boxes in this figure import the downloaded book applications at this location

    `c:/murach/javascript_jquery/book_apps`

into a project named JS_jQuery Book Apps. Once that's done, you can easily access the applications by using the App Explorer window.

The dialog boxes for importing a project in Aptana 3.4 or later

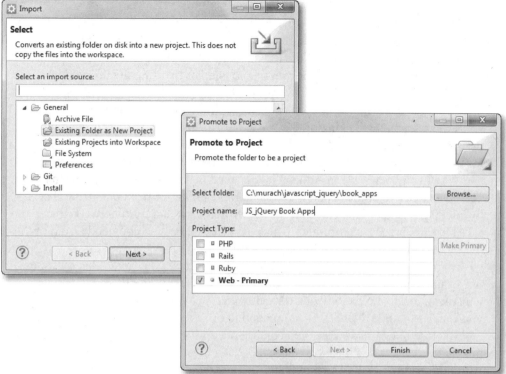

How to create a new project

- Use the File→New→Web Project command.

How to import a project with Aptana 3.4 or later

- Use the File→Import command to display the Import dialog box, click on Existing Folder as New Project, and click Next.
- In the Promote to Project dialog box, browse to the top-level folder for the application, enter a project name, and click the Finish button.

Description

- Aptana works the best when you set up projects for the web applications that you're developing and maintaining.
- In general, each Aptana *project* should contain the folders and files for one web application. For this book, however, you can set up one project for all of the book applications, one project for all exercises, and one project for all exercise solutions.

Figure 1-18   How to create or import a project in Aptana

How to work with files

Figure 1-19 shows how to open or close an HTML, CSS, or JavaScript file after you've created a project. Here, the JS_jQuery Book Apps project is shown in the App Explorer window on the left side of Aptana. If you have created more than one project, you can switch from one to another by using the drop-down project list that's at the top of this window.

Once you have the correct project open, you can drill down to the file that you want to open by clicking on the ▷ symbols for the folders. In this example, the ch01 and email_list folders have been expanded so you can see the four files for the Email List application. Then, to open a file, you just double-click on it.

When you open a file in Aptana, it is opened in a new tab. This means that you can have several files open at the same time and move from one to another by clicking on a tab. This makes it easy to switch back and forth between the HTML, CSS, and JavaScript files. This also makes it easy to copy code from one file to another.

If you want to open a file that isn't part of a project, you can do that by using one of the methods shown in this figure. First, you can use the Project Explorer window to locate the file on your computer and then double-click on it. Second, you can use the File→Open File command to open a file.

To close one or more files, you can use one of the three methods shown in this figure. This makes it easy to close all of the files except the ones that you're currently working with. And that helps you avoid the mistake of making a change to the wrong file.

This figure ends by showing how to start a new file. Most important is to name the file with the appropriate extension (.html, .css, or .js) depending on whether it is going to be an HTML, CSS, or JavaScript file. Then, Aptana will know what type of file it is, and its editor will be adjusted to the syntax of that type of file when it is opened.

As you work with Aptana, you'll see that it has the same type of interface that you've used with other programs. So if you want to do something that isn't presented in this chapter, try right-clicking on an item to see what menu options are available. Check out the other buttons in the toolbar. See what's available from the drop-down menus. With a little experimentation, you'll find that this program is not only powerful, but also easy to use.

Aptana with the App Explorer shown and a JavaScript file in the second tab

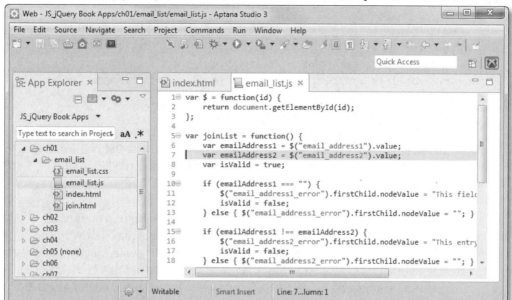

How to open a file within a project

- Use the drop-down list in Aptana's App Explorer to select the project. Then, locate the file in the App Explorer and double-click on it.

Two ways to open a file that isn't in a project

- Use the Project Explorer to locate the file, and double-click on it.
- Use the File→Open File command.

How to close one or more files

- To close one file, click on the X in the tab for the file.
- To close all of the files except one, right click on the tab you don't want to close and select Close Others.
- To close all of the files, right click on any tab and select Close All.

How to start a new file

- To start an HTML, CSS, or JavaScript file, select the File→New→File command. Then, in the New File dialog box, select the folder that the file should be stored in, enter a filename for the new file with an extension (.html, .css, or .js), and click the Finish button.
- To start a new file from another file, use the File→Save As command to save the file with a new name.

Figure 1-19   How to work with files in Aptana

How to edit a file

Figure 1-20 shows how to edit a JavaScript file with Aptana, but editing works the same for HTML and CSS files. When you open a file with an html, css, or js extension, Aptana knows what type of file you're working with so it can use color to highlight the syntax components. The good news is that color coding is also used for CSS that's in a style element of an HTML document or JavaScript that's in a script element of an HTML document.

As you enter a new line of code, the auto-completion feature presents lists of words that start with the letters that you've entered. This type of list is illustrated by this figure. Here, the list shows the JavaScript choices after the letter *t* has been entered. Then, you can select a word and press the Tab key to insert it into your code.

This also works with HTML and CSS entries. If, for example, you type <s in an HTML document, Aptana presents a list of the elements that start with s. Then, if you select one of the elements, Aptana finishes the opening tag and adds the closing tag. This feature also works when you start an attribute.

Similarly, if you enter # to start a CSS style rule, Aptana presents a list of the ids that can be used in an id selector. If you enter *b* to start a property declaration, Aptana presents a list of the properties that start with b. And if you start an entry for a property value, Aptana will present a list of values. In short, this is a powerful feature that can help you avoid many entry errors.

Beyond that, Aptana provides error markers and warning markers that help you find and correct errors. In this figure, for example, you can see two error markers and a warning marker. Then, to get the description for a marker, you can hover the mouse over the marker.

As you're editing, you may want to enlarge the editing area by closing the side pane and restoring that pane later on. Or you may want to close the Project Explorer, as shown in this figure, because you don't use it often. To work with the panes and the Explorers, you can use the third set of procedures in this figure.

Last, if you want to change the colors that are used by the editor, you can use the fourth procedure in this figure. In this book, we use the Dreamweaver theme, but you can experiment with other themes until you find one that you like. If you click the Apply button after you select a theme, you can see the colors that are used in the window behind the dialog box. Then, if you like the colors, you can click the OK button to close the dialog box.

Aptana with an auto-completion list for a JavaScript entry

How to use the auto-completion feature

- The auto-completion feature displays a list of items that start with what you've typed. To insert one of those items, double-click on it or use the arrow keys to highlight it and press the Tab key.
- For some JavaScript statements, like an if-else statement, the editor will insert a snippet that contains the starting code including parentheses and braces.

How to identify the errors that are marked by the Aptana editor

- An error marker is a red circle that contains a white X at the start of a line. A warning marker is a yellow triangle that contains an exclamation mark. These markers are displayed as you enter and edit code.
- To get the description for an error or warning marker, hover the mouse over the marker.

How to hide and restore the Project and App Explorers

- To hide the Project or App Explorer, click on the X in its tab. To display the Project or App Explorer, use the Window→Show ViewApp Explorer or Project Explorer command.
- To hide the pane on the left side of the window, click on its minimize button. To restore the pane, click on the Restore icon at the top of the vertical bar that's to the left or right of the editing window.

How to set the colors that are used to highlight the syntax

- Use the Window→Preferences command to open the Preferences dialog box.
- Click on Aptana Studio, and then click on Themes to display the Themes dialog box.
- Choose a theme from the Editor Theme list. (This book uses the Dreamweaver theme.)

Description

- Aptana provides many features that make it easier to enter and edit JavaScript code.
- Aptana provides many ways to display the panes for its many features.

Figure 1-20   How to edit a file in Aptana

How to run a JavaScript application

Figure 1-21 shows how to run a JavaScript application from Aptana. To do that, you open the HTML file for the application. Or, if the HTML file is already open, you click on its tab to select it as shown in this figure. Then, you click on the Run button. This opens the default browser and runs the file in that browser. You can also run an HTML file in another browser using the drop-down list to the right of the Run button. This list includes any browsers that were installed on your computer when you installed Aptana.

Before you run a JavaScript application, you need to save any changes to the HTML file and its related files. To do that, you can click on the Save or Save All button in the toolbar. If you don't save the files before you click the Run button, though, you'll get a warning message with an option that will save the files for you.

When you run a JavaScript application this way, a new browser or browser tab is opened each time you click the Run button. So, if you click on the Run button 10 times for an application, 10 browsers or tabs will be opened.

Another way to do this, though, is to run an application the first time by clicking on the Run button. Then, after you find and fix the errors in Aptana, you can click on the Save All button in Aptana to save the changes, switch to the browser, and click on the Reload or Refresh button in the browser to reload the application with the changes. That way, you use the same tab or Browser instance each time you test the application.

Aptana's Run button

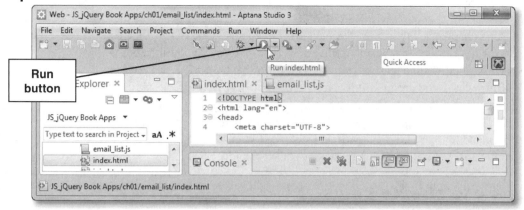

The web page in Chrome

How to run a JavaScript application from Aptana

- Before you run a file, you should save any changes that you've made to it or any of its related files. To do that, you can click on the Save or Save All button in the toolbar.

- To run a JavaScript application in the default browser, open the HTML file for the application or, if it's already open, select its tab. Then, click on the Run button. (The Run button won't work if the HTML file isn't the one that's selected.)

- To run a JavaScript application in another browser, select the tab for its HTML file, click the down-arrow to the right of the Run button, and select the browser.

Description

- When you test an application, you run its HTML page. Then, you can note the errors, fix the errors in Aptana, save the changes, and run the page again.

- Every time you run a page from Aptana, another browser instance or browser tab is opened. Another alternative is to save the corrected files in Aptana, switch to the browser, and click its Reload or Refresh button. That way, another browser or tab isn't opened.

Figure 1-21   How to run a JavaScript application from Aptana

Perspective

This chapter has presented the background concepts and terms that you need for developing JavaScript applications. Now, if you're comfortable with everything that you've learned, you're ready for chapter 2.

But what if you aren't comfortable with your HTML and CSS skills? First, we recommend that you keep going in this book because you don't have to be an HTML or CSS expert to develop JavaScript applications. Second, we recommend that you get a copy of *Murach's HTML5 and CSS3*, because every web developer should eventually master HTML5 and CSS3.

Terms you should know

client	CSS (Cascading Style Sheets)
web browser	DOM scripting
web server	Document Object Model (DOM)
network	HTML5 semantic elements
intranet	HTML5 semantics
local area network (LAN)	attribute
Internet	id attribute
wide area network (WAN)	class attribute
Internet service provider (ISP)	name attribute
HTML (HyperText Markup	for attribute
Language)	title attribute
static web page	external style sheet
HTTP (HyperText Transfer Protocol)	embedded styles
HTTP request	CSS selector
HTTP response	type selector
render a web page	id selector
dynamic web page	class selector
application server	style rule
database server	property declaration
server-side processing	property name
round trip	URL (Uniform Resource Locator)
JavaScript	protocol
JavaScript engine	domain name
scripting language	path
client-side processing	developer tools
image swap	cross-browser compatibility
image rollover	JavaScript shiv
data validation	CDN (Content Delivery Network)
jQuery	transpiler
ECMAScript specification	IDE (Integrated Development
HTML element	Environment)
tag	Aptana project

Summary

- A web application consists of clients, a web server, and a network. *Clients* use *web browsers* to request web pages from the web server. The *web server* returns the requested pages.

- A *local area network* (*LAN*) connects computers that are near to each other. This is often called an *intranet*. In contrast, the *Internet* consists of many *wide area networks* (*WANs*).

- To request a web page, the web browser sends an *HTTP request* to the web server. Then, the web server gets the HTML for the requested page and sends it back to the browser in an *HTTP response*. Last, the browser *renders* the HTML into a web page.

- A *static web page* is a page that is the same each time it's retrieved. In contrast, the HTML for a *dynamic web page* is generated by a server-side program or script, so its HTML can change from one request to another.

- *JavaScript* is a *scripting language* that is run by the *JavaScript engine* of a web browser. It provides for *client-side processing*. *jQuery* is a JavaScript library that makes it easier to code many common functions.

- JavaScript is commonly used to modify the *Document Object Model* (*DOM*) that's built for each web page when it is loaded. This is referred to as *DOM scripting*. When the DOM is changed, the browser immediately changes its display so it reflects those changes.

- The ECMAScript specification provides the standards that JavaScript implements. ECMAScript 5 is the version that's in common use today.

- *HTML* (*HyperText Markup Language*) is the language that defines the structure and contents of a web page. *CSS* (*Cascading Style Sheets*) is used to control how the web pages are formatted.

- You can view a web page that's on your own computer or server or on an Internet server. To view a web page on an Internet server, you can enter the *URL* (*Uniform Resource Locator*) that consists of the *protocol*, *domain name*, *path*, and filename into a browser's address bar.

- To help find errors when you test a JavaScript application, you can use the Console panel in Chrome's *developer tools*.

- When you develop a JavaScript application, you need to provide for *cross-browser compatibility*. That means you have to test your applications on all modern browsers as well as older versions of those browsers.

- To provide compatibility with older browsers like IE7 and IE8, you can use the *JavaScript shiv* for the HTML5 semantic elements and the shim.js and sham.js files for ECMAScript.

- To develop JavaScript applications, you can use a text editor or an *Integrated Development Environment* (*IDE*) like Aptana Studio 3.

Before you do the exercises for this book...

Before you do the exercises for this book, you should download and install the Chrome browser as well as the applications for this book. If you're going to use Aptana, you should also download and install that product. The procedures for installing the software and applications for this book are in appendix A.

Exercise 1-1   Run the Email List application

In this exercise, you'll run the Email List application that's presented in figures 1-6 through 1-8.

Open the application in Chrome

1. Start Chrome if it isn't already open. Then, use the Ctrl+O key combination to open this HTML file:

    ```
    murach\javascript_jquery\book_apps\ch01\email_list\index.html
    ```

2. To test what happens when you don't enter any data, just click the Join our List button without entering any data.

3. Enter an email address in the first text box and invalid data in the second text box and click the Join our List button to see what error messages are displayed.

4. Enter valid data for all three text boxes and click on the button. Then, the data is submitted for processing and a new web page is displayed.

Preview the developer tools

5. To rerun the application, click the Back button. Then, click on the Reload button. This should reset the entries.

6. Enter an email address in the first text box, leave the other text boxes empty, and click the Join our list button. Then, press F12 to open Chrome's developer tools. Display the Console tab by clicking on it, and note that it doesn't contain any error messages.

7. Click on the Sources tab. Then, if it's not already displayed, click on the email_list.js file in the left pane to see the JavaScript code for the page. Do the same for the index.html file to see the HTML for the page.

8. Click on the Elements tab, and drill down to see the HTML elements within the form element for the page. In the span elements, you can see the error messages that are displayed, not the starting values in the HTML. That's because the Elements tab represents the Document Object Model for the page, and JavaScript has changed that model.

9. Do more experimenting if you want. These are powerful debugging tools that you'll use a lot as you go through this book, so it's good to become familiar with them. When you're through, press the F12 button to close the tools.

Exercise 1-2   Run other section 1 applications

This exercise has you run two of the applications presented in chapters 6 and 7. That will give you some idea of what you'll able to do when you complete this section.

Run the FAQs application of chapter 6

1. Open this file in the Chrome browser:

   `murach\javascript_jquery\book_apps\ch06\faqs\index.html`

2. Click on the first heading to display the text for it, and click the heading again to hide the text.

3. Tab to the next heading and press the Enter key to display the text for it, and press the Enter key again to hide the text.

Run the Image Swap application of chapter 7

4. Open this file in the Chrome browser:

   `murach\javascript_jquery\book_apps\ch07\swap\index.html`

   Notice the four small images near the top of the page, and notice that a larger version of the first image is displayed below the smaller images.

5. Click on the second image to see that a larger version of that image is now displayed.

6. Tab to the next image and press the Enter key to display a larger version of that image.

Exercise 1-3   Get started with Aptana

This exercise is for readers who are going to use Aptana with this book. It guides you through the process of creating projects that provide easy access to the book applications and exercises that you've downloaded.

Create the projects

1. Start Aptana, and use the procedure in figure 1-18 to create a project for the book applications that are stored in this folder:

   `murach\javascript_jquery\book_apps`

   This project should be named JS_jQuery Book Apps, and the entries for the last dialog box should be just like those in this figure.

2. Use the same procedure to create a project named JS_jQuery Exercises for the exercises that are stored in this folder:

   `javascript_jquery\exercises`

3. Use the same procedure to again create a project named JS_jQuery Solutions for the exercise solutions that are stored in this folder:

   `murach\javascript_jquery\solutions`

Test the Email List application

4.   Use the drop-down list in the App Explorer to select the JS_jQuery Exercises project. This provides access to all of the exercises that are in this book.

5.   In the App Explorer, click on the ▷ symbol before ch01 to display the email_list folder, and click on the ▷ symbol for the email_list folder to display the files for the Email List application.

6.   Double-click on the file named index.html to open that file. Then, click the Run button in the toolbar to run the application in the default browser. That will automatically switch you to that browser.

7.   Switch back to Aptana, and click on the down arrow to the right of the Run button. If the drop-down list offers Internet Explorer, click on it to run the application in that browser. Then, return to Aptana.

Edit the JavaScript code

8.   In the App Explorer, double click on the file named email_list.js to open that file, and note the colors that are used for syntax highlighting.

9.   If you don't like the colors that are used, use the procedure in figure 1-20 to change them.

10.   In the JavaScript file, delete the right parenthesis in the first line of code. This should display two error markers. Then, hover the mouse over the markers to display the error descriptions. This illustrates Aptana's error-checking feature. Now, undo the change that you made. (To undo a change with the keyboard, press Ctrl+Z.)

11.   In the JavaScript file, after the third statement that starts with var in the joinList() function, start a statement on a new line with these characters:

```
if (e
```

This should insert the closing parenthesis and display a list of the possible entries that start with the letter *e*. Here, you can see that emailAddress1 and emailAddress2 are included in the list. These are the variables that are created by the first two var statements in this function, and this illustrates Aptana's auto-completion feature. Now, undo this change.

12.   Enter this statement on a new line that comes right before the last line of the JavaScript code, which consists of just a right brace (}):

```
alert("The DOM has now been built");
```

In other words, this statement will become the second to last line in the file.

13.   To test the statement that you've added, click on the Save All button in the toolbar to save your changes. Then, switch to your browser and click on the Reload or Refresh button to run the application with this change. This should display a dialog box that you can close by clicking on its OK button. After that, the application should work the same as it did before.

14.   If you're curious, do more experimenting on your own. Then, close the files and exit from Aptana.

2

Getting started with JavaScript

The goal of this chapter is to get you off to a good start with JavaScript, especially if you're new to programming. If you have programming experience with another language, you should be able to move rapidly through this chapter. Otherwise, take it easy and do the exercises at the end of this chapter.

How to include JavaScript in an HTML document

In chapter 1, you saw how the JavaScript for an application can be coded in a separate file. But there are actually three different ways to include JavaScript in an HTML document. You'll learn all three now.

Two ways to include JavaScript in the head of an HTML document

Figure 2-1 presents two of the three ways to include JavaScript in an HTML document. As you saw in the last chapter, one way is to code the JavaScript in a separate *external file*. Then, you code a script element in the head section of the HTML document to include that file.

In the script element, the src attribute is used to refer to the external file. For this element, you can also code a type attribute with the value "text/javascript" to tell the browser what kind of content the file contains. But with HTML5, that attribute is no longer needed because the assumption is that all files that are referred to in script elements contain JavaScript.

In the example in this figure, the src attribute refers to a file named calculate_mpg.js. The assumption here is that this file is in the same folder as the HTML file. Otherwise, you need to code a relative URL that provides the right path for the file. If, for example, the JavaScript file is in a folder named javascript and that folder is in the same folder as the HTML file, the src attribute would be coded this way:

```
<script src="javascript/calculate_mpg.js"></script>
```

This works the same as it does for any other file reference in an HTML document.

The second way to include JavaScript in an HTML document is to code the JavaScript within the script element in the head section. This can be referred to as *embedded JavaScript*. Note, however, that the application will work the same whether the JavaScript is embedded in the head section or loaded into the head section from an external file.

The benefit of using an external file is that it separates the JavaScript from the HTML. Another benefit is that it makes it easier to re-use the code in other pages or applications.

The benefit of using embedded JavaScript is that you don't have to switch between the HTML and JavaScript files as you develop the application. In the examples in this book, you'll see both uses of JavaScript.

As you'll see in the next figure, script elements can be in the body section of the document, too. In fact, some developers prefer to place their script elements just before the closing body tag. This can make the page appear to load faster because the HTML will render before the JavaScript loads. But if you need JavaScript functionality as the HTML renders, scripts at the bottom won't work. Ultimately, you'll make this decision based on your application's needs.

Two attributes of the script element

Attribute	Description
`src`	Specifies the location (source) of an external JavaScript file.
`type`	With HTML5, this attribute can be omitted. If you code it, use "text/javascript" for JavaScript code.

A script element in the head section that loads an external JavaScript file

```
<script src="calculate_mpg.js"></script>
```

A script element that embeds JavaScript in the head section

```
<head>
    ...
    <script>
        alert("The Calculate MPG application");
        var miles = prompt("Enter miles driven");
        miles = parseFloat(miles);
        var gallons = prompt("Enter gallons of gas used");
        gallons = parseFloat(gallons);
        var mpg = miles/gallons;
        mpg = parseInt(mpg);
        alert("Miles per gallon = " + mpg);
    </script>
</head>
```

Description

- A script element in the head section of an HTML document is commonly used to identify an *external JavaScript file* that should be included with the page.

- A script element in the head section can also contain the JavaScript statements that are included with the page. This can be referred to as *embedded JavaScript*.

- If you code more than one script element in the head section, the JavaScript is included in the sequence in which the script statements appear.

- When a script element in the head section includes an external JavaScript file, the JavaScript in the file runs as if it were coded in the script element.

- Some programmers prefer to place their script elements at the bottom of the page, just before the closing body tag. This can make a page seem to load faster, but the JavaScript won't run until after the page is loaded.

Figure 2-1   Two ways to include JavaScript in the head of an HTML document

How to include JavaScript in the body of an HTML document

Figure 2-2 shows a third way to include JavaScript in an HTML document. This time, the two script elements in the first example are coded in the body of the HTML document. When a script element is coded in the body, the script is replaced by the output of the JavaScript code when the page is loaded.

If you want to provide for browsers that don't have JavaScript enabled, you can code a noscript element after a script element as shown in the second example. Then, if JavaScript is disabled, the content of the noscript element will be displayed. But if JavaScript is enabled, the script element is replaced by the output of the JavaScript code and the noscript element is ignored. This way, some output will be displayed whether or not JavaScript is enabled.

In the second example, the noscript element is coded right after a script element, so 2017 will replace the output of the script element if JavaScript isn't enabled in the browser. This means that the result will be the same in the year 2017 whether or not JavaScript is enabled. But after 2017, the year will be updated by the JavaScript if it is enabled.

You can also code a noscript element that doesn't follow a script element. For instance, you can code a noscript element at the top of a page that warns the user that the page won't work right if JavaScript is disabled. This is illustrated by the third example. In this case, nothing is displayed if JavaScript is enabled and the message is displayed if JavaScript is disabled.

In most of the applications in this book, the JavaScript is either embedded in the head section of the HTML or coded in an external file that's identified in the head section of the HTML. However, you shouldn't have any trouble including the JavaScript in the body of an HTML document whenever you want to do that.

JavaScript in the body of an HTML document

```
<p>
    <script>
        var today = new Date();
        document.write("Current date: ");
        document.write(today.toDateString());
    </script>
</p>
<p>&copy; 
    <script>
        var today = new Date();
        document.write( today.getFullYear() );
    </script>
, San Joaquin Valley Town Hall
</p>
```

The result of the JavaScript in a web browser

Current date: Tue Jan 17 2017

© 2017 , San Joaquin Valley Town Hall

A noscript element in the body of an HTML document

```
<p>&copy; 
    <script>
        var today = new Date();
        document.write( today.getFullYear() );
    </script>
    <noscript>2017</noscript>
, San Joaquin Valley Town Hall
</p>
```

A noscript element at the start of an HTML document

```
<h2><noscript>To get the most from this website,
    please enable JavaScript.</noscript></h2>
```

Description

- The JavaScript code in a script element in the body of a document is run when the page is loaded.
- The noscript element can be used to display content when JavaScript is disabled in a user's browser.

Figure 2-2   How to include JavaScript in the body of an HTML document

The JavaScript syntax

The *syntax* of JavaScript refers to the rules that you must follow as you code statements. If you don't adhere to these rules, your web browser won't be able to interpret and execute your statements.

How to code JavaScript statements

Figure 2-3 summarizes the rules for coding *JavaScript statements*. The first rule is that JavaScript is case-sensitive. This means that uppercase and lowercase letters are treated as different letters. For example, *salestax* and *salesTax* are treated as different names.

The second rule is that JavaScript statements should end with a semicolon. That way, it will be easier to tell where one statement ends and the next one begins. To help remind you to include semicolons, some IDEs like Aptana and NetBeans issue a warning if you omit them.

The third rule is that JavaScript ignores extra whitespace in statements. Since *whitespace* includes spaces, tabs, and new line characters, this lets you break long statements into multiple lines so they're easier to read.

Be careful, though, to follow the guidelines in this figure about where to split a statement. If you don't split a statement at a good spot, JavaScript will sometimes try to help you out by adding a semicolon for you, and that can lead to errors.

A block of JavaScript code

```javascript
var joinList = function() {
    var emailAddress1 = $("email_address1").value;
    var emailAddress2 = $("email_address2").value;

    if (emailAddress1 == "") {
        alert("Email Address is required.");
    } else if (emailAddress2 == "") {
        alert("Second Email Address is required.");
    } else if (emailAddress1 != emailAddress2) {
        alert("Second Email entry must equal first entry.");
    } else if ($("first_name").value == "") {
        alert("First Name is required.");
    } else {
        $("email_form").submit();
    }
};
```

The basic syntax rules

- JavaScript is case-sensitive.
- Each JavaScript statement ends with a semicolon.
- JavaScript ignores extra whitespace within statements.

How to split a statement over two or more lines

- Split a statement after:
  - an arithmetic or relational operator such as +, -, *, /, =, ==, >, or <
  - an opening brace ({), bracket ([ ), or parenthesis
  - a closing brace (})
- Do not split a statement after:
  - an identifier, a value, or the *return* keyword
  - a closing bracket ( ]) or closing parenthesis

Description

- A JavaScript *statement* has a syntax that's similar to the syntax of Java.
- *Whitespace* refers to the spaces, tab characters, and return characters in the code, and it is ignored by the compiler. As a result, you can use spaces, tab characters, and return characters to format your code so it's easier to read.
- In some cases, JavaScript will try to correct what it thinks is a missing semicolon by adding a semicolon at the end of a split line. To prevent this, follow the guidelines above for splitting a statement.

Figure 2-3   How to code JavaScript statements

How to create identifiers

Variables, functions, objects, properties, methods, and events must all have names so you can refer to them in your JavaScript code. An *identifier* is the name given to one of these components.

Figure 2-4 shows the rules for creating identifiers in JavaScript. Besides the first four rules, you can't use any of the JavaScript *reserved words* (also known as *keywords*) as an identifier. These are words that are reserved for use within the JavaScript language. You should also avoid using any of the JavaScript global properties or methods as identifiers, which you'll learn more about as you progress through this book.

Besides the rules, you should give your identifiers meaningful names. That means that it should be easy to tell what an identifier refers to and easy to remember how to spell the name. To create names like that, you should avoid abbreviations. If, for example, you abbreviate the name for monthly investment as mon_inv, it will be hard to tell what it refers to and hard to remember how you spelled it. But if you spell it out as monthly_investment, both problems are solved.

Similarly, you should avoid abbreviations that are specific to one industry or field of study unless you are sure the abbreviation will be widely understood. For example, mpg is a common abbreviation for miles per gallon, but cpm could stand for a number of different things and should be spelled out.

To create an identifier that has more than one word in it, many JavaScript programmers use a convention called *camel casing*. With this convention, the first letter of each word is uppercase except for the first word. For example, monthlyInvestment and taxRate are identifiers that use camel casing.

The alternative is to use underscore characters to separate the words in an identifier. For example, monthly_investment and tax_rate use this convention. If the standards in your shop specify one of these conventions, by all means use it. Otherwise, you can use whichever convention you prefer...but be consistent.

In this book, underscore notation is used for the ids and class names in the HTML, and camel casing is used for all JavaScript identifiers. That way, it will be easier for you to tell where the names originated.

Rules for creating identifiers

- Identifiers can only contain letters, numbers, the underscore, and the dollar sign.
- Identifiers can't start with a number.
- Identifiers are case-sensitive.
- Identifiers can be any length.
- Identifiers can't be the same as *reserved words*.
- Avoid using global properties and methods as identifiers. If you use one of them, you won't be able to use the global property or method with the same name.

Valid identifiers in JavaScript

```
subtotal        index_1              $
taxRate         calculate_click      $log
```

Camel casing versus underscore notation

```
taxRate           tax_rate
calculateClick    calculate_click
emailAddress      email_address
futureValue       future_value
```

Naming recommendations

- Use meaningful names for identifiers. That way, your identifiers aren't likely to be reserved words or global properties.
- Be consistent: Either use camel casing (taxRate) or underscores (tax_rate) to identify the words within the variables in your scripts.
- If you're using underscore notation, use lowercase for all letters.

Reserved words in JavaScript

```
abstract     else          instanceof    switch
arguments    enum          int           synchronized
boolean      eval          interface     this
break        export        let           throw
byte         extends       long          throws
case         false         native        transient
catch        final         new           true
char         finally       null          try
class        float         package       typeof
const        for           private       var
continue     function      protected     void
debugger     goto          public        volatile
default      if            return        while
delete       implements    short         with
do           import        static        yield
double       in            super
```

Description

- *Identifiers* are the names given to variables, functions, objects, properties, and methods.
- In *camel casing*, all of the words within an identifier except the first word start with capital letters.

Figure 2-4   How to create identifiers

How to use comments

Comments let you add descriptive notes to your code that are ignored by the JavaScript engine. Later on, these comments can help you or someone else understand the code whenever it needs to be modified.

The example in figure 2-5 shows how comments can be used to describe or explain portions of code. At the start, a *block comment* describes what the application does. This kind of comment starts with /* and ends with */. Everything that's coded between the start and the end is ignored by the JavaScript engine when the application is run.

The other kind of comment is a *single-line comment* that starts with //. In the example, the first single-line comment describes what the JavaScript that comes before it on the same line does. In contrast, the second single-line comment takes up a line by itself. It describes what the function that comes after it does.

In addition to describing JavaScript code, comments can be useful when testing an application. If, for example, you want to disable a portion of the JavaScript code, you can enclose it in a block comment. Then, it will be ignored when the application is run. This can be referred to as *commenting out* a portion of code. Later, after you test the rest of the code, you can enable the commented out code by removing the markers for the start and end of the block comment. This can be referred to *uncommenting*.

Comments are also useful when you want to experiment with changes in code. For instance, you can make a copy of a portion of code, comment out the original code, and then paste the copy just above the original code that is now commented out. Then, you can make changes in the copy. But if the changes don't work, you can restore your old code by deleting the new code and uncommenting the old code.

When should you use comments to describe or explain code? Certainly, when the code is so complicated that you may not remember how it works if you have to maintain it later on. This kind of comment is especially useful if someone else is going to have to maintain the code.

On the other hand, you shouldn't use comments to explain code that any professional programmer should understand. That means that you have to strike some sort of balance between too much and too little. One of the worst problems with comments is changing the way the code works without changing the related comments. Then, the comments mislead the person who is trying to maintain the code, which makes the job even more difficult.

A portion of JavaScript code that includes comments

```
/* this application validates a user's entries for joining
   our email list
*/
var $ = function(id) {                          // the $ function
    return document.getElementById(id);
};
// this function gets and validates the user entries
var joinList = function() {
    var emailAddress1 = $("email_address1").value;
    var emailAddress2 = $("email_address2").value;
    var firstName = $("first_name").value;
    var isValid = true;

    // validate the first entry
    if (emailAddress1 == "") {
        $("email_address1_error").firstChild.nodeValue =
            "This field is required.";
        isValid = false;                        // set valid switch to off
    } else {
        $("email_address1_error").firstChild.nodeValue = "";
    }

    // validate the second entry
    ...
    ...
};
```

The basic syntax rules for JavaScript comments

- Block comments begin with /* and end with */.
- Single-line comments begin with two forward slashes and continue to the end of the line.

Guidelines for using comments

- Use comments to describe portions of code that are hard to understand.
- Use comments to disable portions of code that you don't want to test.
- Don't use comments unnecessarily.

Description

- JavaScript provides two forms of *comments*, *block comments* and *single-line comments*.
- Comments are ignored when the JavaScript is executed.
- During testing, comments can be used to *comment out* (disable) portions of code that you don't want tested. Then, you can remove the comments when you're ready to test those portions.
- You can also use comments to save a portion of code in its original state while you make changes to a copy of that code.

Figure 2-5   How to use comments

How to work with JavaScript data

When you develop JavaScript applications, you frequently work with data, especially the data that users enter into the controls of a form. In the topics that follow, you'll learn how to work with the three types of JavaScript data.

The primitive data types

JavaScript provides for three *primitive data types*. The *number data type* is used to represent numerical data. The *string data type* is used to store character data. And the *Boolean data type* is used to store true and false values. This is summarized in figure 2-6.

The number data type can be used to represent either integers or decimal values. *Integers* are whole numbers, and *decimal values* are numbers that can have one or more decimal digits. The value of either data type can be coded with a preceding plus or minus sign. If the sign is omitted, the value is treated as a positive value. A decimal value can also include a decimal point and one or more digits to the right of the decimal point.

As the last example of the number types shows, you can also include an exponent when you code a decimal value. If you aren't familiar with this notation, you probably won't need to use it because you won't be working with very large or very small numbers. On the other hand, if you're familiar with scientific notation, you already know that this exponent indicates how many places the decimal point should be moved to the left or right. Numbers that use this notation are called *floating-point numbers.*

To represent string data, you code the *string* within single or double quotation marks (quotes). Note, however, that you must close the string with the same type of quotation mark that you used to start it. If you code two quotation marks in a row without even a space between them, the result is called an *empty string*, which can be used to represent a string with no data in it.

To represent Boolean data, you code either the word *true* or *false* with no quotation marks. This data type can be used to represent one of two states.

JavaScript's primitive data types

Data type	Description
Number	Represents an integer or a decimal value that can start with a positive or negative sign.
String	Represents character (string) data.
Boolean	Represents a Boolean value that has two possible states: true or false.

Examples of number values

```
15              // an integer
-21             // a negative integer
21.5            // a decimal value
-124.82         // a negative decimal value
-3.7e-9         // floating-point notation for -0.0000000037
```

Examples of string values

```
"JavaScript"    // a string with double quotes
'String Data'   // a string with single quotes
""              // an empty string
```

The two Boolean values

```
true            // equivalent to true, yes, or on
false           // equivalent to false, no, or off
```

The number data type

- A number value can be an *integer*, which is a whole number, or a *decimal value*, which can have one or more decimal positions to the right of the decimal point.

- In JavaScript, decimal values are stored as *floating-point numbers*. In that format, a number consists of a positive or negative sign, one or more significant digits, an optional decimal point, optional decimal digits, and an optional exponent.

- If a result is stored in a number data type that is larger or smaller than the data type can store, it will be stored as the value Infinity or -Infinity.

The string data type

- A string value is surrounded by double quotes or single quotes. The string must start and end with the same type of quotation mark.

- An *empty string* is a string that contains no characters. It is entered by typing two quotation marks with nothing between them.

The Boolean data type

- A *Boolean value* can be true or false. Boolean values are often used in conditional statements, as you'll see in chapter 3.

Figure 2-6   The primitive data types

How to declare and assign values to variables

A *variable* stores a value that can change as the program executes. When you code a JavaScript application, you frequently declare variables and assign values to them. Figure 2-7 shows how to do both of these tasks.

To *declare* a variable in JavaScript, you code the *var* (for variable) keyword followed by the identifier (or name) that you want to use for the variable. For instance, the first statement in the first example in this figure declares a variable named counter. Note that after you declare a variable, its value and data type are undefined. Before you can use a variable in code, then, you must assign a value to it, which determines its data type.

To assign a value to a variable, you code an *assignment statement* that consists of a variable name, an equals sign (the *assignment operator*), and a value. This is illustrated by the second statement in the first example, which assigns a value of 1 to the counter variable.

The third statement in this example shows that you can declare two or more variables in a single statement. To do that, you code *var* followed by the variable names separated by commas. You can also assign values to two or more variables in a single statement by separating the assignment statements with commas. This is illustrated by the last statement in this example.

You can also declare a variable and assign a value to it using a single statement. To do that, you code the *var* keyword followed by the variable name, an equals sign, and a value. This is illustrated by the second group of examples.

The first two statements in this group show how to declare a variable and assign a numeric value to it. To do that, you can assign a *numeric literal* to the variable, which consists of an integer or decimal value. Here, the first statement assigns an integer value of 1 to a variable named count, and the second statement assigns a decimal value of 74.95 to a variable named subtotal.

The third and fourth statements show how to declare a variable and assign a string value to it. To do that, you can assign a *string literal* to the variable. A string literal consists of a value that's enclosed in single or double quotes. The third statement, for example, assigns a value of "Joseph" to a variable named name. The fourth statement is similar, except no value is included between the quotes. As you learned in the last topic, this represents an empty string that doesn't contain any characters.

The fifth statement shows how to declare a variable and assign a Boolean value to it. To do that, you assign the keyword true or false to the variable. Here, the value false is assigned to a variable named isValid.

The sixth statement shows that, in addition to assigning a *literal value* to a variable, you can assign another variable to it. In this case, the value of the subtotal variable in the second statement is assigned to a variable named total.

Although it's not shown here, you can also assign an expression to a variable. You'll see examples of that in figures 2-9 and 2-10.

The last statement in this group of examples shows that you can declare and assign values to more than one variable in a single statement. To do that, you code *var* followed by the variable name, an equals sign, and a value for each variable separated by commas.

How to declare and assign a value to a variable in two statements

Syntax

```
var variableName;
variableName = value;
```

Examples

```
var counter;                // declaration statement; value is undefined
counter = 1;                // assignment statement; value is 1

var sum, average;           // declares two variables
sum = 0, average = 0;       // assigns values to two variables
```

How to declare and assign a value to a variable in one statement

Syntax

```
var variableName = value;
```

Examples

```
var count = 1;              // integer value of 1
var subtotal = 74.95;       // decimal value of 74.95

var name = "Joseph";        // string value of "Joseph"
var email = "";             // empty string

var isValid = false;        // Boolean value of false

var total = subtotal;       // assigns value of subtotal variable

var x = 0, y = 0;           // declares and assigns values to 2 variables
```

Description

- A *variable* stores a value that can change as the program executes.

- To *declare* a variable, code the keyword *var* and a variable name. To declare more than one variable in a single statement, code *var* and the variable names separated by commas.

- To assign a value to a variable, use an *assignment statement* that consists of the variable name, an equals sign (the *assignment operator*), and a value. The type of a variable is determined by the value that's assigned to it.

- To assign values to two or more variables in a single statement, code the assignment statements separated by commas.

- The value that's assigned to a variable can be a *literal value*, or *literal*, another variable, or an expression like the arithmetic and string expressions that you'll learn how to code in the figures that follow.

- To code a *string literal*, you enclose it in single or double quotes. To code a *numeric literal*, you code an integer or decimal value that isn't enclosed in quotes.

- You can also declare a variable and assign a value to it in a single statement.

- Before you can use a variable, you must assign a value to it. A variable that hasn't been assigned a value has the value *undefined* and its type is undefined.

- To assign a Boolean value to a variable, you use the true and false keywords.

Figure 2-7   How to declare and assign values to variables

How to code arithmetic expressions

An *arithmetic expression* can be as simple as a single value or it can be a series of operations that result in a single value. In figure 2-8, you can see the operators for coding arithmetic expressions. If you've programmed in another language, these are probably similar to what you've been using. In particular, the first four *arithmetic operators* are common to most programming languages.

Most modern languages also have a *modulus operator* that calculates the remainder when the left value is divided by the right value. In the example for this operator, 13 % 4 means the remainder of 13 / 4. Then, since 13 / 4 is 3 with a remainder of 1, 1 is the result of the expression.

In contrast to the first five operators in this figure, the increment and decrement operators add or subtract one from a variable. To complicate matters, though, these operators can be coded before or after a variable name, and that can affect the result. To avoid confusion, then, it's best to only code these operators after the variable names and only in simple expressions like the one that you'll see in the next figure.

When an expression includes two or more operators, the *order of precedence* determines which operators are applied first. This order is summarized in the table in this figure. For instance, all multiplication and division operations are done from left to right before any addition and subtraction operations are done.

To override this order, though, you can use parentheses. Then, the expressions in the innermost sets of parentheses are done first, followed by the expressions in the next sets of parentheses, and so on. This is typical of all programming languages, as well as basic algebra, and the examples in this figure show how this works.

JavaScript's arithmetic operators

Operator	Name	Description
+	Addition	Adds two operands.
-	Subtraction	Subtracts the right operand from the left operand.
*	Multiplication	Multiplies two operands.
/	Division	Divides the right operand into the left operand. The result is always a floating-point number.
%	Modulus	Divides the right operand into the left operand and returns the remainder.
++	Increment	Adds 1 to the operand.
--	Decrement	Subtracts 1 from the operand.

The order of precedence for arithmetic expressions

Order	Operators	Direction	Description
1	++	Left to right	Increment operator
2	--	Left to right	Decrement operator
3	* / %	Left to right	Multiplication, division, modulus
4	+ -	Left to right	Addition, subtraction

Examples of simple arithmetic expressions

Example	Result
5 + 7	12
5 - 12	-7
6 * 7	42
13 / 4	3.25
13 % 4	1
counter++	counter = counter + 1
counter--	counter = counter - 1
3 + 4 * 5	23 (the multiplication is done first)
(3 + 4) * 5	35 (the addition is done first)
13 % 4 + 9	10 (the modulus is done first)
13 % (4 + 9)	0 (the addition is done first)

Description

- An *arithmetic expression* consists of one or more operands that are operated upon by arithmetic *operators*.

- An arithmetic expression is evaluated based on the *order of precedence* of the operators. To override the order of precedence, you can use parentheses.

- Because the use of increment and decrement operators can be confusing, it's best to only use these operators in expressions that consist of a variable name followed by the operator as shown above.

Figure 2-8   How to code arithmetic expressions

How to use arithmetic expressions in assignment statements

Now that you know how to code arithmetic expressions, figure 2-9 shows how to use these expressions with variables and assignment statements. Here, the first two examples show how you can use the multiplication and addition operators in JavaScript statements.

This is followed by a table that presents three of the *compound assignment operators*. These operators provide a shorthand way to code common assignment statements. For instance, the += operator modifies the value of the variable on the left of the operator by adding the value of the expression on the right to the value of the variable on the left. When you use this operator, the variable on the left must already exist and have a value assigned to it.

The other two operators in this table work similarly, but the -= operator subtracts the result of the expression on the right from the variable on the left. And the *= operator multiplies the variable on the left by the result of the expression on the right. The first group of examples after this table illustrate how these operators work.

The second example after the table shows three ways to increment a variable by adding 1 to it. As you will see throughout this book, this is a common JavaScript requirement. Here, the first statement assigns a value of 1 to a variable named counter.

Then, the second statement uses an arithmetic expression to add 1 to the value of the counter. This shows that a variable name can be used on both sides of the = operator. The third statement adds one to the counter by using the += operator. When you use this operator, you don't need to code the variable name on the right side of the = operator, which makes the code more concise.

The last statement in this example uses the ++ operator shown in the previous figure to add one to the counter. This illustrates the best way to use increment and decrement operators. Here, the numeric expression consists only of a variable name followed by the increment operator.

The last example illustrates a potential problem that you should be aware of. Because decimal values are stored internally as floating-point numbers, the results of arithmetic operations aren't always precise. In this example, the salesTax result, which should be 7.495, is 7.495000000000001. Although this result is extremely close to 7.495, it isn't equal to 7.495, which could lead to a programming problem if you expect a comparison of the two values to be equal. The solution is to round the result, which you'll learn how to do in chapter 4.

Code that calculates sales tax

```
var subtotal = 200;
var taxPercent = .05;
var taxAmount = subtotal * taxPercent;      // 10
var total = subtotal + taxAmount;           // 210
```

Code that calculates the perimeter of a rectangle

```
var width = 4.25;
var length = 8.5;
var perimeter = (2 * width) + (2 * length)     // (8.5 + 17) = 25.5
```

The most useful compound assignment operators

Operator	Description
+=	Adds the result of the expression to the variable.
-=	Subtracts the result of the expression from the variable.
*=	Multiplies the variable value by the result of the expression.

Statements that use the compound assignment operators

```
var subtotal = 74.95;
subtotal += 20.00;                 // subtotal = 94.95

var counter = 10;
counter -= 1;                      // counter = 9

var price = 100;
price *= .8;                       // price = 80
```

Three ways to increment a variable named counter by 1

```
var counter = 1;                   // counter = 1
counter = counter + 1;             // counter now = 2
counter += 1;                      // counter now = 3
counter++;                         // counter now = 4
```

A floating-point result that isn't precise

```
var subtotal = 74.95;              // subtotal = 74.95
var salesTax = subtotal * .1;      // salesTax = 7.495000000000001
```

Description

- Besides the assignment operator (=), JavaScript provides for *compound assignment operators*. These operators are a shorthand way to code common assignment operations.

- JavaScript also offers /= and %= compound operators, but you won't use them often.

- When you do some types of arithmetic operations with decimal values, the results aren't always precise, although they are extremely close. That's because decimal values are stored internally as floating-point numbers. The primary problem with this is that an equality comparison may not return true.

Figure 2-9   How to use arithmetic expressions in assignment statements

How to concatenate strings and include special characters in strings

Figure 2-10 presents some special techniques for working with strings. To start, it shows how to *concatenate*, or *join*, two or more strings. This means that one string is added to the end of another string.

To concatenate strings, you can use the + sign as a *concatenation operator*. This is illustrated by the first example in this figure. Here, the first statement assigns string literals to the variables named firstName and lastName. Then, the next statement creates a *string expression* by concatenating lastName, a string literal that consists of a comma and a space, and firstName. The result of this concatenation is

`Hopper, Grace`

which is stored in a new variable named fullName.

In the second example, you can see how the += operator can be used to get the same results. When the expressions that you're working with are strings, this operator does a simple concatenation.

You can also use the + and += operators to concatenate a string and a numeric value. This is illustrated by the third and fourth examples in this figure. In both cases, the number is converted to a string and then the strings are concatenated.

You can also use escape sequences when you work with strings. Three of the many escape sequences that you can use are summarized in the second table in this figure. These sequences let you put characters in a string that you can't put in just by pressing the appropriate key on the keyboard. For instance, the \n escape sequence is equivalent to pressing the Enter key in the middle of a string. And the \' sequence is equivalent to pressing the key for a single quotation mark.

Escape sequences are needed so the JavaScript engine can interpret code correctly. For instance, since single and double quotations marks are used to identify strings in JavaScript statements, coding them within the strings would cause syntax errors. But when the quotation marks are preceded by escape characters, the JavaScript engine can interpret them correctly.

The concatenation operators for strings

Operator	Description
+	Concatenates two values.
+=	Adds the result of the expression to the end of the variable.

Some of the escape sequences that can be used in strings

Operator	Description
\n	Starts a new line in a string.
\"	Puts a double quotation mark in a string.
\'	Puts a single quotation mark in a string.

How to concatenate string variables with the + operator

```
var firstName = "Grace", lastName = "Hopper";
var fullName = lastName + ", " + firstName;   // fullName is "Hopper, Grace"
```

How to concatenate string variables with the += operator

```
var firstName = "Grace", lastName = "Hopper";
var fullName = lastName;                 // fullName is "Hopper"
fullName += ", ";                        // fullName is "Hopper, "
fullName += firstName;                   // fullName is "Hopper, Grace"
```

How to concatenate a string and a number with the + operator

```
var months = 120;
var message = "Months: ";
message = message + months;              // message is "Months: 120"
```

How to concatenate a string and a number with the += operator

```
var months = 120;
var message = "Months: ";
message += months;                       // message is "Months: 120"
```

How escape sequences can be used in a string

```
var message = "A valid variable name\ncannot start with a number.";
var message = "This isn\'t the right way to do this.";
```

Description

- To *concatenate*, or *join*, two or more strings, you can use the + or += operator.
- If you use a plus sign in an expression and both values are strings, JavaScript concatenates them. But if one value is a number and one is a string, JavaScript converts the number to a string and then concatenates the strings.
- *Escape sequences* can be used to insert special characters within a string like a return character that starts a new line or a quotation mark.

Figure 2-10   How to concatenate strings and include special characters in strings

How to use objects, methods, and properties

In simple terms, an *object* is a collection of methods and properties. A *method* performs a function or does an action. A *property* is a data item that relates to the object. When you develop JavaScript applications, you will often work with objects, methods, and properties.

Introduction to objects, methods, and properties

To get you started with objects, methods, and properties, figure 2-11 shows how to use the methods and properties of the window object, which is a common JavaScript object. To *call* (execute) a method of an object, you use the syntax in the summary after the tables. That is, you code the object name, a *dot operator* (period), the method name, and any *parameters* that the method requires within parentheses.

In the syntax summaries in this book, some words are italicized and some aren't. The words that aren't italicized are keywords that always stay the same, like *alert*. You can see this in the first table, where the syntax for the alert() method shows that you code the word *alert* just as it is in the summary. In contrast, the italicized words are the ones that you need to supply, like the string parameter you supply to the alert() method.

In the first example after the syntax summary, you can see how the alert() method of the *window object* is called:

```
window.alert("This is a test of the alert method");
```

In this case, the one parameter that's passed to it is "This is a test of the alert method". So that message is displayed when the alert dialog box is displayed.

In the second example, you can see how the prompt() method of the window object is called. This time, though, the object name is omitted. For the window object (but only the window object), that's okay because the window object is the *global object* for JavaScript applications.

As you can see, the prompt() method accepts two parameters. The first one is a message, and the second one is an optional default value for a user entry. When the prompt() method is executed, it displays a dialog box like the one in this figure. Here, you can see the message and the default value that were passed to the method as parameters. At this point, the user can change the default value or leave it as is, and then click on the OK button to store the entry in the variable named userEntry. Or, the user can click on the Cancel button to cancel the entry, which returns a null value.

The third method in the table doesn't require any parameters. It is the print() method. When it is executed, it issues a request to the browser for printing the current web page. Then, the browser starts its print function, usually by displaying a dialog box that lets the user set some print options.

Common methods of the window object

Method	Description
alert(*string*)	Displays a dialog box that contains the string that's passed to it by the parameter along with an OK button.
prompt(*string, default*)	Displays a dialog box that contains the string in the first parameter, the default value in the second parameter, an OK button, and a Cancel button. If the user enters a value and clicks OK, that value is returned as a string. If the user clicks Cancel, null is returned to indicate that the value is unknown.
print()	Issues a print request for the current web page.

One property of the window object

Property	Description
location	The URL of the current web page.

The syntax for calling a method of an object
```
objectName.methodName(parameters)
```

A statement that calls the alert() method of the window object
```
window.alert("This is a test of the alert method");
```

A statement that calls the prompt() method with the object name omitted
```
var userEntry = prompt("This is a test of the prompt method", 100);
```

The prompt dialog box that's displayed

The syntax for accessing a property of an object
```
objectName.propertyName
```

A statement that displays the location property of the window object
```
alert(window.location);        // Displays the URL of the current page
```

Description

- An *object* has *methods* that perform functions that are related to the object as well as *properties* that represent the data or attributes that are associated with the object.

- When you *call* a method, you may need to pass one or more *parameters* to it by coding them within the parentheses after the method name, separated by commas.

- The *window object* is the *global object* for JavaScript, and JavaScript lets you omit the object name and *dot operator* (period) when referring to the window object.

Figure 2-11   Introduction to objects, methods, and properties

To access a property of an object, you use a similar syntax. However, you code the property name after the dot operator as illustrated by the second syntax summary. Unlike methods, properties don't require parameters in parentheses. This is illustrated by the statement in figure 2-11 that follows the syntax. This statement uses the alert() method of the window object to display the location property of the window object.

As you progress through this book, you'll learn how to use the methods and properties of many objects.

How to use the parseInt() and parseFloat() methods of the window object

The parseInt() and parseFloat() methods are used to convert strings to numbers. The parseInt() method converts a string to an integer, and the parseFloat() method converts a string to a decimal value. If the string can't be converted to a number, the value *NaN* is returned. NaN means "Not a Number". You'll learn one way to check whether a value is a number in the next chapter.

These methods are needed because the values that are returned by the prompt() method and the values that the user enters into text boxes are treated as strings. This is illustrated by the first group of examples in figure 2-12. For this group, assume that the default value in the prompt() method isn't changed by the user. As a result, the first statement in this group stores 12345.6789 as a string in a variable named entryA. Then, the third statement in this group converts the string to an integer value of 12345.

Note that the object name isn't coded before the method name in these examples. That's okay because window is the global object of JavaScript. Note too that the parseInt() method doesn't round the value. It just removes, or truncates, any decimal portion of the string value.

The last four statements in the first group of examples show what happens when the parseInt() or parseFloat() method is used to convert a value that isn't a number. In that case, both of these methods return the value NaN.

Note, however, that these methods can convert values that consist of one or more numeric characters followed by one or more nonnumeric characters. In that case, these methods simply drop the nonnumeric characters. For example, if a string contains the value 72.5%, the parseFloat() method will convert it to a decimal value of 72.5.

The second group of examples in this figure shows how to get the same results by coding the parseInt() and parseFloat() methods as the parameters of the alert() methods. For instance, the third statement in this group uses the parseInt() method as the parameter of the alert() method.

Note in the first set of examples that the values of the entryA, entryB, and entryC variables are all changed by the parseInt() and parseFloat() methods. For instance, entryA becomes the number 12345 and entryC becomes NaN. In contrast, the entries aren't changed by the statements in the second set of examples. That's because the parsed values aren't assigned to the variables; they're just displayed by the alert() methods.

The parseInt() and parseFloat() methods of the window object

Method	Description
`parseInt(`*`string`*`)`	Converts the string that's passed to it to an integer data type and returns that value. If it can't convert the string to an integer, it returns NaN.
`parseFloat(`*`string`*`)`	Converts the string that's passed to it to a decimal data type and returns that value. If it can't convert the string to a decimal value, it returns NaN.

Examples that use the parseInt() and parseFloat() methods

```
var entryA = prompt("Enter any value", 12345.6789);
alert(entryA);                              // displays 12345.6789
entryA = parseInt(entryA);
alert(entryA);                              // displays 12345

var entryB = prompt("Enter any value", 12345.6789);
alert(entryB);                              // displays 12345.6789
entryB = parseFloat(entryB);
alert(entryB);                              // displays 12345.6789

var entryC = prompt("Enter any value", "Hello");
alert(entryC);                              // displays Hello
entryC = parseInt(entryC);
alert(entryC);                              // displays NaN
```

The same examples with the parseInt() and parseFloat() methods embedded in the alert() method

```
var entryA = prompt("Enter any value", 12345.6789);
alert(entryA);                              // displays 12345.6789
alert(parseInt(entryA));                    // displays 12345

var entryB = prompt("Enter any value", 12345.6789);
alert(entryB);                              // displays 12345.6789
alert(parseFloat(entryB));                  // displays 12345.6789

var entryC = prompt("Enter any value", "Hello");
alert(entryC);                              // displays Hello
alert(parseInt(entryC));                    // displays NaN
```

Description

- The window object provides parseInt() and parseFloat() methods that let you convert string values to integer or decimal numbers.

- When you use the prompt() method or a text box to get numeric data that you're going to use in calculations, you need to use either the parseInt() or parseFloat() method to convert the string data to numeric data.

- *NaN* is a value that means "Not a Number". It is returned by the parseInt() and parseFloat() methods when the value that's being parsed isn't a number.

- When working with methods, you can embed one method in the parameter of another. In the second group of examples above, the parseInt() and parseFloat() methods are coded as the parameters for the alert() methods.

Figure 2-12   How to use the parseInt() and parseFloat() methods of the window object

How to use the write() and writeln() methods of the document object

Figure 2-13 shows how to use the write() and writeln() methods of the *document object*. These methods write their data into the body of the document so it's displayed in the browser window.

As the table shows, the only difference between these methods is that the writeln() method ends with a new line character. However, the new line character is ignored by the browser unless it's coded within an HTML pre element. As a result, there's usually no difference in the way these methods work.

This is illustrated by the examples in this figure. Note that you can include HTML tags within the parentheses of these methods. For instance, the first write() method writes the heading at the top of the page because h1 tags were coded around the text. Similarly, the fourth method in that group writes a <br> tag into the document, which is the HTML tag that moves to the next line.

These examples also show that the writeln() method doesn't skip to the next line unless it is coded within a pre element in the HTML. For instance, the first two writeln() methods in the body of the document display the data without skipping to a new line. However, when pre tags are added before and after the output, the writeln() method does skip to a new line.

Note that all of these methods are coded within the body section. Although you could code them in the head section, it makes more sense to code them in the body section since they add content to that section.

The write() and writeln() methods of the document object

Method	Description
write(*string*)	Writes the string that's passed to it into the document.
writeln(*string*)	Writes the string that's passed to it into the document ending with a new line character (see figure 2-10). However, the new line character isn't recognized by HTML except within the HTML pre element.

Examples of the write() and writeln() methods

```html
<body>
    <script>
        var today = new Date();
        document.write("<h1>Welcome to our site!</h1>");
        document.write("Today is ");
        document.write(today.toDateString());
        document.write("<br>");
        document.writeln("Today is ");
        document.writeln(today.toDateString());
        document.write("<br>");
    </script>
    <script>
        document.writeln("Welcome to our site!");
        document.writeln("Today is Monday.");
    </script>
    <script>
        document.writeln("<pre>Welcome to our site!");
        document.writeln("Today is Monday.</pre>");
    </script>
</body>
```

The output in a browser

Welcome to our site!

Today is Tue Jan 17 2017
Today is Tue Jan 17 2017
Welcome to our site! Today is Monday.

```
Welcome to our site!
Today is Monday.
```

Description

- The *document object* is the object that lets you work with the Document Object Model (DOM) that represents all of the HTML elements of the page.
- The write() and writeln() methods are normally used in the body of a document.
- The writeln() method doesn't skip to the next line unless it is coded within a pre element. However, you can code <br> tags to start new lines.

Figure 2-13   How to use the write() and writeln() methods of the document object

Two illustrative applications

This chapter ends by presenting two applications that illustrate the skills that you've just learned. These aren't realistic applications because they get the user entries from prompt statements instead of from controls on a form. However, these applications will get you started with JavaScript.

The Miles Per Gallon application

Figure 2-14 presents a simple application that issues two prompt statements that let the user enter the number of miles driven and the number of gallons of gasoline used. Then, the application calculates miles per gallon and issues an alert statement to display the result in a third dialog box.

Because this application uses prompt() methods to get the input and an alert() method to display the output, the HTML for this application is trivial. It contains one h1 element that is displayed after the JavaScript finishes executing.

In the JavaScript, you can see how the user's entries are stored in variables named miles and gallons and then parsed into decimal values. After that, miles is divided by gallons, and the result is saved in a variable named mpg. Then, the value in that variable is parsed into an integer so any decimal places are removed. Last, an alert statement displays the result that's shown in the third dialog box. When the user clicks on the OK button in that box, the JavaScript ends and the page with its one heading is displayed in the browser.

Can you guess what will happen if the user enters invalid data in one of the prompt dialog boxes? Then, the parseFloat() method will return NaN instead of a number, and the calculation won't work. Instead, the last alert statement will display:

```
Miles per gallon = NaN
```

Unlike other languages, though, the JavaScript will run to completion instead of crashing when the calculation can't be done, so the web page will be displayed.

When you look at the second and third dialog boxes in this figure, you can see that they contain checkboxes with messages that say "Prevent this page from creating additional dialogs." After an application has popped up one dialog box, most modern browsers will include a message like this on any more dialog boxes. This is a security feature designed to prevent endless loops of dialog boxes from locking the browser, and this can't be disabled.

Note that none of the dialog boxes in this figure include the message and Close button that are typically included at the top of a dialog box. You saw these elements in figure 2-11. They've been removed from these dialog boxes to make room on the page.

Incidentally, the dialog boxes in this figure are the ones for a Chrome browser. When you use other browsers, the dialog boxes will work the same but have slightly different appearances.

The dialog boxes for the Calculate MPG application

The first prompt dialog box

Enter miles driven

273

OK   Cancel

The second prompt dialog box

Enter gallons of gas used

12.5

☐ Prevent this page from creating additional dialogs.

OK   Cancel

The alert dialog box that displays the result

Miles per gallon = 21

☐ Prevent this page from creating additional dialogs.

OK

The HTML and JavaScript for the application

```html
<html>
<head>
    <title>The Calculate MPG Application</title>
    <script>
        var miles = prompt("Enter miles driven");
        miles = parseFloat(miles);
        var gallons = prompt("Enter gallons of gas used");
        gallons = parseFloat(gallons);
        var mpg = miles/gallons;
        mpg = parseInt(mpg);
        alert("Miles per gallon = " + mpg);
    </script>
</head>
<body>
    <!-- Will show after the JavaScript has run -->
    <h1>Thanks for using the Miles Per Gallon application!</h1>
</body>
</html>
```

Description

- If an application pops up more than one dialog box, most browsers will give you the option to prevent the page from creating any more. This is a built in security measure that can't be disabled.

Figure 2-14   The Miles Per Gallon application

The Test Scores application

Figure 2-15 presents a simple application that uses prompt() methods to let the user enter three test scores. After the third one is entered, this application calculates the average test score. That ends the JavaScript that's embedded in the head element of the HTML document.

Then, the JavaScript that's coded in the body element is executed. It uses one write() method to write an h1 element at the top of the page. Then, it uses another write() method to write the three test scores and the average score into the body of the document so it is displayed in the browser window. This shows that the variables that were created by the JavaScript in the head element are available to the JavaScript in the body element.

If you take another look at the JavaScript in the head element, you can see that it starts by declaring the variables that are needed to get and process the entries. The entry and average variables are declared but not assigned a value. The entry variable will be used to receive the user entries, and the average variable will receive the calculated average of the scores entered by the user.

In contrast, the total variable is assigned a starting value of zero. Then, each entry is added to this total value, and it is divided by 3 to calculate the average score. In addition, the score1, score2, and score3 variables are declared and assigned values after each score has been entered and parsed.

The results displayed in the browser

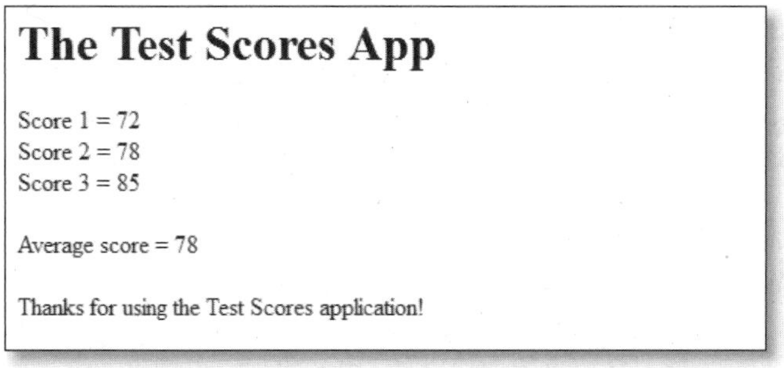

The Test Scores App

Score 1 = 72
Score 2 = 78
Score 3 = 85

Average score = 78

Thanks for using the Test Scores application!

The HTML and JavaScript for the application

```html
<html>
<head>
    <title>Average Test Scores</title>
    <script>
        var entry;
        var average;
        var total = 0;

        //get 3 scores from user and add them together
        entry = prompt("Enter test score");
        entry = parseInt(entry);
        var score1 = entry;
        total = total + score1;

        entry = prompt("Enter test score");
        entry = parseInt(entry);
        var score2 = entry;
        total = total + score2;

        entry = prompt("Enter test score");
        entry = parseInt(entry);
        var score3 = entry;
        total = total + score3;

        //calculate the average
        average = parseInt(total/3);
    </script>
</head>
<body>
    <script>
        document.write("<h1>The Test Scores App</h1>");
        document.write("Score 1 = " + score1 + "<br>" +
            "Score 2 = " + score2 + "<br>" +
            "Score 3 = " + score3 + "<br><br>" +
            "Average score = " + average + "<br><br>");
    </script>
    Thanks for using the Test Scores application!
</body>
</html>
```

Figure 2-15   The Test Scores application

Perspective

If you have programming experience, you can now see that JavaScript syntax is similar to other languages like Java and C#. As a result, you should have breezed through this chapter.

On the other hand, if you're new to programming and you understand all of the code in both of the applications in this chapter, you're off to a good start. Otherwise, you need to study the applications until you understand every line of code in each application. You should also do the exercises that follow.

Terms

external JavaScript file	floating-point number	compound assignment
embedded JavaScript	string data type	operator
JavaScript statement	string	concatenate
syntax	empty string	join
whitespace	Boolean data type	concatenation operator
identifier	Boolean value	string expression
reserved word	variable	escape sequence
keyword	declare a variable	object
camel casing	assignment statement	method
comment	assignment operator	property
block comment	literal value	call a method
in-line comment	literal	dot operator (dot)
comment out	string literal	parameter
uncomment	numeric literal	window object
primitive data type	arithmetic expression	global object
number data type	arithmetic operator	NaN
integer	modulus operator	document object
decimal value	order of precedence	

Summary

- The JavaScript for an HTML document page is commonly coded in an *external JavaScript file* that's identified by a script element. However, the JavaScript can also be *embedded* in a script element in the head or body of a document.

- A JavaScript *statement* has a *syntax* that's similar to Java's. Its *identifiers* are case-sensitive and usually coded with either *camel casing* or underscore notation. Its *comments* can be block or in-line.

- JavaScript provides three *primitive data types*. The *number data type* provides for both *integers* and *decimal values*. The *string data type* provides for character (*string*) data. And the *Boolean data type* provides for true and false values.

- To assign a value to a *variable*, you use the *assignment operator*.

- When you assign a value to a numeric variable, you can use *arithmetic expressions* that include *arithmetic operators*, variable names, and *numeric literals*.

- When you assign a value to a string variable, you can use *string expressions* that include *concatenation operators*, variable names, and *string literals*. Within a string literal, you can use *escape sequences* to provide special characters.

- JavaScript provides many *objects* with *methods* and *properties* that you can *call* or refer to in your applications. Since the *window object* is the *global object* for JavaScript, you can omit it when referring to its methods or properties.

- The *document object* provides some commonly used methods like the write() and writeln() methods.

Before you do the exercises for this book...

If you haven't already done so, you should install the Chrome browser and install the downloads for this book as described in appendix A.

Exercise 2-1   Modify the Miles Per Gallon application

In this exercise, you'll modify the code for the MPG application so the results are displayed in the browser window instead of an alert dialog box. The browser window should look something like this:

> # The Miles Per Gallon Application
>
> Miles driven = 125
> Gallons of gas = 12
>
> Miles per gallon = 10
>
> Thanks for using our MPG application.

1. Open your text editor or IDE. Then, open this HTML file:
   `javascript_jquery\exercises\ch02\mpg.html`

2. Run the application with valid entries, and note the result. Then, run it with invalid entries like zeros or spaces, and note the result.

3. Modify this application so the result is displayed in the browser instead of an alert statement. This result should include the user's entries for miles and gallons as shown above.

4. If you have any problems when you test your exercises, please use Chrome's developer tools as shown in figure 1-16 of the last chapter.

Exercise 2-2   Modify the Test Scores application

In this exercise, you'll modify the Test Scores application so it works the same but uses less code. The output of the application will still be displayed in the browser as it is in figure 2-15.

1. Open your text editor or IDE. Then, open this HTML file:

    `javascript_jquery\exercises\ch02\scores.html`

2. Run the application with valid entries, and note the result.

3. Modify this application so the variable declarations for the three scores parse the entries before storing their values. In other words, the two lines of code for each variable

    ```
    entry = parseInt(entry);
    var score1 = entry;
    ```

    should be combined into one.

4. Change the statements that accumulate the score total so they use the `+=` assignment operator shown in figure 2-9 instead of the equals operator.

Exercise 2-3   Create a simple application

Copying and modifying an existing application is often a good way to start a new application. So in this exercise, you'll modify the Miles Per Gallon application so it gets the length and width of a rectangle from the user, calculates the area and the perimeter of the rectangle, and displays the results in the browser like this:

The Area and Perimeter App

Length = 25
Width = 10

Area = 250
Perimeter = 70

Thanks for using the Area and Perimeter application!

1. Open your text editor or IDE. Then, open this HTML file:

    `javascript_jquery\exercises\ch02\rectangle.html`

    As you can see, this file contains the code for the Miles Per Gallon application.

2. Modify the code for this application so it works for the new application. (The area of a rectangle is length times width. The perimeter is 2 times length plus 2 times width.)

3

The essential JavaScript statements

In the last chapter, you were introduced to the basics of JavaScript coding. Now, you'll learn how to code the JavaScript statements that drive the logic of an application.

How to code conditional expressions

Conditional expressions are expressions that evaluate to either true or false based on the result of a comparison between two or more values. You use these expressions in if statements as well as in looping statements.

How to use the relational operators

Figure 3-1 shows you how to code conditional expressions that use the six *relational operators*. To start, the table summarizes the six relational operators. Then, the examples of conditional expressions show how these operators work.

In the first expression, for example, if the value of lastName is equal to "Hopper", the expression will return true. Otherwise, it will return false. Similarly, in the second expression, if the value of the testScore variable is equal to 10, the expression returns true. Otherwise, it returns false.

The rest of the examples are similar, although they use the other operators. They also show that you can compare a variable with a literal or a variable with another variable. The last example shows that you can compare an arithmetic expression to a variable or another arithmetic expression.

In addition to using the relational operators to code a conditional expression, you can use the global isNaN() method. This method determines whether a string value is a valid numeric value, as illustrated by the next set of examples. To use this method, you pass a parameter that represents the string value that should be tested. Then, this method returns true if the value can't be converted to a number or false if it can be converted.

When you use the equal to operator, you need to remember to use two equals signs, not one. That's because the one equals sign is the assignment operator, not the equal to operator. This is a common mistake when you're learning to program, and it causes a syntax error.

The relational operators

Operator	Name	Description
==	Equal to	Returns true if both operands are equal.
!=	Not equal to	Returns true if the operands are not equal.
>	Greater than	Returns true if the left operand is greater than the right operand.
<	Less than	Returns true if the left operand is less than the right operand.
>=	Greater than or equal to	Returns true if the left operand is greater than or equal to the right operand.
<=	Less than or equal to	Returns true if the left operand is less than or equal to the right operand.

Conditional expressions

```
lastName == "Hopper"
testScore == 10

firstName != "Grace"
months != 0

testScore > 100
age < 18

distance >= limit
stock <= reorder_point

rate / 100 >= 0.1
```

The syntax of the global isNaN() method

```
isNaN(expression)
```

Examples of the isNaN() method

```
isNaN("Hopper") // Returns true since "Hopper" is not a number
isNaN("123.45") // Returns false since "123.45" can be converted to a number
```

Description

- A *conditional expression* uses the *relational operators* to compare the results of two expressions and return a Boolean value.
- Because floating-point numbers aren't stored as exact values, you shouldn't use the equal to (==) or not equal to (!=) operators to compare them.
- The isNaN() method tests whether a string can be converted to a number. It returns true if the string is not a number and false if the string is a number.

Note

- Confusing the assignment operator (=) with the equality operator (==) is a common programming error.

Figure 3-1   How to use the relational operators

How to use the logical operators

To code a *compound conditional expression*, you use the *logical operators* shown in figure 3-2 to combine two conditional expressions. If you use the AND operator (`&&`), the compound expression returns true if both expressions are true. If you use the OR operator (`||`), the compound expression returns true if either expression is true. If you use the NOT operator (`!`), the value returned by the expression is reversed. For instance, !isNaN() returns true if the parameter is a number, so isNaN(10) returns false, but !isNaN(10) returns true.

The examples in this figure show how these operators work. For instance, the first example uses the AND operator to combine two conditional expressions. As a result, it evaluates to true if the expression on its left *and* the expression on its right are both true. Similarly, the second example uses the OR operator to combine two conditional expressions. As a result, it evaluates to true if either the expression on its left *or* the expression on its right is true.

When you use the AND and OR operators, JavaScript evaluates the expressions from left to right, and the second expression is evaluated only if necessary. That's why these operators are known as *short-circuit operators*. If, for example, the first expression in an AND operation is false, the second expression isn't evaluated because the entire expression is going to be false. Similarly, if the first expression in an OR operation is true, the second expression isn't evaluated because the entire expression is going to be true.

The third example in this figure shows how to use the NOT operator to reverse the value of an expression. As a result, this expression evaluates to true if the age variable *is* equal to a number. In this case, using the NOT operator is okay, but often the NOT operator results in code that's difficult to read. In that case, it's a good practice to rewrite your code so it doesn't use the NOT operator.

This figure also shows the order of precedence for the logical operators. That is the order in which the operators are evaluated if more than one logical operator is used in a compound expression. This means that NOT operators are evaluated before AND operators, which are evaluated before OR operators. Although this is normally what you want, you can override this order by using parentheses.

In most cases, the conditional expressions that you use are relatively simple so coding them isn't much of a problem. In the rest of this chapter and book, you'll see some of the types of conditional expressions that are commonly used.

The logical operators

Operator	Name	Description
&&	AND	Returns a true value if both expressions are true. This operator only evaluates the second expression if necessary.
||	OR	Returns a true value if either expression is true. This operator only evaluates the second expression if necessary.
!	NOT	Reverses the value of the Boolean expression.

Conditional expressions that use logical operators

Example 1: The AND operator
```
age > 17 && score < 70
```

Example 2: The OR operator
```
isNaN(rate) || rate < 0
```

Example 3: The NOT operator
```
!isNaN(age)
```

The order of precedence for the logical operators

1. NOT operator
2. AND operator
3. OR operator

Description

- A *compound conditional expression* joins two or more conditional expressions using the *logical operators*.

- If logical operators are used to join two or more conditional expressions, the sequence in which the operations are performed is determined by the *order of precedence* of the operators. To clarify or change the order of precedence, you can use parentheses.

- The AND and OR operators only evaluate the second expression if necessary. As a result, they are known as *short-circuit operators*.

Figure 3-2   How to use the logical operators

How to code the basic control statements

Like all programming languages, JavaScript provides *control statements* that let you control how information is processed in an application. These statements include if statements as well as looping statements.

How to code if statements

If you've programmed in other languages, you won't have any trouble using JavaScript if statements. Just study figure 3-3 to get the syntax and see how the conditions are coded. But if you're new to programming, let's take it slower.

An *if statement* lets you control the execution of statements based on the results of conditional expressions. In a syntax summary like the one in this figure, the brackets [ ] indicate a portion of the syntax that is optional. As a result, this summary means that each if statement must start with an *if clause*. Then, it can have one or more *else if clauses*, but they are optional. Last, it can have an *else clause*, but that clause is also optional.

To code the if clause, you code the keyword *if* followed by a conditional expression in parentheses and a block of one or more statements inside braces. If the conditional expression is true, this block of code will be executed and any remaining clauses in the if statement will be skipped over. If the conditional expression is false, the clause that follows will be executed.

To code an else if clause, you code the keywords *else if* followed by a conditional expression in parentheses and a block of one or more statements inside braces. If the conditional expression is true, its block of code will be executed and any remaining clauses in the if statement will be skipped over. This will continue until one of the else if expressions is true or they all are false.

To code an else clause, you code the keyword *else* followed by a block of one or more statements inside braces. This code will only be executed if all the conditional expressions in the if and else if clauses are false. If those expressions are false and there isn't an else clause, the if statement won't execute any code.

The first example in this figure shows an if statement with an else clause. Here, if the value of the age variable is greater than or equal to 18, the first message will be displayed. Otherwise, the second message will be displayed.

The second example shows an if statement with two else if clauses and an else clause. Here, if the rate is not a number, the first message is displayed. If the rate is less than zero, the second message is displayed. If the rate is greater than 12, the third message is displayed. Otherwise, the message in the else clause is displayed.

The third example shows an if statement with a compound conditional expression that tests whether the value of the userEntry variable is not a number or whether the value is less than or equal to zero. If either expression is true, a message is displayed. If both expressions are false, nothing is done because this if statement doesn't have else if clauses or an else clause.

The syntax of the if statement

```
if ( condition-1 ) { statements }
[ else if ( condition-2 ) { statements }
  ...
  else if ( condition-n ) { statements } ]
[ else { statements } ]
```

An if statement with an else clause

```
if ( age >= 18 ) {
    alert ("You may vote.");
} else {
    alert ("You are not old enough to vote.");
}
```

An if statement with else if and else clauses

```
if ( isNaN(rate) ) {
    alert ("You did not provide a number for the rate.");
} else if ( rate < 0 ) {
    alert ("The rate may not be less than zero.");
} else if ( rate > 12 ) {
    alert ("The rate may not be greater than 12.");
} else {
    alert ("The rate is: " + rate + ".");
}
```

An if statement with a compound conditional expression

```
if ( isNaN(userEntry) || userEntry <= 0 ) {
    alert ("Please enter a valid number greater than zero.");
}
```

Two ways to test whether a Boolean variable is true

```
if ( isValid == true ) { }
if ( isValid ) { }                  // same as isValid == true
```

Three ways to test whether a Boolean variable is false

```
if ( isValid == false ) { }
if ( !isValid == true ) { }
if ( !isValid ) { }                 // same as !isValid == true
```

Description

- An *if statement* always has one *if clause*. It can also have one or more *else if clauses* and one *else clause* at the end.

- The statements in a clause are executed when its condition is true. Otherwise, control passes to the next clause. If none of the conditions in the preceding clauses are true, the statements in the else clause are executed.

- If necessary, you can code one if statement within the if, else if, or else clause of another if statement. This is referred to as *nesting if statements*.

Figure 3-3   How to code if statements

The fourth set of examples in figure 3-3 shows two ways to test whether a Boolean variable is true. Here, both statements are evaluated the same way. That's because a condition that is coded as just a Boolean variable is tested to see whether the variable is equal to true. In practice, this condition is usually coded the way it is in the second statement, with just the name of the variable.

The fifth set of examples is similar. It shows three ways to test whether a Boolean variable is false. Here again, the last statement illustrates the way this condition is usually coded: !isValid.

How to code while and do-while loops

Figure 3-4 starts by presenting the syntax of the *while statement* that is used to create *while loops*. This statement executes the block of code that's in the loop while its conditional expression is true.

The example that follows this syntax shows how a while loop can be used to add the numbers 1 through 5. Before the while statement starts, a variable named sumOfNumbers is set to zero, a variable named numberOfLoops is set to 5, and a variable named counter is set to 1. Then, the condition for the while statement says that the while loop should be repeated as long as the counter value is less than or equal to the numberOfLoops value.

Within the while loop, the first statement adds the counter value to the sumOfNumbers variable. Then, the counter is increased by 1. As a result, this loop is executed five times, one time each for the counter values 1, 2, 3, 4, and 5. The loop ends when the counter is no longer less than or equal to 5, which is when the counter value equals 6.

This example is followed by the syntax for the *do-while statement* that is used to create *do-while loops*. This is like the while statement, but its condition is tested at the end of the loop instead of at the start. As a result, the statements in the loop are always executed at least once. This statement is illustrated by the example that follows the syntax, which gets the same result as the while statement.

In general, you use the do-while statement when you want to execute the statements in the loop at least once, and you use the while statement for other types of loops. Coded correctly, though, you can get the same results with both statements.

The last example in this figure shows another use of a do-while loop. This loop keeps going while the user's entry isn't a number (isNaN()). Within the loop, a prompt statement gets the user's entry, the entry is parsed, and an if statement displays an error message if the entry isn't a number. This loop continues until the user enters a number.

If the condition for a while statement doesn't ever become false, the loop continues indefinitely. This is called an *infinite loop*. When you first start programming, it's common to code an infinite loop by mistake. If you do that, you can end the loop by closing the tab or browser for the application.

The syntax of a while loop

```
while ( condition ) { statements }
```

A while loop that adds the numbers from 1 through 5

```
var sumOfNumbers = 0;
var numberOfLoops = 5;
var counter = 1;
while (counter <= numberOfLoops) {
    sumOfNumbers += counter;    // adds counter to sumOfNumbers
    counter++;                  // adds 1 to counter
}
alert(sumOfNumbers);           // displays 15
```

The syntax of a do-while loop

```
do { statements } while ( condition );
```

A do-while loop that adds the numbers from 1 through 5

```
var sumOfNumbers = 0;
var numberOfLoops = 5;
var counter = 1;
do {
    sumOfNumbers += counter;    // adds counter to sumOfNumbers
    counter++;                  // adds 1 to counter
}
while (counter <= numberOfLoops);
alert(sumOfNumbers);           // displays 15
```

A do-while loop that gets a user entry until it is a number

```
do {
    var investment = prompt("Enter investment amount as xxxxx.xx", 10000);
    investment = parseFloat(investment);
    if ( isNaN(investment) ) {
        alert("Investment must be a number");
    }
}
while ( isNaN(investment) );
```

Description

- The *while statement* creates a *while loop* that contains a block of code that is executed while its condition is true. This condition is tested at the beginning of the loop, and the loop is skipped if the condition is false.

- The *do-while statement* creates a *do-while* loop that contains a block of code that is executed while its condition is true. However, its condition is tested at the end of the loop instead of the beginning, so the code in the loop will always be executed at least once.

- If the condition for a while or do-while loop never evaluates to false, the loop never ends. This is known as an *infinite loop*. You can end an infinite loop by closing the tab or browser window.

Figure 3-4   How to code while and do-while loops

How to code for loops

Figure 3-5 shows how to use the *for statement* to create *for loops*. Within the parentheses of a for statement, you initialize a *counter* (or *index*) variable that will be used within the loop. Then, you code a condition that determines when the loop will end. Last, you code an expression that specifies how the counter should be incremented.

The first example in this figure shows how this works. Here, the first statement in the parentheses of the for statement declares a variable named counter and initializes it to 1. Then, the condition in the parentheses determines that the loop will continue as long as counter is less than or equal to the value in numberOfLoops, and the expression that follows increments the counter by 1 each time through the loop. Within the loop, the value of the counter variable is added to the variable named sumOfNumbers.

If you compare this example to the first two examples in figure 3-4, you can see that all three get the same results. But with the for statement, you don't have to initialize the counter before the statement, and you don't have to increment the counter within the statement.

The next example shows a more realistic use of a for loop. This loop calculates the future value of an investment amount ($10,000) at a specific interest rate (7.0%) for a specific number of years (10). This time, *i* is used as the name for the counter variable, which is a common coding practice, and the loop continues as long as this index is less than or equal to the number of years. In other words, the statement in the loop is executed once for each of the 10 years.

Within the loop, this expression is used to calculate the interest for the year:

```
futureValue * annualRate / 100
```

Then, the += operator adds the interest to the futureValue variable. Note here that the annualRate needs to be divided by 100 for this calculation to work right (7.0 / 100 = .07). Note too in the statements after this example, that this statement could be coded in more than one way and still get the same results.

In both of the examples in this figure, the counter is incremented by 1 each time through the loop, which is usually the way this statement is coded. However, you can also increment or decrement the counter by other amounts. That just depends on what you're trying to do. To increment by 2, for example, you could code the increment expression as:

```
i = i + 2
```

The syntax of a for statement

```
for ( counterInitialization; condition; incrementExpression ) {
    statements
}
```

A for loop that adds the numbers from 1 through 5

```
var sumOfNumbers = 0;
var numberOfLoops = 5;
for ( var counter = 1; counter <= numberOfLoops; counter++ ) {
    sumOfNumbers += counter;      // adds counter to sumOfNumbers
}
alert(sumOfNumbers);                  // displays 15
```

A for loop that calculates the future value of an investment

```
var investment = 10000;
var annualRate = 7.0;
var years = 10;
var futureValue = investment;
for ( var i = 1; i <= years; i++ ) {
    futureValue += futureValue * annualRate / 100;
}
alert (futureValue);                  // displays 19672
```

Other ways that the future value calculation could be coded

```
futureValue = futureValue + (futureValue * annualRate / 100);

futureValue = futureValue * (1 + (annualRate / 100))
```

Description

- The *for statement* is used when you need to increment or decrement a counter that determines how many times the *for loop* is executed.

- Within the parentheses of a for statement, you code an expression that initializes a *counter* (or *index*) variable, a conditional expression that determines when the loop ends, and an increment expression that indicates how the counter should be incremented or decremented each time through the loop.

- The variable name *i* is commonly used for the counter in a for loop.

Figure 3-5   How to code for loops

Three illustrative applications

The three applications that follow illustrate the use of the control statements that you just learned about. These still aren't realistic applications because they get the user entries from prompt statements instead of from controls on a form. But these applications should give you a better understanding of how the control statements work.

The enhanced Miles Per Gallon application

Figure 3-6 presents an enhanced version of the Miles Per Gallon application that you reviewed in chapter 2. This application just gets user entries for miles driven and gallons of gas used and then displays the miles per gallon in an alert dialog box.

This time, though, this application lets the user do the calculation for more than one set of entries. It also checks the entries to make sure that both are valid, and displays an error message if one or both aren't valid.

In the JavaScript, you can see how a do-while loop is used to let the user repeat the calculation. Before entering this loop, a variable named "again" is set to a value of "y". Then, the do-while loop is repeated until that value is changed by the user. The user can do that when the last statement in the loop displays the second prompt dialog box shown in this figure.

Within the do-while loop, you can see how an if-else statement is used to provide the data validation. Here, the condition for the if clause uses the AND (**&&**) operator to check whether the value entered for miles is a number (!isNaN()) and greater than zero and also whether the value entered for gallons is a number and greater than zero. If all four conditions are true, the application calculates miles per gallon and displays the result in an alert dialog box. If any one of the conditions isn't true, the application displays an error message in an alert dialog box.

In other words, this if-else statement tests to see whether both entries are valid. If so, it does the calculation and displays the result. If not, it displays an error message. Note, however, that you could reverse this by testing to see whether one of the entries is invalid by using OR (||) operators. If so, you display the error message. If not, you do the calculation and display the result. This can simplify the coding because you don't have to use the NOT operator with the isNaN() method (!isNaN()).

Two of the dialog boxes for the Miles Per Gallon application

The alert dialog box that displays an invalid data message

The prompt dialog box for continuing the application

The HTML and JavaScript for the application

```html
<head>
    <title>Calculate Miles Per Gallon</title>
    <script>
        var again = "y";
        do {
            var miles = prompt("Enter miles driven");
            miles = parseFloat(miles);
            var gallons = prompt("Enter gallons of gas used");
            gallons = parseFloat(gallons);
            if (!isNaN(miles) && miles > 0
                    && !isNaN(gallons) && gallons > 0)
            {
                var mpg = miles / gallons;
                mpg = parseInt(mpg);
                alert("Miles per gallon = " + mpg);
            }
            else
            {
                alert("One or both entries are invalid");
            }
            again = prompt("Repeat entries?", "y");
        }
        while (again == "y");
    </script>
</head>
<body>
    <main>
        <!-- Will show after JavaScript has run -->
        Thanks for using the Miles Per Gallon application!
    </main>
</body>
```

Figure 3-6   The enhanced Miles Per Gallon application

The Future Value application

Figure 3-7 presents a Future Value application that shows how a for loop can be used to calculate the future value of an investment amount. If you study the code for this application, you can see that prompt statements are used to get the investment amount, interest rate, and number of years. Note, however, that these entries aren't validated. You'll get a chance to add this data validation code in one of the exercises at the end of this chapter.

Next, a for loop uses these entries to calculate the future value of the investment. To do that, it uses i as the name of the index and increments it by 1 each time through the loop. It does that as long as the index is less than or equal to the number of years entered by the user. This means that the loop will be run once for each year. If, for example, the user enters 10 for the number of years, the loop will be run 10 times.

Within the loop, the future value is calculated. To do that, the expression in the parentheses calculates the interest for the year. Then, the interest is added to the current value of the futureValue variable, and the result is stored in the futureValue variable. As figure 3-5 shows, this calculation could also be coded in other ways.

After the for loop finishes, this application parses the future value to an integer so the decimal places will be dropped. Then, the JavaScript in the body of the HTML document displays the results in the browser.

The first of three prompt dialog boxes for the Future Value application

The results in a browser

Investment amount = 10000 Interest rate = 7.5 Years = 10 Future Value is 20610

Thanks for using the Future Value application.

The HTML and JavaScript for the application

```html
<head>
    <meta charset="UTF-8">
    <title>Future Value Application</title>
    <script>
        var futureValue;

        // get user entries
        var investment =
            prompt("Enter investment amount as xxxxx.xx", 10000);
        investment = parseFloat(investment);
        var rate = prompt("Enter interest rate as xx.x", 7.5);
        rate = parseFloat(rate);
        var years = prompt("Enter number of years", 10);
        years = parseInt(years);

        // calulate future value
        futureValue = investment;
        for (var i = 1; i <= years; i++ ) {
            futureValue = futureValue + (futureValue * rate / 100);
        }
        futureValue = parseInt(futureValue);
    </script>
</head>
<body>
    <main>
        <script>
            document.write("Investment amount = " + investment);
            document.write(" Interest rate = " + rate);
            document.write(" Years = " + years);
            document.write(" Future Value is " + futureValue + "<br><br>");
        </script>
        Thanks for using the Future Value application.
    </main>
</body>
```

Figure 3-7   The Future Value application

The enhanced Test Scores application

Figure 3-8 presents an enhanced version of the Test Scores application that you reviewed in chapter 2. This time, the application uses a do-while loop to let the users enter as many scores as they want. Then, when a user enters 999 to end the entries, the application displays the average test score.

This version of the application also tests to make sure that each entry is a valid number from 0 through 100 before it is added to the test score total. If an entry isn't valid, the application displays an error message and issues another prompt statement so the user can either enter another score or 999 to end the entries.

If you look at the JavaScript in the script element of the head section of the HTML, you can see that it starts by declaring the three variables that are needed. The total variable has a starting value of zero, and it will be used to sum the valid test scores. The entryCount variable has a starting value of 0, and it will be used to count the number of valid test scores. The third variable is named entry, and it doesn't have a starting value assigned to it because it will be used to receive the user entries.

After the variables are declared, a do-while loop is used to get the user entries. Because this application has to get at least one user entry, it makes sense to use a do-while loop instead of a while loop.

Within the do-while loop, the prompt method is used to get each user entry. Note that the second parameter is set to 999 so the user can just press the Enter key to end the entries.

After a user makes an entry, the entry is parsed into an integer and an if clause checks to make sure the entry is between 0 and 100. If it is, the entry is valid so the entry value is added to the total variable and 1 is added to the entryCount variable.

If the entry isn't between 0 and 100, the else if clause that follows checks to see whether the entry is not equal to 999. If it isn't, an alert method displays an error message and the entry isn't processed. If the entry is 999, nothing is done.

When the statements in the loop are finished, the condition for the loop is tested. Then, if the entry value is 999, the loop ends. Otherwise, the loop is repeated for the next entry.

When the loop ends, the average test score is calculated by dividing the total variable by the entryCount variable. Then, the parseInt method is used to convert the decimal value to an integer, and an alert statement displays the average score.

The dialog boxes for the Test Scores application

The prompt dialog box for the next test score

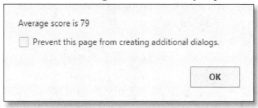

Enter test score
Or enter 999 to end entries

| 999 |

OK   Cancel

The alert dialog box for an entry error

Entry must by a valid number from 0 through 100
Or enter 999 to end entries

☐ Prevent this page from creating additional dialogs.

OK

The alert dialog box that displays the result

Average score is 79

☐ Prevent this page from creating additional dialogs.

OK

The JavaScript in the head section of the HTML file

```
<script>
    var total = 0;
    var entryCount = 0;
    var entry;
    do {
        entry = prompt("Enter test score\n" +
                       "Or enter 999 to end entries", 999);
        entry = parseInt(entry);
        if (entry >= 0 && entry <= 100) {
            total = total + entry;
            entryCount++;
        }
        else if (entry != 999){
            alert("Entry must be a valid number from 0 through 100\n" +
                  "Or enter 999 to end entries");
        }
    }
    while (entry != 999);
    var average = total / entryCount;
    average = parseInt(average);
    alert("Average score is " + average);
</script>
```

Figure 3-8   The enhanced Test Scores application

How to work with arrays

The next two figures present the basic skills for working with arrays. As you will see, arrays are commonly used in JavaScript applications.

How to create and use arrays

An *array* is an object that contains one or more items called *elements*. Each of these elements can be a primitive data type or an object. The *length* of an array indicates the number of elements that it contains.

Figure 3-9 shows two ways to create an array. When you use the first method, you use the *new* keyword followed by the Array object name to create an array with the number of elements that is indicated by the length parameter. This length must be a whole number that is greater than or equal to zero. If you don't specify the length, the array will be empty.

When you use the second method, you just code a set of brackets. This gives you the same result that you get with the first method and no parameter, an empty array.

To refer to the elements in an array, you use an *index* that ranges from zero to one less than the number of elements in an array. In an array with 12 elements, for example, the index values range from 0 to 11.

To use an index, you code it within brackets after the name of the array. In this figure, all of the examples use literal values for the indexes, but an index can also be a variable that contains an index value, as you'll see shortly. If you try to access an element that hasn't been assigned a value, the value of undefined will be returned.

The last two examples in this figure show how to work with the array's length property. The length property returns the number of elements in an array. In the first example, the length property is stored in a variable for later use.

In the second example, the length property is used as the index of a new element. Since this property will always be 1 more than the highest index used in the array, this adds the new element at the end of the array.

The syntax for creating an array

Using the new keyword with the Array object name

```
var arrayName = new Array(length);
```

Using an array literal

```
var arrayName = [];
```

The syntax for referring to an element of an array

```
arrayName[index]
```

The syntax for getting the length property of an array

```
arrayName.length
```

How to add values to an array

```
var totals = [];
totals[0] = 141.95;
totals[1] = 212.25;
totals[2] = 411;
```

How to refer to the elements in an array

```
totals[2]          // refers to the third element - 411
totals[1]          // refers to the second element - 212.25
```

How to determine how many elements are in an array

```
var count = totals.length;          // 3
```

How to add a value to the end of an array

```
totals[totals.length] = 135.75;     // adds a fourth element at index = 3
```

Description

- An *array* can store one or more *elements*. The *length* of an array is the number of elements in the array.

- One way to create an array is to use the new keyword, the name of the object (Array), and an optional length parameter.

- The other way to create an array is to code a set of brackets.

- To refer to the elements in an array, you use an *index* where 0 is the first element, 1 is the second element, and so on.

- One way to add an element to the end of an array is to use the length property as the index.

Figure 3-9   How to create and use arrays

How to use for loops to work with arrays

For loops are commonly used to process one array element at a time by incrementing an index variable. Figure 3-10 shows how this works.

The first example in this figure shows how to create an array and fill it with the numbers 1 through 10. First, this code creates an empty array named numbers. Then, it uses a for loop to add the numbers 1 through 10 to the array. In the body of this loop, one is added to the value in i and the result is stored in the array element. As a result, the element at index 0 stores a 1, the element at index 1 stores a 2, and so on.

Next, this example displays the values in the array. First, this code creates an empty string named numbersString. Then, it uses a for loop to access the elements in the array. In the for loop, the length property of the array is used to control how many times the loop executes. This allows the same code to work with arrays of different lengths. Inside the for loop, the value in the element and a space are concatenated to the end of numbersString. Finally, numbersString is displayed, which shows the ten numbers that were stored in the array.

The next example in this figure shows how to use for loops to add the totals in an array and to display those totals. First, the code puts four values into an array named totals. Then, a for loop adds the four totals in the array to a variable named sum. Last, a for loop concatenates the four totals in the array to a string variable that is displayed when the loop ends.

Code that puts the numbers 1 through 10 into an array

```
var numbers = [];
for (var i = 0; i < 10; i++) {
    numbers[i] = i + 1;
}
```

Code that displays the numbers in the array

```
var numbersString = "";
for (var i = 0; i < numbers.length; i++) {
    numbersString += numbers[i] + " ";
}
alert (numbersString);
```

The message that's displayed

Code that puts four totals in an array

```
var totals = [];
totals[0] = 141.95;
totals[1] = 212.25;
totals[2] = 411;
totals[3] = 135.75;
```

Code that sums the totals in the array

```
var sum = 0;
for (var i = 0; i < totals.length; i++) {
    sum += totals[i];
}
```

Code that displays the totals and the sum

```
var totalsString = "";
for (var i = 0; i < totals.length; i++) {
    totalsString += totals[i] + "\n";
}
alert ("The totals are:\n" + totalsString + "\n" + "Sum: " + sum);
```

The message that's displayed

```
The totals are:
141.95
212.25
411
135.75

Sum: 900.95

                    [ OK ]
```

Description

- When you use a for loop to work with an array, you can use the counter for the loop as the index for the array.

Figure 3-10   How to use for loops to work with arrays

The Test Scores application
with an array

Figure 3-11 presents an enhanced version of the Test Scores application that stores the valid entries in an array. This will give you a better idea of how arrays and for loops can be used.

The user interface

The user interface for this application works the same as the one in figure 3-8. It lets the users enter as many test scores as they want. Then, when a user enters 999 to end the series of entries, the application displays the average score.

The JavaScript

If you look at the JavaScript for this application, you can see that it starts by declaring the variables that are needed to get and process the entries. Here, entry and average variables are declared but not assigned values. The scores variable is declared as an empty array. The total variable is given a starting value of zero. And the show variable is given a starting value of a string that ends with a new line escape sequence. This variable will be used to build the alert message that displays the results at the end of the application.

After the variables are declared, a do-while loop is used to get the user entries. This is like the do-while loop in figure 3-8. The only difference is that the highlighted statement adds each valid entry to the scores array. It doesn't add each value to the total variable.

When the do-while loop ends, an if statement is used to check that the array contains at least one element. If it does, processing continues. If it doesn't, it means that the user entered 999 for the first entry and processing ends.

If the array contains one or more elements, a for loop processes the scores in the array. This loop uses the length property of the scores array to determine how many times to execute the loop, and the loop's index variable (i) is used to retrieve the elements from the scores array. Each time through the loop, the array element is added to the total variable and concatenated to the show variable.

When the for loop ends, the average test score is calculated and stored in the variable named average. This calculation simply divides the total variable by the length of the scores array, which is the number of scores in the array. This calculation is embedded within the parseInt method to convert the result to an integer. Last, an alert method displays the concatenated values of the show variable and the average variable.

The alert dialog box that displays the result

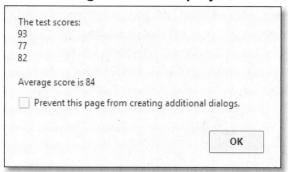

The JavaScript for the enhanced Test Scores application

```
<script>
    var entry;
    var average;
    var scores = [];
    var total = 0;
    var show = "The test scores:\n";

    // use a do-while loop to put the scores in an array
    do {
        entry = prompt("Enter test score\n" +
                        "Or enter 999 to end entries", 999);
        entry = parseInt(entry);
        if (entry >= 0 && entry <= 100) {
            scores[scores.length] = entry;
        }
        else if (entry != 999){
            alert("Entry must by a valid number from 0 through 100\n" +
                "Or enter 999 to end entries");
        }
    }
    while (entry != 999);

    if (scores.length != 0) {
        // use a for loop to process the scores
        for (var i = 0; i < scores.length; i++) {
            total = total + scores[i];      // both are numbers so adds
            show = show + scores[i] + "\n";  // strings & number
                                            // so concatenates
        }

        // calculate the average and display
        average = parseInt(total/scores.length);
        alert(show + "\nAverage score is " + average);
    }
</script>
```

Figure 3-11   The Test Scores application with an array

Perspective

If you have programming experience, you can now see that the JavaScript control statements are similar to those in other languages like Java and C#. As a result, you probably skimmed your way through this chapter. You may also want to skip the exercises.

On the other hand, if you're new to programming and you understand all of the code in the applications in this chapter, you're off to a good start. Otherwise, you need to study the applications until you understand every line of code in each application. You should also do the exercises that follow.

Terms

control statement	while statement
conditional expression	while loop
relational operator	do-while statement
compound conditional expression	do-while loop
logical operator	infinite loop
order of precedence	for statement
short-circuit operator	for loop
if statement	loop counter
if clause	loop index
else if clause	array
else clause	array element
nested if statements	array length

Summary

- When you code a *conditional expression*, you can use *relational operators*, the global isNaN() method, and *logical operators*.

- An *if statement* always starts with an *if clause*. It can also have one or more *else if clauses* and a concluding *else clause*, but those clauses are optional.

- The *while* and *do-while* statements can be used to loop through a series of statements while a condition is true.

- The *for statement* can be used to loop through a series of statements once for each time a *counter* or *index* is incremented or decremented.

- An *array* can store one or more *elements* that you can refer to by the *indexes* of the elements. The *length* property of the array holds the number of elements in the array. To process the elements in an array, you can use a for loop.

Exercise 3-1   Enhance the Future Value application

This exercise will give you a chance to use if statements, do loops, and for loops as you enhance the Future Value application in figure 3-6. The eventual output of this application will be displayed in the browser and should look something like this:

```
Investment amount = 10000 Interest rate = 7.5 Years = 5
Year=1 Interest=750 Value=10750
Year=2 Interest=806.25 Value=11556
Year=3 Interest=866.71875 Value=12422
Year=4 Interest=931.72265625 Value=13354
Year=5 Interest=1001.60185546875 Value=14356

Investment amount = 10000 Interest rate = 8.5 Years = 6
Year=1 Interest=850 Value=10850
Year=2 Interest=922.25 Value=11772
Year=3 Interest=1000.64125 Value=12772
Year=4 Interest=1085.69575625 Value=13858
Year=5 Interest=1177.97989553125 Value=15036
Year=6 Interest=1278.1081866514062 Value=16314

Thanks for using the Future Value application.
```

If you have any problems when you're testing, remember to use Chrome's developer tools as shown in figure 1-16 of chapter 1.

Test the Future Value application

1. Open your text editor or IDE. Then, open this HTML file:

    `javascript_jquery\exercises\ch03\future_value.html`

2. Test the application with valid entries, and note the result. Then, test it with invalid entries, and note the result.

Add a do-while statement for continuing the entries

3. Add a do-while statement to the application like the one in figure 3-6 so the user can repeat the calculation for another series of entries.

Add validation for the investment and rate entries

4. Add a do-while statement like the one in the third example of figure 3-4 so the user will have to enter a valid investment amount before the application will continue with the next entry.

5. Add a similar do-while statement for the interest rate entry. This time, the application shouldn't continue until the user enters a value that's greater than zero and less than 15.

Enhance the display of the results as shown above

6. Modify the for loop that calculates the future value so it displays the interest rate and future value for each year, as shown above. Note that you'll also have to change the location of the existing write() methods to get the display the way it is above.

Exercise 3-2   Enhance the Test Scores application

In this exercise, you'll make an enhancement to the Test Scores application in figure 3-11 that uses an array. What you'll do is add a for loop that gets the highest score in the array and displays it below the average score in the alert dialog box:

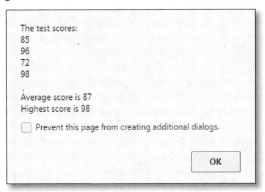

If you have any problems when you're testing, remember to use Chrome's developer tools as shown in figure 1-16 of chapter 1.

1. Open your text editor or IDE. Then, open this HTML file and review its code:
    `javascript_jquery\exercises\ch03\scores_array.html`

2. Test the application with valid entries, and note the result. Then, test it with invalid entries, and note the result.

3. Declare a variable named highestScore at the start of the script that will be used to store the highest score. Its starting value should be zero.

4. Add a second for loop right before the alert statement at the end of the script. This for loop should be executed once for each score in the array. Within the loop, an if statement should replace the value in the highestScore variable with the current score if that score is greater than the value in highestScore. That way, the highestScore variable will eventually store the highest score in the array.

5. Modify the alert statement that follows the for loop so it displays both the average score and highest score as shown above.

6. When you've got that working, comment out the second for loop. Then, modify the first for loop so it not only sums the scores but also puts the highest score in the highestScore variable. After this change, the application should work the same as it did after step 5.

4

How to work with JavaScript objects, functions, and events

In the last two chapters, you learned how to code some simple, but unrealistic, applications using the prompt() and alert() methods. Now, in this chapter, you'll learn how to work with objects, functions, and events. When you finish this chapter, you'll be able to start developing useful applications of your own.

How to use objects to work with data

In chapter 2, you learned the syntax for using the methods and properties of objects. You were also introduced to some of the methods and properties of the window object and document objects. Now, you'll learn how to use the objects, methods, and properties that you need for working with data, starting with a partial review of the methods of the window and document objects.

How to use the window and document objects

In chapter 2, you were introduced to the prompt() and alert() methods of the *window object*. Now, the first table in figure 4-1 presents another method of the window object that can be used to confirm an action.

Then, the second table in this figure summarizes the parseInt() and parseFloat() methods that you learned about in chapter 2. They are also methods of the window object. These methods are needed because the values that are returned by the prompt() method and the values that the user enters into text boxes are treated as strings.

The use of these methods is illustrated by the first group of examples, starting with an example of the confirm() method. For the statements after that, assume that the default values in the prompt() methods aren't changed by the user. As a result, the second statement in this group stores 12345.6789 as a string in a variable named entryA, and the third statement converts the string to an integer value of 12345. Similarly, the fourth statement stores 12345.6789 as a string in a variable named entryB, and the fifth statement converts the string to a decimal value of 12345.6789.

Note that the object name isn't coded before the method name in these examples. That's okay because window is the *global object* of JavaScript. Note too that the parseInt() method doesn't round the value. It just removes, or truncates, any decimal portion of the string.

In contrast to the window object, the *document object* is the highest object in the DOM structure. It represents the document, and you do need to code the object name (document) and the dot when you use one of its methods.

The second group of examples in this figure shows how to use three of the methods of the document object. The first is the getElementById() method. It requires one parameter, which is the id for an element in the HTML document. When it is executed, it returns an object that represents that HTML element. In this example, this object is stored in a variable named rateBox.

The other two methods in this group are the write() and writeln() methods that you learned how to use in figure 2-12 of chapter 2. You saw how these methods work in some of the applications in the last two chapters.

Another method of the window object that displays a dialog box

Method	Description
confirm(*string*)	Displays a dialog box that contains the string in the parameter, an OK button, and a Cancel button. If the user clicks OK, true is returned. If the user clicks Cancel, false is returned.

Two methods of the window object for working with numbers

Method	Description
parseInt(*string*)	Converts the string that's passed to it to an integer data type and returns that value. If it can't convert the string to an integer, it returns NaN.
parseFloat(*string*)	Converts the string that's passed to it to a decimal data type and returns that value. If it can't convert the string to a decimal value, it returns NaN.

Examples of window methods

```
confirm("Are you sure you want to delete it?");

var entryA = prompt("Enter any value", 12345.6789);
entryA = parseInt(entryA);                        // entryA = 12345

var entryB = prompt("Enter any value", 12345.6789);
entryB = parseFloat(entryB);                      // entryB = 12345.6789
```

Three methods of the document object

Method	Description
getElementById(*id*)	Gets the HTML element that has the id that's passed to it and returns that element.
write(*string*)	Writes the string that's passed to it into the document.
writeln(*string*)	Writes the string ending with a new line character.

Examples of document methods

```
// returns the object for the HTML element
var rateBox = document.getElementById("rate");

// writes a line into the document
document.write("Today is " + today.toDateString());
```

Description

- The *window object* is the *global object*, and JavaScript lets you omit the object name and dot operator when referring to the window object.

- The *document object* is the object that lets you work with the Document Object Model (DOM) that represents all of the HTML elements of the page.

- Data in a text box is treated as a string. Before you can use it in a calculation, you need to use either the parseInt() or parseFloat() method to convert it to numeric data.

- *NaN* is a value that means "Not a Number". It is returned by the parseInt() and parseFloat() methods when the value that's being parsed isn't a number.

- The getElementById() method is commonly used to get the object for an HTML element.

Figure 4-1   How to use the window and document objects

How to use Textbox and Number objects

The Textbox object is one of the DOM objects. It represents a text box in the web page that is used to get input from the user or display output to the user. The first two tables in figure 4-2 summarize one of its methods and two of its properties. Then, this figure shows the HTML code for two text boxes that have "first_name" and "sales_amount" as their ids. These text boxes will be used by the examples that follow.

The first group of examples in this figure shows two ways to get the value from the text box with "first_name" as its id. To do that with two statements, the first statement uses the getElementById() method of the document object to get the Textbox object for that text box. Then, the second statement uses the value property of the Textbox object to get the value that the user entered into the text box.

In practice, though, you would do that with just one statement by using *method chaining*, or just *chaining*. In that case, a single statement first uses the getElementById() method to get the Textbox object, and then uses the value property of the Textbox object to get the value from the text box. In other words, you combine the use of the two methods into a single statement.

The second group of examples takes chaining to a third level. Without chaining, it takes three statements to get a valid number from a text box. First, the getDocumentById() method gets the Textbox object for the text box with "sales_amount" as its id. Second, the value property of the Textbox object gets the value that the user entered into the text box. Third, the parseFloat() method of the window object converts the string value to a decimal number. If the user entry is a valid number, this stores the number in the salesAmount variable, so it becomes a Number object.

With chaining, though, this requires only one statement. Code like this is sometimes called *fluent,* because it's more like a sentence and thus more readable to a human eye. It can also make your code shorter, and shorter code is usually easier to understand. You'll want to be careful with this, though. Like a run-on sentence in a book, if you get to the end of the statement and can't remember what the beginning was doing, you might have chained too much.

The third table in this figure summarizes the toFixed() method of a Number object. When a user enters a valid number in a text box and the parseInt() or parseFloat() method is used to parse it before it is stored in a variable, the variable becomes a Number object. Then, you can use properties and methods of that object to work with the number. For example, you can use the toFixed() method of a Number object to round the number to a specific number of decimal places.

This is illustrated by the first statement in the third group of examples. This statement takes chaining to a fourth level by adding the toFixed() method to the chain. As a result, the number that's stored in the salesAmount variable is rounded to two decimal places. Some might consider this an example of chaining taken too far.

The last two statements in this group present two more examples of chaining. The first one shows how to assign a value to a text box. In this case,

One method of the Textbox object

Method	Description
focus()	Moves the cursor into the text box, but doesn't return anything.

Two properties of the Textbox object

Property	Description
value	A string that represents the contents of the text box.
disabled	A Boolean value that controls whether the text box is disabled.

One method of the Number object

Method	Description
toFixed(*digits*)	Returns a string representation of the number after it has been rounded to the number of decimal places in the parameter.

HTML tags that define two text boxes

```
<input type="text" id="first_name">
<input type="text" id="sales_amount">
```

How to use the value property to get the value from a text box

Without chaining

```
var firstName = document.getElementById("first_name");
firstName = firstName.value;
```

With chaining

```
var firstName = document.getElementById("first_name").value;
```

How to use the parseFloat() method to get a number value from a text box

Without chaining

```
var salesAmount = document.getElementById("sales_amount");
salesAmount = salesAmount.value;
salesAmount = parseFloat(salesAmount);
```

With chaining

```
var salesAmount = parseFloat(document.getElementById("sales_amount").value);
```

Other examples of chaining

```
var salesAmount =
    parseFloat(document.getElementById("sales_amount").value).toFixed(2);
document.getElementById("first_name").value = ""; // clear a text box
document.getElementById("first_name").focus();     // move focus to a text box
```

Description

- When you use the getElementById() method to get a text box, the method returns a Textbox object. Then, you can use its value property to get the value in the box.

- When you assign a numeric value to a variable, a Number object is created. Then, you can use the Number methods with the variable.

Figure 4-2   How to use Textbox and Number objects

the value is an empty string, which in effect clears the text box of any data. The second statement shows how to move the focus to a text box.

How to use Date and String objects

When you store a numeric or string value in a variable, it is automatically converted to a Number or String object. This lets you use the properties and methods of the Number and String objects without having to explicitly create the objects.

However, there isn't a primitive data type for dates. As a result, you need to create a Date object before you can use its methods. To do that, you can use the syntax shown in figure 4-3. When you create a Date object, it is initialized with the current date and time, which is the date and time on the user's computer.

After you create a Date object, you can use the methods in this figure to work with it. These methods are illustrated by the first group of examples, assuming that the date is March 9, 2017. Here, the toDateString() method converts the date to a string. The getFullYear() method gets the four-digit year from the date. The getDate() method gets the day of the month. And the getMonth() method gets the month, counting from 0, not 1. As a result, the getMonth() method returns 2 for March, not 3.

This figure also presents one property and five methods of a String object. Then, the last group of examples presents some statements that show how these properties work. For example, the second statement uses the toUpperCase() method to convert a string to uppercase, and the third statement uses the length property to get the number of characters in a string.

The last two statements show how the indexOf() and substr() methods of a String object can be used to extract a substring from a string. Here, the indexOf() method is used to get the position (index) of the first space in the string, counting from zero. Since the space is in the sixth position, this method returns 5. Then, the substr() method gets the substring that starts at the first position and has a length of 5. As a result, this method returns "Grace".

It's important to note the difference between the substr() and substring() methods. If you start from the first position, as in the example, there is no difference. In that case, both methods will return "Grace". However, if you start anywhere else, you'll get different results depending on which method you use.

For example, if you start at the third position (with an index of 2), the substr() method will still return five characters, and you'll get the string "ace H". The substring() method, on the other hand, will stop at the sixth position (with an index of 5). This means it will only return 3 characters, the string "ace". (It doesn't return the character at the stop position.)

Incidentally, JavaScript provides many more methods and properties for Date and String objects, but these will get you started. You can learn about the others in chapter 13.

The syntax for creating a JavaScript object and assigning it to a variable

```
var variableName = new ObjectType();
```

A statement that creates a Date object

```
var today = new Date();
```

A few of the methods of a Date object

Method	Description
`toDateString()`	Returns a string with the formatted date.
`getFullYear()`	Returns the four-digit year from the date.
`getDate()`	Returns the day of the month from the date.
`getMonth()`	Returns the month number from the date. The months are numbered starting with zero. (January is 0 and December is 11).

Examples that use a Date object

```
var today = new Date();            // creates Date object with current date
alert( today.toDateString() );     // displays Thu Mar 09 2017 on 3/9/2017
alert( today.getFullYear() );      // displays 2017
alert( today.getDate() );          // displays 9
alert( today.getMonth() );         // displays 2, not 3 for March
```

One property of a String object

Property	Description
`length`	Returns the number of characters in the string.

A few of the methods of a String object

Method	Description
`indexOf(search, position)`	Searches for the first occurrence of the search string starting at the position specified or zero if position is omitted. If found, it returns the position of the first character, counting from 0. If not found, it returns -1.
`substr(start, length)`	Returns the substring that starts at the specified position (counting from zero) and contains the specified number of characters.
`substring(start, stop)`	Returns the substring that starts at the specified position (counting from zero) and stops at the specified position (counting from zero).
`toLowerCase()`	Returns a new string with the letters converted to lowercase.
`toUpperCase()`	Returns a new string with the letters converted to uppercase.

Examples that use a String object

```
var name = "Grace Hopper";
var nameUpper = name.toUpperCase();      // nameUpper = GRACE HOPPER
var nameLength = name.length;            // nameLength = 12
var index = name.indexOf(" ");           // index = 5
var firstName = name.substr(0, index);   // firstName = Grace
```

Description

- To create a Date object and assign it to a variable, use the syntax shown above.
- When you assign a string value to a variable, a String object is automatically created.

Figure 4-3   How to use Date and String objects

How to use functions

When you develop JavaScript applications, you need to handle events like a user clicking on a button. To do that, you need to code and call functions that handle the events. As you will see, you can also use functions in other ways.

How to create and call a function expression

A *function* is a block of statements that performs an action. It can receive *parameters* and return a value by issuing a *return statement*. Once you've defined a function, you can call it from other portions of your JavaScript code. In figure 4-4, you can see how to create and call a *function expression*.

To start a function expression, you code the keyword var followed by the name of the variable that will store the function. With one exception, we recommend you use variable names that consist of verbs and nouns that indicate the type of processing the function will do. The exception is the $ function, which is always used as shown in the second example in this figure.

Following the variable name, you code an assignment operator, the keyword function, a list of parameters in parentheses, and a block of code in braces. Functions coded this way are called function expressions because they're assigned to a variable.

To *call* a function expression, you code the name of the variable that the function is stored in, followed by the parameters in parentheses. Then, the function uses the data that's passed to it in the parameters as it executes its block of code. Here again, the parentheses are required even if there are no parameters.

The first example in this figure creates a function that's stored in a variable named showYear. This function doesn't require any parameters and doesn't return a value. When called, this function displays a dialog box that shows the current year.

The second example creates a function that's stored in a variable named $. This function takes one parameter, which is the value of the id attribute of an HTML element. This function returns an object that represents the HTML element. In this example, the call statement gets the object for the HTML text box with "email_address1" as its id, and then uses the value property of that object to get the value that the user entered.

The third example in this figure creates a function that's stored in a variable named calculateTax that requires two parameters and returns a value. It calculates sales tax, rounds it to two decimal places, and returns that rounded value to the statement that called it.

To call this function, the statement passes two variables named subtotal and taxRate. In this case, the variable names for these values are the same as the parameter names in the function, but that isn't necessary. What is required is that the calling statement must pass parameters with the same data types and in the same sequence as the parameters in the function.

Incidentally, some programmers treat *parameter* and *argument* as synonyms. Others use *parameter* to refer to a parameter in a function and *argument* to refer to the value that is passed to the function. In this section of the book, we use *parameter* for both purposes.

The syntax for a function expression

```
var variableName = function(parameters) {
    // statements that run when the function is executed
};
```

A function expression with no parameters that doesn't return a value

```
var showYear = function() {
    var today = new Date();
    alert( "The year is " + today.getFullYear() );
};
```

How to call the function

```
showYear();
```

A function expression with one parameter that returns a DOM element

```
var $ = function(id) {
    return document.getElementById(id);
};
```

How to call the function

```
var emailAddress1 = $("email_address1").value;
```

A function expression with two parameters that returns a value

```
var calculateTax = function( subtotal, taxRate ) {
    var tax = subtotal * taxRate;
    tax = tax.toFixed(2);
    return tax;
};
```

How to call the function

```
var subtotal = 85.00;
var taxRate = 0.05;
var salesTax = calculateTax( subtotal, taxRate );    // calls the function
alert(salesTax);                                     // displays 4.25
```

Description

- A *function* is a block of code that can be *called* (or *invoked*) by other statements in the program. When the function ends, the program continues with the statement that comes after the statement that called the function.

- A function can require that one or more *parameters* be passed to it when the function is called. In the calling statement, these parameters can also be referred to as *arguments*.

- To return a value to the statement that called it, a function uses a *return statement*. When the return statement is executed, the function returns the specified value and ends.

- A *function expression* is assigned to a variable and is referred to by the variable name.

- Function expressions are sometimes called *anonymous functions* because they don't have names. Technically, function expressions can have names, but usually they don't.

- In the JavaScript for an application, a function expression must be coded before any statements that call it. Otherwise, an error will occur.

Figure 4-4   How to create and call a function expression

How to create and call a function declaration

Since function expressions are commonly used to handle the events that occur in JavaScript applications, you'll use them most of the time. However, you should know that JavaScript also lets you code *function declarations*.

Figure 4-5 shows you how to create and call a function declaration. It uses the same examples as the previous figure but with function declarations instead of function expressions. As the syntax shows, a function declaration isn't stored in a variable, and its name is coded after the keyword *function* and before the parameters.

Notice that it isn't necessary to code a semicolon following the closing brace of a function declaration. That's because a function declaration isn't an executable statement. Instead, it just declares the function. In contrast, a function expression is part of a statement that assigns the function to a variable, so you do code a semicolon after it.

As in the previous figure, the showYear() function doesn't have any parameters and doesn't return a value. The $ function requires one parameter with the value of the id attribute of an HTML element and returns that element. And the calculateTax() function requires two parameters and returns the sales tax value rounded to two decimal places. In these examples, using function declarations is just another way to get the same results as function expressions.

The one benefit of using function declarations is that they can be coded after any statements that call them. That's because the JavaScript interpreter reads ahead and moves, or *hoists*, all function declarations to the top of the scope that contains them. You'll learn more about scope in just a minute.

In contrast, function expressions aren't hoisted, and so must be coded before any statements that call them. Nevertheless, most programmers use function expressions. And some programmers think that coding function declarations after they are called is a confusing practice that should be avoided.

The syntax for a function declaration

```
function functionName(parameters) {
    // statements that run when the function is executed
}
```

A function declaration with no parameters that doesn't return a value

```
function showYear() {
    var today = new Date();
    alert( "The year is " + today.getFullYear() );
}
```

How to call the function

```
showYear();
```

A function declaration with one parameter that returns a DOM element

```
function $(id) {
    return document.getElementById(id);
}
```

How to call the function

```
var emailAddress1 = $("email_address1").value;
```

A function declaration with two parameters that returns a value

```
function calculateTax( subtotal, taxRate ) {
    var tax = subtotal * taxRate;
    tax = tax.toFixed(2);
    return tax;
}
```

How to call the function

```
var subtotal = 85.00;
var taxRate = 0.05;
var salesTax = calculateTax( subtotal, taxRate );    // calls the function
alert(salesTax);                                     // displays 4.25
```

Description

- A *function declaration* is one that is coded with a name and isn't assigned to a variable. This is just another way to code functions.

- In contrast to a function expression, a function declaration is *hoisted* to the top of the scope that contains it. That means that it doesn't have to be coded before any statements that call it.

Figure 4-5   How to create and call a function declaration

When and how to use local and global variables

Scope in a programming language refers to the visibility of variables and functions. That is, it tells you where in your program you are allowed to use the variables and functions that you've defined.

When you use JavaScript, *local variables* are variables that are defined within functions. They have *local scope*, which means that they can only be used within the functions that define them.

In contrast, *global variables* are variables that are defined outside of functions. These variables have *global scope*, so they can be used by any function without passing them to the function as parameters.

The first example in figure 4-6 illustrates the use of a local variable. Here, the calculateTax() function creates a variable named tax and returns that variable to the calling statement. Then, that statement can store the variable in another variable. Note, however, that a statement outside of the function can't refer to the variable named tax without causing an error. That's because it has local scope.

In contrast, the second example first creates a global variable named tax. Then, the function calculates the sales tax and stores the result in that global variable. As a result, the function doesn't have to return the tax variable. Instead, a statement outside of the function can refer to the variable because it's global.

Although it may seem easier to use global variables than to pass data to a function and return data from it, global variables often create problems. That's because any function can modify a global variable, and it's all too easy to misspell a variable name or modify the wrong variable, especially in large applications. That in turn can create debugging problems.

In contrast, the use of local variables reduces the likelihood of naming conflicts. For instance, two different functions can use the same names for local variables without causing conflicts. That of course means fewer errors and debugging problems. With just a few exceptions, then, all of the code in your applications should be in functions so all of the variables are local.

To complicate the use of variables, the JavaScript engine assumes that a variable is global if you accidentally omit the var keyword when you declare it. This is illustrated by the third example in this figure. Here, the var keyword is missing before the first assignment statement, so tax is assumed to be a global variable.

This is a weakness of JavaScript that you need to be aware of because it can lead to coding errors. If, for example, you misspell the name of a variable that you've already declared when you code an assignment statement, it will be treated as a new global variable. With this in mind, be sure to include the var keyword when you declare new variables and always declare a variable before you refer to it in your code. With ECMAScript 5, you can also address this weakness by using strict mode, as explained in the next figure.

A function that uses a local variable named tax

```
var calculateTax = function( subtotal, taxRate ) {
    var tax = subtotal * taxRate;      // tax is a local variable
    tax = tax.toFixed(2);
    return tax;
};
```

Referring to a local variable from outside the function causes an error

```
alert("Tax is " + tax);                // causes error
```

A function that uses a global variable named tax

```
var tax;                               // tax is a global variable
var calculateTax = function( subtotal, taxRate ) {
    tax = subtotal * taxRate;
    tax = tax.toFixed(2);
};
```

Referring to a global variable from outside the function doesn't cause an error

```
alert("Tax is " + tax);                // will not cause error
```

A function that inadvertently uses a global variable named tax

```
var calculateTax = function( subtotal, taxRate ) {
    tax = subtotal * taxRate;  // no var keyword so tax is treated as global
    tax = tax.toFixed(2);
};
```

Referring to the tax variable from outside the function doesn't cause an error... but it should!

```
alert("Tax is " + tax);                // will not cause error
```

Discussion

- The *scope* of a variable or function determines what code has access to it.

- Variables that are created inside a function are *local variables*, and local variables can only be referred to by the code within the function.

- Variables created outside of functions are *global variables*, and the code in all functions has access to all global variables.

- If you forget to code the var keyword in a variable declaration, the JavaScript engine assumes that the variable is global. This can cause debugging problems.

- In general, it's better to pass local variables from one function to another as parameters than it is to use global variables. That will make your code easier to understand with less chance for errors.

Figure 4-6   When and how to use local and global variables

When and how to use strict mode

To address the problem of JavaScript creating unwanted variables when you misspell an identifier or omit the var keyword, ECMAScript 5 provides a mode of operation called *strict mode*. To use strict mode, you code the strict mode directive shown in figure 4-7 at the start of your JavaScript code. Then, the JavaScript engine in a modern browser will throw an error if a variable name is used before it has been declared in a statement that uses the var keyword.

This is illustrated by the first two examples. In the first example, strict mode isn't used so omitting the var keyword will cause a debugging problem, but the application will continue running. In the second example, strict mode is used so the same omission will cause the JavaScript engine to throw an error and stop running the JavaScript code. That alerts you to the problem and forces you to fix it.

Note, however, that this feature of ECMAScript 5 isn't supported by older browsers like IE7, IE8, and IE9. That's okay, though, because if you fix the problems in a modern browser, the problems won't be there for older browsers either.

With that in mind, this figure summarizes the best coding practices for working with local and global variables. First, use local variables whenever possible. Second, use the var keyword to declare all variables. Third, always use strict mode. Fourth, declare the variables that are used by a function at the start of the function, before you use them.

You'll see these practices illustrated in the applications at the end of this chapter and throughout this book. If the code doesn't always show the strict mode declaration or declare all of the variables at the start of a function, it's just to fit the coding onto a single page.

The strict mode directive

```
"use strict";   // goes at the top of a file or function
```

A function that inadvertently uses a global variable named tax

```
var calculateTax = function( subtotal, taxRate ) {
    tax = subtotal * taxRate; // no var keyword so tax is treated as global
    tax = tax.toFixed(2);
};
```

Referring to the tax variable from outside the function doesn't cause an error...but it should!

```
alert("Tax is " + tax);              // will not cause error
```

The same function in strict mode

```
"use strict";
var calculateTax = function( subtotal, taxRate ) {
    tax = subtotal * taxRate; // in strict mode so error is thrown
    tax = tax.toFixed(2);
};
```

Referring to the tax variable causes a JavaScript error

```
alert("Tax is " + tax);              // causes error
```

Best coding practices

- Use local variables whenever possible.
- Use the var keyword to declare all variables.
- Use strict mode.
- Declare the variables that are used in a function at the start of the function.

Description

- The strict mode directive goes at the top of a file or function, before any other code.
- When you're coding in strict mode, if you forget to code the var keyword in a variable declaration or if you misspell a variable name that has been declared, the JavaScript engine will throw an error.
- Because strict mode became available with ECMAScript 5, it won't work with IE7, IE8, and IE9. However, if you test your applications in strict mode in a modern browser, you'll catch all of your omissions of the var keyword so they won't cause debugging problems in older browsers.

Figure 4-7   When and how to use strict mode

How to handle events

JavaScript applications commonly respond to user actions like clicking on a button. These actions are called *events*, and the function expressions that handle the events are called *event handlers*. To make that happen, you have to *attach* the functions to the events.

How to attach an event handler to an event

The table in figure 4-8 summarizes some of the events that are commonly handled by JavaScript applications. For instance, the load event of the window object occurs when the browser finishes loading the HTML for a page. The click event of a button object occurs when the user clicks on the button. And the mouseover action of an element like a heading or link occurs when the user hovers the mouse over the element.

After this table, you can see the syntax for attaching a function to an event. To do that, you code the object name, a dot, and the event name preceded by the word *on*. Then, you code an equals sign followed by the name of the variable for the function expression that's going to handle the event.

In the group of examples that follows the syntax summary, the first example starts with a function expression that can be used as an event handler. This function is stored in a variable named joinList, and all it does is display a message. In an actual application, of course, this function would perform the actions needed for handling the event.

The second example in this first group shows a JavaScript statement that attaches the joinList() function to the click event of a button that has "submit_button" as its id. To do that, this statement first uses the $ function that you saw in figure 4-5, which uses the getElementById() method to get the object for the button. This is followed by the dot operator and the event name preceded by *on* (onclick). Then, an equals sign is followed by joinList, which is the variable name for the function that will handle the click event.

Note here that you don't code the parentheses after the name of the variable that's used for the function like you do in the examples in figure 4-5. That's because you're *attaching* the event handler, not *calling* it. That's why the function won't be called until the click event is fired. If you were to put parentheses after joinList, the function would be called right away, and the function wouldn't be attached to the event.

The next statement in this group attaches the joinList event handler to the double-click event of a text box that has "text_box_1" as its id. This means that the same event handler will be used for two different events. Here again, you don't code the parentheses because you're attaching, not calling, the function.

The last example in this figure illustrates how to create an event handler and attach it to the window.onload event in one step. This is a common way to attach an onload event handler.

Common events

Object	Event	Occurs when...
`window`	`load`	The document has been loaded into the browser.
`button`	`click`	The button is clicked.
`control or link`	`focus`	The control or link receives the focus.
	`blur`	The control or link loses the focus.
`control`	`change`	The user changes the value in the control.
	`select`	The user selects text in a text box or text area.
`element`	`click`	The user clicks on the element.
	`dblclick`	The user double-clicks on the element.
	`mouseover`	The user moves the mouse over the element.
	`mousein`	The user moves the mouse into the element.
	`mouseout`	The user moves the mouse out of the element.

The syntax for attaching an event handler

```
objectVariable.oneventName = eventHandlerName;
```

An event handler named joinList

```
var joinList = function() {
    alert("The statements for the function go here");
};
```

How to attach the event handler to the click event of a button

```
$("submit_button").onclick = joinList;
```

How to attach the event handler to the double-click event of a text box

```
$("text_box_1").ondblclick = joinList;
```

How to create and attach an event handler in one step

```
window.onload = function() {
    alert("This is the window onload event handler function.");
};
```

Description

- An *event handler* is a function that's executed when an *event* occurs, so it "handles" the event. As a result, you code an event handler just like any other function.

- To *attach* an event handler to an event, you must first specify the object and the event that triggers the event handler. Then, you assign the event handler function to that event.

- When you code the event for an event handler, you precede the event name with *on*. So, for example, onclick is used for the click event.

- You can create a function expression as an event handler and then attach it to an event. This is useful when you want to use the same function for more than one event, as shown above. When you do this, you don't code the parentheses after the variable name.

- You can also create and attach an event handler function in one step, as in the last example above. This is commonly done for the load event as you'll see in the next figure.

Figure 4-8   How to attach an event handler to an event

How to use an onload event handler to attach other event handlers

When do you attach an event handler like the one in the previous figure? You attach it after all the HTML has been loaded into a user's browser and the DOM has been built. To do that, you code an event handler for the load event of the window object as shown in figure 4-9.

In the HTML for this example, you can see a label, a text box, a label that contains one space, and a button. This simple application is supposed to display a message when the button is clicked or when the user changes the value in the text box.

In the JavaScript code, you can see three function expressions. The first one is stored in a variable named $. This function uses the getElementById() method of the document object to get an element object when the id of an HTML element is passed to it. This function makes it easy to get an element object without coding the document.getElementById() method every time.

The second function is the event handler for the click event of the button, and the third function is the event handler for the change event of the text box. Both of these functions just display a message.

The fourth function is the event handler for the load event. It is used to attach the other event handlers to the click and change events. Note that this function starts with

`window.onload`

so it is attached to the load event of the window object. As a result, this event handler is executed after the page is loaded and the DOM has been built. (Remember from chapter 1 that the DOM, or Document Object Model, is generated by the browser when a page is loaded and represents all the elements and attributes that are coded in the HTML.)

Within the event handler for the load event are the two statements that attach the other event handlers. The first one attaches the joinList() function to the click event of the button. The second one attaches the changeValue() function to the change event of the text box. Both of these statements use the $ function to get the object that the event applies to, which makes the code easier to read and understand.

Incidentally, the event handler for the window.onload event can do more than assign functions to events. In fact, it can do whatever needs to be done after the DOM is loaded.

The web browser after the Email Address has been changed

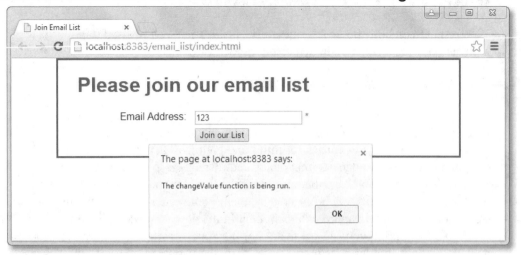

The HTML

```
<h1>Please join our email list</h1>
<label for="email_address">Email Address:</label>
<input type="text" id="email_address" name="email_address"><br>
<label> </label>
<input type="button" id="join_list" value="Join our List"><br>
```

The JavaScript

```
// the $ function
var $ = function(id) {
    return document.getElementById(id);
};
// the event handler for the click event of the button
var joinList = function() {
    alert("The joinList function is being run.");
};
// the event handler for the change event of the text box
var changeValue = function() {
    alert("The changeValue function is being run.");
};
// the event handler for the load event that attaches two event handlers
window.onload = function() {
    $("join_list").onclick = joinList;           // attaches 1st handler
    $("email_address").onchange = changeValue;    // attaches 2nd handler
};
```

Description

- The event handler for the onload event of the window object can be used to attach the event handlers for other events after the DOM has been built.

Figure 4-9   How to use an onload event handler to attach other event handlers

Two illustrative applications

To show you how the JavaScript you've just learned can be used to build applications, this chapter ends by presenting two of them.

The Miles Per Gallon application

Figure 4-10 presents the Miles Per Gallon application from chapter 2, but this time it uses text boxes and a button, rather than prompt and alert dialog boxes. This version gets the user entries for miles and gallons. Then, it calculates miles per gallon, rounds it to one decimal place, and displays it in the third text box.

Note that the disabled attribute is set for the third text box in the HTML. This disables and shades this text box so the user can't enter data into it. Although the CSS isn't shown in this figure, you can see it in the downloaded application.

In the JavaScript, you can see that all of the code is within four functions. As a result, all the variables have local scope. Also, the variables for each function are declared at the start of the function, and strict mode is used. These are all best coding practices.

You should also note the sequence of the functions. Here, the first function is the $ function. The second function is the calculateMpg() function, which calculates the miles per gallon. The third function is the processEntries() function, which calls both the $ function and the calculateMpg() function. And the fourth function is the event handler for the load event, which attaches the processEntries() function and moves the focus to the first text box.

In short, each function only calls functions that precede it in the code. This is a logical sequence that makes your code easier to read and understand.

In the processEntries() function, the user entries are retrieved using the $ function and then parsed into the miles and gallons variables. Then, an if statement tests whether either entry is invalid because it isn't numeric. If so, an error message is displayed. If both entries are valid, the one statement in the else clause calls the calculateMpg() function and passes it the valid entries.

The calculateMpg() function calculates the miles per gallon by dividing miles by gallons. Then, it rounds the result to one decimal place and returns the result to the calling statement, which stores it in the value property of the text box with "mpg" as its id.

When the web page is loaded, the onload event handler is executed first, even though it comes last in the script. It attaches the event handler for the click event of the Calculate MPG button. After that, the browser waits until the user clicks on that button. Then, the processEntries() function validates the entries, calls the calculateMpg() function if the entries are valid, and displays the rounded result when it is returned.

In this application, the calculateMpg() function illustrates a function that isn't an event handler. Because this function consists of just three statements, you could delete this function and put the two statements that calculate and round the result into the else clause of the processEntries() function. But when a calculation is more complicated, moving its code into a function like this can simplify the code in the calling function and make the code easier to maintain.

The Miles Per Gallon application in a browser

The HTML and JavaScript for the application

```
<head>
    <title>Calculate MPG</title>
    <link rel="stylesheet" href="mpg.css">
    <script>
        "use strict";
        var $ = function(id) {
            return document.getElementById(id);
        };
        var calculateMpg = function(miles, gallons) {
            var mpg = (miles / gallons);
            mpg = mpg.toFixed(1);
            return mpg;
        };
        var processEntries = function() {
            var miles = parseFloat($("miles").value);
            var gallons = parseFloat($("gallons").value);
            if (isNaN(miles) || isNaN(gallons)) {
                alert("Both entries must be numeric");
            } else if (miles <= 0 || gallons <= 0) {
                alert("Both entries must be greater than zero");
            } else {
                $("mpg").value = calculateMpg(miles, gallons);
            }
        };
        window.onload = function() {
            $("calculate").onclick = processEntries;
            $("miles").focus();
        };
    </script>
</head>
<body>
    <main>
        <h1>Calculate Miles Per Gallon</h1>
        <label for="miles">Miles Driven:</label>
        <input type="text" id="miles"><br>
        <label for="gallons">Gallons of Gas Used:</label>
        <input type="text" id="gallons"><br>
        <label for="mpg">Miles Per Gallon</label>
        <input type="text" id="mpg" disabled><br>
        <label> </label>
        <input type="button" id="calculate" value="Calculate MPG"><br>
    </main>
</body>
```

Figure 4-10   The Miles Per Gallon application

The Email List application

Figure 4-11 presents an Email List application like the one that you were introduced to in chapter 1. In this application, the user enters the data for three text boxes and clicks the Join our List button. Then, the JavaScript application checks the data for validity. If any entry is invalid, this application displays a dialog box with an error message for the first invalid entry. If all entries are valid, the data is submitted to the server for server-side processing.

The data validation that's done in this application is typical of the client-side validation that's done for any form before its data is submitted to the server for processing.

In the head section of the HTML, you can see that a link element is used to include a CSS file for this page. You can also see a script element that includes an external JavaScript file for this page. Here again, the CSS isn't shown because it's irrelevant to the operation of the application.

In the body of the HTML, you can see the form, label, and input elements for this page. You might also notice the id attributes for the form and text boxes. The id for the form is "email_form", and the ids for the text boxes are "email_address1", "email_address2", and "first_name". These are the ids that will be passed to the $ function in the JavaScript.

Note too that the values for the name attributes of the form and text boxes are the same as the values for their id attributes. The name attributes for the text boxes are used by the server-side code to get the user entries that are passed to it when the form data is submitted to the server.

The Email List application in a web browser

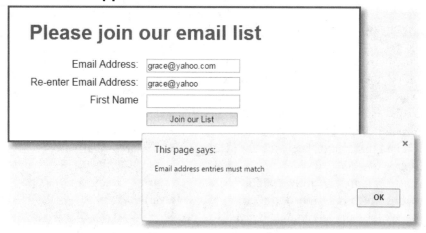

The HTML file for the page

```html
<!DOCTYPE html>
<html>
<head>
    <title>Join Email List</title>
    <link rel="stylesheet" href="email_list.css">
    <script src="email_list.js"></script>
</head>
<body>
    <main>
        <h1>Please join our email list</h1>
        <form id="email_form" name="email_form"
            action="join.html" method="get">
            <label for="email_address1">Email Address:</label>
            <input type="text" id="email_address1" name="email_address1">
            <br>
            <label for="email_address2">Re-enter Email Address:</label>
            <input type="text" id="email_address2" name="email_address2">
            <br>
            <label for="first_name">First Name</label>
            <input type="text" id="first_name" name="first_name">
            <br>
            <label> </label>
            <input type="button" id="join_list" value="Join our List">
        </form>
    </main>
</body>
</html>
```

Figure 4-11   The HTML for the Email List application

Figure 4-12 shows one way that the JavaScript for this application can be coded. Here again, the functions are coded in a sequence that's easy to read because the function definitions precede the function calls. And here again, the best practices for declaring variables are used.

In this application, the event handler for the onload event attaches the joinList() function to the click event of the button with "join_list" as its id. Then, the event handler moves the focus to the first text box.

When the joinList() function is called, its first three statements use the $ function to store the user's text box entries in variables named emailAddress1, emailAddress2, and firstName. Then, the fourth statement declares a variable named errorMessage and sets it to an empty string.

The if-else statement that follows validates the three entries. If any entry is invalid, an error message is assigned to the errorMessage variable and the focus is moved to the text box that contains the invalid value.

After the three entries are checked for validity, another if statement tests the errorMessage variable to see if it contains an empty string. If it does, that means that all of the entries are valid. As a result, the if clause uses the submit() method of the form object to send the data to the server. Although this method hasn't been presented yet, you'll learn more about it in chapter 6. If the errorMessage variable isn't equal to an empty string, it means that at least one of the entries is invalid. In that case, the errorMessage variable is displayed.

If you study this code, you can see that the first if statement checks the second email address entry for two types of validity. First, it checks to make sure an entry has been made. Second, if an entry has been made, it checks to make sure that the second email address entry is equal to the first email address entry.

You might notice, though, that the code for this application doesn't provide all of the validity checking that you might want. For instance, it doesn't test whether the entries in the first two text boxes are valid email addresses. In chapters 10 and 14, though, you'll learn how to provide more extensive data validation.

The JavaScript for the Email List application

```javascript
"use strict";

var $ = function(id) {
    return document.getElementById(id);
};

var joinList = function() {
    var emailAddress1 = $("email_address1").value;
    var emailAddress2 = $("email_address2").value;
    var firstName = $("first_name").value;
    var errorMessage = "";

    // validate the entries
    if (emailAddress1 == "") {
        errorMessage = "First email address entry required";
        $("email_address1").focus();
    }
    else if (emailAddress2 == "") {
        errorMessage = "Second email address entry required";
        $("email_address2").focus();
    }
    else if (emailAddress2 != emailAddress1) {
        errorMessage = "Email address entries must match";
        $("email_address2").focus();
    }
    else if (firstName == "") {
        errorMessage = "First name entry required";
        $("first_name").focus();
    }

    // submit the form if all entries are valid
    // otherwise, display an error message
    if (errorMessage == "") {
        $("email_form").submit();
    }
    else {
        alert(errorMessage);
    }
};

window.onload = function() {
    $("join_list").onclick = joinList;
    $("email_address1").focus();
};
```

Figure 4-12   The JavaScript for the Email List application

Perspective

In this chapter, you've seen the way real-world JavaScript applications use objects and respond to events. Now, if you understand everything in this chapter, you should be ready to start developing useful applications of your own.

Terms

window object	argument
global object	function declaration
document object	hoist
NaN	scope
method chaining	local variable
chaining	local scope
fluent coding	global variable
function	global scope
function expression	strict mode
call a function	event
return statement	event handler
parameter	attach an event handler

Summary

- The Textbox, Number, Date, and String objects provide methods and properties for text boxes, number data types, dates, and string data types. When working with the methods and properties of these objects, you often use *method chaining*.

- A *function* consists of a block of code that is executed when the function is *called* (or *invoked*). The function can require one or more *parameters* that are passed to it by the calling statement.

- A *function expression* is stored in a variable, and a *function declaration* is given a name but not stored in a variable.

- *Local variables* are defined within a function and can only be accessed by statements within the function. *Global variables* are defined outside of all functions and can be accessed by any of the other code.

- *Strict mode* is an ECMAScript 5 feature that causes the JavaScript engine to throw an error if a variable name is used before it has been declared.

- An *event handler* is a function that is called when an *event* like clicking on a button occurs. To make this work, the function must be *attached* to the event.

Exercise 4-1   Enhance the MPG application

In this exercise, you'll enhance the validation for the MPG application, and you'll provide for clearing the entries from the form.

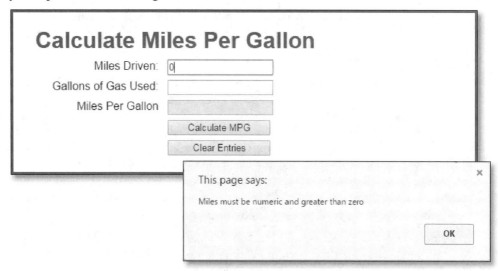

If you have any problems when you're testing, remember to use Chrome's developer tools as shown in figure 1-16 of chapter 1.

Test the application

1. Open your text editor or IDE, and open this HTML file:

    `c:\javascript_jquery\exercises\ch04\mpg\index.html`

    Then, review the JavaScript code to see that it's the same as in figure 4-10.

2. Test this application with valid data to see how it works. When you click the Calculate MPG button, the correct result should be displayed.

3. Test the data validation routine. Note that one error message is displayed in an alert dialog box if either entry is nonnumeric or if either entry is less than or equal to zero.

Enhance the data validation

4. Modify the if-else statement that provides the data validation so it checks each text box separately. If the data in a text box is invalid, an error message should be displayed and the focus should be moved to that text box.

5. Test this change to be sure that a separate error message is displayed for a text box if it contains invalid data.

Provide for clearing the entries from the form

6. Add a Clear Entries button below the Calculate MPG button. To do that, copy the HTML for the label and input elements for the Calculate button, and paste it after the input element for the Calculate button. Then, modify the HTML for the Clear Entries button so it has a unique id and an appropriate value attribute.

7. Add a function expression named clearEntries() that clears the entries in the four text boxes. Then, add a statement in the onload event handler that attaches the clearEntries() function to the click event of the Clear Entries button.

8. Add a statement to the onload event handler that attaches the clearEntries() function to the double-click event of the miles text box. Then, test this change.

See what happens when you remove strict mode

9. Change the second statement in the calculateMpg() function as follows so the variable name is misspelled as *Mpg* instead of *mpg*.

```
var mpg = (miles / gallons);
Mpg = mpg.toFixed(1);
return mpg;
```

10. Test this application with valid entries, and note that it doesn't work. Then, press F12 to display the developer tools, click on the Console tab, and see this error message: Mpg is not defined. This shows that strict mode prevents the declaration of a variable without using the var keyword.

11. Delete the strict mode declaration, and test again with the 1000 for miles and 33 for gallons. This time, the application works, but the result isn't rounded. That's because the JavaScript engine treated Mpg as a new variable.

12. Restore the strict mode declaration and return the variable name to mpg. Then, test again to make sure the application is working.

Exercise 4-2   Build a new Future Value application

In this exercise, you will build a new version of the Future Value application of chapter 3. Its user interface will look like this:

If you have any problems when you're testing, remember to use Chrome's developer tools as shown in figure 1-16 of chapter 1.

Open and review the starting files

1. Open your text editor or IDE, and open the HTML and JavaScript files in this folder:

```
javascript_jquery\exercises\ch04\future_value\
```

2. Run the HTML file to see that it provides the user interface, but nothing works.

3. Review the JavaScript file. Note that it contains just the $ function.

Create a function for the Future Value calculation

4. Create a function expression named calculateFV(). It should have three parameters that receive the user's entries: investment amount, interest rate, and number of years. It should calculate the future value based on these parameter values, round the result to two decimal places, and return the rounded result. If you need help with this calculation, you can refer back to the Future Value application in figure 3-7.

Create the event handler for the click event of the Calculate button

5. Create a function expression named processEntries() that gets the user entries with no data validation. Use strict mode, and start by declaring the variables that will hold the user's entries and assigning the user's entries to these variables.

6. Code a statement that calls the calculateFV() function and stores the result that's returned in the fourth text box.

7. Create an event handler for the onload event that attaches the processEntries() function to the click event of the Calculate button. This handler should also move the focus to the first text box.

8. Test this application with valid entries, and debug until this works correctly.

Add data validation

9. Declare a variable that will be used to store an error message right after the other variable declarations.

10. Add an if-else statement that tests whether each entry is valid. If an entry is invalid, assign an error message to the variable you declared in step 9 and move the focus to the text box that contains the error. The values for the three entries should be as follows:

   Investment is a number that's greater than zero and less than or equal to 100,000;

   Interest rate is a number that's greater than zero and less than or equal to 15;

   Years is a number that's greater than zero and less than or equal to 50.

11. Add another if-else statement that tests whether any errors were detected. If not, the statement that you coded in step 6 should be executed. Otherwise, the error message should be displayed. Now, test this change.

5

How to test and debug a JavaScript application

As you build a JavaScript application, you need to test it to make sure that it performs as expected. Then, if there are any problems, you need to debug your application to correct those problems. This chapter shows you how to do both.

An introduction to testing and debugging

When you *test* an application, you run it to make sure that it works correctly. As you test the application, you try every possible combination of input data and user actions to be certain that the application works in every case. In other words, the goal of testing is to make an application fail.

When you *debug* an application, you fix the errors (*bugs*) that you discover during testing. Each time you fix a bug, you test again to make sure that the change you made didn't affect any other aspect of the application.

The three types of errors that can occur

As you test an application, three types of errors can occur. These errors are described in figure 5-1.

Syntax errors violate the rules for coding JavaScript statements. These errors are detected by the JavaScript engine as a page is loaded into the browser. As you learned in chapter 1, some syntax errors are also detected by IDEs like Aptana. Syntax errors are the easiest to fix, because web browsers and IDEs provide error messages that help you do that.

A *runtime error* occurs after a page has been loaded and the application is running. Then, when a statement can't be executed, the JavaScript engine *throws an exception* (or *error*) that stops the execution of the application.

Logic errors are errors in the logic of the coding: an arithmetic expression that delivers the wrong result, using the wrong relational operator in a comparison, and so on. This type of error is often the most difficult to find and fix. For example, the Future Value application in this figure has a logic error that results in an incorrect result. In this case, though, it's hard to tell what the right future value should be. Later in this chapter, you'll learn one way to do that by tracing the execution of your code.

The Future Value application with a logic error

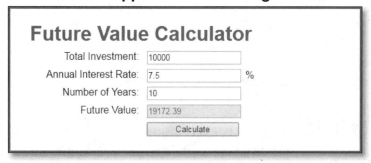

The goal of testing

- To find all errors before the application is put into production.

The goal of debugging

- To fix all errors before the application is put into production.

The three types of errors that can occur

- *Syntax errors* violate the rules for how JavaScript statements must be written. These errors are caught by the JavaScript engine as a page is loaded into the web browser.

- *Runtime errors* occur after a page is loaded and the application is being run. When a runtime error occurs, the JavaScript engine throws an error that stops the execution of the application.

- *Logic errors* are statements that don't cause syntax or runtime errors, but produce the wrong results.

Description

- To *test* a JavaScript application, you run it to make sure that it works properly no matter what data you enter or what events you initiate.

- When you *debug* an application, you fix all of the errors (*bugs*) that you find when you test the application.

Figure 5-1   An introduction to testing and debugging

Common JavaScript errors

Figure 5-2 presents some of the coding errors that are commonly made as you write a JavaScript application. If you've been doing the exercises, you most likely have encountered several of these errors already. Now, if you study this figure, you'll have a better idea of what to watch out for.

If you're using a good text editor or IDE, you can avoid most of these errors by noting the error markers and warnings that are displayed as you enter the code. For instance, Aptana will help you avoid most of the errors in the first two groups in this figure. However, it won't help you avoid the errors in the third group.

The fourth group in this figure addresses the problem with floating-point arithmetic that was mentioned in chapter 2. In brief, JavaScript uses the IEEE 754 standard for floating-point numbers, and this standard can introduce inexact results, even for simple calculations. Although these results are extremely close to the exact results, they can cause problems, especially in comparisons. For instance, the number 7.495 is not equal to 7.495000000000001.

To get around this problem, you can round the result as shown by the examples. Here, the first statement rounds the salesTax value to two decimal places by using the toFixed method of the number. In this case, the result is stored as a string because the toFixed method returns a string.

In contrast, the second statement gets the rounded result and then uses the parseFloat method to store it as a number. The approach you use depends on whether you need the result to be a string or a number.

The last group in this figure illustrates the type of problem that can occur when JavaScript assumes that a variable is global. In this example, the salesTax variable is declared properly by using the var keyword. But the next statement misspells salesTax as salestax when it tries to assign a rounded and parsed value to salesTax. As a result, salestax is treated as a global variable, and the rounded and parsed value goes into salestax, not salesTax, which of course causes a bug.

As you learned in chapter 4, though, you can avoid that type of error by using strict mode for all of your JavaScript files. Then, the JavaScript engine will throw an error if you use a variable before it's declared so you'll have to fix the error. Otherwise, an error like this will go undetected, which may lead to a difficult debugging problem.

Common syntax errors

- Misspelling keywords, like coding getElementByID instead of getElementById.
- Omitting required parentheses, quotation marks, or braces.
- Not using the same opening and closing quotation mark.
- Omitting the semicolon at the end of a statement.
- Misspelling or incorrectly capitalizing an identifier, like defining a variable named salesTax and referring to it later as salestax.

Problems with HTML references

- Referring to an attribute value or other HTML component incorrectly, like referring to an id as "salesTax" when the id is "sales_tax".

Problems with data and comparisons

- Not making sure that a user entry is the right data type before processing it.
- Not using the parseInt() or parseFloat() method to convert a user entry into a numeric value before processing it.
- Using one equals sign instead of two when testing for equality.

Problems with floating-point arithmetic

- The number data type in JavaScript uses floating-point numbers, and that can lead to arithmetic results that are imprecise. For example,

```
var salesAmount = 74.95;
salesTax = salesAmount * .1;              // result is 7.495000000000001
```

- One way to fix this potential problem is to round the result to the right number of decimal places. If necessary, you can also convert it back to a floating-point number:

```
salesTax = salesTax.toFixed(2)            // result is 7.50 as a string
salesTax = parseFloat(salesTax.toFixed(2)); // result is 7.50 as a number
```

Problems with undeclared variables that are treated as global variables

- If you don't use strict mode and you assign a value to a variable that hasn't been declared, the JavaScript engine treats it as a global variable, as in this example:

```
var calculateTax = function(subtotal, taxRate) {
    var salesTax = subtotal * taxRate;        // salesTax is local
    salestax = parseFloat(salesTax.toFixed(2));  // salestax is global
    return salesTax;        // salesTax isn't rounded but salestax is
};
```

- The solution to this type of problem is to always use strict mode.

Description

- When the JavaScript engine in a browser comes to a JavaScript statement that it can't execute, it *throws an exception* (or *error*) and skips the rest of the JavaScript statements.

Figure 5-2   Common JavaScript errors

How to plan the test runs

When you test an application, you typically do so in at least two phases. In the first phase, you test the application with valid data. In the second phase, you test the application with invalid data. This is illustrated in figure 5-3.

As your applications become more complex, it helps to create a test plan for testing an application. This is simply a table or spreadsheet that shows what test data you're going to enter and what the results should be.

In the valid testing phase, you should start with test data that produces results that can be easily verified. This is illustrated by the Future Value application in this figure. Here, the first test data entries are for a $1000 investment at an annual interest rate of 10% for 1 year. The result should clearly be 1100, and it is.

Next, you should use test data that is more likely to produce an inaccurate result. That involves using a range of valid entries and verifying that the results are accurate. To do that, of course, you need to know what the results should be. For applications like the Calculate MPG application that perform simple calculations, that's not a problem. For applications like the Future Value application that perform more complex calculations, though, it can be difficult to determine what the results should be. In that case, you can use some of the debugging techniques that you'll learn about later in this chapter to determine if the result of a calculation is correct.

For the invalid testing phase, your test data should include all varieties of invalid entries. This is illustrated by the second example in this figure. This shows a test run of the Future Value application when zeros are entered for all three values. As you can see, an error is displayed for the first entry because the value must be greater than zero. If you fix this entry, a similar error will be displayed for the second entry. And if you fix that entry, a similar error will be displayed for the third entry. When you create a test plan for invalid data, you try to make the program fail by testing every combination of invalid data and user actions that you can think of. That should include random actions like pressing the Enter key or clicking the mouse at the wrong time or place.

The Future Value application as it's tested with valid data

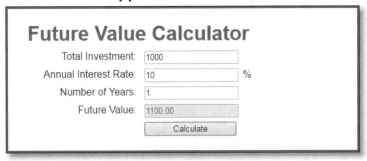

The Future Value application as it's tested with invalid data

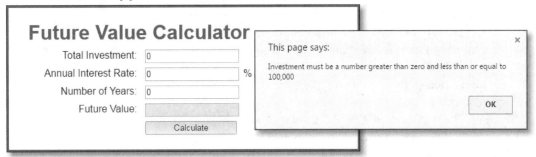

The two critical test phases

1. Test the application with valid input data to make sure the results are correct.
2. Test the application with invalid data or unexpected user actions. Try everything you can think of to make the application fail.

How to make a test plan for the critical phases

1. List the valid entries that you're going to make and the correct results for each set of entries. Then, make sure that the results are correct when you test with these entries.
2. List the invalid entries that you're going to make. These should include entries that test the limits of the allowable values.

Two common testing problems

- Not testing a wide enough range of entries.
- Not knowing what the results of each set of entries should be and assuming that the results are correct because they look correct.

Description

- It's easy to find and fix syntax and runtime errors because the application won't run correctly until you fix them.
- Logic errors can slip through your test runs if you don't check that the results are correct, or if you don't test a wide enough range of entries.

Figure 5-3   How to plan the test runs

How to use top-down coding and testing to simplify debugging

One way to simplify debugging is to code and test just a small portion of code at a time. This can be referred to as *top-down coding and testing* or just *top-down testing*. The implication is that you test the most important operations first and work your way down to the least important operations and the finishing touches.

This is illustrated by the example in figure 5-4. Here, the first testing phase consists of 15 lines of code that provide an event handler for the click event of the Calculate button. However, that event handler doesn't do any data validation. It just calls the calculateFV() function to calculate the future value of the investment amount, which is the essence of this application.

Then, phase 2 adds to this code by doing the data validation for just the first entry. Phase 3 adds the data validation for the other two entries. And phase 4 adds finishing touches like moving the focus to the first text box when the application starts and moving the focus to the appropriate text box when an error is detected.

The result is that you're testing a small amount of code at a time. That makes debugging easy because you know that any errors were introduced by the lines of code that you've just added. This also makes developing an application more enjoyable because you're making continuous progress without the frustration of complex debugging problems.

The user interface for a Future Value application

Future Value Calculator

Total Investment:	75000
Annual Interest Rate:	5.5 %
Number of Years:	7
Future Value:	109100.94
	Calculate

Testing phase 1: No data validation

```javascript
var $ = function(id) {
    return document.getElementById(id);
};
var calculateFV = function(investment,rate,years) {
    // calculate and return future value
};
var calculateClick = function() {
    var investment = parseFloat( $("investment").value );
    var rate = parseFloat( $("rate").value );
    var years = parseInt( $("years").value );
    $("future_value").value = calculateFV(investment,rate,years);
};
window.onload = function() {
    $("calculate").onclick = calculateClick;
};
```

Testing phase 2: Add data validation for just the first entry

```javascript
var error = "";
if (isNaN(investment) || investment <= 0 || investment > 100000) {
    error = "Investment must be a number greater than zero"
        + " and less than or equal to 100,000";
}
else {
    $("future_value").value = calculateFV(investment,rate,years);
}
```

Testing phase 3: Add data validation for the other entries

```javascript
// Add data validation for the other entries
```

Testing phase 4: Add the finishing touches

```javascript
// Add finishing touches like moving the focus to the first text box
// or the text box that contains an error
```

Description

- When you use *top-down coding and testing*, you start by coding and testing a small portion of code. Then, you build on that base by adding the code for an operation or two at a time and testing after each addition.

- Top-down testing simplifies debugging because you know that the errors are caused by the code that you've just added. As a result, it's relatively easy to find the errors.

Figure 5-4   How to use top-down coding and testing to simplify debugging

How to debug with Chrome's developer tools

In chapter 1, you were introduced to the Console panel of Chrome's *developer tools* as a way to find errors. Besides that, though, Chrome offers some excellent debugging features for more complicated problems.

Since Chrome's developer tools are relatively easy to use, the topics that follow don't present the procedures for using all of its features. Instead, they present the skills that you're going to use the most. Then, if you decide that you want to use some of the other features, you can experiment with them on your own.

How to use Chrome to find errors

As figure 5-5 shows, there are several ways to open and close the developer tools, but most of the time you'll use the F12 key. That's why the developer tools for Chrome and other browsers are often referred to as the *F12 tools*.

One of the primary uses of Chrome's developer tools is to get error messages when a JavaScript application throws an error and stops running. To get the error message, you open the developer tools and click on the Console tab to display the Console panel, which will show the error message. Then, you can click on the link to the right of the message to switch to the Sources panel with the JavaScript code for the error statement highlighted.

In the example in this figure, the problem is that the *isNaN* in the statement is spelled wrong. It is *isNan* when it should be *isNaN*. This shows how easy it can be to find an error. Often, the statement that's highlighted isn't the one that caused the error, but at least you have a clue that should help you find the actual error.

Incidentally, the error message that's displayed is for the first error that's detected, but there can be other errors in the code. To catch them, you have to correct the first error and run the application again. Then, if there are other errors, you repeat the process until they're all fixed and the application runs to completion.

Chrome with an open Console panel that shows an error

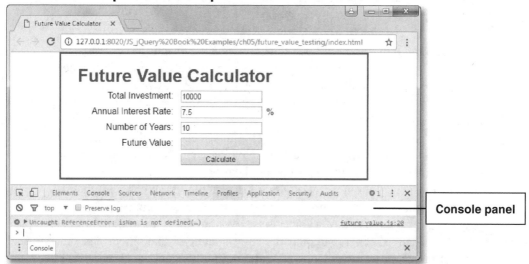

Console panel

The Sources panel after the link in the Console panel has been clicked

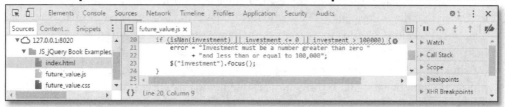

How to open or close Chrome's developer tools

- To open the developer tools, press F12 or Ctrl+Shift+I. Or, click on the Menu button in the upper right corner of the browser, and select More Tools→Developer Tools.

- To close the developer tools, click on the X in the upper right corner of the tools panel or press F12.

How to find the JavaScript statement that caused the error

- Open the Console panel by clicking on the Console tab. You should see an error message like the one above along with the line of code that caused the error.

- Click on the link to the right of the error message that indicates the line of code. That will open the Sources panel with the portion of JavaScript code that contains the statement displayed and the statement highlighted.

Description

- Chrome's *developer tools* provide some excellent debugging features, like identifying the JavaScript statement that caused an error.

- Because you usually start the developer tools by pressing the F12 key, these tools are often referred to as the *F12 tools*.

Figure 5-5   How to use Chrome to find errors

How to use breakpoints and step through your code

A *breakpoint* is a point in your code at which the execution of your application will be stopped. Then, you can examine the contents of variables to see if your code is executing as expected. You can also *step through* the execution of the code from that point on. These techniques can help you solve difficult debugging problems.

Figure 5-6 shows you how to set breakpoints, step through the code, and view the contents of variables. In this example, you can see that a breakpoint has been set on line 20 of the Future Value application.

When you run your application, it will stop at the first breakpoint that it encounters and highlight the line of code next to the breakpoint. While your code is stopped, you can hover your mouse over an object's name in the center pane of the Sources panel to display the current value of that object. The current values of variables are also displayed to the right of the statement that declares them.

At a breakpoint, you can also view the current variables in the Scope pane on the right side of the panel. That pane has two sections, Local and Global. The Local section contains the variables that are used by the function that is being executed. You can also see the values of other variables and expressions by clicking the ▶ symbol to the left of Watch at the top of the pane, clicking the plus sign that appears, and typing the variable name or expression that you want to watch.

To step through the execution of an application after a breakpoint is reached, you can use the Step Into, Step Over, and Step Out buttons. These buttons are just above the Watch Expressions pane. Or, you can press the key associated with these operations, as shown in the table in this figure.

If you repeatedly click or press Step Into, you will execute the code one line at a time and the next line to be executed will be highlighted. After each line of code is executed, you can use the Local or Watch pane to observe any changes in the variables.

As you step through an application, you can use Step Over if you want to execute a called function without taking the time to step through it. Or, you can use Step Out to step out of a function that you don't want to step all the way through. When you want to return to normal execution, you can use Resume. Then, the application will run until the next breakpoint is reached.

These are powerful debugging features that can help you find the causes of serious debugging problems. Stepping through an application is also a good way to understand how the code in an existing application works. If, for example, you step through the for loop in the Future Value application, you'll get a better idea of how it works.

A breakpoint in the Sources panel

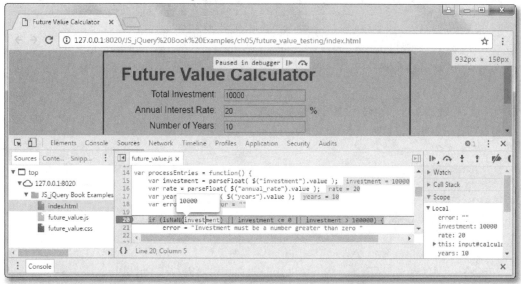

How to set or remove a breakpoint in the Sources panel

- Click on the Sources tab to display the Sources panel. Then, click on the JavaScript file in the left pane that you want to debug.

- In the center pane, click on a line number in the bar to the left of a statement. This will either add a breakpoint or remove an existing one.

The buttons and keys for stepping through the JavaScript code

Button	Key	Description
Step Into	F11	Step through the code one line at a time.
Step Over	F10	Run any called functions without stepping through them.
Step Out	SHIFT+F11	Execute the rest of a function without stepping through it.
Resume	F8	Resume normal execution.

How to view the current data values at each step

- Hover the mouse pointer over a variable name in the center pane of the Sources panel.

- View the current variables in the Scope→Local section of the right-hand pane.

- Click the ▶ symbol in the Watch section of the right-hand pane, click the plus sign that appears, and type the variable name or expression that you want to watch.

- The values are also displayed to the right of the variable declarations in the center pane.

Description

- You can set a *breakpoint* on any line except a blank line. When the JavaScript engine encounters a breakpoint, it stops before executing the statement with the breakpoint.

- A light blue arrow around the line number marks a breakpoint, and a light blue highlight marks the next statement to be executed as you *step through* your code.

Figure 5-6   How to use breakpoints and step through your code

Other debugging methods

Because Chrome has excellent developer tools, you should use them for most of your debugging. Here, though, are other debugging methods that you should be aware of.

How to trace the execution of your JavaScript code

When you *trace* the execution of an application, you determine the sequence in which the statements in the application are executed. An easy way to do that is to add statements to your code that log messages or variable values at key points in the code. You can then view this information in the Console panel of Chrome's developer tools.

This is illustrated by the example in figure 5-7. Here, two log statements are added to the calculateFV() function for the Future Value application. The first one is coded at the beginning of the function and lets you know that the calculateFV() function has been started. The second one is coded at the end of the for loop and displays the value of the counter variable and the current future value.

If you review that output from the log statements, you should be able to tell why the result of the future value calculation is incorrect. (This application has the same logic error as the one that you saw in figure 5-1.) Here, the loop is only executed nine times, but the Number of Years entry is 10. That means that the conditional expression that determines when the loop should end is incorrect. In this case, the loop should be executed until i is less than or equal to ten.

In this example, tracing helps you find a bug. However, you can also use tracing to make sure that the results are correct. For instance, you could easity assume that the future value result is correct without checking further. However, tracing the execution of the statements in the loop shows that the result can't possibly be correct.

When you use this technique, you usually start by adding just a few log statements to the code. Then, if that doesn't help you solve the problem, you can add more. Often, this is all you need for solving simple debugging problems, and this is quicker than setting breakpoints and stepping through the code.

One way that tracing is better than stepping through code is when you're dealing with code that is executed many times. Say, for example, you've got an error that occurs somewhere inside a loop that performs a calculation on each element of an array with 1000 elements. Then, it would be daunting to step through the entire array to find the calculation that fails. With the console.log() method, though, you can send the loop's index and the element's value to the console on each iteration, and then look at the complete log when the script has stopped running.

You can also use the alert() method to trace the execution of an application. This has the benefit of displaying the trace data directly in the browser, rather than having to open the Console panel. But it has the drawback of being intrusive.

JavaScript with two log statements that trace the execution of the code

```javascript
var calculateFV = function(investment,rate,years) {
    console.log("calculateFV function has started");
    var futureValue = investment;
    for (var i = 1; i < years; i++ ) {
        futureValue += futureValue * rate / 100;
        console.log("i = " + i + " future value = " + futureValue);
    }
    futureValue = futureValue.toFixed(2);
    return futureValue;
};
```

The messages in the Console panel of Chrome's developer tools

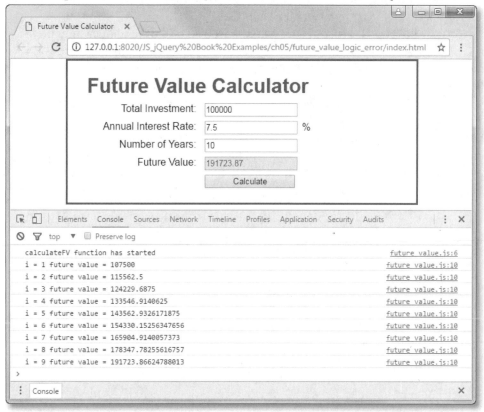

Description

- A simple way to *trace* the execution of a JavaScript application is to insert console.log() method calls at key points in the code. Then, the messages specified in these method calls are displayed in the Console panel.

- The log statements can display messages that indicate what portion of the code is being executed or display the values of variables.

- You can also use the alert() method for tracing, but the resulting popups can be intrusive, especially if you're tracing something extensive like a loop.

Figure 5-7   How to trace the execution of your JavaScript code

In the example in figure5-7, for instance, you would need to close an alert dialog box once when the calculateFV() function first starts and then once each time through the loop. That may not seem like much, but that can quickly become annoying, especially if you're tracing something extensive. Imagine tracing the loop that I just described with alert statements! Of course, if you just want to check one or two values, the alert() method might be all that you need.

How to view the source code

Occasionally, when nothing seems to be working right as you test an application, you may want to view the source code for the application. That will at least confirm that you're testing the right files.

To view the HTML source code, you can use one of the techniques in figure 5-8. Be aware, however, that the HTML source code is the code that is initially loaded into the browser, so it doesn't reflect any changes made to the DOM by the JavaScript. You'll learn how to view those changes in the next chapter.

If the JavaScript for an HTML page is stored in an external file, you can sometimes use the Chrome or Firefox browser to open that file by clicking on the path in the HTML code. In the code in this figure, for example, you can click on future_value.js to display the JavaScript file that this page uses. This lets you review the code in the JavaScript file.

Some of the HTML and JavaScript code for the Future Value application

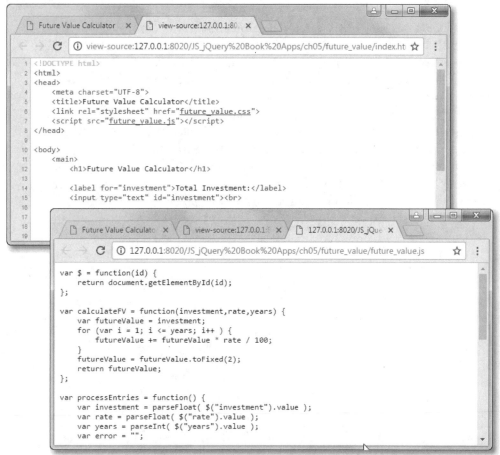

How to view the source code for a web page in any browser

- If it's available, use a menu command like View→Source or View→Page Source.
- You can also right-click on the page and select a command like Source, View Source, or View Page Source.

How to view the JavaScript code in an external file

- In Chrome or Firefox, click on the script element that refers to it.

Description

- When you're debugging, it can be useful to view the page's HTML.
- If the JavaScript is stored in the HTML file, you'll be able to see both the HTML and JavaScript code in the one file.

Figure 5-8   How to view the source code for a web page

When and how to validate the HTML

In some cases, an HTML error will cause a JavaScript error. Then, if you suspect that might be happening, it's worth taking the time to *validate* the HTML code. To do that, you can use the technique in figure 5-9.

Suppose, for example, that you accidentally use the same id attribute for more than one element in an HTML document. Then, when the JavaScript refers to that id, it won't run correctly, although it may not throw an error. If you validate the HTML, though, the problem with duplicate ids will be identified, so you can fix the ids in the HTML as well as the JavaScript that refers to those ids.

In fact, we recommend that you validate the HTML for all of the pages in an application. Of course, this isn't necessary when you're doing exercises or developing applications for a class, but this may help you fix a problem that is affecting your JavaScript.

The home page for the W3C validator

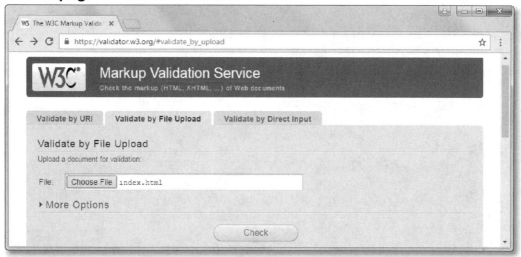

The validation results with one error

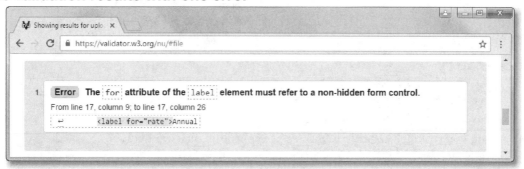

How to use the W3C Markup Validation Service

- Go to the URL that follows, identify the file to be validated, and click the Check button:
  http://validator.w3.org/

How to validate an HTML file from Aptana

- Select the file. Then, select the Commands→HTML→Validate Syntax (W3C) command.

Description

- Occasionally, an error in the HTML for a page will affect the operation of the JavaScript for that page. If you suspect that could be happening, *validating* the HTML for the page will sometimes expose the error.

- To validate the HTML for a page, you can use a program or website for that purpose. One of the most popular websites is the W3C Markup Validation Service.

- When you use the W3C Markup Validation Service, if the file you want to validate has already been uploaded to a web server, you can validate it by entering its URL on the Validate by URI tab. If the file you want to validate hasn't been uploaded to a web server, you can validate it by locating it on the Validate by File Upload tab.

- If you're using Aptana, you can validate an HTML file by using the command above.

Figure 5-9   When and how to validate the HTML

Perspective

All too often, JavaScript applications are put into production before they have been thoroughly tested and debugged. In the early days of JavaScript programming, that was understandable because the tools for testing and debugging were limited. Today, however, you have all the tools that you need for thoroughly debugging an application before you put it into production.

Terms

test	top-down coding and testing
debug	top-down testing
bug	developer tools
syntax error	F12 tools
runtime error	breakpoint
throw an exception	step through code
throw an error	trace
logic error	validate the HTML

Summary

- When you *test* an application, you try to make it fail. When you *debug* an application, you fix all of the problems that you discover during testing.

- When you write the code for a JavaScript application, you are likely to introduce three types of errors: *syntax errors*, *runtime errors*, and *logic errors*.

- *Top-down coding and testing* simplifies debugging because you build an application by coding and testing a small number of statements at a time.

- Chrome's *developer tools* (or *F12 tools*) can help you debug an application when it stops running. First, the Console panel displays an error message. Then, the link in the message goes to the statement where the error occurred in the Sources panel.

- In the Sources panel of Chrome's developer tools, you can set *breakpoints* that stop the execution of code. Then, you can *step through* the code starting from a breakpoint and view the changes in the variables at each step.

- An easy way to *trace* the execution of an application is to call the console.log() method at key points in the JavaScript code. This method logs the specified data in Chrome's Console panel. You can also use alert() methods for tracing.

- As you debug, you may occasionally want to view the HTML and JavaScript that have been loaded into the browser.

- *Validating* the HTML for a page will occasionally help you debug an application.

Exercise 5-1 Use Chrome's developer tools

In this exercise, you'll use Chrome's developer tools to find a syntax error and a logic error, set a breakpoint, and step through the Email List application.

1. Open the HTML and JavaScript files for the Email List application in this folder:

   `javascript_jquery\exercises\ch05\email_list`

2. Run the application in Chrome, enter valid values in all three text boxes, and click on the Join our List button. Then, note that nothing happens.

3. Open the developer tools and use the Console panel to display the error that caused the problem, as shown in figure 5-5. Then, click the link for the error to find the statement that caused the error.

4. Switch to your text editor or IDE and fix the code. The correction should be fairly obvious. Then, test the application again with valid values in all three text boxes. This time, an alert dialog box should be displayed with no message.

5. Click the OK button in the dialog box, and notice that there are no error messages in the Console panel. That's because a logic error has occurred.

6. Still in the developer tools, switch to the Sources panel. Then, if necessary, click on the email_list.js file in the Sources pane on the left to display the JavaScript code in the email_list.js file.

7. Set a breakpoint on the first statement in the joinList() function, as shown in figure 5-5. Then, with valid values still in the three text boxes, click the Join our List button again. The application should stop at the breakpoint.

8. Use the Step Into button or F11 key to step through the application. At each step, notice the values that are displayed in the local variables pane. Also, hover the mouse over a variable in the JavaScript code to see what its value is.

9. Experiment with the Step Over and Step Out buttons as you step through the application. When you get to the second if-else statement in the function, watch carefully to see what statements are executed. That should help you determine the cause of the logic error.

10. Switch to your text editor or IDE and fix the code. Then, test the application with valid data one more time. When the breakpoint is reached, remove it and then continue execution. This time, the application should execute to completion.

Exercise 5-2 Use other debugging methods

In this exercise, you'll use the other debugging methods that you learned in this chapter.

1. Open this HTML file, and notice that it includes calls to console.log() methods for tracing the execution of this application, as shown in figure 5-7:

   `javascript_jquery\exercises\ch05\mpg\index.html`

2. Run this application in Chrome, don't enter anything into the text boxes, and click on the Calculate button. Note that an error message is displayed in an alert dialog box.

3. Close the dialog box, and then switch to the Console panel and review the information in the log.

4. Enter valid values in the two text boxes, and click on the Calculate button. Then, go to the Console panel to review the new information.

5. In the JavaScript for this application, replace each console.log() method with an alert() method. Then, run the application to see how this works.

6. Use one of the methods in figure 5-8 to display the source code for the page. Notice that since the JavaScript is included in the HTML document, you can see both the HTML and JavaScript code.

7. In the HTML, change the name in the for attribute for the Miles Per Gallon label from *mpg* to *mpgx*. This may not be identified as an error by your text editor or IDE. Then, use one of the methods in figure 5-9 to validate the HTML for the page, which should identify this error.

6

How to script the DOM with JavaScript

At this point, you have all of the JavaScript skills that you need for some serious DOM scripting. You just need to learn how to use some of the properties and methods that are provided by the DOM specifications, as well as some special skills for working with forms and controls.

DOM scripting properties and methods

To script the DOM, you use properties and methods of the objects that make up the DOM. These properties and methods are defined by the *DOM Core specification* that is implemented by all current browsers, as well as by the *DOM HTML specification*.

DOM scripting concepts

Before you learn the properties and methods of the *DOM Core specification*, figure 6-1 presents the DOM scripting concepts that you should understand. First, the *Document Object Model*, or *DOM*, is built as an HTML page is loaded into the browser. It contains *nodes* that represent all of the HTML elements and attributes for the page. This is illustrated by the HTML and diagram in this figure.

Besides the *element nodes* that are represented by ovals in this diagram, the DOM includes *text nodes* that hold the data for the HTML elements. In this diagram, these text nodes are rectangles. For instance, the first text node contains the text for the title element in the head section: "Join Email List". The one to the right of that contains the text for the h1 element in the body: "Please join our email list". And so on.

For simplicity, this diagram only includes the element and text nodes, but the DOM also contains *attribute nodes*, and each attribute node can have a text node that holds the attribute value. Also, if the HTML includes comments, the DOM will include *comment nodes*.

If you study the table in this figure, you can see that an element node can have element, text, and comment nodes as child nodes. An attribute node can have a text node as a child node. And a text node can't have a child node. Even though an attribute node is attached to an element node, it isn't considered to be a child node of the element node.

The properties and methods for working with DOM nodes are defined by a specification called an *interface*. In the topics that follow, you'll learn how to work with the properties and methods of the Node, Document, and Element interfaces.

As you work with these interfaces, you'll come across terms like *parent*, *child*, *sibling*, and *descendant*. These terms are used just as they are in a family tree. In the diagram in this figure, for example, the form element is the parent of the label, input, and span elements, and the label, input, and span elements are children of the form element. The label, input, and span elements are also siblings because they have the same parent. Similarly, the h1 and form elements are children of the body element, and the h1, form, label, input, and span elements are all descendants of the body element.

You should also be able to see these relationships in the HTML for a web page. In the HTML in this figure, for example, the indentation clearly shows the children and descendants for each element.

The code for a web page

```html
<!DOCTYPE html>
<html>
<head>
    <title>Join Email List</title>
</head>
<body>
    <h1>Please join our email list</h1>
    <form id="email_form" name="email_form" action="join.html" method="get">
        <label for="email_address">Email Address:</label>
        <input type="text" id="email_address" name="email_address">
        <span id="email_error">*</span><br>
    </form>
</body>
</html>
```

The DOM for the web page

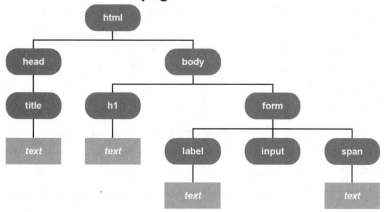

The DOM nodes that you commonly use

Type	Description
Document	Root node of the DOM. It can only have one Element node as a child node.
Element	An element in the web page. It can have Element, Text, and Comment nodes as child nodes.
Attr	An attribute of an element. Although it is attached to an Element node, it isn't considered a child node. It can have a Text node as a child node.
Text	The text for an element or attribute. It can't have a child node.

Description

- The *DOM* (*Document Object Model*) is a hierarchical collection of *nodes* in the web browser's memory that represents the current web page.
- The DOM for a web page is built as the page is loaded by the web browser.
- JavaScript can modify the web page in the browser by modifying the DOM. Whenever the DOM is changed, the web browser displays the results of the change.
- To modify the DOM, you can use the properties and methods that are defined by the *DOM Core specification*.

Figure 6-1   DOM scripting concepts

The properties of the Node interface

Figure 6-2 describes six properties that you can use for working with nodes. These properties are defined by the Node interface. All the examples in this figure assume the use of the $ function that gets an element by id.

The first JavaScript example shows how to use the firstChild and nodeValue properties to get the text of an HTML element. In this case, this statement will store an asterisk (*) in the variable named errorText if the statement is run before the node is changed. That's because this node is set to the asterisk by the HTML.

If you refer back to the diagram in the previous figure, you can see that the firstChild property is needed to get the text node for the span element. Then, the nodeValue property gets the text from that text node.

The second JavaScript example shows how to use the firstChild and nodeValue properties to put text into the text node of an HTML element. Like the first example, the firstChild property gets the text node for the span element. Then, a value is assigned to the nodeValue property of that element.

The third JavaScript example shows how to use three properties of the input element with "email_address" as its id to set the text for the span element that follows it to an empty string. First, the nextElementSibling property gets the span element that is the next sibling of the input element. Then, the firstChild and nodeValue properties get the text.

You should know that, in all of these examples, you'll need to make sure that the text node contains a text value when it initially loads. Otherwise, the element won't have a firstChild property. You'll learn one way to add text to a node later in this chapter.

Some of the properties of the Node interface

Property	Description
`nodeValue`	For a Text, Comment, or Attribute node, this property returns the text that's stored in the node. Otherwise, it returns a null value.
`parentNode`	Returns the parent node of a node if one exists. Otherwise, this property returns a null value.
`childNodes`	Returns an array of Node objects representing the child nodes of a node. If the node doesn't have child nodes, the array contains no elements.
`firstChild`	Returns a Node object for the first child node of a node. If the node doesn't have child nodes, this property returns a null value.
`lastChild`	Returns a Node object for the last child node of a node. If the node doesn't have child nodes, this property returns a null value.
`nextElementSibling`	Returns a Node object for the next sibling of a node. If the node doesn't have a sibling element that follows it, this property returns a null value.

HTML that contains element and text nodes

```
<body>
    <h1>Please join our email list</h1>
    <form id="email_form" name="email_form" action="join.html"
        method="get">
        <label for="email_address">Email Address:</label>
        <input type="text" id="email_address" name="email_address">
        <span id="email_error">*</span><br>
        <label> </label>
        <input type="button" id="join_list" value="Join our List">
    </form>
</body>
```

How to get the text of an HTML element with "email_error" as its id

```
var errorText = $("email_error").firstChild.nodeValue;
```

How to set the text of an HTML element with "email_error" as its id

```
$("email_error").firstChild.nodeValue = "Entry is invalid.";
```

How to set the text of an HTML element without using its id

```
$("email_address").nextElementSibling.firstChild.nodeValue = "";
```

Description

- An *interface* describes the properties and methods for an object.
- When DOM scripting, you often use the properties of the Node interface. Some of the most useful ones are summarized in the table above.
- In the examples above, the **$** sign calls the function that gets the element that has the id that's passed to it as the parameter.

Figure 6-2   The properties of the Node interface

The methods of the Document and Element interfaces

The first table in figure 6-3 summarizes three methods that are in both the Document and Element interfaces. All three of these methods return arrays. For instance, the getElementsByTagName() method returns an array that contains all of the Element nodes with the specified tag name.

If these methods are used with the document object, they get all of the elements in the document. This is illustrated by the first example that gets all of the <a> elements in the document and puts them in an array named links.

If these methods are used with an element as the object, they get all of the elements that are descendants of that element. For instance, the first statement in the second example gets the element with "image_list" as its id. Then, the second statement gets an array of all of the li elements that are descendants of the image_list element.

The second table in this figure summarizes some of the methods of the Element interface that work with attributes. For instance, the third example in this figure uses the hasAttribute() method to find out whether an element has a class attribute. If it does, it uses the getAttribute() method to get the value of that attribute.

The fourth example shows how to use the setAttribute() method to set an attribute. Here, the second statement sets the class attribute to "open". When this method is used, if the attribute doesn't already exist, the method adds it to the element before setting its value. Then, the last example in this figure uses the removeAttribute() method to remove the class attribute from the element.

Common methods of the Document and Element interfaces

Method	Description
getElementsByTagName(*tagName*)	Returns an array of all Element objects descended from the document or element that have a tag that matches the specified tag.
getElementsByName(*name*)	Returns an array of all Element objects descended from the document or element that have a name attribute that matches the specified name.
getElementsByClassName(*classNames*)	Returns an array of all Element objects descended from the document or element that have a class attribute with a name or names that match the parameter. The classNames parameter can be a single name or a space-separated list of class names.

Common methods of the Element interface

Method	Description
hasAttribute(*name*)	Returns true if the Element has the attribute specified in name.
getAttribute(*name*)	Returns the value of the attribute specified in name or an empty string if an attribute of that name isn't set.
setAttribute(*name*, *value*)	Sets the attribute specified in name to the specified value. If the attribute doesn't already exist, it creates the attribute too.
removeAttribute(*name*)	Removes the attribute specified in name.

How to create an array of all <a> tags in a document

```
var links = document.getElementsByTagName("a");
```

How to create an array of all li tags within a ul element (image_list)

```
var list = document.getElementById("image_list");
var items = list.getElementsByTagName("li");
```

How to test for and get an attribute

```
var list = document.getElementById("image_list");
if ( list.hasAttribute("class") ) {
    var classAttribute = list.getAttribute("class"));
}
```

How to set an attribute

```
var list = document.getElementById("image_list");
list.setAttribute("class", "open");
```

How to remove an attribute

```
var list = document.getElementById("image_list");
list.removeAttribute("class");
```

Description

- The methods of the Document and Element interfaces let you get arrays of elements.
- The methods of the Element interface also let you work with attributes.

Figure 6-3   The methods of the Document and Element interfaces

The properties of the DOM HTML specification

The properties and methods that you've seen so far are part of the DOM Core specification. But there's also a *DOM HTML specification* that provides properties that make it easier to work with HTML elements. Figure 6-4 summarizes some of these properties and shows you how to use them.

When you work with the DOM HTML specification, you should remember that its properties don't provide new functionality. Instead, they provide shortcuts that make it easier to work with the DOM nodes of an HTML document.

The differences are illustrated by the first set of examples in this figure, which get and set the src attribute for an img element. With the DOM core specification, the getAttribute() and setAttribute() methods are used. With the DOM HTML specification, the src property is used, which shortens and simplifies the code.

The other examples in this figure show how to use some of the other properties of the DOM HTML specification. You'll also see some other properties used in the applications in this book. Usually, the property name is the same as the attribute name, but sometimes the property name is different. For instance, as one of the examples shows, the className property is used to get and set the class attribute.

If you want to use the online documentation for the DOM HTML specification, it helps to know that this specification is composed of several *interfaces* that describe the properties and methods of an object type. The base interface is HTMLElement, which describes a base HTML element. In addition, the HTMLElement interface *inherits* properties and methods from the DOM Core Element interface, which in turn inherits from the DOM Core Node interface. This means that all the Node, Element, and HTMLElement properties and methods are available to you when you work with HTML elements in JavaScript.

Beyond that, specific HTML elements use specific DOM HTML interfaces that inherit from the base HTMLElement interface. For example, an img element uses the HTMLImageElement interface, and an input element uses the HTMLInputElement interface.

Most of the time, you won't need to know which interface an element uses. Usually, you'll be able to use the element's attribute name as the DOM HTML property name in your code. But if that doesn't work, you can use the URL at the top of this figure to look up the correct property name. In the table of contents that you'll find there, you can find subheadings for the base HTMLElement interface, and for the more specific interfaces that inherit from HTMLElement, like HTMLLinkElement, HTMLImageElement, and HTMLInputElement.

The URL for the DOM HTML specification

`www.w3.org/TR/DOM-Level-2-HTML/html.html`

Typical properties available with the DOM HTML specification

Element	Property	Attribute
all	id	The id attribute
	title	The title attribute
	className	The class attribute. To set multiple class names, separate the names with spaces.
	tagName	The name of the tag, like div, h1, h2, a, or img.
<a>	href	The href attribute
img	src	The src attribute
	alt	The alt attribute
input	disabled	The disabled attribute

How the DOM HTML specification can simplify your code

How to get and set an img tag src attribute with the DOM core specification

```
var imageElement = $("image");
alert(imageElement.getAttribute(src));      // displays the src attribute
imageElement.setAttribute(src, "lures.jpg"); // sets the src attribute
```

How to get and set the same attribute with the DOM HTML specification

```
alert(imageElement.src);                    // displays the src attribute
imageElement.src = "lures.jpg";             // sets the src attribute
```

Other examples of using the DOM HTML specification

How to get the id attribute of the first element in an array

```
links = document.getElementsByTagName("a");
var firstLinkId = links[0].id);
```

How to get the href attribute of an <a> element

```
var target = $("first_link").href;
```

How to set and get the class attribute of an element with two class names

```
$("div").className = "open plus";
var classNames = $("div").className;        // classNames = "open plus"
```

How to get the tag attribute of the first element in an array

```
links = document.getElementsByTagName("a");
var tagName = links[0].tagName;             // tagName = "a"
```

How to disable and enable an element

```
$("btnPlay").disabled = true;
$("btnPlay").disabled = false;
```

Description

- The HTML specification provides shortcuts that make it easier to work with DOM nodes.

- The HTML specification is composed of *interfaces* that *inherit* properties and methods from other interfaces. The HTMLElement interface represents a base HTML element.

Figure 6-4   The properties of the DOM HTML specification

The FAQs application

Now, you'll see how the properties and methods of the Node, Document, and Element interfaces are used in a typical DOM scripting application. We call this the FAQs (Frequently Asked Questions) application, and you can see its user interface in figure 6-5.

Quite simply, if the user clicks on a heading with a plus sign before it, the text below it is displayed and the plus sign is changed to a minus sign. Similarly, if the user clicks on a heading with a minus sign before it, the text below it is hidden and the minus sign is changed to a plus sign. The user can display the text below all three headings at the same time, and the user can hide the text below all three headings at the same time.

The HTML and CSS

In the HTML in this figure, you can see that each of the questions is coded in an <a> element within an h2 element, and each h2 element is followed by a div element that contains the answer. Note that the href attributes in these elements are coded as # signs so these links don't go anywhere.

Because <a> elements are coded within the h2 elements, a user can tab from one heading to the next. Then, when a user tabs to a heading and presses the Enter key, the effect is the same as clicking on the heading. This makes this app easier to use for motor-impaired users who can't handle a mouse.

In the CSS, you can see that both the focus and hover pseudo-classes are set to the color blue. That way, the <a> elements will look the same whether the user hovers the mouse over a link or tabs to the link.

Next, look at the two style rules for the h2 elements. The first one applies to all h2 elements, and it sets the cursor to a pointer when the user hovers the mouse over an h2 element. It also applies a background property that includes an image named plus.png. This image is displayed just once (no-repeat) to the left of the element and it is vertically centered.

The second style rule for the h2 elements applies to elements that have a class property set to "minus". This style rule applies a background property like the one for all h2 elements, but this time it uses an image named minus.png. That's the image that's used when the text below a heading is displayed.

Now, look at the two style rules for the div elements. The first one sets the display property to "none", which hides the contents of the div element. In contrast, the second style rule applies to div elements that have a class attribute set to "open". It sets the display property to block, which means that the contents of the div element are displayed.

With the HTML and CSS set up this way, all the JavaScript has to do is turn these classes on and off as the user clicks on a heading. If, for example, the user clicks on the middle h2 heading when its text is hidden, the JavaScript needs to set the class attribute for the clicked h2 element to "minus" and the class attribute for its sibling div element to "open".

The FAQs application in a browser

JavaScript FAQs

− **What is JavaScript?**

JavaScript is a browser-based programming language that makes web pages more responsive and saves round trips to the server.

⊕ **What is jQuery?**

⊕ **Why is jQuery becoming so popular?**

The HTML

```
<body>
    <main id="faqs">
        <h1>JavaScript FAQs</h1>
        <h2><a href="#">What is JavaScript?</a></h2>
        <div>
            <p>JavaScript is a browser-based programming language that makes
                web pages more responsive and saves round trips to the
                server.</p>
        </div>
        <h2><a href="#">What is jQuery?</a></h2>
        <div>
            <p>jQuery is a library of the JavaScript functions that you're
                most likely to need as you develop websites.</p>
        </div>
        <h2><a href="#">Why is jQuery becoming so popular?</a></h2>
        <div>
            <p>Three reasons:</p>
            <ul>
                <li>It's free.</li>
                <li>It lets you get more done in less time.</li>
                <li>All of its functions are cross-browser compatible.</li>
            </ul>
        </div>
    </main>
</body>
```

The CSS

```
a {
    color: black;
    text-decoration: none; }
a:focus, a:hover {
    color: blue; }
h2 {
    cursor: pointer;
    background: url(images/plus.png) no-repeat left center; }
h2.minus {
    background: url(images/minus.png) no-repeat left center; }
div {
    display: none; }
div.open {
    display: block; }
```

Figure 6-5   The HTML and CSS for the FAQs application

The JavaScript

Figure 6-6 shows the JavaScript for this application. Here, the event handler for the onload event attaches the event handlers for each of the h2 elements. To do that, its first statement gets the object for the element that has "faqs" as its id. That's the main element in the HTML code. Then, the second statement uses the getElementsByTagName() method to get an array of the h2 elements within that section. This array is stored in a variable named h2Elements.

This is followed by a for statement that attaches the event handler for each h2 element. Its loop is executed once for each element in the h2Elements array. The only statement in this loop attaches the event handler named "toggle" to the current h2 element in the array.

The onload event handler ends by setting the focus to the <a> element in the first h2 element in the array of h2 elements. It does that with this code:

```
h2Elements[0].firstChild.focus();
```

This refers to the first child of the first h2 element in the array (index zero), which is its <a> element.

Now, look at the toggle() function that is the event handler for the click event of each h2 element. Remember that it is assigned to each h2 element in the array.

The first statement within this function declares a new variable named h2 and assigns the *this* keyword to it. This is the critical statement in this function, because the *this* keyword refers to that specific h2 object in the DOM. As a result, one event handler is created for each h2 element in the DOM.

Without this statement, the loop would create just one event handler and attach it to each h2 element. That's because the statements in the event handler would be replaced each time through the loop, ending up with the statements for the last heading. As a result, clicking on any h2 heading would only toggle the last heading. You'll learn more about this in chapter 18.

The second statement in the toggle() function gets the div element below the current h2 element by using the nextElementSibling() method. Then, the if statement that follows tests whether the h2 element has a class attribute. If it does, it removes that attribute. If it doesn't, it adds a class attribute with a value of "minus". That means that the CSS will change the background image from a plus sign to a minus sign, or vice versa.

Then, the second if statement uses similar coding to add an "open" class if the div element doesn't have one and to remove the class if it does. That means that the CSS will change the display property from none to block, or vice versa.

Now that you've reviewed this code, you should note that it will work for any number of h2 and div elements that are defined by the HTML. You should also note that the div elements can contain whatever HTML elements the application requires, including img, <a>, and list elements.

This application should also give you some idea of what JavaScript and DOM scripting can do. As you progress through this chapter, you'll learn some additional skills for DOM scripting. Then, in section 2, you'll see how jQuery makes it easier to do this kind of DOM scripting.

The JavaScript for the FAQs application

```javascript
"use strict";
var $ = function(id) { return document.getElementById(id); };

// the event handler for the click event of each h2 element
var toggle = function() {
    var h2 = this;                      // this refers to the clicked h2 tag
    var div = h2.nextElementSibling;    // div = h2's sibling div

    // toggle + and - image in h2 elements by adding or removing a class
    if (h2.hasAttribute("class")) {
        h2.removeAttribute("class");
    } else {
        h2.setAttribute("class", "minus");
    }

    // toggle div visibility by adding or removing a class
    if (div.hasAttribute("class")) {
        div.removeAttribute("class");
    } else {
        div.setAttribute("class", "open");
    }
};

window.onload = function() {
    // get the h2 tags
    var faqs = $("faqs");
    var h2Elements = faqs.getElementsByTagName("h2");

    // attach event handler for each h2 tag
    for (var i = 0; i < h2Elements.length; i++ ) {
        h2Elements[i].onclick = toggle;
    }
    // set focus on first h2 tag's <a> tag
    h2Elements[0].firstChild.focus();
};
```

Notes

- The first two statements in the onload event handler create an array of the h2 elements in the section with "faqs" as its id.

- The for loop in the onload event handler is executed once for each of the h2 elements. It attaches the toggle event handler to the onclick event of each h2 element.

- In the code for the toggle event handler, the *this* keyword refers to the h2 element that has been clicked. You'll learn more about the *this* keyword in chapter 12.

Figure 6-6   The JavaScript for the FAQs application

How to script forms and controls

A *form* contains one or more *controls* such as text boxes and buttons. The controls that accept user entries are also known as *fields*. In the topics that follow, you'll learn how to work with forms and controls.

How forms work

Figure 6-7 shows how to create a form that contains three controls: two text boxes and a button. To start, you code the form element. On the opening tag for this element, you code the action and method attributes. The action attribute specifies the file on the web server that will be used to process the data when the form is submitted. The method attribute specifies the HTTP method that will be used for sending the form to the web server.

In the example in this figure, the form will be submitted to the server using the HTTP "get" method when the user clicks the Join our List button. Then, the data in the form will be processed on the server by the code that's in the file named join.php. That file will use PHP as the scripting language.

When you use the "get" method, the form data is sent as part of the URL for the HTTP request. That means that the data is visible in the address bar of the browser. This is illustrated by the URL in this figure. Here, the URL is followed by a question mark and name/value pairs separated by ampersands that present the name attributes and field values. In this case, two values are submitted: the email address and first name entries.

When you use the "post" method, by contrast, the form data is packaged as part of an HTTP request and isn't visible in the browser. Because of that, the submission is more secure than it is when you use the "get" method.

Within the opening and closing tags of the form element, you code the controls for the form. In this example, the first two input elements are for text boxes that will receive the user's email address and first name. The third input element has "submit" as the value for its type attribute, which means it is a *submit button*. When it is clicked, the data in the form will automatically be submitted to the server.

If the type attribute of an input element is "reset", the button is a *reset button*. When that type of button is clicked, all of the values in the controls of the form will be reset to their starting HTML values.

When a form is submitted to the server, the data in the form should be completely validated on the server before the data is processed. Then, if any of the data isn't valid, the form is sent back to the browser with appropriate error messages so the entries can be corrected. This is referred to as *data validation*.

Usually, the form data is validated by the browser too before it is submitted to the server. Note, however, that the browser validation doesn't have to be as thorough as the server-side validation. If the browser validation catches 80 to 90% of the entry errors, it will save many round trips to the server.

A form in a web browser

Email Address:	grace@yahoo.com
First Name:	Grace
	Join our List

The HTML for the form

```
<form id="email_form" name="email_form" action="join.php" method="get">
    <label for="email_address">Email Address:</label>
    <input type="text" id="email_address" name="email_address"><br>
    <label for="first_name">First Name:</label>
    <input type="text" id="first_name" name="first_name"><br>
    <label> </label>
    <input type="submit" id="join_list" value="Join our List"><br>
</form>
```

The URL that's sent when the form is submitted with the "get" method

```
join.php?email_address=grace%40yahoo.com&first_name=Grace
```

Attributes of the form element

Attribute	Description
name	A name that can be referred to by client-side or server-side code.
action	The URL of the file that will process the data in the form.
method	The HTTP method for submitting the form data. It can be set to either "get" or "post". The default value is "get".

Description

- A *form* contains one or more *controls* (or *fields*) like text boxes, radio buttons, lists, or check boxes that can receive data.

- When you click on a *submit button* for a form (type is "submit"), the form data is sent to the server as part of an HTTP request. When you click on a *reset button* for a form (type is "reset"), the form data is reset to its default values.

- When a form is submitted to the server for processing, the data in the controls is sent along with the HTTP request.

- When you use the "get" method to submit a form, the URL that requests the file is followed by a question mark and name/value pairs that are separated by ampersands. These pairs contain the name attributes and values of the data that is submitted. When you use the "post" method, the data is hidden.

- *Data validation* refers to checking the data collected by a form to make sure it is valid, and complete data validation is always done on the server. Then, if any invalid data is detected, the form is returned to the client so the user can correct the entries.

- To save round trips to the server when the data is invalid, some validation is usually done on the client before the data is sent to the server. However, this validation doesn't have to be as thorough as the validation that's done on the server.

Figure 6-7   How forms work

How to script Textbox, Textarea, and Select objects

Text boxes, text areas, and select lists are common controls that you should be familiar with. A Textbox object provides a single line for an entry, a Textarea object provides multiple lines for an entry, and a Select object provides a list of options that the user can select from, usually in a drop-down list.

The table in figure 6-8 shows the value property that's common to all three of these HTML objects. It returns a string containing either the entry that the user made or the option that the user selected from the list.

The HTML code in this figure uses these controls to get a user's name, comments, and country. Note that the select control's initial option has no display string and a value of an empty string. This is a common way to make the control appear as if no selection has been made when the page first loads. Another way to do this is to have the display string say something like "Select One" instead of being blank. If, however, you want to make sure that the user makes a selection, you can remove this blank option. This forces the user to either accept the default option or select a different one.

The first JavaScript example in this figure shows how to use the value property of these controls to get the values the user entered or selected. The first two statements use the $ function to store the text box and text area values in variables named name and comment. Then, because the value property returns strings, the next two lines use the length property of the value string to make sure the user entered a value.

When doing this kind of check for a text area, though, you'll need to think about line returns. For instance, if the user presses just the Enter key, a *hard return* is entered and becomes a character in the value property, even though the user didn't type any other text. In contrast, *soft returns* are the automatic returns that occur when the line the user is entering overflows to the next line. These returns don't become characters in the value property.

The last portion of code in this example works with the select element. First, it uses the value property to retrieve the user's selection and store it in a variable named country. Then, it checks the value of the variable and performs different processing depending on which country was chosen, or it notifies the user if no country was chosen.

In addition to using the value property to retrieve the content of these controls, you can use it to set the content of the controls. The second JavaScript example in this figure shows how this works. In this case, each of the controls on the form has its value property set to an empty string. This is a common way to clear a form, but you can set the value property to any string.

When you set the value property for a Textbox or Textarea object, the value will replace the contents of the value property. But when you set the value of a Select object, it selects the option in the list with that value. For example, setting the value property of the Select object to "can" will select the Canada option. If you set the value property to a value that isn't in the option list, nothing is selected, not even the Select object's default value. (The default value is the value of the first option in the list, or the option that has a selected attribute.)

Property of a Textbox, Textarea, or Select object

Property	Description
`value`	The content of the value attribute for the entered text or selected option. Returns a string.

HTML code for a text box, text area, and select list

```
<label for="name">First Name:</label>
<input type="text" name="name" id="name"><br>
<label for="comment">Comment:</label>
<textarea name="comment" id="comment" rows="5" cols="40"></textarea><br>
<label for="country">Country:</label>
<select name="country" id="country">
    <option value=""></option>
    <option value="usa">USA</option>
    <option value="can">Canada</option>
    <option value="mex">Mexico</option>
</select>
```

JavaScript code to get the text box, text area, and select list values

```
var name = $("name").value;
var comment = $("comment").value;

if (name.length == 0) { alert("Please enter a name."); }
if (comment.length == 0) { alert("Please enter a comment."); }

var country = $("country").value;
if ( country == "usa" ) { /* USA processing */ }
else if ( country == "can" ) { /* Canada processing */ }
else if ( country == "mex" ) { /* Mexico processing */ }
else { alert("Please select a country."); }
```

JavaScript code to set the text box, text area, and select list values

```
$("country").value = "";
$("name").value = "";
$("comment").value = "";
```

Description

- The name and id attributes of these controls should be set to the same value.

- After you use the value property of one of these objects to get the value string, you can use the length property of the String object to get the number of characters in the string.

- Setting the value property of a Textbox or Textarea object replaces the text contents.

- Setting the value property of a Select object selects the option with the corresponding value.

- When the user presses the Enter key while typing in a text area, a *hard return* is entered into the text. Hard returns appear as characters in the value property.

- When the user types past the end of a line in a text area and a new line is automatically started, a *soft return* occurs. Soft returns do not appear as characters in the value property.

Figure 6-8   How to script Textbox, Textarea, and Select objects

How to script Radio and Checkbox objects

Two other types of controls that you should be familiar with are radio buttons and check boxes. Both of these controls let a user select an option. A group of radio buttons in a web page lets a user select one of several options. When the user clicks one button in a group, the other buttons in the group are deselected. By contrast, each check box on a page is independent. Selecting one check box has no effect on any other check box.

The table in figure 6-9 shows two of the properties common to these HTML objects. The value property returns a string containing the contents of the control's value attribute. The checked property returns a Boolean value indicating whether or not the radio button or check box is checked.

The HTML example in this figure contains two radio buttons and a check box. When you create a group of radio buttons, they must have the same name so the web browser knows they are in the same group. However, they must have different id values. In the example, both radio buttons have the name "contact", but one has an id of "text" and a value of "text" while the other has an id of "email" and a value of "email". Note that the id and value attributes don't have to be the same, but they often are.

Unlike radio buttons, when you create a check box, it must have a unique name and the name and id attributes must be set to the same value. In the example, the check box has a name and id of "accept".

The first JavaScript example in this figure shows how to get the user's choices from radio buttons and check boxes. First, it declares a variable named contact. Then, it checks to see to see if the radio button with an id of "text" is checked. If it is, it gets the contents of the radio button's value property and stores it in the contact variable.

Next, the code checks to see if the radio button with an id of "email" is checked. If it is, it gets the contents of the radio button's value property and stores it in the contact variable. Remember, though, that only one member of a radio button group can be checked. This means that only one of these radio buttons is going to have its checked property set to true.

Then, the code checks the value of the contact variable and does either text or email processing based on that value. If no radio button was selected, the code notifies the user to make a selection.

Finally, the code gets the value of the check box's checked property and stores it in a variable called accept. Then, the code checks to see if the value of the accept variable is true. If it is, the code processes the acceptance. If it isn't, the code notifies the user that the box needs to be checked.

The second JavaScript example in this figure shows how to set the checked property of radio buttons and check boxes. In this example, the radio buttons are unchecked and the check box is checked.

Two properties of a Radio or Checkbox object

Property	Description
value	The contents of the value attribute for the button or check box. Returns a string.
checked	If set to true, the button or check box is selected. If set to false, it isn't selected.

HTML code for two radio buttons and a check box

```
<label>Contact me by:</label>
<input type="radio" name="contact" id="text" value="text" checked>Text
<input type="radio" name="contact" id="email" value="email">Email<br>
<label>Terms of Service:</label>
<input type="checkbox" name="accept" id="accept" value="accept">I accept<br>
```

JavaScript code to get the radio button and check box values

```
var contact;
if ( $("text").checked ) { contact = $("text").value; }
if ( $("email").checked ) { contact = $("email").value; }

if ( contact == "text" ) { /*text processing*/ }
else if ( contact == "email" ) { /*email processing*/ }
else { alert("You must select a contact method"); }

var accept = $("accept").checked;
if ( accept ) {
    /*accept processing*/
} else { alert("You cannot use the web store at this time."); }
```

JavaScript code to set the radio button and check box values

```
$("text").checked = false;
$("email").checked = false;
$("accept").checked = true;
```

Description

- All radio buttons in a group must have the same name, but different ids. Only one button in a group may be checked at a time, but none of the buttons has to be checked.

- Each check box is independent of the other check boxes on the page. They aren't treated as a group. The name and id attributes of a check box should be set to the same value.

- To select a radio button, set its checked property to true. When you select a radio button, any other checked button in the same group will be cleared.

- To clear a radio button, set its checked property to false. When you clear a radio button, no other button will become checked.

- To select a check box, set its checked property to true. To clear a check box, set its checked property to false.

Figure 6-9   How to script Radio and Checkbox objects

How to use the methods and events for forms and controls

Figure 6-10 presents some of the common methods and events that you are likely to use with forms and controls. The first table summarizes two methods that are commonly used with forms.

The first method submits the form to the web server for processing. That's usually done after the user clicks a button to submit the form and all of the data is valid. The second method resets the data in the controls. That's usually done when the user clicks a button.

If you're familiar with HTML buttons, you know that input elements with their type attributes set to "submit" or "reset" call the submit() and reset() methods automatically with no JavaScript. If you want to validate the data in a form before you submit it to the server, though, you don't want that. As a result, you should use a regular input button.

The same is true for reset buttons. You'll often want to use a regular button as the reset button and issue the reset() method from your JavaScript. You'll see this illustrated for both submit and reset buttons in the application that follows.

The second table in this figure summarizes two methods that are commonly used with controls. In chapter 4, you learned how to use the focus() method to move the focus to a control. But you can also use the blur() method to remove the focus from a control.

The third table summaries six events that are commonly used with controls. In chapter 4, you learned how to use the onclick and ondblclick events to start event handlers. But you can also use other events to work with controls like text boxes, select lists, text areas, and links. For instance, you can write an event handler for the onchange event of a text box or the onblur event of an <a> element.

The examples in this figure illustrate how these methods and events can be used. You code the reset() and submit() methods for forms, not controls. You write the event handlers for the controls. And you use the event handler for the window.onload event to attach the event handlers for the controls.

Two methods that are commonly used with forms

Method	Description
`submit()`	Submits the form and its data to the server.
`reset()`	Resets the controls in the form to their starting values.

Two methods that are commonly used with controls

Method	Description
`focus()`	Moves the focus to the control.
`blur()`	Removes the focus from the control.

Common control events

Event	Description
`onfocus`	The control receives the focus.
`onblur`	The control loses the focus.
`onclick`	The user clicks the control.
`ondblclick`	The user double-clicks the control.
`onchange`	The value of the control changes.
`onselect`	The user selects text in a text box or text area.

Statements that use the reset() and submit() methods

```
$("registration_form").reset();
$("registration_form").submit();
```

An event handler for the onchange event of a select list

```
var investmentChange = function() {
    calculateClick();          // call the calculateClick function
    $("investment").blur();  // remove the focus from the select list
};
```

An event handler for the dblclick event of a text box

```
var yearsDblclick = function() {
    $("years").value = "";    // clear text box when double clicked
};
```

An onload event handler that assigns event handlers to events

```
window.onload = function() {
    $("investment").onchange = investmentChange;
    $("years").ondblclick = yearsDblclick;
    $("years").focus();
};
```

Description

- Input elements with the type attribute set to "submit" or "reset" automatically submit or reset a form. When validating data, though, regular buttons are often used and the form is submitted or reset by using the JavaScript submit() or reset() method.

Figure 6-10   How to use the methods and events for forms and controls

The Register application

Figure 6-11 presents a Register application that consists of several controls on a form. If an entry is required, a red asterisk is displayed to the right of the control. Then, when the user clicks the Register button, the application checks the entries to make sure they're valid. If any of them aren't valid, the application displays error messages to the right of the fields. If all are valid, the application submits the form.

If the user clicks the Reset button somewhere along the way, the application resets the controls on the form to their starting values. That's done by issuing the reset() method for the form. But this application also clears any error messages and restores the starting asterisks, which isn't done by the reset() method.

The HTML and CSS

In the HTML, you can see a form named registration_form. This form uses the "get" method to submit the values of the controls to register_account.html. In real life, though, a registration page would use the "post" method because it's more secure.

Inside the form, there are two text boxes named "email_address" and "phone", a select element named "country", a radio button group named "contact", and a check box named "terms". Within the radio button group are three radio buttons with ids of "text", "email", and "none". Below these controls are two button elements named "register" and "reset_form".

After some of the controls, you can see span elements. The starting values of these controls are asterisks (*) to indicate that these entries are required.

Below the HTML in this figure, you can see the CSS for these span elements. This style rule selects the span elements that are within the form that has "registration_form" as its id attribute. It sets the color for the asterisks and any subsequent error messages in the span elements to red.

The Register application in a browser

The HTML

```
<main>
    <h1>Register for an Account</h1>
    <form action="register_account.html" method="get"
        name="registration_form" id="registration_form">
        <label for="email_address">E-Mail:</label>
            <input type="text" name="email_address" id="email_address">
            <span>*</span><br>
        <label for="phone">Mobile Phone:</label>
            <input type="text" name="phone" id="phone">
            <span>*</span><br>
        <label for="country">Country:</label>
            <select name="country" id="country">
                <option value="">Select a country</option>
                <option>USA</option>
                <option>Canada</option>
                <option>Mexico</option>
            </select>
            <span>*</span><br>
        <label>Contact me by:</label>
            <input type="radio" name="contact" id="text"
                value="text" checked>Text
            <input type="radio" name="contact" id="email"
                value="email">Email
            <input type="radio" name="contact" id="none"
                value="none">Don't contact me<br>
        <label>Terms of Service:</label>
            <input type="checkbox" name="terms" id="terms"
                value="yes">I accept
            <span>*</span><br>
        <input type="button" id="register" value="Register">
        <input type="button" id="reset_form" value="Reset"><br>
    </form>
</main>
```

The CSS for the span elements in the registration form

```
#registration_form span {
    color: red;
}
```

Figure 6-11   The HTML and CSS for the Register application

The JavaScript

Figure 6-12 presents the JavaScript for this application, which consists of four functions starting with the $ function. Then, the second function is an event handler named processEntries() that does the data validation for the controls and submits the form when all of the controls are valid. The third function is an event handler named resetForm() that resets the form. And the fourth function is the event handler for the onload event that attaches the processEntries() and resetForm() event handlers to the click events of the Register and Reset buttons.

The processEntries() function is executed when the user clicks the Register button. It starts by declaring a Boolean variable named isValid that is assigned a starting value of true. Then, the next statements declare the variables that are assigned the values for the email, phone, country, contact, and terms controls. Note that the contact value is set to either Text, Email, or None, based on which radio button is checked.

After the user's data has been stored in the variables, an if statement is used for each of the entries to check that entry for validity. If any of the variables is invalid, an error message is moved into the span element that follows the related control. It does that by using code like this:

```
$("email_address").nextElementSibling.firstChild.nodeValue
    = "This field is required.";
```

This puts the message into first child element (the text node) of the next sibling element after the control (the span element). If the entry is valid, the code puts an empty string into the span element, which removes the asterisk. If an entry is invalid, the code also sets the isValid variable to false.

After the data validation, another if statement checks whether the isValid variable is true. If so, it submits the form to the server for processing by issuing the submit() method of the form. If the isValid variable is false, the form isn't submitted so the user can correct the entries.

The resetForm() function is executed when the user clicks the Reset button. It starts by calling the form's reset() method, which resets all of the values in the controls to their starting HTML values. But more needs to be done. So the next four statements reset the values in the span elements to asterisks, and the last statement moves the focus to the first text box.

The last function is the event handler for the onload event. It just attaches the two event handlers to the Register and Reset buttons. Then, it moves the focus to the first text box.

Now, take a moment to look at the naming conventions used for the event handlers for the click events of the Register and Reset buttons. Here again, they consist of verbs and nouns that indicate what type of processing they're going to do.

The JavaScript for the Register application

```
"use strict";
var $ = function(id) { return document.getElementById(id); };

var processEntries = function() {
    var isValid = true;

    // get values for user entries
    var email = $("email_address").value;
    var phone = $("phone").value;
    var country = $("country").value;
    var contact = "Text";
    if ($("email").checked) { contact = "Email"; }
    if ($("none").checked) { contact = "None"; }
    var terms = $("terms").checked;

    // check user entries for validity
    if (email == "") {
        $("email_address").nextElementSibling.firstChild.nodeValue
            = "This field is required.";
        isValid = false; }
    else {
        $("email_address").nextElementSibling.firstChild.nodeValue = ""; }
    if (phone == "") {
        $("phone").nextElementSibling.firstChild.nodeValue
            = "This field is required.";
        isValid = false; }
    else { $("phone").nextElementSibling.firstChild.nodeValue = "";}
    if (country == "") {
        $("country").nextElementSibling.firstChild.nodeValue
            = "Please select a country.";
        isValid = false; }
    else { $("country").nextElementSibling.firstChild.nodeValue = "";}
    if (terms == false) {
        $("terms").nextElementSibling.firstChild.nodeValue
            = "This box must be checked.";
        isValid = false; }
    else { $("terms").nextElementSibling.firstChild.nodeValue = "";}

    // submit the form if all fields are valid
    if (isValid == true) {
        $("registration_form").submit(); }
};
var resetForm = function() {
    $("registration_form").reset();
    $("email_address").nextElementSibling.firstChild.nodeValue = "*";
    $("phone").nextElementSibling.firstChild.nodeValue = "*";
    $("country").nextElementSibling.firstChild.nodeValue = "*";
    $("terms").nextElementSibling.firstChild.nodeValue = "*";
    $("email_address").focus();
};
window.onload = function() {
    $("register").onclick = processEntries;
    $("reset_form").onclick = resetForm;
    $("email_address").focus();
};
```

Figure 6-12   The JavaScript for the Register application

How to add and remove nodes from the DOM

Besides working with existing nodes, JavaScript lets you add nodes to and remove nodes from the DOM. You'll learn the easiest way to perform these operations in the next figure. Then, you'll learn how to view the changes to the DOM in Chrome.

How to use the innerHTML property of the Element interface

Figure 6-13 presents the innerHTML property of the Element interface. This property lets you set or return the contents of the HTML element you specify. This is illustrated by the examples in this figure.

The first example shows how to add content to an HTML element. In this case, four images will be added to a ul element with an id of "image_list". If you review the starting HTML for the page that contains this element, you'll see that the element contains no content.

When the page is loaded, though, its JavaScript adds the images to the list. To do that, it creates a string for each item to be added to the list that contains the HTML for that item. Since each list item contains an image, the HTML consists of an img element within an li element. Then, the first string is assigned to the innerHTML property of the element with an id of "image_list". Then, the next three strings are added to the content of that element. The result is a list of four images formatted as shown in this figure.

The second example in this figure shows how to get the HTML content of an element. To do that, you simply refer to the innerHTML property of the element. In this example, the HTML content that was added to the "image_list" element of the first example is assigned to a variable named listHTML.

You can also use the innerHTML property to remove the HTML content of an element. To do that, you simply assign an empty string to the property as shown in the third example.

One property of the Element interface for setting or returning HTML content

Property	Description
`innerHTML`	Sets or returns the HTML content of an element.

An application that displays a list of images

The starting HTML for the application

```html
<body>
    <main>
        <h1>Create Image List</h1>
        <ul id="image_list"></ul>
    </main>
</body>
```

The JavaScript that adds the images to the list

```javascript
<script>
    "use strict";
    var $ = function(id) {
        return document.getElementById(id);
    };
    window.onload = function() {
        $("image_list").innerHTML =
            "<li><img src='images/image1.jpg'></li>";
        $("image_list").innerHTML +=
            "<li><img src='images/image2.jpg'></li>";
        $("image_list").innerHTML +=
            "<li><img src='images/image3.jpg'></li>";
        $("image_list").innerHTML +=
            "<li><img src='images/image4.jpg'></li>";
    };
</script>
```

How to get the HTML content of an element

```javascript
var listHTML = $("image_list").innerHTML;
```

How to remove the HTML content of an element

```javascript
$("image_list").innerHTML = "";
```

Description

- To set the HTML content of an element, assign the content to the innerHTML property of the element. If you assign an empty string, the content is removed.
- You can also use the innerHTML property to return the content of an element. Then, you can assign that content to a variable or another element.

Figure 6-13   How to add nodes to and remove nodes from the DOM

How to view the changes to the DOM in Chrome

In the last chapter, you learned how to view the source code for a web page in a browser. You also learned that the code you'll see is the code that was initially loaded into the browser. In other words, it doesn't reflect any changes made to the DOM by JavaScript. If you looked at the source code for the application shown in the previous figure, for example, you'd see a ul element with no content even after the li elements have been added to the list.

To see these changes to the DOM, you can use the Elements panel in Chrome's developer tools as shown in figure 6-14. By using the techniques described in this figure, you can drill down into the document's elements. In this figure, for example, you can see that the body, main, ul, and li elements have been expanded so you can see their content. This shows that the li elements that contain the img elements have been added to the DOM.

In the Styles pane to the right of the Elements pane, you can also see the CSS that has been applied to the selected element. This pane shows all of the styles that have been applied from all of the style sheets that are attached to the web page. If a style in this pane has a line through it, that means it has been overridden by another style. This pane can be invaluable when you're trying to solve complicated formatting problems with cascading style sheets.

The Elements panel after JavaScript has changed the DOM

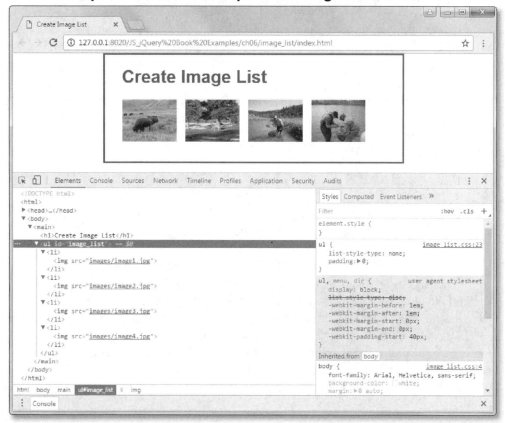

Description

- If you're using Chrome, you can use the Elements panel of the developer tools to see the changes to the DOM that your JavaScript has made.

- To open the developer tools, press F12. Then, click on the Elements tab to display the Elements panel.

- The Elements panel displays the HTML nodes for a document. You can expand these nodes until you can see the changes made to the DOM by JavaScript.

- To select a node, click on it. Then, you can see the CSS that's applied to the element in the Styles pane at the right side of the panel.

Figure 6-14   How to view the changes to the DOM in Chrome

The Register application with a table

Figure 6-15 illustrates a Register application that has controls on a form. When the user clicks the Register button, the application performs data validation to make sure all the fields are filled out correctly. If they are, the application submits the form. If they aren't, the application displays a table that shows what values have been entered and what values didn't pass validation. When the user clicks the Reset button, the application resets the controls on the form and clears the table of information.

The HTML and CSS

The HTML for this application is the same as the HTML in figure 6-11, but with two exceptions. First, the h2 and table elements shown in figure 6-15 are added to the end of the HTML in the main element.

Second, the span elements after the controls have been deleted because they aren't used in this application. Instead, the validation results and messages are shown in the table below the form. Please note, however, that the HTML for the table has no rows. That's because the rows will be added by the JavaScript.

In the CSS in this figure, you can see one change to the CSS for the earlier Register application. Instead of setting the font color for the span elements in the form to red, it sets the font color for the span elements in the table to red. You'll see that these span elements are added to the table by the JavaScript in the next figure.

The Register application with a table that's created for the user's entries

Register for an Account

E-Mail: ben@yahoo.com

Mobile Phone:

Country: Select a country

Contact me by: ● Text   ○ Email   ○ Don't contact me

Terms of Service: ☐ I accept

Register   Reset

Please review your entries and complete all required fields

Email: ben@yahoo.com
Phone: Required field
Country: Required field
Contact: Text
Terms: Required field

The HTML for the two elements below the form

```
        </form>
        <h2 id="registration_header"> </h2>
        <table id="registration_info"></table>
    </main>
```

The CSS for the span elements in the table

```
#registration_info span {
    color: red;
}
```

Description

- When the user clicks the Register button, this application displays a table below the form that shows the data for valid entries and error messages for invalid entries. If all of the entries are valid, this application calls the submit() method to submit the form to the server.

- When the user clicks the Reset button, this application calls the reset() method to reset the values in the controls. But it also removes the table below the form.

- Besides the two elements shown above that have been added to the HTML, the span elements after the controls have been removed because the asterisks and error messages aren't displayed to the right of the controls.

- In the CSS, the selector for the rule set that sets the color of the error messages to red has been changed to the one shown above. It selects all span elements in the table, which has an id of "registration_info".

Figure 6-15   The HTML and CSS for the Register application with a table

The JavaScript

Figure 6-16 presents the JavaScript for this application. It illustrates some interesting code that shows another way to apply some of the skills that you learned in this chapter.

Here, as a best practice, the processEntries() function starts by declaring the variables that will be used by the function. In this case, the first two statements declare variables named header and html and assigns empty strings to them. The header variable will be used to store the header for the table that is displayed below the form. The html variable will be used to store the content for the innerHTML property that will fill the table element with the user's entries.

The next two statements declare variables named required and msg. The required variable is set to a span element with "Required field" as its content. It will be placed in the table when the user doesn't enter a required field. Because this is a span element, the CSS will set the color for the message to red. The msg variable contains the header that will be printed before the table if one or more errors are detected.

The next seven statements are just like those in the earlier version of this application. They get the user's entries from the form and store them in variables.

This is followed by four if statements that check the validity of four of the entries to make sure they aren't empty strings. If an entry is an empty string, the related variable is changed to the value of the required variable. So instead of an entry, the variable will be set to a span element that contains "Required field". Then, the value of the header variable is replaced with the text in the msg variable. That will become the heading that's displayed before the table.

After the data validation, the nodeValue property of the firstChild property of the h2 element with "registration_header" as its id is set to the value of the header variable. This will either be an empty string or the starting value of the msg variable. If it's the value of the msg variable, the heading will be displayed after the form.

This is followed by an if statement that checks whether the header variable is equal to the msg variable. If it is, that means one or more fields are invalid because the header variable was changed from its starting value of an empty string. In that case, the next five statements add the HTML for five rows to the html variable. Then, the sixth statement puts the value of the html variable into the innerHTML property of the table. As soon as that's done, the table is displayed.

On the other hand, if none of the entries is invalid, the else clause of the if statement clears any previous values from the table element by setting its innerHTML property to an empty string. Then, it submits the form by issuing the submit() method of the form.

After that explanation, you shouldn't have any trouble understanding the code for the resetForm and the onload event handlers. The resetForm() function uses the reset() method to reset the controls on the form, sets the h2 element and table that are after the form to empty strings, and sets the focus to the first control on the form. The onload event handler just attaches the event handlers to the right events and sets the focus to the first control on the form.

The JavaScript for the Register application

```
"use strict";
var $ = function(id) { return document.getElementById(id); };

var processEntries = function() {
    var header = "";
    var html = "";
    var required = "<span>Required field</span>";
    var msg = "Please review your entries and complete all required fields";

    var email = $("email_address").value;
    var phone = $("phone").value;
    var country = $("country").value;
    var contact = "Text";
    if ($("email").checked) { contact = "Email"; }
    if ($("none").checked) { contact = "None"; }
    var terms = $("terms").checked;

    if (email == "") {
        email = required;
        header = msg; }
    if (phone == "") {
        phone = required;
        header = msg; }
    if (country == "") {
        country = required;
        header = msg; }
    if (terms == false) {
        terms = required;
        header = msg; }

    $("registration_header").firstChild.nodeValue = header;
    if (header == msg) {
        html = "<tr><td>Email:</td><td>" + email + "</td></tr>";
        html += "<tr><td>Phone:</td><td>" + phone + "</td></tr>";
        html += "<tr><td>Country:</td><td>" + country + "</td></tr>";
        html += "<tr><td>Contact:</td><td>" + contact + "</td></tr>";
        html += "<tr><td>Terms:</td><td>" + terms + "</td></tr>";
        $("registration_info").innerHTML = html;
    } else {
        $("registration_info").innerHTML = "";
        $("registration_form").submit();
    }
};
var resetForm = function() {
    $("registration_form").reset();
    $("registration_header").firstChild.nodeValue = "";
    $("registration_info").innerHTML = "";
    $("email_address").focus();
};
window.onload = function() {
    $("register").onclick = processEntries;
    $("reset_form").onclick = resetForm;
    $("email_address").focus();
};
```

Figure 6-16   The JavaScript for the Register application with a table

Perspective

The goal of this chapter has been to introduce you to some of the capabilities of DOM scripting with JavaScript. As a result, three different types of applications were presented. The FAQs application showed how you can use common properties and methods of the Document, Element, and Node interfaces. The Register application showed how JavaScript is commonly used for data validation. And the Register application with the table showed how HTML elements like a table can be added to the DOM.

Before you continue, you should know that there's a limit to how much DOM scripting you should do with JavaScript. That's because jQuery is a JavaScript library that is designed to make DOM scripting easier. As a result, most DOM scripting is done with a combination of JavaScript and jQuery. You'll learn more about jQuery in section 2.

Terms

DOM (Document Object Model)	form
DOM Core specification	control
DOM HTML specification	field
DOM node	submit button
element node	reset button
text node	data validation
attribute node	hard return
comment node	soft return
interface	

Summary

- The *Document Object Model*, or *DOM*, is built when a page is loaded into a browser. It consists of various types of *nodes*.

- In the DOM, *element nodes* represent the elements in an HTML document and *text nodes* represent the text within those elements. The DOM can also contain *comment nodes*, and it can contain *attribute nodes* that have text nodes that store the attribute values.

- JavaScript provides properties and methods for the objects of the DOM that are described in the *DOM Core Specification*. These include the properties and methods that are described by the Node, Document, and Element *interfaces*.

- JavaScript also provides properties for the objects of the DOM that are described in the *DOM HTML Specification*. Although these properties don't provide new functionality, they do provide shortcuts that make it easier to work with the DOM nodes of an HTML document.

- A *form* contains one or more *controls* such as text boxes and buttons. The controls that accept user entries are also known as *fields*. Some common controls are text boxes, text areas, select lists, radio buttons, and check boxes.

- When you work with controls, you use properties like value and checked, methods like focus() and blur(), and events like onfocus, onclick, and onblur.

- When you work with forms, you can use the submit() method to submit a form and the reset() method to reset the values in the controls of the form.

- To add nodes to or remove nodes from the DOM, you can use the innerHTML property of the Element interface.

- You can use the Elements panel of Chrome's developer tools to view the changes that are made to the DOM as an application executes.

Exercise 6-1   Experiment with the FAQs application

This exercise will give you a chance to better understand the FAQs application as you work with its code. It will also give you a chance to use one of the properties of the DOM HTML specification.

If you have any problems when you're testing, remember to use Chrome's developer tools as shown in chapter 5.

Test and review the application

1. Use your text editor or IDE to open the HTML and JavaScript files in this folder:

   `javascript_jquery\exercises\ch06\faqs`

   Then, test this application to see how it works, and review its code.

Attach the event handlers to the <a> elements instead of the h2 elements

2. Change this application so the toggle event handlers are attached to the <a> elements within the h2 elements instead of to the h2 elements themselves.

3. Test this change. When you do that, clicking on the headings should work, but clicking on the plus or minus signs before them shouldn't work.

Use the className property of the DOM HTML specification

4. Comment out the two if statements in the toggle event handler.

5. Below each commented out statement, code an if statement that gets the same result by using the className property instead of the hasAttribute(), removeAttribute(), and setAttribute() methods. For instance, you can check for a class by testing the value of the className property, and you can remove a class by setting the className property to an empty string (`""`).

6. Test this change.

Exercise 6-2   Add controls to the Register application

In this exercise, you'll add another radio button and a comments control to the form for the Register with table application, so the form looks like this:

If you have any problems when you're testing, remember to use Chrome's developer tools as shown in chapter 5.

1. Use your text editor or IDE to open the index.html and register.js files that are in this folder:

    `javascript_jquery\exercises\ch06\register_table`

2. Test this application with both invalid and valid data.

3. In the HTML file, add a radio button for Mobile phone and a text area for Comments, but watch out for duplicate id attributes. For the text area, you can use the example in figure 6-8 as your guide, but note that the width of the area will be set by the CSS.

4. In the JavaScript file, add the code that gets the data entered in the two new controls. Then, modify the code that builds the html table rows by adding a row for the comments entry. Note, however, that this entry is optional so no validation is required.

5. Test the application to see how a comment is displayed in the table below the form. Remember, though, that if all the entries are valid, the application will go to a new page and not display the table. So at least leave the Terms box unchecked.

6. Test the application again, but enter just two hard returns in the comments area by pressing the Enter key twice. Then, note that the table shows no entry.

7. Change the code in the JavaScript file so instead of displaying the comments in the table, the length of the comments entry is displayed, like this: Entry length = 41. You can use the length property of the entry to get the length. Then, test this change with hard return entries, text entries, and no entry.

8. Test the Reset button for the new fields. If changes are required, make them.

9. Enter all valid data, and click the Register button to submit the form. Because the "get" method is used, the entries are added to the URL for the next page.

Exercise 6-3   Enhance the Email List application

In this exercise, you'll enhance an Email List application that's similar to the one you saw in chapter 4 by providing better data validation with error messages to the right of the entries:

If you have any problems when you're testing, remember to use Chrome's developer tools as shown in chapter 5 and figure 6-14 of this chapter.

Test the application

1. Open your text editor or IDE, and open this HTML file:

    ```
    javascript_jquery\exercises\ch06\email\index.html
    ```

    Then, review the JavaScript code.

2. Test this application with valid data to see how it works. When you click the Join our List button, another page should be displayed.

3. Click the back button in your browser, then test the application with invalid data. Note that the errors are displayed in alert dialog boxes.

Enhance the data validation

4. Review the HTML and notice that span elements that contain asterisks have been added right after the first two input controls. Also notice that these span elements don't have ids. When you enhance the data validation, these elements should receive your error messages.

5. Enhance the data validation so it displays the error messages in the span elements. For this to work, you will need to code the data validation for each entry in a separate if statement. Use a Boolean variable to keep track of whether any entries are invalid. Then, if all of the entries are valid, you can submit the form. If you need help, you can refer to the code for the Register application in figure 6-12.

6. Test the application with valid data to be sure it still works. If it does, click the back button in your browser to return to the previous page and then refresh the page.

7. Click the Join our List button without entering any data. Then, use Chrome's developer tools to view the changes that have been made to the DOM to display the error messages. When you're done, close the developer tools.

See what happens when the span elements in the HTML are empty

8. In the HTML, delete the asterisk from the first span element. Then, test the application in Chrome by clicking on the Join our List button before making an entry. Nothing will happen.

9. Press the F12 key to display the developer tools, click on the Console tab, and you should see this error message: Cannot set property 'nodeValue' of null. This shows that the text node of the first span element hasn't been added to the DOM because it didn't have a starting value.

10. Restore the asterisk in the span element, and test again to make sure the application is working.

7

How to work with links, images, and timers

In the last chapter, you learned some of the most important DOM scripting skills. Now, this chapter presents some additional skills for working with links, images, and timers. Because jQuery doesn't provide for all of the functionality that's presented here, it's important to know how to implement this functionality in JavaScript.

How to work with links and images

A common task when working with links and images is cancelling the default action of the click event. Another common task is preloading images. In the following topics, you'll learn both skills.

How to cancel the default action of an event

Most of the time, when a user clicks on an element, nothing happens unless a JavaScript event handler has been attached to that element. In other words, there is no default action for most elements. However, when a user clicks on some elements of a web page, the browser performs a *default action*.

Figure 7-1 lists the default action for several elements. If, for example, a user clicks on a link, the browser loads the URL specified by the link. Similarly, if a user clicks on a button of the submit type, the browser submits the form to the server.

Although these default actions usually work the way you want, you may occasionally need to cancel a default action. If, for example, the user clicks on a link with an href attribute that points to an image, the browser by default loads the specified image, which displays the image and exits from the application. But if the application is doing an image swap, for example, you don't want that. As a result, you need to cancel the default action for this event.

When an event occurs, an *event object* is created. This object contains information about the event that occurred and provides methods that let you control the behavior of the event. To cancel the default action of an event, for example, you need to create an event handler that accesses the event object and uses one of its methods to cancel the default action.

As the first example in this figure shows, most web browsers are DOM-compliant so they pass the event object as the first parameter to the event handler. In addition, this event object has a method named preventDefault() that you can use to prevent the default action from occurring.

Unfortunately, older versions of Internet Explorer weren't completely DOM-compliant. So, as the second example shows, you get the event object by using the global window.event property. In addition, you set the returnValue property of this event object to false to prevent the default action from occurring.

To make your applications compatible with all browsers, you can combine the two techniques, as shown in the third example. Here, the function has a parameter that will receive the event object in a DOM-compliant browser. Then, the first if statement in the function tests the evt parameter to see if it's undefined. If so, the browser is IE, so this code assigns the event object in the window.event property to the evt parameter. Otherwise, the browser is DOM-compliant, so the evt parameter already contains the event object.

Then, the second if statement tests the evt parameter to see if it provides a preventDefault() method. Note that this code doesn't call the preventDefault() method, which it would if parentheses were included. If the evt parameter

Common HTML elements that have default actions for the click event

Element	Default action for the click event
`<a>`	Load the page in the href attribute.
`<input>`	Submit the form if the type attribute is set to submit.
`<input>`	Reset the form if the type attribute is set to reset.
`<button>`	Submit the form if the type attribute is set to submit.
`<button>`	Reset the form if the type attribute is set to reset.

DOM-compliant code that cancels the default action

```
var eventHandler = function(evt) {
    evt.preventDefault();
};
```

Older IE code that cancels the default action

```
var eventHandler = function() {
    var evt = window.event;
    evt.returnValue = false;
};
```

Cross-browser compatible code that cancels the default action

```
var eventHandler = function(evt) {
    // If the event object is not sent, get it from the window object
    if (!evt) { evt = window.event; }      // for IE

    // Cancel the default action
    if (evt.preventDefault) {
        evt.preventDefault();              // for most browsers
    }
    else {
        evt.returnValue = false;           // for IE
    }
};
```

Description

- Modern browsers send an *event object* to the event handler that's handling the event. They also provide a DOM-compliant preventDefault() method for the event object. When called, this method prevents the *default action* of the event from occurring.

- Older versions of IE store the event object in the global window.event property. When the returnValue property of this event object is set to false, it prevents the default action of the event from occurring.

- To ensure cross-browser compatibility, you need to provide for both ways of cancelling a default action.

Figure 7-1   How to cancel the default action of an event

includes a preventDefault() method, the code calls that method. Otherwise, the else clause sets the returnValue property of the window.event object to false.

Because cross-browser compatible code like this can be unwieldy, you can include just the DOM-compliant code if you know that you don't need to support older browsers. If you do need to support older browsers, though, you'll see an easier way to do that with jQuery in the next section of this book.

How to preload images

In JavaScript applications that load an image in response to a user event, the image isn't loaded into the browser until the JavaScript code changes the src attribute of the img tag. For large images or slow connections, this can cause a delay of a few seconds before the browser is able to display the image.

To solve this problem, an application can load the images before the user event occurs. This is known as *preloading images*. Then, the browser can display the images without noticeable delays. Although this may result in a longer delay when the page is initially loaded, the user won't encounter any delays when using the application.

Figure 7-2 shows how to preload images. To start, the first line of code creates a new Image object and stores it in a variable named image. This creates a new image node that's empty. Then, the second line of code sets the src property to the URL of the image to be preloaded. This causes the web browser to preload the image. Note here that you don't need to use the Image object after you've set the src property. The act of setting the src property is what causes the browser to preload the image.

The example in this figure shows how to preload the images for all the links on a page. This assumes that the href attribute in each link contains the location of each image that needs to be preloaded. First, the getElementsByTagName() method is used to get an array of all the links, and this array is stored in a variable named links. Then, a for loop is used to process each link in the array.

Within the loop, the first statement assigns the current link to the link variable, and the second statement creates a new Image object. Then, the third statement sets the src property of the Image object to the href property of the link. This preloads the image. As a result, all of the images will be preloaded in the browser's cache when the loop finishes.

How to preload an image with the Image object

How to create an Image object

```
var image = new Image();
```

How to load an image in an Image object

```
image.src = "image_name.jpg";
```

How to preload all images referenced by the href attributes of <a> tags

```
var links = document.getElementsByTagName("a");
var i, link, image;
for ( i = 0; i < links.length; i++ ) {
    link = links[i];
    image = new Image();
    image.src = link.href;
}
```

Description

- When an application *preloads images*, it loads all of the images that it's going to need when the page loads, and it stores these images in the web browser's cache for future use.

- When the images are preloaded, the browser can display them whenever they're needed without any noticeable delay.

- To preload an image, you start by using the new keyword to create an empty Image object. Then, you set the src attribute of the Image object to the URL for the image you want to preload.

Figure 7-2   How to preload images

The Image Swap application

Figure 7-3 shows an *image swap* application, which is a common type of JavaScript application. Here, the main image is swapped whenever the user clicks on one of the small (thumbnail) images. In this example, the user has clicked on the third thumbnail so the larger version of that image is displayed. In this application, the caption above the large image is also changed as part of the image swap, but that isn't always done in image swaps.

The HTML and CSS

In the HTML for this application, img elements are used to display the four thumbnail images. However, these elements are coded within <a> elements so the images are clickable and they can receive the focus. In the <a> elements, the href attributes identify the images to be swapped when the links are clicked and the title attributes provide the text for the related captions. In this case, both the <a> elements and the img elements are coded within a ul element.

After the ul element, you can see the h2 element for the caption and the img element for the main image on the page. The contents of the h2 element provides the caption for the first image, and the src attribute of the img element provides the location for the first image. That way, when the application first starts, the first caption and image are displayed.

The three ids that are used by the JavaScript are highlighted here. First, the id of the ul element is set to "image_list" so the JavaScript can get its child <a> elements. Second, the id of the h2 element is set to "caption" so the JavaScript can change the caption. And third, the id of the main img element is set to "main_image" so the JavaScript can change the image.

For the motor-impaired, this HTML provides accessibility by coding the img elements for the thumbnails within <a> elements. Then, as you'll see in the next figure, the JavaScript sets the focus on the first <a> element. That way, the user can access the thumbnail links by pressing the Tab key, and the user can swap the main image by pressing the Enter key when a thumbnail has the focus, which starts the onclick event handler.

Of note in the CSS for this page is the rule set for the li elements. As this figure shows, their display properties are set to inline so the thumbnail images go from left to right instead of from top to bottom.

The user interface for the Image Swap application

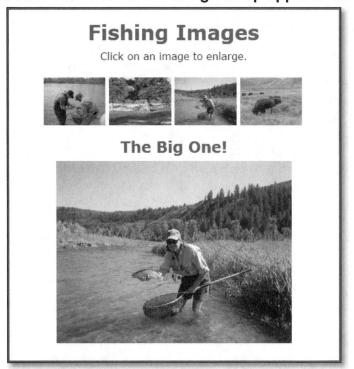

The HTML

```
<main>
    <h1>Fishing Images</h1>
    <p>Click on an image to enlarge.</p>
    <ul id="image_list">
        <li><a href="images/release.jpg" title="Catch and Release">
            <img src="thumbnails/release.jpg" alt=""></a></li>
        <li><a href="images/deer.jpg" title="Deer at Play">
            <img src="thumbnails/deer.jpg" alt=""></a></li>
        <li><a href="images/hero.jpg" title="The Big One!">
            <img src="thumbnails/hero.jpg" alt=""></a></li>
        <li><a href="images/bison.jpg" title="Grazing Bison">
            <img src="thumbnails/bison.jpg" alt=""></a></li>
    </ul>
    <h2 id="caption">Catch and Release</h2>
    <p><img id="main_image" src="images/release.jpg" alt=""></p>
</main>
```

The CSS for the li elements

```
li { display: inline; }
```

Figure 7-3   The user interface, HTML, and CSS for the Image Swap application

The JavaScript

Figure 7-4 presents the JavaScript for this application. In the onload event handler, the first three statements get the objects for the ul element (image_list), the h2 element for the caption, and the img element that displays the enlarged image. These objects are for the nodes in the DOM. Then, the fourth statement creates an array of the <a> elements within the image list and saves it in a variable named imageLinks. The code then uses a for loop to process each of the links in the array.

The for loop starts by preloading the image that will be swapped. Next, an event handler is created for the click event of each link. Note here that the function that creates each event handler has an evt parameter that will receive the event object for each link in a DOM-compliant browser. Note too that the first statement in this function assigns the *this* keyword to the link variable. This is the critical statement in this function, because the *this* keyword refers to that specific <a> object in the DOM. As a result, one event handler is created for each <a> object in the DOM.

Without this statement, the loop would create just one event handler and attach it to each <a> element. If, for example, you assigned linkNode to the link variable instead of the *this* keyword, clicking on any thumbnail image would display the last image. That's because the statements in the event handler would be replaced each time through the loop, ending up with the statement for the last link.

After that, the next statement changes the src attribute in the image node to the href attribute of the link. Then, the next statement changes the value of the first child of the caption node to the title attribute of the link. Later, when the application is run and the user clicks on a thumbnail, these statements will change the DOM so the image and caption are immediately changed in the display.

This event handler ends by cancelling the default action of the event for the link using the code in figure 7-1. Since the default action is to display the file identified by the href attribute, cancelling this action is essential. Otherwise, clicking on the link would open a new browser window or tab and display the image that's specified by the href attribute.

When the for loop ends, the code moves the focus to the first link. This allows the user to tab through the thumbnail images and swap the main image, as described in the previous topic.

The swap.js file

```javascript
var $ = function(id) {
    return document.getElementById(id);
};

window.onload = function() {
    var listNode = $("image_list");         // the ul element
    var captionNode = $("caption");         // the h2 element
    var imageNode = $("main_image");        // the main img element

    var imageLinks = listNode.getElementsByTagName("a");

    // process image links
    var i, image, linkNode, link;
    for ( i = 0; i < imageLinks.length; i++ ) {
        linkNode = imageLinks[i];

        // preload image
        image = new Image();
        image.src = linkNode.getAttribute("href");

        // attach event handler
        linkNode.onclick = function(evt) {
            link = this;    // "this" is the link that was clicked

            // set new image and caption
            imageNode.src = link.getAttribute("href");
            captionNode.firstChild.nodeValue = link.getAttribute("title");

            // cancel the default action of the event
            if (!evt) {
                evt = window.event;
            }
            if (evt.preventDefault) {
                evt.preventDefault();
            }
            else {
                evt.returnFalse = false;
            }
        };
    }

    // set focus on first image link
    imageLinks[0].focus();
};
```

Figure 7-4   The JavaScript for the Image Swap application

How to use timers

A *timer* lets you execute a function after a specified period of time has elapsed. Timers are provided by web browsers rather than the DOM or ECMAScript standards. Timers are often useful in DOM scripting applications like the Slide Show application you'll see at the end of this chapter. Here, you'll learn about the two types of timers.

How to use a one-time timer

The first type of timer calls its function only once. To create this type of timer, you use the global setTimeout() method that's shown in figure 7-5. Its first parameter is the function that the timer calls. Its second parameter is the number of milliseconds to wait before calling the function.

When you use the setTimeout() method to create a timer, it returns a reference to the timer that's created. Then, if necessary, you can use this reference to cancel the timer. To do that, you pass this reference to the clearTimeout() method.

The example in this figure is another version of the FAQs application that you saw in the last chapter. This application uses a one-time timer to start the download and installation of an upgrade after a delay of five seconds. The user can cancel the upgrade by clicking the Cancel Upgrade button before the five seconds have elapsed.

The HTML for this application includes a fieldset element that contains a legend element, a <p> element that explains what's going to happen, a button to cancel the upgrade, and a span element where messages will be displayed. Also, a CSS class named hidden has been added to the CSS file. It will be used to hide elements by setting their display properties to none.

The JavaScript code starts by declaring a global variable for the timer. This is followed by functions named startUpgrade() and cancelUpgrade(). The startUpgrade() function starts by setting the class attribute of the button to "hidden" so it's no longer displayed. That way, the user can't click this button once the upgrade has started. Next, this function sets the content of the span element to notify the user of the progress of the upgrade. This is followed by the code that performs the upgrade. When the update is complete, this function hides the fieldset element by setting its class attribute to "hidden".

The cancelUpgrade() function uses the clearTimeout() method to stop the timer that's started by the setTimeout() method. If this function is called before the timer calls the startUpgrade() function, it will keep the code in the startUpgrade() function from running. Then, this function hides the fieldset element by setting its class attribute to "hidden".

This is followed by the onload event hander. It uses the setTimeout() method to set the global timer variable to a timer that calls the startUpgrade() function after a delay of 5 seconds (5000 milliseconds). Then, it attaches the cancelUpgrade() function to the Cancel Upgrade button so the upgrade can be cancelled before those 5 seconds elapse.

Two methods for working with a timer that calls a function once

```
setTimeout( function, delayTime )      // creates a timer
clearTimeout( timer )                  // cancels a timer
```

The FAQs application with an upgrade that starts after 5 seconds

JavaScript FAQs

A new version is available!

Upgrade will start in 5 seconds! [Cancel Upgrade]

✦ **What is JavaScript?**

The HTML that provides for the upgrade

```
<fieldset id="upgrade">
    <legend>A new version is available!</legend>
    <p>Upgrade will start in 5 seconds!
        <input type="button" id="cancel" value="Cancel Upgrade">
        <span id="message"> </span></p>
</fieldset>
```

The CSS for the hidden class

```
.hidden { display: none; }
```

How to use a one-time timer to start or cancel the upgrade

```
// declare a variable to hold the reference to the timer; make it
// global so all the functions can access it
var timer;

var startUpgrade = function() {
    $("cancel").setAttribute("class", "hidden");
    $("message").firstChild.nodeValue = "Download starting...";

    /* code to perform the upgrade goes here */

    $("upgrade").setAttribute("class", "hidden");
};
var cancelUpgrade = function() {
    clearTimeout( timer );
    $("upgrade").setAttribute("class", "hidden");
};
window.onload = function() {
    timer = setTimeout( startUpgrade, 5000 );
    $("cancel").onclick = cancelUpgrade;
};
```

Description

- The setTimeout() method creates a *timer* that calls the specified function once after the specified delay in milliseconds has elapsed. This method returns a reference to the new timer that can be used to cancel the timer.

- The clearTimeout() method cancels the timer that was created with the setTimeout() method.

Figure 7-5   How to use a one-time timer

How to use an interval timer

The second type of timer calls its function repeatedly. To create this type of timer, you use the global setInterval() method shown in figure 7-6. Its first parameter is the function to be called. Its second parameter is the time interval between function calls. To cancel this type of timer, you pass the timer to the clearInterval() method.

The example in this figure shows how to use an interval timer to create a counter that is incremented every second. This counter value is displayed in a span element within an h3 element at the bottom of the page.

The first JavaScript example in this figure shows one way to create and use the timer. Here, global timer and counter variables are declared with the counter set to a starting value of zero. Then, the updateCounter() function increases this counter by 1 and displays the new value in the span element. Last, the onload event handler creates the timer by using the updateCounter() function as the function parameter of the setInterval() method and 1000 (one second) as the interval time.

If you want to cancel an interval timer that's stored in a global variable, you can use the clearInterval() method that's right after this example. This is useful when you want to modify a timer. To do that, you need to cancel the old timer and create a new one that works the way you want it to.

The second JavaScript example shows another way you can code the setInterval() method. Here, the function that the setInterval() method will call is coded at the same time that it's passed to the method. This is called an *anonymous function*, and coding it this way means that you don't have to code a variable to hold it. This is a common way to code both the setInterval() method and the setTimeout() method of the last figure.

When you use the setInterval() method to create a timer, the timer waits for the specified interval to elapse before calling the function the first time. So, if you want the function to be called immediately, you need to call the function before you create the timer.

Two methods for working with a timer that calls a function repeatedly

```
setInterval( function, intervalTime )    // creates a timer
clearInterval( timer )                   // cancels a timer
```

The FAQs application with a counter at the bottom

jQuery FAQs
✦ What is jQuery?
✦ Why is jQuery becoming so popular?
✦ Which is harder to learn: jQuery or JavaScript?

Number of seconds on page: 8

The HTML for the counter

```
<h3>Number of seconds on page: <span id="counter">0</span></h3>
```

How to use the setInterval() method to add a counter to a page

```
// create global variables to hold the timer and the current count
var timer;
var counter = 0;

// create the function that the timer calls
var updateCounter = function() {
    counter++;
    $("counter").firstChild.nodeValue = counter;
};
// create a timer that calls the updateCounter function repeatedly
window.onload = function() {
    timer = setInterval ( updateCounter, 1000 );
};
```

How to cancel the timer

```
clearInterval( timer );
```

How to use an anonymous function with the setInterval() method

```
var timer;
var counter = 0;
window.onload = function() {
    timer = setInterval( function() {      // the function parameter
        counter++;
        $("counter").firstChild.nodeValue = counter;
    },
    1000 );                                // the time interval parameter
};
```

Description

- The setInterval() method creates a timer that calls a function each time the specified interval in milliseconds has elapsed. This method returns a reference to the new timer that can be used by the clearInterval() method to cancel the timer.

- Although you can't modify an interval timer, you can cancel it and create a new one.

Figure 7-6   How to use an interval timer

The Slide Show application

Figure 7-7 illustrates a Slide Show application that requires the use of an interval timer. When the user starts this application, it displays a new caption and image every two seconds.

The HTML and CSS

If you look at the HTML, you can see that four <a> elements are coded within a ul element. The href attribute for each <a> element provides the location for one of the images in the slide show. The title attribute provides the caption for the slide.

After the unordered list is the img element that will display the image for each slide. Its src attribute provides the location of the first slide. It's followed by the h2 element that will display the caption for each slide. Its contents provide the caption for the first slide. That way, the first slide and caption are displayed when the application starts.

To keep this application simple, no controls are provided for stopping the slide show or moving through the slides manually. As a result, this slide show doesn't meet the best standards for usability or accessibility.

Of note in the CSS is the style rule for the ul element that contains the list. Since the purpose of this list is to provide the captions and images for the slide show, the list shouldn't be displayed. That's why its display property is set to none.

The user interface for the Slide Show application

The HTML for the application

```
<main>
    <h1>Fishing Slide Show</h1>
    <ul id="image_list">
        <li><a href="images/release.jpg" title="Catch and Release"></a></li>
        <li><a href="images/deer.jpg" title="Deer at Play"></a></li>
        <li><a href="images/hero.jpg" title="The Big One!"></a></li>
        <li><a href="images/bison.jpg" title="Roaming Bison"></a></li>
    </ul>

    <p><img src="images/release.jpg" alt="Catch and Release" id="image"></p>
    <h2 id="caption">Catch and Release</h2>
</main>
```

The CSS of the ul element

```
ul { display: none; }
```

Figure 7-7   The user interface, HTML, and CSS for the Slide Show application

The JavaScript

Figure 7-8 presents the JavaScript for this application. Here, you can see that the onload event handler starts by declaring variables that contain the nodes for the ul element, the h2 element for the caption, and the img element for the slide show. Then, the getElementsByTagName() method is used to create an array named links that contains one object for each <a> element in the ul element.

Each of these links is processed by the for loop that follows. This loop preloads the images and sets the title property of each image to the title property of the current link. Then, it adds the image object to the imageCache array so it can be used later.

At this point, the onload event handler starts the slide show. To do that, it creates an interval timer with a function that's embedded in the first parameter and 2000 (2 seconds) as the second parameter. It is the embedded function that displays the next slide when the interval time is up.

Within this function, the variable named imageCounter determines which slide in the imageCache array will be displayed next. The first statement in this function adds one to the imageCounter, and then uses the modulus operator (%) to get the remainder when the imageCounter property is divided by the length of the imageCache array. This means the imageCounter property will range from 0 through one less than the length of the array.

If, for example, the imageCache array contains 4 images, the counter values will range from 0 through 3 (1%4=1; 2%4=2; 3%4=3; 4%4=0). So, if the imageCounter value is used as the index of the imageCache array, the function will loop through the elements of the array and the index will never be larger than 3.

After the value of the imageCounter variable is set, the second statement in this function uses the imageCounter as the index for the imageCache array and stores that image object in the image variable. The third statement sets the src attribute of the img node to the src attribute of the Image object. The last statement sets the text for the caption node to the title attribute of the Image object. As soon as these changes are made to the DOM, the image and caption are changed in the browser display.

You might notice that this code doesn't set up any event handlers for user events. Instead, the slide show is driven by the interval timer, which issues timer events. Then, after each time interval passes, the function in the first parameter is executed again, which changes the src attribute of the img element in the DOM and the text of the h2 element.

The JavaScript for the Slide Show application

```javascript
var $ = function (id) { return document.getElementById(id); };

window.onload = function () {
    var listNode = $("image_list");      // the ul element
    var captionNode = $("caption");      // the h2 element for the caption
    var imageNode = $("image");          // the img element for the show

    var links = listNode.getElementsByTagName("a");

    // Process image links
    var i, linkNode, image;
    var imageCache = [];
    for ( i = 0; i < links.length; i++ ) {
        linkNode = links[i];

        // Preload image and copy title properties
        image = new Image();
        image.src = linkNode.getAttribute("href");
        image.title = linkNode.getAttribute("title");
        imageCache[imageCache.length] = image;
    }

    // Start slide show
    var imageCounter = 0;
    var  timer = setInterval(
        function () {
            imageCounter = (imageCounter + 1) % imageCache.length;
            image = imageCache[imageCounter];
            imageNode.src = image.src;
            captionNode.firstChild.nodeValue = image.title;
        },
        2000);
};
```

Figure 7-8   The JavaScript for the Slide Show application

Perspective

Now that you've completed this chapter, you should know how to use JavaScript to create simple applications that work with links, images, and timers. When your applications get more complicated than the ones in this chapter, though, you should consider using jQuery instead of JavaScript. As you'll see in the next section of this book, jQuery makes it much easier to develop applications like the ones you've just seen.

Terms

default action	image swap
event object	timer
preload an image	anonymous function

Summary

- For some JavaScript applications, you need to cancel the *default action* of an event, like clicking on a link or button. For modern browsers, you can do that by calling the preventDefault() method of the *event object* that's passed to the event handler. For older IE browsers, you have to get the event object using the global window.event property. Then, you have to set the returnValue property of that object to false.

- To *preload* an image, you create a new Image object and set its src attribute to the URL for the image. When you preload images, the page may take longer to load, but the image changes will take place immediately.

- Browsers provide two types of *timers*. A one-time timer executes a function just once after the specified interval of time. An interval timer executes a function each time the specified time interval elapses.

- JavaScript provides methods to cancel a one-time timer before it executes for the first time, or to cancel an interval timer before the next scheduled execution.

Exercise 7-1   Develop a rollover application

In this exercise, you'll create an application with two images that change when you roll over them with the mouse.

Fishing Images

Move your mouse over an image to change it and back out of the image to restore the original image.

Open, test, and review the application

1. Use your text editor or IDE to open the files in this folder:

    `javascript_jquery\exercises\ch07\rollover\`

2. Review the code in the index.html file, and note that each li element within the ul element contains an <a> element whose href attribute refers to one of the images used by this application. Also note that the <p> element at the bottom of the page contains two img elements with ids "image1" and "image2" whose src attributes determine the images that are currently displayed.

3. Review the code in the rollover.css file, and note that it contains a style rule that keeps the ul element in the index.html file from being displayed in the browser.

4. Review the code in the rollover.js file, and note that the images with ids "image1" and "image2" are stored in variables named image1 and image2. In addition, the <a> elements in the ul element are stored in an array named links.

5. Use Chrome to test this application. Notice that the images shown above are displayed, but nothing happens when you move your mouse over them.

Add code to preload the images and implement the rollovers

6. In the onload event handler, add code that uses the links array to preload the four images used by this application.

7. Add code to the mouseover and mouseout event handlers for the two image elements that are displayed on the page. The image element with id "image1" should display the release.jpg image when the mouse is over it and the hero.jpg image otherwise. The image element with id "image2" should display the deer.jpg image when the mouse is over it and the bison.jpg image otherwise.

8. Test the application to be sure that the rollovers are working and that the correct images are being displayed.

Exercise 7-2   Enhance the Slide Show application

In this exercise, you'll enhance the Slide Show application by adding buttons to start and pause the slide show.

Open and test the application

1. Use your text editor or IDE to open the HTML and JavaScript files in this folder:

    `javascript_jquery\exercises\ch07\slideshow\`

2. Use Chrome to test this application. Notice that the slideshow isn't running, the Pause button is disabled, and nothing happens when you click on the Start button.

Add code to start the slide show when the Start button is clicked

3. Review the code in the index.html file, and notice that the disabled attribute of the Pause button is set to "true". That makes sense because the user shouldn't be able to click this button if the slide show isn't running.

4. Review the code in the slide_show.js file, and note that the code for running the slide show is coded in a function named runSlideShow() and the imageCache, imageCounter, and timer variables are coded as global variables so they can be accessed by the runSlideShow() and onload() functions.

5. Within the onload event handler, add code to the click event handler of the Start button that creates a timer that runs the slide show and changes the slide every 2 seconds. In addition, add code that disables the Start button and enables the Pause button. To disable a button, you can set its disabled attribute to true. To enable a button, you can remove its disabled attribute.

6. Test the application again and click the Start button to make sure the slide show is working. Notice that there's a delay of 2 seconds before the next slide is displayed.

7. Add code to the click event handler of the Start button that calls the runSlideShow() function before the timer is started. Then, test the application again to see that the next slide is displayed immediately when the Start button is clicked.

Add code to pause the slide show when the Pause button is clicked

8. Add code to the click event handler of the Pause button that cancels the timer. In addition, add code that enables the Start button and disables the Pause button.

9. Test the application again, click the Start button to start the slide show, and then click the Pause button to pause the slide show. Click the Start button again to re-start the slide show. When you're done testing, close the browser.

Section 2

jQuery essentials

Now that you have some JavaScript skills, you're ready to learn jQuery. So, in chapter 8, you'll learn a working subset of jQuery that will get you off to a fast start. By the time you finish that chapter, you'll be able to build jQuery applications like image swaps, image rollovers, and the FAQs application.

Then, to complete your jQuery skills, chapter 9 shows you how to use the jQuery effects and animations that can bring a web page to life. Chapter 10 shows you how to use the jQuery features for working with forms. Chapter 11 shows you how to use jQuery plugins and jQuery UI widgets to improve your productivity. And chapter 12 shows you how to use Ajax and JSON to get data from a web server without refreshing the page.

8

Get off to a fast start with jQuery

In this chapter, you'll quickly see how jQuery makes JavaScript programming easier. Then, you'll learn a working subset of jQuery that will get you off to a fast start. Along the way, you'll study four complete applications that will show you how to apply jQuery.

Introduction to jQuery

In this introduction, you'll learn what jQuery is, how to include it in your applications, and how jQuery, jQuery UI, and plugins can simplify JavaScript development.

What jQuery is

As figure 8-1 summarizes, *jQuery* is a free, open-source, JavaScript library that provides dozens of methods for common web features that make JavaScript programming easier. Beyond that, the jQuery functions are coded and tested for cross-browser compatibility, so they will work in all browsers.

Those are just two of the reasons why jQuery is used by the majority of the one million most-visited websites today. And that's why jQuery is commonly used by professional web developers. In fact, you can think of jQuery as one of the four technologies that every web developer should know how to use: HTML, CSS, JavaScript, and jQuery. But don't forget that jQuery is actually JavaScript.

The jQuery website at jquery.com

What jQuery offers

- Dozens of selectors, methods, and event methods that make it easier to add JavaScript features to your web pages
- Cross-browser compatibility
- Selectors that are compliant with CSS3
- A compressed library that loads quickly so it doesn't degrade performance

Description

- *jQuery* is a free, open-source, JavaScript library that provides methods that make JavaScript programming easier.
- Today, jQuery is used by the majority of the one million most-visited websites, and its popularity is still growing.

Figure 8-1   What jQuery is

How jQuery can simplify JavaScript development

To show you how jQuery can simplify JavaScript development, figure 8-2 shows the jQuery for the FAQs application that you learned how to develop in chapter 6. If you're like most people, you probably found the JavaScript code for that application both complicated and confusing.

In contrast, this jQuery code takes significantly fewer lines of code. You'll also find that it is much easier to understand once you learn how to use the JQuery selectors, methods, and event methods. And you'll start learning those skills right after this introduction.

Incidentally, jQuery uses CSS selectors to select the HTML elements that the methods should be applied to. For instance,

```
$("#faqs h2")
```

is a jQuery selector for the CSS selector

```
#faqs h2
```

which selects all of the h2 elements in the element with "faqs" as its id. In fact, jQuery supports all of the CSS selectors including the CSS3 selectors, even in browsers that don't support all of the CSS3 selectors. This is another reason why developers like jQuery.

The FAQs application in a browser

> ### jQuery FAQs
> ✦ **What is jQuery?**
> ─ **Why is jQuery becoming so popular?**
> Three reasons:
> • It's free.
> • It lets you get more done in less time.
> • All of its functions are cross-browser compatible.
>
> ✦ **Which is harder to learn: jQuery or JavaScript?**

The HTML

```
<main id="faqs">
    <h1>jQuery FAQs</h1>
    <h2><a href="#">What is jQuery?</a></h2>
    <div>
        <p>jQuery is a library of the JavaScript functions that you're most
            likely to need as you develop websites.</p>
    </div>
    <h2><a href="#">Why is jQuery becoming so popular?</a></h2>
    <div>
        ...
    </div>
    ...
    ...
</main>
```

The critical CSS

```
h2 { background: url(images/plus.png) no-repeat left center; }
h2.minus { background: url(images/minus.png) no-repeat left center; }
div { display: none; }
```

The jQuery for the application

```
$(document).ready(function() {
    $("#faqs h2").click(function() {
        $(this).toggleClass("minus");
        if ($(this).attr("class") != "minus") {
            $(this).next().hide();
        }
        else {
            $(this).next().show();
        }
    }); // end click
}); // end ready
```

Description

• The application illustrates the use of the ready() event method, a jQuery selector that's just like a CSS selector (#faqs h2"), and five jQuery methods. All of these make jQuery programming easier than JavaScript programming.

Figure 8-2   How jQuery can simplify JavaScript development

The basics of jQuery programming

In the next four figures, you're going to learn the basics of jQuery programming. Then, you'll study an application that uses these skills. That will show you how jQuery simplifies JavaScript programming.

How to include jQuery in your web pages

If you go to the web page that's shown in figure 8-3, you'll see that it contains links that let you download various releases of the jQuery core library. At this writing, the most current release is jQuery 3.1.1, and it comes in four versions: uncompressed, compressed, slim uncompressed, and slim compressed.

The uncompressed versions allow you to study the JavaScript code that's used in the library. But beware, this code is extremely complicated. In contrast, all whitespace has been removed from the compressed versions, which makes it almost impossible for a human to read them. But they are much smaller, which improves performance. The slim version of jQuery was introduced with jQuery 3.0. It doesn't include the ajax or effects modules, so it's even smaller.

Once you've downloaded the jQuery library you want, you can include it in a web page by coding a script element like the first one in this figure. Then, if you store the file on your own computer or a local web server, you'll be able to develop jQuery applications without being connected to the Internet.

The other way to include the jQuery library in your web applications is to get the file from a *Content Delivery Network* (*CDN*). A CDN is a web server that hosts open-source software, and the download page shown here contains a link to the jQuery CDN. The next two examples in this figure show script elements that use the jQuery CDN with URLs that get version 3.1.1. Because using a CDN is a best practice, all the applications in this book use this technique.

Although you might think that you should always use the most current release of jQuery, that's not necessarily the case. As you can see in the table in this figure, different versions of jQuery implemented various changes over time. For example, the 2.x and 3.x branches of jQuery don't provide support for IE6, IE7, or IE8. So if you think that some of your users may be using those browsers, you'll want to use jQuery 1.12.4 since it's the most current release of the 1.x branch that supports them.

Also, jQuery versions 1.9 and 3.0 dropped certain features that were included in earlier versions. So if you have old code that uses those features, you'll need to keep using the older versions of the library. Or, you can use the jQuery Migrate plugins presented here to upgrade your application. To use these plugins, go to jquery.com/upgrade-guide, click on the upgrade you want, and then follow the step-by-step instructions.

Finally, you should know that jQuery recommends that you use *Subresource Integrity (SRI) checking* when you link to files on their CDN. This helps ensure that resources hosted on the CDN haven't been tampered with. The last example in this figure shows how this works. You can get more information on the jQuery CDN website and at https://www.srihash.org/. For brevity, the applications in this book don't use SRI checking.

The jQuery download page at jquery.com/download

How to include jQuery 3.1.1 after you've downloaded it to your computer

```
<script src="jquery-3.1.1.min.js"></script>
```

How to include jQuery 3.1.1 from a Content Delivery Network (CDN)

```
<script src="https://code.jquery.com/jquery-3.1.1.min.js"></script>
```

How to include the slim version of jQuery 3.1.1 from a CDN

```
<script src="https://code.jquery.com/jquery-3.1.1.slim.min.js"></script>
```

The most important releases of jQuery

Version	Release date	Description
1.0	Aug 2006	First stable release.
1.9.1	Feb 2013	Deprecated interfaces removed.
1.12.4	May 2016	Last updated version of 1.x branch, which supports IE6-8.
2.0	April 2013	First version of 2.x branch. Dropped support for IE6-8.
2.2.4	May 2016	Last updated version of 2.x branch.
3.0	June 2016	First version of 3.x branch. A smaller, faster version of the 2.x branch, but with some breaking changes. Adds a slim version.
3.1.1	Sept 2016	Current version of jQuery.

Two jQuery migrate plugins

Version	Description
1.4.1	Restores features dropped by version 1.9.
3.0.0	Restores features dropped by version 3.0.

How to include SRI checking with the jQuery CDN

```
<script src="https://code.jquery.com/jquery-3.1.1.min.js"
integrity="sha256-hVVnYaiADRTO2PzUGmuLJr8BLUSjGIZsDYGmIJLv2b8="
crossorigin="anonymous"></script>
```

Figure 8-3   How to include jQuery in your web pages

How to code jQuery selectors

When you use jQuery, you start by selecting the element or elements that you want to apply a jQuery method to. To do that, you can use jQuery *selectors* as shown in figure 8-4.

To code a jQuery selector, you start by coding the dollar sign (**$**) followed by a set of parentheses that contains a set of quotation marks. Then, within the quotation marks, you code the CSS selector for the element or elements that you want to select. This is shown by the syntax summary at the top of this figure.

The HTML and the examples that follow show how easy it is to select one or more elements with jQuery. For instance, the first selector in the first group of examples selects all <p> elements within the entire document. The second selector selects the element with "faqs" as its id. And the third selector selects all elements with "minus" as the value of its class attribute.

In the second group of examples, you can see how other types of CSS selectors are coded with jQuery. Here, you can see how descendants, adjacent siblings, general siblings, and children are coded. For instance, the first selector gets all <p> elements that are descendants of the element with "faqs" as its id. That includes all of the <p> elements in the HTML in this figure.

In contrast, the second selector gets the div elements that are adjacent siblings to the h2 elements, which includes all of the div elements. The third selector gets all <p> elements that are siblings of ul elements, which selects the one <p> element in the second div element. And the fourth selector gets all ul elements that are children of div elements, which selects the ul element in the second div element.

The third group of examples shows how to code multiple selectors. To do that, you separate them with commas, just as you do with CSS.

The syntax for a jQuery selector

```
$("selector")
```

The HTML for the elements that are selected by the examples

```
<main id="faqs">
    <h1>jQuery FAQs</h1>
    <h2 class="minus"><a href="#">What is jQuery?</a></h2>
    <div>
        <p>jQuery is a library of the JavaScript functions that you're most
            likely to need as you develop websites.
        </p>
    </div>
    <h2><a href="#">Why is jQuery becoming so popular?</a></h2>
    <div>
        <p>Three reasons:</p>
        <ul>
            <li>It's free.</li>
            <li>It lets you get more done in less time.</li>
            <li>All of its functions are cross-browser compatible.</li>
        </ul>
    </div>
</main>
```

How to select elements by element, id, and class

By element type: All <p> elements in the entire document

```
$("p")
```

By id: The element with "faqs" as its id

```
$("#faqs")
```

By class: All elements with "minus" as a class

```
$(".minus")
```

How to select elements by relationship

Descendants: All <p> elements that are descendants of the main element

```
$("#faqs p");
```

Adjacent siblings: All div elements that are adjacent siblings of h2 elements

```
$("h2 + div")
```

General siblings: All <p> elements that are siblings of ul elements

```
$("ul ~ p")
```

Children: All ul elements that are children of div elements

```
$("div > ul")
```

How to code multiple selectors

```
$("#faqs li, div p")
$("p + ul, div ~ p")
```

Description

- When you use jQuery, the dollar sign (**$**) is used to refer to the jQuery library. Then, you can code *selectors* by using the CSS syntax within quotation marks within parentheses.

Figure 8-4   How to code jQuery selectors

How to call jQuery methods

Once you've selected the element or elements that you want to apply a *method* to, you call the method using the syntax shown at the top of figure 8- 5. This is the same way that you call a method of any object. You code the selector that gets the element or elements, the dot, the method name, and any parameters within parentheses.

To get you started with jQuery, the table in this figure summarizes some of the jQuery methods that you'll use the most. For instance, the val() method without a parameter gets the value from a selected text box or other form control, and the val() method with a parameter sets the value in a selected text box or other form control. The first two examples after the table show how this works.

Similarly, the text() method without a parameter can be used to get the text of a selected element, and the text() method with a parameter can be used to set the text of a selected element. Methods like these are often referred to as *getter* and *setter* methods. Here, the third example illustrates the setter version of the text() method, which sets the text of an element to "Email address is required".

The fifth method in the table is the next() method, which is used to get the next (or adjacent) sibling of an element. This method is often followed by another method. To do that, you use *object chaining*, which works just as it does with JavaScript. This is illustrated by the fourth example. Here, the next() method gets the next sibling after the element that has been selected, and the text() method sets the text for that sibling.

In most cases, you'll use the val(), text(), and next() methods with selectors that select a single control or element. However, you can also use them with selectors that select two or more controls or elements. In that case, the set form of the val() and text() methods set the values of all the matching controls or elements. In contrast, the get form of the val() method gets the value of just the first matching form control. The get form of the text() method gets the combined text of all the matching elements. And the next() method gets the siblings of all the matched elements.

The last two methods in the table are the submit() and focus() methods, which are just like the JavaScript submit() and focus() methods. The submit() method submits the data for a selected form to the server, and the focus() method moves the focus to the selected form control or link.

In a moment, you'll see how these selectors and methods work in an application. But first, you need to learn how to set up the event handlers for an application.

The syntax for calling a jQuery method

```
$("selector").methodName(parameters)
```

Some common jQuery methods

Method	Description
`val()`	Get the value of a text box or other form control.
`val(value)`	Set the value of a text box or other form control.
`text()`	Get the text of an element.
`text(value)`	Set the text of an element.
`next([type])`	Get the next sibling of an element or the next sibling of a specified type if the parameter is coded.
`submit()`	Submit the selected form.
`focus()`	Move the focus to the selected form control or link.

Examples

How to get the value from a text box

```
var gallons = $("#gallons").val();
```

How to set the value for an input element

```
$("#gallons").val("");
```

How to set the text in an element

```
$("#email_address_error").text("Email address is required");
```

How to set the text for the next sibling with object chaining

```
$("#last_name").next().text("Last name is required");
```

How to submit a form

```
$("#join_list").submit();
```

How to move the focus to a form control or link

```
$("#email_address").focus();
```

Description

- To call a jQuery *method*, you code a selector, the dot operator, the method name, and any parameters within parentheses. Then, that method is applied to the element or elements that are selected by the selector.

- When you use *object chaining* with jQuery, you code one method after the other. This works because each method returns the appropriate object.

- Although you'll typically use the val(), text(), and next() methods with selectors that select a single form control or element, you can also use them with selectors that select two or more form controls or elements. The result depends on the method you use.

Figure 8-5   How to call jQuery methods

How to use jQuery event methods

When you use jQuery, you use *event methods* to attach event handlers to events. To do that, you use the syntax shown at the top of figure 8-6. First, you code the selector for the element that will initiate the event like a button that will be clicked. Then, you code the name of the event method that represents the event that you want to use. Last, you code a function that will be the event handler for the event within parentheses.

In the table in this figure, the two event methods that you'll use the most are summarized. The ready event is the jQuery alternative to the JavaScript load event. The ready event works better than the load event, though, because it's triggered as soon as the DOM is built, even if other elements like images are still being loaded into the browser. This means that the user can start using the web page faster.

Because the DOM usually has to be built before you can use JavaScript or jQuery, you'll probably use the ready() event method in every JavaScript application that you develop. The examples in this figure show two ways to do that. In the long form, you use document as the selector for the web page followed by the dot, the method name (ready()), and the function for the event handler.

In the short form, you can omit the selector and event method name and just code the function in parentheses after the dollar sign. Although this form is often used by professional developers, all of the examples in this book use the long form. That way, it's clear where the ready event handler starts.

The next example in this figure shows an event handler for the click event of all h2 elements. This is coded just like the event handler for the ready event except h2 is used as the selector and click() is used as the name of the event method.

The last example in this figure shows how you code an event handler within the ready() event handler. Note here that the closing brace, parenthesis, and semicolon for each event handler is critical. As you can guess, it's easy to omit one of these marks or get them out of sequence, so this is a frequent source of errors. That's why professional programmers often code inline comments after the ending marks for each event handler to identify which event handler the marks are for.

The syntax for a jQuery event method

```
$(selector).eventMethodName(function() {
    // the statements of the event handler
});
```

Two common jQuery event methods

Event method	Description
ready(handler)	The event handler runs when the DOM is ready.
click(handler)	The event handler runs when the selected element is clicked.

Two ways to code an event handler for the jQuery ready event

The long way

```
$(document).ready(function() {
    alert("The DOM is ready");
});
```

The short way

```
$(function(){                    // (document).ready is assumed
    alert("The DOM is ready");
});
```

An event handler for the click event of all h2 elements

```
$("h2").click(function() {
    alert("This heading has been clicked");
});
```

The click event handler within the ready event handler

```
$(document).ready(function() {
    $("h2").click(function() {
        alert("This heading has been clicked");
    }); // end of click event handler
}); // end of ready event handler
```

Description

- To code a jQuery event handler, you code a selector, the dot operator, the name of the jQuery *event method*, and an anonymous function that handles the event within parentheses.

- The event handler for the ready event will run any methods that it contains as soon as the DOM is ready, even if the browser is loading images and other content for the page. This works better than the JavaScript onload event, which doesn't occur until all of the content for the page is loaded.

- In this book, the ready event is always coded the long way that's shown above. In practice, though, many programmers use the short way.

- When coding one event handler within another, the use of the closing braces, parentheses, and semicolons is critical. To help get this right, many programmers code inline comments after these punctuation marks to identify the ends of the handlers.

Figure 8-6   How to use jQuery event methods

The Email List application in jQuery

With that as background, you're ready to see how jQuery can be used in the Email List application that you studied in section 1. That will show you how jQuery can simplify coding.

The user interface and HTML

To refresh your memory, figure 8-7 presents the user interface and HTML for the Email List application. To use the application, the user enters text into the first three text boxes and clicks on the Join our List button. Then, the JavaScript validates the entries and displays appropriate error messages if errors are found. If no errors are found, the data in the form is submitted to the web server for processing.

In the HTML, note first the script element that loads jQuery. It is followed by the script element that identifies the file that holds the JavaScript for this application. That sequence is essential because the JavaScript file is going to use the jQuery file.

Also note that the span elements are adjacent siblings to the input elements for the text boxes. The starting text for each of these span elements is an asterisk that indicates that the text box entry is required. Later, if the JavaScript finds errors in the entries, it displays error messages in these span elements.

Finally, note that, unlike the Email List application you saw earlier, the span elements in this version don't have id attributes. That's because the jQuery code will use some of the methods you just learned to locate the span element it needs. You'll see how that works next.

The user interface for the Email List application

The HTML

```
<!DOCTYPE html>
<html>
<head>
    <meta charset="UTF-8">
    <title>Join Email List</title>
    <link rel="stylesheet" href="email_list.css">
    <script src="https://code.jquery.com/jquery-3.1.1.min.js"></script>
    <script src="email_list.js"></script>
</head>
<body>
    <main>
        <h1>Please join our email list</h1>
        <form id="email_form" name="email_form"
            action="join.html" method="get">
            <label for="email_address1">Email Address:</label>
            <input type="text" id="email_address1">
            <span>*</span><br>

            <label for="email_address2">Re-enter Email Address:</label>
            <input type="text" id="email_address2">
            <span>*</span><br>

            <label for="first_name">First Name:</label>
            <input type="text" id="first_name">
            <span>*</span><br>

            <label> </label>
            <input type="button" id="join_list" value="Join our List">
        </form>
    </main>
</body>
</html>
```

Figure 8-7   The user interface and HTML for the Email List application

The jQuery

Figure 8-8 presents the jQuery for this application. This is the code in the email_list.js file that's included by the HTML. Here, all of the jQuery is highlighted. The rest of the code is JavaScript code.

To start, you can see that an event handler for the click event of the Join our List button is coded within the event handler for the ready event. Then, if you look at the last three lines of code, you can see the ending punctuation marks for these handlers. Within the click event handler, the first two statements show how jQuery selectors and the val() method can be used to get the values from text boxes.

In the first if statement, you can see how an error message is displayed if the user doesn't enter an email address in the first text box. Here, the next() method gets the adjacent sibling for the text box, which is the span element, and then the text() method puts an error message in that span element. This changes the DOM, and as soon as it is changed, the error message is displayed in the browser.

The next(), text(), and val() methods are used in similar ways in the next two if statements. Then, the fourth if statement tests to see whether the isValid variable is still true. If it is, the submit() method of the form is issued, which sends the data to the web server.

That ends the event handler for the click event of the Join our List button. But that handler is followed by one more statement. It moves the focus to the first text box, the one with "email_address1" as its id.

As you review this code, note that it doesn't require the standard $ function that gets an element object when the element's id is passed to it. Instead, the $ sign is used to start a jQuery selector that gets elements by their ids. This simplifies the coding.

Although this jQuery code illustrates how jQuery can simplify a data validation application, it doesn't begin to show the power of jQuery. For that, you need to learn more selectors, methods, and event methods, and then see how they can be used in other types of applications. You'll do that next.

The jQuery for the Email List application (email_list.js)

```javascript
$(document).ready(function() {
    $("#join_list").click(function() {
        var emailAddress1 = $("#email_address1").val();
        var emailAddress2 = $("#email_address2").val();
        var isValid = true;

        // validate the first email address
        if (emailAddress1 == "") {
            $("#email_address1").next().text("This field is required.");
            isValid = false;
        } else {
            $("#email_address1").next().text("");
        }

        // validate the second email address
        if (emailAddress2 == "") {
            $("#email_address2").next().text("This field is required.");
            isValid = false;
        } else if (emailAddress1 != emailAddress2) {
            $("#email_address2").next().text(
                "This entry must equal first entry.");
            isValid = false;
        } else {
            $("#email_address2").next().text("");
        }

        // validate the first name entry
        if ($("#first_name").val() == "") {
            $("#first_name").next().text("This field is required.");
            isValid = false;
        }
        else {
            $("#first_name").next().text("");
        }

        // submit the form if all entries are valid
        if (isValid) {
            $("#email_form").submit();
        }
    }); // end click
    $("#email_address1").focus();
}); // end ready
```

Figure 8-8   The jQuery for the Email List application

A working subset of selectors, methods, and event methods

The next three figures present a working subset of the most useful jQuery selectors, methods, and event methods. This is a lot to take in, but once you understand them, you'll be able to write practical jQuery applications of your own.

The most useful selectors

In figure 8-4, you were introduced to the basic selectors that you can use with jQuery. Now, figure 8-9 presents the other selectors that you're most likely to use in your jQuery applications. The only selectors of significance that are missing are ones that you'll learn about in later chapters, like the animate selector that you use with animations and the form control selectors that you use with forms.

If this summary seems daunting, just read the list and realize that these selectors let you select just about any element that you need to select. Then, make sure that you understand the examples in this figure. Later, when you need to make a specific type of selection for an application, you can refer back to this summary and to figure 8-4.

To illustrate the use of these selectors, the first example shows a selector that gets the li elements that are the first children of their parent elements. If the HTML contains more than one list, this selects the first li element of each list. The second example shows how to get the even tr (row) elements in an HTML table.

The third example shows how to use the :eq selector to get a specific element within an array of elements. If, for example, there are four <p> elements that are descendants of the "faqs" element, :eq(2) will return the third <p> element because the index values start with zero.

The last example shows a selector that gets all input elements with type attributes that have "text" as the value. In other words, this selector gets all text boxes. Note, however, that you can also get the text boxes by using this selector:

```
$("input[type=text]")
```

This just shows that you can often select the elements that you want in more than one way.

A summary of the most useful jQuery selectors

Selector	Selects
[*attribute*]	All elements with the named attribute.
[*attribute=value*]	All elements with the named attribute and value.
:contains(*text*)	All elements that contain the specified text.
:empty	All elements with no children including text nodes.
:eq(*n*)	The element at index n within the selected set.
:even	All elements with an even index within the selected set.
:first	The first element within the set.
:first-child	All elements that are first children of their parent elements.
:gt(*n*)	All elements within the selected set that have an index greater than n.
:has(*selector*)	All elements that contain the element specified by the selector.
:header	All elements that are headers (h1, h2, ...).
:hidden	All elements that are hidden.
:last	The last element within the selected set.
:last-child	All elements that are the last children of their parent elements.
:lt(*n*)	All elements within the selected set that have an index less than n.
:not(*selector*)	All elements that aren't selected by the selector.
:nth-child	All elements that are the nth children of their parent elements.
:odd	All elements with an odd index within the selected set.
:only-child	All elements that are the only children of their parent elements.
:parent	All elements that are parents of other elements, including text nodes.
:text	All input elements with the type attribute set to "text".
:visible	All elements that are visible.

Examples

How to select the li elements that are the first child of their parent element
```
$("li:first-child")
```

How to select the even tr elements of a table
```
$("table > tr:even")     // numbering starts at 0, so first tag is even
```

How to select the third descendant <p> element of an element
```
$("#faqs p:eq(2)")       // numbering starts at 0
```

How to select all input elements with "text" as the type attribute
```
$(":text")
```

Description

- Figure 8-4 and the table above summarize the selectors that you are most likely to need.
- Not included are six attribute selectors that let you select attributes with attribute values that contain specific substrings.
- In chapter 9, you'll learn about a selector that's used with animation, and in chapter 10, you'll learn about other selectors that are used for form controls.

Figure 8-9   The most useful selectors

The most useful methods

The table in figure 8-10 represents a collection of methods that are taken from several jQuery categories. For instance, the prev(), next(), and find() methods are DOM traversal methods. The attr(), css(), addClass(), removeClass(), toggleClass(), and html() methods are DOM manipulation methods. The hide() and show() methods are effect methods. And the each() method is a miscellaneous method.

These are some of the most useful jQuery methods, and they will get you off to a fast start with jQuery. Then, you'll add methods to your repertoire as you read the rest of the chapters in this section.

Here again, if this table seems daunting, just read through these methods to see what's available. Then, study the examples to see how they can be used. Later, when you need a specific method for an application, you can refer back to this summary.

In the first example, the attr() method is used to get the src attribute of an element with "image" as its id. The second example uses the attr() method to add an src attribute to the selected element with the value that's stored in the variable named imageSource. If the element already has an src attribute, this method changes its value. The third example uses the css() method to change the color property of the selected elements to blue.

In the fourth example, the addClass() method is used to add a class to all of the h2 elements within the element that has "faqs" as its id. That's similar to what you've done using JavaScript.

In the fifth example, the html() method adds an h2 element to an aside element. This jQuery method works like the innerHTML property that you learned how to use in chapter 6.

In the last example, the each() method is used to perform a function for each element in an array. In this case, the array contains all of the <a> elements within the element with "image_list" as its id, and the each() method loops through these elements. As you will see, this simplifies the handling of the elements in the array.

In most cases, the jQuery methods operate on all of the selected elements. There are some exceptions, however. For example, if you use the attr() method to get the value of an attribute, it will get the value only for the first selected element. Similarly, the css() method will get the value of a property only for the first selected element.

A summary of the most useful jQuery methods

Method	Description
next([*selector*])	Get the next sibling of each selected element or the first sibling of a specified type if the parameter is coded.
prev([*selector*])	Get the previous sibling of each selected element or the previous sibling of a specified type if the parameter is coded.
find(*selector*)	Search the selected element and return descendant elements.
attr(*attributeName*)	Get the value of the specified attribute from the first selected element.
attr(*attributeName, value*)	Set the value of the specified attribute for each selected element.
css(*propertyName*)	Get the value of the specified property from the first selected element.
css(*propertyName, value*)	Set the value of the specified property for each selected element.
addClass(*className*)	Add one or more classes to the selected elements and, if necessary, create the class. If you use more than one class as the parameter, separate them with spaces.
removeClass([*className*])	Remove one or more classes. If you use more than one class as the parameter, separate them with spaces.
toggleClass(*className*)	If the class is present, remove it. Otherwise, add it.
html(*htmlString*)	Sets the HTML contents of each selected element to the specified HTML string.
hide([*duration*])	Hide the selected elements. The duration parameter can be "slow", "fast", or a number giving the time in milliseconds. By default, the duration is 400 milliseconds, "slow" is 600 milliseconds, and "fast" is 200 milliseconds.
show([*duration*])	Show the selected elements. The duration parameter is the same as for the hide() method.
each(*function*)	Run the function for each element in an array.

Get the value of the src attribute of an image

```
$("#image").attr("src");
```

Set the value of the src attribute of an image to the value of a variable

```
$("#image").attr("src", imageSource);
```

Set the value of the color property of the h2 elements to blue

```
$("h2").css("color", "blue");
```

Add a class to the h2 descendants of the "faqs" element

```
$("#faqs h2").addClass("minus");
```

Put an h2 element into an aside element

```
$("aside").html("<h2>Table of Contents</h2>");
```

Run a function for each <a> element within an "image_list" element

```
$("#image_list a").each(function() {
    // the statements of the function
});
```

Figure 8-10   The most useful methods

The most useful event methods

Figure 8-11 summarizes some of the most useful event methods, and this summary includes the ready() and click() methods that were introduced in figure 8-6. As you can see, most of these event methods provide for a single event handler that runs when the event occurs. Those event methods work like the ready() and click() methods, but with different events.

This is illustrated by the first example, which works just like the click() event method except that it handles the double-click event. Of note here is the use of the *this* keyword within the handler. It is coded as a jQuery selector, and it refers to the text box that has been double-clicked. This is similar to the way the *this* keyword works with JavaScript. Note that it isn't enclosed within quotation marks, even though it's a selector. What this function does is use the val() method to set the value of the double-clicked text box to an empty string.

In contrast, the hover() event method provides for two event handlers: one for when the mouse pointer moves into an element and another for when the mouse pointer moves out of an element. This is illustrated by the second example in this figure. Note here that the first function is the first parameter of the hover() method, and it is followed by a comma. Then, the second function is the second parameter of the hover() method. To end the parameters, the last line of code consists of a right parenthesis followed by a semicolon.

The hover() method is typical of jQuery coding, which often requires the use of one or more functions within another function. That's why you need to code the functions in a way that helps you keep the punctuation straight. It also helps to code inline comments that mark the ends of functions and methods.

In these examples, note that when a selector gets more than one element, the event method sets up the event handler for each of the selected elements. This makes it much easier to set up event handlers with jQuery than it is with JavaScript.

The last example in this figure shows how to use the preventDefault() method of the event object that's passed to the event handler to cancel the default action of the event. When you include the jQuery library, this jQuery method is executed in place of the preventDefault() method of the browser that you learned about in figure 7-1. Then, because the jQuery version of this method is cross-browser compatible, it simplifies the JavaScript code. You'll see how this method is used in some of the applications that are presented later in this chapter.

A summary of the most useful jQuery event methods

Event method	Description
ready(*handler*)	The handler runs when the DOM is ready.
click(*handler*)	The handler runs when the selected element is clicked.
dblclick(*handler*)	The handler runs when the selected element is double-clicked.
mouseenter(*handler*)	The handler runs when the mouse pointer enters the selected element.
mouseover(*handler*)	The handler runs when the mouse pointer moves over the selected element.
mouseout(*handler*)	The handler runs when the mouse pointer moves out of the selected element.
hover(*handlerIn*, *handlerOut*)	The first event handler runs when the mouse pointer moves into an element. The second event handler runs when the mouse pointer moves out.
event.preventDefault()	Stops the default action of an event from happening.

A handler for the double-click event of all text boxes that clears the clicked box

```
$(":text").dblclick(function () {
    $(this).val("");
});
```

A handler for the hover event of each img element within a list

```
$("#image_list img").hover(
    function() {
        alert("The mouse pointer has moved into an img element");
    },
    function() {
        alert("The mouse pointer has moved out of an img element");
    }
);  // end hover
```

A preventDefault() method that stops the default action of an event

```
$("#faqs a").click(function(evt) {  // the event object is named evt
    evt.preventDefault();             // the method is run on the event object
}); // end click
```

Description

- The table above presents the event methods that you'll use the most. Not included are: keydown, keypress, keyup, mousedown, mouseup, mouseleave, and mousemove.

- The preventDefault() method is executed on the event object that gets passed to a function when an event occurs. You can name this object whatever you want.

- Event methods named load(), unload(), and error() were deprecated in version 1.8 and removed in version 3.0. You may see them sometimes in older code examples online, but you shouldn't try to use them.

Figure 8-11   The most useful event methods

Other event methods that you should be aware of

For most applications, you'll use the event methods that have already been presented. You'll also code the function or functions for the event handlers as the parameters of the event methods.

Sometimes, though, you'll want to attach event handlers in other ways, remove an event handler, or trigger an event that starts an event handler. Then, you can use the methods that are presented in the table in figure 8-12.

The on() method lets you attach an event handler to one or more events. In the first set of examples, it's used to attach an event handler to the click event of an element with "clear" as its id. You can also do this using the click() event method as shown here. A method like this is called a *shortcut method* because it actually uses the on() method internally. In a case like this where you're attaching a single event handler, you can use either the on() method or the shortcut method.

One advantage of the on() method is that you can use it to attach an event handler to two different events. This is illustrated by the first statement in the second set of examples. Here, two events—click and mouseover—are included in the first parameter of the on() method. That means that the event handler will be triggered whenever either of these events occurs on the selected elements.

In contrast, if you want to attach the same event handler to two different events of two different elements, you can use shortcut events as shown here. Notice that because both event methods refer to the same event handler, you typically assign the event handler to a variable. Then, you can use the name of that variable as the parameter of the shortcut methods. In this example, the event handler is assigned to a variable named clearClick. Then, the click() method is used to attach this event handler to an element with "clear" as its id, and the dblclick() method is used to attach this event handler to all text boxes.

For some applications, you may want to remove an event handler when some condition occurs. To do that, you can use the off() method, as illustrated by the third example in this figure. If the event handler is assigned to a variable, you can also name the variable on the handler parameter of the off() method.

Or, if you want to remove an event handler after it runs just one time, you can use the one() event method. This is illustrated by the fourth example.

If you want to initiate an event from your jQuery code, you can use the trigger() method in either the long or short form, as illustrated by the fifth set of examples. Both of those examples trigger the click event of the element with "clear" as its id, which in turn causes the event handler for that event to be run.

That provides another way to run the same event handler for two different events. All you have to do is trigger the event for one event handler from another event handler. That's illustrated by the last example in this figure. There, the event handler for the double-click event of all text boxes triggers the click event of the element with "clear" as its id, and that starts the event handler.

Other event methods that you should be aware of

Event method	Description
on(*events, handler*)	Attach an event handler to one or more events.
off(*events, [handler]*)	Remove an event handler from one or more events.
one(*event, handler*)	Attach an event handler and remove it after it runs one time.
trigger(*event*)	Trigger the event for the selected element.

How to attach an event handler to an event

With the on() method
```
$("#clear").on("click", function() {...});
```

With the shortcut method
```
$("#clear").click(function() {...});
```

How to attach an event handler to two different events

Of the same element
```
$("image_list img").on("click mouseover", function() {...});
```

Of two different elements
```
var clearClick = function() {...};
$("#clear").click(clearClick);
$(":text").dblclick(clearClick);
```

How to remove an event handler from an event
```
$("#clear").off("click");
```

How to attach and remove an event handler so it runs only once
```
$("#clear").one("click", function() {...});
```

How to trigger an event

With the trigger() method
```
$("#clear").trigger("click");
```

With the shortcut method
```
$("#clear").click();
```

How to use the shortcut method to trigger an event from an event handler
```
$(":text").dblclick(function() {
    $("#clear").click();     // triggers the click event of the clear button
});
```

Description

- When you use a *shortcut method* to attach an event handler to an event, you're actually using the on() method.

- Event methods named bind() and unbind() were deprecated in version 3.0. You may see them sometimes in older code examples online, but you shouldn't try to use them.

Figure 8-12   Other event methods that you should be aware of

Three illustrative applications

Now, to help you see how the selectors, methods, and event methods work in actual applications, this chapter presents three typical JavaScript applications.

The FAQs application in jQuery

Figure 8-13 presents a FAQs application similar to the one that you studied in chapter 6, but this time it uses jQuery. When this applications starts, the div elements after the h2 elements are hidden by the CSS, and the h2 elements are preceded by a plus sign. Then, if the user clicks on an h2 element, the div element below it is displayed and the plus sign is changed to a minus sign. And if the user clicks on the heading again, the process is reversed.

The jQuery code for this application consists of a click() event method that's within the ready() method. This click() event method sets up the event handlers for every h2 element within the section that has "faqs" as its id:

```
$("#faqs h2").click
```

Within the function for the event handler, the *this* keyword is used to refer to the current h2 element because that's the object of the click() method. Then, the toggleClass() method is used to add a class named "minus" to the h2 element if it isn't present or to remove it if it is. If you refer to the CSS that's shown here, you can see that this class determines whether a plus or minus sign is displayed before the heading.

Next, an if statement is used to check the value of the class attribute of the h2 element. To do that, it uses the attr() method. If the class isn't equal to "minus", it means that the div element that follows the h2 element shouldn't be displayed. Then, the statement within the if clause chains the next() and hide() methods to hide the div element that is a sibling to the h2 element.

If the class attribute of the h2 element is equal to "minus", it means that the div element that follows the h2 element should be displayed. Then, the statement within the else clause uses the next() and show() methods to show the div element that is a sibling to the h2 element.

The click event ends by cancelling the default action of the <a> element that's within the h2 element. The next application will discuss how this works in more detail. For now, just know that this line of code, which is similar to the code you saw in figure 7-1, works across browsers, not just on DOM-compliant browsers.

Finally, the ready event ends by using the find() method to get the <a> elements that are descendants of the element whose id is "faqs". It then uses the first selector to get the first <a> element, and it sets the focus on that element.

This application begins to show the power of jQuery. Here, it takes just 13 lines of code to do the same thing that the JavaScript application in figure 6-6 needed 23 lines of code to do. Furthermore, these lines of code are easier to read because jQuery methods like show(), hide(), and find() are more descriptive and therefore easier to understand.

The FAQs application in a browser

The HTML

```html
<main id="faqs">
    <h1>jQuery FAQs</h1>
    <h2><a href="#">What is jQuery?</a></h2>
    <div>
        <p>jQuery is a library of the JavaScript functions that you're most
            likely to need as you develop websites.
        </p>
    </div>
    <h2><a href="#">Why is jQuery becoming so popular?</a></h2>
    <div>
        <p>Three reasons:</p>
        <ul>
            <li>It's free.</li>
            <li>It lets you get more done in less time.</li>
            <li>All of its functions are cross-browser compatible.</li>
        </ul>
    </div>
    ...
    ...
</main>
```

The critical CSS

```css
h2 { background: url(images/plus.png) no-repeat left center; }
h2.minus { background: url(images/minus.png) no-repeat left center; }
div { display: none; }
```

The jQuery

```javascript
$(document).ready(function( evt ) {
    $("#faqs h2").click(function() {
        $(this).toggleClass("minus");
        if ($(this).attr("class") != "minus") {
            $(this).next().hide();
        }
        else {
            $(this).next().show();
        }
        evt.preventDefault();               // cancel default action
    }); // end click
    $("#faqs").find("a:first").focus();   // set focus on first <a> tag
}); // end ready
```

Figure 8-13   The FAQs application in jQuery

The Image Swap application in jQuery

Figure 8-14 presents another application that shows the power of jQuery. It is the Image Swap application that you studied in chapter 7. In this application, when the user clicks on one of the thumbnail images at the top of the browser window, the caption and image below the thumbnails are changed.

In the HTML shown here, img elements are used to display the four thumbnail images. However, these elements are coded within <a> elements so the images are clickable and they can receive the focus. In the <a> elements, the href attributes identify the images to be swapped when the links are clicked, and the title attributes provide the text for the related captions. In this case, both the <a> elements and the img elements are coded within a ul element.

After the ul element, you can see the h2 element for the caption and the img element for the main image on the page. The ids of these elements are highlighted because the jQuery will use those ids as it swaps captions and images into them.

For the motor-impaired, this HTML provides accessibility by coding the img elements for the thumbnails within <a> elements. That way, the user can access the thumbnail links by pressing the Tab key, and the user can swap the image by pressing the Enter key when a thumbnail has the focus, which starts the click event.

Of note in the CSS for this page is the rule set for the li elements. Their display properties are set to inline so the images go from left to right instead of from top to bottom.

The user interface for the Image Swap application

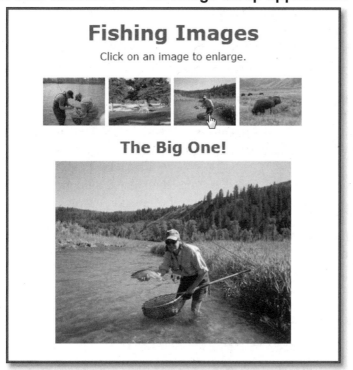

The HTML

```
<main>
    <h1>Fishing Images</h1>
    <p>Click on an image to enlarge.</p>
    <ul id="image_list">
        <li><a href="images/release.jpg" title="Catch and Release">
            <img src="thumbnails/release.jpg" alt=""></a></li>
        <li><a href="images/deer.jpg" title="Deer at Play">
            <img src="thumbnails/deer.jpg" alt=""></a></li>
        <li><a href="images/hero.jpg" title="The Big One!">
            <img src="thumbnails/hero.jpg" alt=""></a></li>
        <li><a href="images/bison.jpg" title="Grazing Bison">
            <img src="thumbnails/bison.jpg" alt=""></a></li>
    </ul>
    <h2 id="caption">Catch and Release</h2>
    <p><img id="main_image" src="images/release.jpg" alt=""></p>
</main>
```

The CSS for the li elements

```
li {
    display: inline;
}
```

Figure 8-14   The user interface, HTML, and CSS for the Image Swap application

Figure 8-15 presents the JavaScript and jQuery for this application. Within the ready event handler, the each() method is used to run a function for each <a> element in the unordered list. This function preloads the images that will be swapped so they are in the browser cache when the user starts using the application. If an application uses many images, this can make the application run faster.

Within the function for each <a> element, the first statement creates a new Image object. Then, the second statement uses the *this* keyword and the attr() method to set the src attribute of the Image object to the value of the href attribute in the <a> element. As soon as that's done, the image is loaded into the browser.

The each() method is followed by a click() event method that sets up the event handlers for the click events of the <a> elements that contain the thumbnail images. Note here that evt is coded as the parameter for the click() event method, which receives the event object when the event occurs. This object will be used later to cancel the default action of each link.

The first two statements in this event handler swap the image in the main portion of the browser window. The first statement uses the *this* keyword and attr() method to get the value of the href attribute of the <a> element. This value gives the location of the image to be swapped. Then, the second statement sets the src attribute of the main img element to this value. As soon as that's done, the image is swapped in the browser.

The next two statements work similarly. They swap the caption of the image in the main portion of the browser window. This time, the caption is taken from the title attribute of the <a> element.

The last statement in the click event handler uses the preventDefault() method of the evt object that is passed to the event handler to cancel the default action of clicking on the link. This is the same statement you saw in the FAQs application, but it's more important here. If you didn't cancel the default action of clicking on the <a> element in the FAQs application, the application would still work. The page would just be reloaded, which would make it less efficient. If the default action isn't cancelled when you click on a link in this application, though, the image that's referred to by the href attribute will be displayed in a new window or tab, which isn't what you want.

After the click event handler, the last statement in the ready() method shows another way to set the focus to the first <a> element. Because that element contains the first thumbnail image, that will make it easier for the users to tab to the thumbnails that they want to swap. To identify the first <a> element, the :first-child selector is used to get the first li element of the unordered list. Then, a descendant selector is used to get the <a> element within the li element.

The JavaScript

```
$(document).ready(function() {
    // preload images
    $("#image_list a").each(function() {
        var swappedImage = new Image();
        swappedImage.src = $(this).attr("href");
    });

    // set up event handlers for links
    $("#image_list a").click(function(evt) {
        // swap image
        var imageURL = $(this).attr("href");
        $("#main_image").attr("src", imageURL);

        //swap caption
        var caption = $(this).attr("title");
        $("#caption").text(caption);

        // cancel the default action of the link
        evt.preventDefault();  // jQuery cross-browser method
    }); // end click

    // move focus to first thumbnail
    $("li:first-child a").focus();
}); // end ready
```

Description

- When you attach an event handler to a link, you often need to cancel the default action of the link, which is to open the page or image that's identified by its href attribute.

- To cancel the default action of a link, you can use the jQuery preventDefault() method of the event object that is passed to the event handler. The jQuery version of this method is cross-browser compatible.

- To get the event object that's passed to a method, you need to code a parameter for the event handler function. You can use whatever name you want for this parameter, like evt or event. Then, you must use that name whenever you refer to the event object.

- When you use jQuery to work with images that aren't included in the HTML, preloading the images can improve the performance of the application because the user doesn't have to wait for a new image to be loaded into the browser.

- To preload an image, you create a new Image object and assign the URL for the image to the Image object's src attribute. As soon as that's done, the image is loaded into the browser.

Figure 8-15   The JavaScript for the Image Swap application

The Image Rollover application in jQuery

Figure 8-16 presents another application that shows the power of jQuery. It's the Rollover application from the exercises for chapter 7. In this application, when the user hovers the mouse pointer over one of the starting images in the Rollover application, it's replaced by another image. And when the user moves the mouse pointer out of the image, the original image is again displayed.

In the HTML shown here, img elements are coded within the li elements of an unordered list. In these img elements, the src attribute identifies the image that is displayed when the application is loaded into the browser, and the id attribute identifies the image that should be displayed when the mouse hovers over the img element.

In the JavaScript shown here, an each() method is used to perform a function for each occurrence of an img element within the ul element that has "image_rollovers" as its id:

```
$("#image_rollovers img").each
```

The function for the each() method starts by using the *this* keyword and the attr() method to get the values of the src and id attributes of the current image and store them in variables named oldURL and newURL. Remember that these attributes hold the values that locate the starting image and its rollover image. Then, these variables can be used to preload the rollover image and to set up the hover event handlers for each image.

Note that the each() method applies the function to all img elements in the element whose id is "image_rollovers". That means that you can add more images to this element, and as long as the img elements have an src attribute with the original image and an id attribute with the new image, they will work as rollovers without adding any more jQuery or JavaScript code.

The next two statements preload the rollover image by creating a new Image object and assigning the value of the newURL variable to its src attribute. As soon as the src attribute is set, the browser loads the image. Although preloading isn't essential, it can improve the user experience because the users won't have to wait for a rollover image to be loaded.

Next, the hover() event method is used to set up the event handlers for the current image (this). Remember, this event method has two event handlers as its parameters. The first event handler is run when the mouse pointer moves into the element, and the second is run when the mouse pointer moves out of the element.

In the function for the first event handler, you can see that the *this* keyword and the attr() method are used to set the src attribute of the image to the value of the newURL variable. That causes the rollover image to be displayed. The function for the second event handler reverses this process by restoring the src attribute of the image to the value of the oldURL variable.

Of course, there's more than one way to code an application like this. For instance, you could implement this application by using the mouseover and mouseout events, similar to how the chapter 7 exercise worked. Then, you'd code the mouseover event like the first function of the hover() event method, and the mouseout event like the second function of the hover() event method.

Two images with the second image rolled over

The HTML

```
<main>
    <h1>Fishing Images</h1>
    <p>Move your mouse over an image to change it and back out of the
        image to restore the original image.</p>
    <ul id="image_rollovers">
        <li><img src="images/release.jpg" alt="" id="images/deer.jpg"></li>
        <li><img src="images/hero.jpg" alt="" id="images/bison.jpg"></li>
    </ul>
</main>
```

The JavaScript

```
$(document).ready(function() {
    $("#image_rollovers img").each(function() {
        var oldURL = $(this).attr("src");      // gets the src attribute
        var newURL = $(this).attr("id");       // gets the id attribute

        // preload rollover image
        var rolloverImage = new Image();
        rolloverImage.src = newURL;

        // set up event handlers
        $(this).hover(
            function() {
                $(this).attr("src", newURL);   // sets the src attribute
            },
            function() {
                $(this).attr("src", oldURL);   // sets the src attribute
            }
        );   // end hover
    });  // end each
});  // end ready
```

Figure 8-16   The Image Rollover application in jQuery

Perspective

To get you off to a fast start, this chapter has presented a working subset of the most useful jQuery selectors, methods, and event methods. That should give you some idea of what you have to work with when you use jQuery. And you'll add to those selectors and methods as you read other chapters in this book.

The trick of course is being able to apply the right selectors, methods, and event methods to the application that you're trying to develop. To get good at that, it helps to review many different types of jQuery applications. That's why this chapter has presented four applications, and that's why you'll see many more before you complete this book.

Terms

jQuery   getter method
CDN (Content Delivery Network)   setter method
Subresource Integrity (SRI) checking   object chaining
selector   event method
method   shortcut method

Summary

- *jQuery* is a JavaScript library that provides methods that make JavaScript programming easier. These methods have been tested for cross-browser compatibility.

- To use jQuery, you code a script element in the head section that includes the file for the jQuery core library. This file can be downloaded and stored on your computer or server, or you can access it through a *Content Delivery Network (CDN)*.

- If you use the jQuery CDN, the jQuery website recommends that you use *Subresource Integrity (SRI) checking* to help ensure that resources from a third-party server aren't tampered with.

- When you code statements that use jQuery, you use *selectors* that are like those for CSS. You also use a dot syntax that consists of the selector for one or more elements, the dot, and the name of the *method* that should be executed.

- You can use *object chaining* to call a jQuery method on the object that's returned by another method.

- To set up event handlers in jQuery, you use *event methods*. Most of these methods have one parameter that is the event handler that will be run when the event occurs. But some event methods like the hover() method take two event handler parameters.

Exercise 8-1   Add a Clear button to the Email List application

In this exercise, you'll add a Clear button to the Email List application of figures 8-7 and 8-8. That will give you practice creating and attaching another event handler.

1. Use your text editor or IDE to open the index.html and email_list.js files in this folder:

    `javascript_jquery\exercises\ch08\email_list\`

2. Run the application to refresh your memory about how it works. Note that a Clear button has been added below the Join our List button, but the button doesn't work.

3. Add an event handler for the click event of the Clear button that clears all of the text boxes by setting them to an empty string (""). This can be done in one statement. To select just the text boxes, you use a selector like the one in the last example in figure 8-9. To set the values to empty strings, you use the val() method like the second example in figure 8-5. Now, test this change.

4. This event handler should also put the asterisks back in the span elements that are displayed to the right of the text boxes to show that entries are required. That requires just one statement that uses the next() and the text() methods.

5. Add one more statement to this event handler that moves the focus to the first text box. Then, test this change.

6. Add another event handler to this application for the double-click event of any text box. This event handler should do the same thing that the event handler for the click event of the Clear button does. The easiest way to do that is to trigger the click event of the Clear button from the handler for the double-click event, as in the last example in figure 8-12. Test this change.

7. Comment out the line of code that you just used to trigger the click event of the Clear button. Then, add a statement to the double-click event handler that only clears the text from the text box that the user double-clicks in. To do that, you'll have to use the *this* keyword, as in the first example in figure 8-11. Test the application one more time to make sure this works.

Exercise 8-2   Use different event methods for the Image Rollover application

This exercise asks you to modify the Image Rollover application of figure 8-16 so it uses different events for the event handlers.

1. Use your text editor or IDE to open the HTML and JavaScript files that are in this folder:

    `javascript_jquery\exercises\ch08\rollover\`

2. Run the application to refresh your memory about how it works.

3. Comment out the hover() method in the JavaScript, and rewrite the code so it uses the mouseover() and mouseout() event methods to implement this application.

4. Add the two images that are displayed when the two existing images are rolled over to the ul element whose id is image_rollovers. Make sure that the src attributes of the img elements contain the original image for the rollover, and that the id attributes contain the image that should display when the mouse is over the image.

Exercise 8-3   Develop a Book List application

In this exercise, you'll start with the HTML and CSS for the user interface that follows. Then, you'll develop the jQuery code that makes it work.

Murach products

− **Books for open-source web developers**
- Murach's HTML5 and CSS3 (3rd Edition)
- Murach's JavaScript and jQuery
- Murach's JavaScript (2nd Edition)
- Murach's jQuery (2nd Edition)
- Murach's PHP and MySQL (2nd Edition)

✛ **Books for Java programmers**

✛ **Books for .NET developers**

✛ **Books for database programmers**

Development guidelines

1. You'll find the HTML, CSS, and image files for this application in this folder:

   `javascript_jquery\exercises\ch08\book_list\`

   You'll also find an empty JavaScript file named book_list.js. You can add your code to this file.

2. This application works like the FAQs application you saw in this chapter, except that a list of book links is displayed below each heading. If the user clicks on one of these links, an image for the book is displayed to the right of the list. In addition, any time the user clicks on a heading with a plus or minus sign before it, the image should no longer be displayed.

3. The HTML for the links of this application is like the HTML for the Image Swap application. However, the links for this application don't require the title attribute since no caption is displayed for the image.

4. The images that are referred to by the href attributes of the links in this application should be preloaded. To do that, you can loop through all the links in the main element. Also, be sure to cancel the default actions of the links.

5. Feel free to copy and paste code from any of the applications that are available to you. That's the most efficient way to build a new application.

9

How to use effects
and animations

Now that you know the basics of using jQuery, this chapter presents the methods for effects and animations. Many developers like these jQuery methods the best because effects and animations are fun to develop and can add interest to a page. As you study these methods, though, remember that the primary goal of a website is usability, so make sure that your effects and animations don't detract from that goal.

Keep in mind too that it may be difficult to understand how some of these methods work until you see them in action. To help you with that, we've included most of the examples in this chapter in the downloadables for this chapter. So, you may want to run these examples as you progress through this chapter to see how they work.

How to use effects

This chapter starts by presenting the basic methods for effects that are provided by jQuery. After you learn how to use them, you'll learn how to use what the jQuery documentation refers to as custom effects. In practice, though, any illusion of movement on a web page can be referred to as *animation*, so you can think of all the examples in this chapter as animation.

The jQuery methods for effects

Figure 9-1 summarizes the jQuery methods for *effects*. These include the show() and hide() methods that were presented in chapter 8.

For all of the methods except the fadeTo() method, the primary parameter is the duration parameter that determines how long the effect will take. If, for example, the duration parameter for the fadeOut() method is 5000, the selected element or elements will be faded out over 5 seconds (5000 milliseconds). If the duration parameter is omitted, the effect takes place immediately so there is no animation.

In contrast, the fadeTo() method not only requires the duration parameter but also an opacity parameter. The opacity parameter must be a value from 0 through 1, where 1 is the full (normal) opacity and 0 is invisible.

The examples in this figure show how these methods work. Here, the first example uses the fadeOut() method to fade out a heading over 5 seconds. Then, the second example chains the fadeOut() and slideDown() methods to first fade out the heading over five seconds and then redisplay it by increasing its height over one second so it appears to slide down. As you will see, chaining is commonly used with effects to get the desired animation.

The next example shows how fadeTo() methods can be chained. Here, the heading is first faded to an opacity of .2 over 5 seconds. Then, the heading is faded to an opacity of 1 over 1 second. This has the effect of the heading almost fading away completely and then being restored to its full opacity.

The last example shows how a *callback function* can be used with any of these methods. To use a callback function, you code a function as the last parameter of the method. Then, that function is called after the method finishes.

In this example, the fadeTo() method is used to fade a heading to .2 opacity. Then, the callback function fades the heading back to full opacity. Note in the callback function that the *this* keyword is used to refer to the heading that's selected for the first fadeTo() method. As you will see, though, the callback method often selects other elements for its operations.

Please note that the last two examples in this figure get the same result. However, chaining is the better way to get this result.

Before going on, you may be interested to know that when you specify a duration with the hide() or show() method, the effect is implemented by changing the height, width, and opacity properties of the elements. To show an element, for example, its height, width, and opacity are increased so it appears to grow from its upper left corner. Conversely, to hide an element, its height, width, and opacity are decreased so it appears to shrink from its lower right corner.

The basic methods for jQuery effects

Method	Description
show()	Display the selected elements from the upper left to the lower right.
hide()	Hide the selected elements from the lower right to the upper left.
toggle()	Display or hide the selected elements.
slideDown()	Display the selected elements with a sliding motion.
slideUp()	Hide the selected elements with a sliding motion.
slideToggle()	Display or hide the selected elements with a sliding motion.
fadeIn()	Display the selected elements by fading them in to opaque.
fadeOut()	Hide the selected elements by fading them out to transparent.
fadeToggle()	Display or hide the selected elements by fading them in or out.
fadeTo()	Adjust the opacity property of the selected elements to the opacity set by the second parameter. The duration parameter must be specified with this method.

The basic syntax for all of the methods except the fadeTo() method

```
methodName([duration][, callback])
```

The basic syntax for the fadeTo() method

```
fadeTo(duration, opacity[, callback])
```

HTML for a heading that is animated after the web page is loaded

```
<h1 id="startup_message">Temporarily under construction!</h1>
```

jQuery that fades the heading out over 5 seconds

```
$("#startup_message").fadeOut(5000);
```

jQuery that uses chaining to fade the heading out and slide it back down

```
$("#startup_message").fadeOut(5000).slideDown(1000);
```

Chaining with fadeTo() methods

```
$("#startup_message").fadeTo(5000, .2).fadeTo(1000, 1);
```

jQuery with a callback function that gets the same result as the chaining

```
$("#startup_message").fadeTo(5000, .2,
    function() {                        // start callback function
        $(this).fadeTo(1000, 1);
    }                                   // end callback function
);
```

Description

- The duration parameter can be "slow", "fast", or a number giving the time in milliseconds. By default, the duration is 400 milliseconds, "slow" is 600 milliseconds, and "fast" is 200 milliseconds.

- The callback parameter is for a function that is called after the effect has finished. If more than one element is selected, the *callback function* is run once for each element.

- Chaining is commonly used with effects. This works because each effect method returns the object that it performed the effect on.

Figure 9-1   The jQuery methods for effects

The FAQs application with jQuery effects

Remember the FAQs application from the last chapter? That application used the show() and hide() methods without duration parameters to show and hide the answers to the questions in h2 elements. Now, figure 9-2 shows two ways that you can apply animation to that application.

The first example uses code similar to the code you saw in chapter 8. Here, when the user clicks on an h2 element, the function for the click event uses the toggleClass() method to add or remove a class named "minus". Then, the div element that's adjacent to the h2 element is displayed or hidden depending on whether the h2 element includes the "minus" class. In this case, though, the show() and hide() methods are replaced by slideDown() and fadeOut() methods with duration parameters to add animation to the application.

The second example shows another way to get the same results. Just as in the first example, the function for the click event starts by using the toggleClass() method to add or remove a class named "minus". Then, the slideToggle() method is used to toggle the slideUp() and slideDown() methods on each click. This works just like the first example, except the slideUp() method is used instead of the fadeOut() method. It also requires fewer lines of code.

The FAQs application as the text for a heading is displayed

jQuery FAQs

+ **What is jQuery?**

− **Why is jQuery becoming so popular?**
Three reasons:
- It's free.
- It lets you get more done in less time

+ **Which is harder to learn: jQuery or JavaScript?**

The HTML

```html
<main id="faqs">
    <h1>jQuery FAQs</h1>
    <h2><a href="#">What is jQuery?</a></h2>
    <div>
        <!-- div content -->
    </div>
    <h2><a href="#">Why is jQuery becoming so popular?</a></h2>
    <div>
        <!-- div content -->
    </div>
    <h2><a href="#">Which is harder to learn: jQuery or JavaScript?</a>
    </h2>
    <div>
        <!-- div content -->
    </div>
</main>
```

The jQuery with slideDown() and fadeOut() methods

```javascript
$(document).ready(function() {
    $("#faqs h2").click(
        function() {
            $(this).toggleClass("minus");
            if ($(this).attr("class") != "minus") {
                $(this).next().fadeOut(1000);
            }
            else {
                $(this).next().slideDown(1000);
            }
        }
    );    // end click
});        // end ready
```

The jQuery with the slideToggle() method

```javascript
$(document).ready(function() {
    $("#faqs h2").click(
        function() {
            $(this).toggleClass("minus");
            $(this).next().slideToggle(1000);
        }
    );    // end click
});        // end ready
```

Figure 9-2   The FAQs application with jQuery effects

A Slide Show application with effects

To give you a better idea of how effects can be used, you will now review two different ways that a Slide Show application can be coded.

The user interface, HTML, and CSS

In figure 9-3, the screen capture shows the third slide in a slide show as it is being faded in. In the div element in the HTML, you can see that five img elements provide the slides for the show, and each of these has an alt attribute that provides the caption that is shown above the slide.

In the HTML, note that an h2 element is used for the caption, an img element is used for the slide show, and the div element that follows contains the img elements for the slides. The id attributes for these elements are "caption", "slide", and "slides", and the "caption" and "slide" elements contain the caption and slide for the first slide in the series.

In the CSS that's shown for this application, you can see that the height of the images is set to 250 pixels. In practice, all of the images for a slide show would usually be the same size, but setting the height for all of them ensures that the heights will be the same, even if the widths aren't.

Note too that the CSS sets the display property of all of the img elements in the div element named "slides" to "none". This means that those img elements won't be displayed in the browser, even if they're preloaded. Instead, they will be displayed one at a time as they're moved into the "slide" img element by the jQuery.

A Slide Show application with fading out and fading in

The HTML for the slide show

```
<main>
    <h1>Fishing Slide Show</h1>
    <h2 id="caption">Casting on the Upper Kings</h2>
    <img id="slide" src="images/casting1.jpg" alt="">
    <div id="slides">
        <img src="images/casting1.jpg" alt="Casting on the Upper Kings">
        <img src="images/casting2.jpg" alt="Casting on the Lower Kings">
        <img src="images/catchrelease.jpg"
            alt="Catch and Release on the Big Horn">
        <img src="images/fish.jpg" alt="Catching on the South Fork">
        <img src="images/lures.jpg" alt="The Lures for Catching">
    </div>
</main>
```

The critical CSS for the slide show

```
img {
    height: 250px;
}
#slides img {
    display: none;
}
```

Description

- The images in the "slides" div element will be used in the slide show.
- The caption for each image will come from its alt attribute.

Figure 9-3   The user interface, HTML, and CSS for a slide show

Two ways to code the jQuery

It should be obvious by now that most jQuery applications can be coded in many different ways. In fact, the biggest problem when learning jQuery is figuring out how to apply jQuery to get the result that you want. That's why this book frequently shows more than one way to get a result, and that's why figure 9-4 shows two ways to code the Slide Show application.

In the first example, the code starts by creating an array of Image objects that store the src and alt attributes of the five img elements in the "slides" div of the HTML. That's done by using the each() method to process each of the five elements. Within the processing loop, the attr() method is used to get the src and alt attributes from each img element and store them in the src and title properties of each Image object. Then, the Image object is added to the array.

After the array has been created, the setInterval() method is used to perform its function (the first parameter) every 3000 milliseconds (the second parameter). Within that function, the first statement selects the caption and fades it out over 1000 milliseconds. Then, the second statement selects the slide and fades it out. But note that this statement includes a callback function.

Within the callback function, the first statement gets a new value for the imageCounter variable, which was initially set to zero. To do that, it increases the counter value by 1 and uses the modulus operator to get the remainder that's left when the counter is divided by the length of the array. For the second slide in the show, that means the counter is increased to 1 and divided by 5 so the remainder is 1. For the fifth slide, the counter is increased to 5 and divided by 5 so the remainder is 0. Since this remainder is assigned back to the imageCounter variable, this means that variable will range from 0 to 5 as the slide show progresses.

Once the imageCounter value is set, the rest is easy. First, the nextImage variable is set to the next image in the array. Second, the src attribute for the "slide" img element is set to the src property of the next image object in the array, and that slide is faded in. Last, the text for the caption is set to the title property of the next image object in the array, and that caption is faded in.

In the second example, the code starts by setting the nextSlide variable to the first img element in the "slides" division. Then, the function for the setInterval timer fades out the starting slide and caption, just as it did in the first example. However, the code in the callback function for the fadeOut() method is completely different.

It starts by testing whether the next img element in the "slides" div has a length of zero. If so, that means that there isn't a next slide, and the nextSlide variable is set to the first img element in that div. Otherwise, the next slide is set to the next img element in the "slides" div.

Once the next slide is established, the code sets variables for the next slide's src and alt attributes. Then, it uses the first variable to set the src attribute for the img element that is displaying the slide show and fades it in, and it uses the second variable to set the text for the next caption and fades that in.

This shows just two of the ways that an application like this can be coded, and you'll see a few more in subsequent chapters. When you develop any

One way to code the jQuery

```
$(document).ready(function() {
    // create an array of the slide images
    var image, imageCounter = 0, imageCache = [];
    $("#slides img").each(function() {
        image = new Image();
        image.src = $(this).attr("src");
        image.title = $(this).attr("alt");
        imageCache[imageCounter] = image;
        imageCounter++;
    });
    // start slide show
    imageCounter = 0;
    var nextImage;
    setInterval( function(){
        $("#caption").fadeOut(1000);
        $("#slide").fadeOut(1000
            function() {
                imageCounter = (imageCounter + 1) % imageCache.length;
                nextImage = imageCache[imageCounter];
                $("#slide").attr("src", nextImage.src).fadeIn(1000);
                $("#caption").text(nextImage.title).fadeIn(1000);
            }
        );    // end callback
    },
    3000);
});    // end ready
```

Another way to code the jQuery

```
$(document).ready(function() {
    var nextSlide = $("#slides img:first-child");
    var nextCaption;
    var nextSlideSource;
    // start slide show
    setInterval( function(){
        $("#caption").fadeOut(1000);
        $("#slide").fadeOut(1000,
            function () {
                if (nextSlide.next().length == 0) {
                    nextSlide = $("#slides img:first-child");
                }
                else {
                    nextSlide = nextSlide.next();
                }
                nextSlideSource = nextSlide.attr("src");
                nextCaption = nextSlide.attr("alt");
                $("#slide").attr("src", nextSlideSource).fadeIn(1000);
                $("#caption").text(nextCaption).fadeIn(1000);
            }
        );    // end callback
    },
    3000);
});    // end ready
```

Figure 9-4   Two ways to code the jQuery for the slide show

application, one of the goals is to write code that is easy to read, maintain, and reuse in other web pages. The other is to write code that's efficient. Judging by those goals, the second example in figure 9-4 is better because its code is relatively straightforward, and it doesn't require an array of Image objects.

Regardless of how you code this application, though, you'll notice that when you run it, the captions and slides are faded out almost simultaneously, not one after the other. That's because the effects for two different elements run as soon as they're started. In this case, that means that one effect is started a few milliseconds after the other, so the fade out and in for the caption runs at almost the same time that the fade out and fade in for the slide runs.

How to stop and start a slide show

To improve the usability of a slide show, you usually provide some way for the user to stop and restart the show. Figure 9-5 shows one way to do that. It stops on the current slide when the user clicks on it, and it restarts when the user clicks on it again.

First, this code sets up a function expression for running the slide show and stores it in a variable named runSlideShow. If you look at the code in this function, you can see that it's the same as the code in the second example in the previous figure.

Second, this function is followed by a statement that creates a timer variable that calls the runSlideShow() function every 3 seconds. Note, however, that this must be coded after the runSlideShow() function. If this statement is coded before the function, the JavaScript engine will throw an error.

Third, the last event handler uses the click() event method to cancel and restore the timer on alternate clicks of the current slide. When a slide is clicked and the timer isn't null, the function uses the clearInterval() method to cancel the timer and thus stop the slide show. Otherwise, the timer is created again so the show restarts.

You'll also notice that the slide show stops on a full image, not one that is fading out or fading in. That's because the timer for the slide show isn't cancelled until the current interval ends. Also, the slide show restarts with the next image in sequence. That's because the values of the nextSlide, nextCaption, and nextSlideSource variables are retained, even though the timer has been cancelled.

Of course, there are many other ways that you can stop and restart a slide show. For instance, you could provide a stop/start button that works the same way that clicking on a slide works. You could also add next and previous buttons that would let the user manually move from one slide to the next while the slide show is stopped. Now that you know the basic code for running, stopping, and starting a slide show, you should be able to add these enhancements on your own.

The jQuery for stopping and restarting a slide show

```javascript
$(document).ready(function() {
    var nextSlide = $("#slides img:first-child");
    var nextCaption;
    var nextSlideSource;

    // the function for running the slide show
    var runSlideShow = function() {
        $("#caption").fadeOut(1000);
        $("#slide").fadeOut(1000,
            function () {
                if (nextSlide.next().length == 0) {
                    nextSlide = $("#slides img:first-child");
                }
                else {
                    nextSlide = nextSlide.next();
                }
                nextSlideSource = nextSlide.attr("src");
                nextCaption = nextSlide.attr("alt");
                $("#slide").attr("src", nextSlideSource).fadeIn(1000);
                $("#caption").text(nextCaption).fadeIn(1000);
            }
        );    // end callback
    };

    // start slide show
    var timer1 = setInterval(runSlideShow, 3000);

    // starting and stopping the slide show
    $("#slide").click(function() {
        if (timer1 != null) {
            clearInterval(timer1);
            timer1 = null;
        }
        else {
            timer1 = setInterval(runSlideShow, 3000);
        }
    });
});    // end ready
```

Description

- With this code, the user can stop a slide show by clicking on a slide and restart the slide show by clicking on it again.

- So the code for the slide show doesn't have to be repeated, it is coded in a function expression and stored in the variable named runSlideShow.

- Because the runSlideShow() function is a function expression, it must come before the setInterval() method that calls it. Otherwise, the JavaScript engine will throw an error.

Figure 9-5   How to stop and start a slide show

How to use animation

Now that you know how to use the basic jQuery effects, you'll learn how to use what the jQuery website refers to as custom effects. We refer to these custom effects as animation, and that starts with the animate() method.

How to use the basic syntax of the animate() method

Figure 9-6 presents the basic syntax of the animate() method. Here, the first parameter is a *properties map* that's coded in braces. This map consists of name/value pairs. For instance, the first example in this figure sets the fontSize property to 275%, the opacity property to 1, and the left property to 0. Then, the second parameter is the duration for the animation, which in the first example is 2 seconds.

When the animate() method is executed, it modifies the selected element or elements by changing their properties to the ones in the properties map over the duration specified. This gives the illusion of animation.

If you look at the starting CSS for the heading that is animated in the examples, you can see that the heading starts with its font size at 75% of the browser default, its opacity at .2 (faded out), and its left position at -175 pixels, which is 175 pixels to the left of its normal position. Then, when the animate() method in the first example is run, the heading's font size is increased to 275%, its opacity is increased to 1, and its left position is changed to zero, which is its normal position. Since this is done over 2 seconds, the result is an interesting animation, with the heading moving to the right and increasing in size and opacity.

Incidentally, to make this work correctly, the position property for the heading must be set to relative. That means that the settings for the left and top properties are relative to the position the element would be in with normal flow. That position has left and top properties of 0.

The second example is like the first one, but it includes a callback function. Here, the callback function selects the h2 headings on the page and then uses the next(), fadeIn(), and fadeOut() methods to fade in and out the div elements that follow the h2 headings. The one difference in the properties map is that the left property is set to "+=175" which moves the heading 175 pixels to the right of where it started. This gets the same results as the properties map in the first example.

When you code the properties map for a function, you must obey the rules that are described in this figure. For instance, you either use camel casing for the property names, like fontSize instead of font-size, or you code the property names in quotation marks. You code numeric values as numbers or decimal values, but otherwise you code the values in quotation marks. And when you code a numeric value for a property like left, pixels are assumed, unless you specify the unit of measurement and enclose the entire value in quotation marks.

The basic syntax for the animate() method

```
animate({properties}[, duration][, callback])
```

An animated heading that is moving into the "faqs" section

The CSS for the h1 heading

```
#faqs h1 {
    position: relative;
    left: -175px;
    font-size: 75%;
    opacity: .2;
}
```

An animate() method for the h1 heading without a callback function

```
$("#faqs h1").animate(
    { fontSize: "275%", opacity: 1, left: 0 },    // the properties map
    2000
);                                                 // end animate
```

An animate() method for the h1 heading with a callback function

```
$("#faqs h1").animate(
    { fontSize: "275%", opacity: 1, left: "+=175" },
    2000,
    function() {
        $("#faqs h2").next().fadeIn(1000).fadeOut(1000);
    }
);                                                 // end animate
```

Description

- When the animate() method is run, the CSS properties for the selected elements are changed to the properties in the *properties map* that is coded as the first parameter of the method. The animation is done in a phased transition based on the duration parameter.

- To specify a property name in the properties map, you can use camel casing instead of the CSS hyphenation (as above) or you can enclose the property name in quotes.

- To specify a non-numeric property value, enclose the value in quotes.

- To specify a numeric property value, just code the value. For measurements, pixels are assumed. You can also use the += and -= operators with numeric values, but these expressions must be enclosed in quotes.

- For some properties, like width, height, and opacity, you can use "show", "hide", or "toggle" as the property values. These will show, hide, or toggle the element by setting the property appropriately.

- Although color transitions aren't handled properly by jQuery, they are by jQuery UI.

Figure 9-6   How to use the basic syntax of the animate() method

For some properties, like width, height, and opacity, you can use "show", "hide", or "toggle" as the property values. If, for example, you code "hide" for the width or opacity value, it is decreased to zero. If you code "show", the width is increased to its normal width or the opacity is increased to 1. And if you code "toggle", the values toggle between the show and hide values.

How to chain animate() methods

To chain animations, you use the same technique that you use for chaining effects or any other methods. You code a dot operator after the first animate() method and then code the second animate() method.

This is illustrated by the first example in figure 9-7, which chains two animate() methods in the click event handler for a heading. Here, the indentation and alignment of the code are meant to show that the two animate() methods are chained. The first method increases the font size and opacity and moves the heading 275 pixels to the right. Then, the second method reduces the font size and moves the heading 275 pixels to the left so it's back where it started.

When you chain effects or animations for a selected element, they are placed in the *queue* for that element. Then, the effects and animations are run in sequence. This makes it easy for you to create some interesting animations.

Note, however, that animations that are coded separately are also placed in queues. This is illustrated by the second example in this figure. Here, the first statement is for one animate() method that is applied to the heading (this). The second statement is for another animate() method that is applied to the same heading (this). Then, when the user clicks the heading, these animations are placed in a queue and run in succession just as though they were chained, so the result is the same as for the chained methods in the first example.

Now, what happens if you click on the heading two or three times in quick succession? Either way, the animate() methods are put in the queue for the heading so they will run two or three times in a row.

In contrast, the third example uses a callback function for the first animate() method to provide the second animate() method. Then, if the user clicks on the heading just once, it works the same as the other two examples. But if the user clicks on it twice in succession, the second click will queue the second animate() method so it runs right after the first. But this may mean that the second animate() method will start before the callback method of the first animate() method is finished.

As you will see, the concept of queuing is important for some applications, especially when you want to stop the methods in the queue from running. Remember too that there is a separate queue for each element. That's why the fading in and fading out of the captions and slides in the Slide Show application are almost simultaneous.

A heading with two animations started by its click event

Chained animations

```
$("#faqs h1").click(function() {
    $(this).animate(
            { fontSize: "650%", opacity: 1, left: "+=275" }, 2000 )
        .animate(
            { fontSize: "175%", left: "-=275" }, 1000 );
});    // end click
```

Queued animations

```
$("#faqs h1").click(function() {
    $(this).animate(
        { fontSize: "650%", opacity: 1, left: "+=275" }, 2000 );
    $(this).animate(
        { fontSize: "175%", left: "-=275" }, 1000 );
});    // end click
```

An animation with a second animation in its callback function

```
$("#faqs h1").click(function() {
    $(this).animate(
        { fontSize: "650%", opacity: 1, left: "+=275" },
        2000,
        function() {
            $(this).animate(
                { fontSize: "175%", left: "-=275" }, 1000
            );
        }    // end function
    );
});          // end click
```

Description

- When you chain the effects and animations for an element, they are placed in a *queue* for that element and run in sequence, not at the same time.

- When separate effects and animations are started for an element, they are also placed in a queue for that element and run in sequence.

- When you use a callback function with an animate() method, the callback function is run after the animation is finished.

- In some cases, a problem will occur if the user starts a second animation for an element before the callback function for the first animation has finished.

Figure 9-7   How to chain animate() methods

How to use the delay(), stop(), and finish() methods

Figure 9-8 shows how to use the delay(), stop(), and finish() methods for effects and animations. As the first example shows, the delay() method delays the start of the next animation in the queue for the number of milliseconds that are specified. Here, the fadeOut effect of the selected heading is delayed for five seconds.

In contrast, the stop() method stops the animations in the queue for the selected element. This is illustrated by the second example. Here, the animation is for the hover event of the <a> elements in the HTML. This animation moves an <a> element down 15 pixels when the mouse pointer moves into the element, and it moves it back to its starting location when the mouse pointer moves out of the element.

But what if the user swipes the mouse pointer back and forth over the <a> elements several times in succession? As you've just learned, this will queue multiple animations for each <a> element that will run in succession. This will cause a bouncing effect after the user stops using the mouse, and that's not what you want.

To fix this, you can use the stop() method as shown in this figure. As the summary shows, this method stops the current animation for the selected elements. In addition, when the first parameter is set to true, the queues for the elements are cleared. As a result, all of the animations for an element in the example are stopped and the queue is cleared before another animation is added to the queue. This stops the bouncing of the <a> elements, which makes the application easier to use.

The second parameter for the stop() method causes the current animation to be completed immediately. For example, suppose an element is being faded in when the stop() method is executed. In that case, the element is left at its current opacity. If that's not what you want, you can code true for the second parameter so the end result of the animation is displayed. In the case of the fadeIn() method, that means that the element is displayed with an opacity of 1.

The finish() method is similar to the stop() method with both of its parameters set to true. The difference is that the properties of *all* queued animations, not just the current animation, are immediately set to their end values when you use finish.

The delay(), stop(), and finish() methods

Method	Description
`delay(duration)`	Delay the start of the next animation in the queue.
`stop([clearQueue] [, jumpToEnd])`	Stop the current animation for the selected element. The two parameters are Boolean with false default values. If set to true, the first parameter clears the queue so no additional animations are run. The second parameter causes the current animation to be completed immediately.
`finish([queue])`	Stop the current animation for the selected element, clear the queue, and complete all animations for the selected elements.

HTML for a heading that is displayed when the web page is loaded

```
<h1 id="startup_message">Temporarily under construction!</h1>
```

jQuery that fades the heading out after 5 seconds

```
$("#startup_message").delay(5000).fadeOut(1000);
```

Thumbnail images with queues that are still running

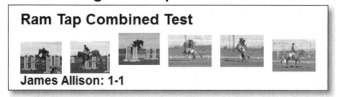

The HTML for the thumbnail images

```
<ul id="image_list">
    <li><a href="images/h1.jpg" title="James Allison: 1-1">
        <img src="thumbnails/t1.jpg" alt=""></a></li>
    // four more li elements that contain thumbnail images
    <li><a href="images/h6.jpg" title="James Allison: 1-6">
        <img src="thumbnails/t6.jpg" alt=""></a></li>
</ul>
```

The CSS for the <a> elements

```
a { position: relative; }
```

The stop() method stops the queued animations before starting a new one

```
$("#image_list a").hover(
    function(evt) { $(this).stop(true).animate({ top: 15 }, "fast"); },
    function(evt) { $(this).stop(true).animate({ top: 0 }, "fast"); }
);    // end hover
```

Description

- The delay() method in the first example above works as an alternative to the use of a one-time timer.

- The stop() method in the second example above stops the current animation for each <a> element and clears the queue. This will stop the bouncing effect that occurs when the user moves the mouse pointer rapidly back and forth over the thumbnails.

- The finish() method is similar to the stop() method with true coded for both parameters, except that the properties of all queued animations jump to their end values.

Figure 9-8   How to use the delay(), stop(), and finish() methods

How to use easings with effects and animations

Figure 9-9 shows how to use easings with effects and animations. An *easing* determines the way an animation is performed. For instance, an animation can start slowly and pick up speed as it goes. Or, an animation can start or end with a little bounce.

Right now, jQuery only provides two easings: linear and swing. As you might guess, the linear easing moves an animation at a uniform speed, but the swing easing varies the speed in a way that is more interesting. Fortunately, swing is the default, so you don't need to change that.

If you want to use other easings, you can use a plugin like the jQuery easing plugin shown in this figure. To use this plugin, you start by coding a script element for it. In the example in this figure, the script element gets the jQuery easing plugin from the Cloudflare CDN. Note that this script element must be coded after the script element for jQuery because the plugin uses jQuery.

Then, to use one of the easings that this plugin provides, you code the easing parameter for an effect or animation. The location of this parameter in each type of statement is shown in the syntax summaries at the top of this figure.

To code this parameter, of course, you need to know the names of the easings that you want to use. Perhaps the best way to find out what's available is to go to the URL that's specified at the bottom of this figure. This page not only provides information about using the plugin, but also lets you see each one in action. That will help you select the easings that you want to use for each type of animation.

The syntax for using easing with effects and animations

The syntax for all of the basic methods except the fadeTo() method

```
methodName([duration][, easing][, callback])
```

The syntax for the fadeTo() method

```
fadeTo(duration, opacity[, easing][, callback])
```

The syntax for the basic animate() method

```
animate({properties}[, duration][, easing][, callback])
```

A script element for getting the jQuery easing plugin from a CDN

```
<!-- the element for jquery easings must come after the one for jquery -->
<script src="https://cdnjs.cloudflare.com/ajax/libs/jquery-easing/1.3/
jquery.easing.min.js"></script>
```

Two easings used by the FAQs application

```
$("#faqs h2").click(function() {
    $(this).toggleClass("minus");
    if ($(this).attr("class") == "minus") {
        $(this).next().slideDown(1000, "easeOutBounce");
    }
    else {
        $(this).next().slideUp(1000, "easeInBounce");
    }
});    // end click
```

Two easings for an animated heading

```
$("#faqs h1").click(function() {
    $(this).animate(
        { fontSize: "650%", opacity: 1, left: "+=275" }, 2000, "easeInExpo" )
    .animate(
        { fontSize: "175%", left: "-=275" }, 1000, "easeOutExpo" );
});    // end click
```

Description

- *Easing* refers to the way an animation is performed. jQuery provides only two easings: swing and linear. Swing is the default, and it's the animation that you usually want.

- Plugins provide many other types of easings. Four of the easings in the jQuery easing plugin are shown in the examples above.

- To use an easing, you code a script element for the plugin library. Then, you code the easing parameter for a method with the name of any easing that the plugin supports.

- For a full list and demonstration of all the easings in the jQuery easing plugin, you can go to:
  http://gsgd.co.uk/sandbox/jquery/easing/

- You'll learn more about using other plugins in chapter 11.

Figure 9-9   How to use easings with effects and animations

How to use the advanced animate syntax and the methods for working with queues

At this point, you've probably already learned all of the methods and skills that you're going to want to use for your effects and animations. But in case you are trying to build applications that require more control over the queues, figure 9-10 presents the advanced syntax of the animate() method and the methods for working with queues.

When you use the advanced syntax of the animate() method, you code two parameters within braces and separated by a comma. In the first set of braces, you code the properties map just as you do in the basic syntax. In the second set of braces, you code one or more of the options that are summarized in the first table in this figure.

The first example in this figure shows how this works with three options: duration, specialEasing, and complete. Here, the duration option is like the duration parameter in the basic syntax, and the complete option is like the callback parameter in the basic syntax. However, the special easing parameter lets you specify a different easing for each property that is being animated.

Although the use of special easings may be more than you need, you should know that you can also use them with the basic syntax. That is illustrated by the second example in this figure. Here, you just code each property and its easing within brackets within the properties map.

The step option of the advanced animate() method lets you run a function after each step of the animation. This makes you realize that an animation is actually broken down into small steps that give the illusion of continuous progress. If, for example, you code the step option with a function that displays an alert message after each step of the first example, you'll see how many steps this animation is broken down into.

The queue option of the advanced animate() method lets you execute an animation immediately without placing it in the queue. You can also use the methods in the second table in this figure to work with the animations in a queue. But as I said at the start of this topic, you may never find the need for the advanced animate syntax or the methods for working with queues.

The advanced syntax for the animate() method

```
animate({properties}, {options})
```

Some of the options for the advanced syntax

Option	Description
`duration`	A string or number that specifies the duration of the animation.
`easing`	A string that specifies an easing function.
`complete`	A callback function that runs when the animation is complete.
`step`	A function to call after each step that the animation is broken down into.
`queue`	A Boolean value. If true, the animation will be placed in the queue. If false, the animation will start immediately.
`specialEasing`	A map of one or more of the properties in the properties map with their corresponding easings.

The methods for working with animation queues

Method	Description
`queue([name])`	Get the queue for the selected element.
`queue([name], newQueue)`	Replace the queue for the selected element with a new queue.
`queue([name], callback)`	Add a new function (callback) to the end of the queue for the selected element.
`dequeue([name])`	Run the next item in the queue for the selected element.
`clearQueue([name])`	Remove all items that haven't yet been run from the queue.

An animate() method that uses the advanced syntax

```
$("#faqs h1").animate(
    { fontSize: "650%", opacity: 1, left: "+=175" },
    { duration: 2000,
      specialEasing: { fontSize: "easeInExpo", left: "easeOutExpo" },
      complete: function() {
          $("#faqs h2").next().fadeIn(1000).fadeOut(1000); }
    }
);    // end animate
```

How to provide easings by property with the basic syntax

```
$("#faqs h1").animate(
    { fontSize: ["650%", "easeInExpo"],
      opacity: [1, "swing"],
      left: ["+=275", "easeOutExpo"] }, 2000
);    // end animate
```

Description

- The specialEasing option of the advanced syntax of the animate() method lets you specify easings by property, as shown by the first example. However, you can also do that with the basic syntax as shown by the second example.

- The name parameter in the methods for working with queues isn't needed for the default queue (fx). It's only needed for custom queues that you create.

Figure 9-10   How to use the advanced animate syntax and the methods for queues

A Carousel application with animation

This chapter ends by presenting a common application called a Carousel application. It makes use of a simple animate() method, but the setup for using that method is extensive.

The user interface, HTML, and CSS

Figure 9-11 presents the user interface, HTML, and CSS for the Carousel application. Because carousels are so common, you've most likely used one on more than one website. If you click on the button to the right of the three books in the carousel shown here, the books slide left and three more are shown. If you click on the button to the left of the books, the books slide right to the previous three books.

In the HTML, you can see that three div elements are coded within a div element for the entire carousel. The first of these div elements contains the left button; the second contains all nine of the books that will be used in the carousel; and the third contains the right button.

Within the second div element, you can see a ul element that contains nine li elements. Then, within each li element, there is an img element for each book within an <a> element. That means that the user can click on each book to go to the page for that book. In this example, the values of all the href attributes are coded as "newpage.html", but these values would refer to the actual pages for the books in a real-world application.

In the critical CSS for this application, you can see that the width of the middle div element (id is "display_panel") is set to 300 pixels, which is the width of three list items. Also, its overflow property is set to hidden, which means that anything that goes beyond 300 pixels (the other books) will be hidden.

Next, the CSS for the ul element (id is "image_list") sets the position property to relative, which means that any settings for the top or left properties will be relative to the normal position of this element. As you'll see in the jQuery for this application, the books that are displayed in the carousel are determined by the value of the left property. The CSS for this element also sets the width to 900 pixels, and the list-style to "none", which removes the bullets from the list items. The left property for this ul element illustrates one of the browser incompatibilities. With IE, this property must be set to 0. With other browsers, 0 is assumed.

Then, the CSS for the list items floats them to the left. This means that the items in the ul element will be displayed horizontally, but the 900 pixel width (100 pixels for each item) will exceed the width of its div container by 600 pixels. Remember, though, that this overflow will be hidden.

The last CSS style rule sets the width of the img elements within the li elements to 95 pixels. That means that there should be 5 pixels to the right of each image within each of the li items.

Since there are nine images in total and each list item is set to a width of 100 pixels, nine images require 900 pixels and that's the width that the ul element

A Carousel application

The HTML for the application

```html
<main>
    <h1>View our Books</h1>
    <div id="carousel">
        <div id="left_button" class="button_panel">
            <img src="images/left.jpg" alt=""></div>
        <div id="display_panel">
            <ul id="image_list">
                <li><a href="newpage.html">
                    <img src="images/book1.jpg" alt=""></a></li>
                <li><a href="newpage.html">
                    <img src="images/book2.jpg" alt=""></a></li>
                // 5 more li elements that contain images
                <li><a href="newpage.html">
                    <img src="images/book8.jpg" alt=""></a></li>
                <li><a href="newpage.html">
                    <img src="images/book9.jpg" alt=""></a></li>
            </ul>
        </div>
        <div id="right_button" class="button_panel">
            <img src="images/right.jpg" alt=""></div>
    </div>
</main>
```

The critical CSS for the application

```css
#display_panel {
    width: 300px;
    overflow: hidden;
    float: left;
    height: 125px; }
#image_list {
    position: relative;
    left: 0px;              // required for IE
    width: 900px;
    list-style: none; }
#image_list li {
    float: left;
    width: 100px; }
#image_list li img {
    width: 95px; }
```

Figure 9-11   The user interface, HTML, and CSS for the Carousel application

has been set to. For this application to work properly, of course, the widths of the div, ul, and li elements have to be properly coordinated.

The jQuery

If you look at the jQuery code for this application in figure 9-12, you can see that it consists of two event handlers: one for the right button, and one for the left button. You can also see that the last line in each event handler uses the animate() method to change the left property of the slider variable to the value of the variable named newLeftProperty. Since the first line of code in the ready event handler sets the slider variable to the ul element, this means that the ul element is moved right or left based on the value in the newLeftProperty variable.

The trick, then, is setting the value of the newLeftProperty variable each time the right or left button is clicked. That's what the rest of the code in each event handler does. As you study this code, keep in mind that the ul element must move to the left to display the images in the li elements, so the left property will either be zero (the starting position) or a negative number.

Now, look at the event handler for the right button. There, the first statement gets the value of the current left property by using the css() method. Then, it uses the parseInt() method to convert that value to an integer. The first time the button is clicked, for example, the value will be zero.

The if statement that follows sets the value of the newLeftProperty variable that's used by the animate() method. If the current value of the left property (which is either 0 or a negative number) minus 300 (which is the width of three list items) is less than or equal to -900, the new left property is set to zero. Then, the animate() method will slide the images all the way back to the right so the first three images will be displayed. Otherwise, 300 is subtracted from the new left property so the animate() method will move the slider three images to the left.

The click event handler for the left button works similarly. After it gets the value of the current left property, it uses an if statement to set the new left property. This time, if the current property is less than zero, the new left property is increased by 300. This means that the animate() method will move the slider three images to the right. Otherwise, the first three images are already displayed and the slider shouldn't be moved. To indicate that, the new left property is set to zero.

The jQuery for the Carousel application

```
$(document).ready(function() {
    var slider = $("#image_list");  // slider = ul element
    var leftProperty, newleftProperty;

    // the click event handler for the right button
    $("#right_button").click(function() {

        // get value of current left property
        leftProperty = parseInt(slider.css("left"));

        // determine new value of left property
        if (leftProperty - 300 <= -900) {
            newLeftProperty = 0;
        }
        else {
            newLeftProperty = leftProperty - 300;
        }

        // use the animate method to change the left property
        slider.animate( {left: newLeftProperty}, 1000);

    });    // end click

    // the click event handler for the left button
    $("#left_button").click(function() {

        // get value of current left property
        leftProperty = parseInt(slider.css("left"));

        // determine new value of left property
        if (leftProperty < 0) {
            newLeftProperty = leftProperty + 300;
        }
        else {
            newLeftProperty = 0;
        }

        // use the animate method to change the left property
        slider.animate( {left: newLeftProperty}, 1000);

    });    // end click
});    // end ready
```

Description

- To get the value of the left property of the ul element, the css() method is used.
- The value of the left property for the ul element will range from 0 to -600.

Figure 9-12   The jQuery for the Carousel application

Perspective

Now that you've completed this chapter, you should be able to add some of the common animations to your web pages, like a slide show or a carousel. In the next chapter, though, you'll learn how to use jQuery plugins to create these as well as other types of animations. Because plugins are typically easy to use and because they typically work better than code you could write yourself, you should use them whenever possible.

Terms

animation	properties map
effect	queue
callback function	easing

Summary

- jQuery provides methods for *effects*, like fading in and fading out, that let you add *animation* to your web pages.

- The jQuery animate() method lets you change the CSS properties for an element over a specific duration. This lets you create interesting animations.

- To get the animation that you want, you often chain one effect after another. This places the effects in a *queue* so the effects are executed in sequence.

- If a user starts an effect for an element several times in quick succession, the effects are placed in a queue for that element. In some cases in which a user is likely to do that, you may want to use the stop() or finish() method to stop the effects and clear the queue.

- *Easings* refer to the ways that effects and animations are executed over time. Although jQuery provides for only two easings, linear and swing, the jQuery easing plugin provides for many more.

Exercise 9-1   Experiment with animation

In this exercise, you'll experiment with effects, animations, and easings.

Review the application

1. Use your text editor or IDE to open the HTML, CSS, and JavaScript files in this folder:

   `javascript_jquery\exercises\ch09\animation\`

2. Run the application to see how it works. Note how the top-level heading is animated into view from off the page. Then, click on the FAQ headings to see what happens.

Experiment with the effects for the FAQ headings

3. In the jQuery code, change the effects for the FAQ headings so the answers fade in and fade out of view when the headings are clicked.

4. Now, change the effects for the FAQ headings so the answers slide down and slide up when the headings are clicked.

5. Experiment with the durations and effects to see which ones you think are best for usability.

Experiment with the h1 heading

6. Check the CSS for the h1 heading to see that it starts with its left property at minus 175 pixels. Then, check the jQuery code to see that it moves the left property 375 pixels to the right and then 200 pixels to the left, which means the left property ends at zero pixels.

7. Restart the application and note the animation as the h1 heading moves from off the page into its proper location. Then, click the heading to see that the animation is repeated, which moves the heading farther to the right. Click on it again to see that it's repeated, which moves the heading still farther.

8. Restart the application. Then, click on the top-level heading twice in rapid succession. This should run the animations twice in a row, which shows that the animations are queued.

9. Fix the animation for the top-level heading so it always returns to its proper location above the FAQs at the end of the animation. That way, it won't move across the page. To do that, set its ending left property to zero pixels.

Add jQuery UI easings to the application

10. Note that there's a script element for the jQuery easing plugin in the HTML for the page. Then, add the easings shown in figure 9-9 to the effects and animations. Does that improve them?

11. After you run the application to see how those easings work, click on the link at the bottom of the page to view information about using the jQuery easing plugin. Note that this opens a new page or tab in your browser. Then, try some of the other easings to see how you like them.

Exercise 9-2   Modify the Slide Show application

This is a simple exercise that has you experiment with the effects that can be used with the slide show in figure 9-3. It uses the second block of jQuery code that's shown in figure 9-4.

1. Use your text editor or IDE to open the HTML, CSS, and JavaScript files in this folder:

    ```
    javascript_jquery\exercises\ch09\slide_show\
    ```

    Then, run the application to see how it works.

2. Modify the jQuery so the caption and the image slide up and then back down as the show moves from one slide to the next. Then, test to see how you like this.

3. Modify the jQuery so the caption is hidden by the hide() method and displayed by the show() method, both over an interval of one second. Also, increase the time for displaying and hiding the slide to two seconds, and increase the interval for the timer to five seconds. Then, test these changes.

4. If you're curious, experiment with effects, durations, and easings until you get the slide show to work in a way that you like.

Exercise 9-3   Modify the Carousel application

This is a simple exercise that will test whether you understand the code for the Carousel application in figures 9-11 and 9-12.

1. Use your text editor or IDE to open the HTML, CSS, and JavaScript files in this folder:
   ```
   javascript_jquery\exercises\ch09\carousel\
   ```

2. The way it is now, nothing happens if you click on the left button when the first three books are displayed. Change this so the last three books are displayed when you click on the left button while the first three books are visible.

3. Modify the jQuery code so the carousel moves one book at a time when you click on one of the buttons instead of three books at a time. Now, what happens when you click on the right button when the last three books are displayed?

4. Modify the CSS and jQuery code so only one book is displayed. Otherwise, the application should work the same way.

10

How to work with forms and data validation

To create dynamic web pages, you use HTML to create forms that let the user enter data. Then, the user can click on a button to submit the data to a web server for processing. Before the data is submitted, though, the data is usually validated by JavaScript in the browser. In this chapter, you'll learn how to use jQuery to work with forms, and you'll learn some basic skills for using JavaScript for data validation in the browser.

Introduction to forms and controls

In chapter 6, you learned that a *form* contains one or more *controls* such as text boxes and buttons. The controls that accept user entries are also known as *fields*. In the three topics that follow, you'll review how forms work and how to use the HTML5 features for working with forms.

How forms work

Figure 10-1 shows how to create a form that contains three controls: two text boxes and a button. To start, you code the form element. On the opening tag for this element, you code the action and method attributes. The action attribute specifies the file on the web server that will be used to process the data when the form is submitted. The method attribute specifies the HTTP method that will be used for sending the form to the web server.

In the example in this figure, the form will be submitted to the server using the HTTP "get" method when the user clicks the Join our List button. Then, the data in the form will be processed on the server by the code that's in the file named join.php. That file will use PHP as the scripting language.

When you use the "get" method, the form data is sent as part of the URL for the HTTP request. That means that the data is visible and the page can be bookmarked. This is illustrated by the URL in this figure. Here, the URL is followed by a question mark and name/value pairs separated by ampersands that present the name attributes and field values. In this case, two values are submitted: the email address and first name entries.

When you use the "post" method, the form data is packaged as part of an HTTP request and isn't visible in the browser. Because of that, the submission is more secure than it is when you use the "get" method, but the resulting page can't be bookmarked.

Within the opening and closing tags of the form element, you code the controls for the form. In this example, the first two input elements are for text boxes that will receive the user's email address and first name. The third input element has "submit" as the value for its type attribute, which means it is a *submit button*. When it is clicked, the data in the form will automatically be submitted to the server.

If the type attribute of an input element is "reset", the button is a *reset button*. When that type of button is clicked, all of the values in the controls of the form will be reset to their starting HTML values.

When a form is submitted to the server, the data in the form is completely validated on the server before the data is processed. Then, if any of the data isn't valid, the form is sent back to the browser with appropriate error messages so the entries can be corrected. This is referred to as *data validation*.

Usually, the form data is validated by the browser too before it is submitted to the server. Note, however, that the browser validation doesn't have to be as thorough as the server-side validation. If the browser validation catches 80 to 90% of the entry errors, it will save many round trips to the server.

A form in a web browser

The HTML for the form

```
<form id="email_form" name="email_form" action="join.php" method="get">
    <label for="email_address">Email Address:</label>
    <input type="text" id="email_address" name="email_address"><br>
    <label for="first_name">First Name:</label>
    <input type="text" id="first_name" name="first_name"><br>
    <label> </label>
    <input type="submit" id="join_list" value="Join our List"><br>
</form>
```

The URL that's sent when the form is submitted with the "get" method

```
join.php?email_address=judy%40murach.com&first_name=Judy
```

Attributes of the form element

Attribute	Description
name	A name that can be referred to by client-side or server-side code.
action	The URL of the file that will process the data in the form.
method	The HTTP method for submitting the form data. It can be set to either "get" or "post". The default value is "get".

Description

- A *form* contains one or more *controls* (or *fields*) like text boxes, radio buttons, lists, or check boxes that can receive data.

- When you click on a *submit button* for a form (type is "submit"), the form data is sent to the server as part of an HTTP request. When you click on a *reset button* for a form (type is "reset"), the form data is reset to its default values.

- When a form is submitted to the server for processing, the data in the controls is sent along with the HTTP request.

- When you use the "get" method to submit a form, the URL that requests the file is followed by a question mark and name/value pairs that are separated by ampersands. These pairs contain the name attributes and values of the data that is submitted. When you use the "post" method, the data is hidden.

- *Data validation* refers to checking the data collected by a form to make sure it is valid, and complete data validation is always done on the server. Then, if any invalid data is detected, the form is returned to the client so the user can correct the entries.

- To save round trips to the server when the data is invalid, some validation is usually done on the client before the data is sent to the server. However, this validation doesn't have to be as thorough as the validation that's done on the server.

Figure 10-1   How forms work

The HTML5 controls for working with forms

In case you aren't familiar with the HTML5 input controls, the first table in figure 10-2 summarizes the ones you'll use most often. When you use these controls, the type attribute indicates what type of data should be entered in the control. Then, in some cases, the browser will validate the data that's entered into the text box that's displayed to be sure it's the right type. In other cases, the browser will display other types of controls to assist users in entering a valid value.

If, for example, you use "email" for the type attribute, all of the major browsers except Safari (Chrome, IE, Edge, Firefox, and Opera) will provide data validation for the email address that's entered into the text box. If you use "number" for the type attribute, all of the major browsers except IE and Edge will implement the control as a text box with up and down arrows that let the user increase or decrease the current value. And if you use "date" as the type attribute, Chrome and Opera will display a popup calendar that lets the user select a date, and Edge will display drop-down lists that let the user select the month, day, and year. At the least, these attributes indicate the type of data that the control is for, and that's good for semantic reasons.

HTML5 also provides new attributes for working with controls, and two of the basic attributes are summarized in the second table in this figure. The autofocus attribute moves the focus to the control when the form is loaded. This means that you don't need to use JavaScript to do that. Also, the placeholder attribute can be used to put starting text in a control to help the user enter the data in the correct format. When the user starts to enter a value in the control, that text is removed.

Some of these controls and attributes are illustrated in the code example in this figure. Here, the type attribute for the input control that accepts an email address is set to "email". In addition, since this is the first input control in the form, the autofocus attribute is included so the control will have the focus when the page is first displayed. In the form below the code example, you can see the error message that's displayed in Chrome when an invalid entry is made in the email field.

Because the third input field in this example is for a telephone number, its type attribute is set to "tel". Although none of the current browsers provide data validation for this type, it's good to use it for semantic reasons. This control also uses the placeholder attribute to indicate the format of the phone number that should be entered. You can see part of this placeholder in the form in this figure.

Common HTML5 controls for input data

Control	Description
email	Gets an email address with validation done by the browser.
url	Gets a URL with validation done by the browser.
tel	Gets a telephone number with no validation done by the browser.
number	When supported, gets a numeric entry with min, max, and step attributes, browser validation, and up and down arrows.
range	When supported, gets a numeric entry with min, max, and step attributes, browser validation, and a slider control.
date	When supported, gets a date entry with min and max attributes and may include a popup calendar or up and down arrows.
time	When supported, gets a time entry with min and max attributes and may include up and down arrows.

The basic HTML5 attributes for working with forms

Attribute	Description
autofocus	A Boolean attribute that tells the browser to set the focus on the field when the page is loaded.
placeholder	A message in the field that is removed when an entry is made in the field.

The HTML for a form that uses some of these controls and attributes

```
<form id="email_form" name="email_form" action="join.php" method="get">
    <label for="email_address">Email Address:</label>
    <input type="email" id="email_address" name="email_address" autofocus><br>
    <label for="name">Name:</label>
    <input type="text" id="name" name="name"><br>
    <label for="phone">Phone Number:</label>
    <input type="tel" id="phone" name="phone" placeholder="999-999-9999"><br>
    <label> </label>
    <input type="submit" id="join_list" value="Join our List"><br>
</form>
```

The form in Chrome with an error message for the email address

Description

- Many of the HTML5 input controls provide for basic data validation. You can also use the HTML5 attributes in figure 10-3 for data validation.

- For a complete description of the HTML5 and CSS3 features for working with forms, please refer to *Murach's HTML5 and CSS3*.

Figure 10-2   The HTML5 controls for working with forms

The HTML5 and CSS3 features for data validation

In addition to the HTML5 controls you saw in the last figure, HTML5 and CSS3 provide some features specifically for data validation. These features are presented in figure 10-3.

The table at the top of this figure summarizes the HTML5 attributes for data validation. To start, the required attribute causes the browser to check whether a field is empty before it submits the form for processing. If the field is empty, it displays a message and the form isn't submitted. The browser also highlights all of the other required fields that are empty when the submit button is clicked.

If you code a title attribute for a field, the value of that attribute is displayed when the mouse hovers over the field. It is also displayed at the end of the browser's standard error message for a field.

The pattern attribute provides for data validation through the use of regular expressions. A *regular expression* provides a way to match a user entry against a *pattern* of characters. As a result, regular expressions can be used for validating user entries like credit card numbers, zip codes, dates, or phone numbers. Regular expressions are supported by many programming languages including JavaScript and PHP, and now regular expressions are supported by HTML5. The trick of course is coding the regular expressions that you need, but you can learn how to do that in chapter 14.

If you want to stop a control from being validated, you can code the novalidate attribute for that control. And if you want to turn the auto-completion feature off for a control, you can set its autocomplete attribute to "off". The *auto-completion feature* is on by default in all modern browsers, which means that a browser will display a list of entry options when the user starts the entry for a field. These options will be based on the entries the user has previously made for fields with similar names.

The code example in this figure illustrates how you can use some of these attributes. This is the same form that was presented in the previous figure except this time, the required attribute is coded for each input field so the user must make an entry. In addition, the auto-completion feature is turned off for the email field, and a pattern and title are specified for the phone field. In the form below this code, you can see the error message that's displayed if the user enters a phone number with an invalid format. It includes the browser's standard error message as well as the text that's specified by the title attribute for this field.

This figure also presents three CSS3 pseudo-classes that you can use to format required, valid, and invalid fields. For instance, you can use the :required pseudo-class to format all required fields, and you can use the :invalid pseudo-class to format all invalid fields.

For simple forms, you may be able to get by with just HTML5 controls and data validation attributes. For most forms, though, you are going to need JavaScript. That's because the HTML5 features don't provide for all of the types of validation that most forms need.

The HTML5 attributes for data validation

Attribute	Description
required	A Boolean attribute that indicates that a value is required for a field.
title	Text that is displayed in a tooltip when the mouse hovers over a field. This text is also displayed after the browser's default error message.
pattern	A regular expression that is used to validate the entry in a field.
novalidate	A Boolean attribute that tells the browser that it shouldn't validate the form or control that it is coded for.
autocomplete	Set this attribute to "off" to tell the browser to disable auto-completion. This can be coded for a form or a control.

CSS3 pseudo-classes for required, valid, and invalid fields

```
:required        :valid        :invalid
```

The HTML for a form that uses some of these attributes

```
<form id="email_form" name="email_form" action="join.php" method="get">
    <label for="email_address">Email Address:</label>
    <input type="email" id="email_address" name="email_address"
            required autofocus autocomplete="off"><br>
    <label for="name">Name:</label>
    <input type="text" id="name" name="name" required><br>
    <label for="phone">Phone Number:</label>
    <input type="tel" id="phone" name="phone" required
            pattern="\d{3}[\-]\d[3][\-]\d{4}"
            title="Must be 999-999-9999"><br>
    <label> </label>
    <input type="submit" id="join_list" value="Join our List"><br>
</form>
```

The form in Chrome with an error message for the phone field

Two of the reasons why you need JavaScript for data validation

- The HTML5 input controls and attributes for data validation aren't implemented by all current browsers, and the ones that are may not be implemented the same way.

- HTML5 is limited in the types of validation it can do. For instance, HTML5 can't check whether a field is equal to another one or look up a state code in a table.

Description

- At this writing, Chrome, IE, Edge, Firefox, and Opera all support the HTML5 attributes and CSS3 pseudo-classes shown above. Even so, you typically need to use JavaScript and jQuery to do an adequate job of client-side validation.

Figure 10-3   The HTML5 and CSS3 features for data validation

How to use jQuery to work with forms

To make it easier to work with forms, jQuery provides selectors, methods, and event methods that are designed for that purpose. However, as the next two figures show, jQuery doesn't provide specific features for data validation.

The jQuery selectors and methods for forms

The first table in figure 10-4 summarizes the jQuery selectors that you can use with forms. As you can see, these selectors make it easy to select the various types of controls. They also make it easy to select disabled, enabled, checked, and selected controls.

The second table in this figure summarizes the val() methods that you are already familiar with. They let you get and set the value in a control. For instance, the first example in this figure gets the entry in the control with "age" as its id. The code also parses this entry into an integer before saving it in the variable named age.

The third table summarizes the trim() method, which is one of the miscellaneous jQuery methods. It is useful because JavaScript doesn't provide its own trim() method. In the second example in this figure, you can see how this method is used to trim the entry in the control with "first_name" as its id before the entry is saved in the variable named firstName. The second statement in this example puts that trimmed entry back into the control.

The third example in this figure shows how to get the value of the checked radio button in a named group. Here, an attribute selector is used to select all of the input elements whose name attribute is set to "contact_by". That includes all the radio buttons in the group, since they all must have the same name. Then, it uses the :checked selector to get the radio button within that group whose checked attribute has a value of true. This works because only one radio button in a named group can be selected. Finally, the val() method is used to get the value of the radio button's value attribute, and that value is saved in the variable named radioButton.

The last example shows how to get an array of the selected options in a select list that allows multiple selections. First, an empty array named selectOptions is created. Next, the :selected selector is used to get all of the selected options in a select list with "select_list" as its id. These options are then saved in the selectOptions variable.

Notice in this example that there's a space between the id of the select list and the :selected selector. That's because a select list consists of a select element that contains option elements. So the selector in this example selects all the descendant option elements that are selected. Another way to code this statement would be like this:

```
selectOptions = $("#select_list option:selected");
```

In contrast, there's no space before the :checked selector in the third example. That's because a group of radio buttons consists of independent input elements with the same name attribute. So the selector in this example selects the radio button that's checked in the group.

The jQuery selectors for form controls

Selector	Selects
`:input`	All input, select, textarea, and button elements.
`:text`	All text boxes: input elements with type equal to "text".
`:radio`	All radio buttons: input elements with type equal to "radio".
`:checkbox`	All check boxes: input elements with type equal to "checkbox".
`:file`	All file upload fields: input elements with type equal to "file".
`:password`	All password fields: input elements with type equal to "password".
`:submit`	All submit buttons and button elements: input elements with type equal to "submit" and button elements.
`:reset`	All reset buttons: input elements with type equal to "reset".
`:image`	All image buttons: input elements with type equal to "image".
`:button`	All buttons: button elements and input elements with type equal to "button".
`:disabled`	All disabled elements: elements that have the disabled attribute.
`:enabled`	All enabled elements: elements that don't have the disabled attribute.
`:checked`	All check boxes and radio buttons that are checked.
`:selected`	All options in select elements that are selected.

The jQuery methods for getting and setting control values

Method	Description
`val()`	Gets the value of a text box or other form control.
`val(value)`	Sets the value of a text box or other form control.

The jQuery method for trimming an entry

Method	Description
`trim()`	Removes all spaces at the start and end of the string.

How to get the value of a numeric entry from a text box
```
var age = parseInt($("#age").val());
```

How to trim the value of an entry and put it back into the same text box
```
var firstName = $("#first_name").val().trim();
$("#first_name").val(firstName);
```

How to get the value of the checked radio button in a group
```
var radioButton = $("input[name='contact_by']:checked").val();
```

How to get an array of the selected options from a list
```
var selectOptions = [];
selectOptions = $("#select_list :selected");
```

Description
* jQuery provides special selectors for selecting the controls on a form, the val() method for getting and setting the value in a control, and a trim() method for trimming an entry.

Figure 10-4 The jQuery selectors and methods for forms

The jQuery event methods for forms

The first table in figure 10-5 summarizes the jQuery event methods for working with forms, and you have already been introduced to some of these. For instance, the handler for the focus() event method is run when the focus moves to the selected element, and the handler for the change() event method is run when the value in the selected element is changed.

The last event method in this table runs when the submit event occurs. That event occurs when the user clicks on a submit button or when the user moves the focus to the submit button and presses the Enter key. But it also occurs when the submit() method is used to trigger the event.

The second table in this figure summarizes the jQuery methods for triggering (starting) events. If, for example, you code the focus() method for a text box, the focus is moved to that text box and the focus event is triggered. However, if a handler hasn't been assigned to that event, that event isn't processed. Please note that the names of these triggering methods are the same as the ones for the event methods.

The examples in this figure show how you can use these event methods. In the first example, the change() event method is used to create an event handler for the change event of a check box with "contact_me" as its id. Then, the function within this handler checks the value of the check box's checked attribute to see if the check box is checked. If it is checked, the code turns off the disabled attribute of all of the radio buttons on the form. Otherwise, the code turns on the disabled attribute for all of the radio buttons.

This is useful in an application in which the radio buttons should only be enabled if the check box is checked. If, for example, the user checks the Contact Me box, the radio buttons should be enabled so the user can click the preferred method of contact. Otherwise, the radio buttons should be disabled.

The second example in this figure shows how you can trigger the submit event at the end of an event handler for the click event of an input button with "button" as its type attribute. Here, the function for the event handler starts by validating the code in all of the entries. Then, if all the entries are valid, it uses the submit() method to initiate the submit event of the form, and that will send the form to the server. This is the method that you've been using in the Email List application in earlier chapters.

The other way to provide for data validation is to use a submit button instead of a regular button. Then, you can code an event handler for the submit event of the form. Within that handler, you can test all of the entries for validity. If they are all valid, you can end the handler, so the form will be submitted. But if one or more entries are invalid, you can issue the preventDefault() method of the event object for the submit event to cancel the submission of the form. You'll see this illustrated in figure 10-7.

The jQuery event methods for forms

Event method	Description
focus(*handler*)	The handler runs when the focus moves to the selected element.
blur(*handler*)	The handler runs when the focus leaves the selected element.
change(*handler*)	The handler runs when the value in the selected element is changed.
select(*handler*)	The handler runs when the user selects text in a text or textarea box.
submit(*handler*)	The handler runs when a submit button is clicked.

The jQuery methods for triggering events

Event method	Description
focus()	Moves the focus to the selected element and triggers the focus event.
blur()	Removes the focus from the selected element and triggers the blur event.
change()	Triggers the change event.
select()	Triggers the select event.
submit()	Triggers the submit event for a form.

A handler that disables or enables radio buttons when a check box is checked or unchecked

```
$("#contact_me").change(                      // the change event for a check box
    function(){
        if ($("#contact_me").attr("checked")) {
            $(":radio").attr("disabled", false) }  // enables radio buttons
        else {
            $(":radio").attr("disabled", true)}    // disables radio buttons
});
```

A handler that triggers the submit event after some data validation

```
$(document).ready(function() {
    $("#join_list").click(    // join_list is a button, not a submit button
        function() {
            // the data validation code goes here
            $("#email_form").submit();
        } // end function
    ); // end click
}); // end ready
```

Description

- You can use event handlers for the focus, blur, change, and select events to process data as the user works with individual controls.

- You can use an event handler for the click event of a regular button, not a submit button, to validate the data in a form. Then, if the data is valid, you can use the submit() method to submit the form.

- You can also use an event handler for the submit event of a form to validate data before it is sent to the server. Then, if any of the data is invalid, you can issue the preventDefault() method of the event object to cancel the submission of the data to the server.

Figure 10-5   The jQuery event methods for forms

A Validation application that uses JavaScript

To show you how you can use jQuery to work with forms, you will now study a simple Validation application. As you will see, jQuery makes it easy to access the user entries and display error messages. To test the validity of the user entries, though, you need to use JavaScript.

The user interface and HTML

Figure 10-6 presents the user interface and HTML for the Validation application. To use the form, the user enters data into the text boxes. The user can also use the radio buttons to determine if the membership is for an individual or a company. By default, the Individual radio button is selected and the Company Name text box is disabled. If the user selects the Corporate radio button, though, the Company Name text box is enabled.

Once the form is complete, the user can click on the Submit button. Or, if the user wants to start over, she can click on the Reset button to return the fields to their original values.

In the HTML for this form, you can see that the id of the form is "member_form" and the Submit button at the bottom of the form is the "submit" type. This means that it will automatically submit the form to the server when it is clicked. As you will see, though, the JavaScript for this form will validate the entries before the form is actually submitted and cancel the submission if any entries are invalid.

Like the Email List application that you've seen in previous chapters, each text box in this application is followed by a span element. These span elements will be used to display error messages to the right of the user entries as shown here. When the form is first loaded, the initial value of all but one of these span elements is an asterisk. The exception is the span element for the Company Name text box. Because this text box is disabled by default, the span element that follows it has no initial value.

Notice that HTML5 placeholder attributes are used for the password and phone number fields on this form. This attribute is used for the phone number field to show the user the entry format that should be used. And it's used for the password field to provide an entry hint. Remember, though, that as soon as the user starts entering a value into a field with a placeholder, the placeholder text disappears.

On the other hand, this HTML doesn't use the HTML5 type attributes for email, phone, and date entries. That way, you don't have to worry about getting some unexpected validation messages from the browser, like a message that indicates an invalid email address. Instead, the JavaScript will have complete control of the validation that's done.

The form for a Validation application

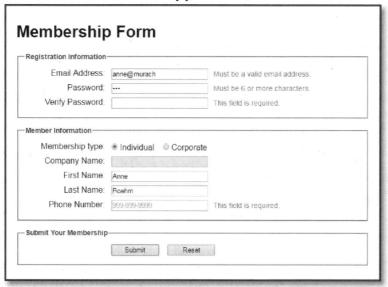

The HTML

```
<form action="register.html" method="get" name="member_form" id="member_form">
    <fieldset>
        <legend>Registration Information</legend>
        <label for="email">Email Address:</label>
        <input type="text" id="email" name="email"><span>*</span><br>
        <label for="password">Password:</label>
        <input type="password" id="password" name="password"
               placeholder="At least 6 characters"><span>*</span><br>
        <label for="verify">Verify Password:</label>
        <input type="password" id="verify" name="verify"><span>*</span><br>
    </fieldset>
    <fieldset>
        <legend>Member Information</legend>
        <label>Membership type:</label>
        <input type="radio" name="type" id="individual" value="individual"
               checked>Individual
        <input type="radio" name="type" id="corporate" value="corporate">
               Corporate<br>
        <label for="company_name">Company Name:</label>
        <input type="text" id="company_name" name="company_name" disabled>
        <span></span><br>
        <!-- Two fields are omitted here -->
        <label for="phone">Phone Number:</label>
        <input type="text" id="phone" name="phone" placeholder="999-999-9999">
        <span>*</span><br>
    </fieldset>
    <fieldset id="buttons">
        <legend>Submit Your Membership</legend>
        <label> </label>
        <input type="submit" id="submit" name="submit" value="Submit">
        <input type="reset" id="reset" name="reset" value="Reset"><br>
    </fieldset>
</form>
```

Figure 10-6   The user interface and HTML for the Validation application

Some of the JavaScript for the application

Figure 10-7 presents some of the JavaScript in the ready() event handler for this application. This event handler contains two additional event handlers. The first one is for the change event of the two radio buttons, and the second one is for the submit button of the form.

To select the two radio buttons, the change() event handler uses the :radio selector. This works because the form contains only one group of radio buttons. If there was more than one group, you'd need to code an attribute selector similar to the one in the third example in figure 10-4 that selects elements by name.

Within the change() event handler, the val() method is used to get the value of the checked radio button, and that value is assigned to a variable named radioButton. Then, that value is used to determine whether the company-name field is enabled or disabled and whether the span element that follows this field contains an asterisk.

To get the checked radio button, both the :radio and :checked selectors are used. Note that because the two radio buttons are the only controls on the form that can have the checked attribute, though, you could omit the :radio selector. It's included here only for clarity.

The event handler for the submit event of the form contains the validation routines for all of the text boxes on the form. The validation code for just three of those fields is shown here, but that should give you a better idea of how jQuery and JavaScript can be used for data validation.

The validation for the email entry shows how you can use a regular expression for validation. You'll learn more about regular expressions in chapter 14. For now, you just need to know that the test() method of a regular expression checks that a value has the specified pattern. In this case, the test() method is used to check that the value the user entered in the email field matches the pattern in the emailPattern variable. If it doesn't, the jQuery next() and text() methods are used to display an error message in the span element that follows the email field.

The validation for the password and company name follow. To validate the password, the length property of a string is used to test whether the length of the entry is less than 6. Note that in a more realistic application, though, extensive string handling would be used to validate this entry. To validate the company name, the control is first checked to be sure it's enabled. If it is, the entry is validated to be sure it isn't equal to an empty string.

Notice that the jQuery trim() method is used to trim each entry before it's tested to see whether it's equal to an empty string. If you don't use the trim() method, an entry of one or more spaces won't be equal to an empty string so the entry will be treated as valid. After the validation is complete, the val() method is used to assign the trimmed value back to the field. That way, the value is always displayed without any leading or trailing spaces.

After the validation, a final if statement is used to test the isValid variable. If it's false, it means that one or more of the fields are invalid. In that case, the preventDefault() method of the event object that's passed to the submit() event handler is executed. If you don't use the preventDefault() method when one or more fields are invalid, the form will be submitted to the server by default.

JavaScript validation

```javascript
$(document).ready(function() {
    $(":radio").change(                        // change event of radio buttons
        function() {
            var radioButton = $(":radio:checked").val();
            if (radioButton == "corporate") {
                $("#company_name").attr("disabled", false);
                $("#company_name").next().text("*");
            } else {
                $("#company_name").attr("disabled", true);
                $("#company_name").next().text("");
            }
        } // end function
    ); // end change

    $("#member_form").submit(                   // submit event of form
        function(event) {
            var isValid = true;

            // validate the email entry with a regular expression
            var emailPattern =
                /\b[A-Za-z0-9._%+-]+@[A-Za-z0-9.-]+\.[A-Za-z]{2,4}\b/;
            var email = $("#email").val().trim();
            if (email == "") {
                $("#email").next().text("This field is required.");
                isValid = false;
            } else if ( !emailPattern.test(email) ) {
                $("#email").next().text("Must be a valid email address.");
                isValid = false;
            } else {
                $("#email").next().text("");
            }
            $("#email").val(email);
            // validate the password entry
            var password = $("#password").val().trim();
            if ( password.length < 6 ) {
                $("#password").next().text("Must be 6 or more characters.");
                isValid = false;
            } else {
                $("#password").next().text("");
            }
            $("#password").val(password);
            ...
            // validate the company name entry
            if ( !$("#company_name").attr("disabled")) {
                var companyName = $("#company_name").val().trim();
                if (companyName == "") {
                    $("#company_name").next().text("This field is required.");
                    isValid = false;
                } else {
                    $("#company_name").next().text("");
                }
                $("#company_name").val(companyName);
            }
            ...
            // prevent the submission of the form if any entries are invalid
            if (isValid == false) { event.preventDefault(); }
        } // end function
    ); // end submit
}); // end ready
```

Figure 10-7   The JavaScript for validating three entries and submitting the form

Perspective

At this point, you should be comfortable with the jQuery features for working with forms. You should also realize that you need both JavaScript and jQuery to validate the data on a form. In this chapter, you learned some of the basic JavaScript skills for data validation, and you'll learn more in the chapters in section 3.

Terms

form	data validation
control	regular expression
field	pattern
submit button	auto-completion feature
reset button	conditional operator

Summary

- A *form* contains one or more *controls* like text boxes, radio buttons, and check boxes that can receive data. These controls are also referred to as *fields*. When a form is submitted to the server for processing, the data in the controls is sent along with the HTTP request.

- A *submit button* submits the form data to the server when the button is clicked. A *reset button* resets all the data in the form when it is clicked.

- HTML5 introduces some input controls like the email, url, tel, and date controls that are good semantically because they indicate what types of data the controls are for. HTML5 also introduces some attributes for *data validation*, and CSS3 introduces some pseudo-classes for formatting required, valid, and invalid fields.

- When a form is submitted to the server, the server script should provide complete validation of the data in the form and return the form to the client if any errors are found.

- Before a form is submitted to the server, JavaScript should try to catch 80% or more of the entry errors. That will reduce the number of trips to the server and back that are required to process the form.

- jQuery provides some selectors, methods, and event methods for working with forms, but nothing for data validation. So, to validate the entries that a user makes, many developers use JavaScript features like *regular expressions* and string methods.

Exercise 10-1   Validate with JavaScript

Since you already know how to validate some types of fields with JavaScript, most of the code for this exercise is provided for you. However, you will make some enhancements to this code. The form that you will be working with looks like this:

Please join our email list

Email Address:	anne@murachcom	Must be a valid email address.
Re-enter Email Address:	anne@murach.com	Must equal first email entry.
First Name:		This field is required.
Last Name:	Boehm	
State Code:	California	Use 2-character code.
Zip Code:	93722-1234	Use 99999 format.
Email me about:	☐ Web books ☐ Java books ☐ .NET books Select at least one.	

[Join our List]   [Reset]

1. Use your text editor or IDE to open the HTML and JavaScript files in this folder:

    ```
    javascript_jquery\exercises\ch10\email_list\
    ```

2. Test the application, and notice that the focus isn't in the first text box. Modify the JavaScript so it moves the focus to the first text box when the document is loaded, and then test again.

3. Review the code in the JavaScript file and note that it contains validation routines for the first five fields. Then, test this form by clicking the Join our List button before you enter any data in this form. Oops! The data is submitted even though no entries have been made.

4. To fix this, you must stop the default action of the submit button. To do that, code the preventDefault() method of the event object in the if statement at the end of the file, as in figure 10-7. Remember that the name that you use for the event object must be the same as the name of the parameter that's used for the submit() event handler. Now, test again with empty fields. This should display "This field is required." to the right of each field except the zip-code and email-me-about fields.

5. Enter four spaces in the first-name field and click the Join our List button again. Note that the error message is removed, which means the four spaces have been accepted as a valid entry.

6. Fix this problem by trimming the first-name entry before it is validated, as in the code for the last-name entry. This trimmed value should also be placed in the text box whether or not the entry is valid. Test this enhancement by first entering just four spaces in this field and then by entering four spaces followed by a first name.

7. Add the code for validating the zip-code field by testing to make sure it consists of five characters. To do this, you can copy and modify the code that's used to validate the state-code field. Now, test this change.

8. Add the code for validating the check boxes. For this application, at least one check box must be selected. To perform this validation, you'll need to create a variable that holds an array. Then, you'll need to get all the check boxes that are selected. To do that, you can use the :checkbox and :checked selectors. If none of the check boxes are selected, display an error message in the span element that follows the last check box. Otherwise, clear that span element.

11

How to use jQuery plugins and jQuery UI widgets

The easiest way to add common features like accordions, tabs, and carousels to your web pages is to use jQuery plugins and jQuery UI widgets. In this chapter, you'll learn how to do that.

Introduction to jQuery plugins

In this introduction, you'll learn how to find and use jQuery plugins. A *jQuery plugin* is just a jQuery application that does one web task or a set of related web tasks. A plugin makes use of the jQuery library, and most plugins can be used with limited knowledge of JavaScript and jQuery.

How to find jQuery plugins

Figure 11-1 starts with a screen capture that shows the results of a Google search for "jquery rotator plugin". Often, doing a search like this is the best way to find what you're looking for. Note, however, that the search entry includes the word *jquery* because there are other types of plugins.

Another way to find the type of plugin that you're looking for is to go to the URLs for the websites in the table in this figure. The first one is for the jQuery Plugin Registry, which is part of the jQuery website, and the second one is for a site that is only for jQuery plugins.

In contrast, the next three websites are repositories for many types of code, including jQuery plugins. As a result, you must search for jQuery plugins to find what you want on these sites.

In most cases, jQuery plugins are free or are available for a small price or donation. Besides that, jQuery plugins can often be used by non-programmers, and they can save you many hours of development time if you are a JavaScript programmer. For those reasons, it makes sense to look for a plugin whenever you need to add a common function to your website.

This figure also summarizes some of the most useful plugins for displaying images and running slide shows and carousels. You'll see three of these illustrated in the pages that follow.

A Google search for a jQuery plugin

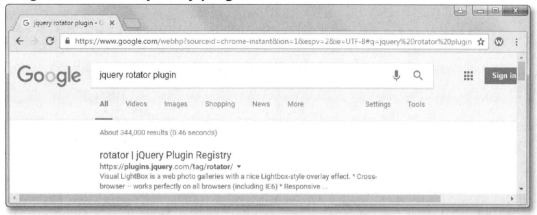

Websites for finding jQuery plugins

Site name	URL
jQuery Plugin Registry	http://plugins.jquery.com
jQuery Plugins	http://jquery-plugins.net
Google Code	http://code.google.com
GitHub	https://github.com
Sourceforge	http://sourceforge.net

Popular plugins for displaying images

Lightbox	http://lokeshdhakar.com/projects/lightbox2/
Fancybox	http://fancybox.net
ThickBox	http://codylindley.com/thickbox/
ColorBox	http://www.jacklmoore.com/colorbox

Popular plugins for slide shows and carousels

bxSlider	http://bxslider.com
Malsup jQuery Cycle 2	http://jquery.malsup.com/cycle2
jCarousel	http://sorgalla.com/jcarousel

Description

- jQuery *plugins* are JavaScript applications that extend the functionality of jQuery. These plugins require the use of the core jQuery library.

- Plugins are available for hundreds of web functions like slide shows, carousels, tabs, menus, text layout, data validation, and mobile application development.

- Some of the websites that provide jQuery plugins are listed above. Often, though, you can find what you're looking for by searching the Internet.

- In general, if you can find a plugin for doing what you want, that's usually better than writing the jQuery code yourself.

Figure 11-1   How to find jQuery plugins

How to use any jQuery plugin

Figure 11-2 shows how to use any plugin after you find the one you want. First, you study the documentation for the plugin so you know what HTML and CSS it requires and what methods and options it provides. Usually, you'll do this as you evaluate the plugin to see if it does what you want and if its documentation tells you everything you need to know.

Second, you usually download the files for the plugin and save them on your web server. This download is often in the form of a zip file, and it will always include at least one JavaScript file. In addition, it may include CSS or image files that are used by the plugin.

The download may also include two versions of the main JavaScript file for the plugin. If you want to review the code for the file, you can open the full version in your text editor. But the one you should use for your applications is the compressed version, which usually has a name that ends with min.js.

For some plugins, the files are also available from a Content Delivery Network (CDN). If you want to access the files that way, you can record the URLs for the files. Then, you can use those URLs in the link and script elements for the files.

Third, if a plugin requires one or more CSS files, you code the link elements for them in the head element of the HTML. Then, you code the script elements for the JavaScript files for the plugin. Usually, only one JavaScript file is required, but some plugins require more than one.

Fourth, if the download includes a folder for images, you need to make sure the folder has the right structural relationship with the CSS and JavaScript files for the plugin. Otherwise, you may have to adjust the CSS or JavaScript code so it can find the images folder (and you probably don't want to do that).

At this point, you're ready to use the plugin. So, fifth, you code the HTML and CSS for the plugin. And sixth, you code the jQuery for using the plugin. This can be in an external file or it can be within the head element of the HTML.

This procedure is illustrated by the example in this figure, which uses the bxSlider plugin. Here, the script elements show that the element for the plugin must come after the element for the jQuery library. That's because all jQuery plugins use the jQuery library. As the first caution in this figure points out, not coding these script elements in this sequence is a common error.

The HTML that follows shows the elements that the plugin requires. In particular, the id attribute for the unordered list is set to "slider" so the jQuery code can select that element when it calls the bxSlider() method of the plugin. Also, the title attributes for the img elements are set to the captions for the slides.

This is followed by the jQuery code for using this plugin. Here, the bxSlider() method is called as the first statement within the function for the ready() method for the document. This method name is followed by a set of braces that contains the code for setting four options for this method.

Before you continue, note the second caution in this figure, which is that some plugins won't work with the latest version of jQuery. So if a plugin doesn't work, you should check its documentation to see what version of jQuery it uses. For example, the documentation for the bxSlider plugin says to use jQuery 1.8.2.

General steps for using a plugin within your web pages

1. Study the documentation for the plugin so you know what HTML and CSS it requires as well as what methods and options it provides.

2. If the plugin file or files are available via a Content Delivery Network (CDN) and you want to access them that way, get the URLs for them. Otherwise, download the file or files for the plugin, and save them in one of the folders of your website.

3. In the head element of the HTML for a page that will use the plugin, code the link elements for any CSS files that are required. Also, code the script elements for the JavaScript files that are required. These script elements must be after the one for the jQuery library because all jQuery plugins use that library.

4. If the download for a plugin includes an images folder, make sure the folder has the right structural relationship with both the CSS and JavaScript files for the plugin.

5. Code the HTML and CSS for the page so it is appropriate for the plugin.

6. If necessary, write the jQuery code that uses the methods and options of the plugin.

The script elements for the jQuery library and the bxSlider plugin

```
<!-- the script element for the core jQuery library -->
<script src="http://code.jquery.com/jquery-1.8.2.min.js"></script>
<!-- the script element for the plugin when it has been downloaded -->
<script src="js/jquery.bxSlider.min.js"></script>
```

The HTML for the bxSlider plugin

```
<ul id="slider">
    <li><img src="images/building_01.jpg" alt="" title="Front"></li>
    <li><img src="images/building_02.jpg" alt="" title="Left side"></li>
    ...
</ul>
```

The jQuery for using the bxSlider plugin

```
$(document).ready(function(){
    $("#slider").bxSlider({
        minSlides: 2,
        maxSlides: 2,
        slideWidth: 250,
        slideMargin: 10
    });
});
```

Two cautions

- Make sure that you include a script element for jQuery and make sure that the script element for the plugin comes after it. Not doing one or the other is a common error.

- Some plugins, like the bxSlider plugin shown above, won't work with the latest version of jQuery. So if you have any problems with a plugin, check its documentation to see which version of jQuery it requires.

Description

- Some plugins can be accessed via a CDN, but most must be downloaded and stored on your server.

Figure 11-2   How to use any jQuery plugin

How to use three
of the most popular plugins

Now, you'll get a close-up view of three of the most useful plugins. This will introduce you to the power of plugins. It will also show you how the procedure in the last figure works with specific plugins.

How to use the Lightbox plugin for images

Figure 11-3 presents the Lightbox plugin. This is a popular plugin that displays a larger version of a thumbnail image when the user clicks the thumbnail image. This image is displayed in a *modal dialog box*, which means that it must be closed before the user can continue. The image in this box has a thick white border, and it may have a caption below it. The part of the web page that's outside of the dialog box is darkened. To close the dialog box, the user clicks on the "X" in the bottom right corner.

If images are grouped in sets, this plugin not only displays the dialog box for the thumbnail, it also displays the image number and total number of images below the image, as in "Image 3 of 5". Also, when the mouse hovers over the left or right side of an image, previous and next icons are displayed. Then, if the user clicks on an icon, the display is moved to the previous or next image.

As the link and script elements in this example show, this plugin requires both CSS and JavaScript files. These elements use the names of the downloaded files. Remember, though, that the script element for the plugin must come after the script element for the jQuery library.

The download also includes an images folder that contains the images used by the plugin. Here again, you must maintain the proper relationship between the images folder and the JavaScript and CSS files for this plugin.

Next, this figure shows the HTML for using this plugin. Here, img elements that represent the thumbnail images are coded within <a> elements. To make this work, each <a> element must have an href attribute that identifies the related large image and a data-lightbox attribute that activates the Lightbox plugin.

If you're using the Lightbox plugin with independent images, the value of the data-lightbox attribute should be unique for each <a> element. On the other hand, if you're using this plugin with a set of related images as shown here, the value of this attribute should be the same for all <a> elements. The last attribute shown here, data-title, provides a caption for each image.

Once all of that's done, you're done, because you don't have to initiate the Lightbox plugin by calling one of its methods. In other words, no JavaScript code is required. It just works!

A Lightbox after the user has clicked on a thumbnail image to start it

The URL for the Lightbox website

http://lokeshdhakar.com/projects/lightbox2/

The link and script elements for the Lightbox plugin

```
<link href="styles.css" rel="stylesheet">
<link href="css/lightbox.css" rel="stylesheet">
<script src="http://code.jquery.com/jquery-3.1.1.min.js"></script>
<script src="js/lightbox.min.js"></script>
```

The HTML for the images used by the Lightbox plugin

```
<a href="images/building_01.jpg" data-lightbox="vecta" data-title="Front">
    <img src="images/building_01_thumb.jpg" alt=""></a>
<a href="images/building_02.jpg" data-lightbox="vecta" data-title="Left side">
    <img src="images/building_02_thumb.jpg" alt=""></a>
...
```

Description

- The Lightbox plugin can be used to display larger versions of thumbnail images. The Lightbox starts when the user clicks one of the thumbnail images.

- When the user clicks on a thumbnail image within a set of images, the rest of the page is darkened and a larger version of the image is displayed with a counter and a caption. Then, if the mouse pointer moves over the larger image, next or previous icons appear.

- The Lightbox download includes a CSS file, a plugin file, and an images folder that contains an image for loading and images for the close, next, and previous icons.

- The HTML for a Lightbox consists of img elements within <a> elements. The src attributes of the img elements identify the thumbnail images, and the href attributes of the <a> elements identify the larger images.

- The data-lightbox attributes of the <a> elements activate Lightbox. Their values should be unique for independent images but the same for a group of images.

- The data-title attributes of the <a> elements can be used to provide captions.

Figure 11-3   How to use the Lightbox plugin for images

How to use the bxSlider plugin for carousels

Figure 11-4 shows how to use the bxSlider plugin for creating carousels. In this example, this plugin displays two images at a time, it slides from one set of images to the next automatically, it provides captions in the slides, it provides controls below the carousel, and you can move to the next or previous image by clicking on the right or left icon that's displayed.

If you download the JavaScript file for this plugin, the script element can refer to it as shown in this figure. As part of this download, you also get a CSS file and an images folder that contains the images that can be used with this plugin.

One way to set up the HTML for use with this plugin is shown in this figure. Here, img elements are coded within the li elements of an unordered list. Then, the src attributes of the img elements identify the images that are displayed, and the title attributes provide the captions.

To run the bxSlider plugin, you use the jQuery code in this figure. Within the ready() function, the selector selects the ul element that contains the slides and executes the bxSlider() method.

Within that method, several options are set. The auto option makes the carousel run automatically, the autoControls option puts the controls below the carousel, the captions option causes the title attributes to be used for captions, the minSlides and maxSlides options set the carousel so 2 slides are always displayed, and the slideWidth and slideMargin options set the size of the slides and the space between them.

These options show just some of the capabilities of this plugin. To learn more, you can go to the website for this plugin and review its demos and option summaries.

By the way, if you try to run a page that contains a bxSlider plugin from Aptana, you'll see that the plugin doesn't work. Because of that, you'll need to run the page from outside of Aptana.

When you use this plugin, you will often want to change the location of components like the left and right icons, the captions (which were adjusted for this example), and the controls below the carousel. To do that, you can adjust the styles in the CSS file for this plugin.

If, for example, you want to adjust the location of the left and right icons, like moving them outside of the slider, you can modify the CSS for the bx.next and bx.prev classes. You won't find these classes in the HTML, though, because they're added to the DOM by the plugin. Usually, you'll learn a lot by studying the code in the CSS files for plugins and by making adjustments to that code.

A web page that uses the bxSlider plugin for a carousel

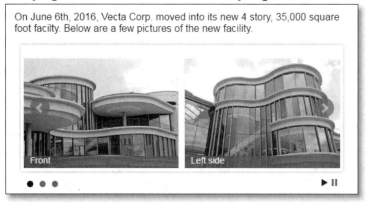

The URL for the bxSlider website

```
http://bxslider.com
```

The link and script elements for the bxSlider plugin

```html
<link href="styles.css" rel="stylesheet">
<link href="jquery.bxslider.css" rel="stylesheet">
<script src="http://code.jquery.com/jquery-1.8.2.min.js"></script>
<script src="js/jquery.bxSlider.min.js">
```

The HTML for the bxSlider plugin

```html
<ul id="slider">
    <li><img src="images/building_01.jpg" alt="" title="Front"></li>
    <li><img src="images/building_02.jpg" alt="" title="Left side"></li>
    ...
</ul>
```

The jQuery for using some of the bxSlider options

```javascript
$(document).ready(function(){
    $("#slider").bxSlider({
        auto: true,
        autoControls: true,
        captions: true,
        minSlides: 2,
        maxSlides: 2,
        slideWidth: 250,
        slideMargin: 10
    });
});
```

Description

- The bxSlider plugin makes it easy to develop a carousel. The HTML is an unordered list with one list item for each slide that contains images or other HTML.

- The bxSlider website provides excellent examples and option summaries.

- If the slide images contain title attributes, the captions option will make them captions.

- The bxSlider download consists of a JavaScript file, a CSS file, and an images folder that contains the images that are used by the plugin.

Figure 11-4   How to use the bxSlider plugin for carousels

How to use the Cycle 2 plugin for slide shows

Figure 11-5 shows how to use the Cycle 2 plugin for slide shows. The easiest way to include this plugin in your web pages is to use the URL for the CDN that's shown in this figure. This plugin doesn't require a CSS file or any images.

The HTML for this plugin works with the children of a selected div element. These children are usually img or div elements. When you use div elements, you can code whatever you want within them, including headings, text, lists, and images. In this example, there is one img element for each slide that's contained within a div element for the slide show. The class attribute for this div element must be set to "cycle-slideshow" to initialize the slide show.

If you don't want to set any options for the slide show, that's all you need. Otherwise, you can set options by coding data-cycle attributes for the main div element. In this example, options are set for the effect (fx) that's used to move from slide to slide, how many milliseconds each slide should be displayed, where the captions should be displayed, and what caption template should be used. Here, the caption option points to the div that has been added after the img elements.

If you go to the Cycle 2 website, you'll find demos that show the many ways that this plugin can be used. You'll also find a complete summary of its options. Incidentally, instead of using the "cycle-slideshow" class to initialize a slide show and setting options using data-cycle attributes, you can call the cycle() method of the div element that contains the slides and code the options like you do for the bxSlider plugin. The preferred method, though, is the one shown here.

A web page that uses the Cycle 2 plugin for slide shows

On June 6th, 2016, Vecta Corp. moved into its new 4 story, 35,000 square foot facilty. Below are a few pictures of the new facility.

Slide 2: Left side

The URL for the Cycle 2 website

```
http://jquery.malsup.com/cycle2/
```

The script elements for the Cycle 2 plugin

```
<script src="http://code.jquery.com/jquery-3.1.1.min.js"></script>
<script src="http://malsup.github.com/jquery.cycle2.js"></script>
```

The HTML for the Cycle 2 plugin

```
<div class="cycle-slideshow"
        data-cycle-fx="scrollHorz"
        data-cycle-timeout="2000"
        data-cycle-caption="#adv-custom-caption"
        data-cycle-caption-template="Slide {{slideNum}}: {{cycleTitle}}" >
    <img src="images/building_01.jpg" alt="" data-cycle-title="Front">
    <img src="images/building_02.jpg" alt="" data-cycle-title="Left side">
    ...
    <!-- empty element for caption -->
    <div id="adv-custom-caption"></div>
</div>
```

Description

- The Cycle 2 plugin treats the children of a div element as the slides. Those children are usually img elements, but they can be div elements that contain both text and images.
- The best way to include this plugin in your web pages is to use the GitHub CDN for it.
- The Cycle 2 website provides excellent demos and summaries that let you enhance a slide show in many ways.
- To set options for a slide show, you can code data-cycle attributes for the div element.
- To provide captions below the slides, you can code data-cycle-title attributes for the img elements, data-cycle-caption attributes for the div element, and an empty div element for the captions below the slides.

Figure 11-5   How to use the Cycle 2 plugin for slide shows

Introduction to jQuery UI

To get you started with jQuery UI, you'll first learn what it is, where to get it, how to download it, and how to add it to your web pages.

What jQuery UI is and where to get it

jQuery UI (User Interface) is a free, open-source, JavaScript library that extends the use of the jQuery library by providing higher-level features that you can use with a minimum of code. To provide those features, the jQuery UI library uses the jQuery library. In fact, you can think of jQuery UI as the official plugin library for jQuery.

Figure 11-6 shows the home page and the URL for the jQuery UI website. That's the site where you can download jQuery UI. The quickest way to do that is to just click on the Stable button in the Quick Downloads box on the right of the page.

This figure also summarizes the four types of features that jQuery UI provides. *Widgets* are features like accordions, tabs, and date pickers. These are the jQuery features that developers use the most, and you'll learn how to use five of the widgets in this chapter.

Themes provide the formatting for widgets, and they are implemented by a CSS style sheet that's part of the jQuery UI download. Interactions and effects are less-used features, so you won't learn how to use them in this book.

The jQuery UI website

The URL for jQuery UI
`http://jqueryui.com/`

The four types of features provided by jQuery UI

Name	Description
Widgets	Accordions, tabs, date pickers, and more.
Themes	25 predefined themes as well as a ThemeRoller application that lets you create a custom theme. A theme is implemented by a CSS style sheet.
Interactions	Draggable, droppable, resizable, and more.
Effects	Color animations, class transitions, and more.

Description

- *jQuery UI* is a free, open-source, JavaScript library that extends the jQuery library by providing higher-level features. jQuery UI uses jQuery and can be thought of as the official plugin library for jQuery.

- The jQuery UI website can be accessed by the URL above.

Figure 11-6   What jQuery UI is and where to get it

How to download jQuery UI

Figure 11-7 shows how to build a custom jQuery UI download and download it to your computer. When you're learning how to use jQuery UI, though, you can just click the Stable button under Quick Downloads on the right side of the home page that's shown in the previous figure. Then, you can experiment with all of the jQuery UI features.

For production websites, it's better to build a custom download that includes only the components that are required. That will reduce the time that it takes to load jQuery UI into a browser. If, for example, you're only going to use a few of the widgets and you're not going to use the Dialog widget, you can uncheck all of the other widgets, the interactions, and the effects. However, if a component like a widget requires other components like interactions or effects, a message will be displayed that lets you know what you need. Then, you can respond accordingly.

In this figure, you can see some of the folders and files that are included in a typical jQuery download. For widgets, you only need the jquery-ui.min.css file, the jquery-ui.min.js file (the jQuery UI library), and the images in the images folder. The min files are compressed versions of the CSS and jQuery UI files, which are smaller than the uncompressed versions.

A jQuery UI download also includes the jQuery library in the external folder, an index.html file that displays a page that demonstrates the features that your download includes, and uncompressed versions of the CSS and jQuery files. You can use these versions if you want to see the code in these files. And you can use the jQuery library file if you haven't already downloaded jQuery and aren't using a CDN to get the jQuery library.

Last, the download includes structure and theme CSS files. However, all of the rule sets for these files are included in the core CSS file. As a result, you don't need these files unless you want to use only the structure or theme rule sets.

How to include jQuery UI in your web pages

To include the jQuery UI CSS and JavaScript files in a web page, you use the link and script elements that are shown in this figure. Here, the link element points to the min version of the CSS file. Then, the first script element points to the CDN address for the jQuery library (it doesn't use the downloaded jQuery file). And the second script element points to the min version of the jQuery UI file. But note that the script element for the jQuery UI file must follow the script element for the jQuery file because jQuery UI uses jQuery.

The last script element either points to the developer's external JavaScript file or it contains the JavaScript code. If the code that's needed is short, it is often embedded within the script element in the HTML document. Otherwise, an external JavaScript file can be used.

The link and script elements in this example assume that the jQuery UI folders and files are kept in the top-level folder that's downloaded. But you can organize the downloaded files in the way that you think is best for your applications. You can see this in the downloaded applications for this chapter.

The primary folders and files in a full jQuery UI download

Name	Type	Size	Date modified
external	File folder		12/8/2016 11:39 AM
images	File folder		12/8/2016 11:39 AM
index.html	Chrome HTML Document	32 KB	9/14/2016 6:34 PM
jquery-ui.css	Cascading Style Sheet Document	37 KB	9/14/2016 6:34 PM
jquery-ui.js	JScript Script File	509 KB	9/14/2016 6:34 PM
jquery-ui.min.css	Cascading Style Sheet Document	32 KB	9/14/2016 6:34 PM
jquery-ui.min.js	JScript Script File	248 KB	9/14/2016 6:34 PM

How to build a custom jQuery UI library and download its files

1. From the home page, click the Download link in the navigation bar or the Custom Download button. That will take you to the Download Builder page.

2. Select or deselect the interactions, widgets, and effects until the checked boxes identify the components that you want in your download.

3. If you want to select a theme for the download, use the drop-down list at the bottom of the page. Or, if you want to build a custom theme, click on the link above the list.

4. After you select a theme or design a custom theme, click the Download button to download a zipped folder that contains the jQuery UI files.

How to include the downloaded files in your application

```
<!-- link elements for the jQuery UI stylesheets -->
<link rel="stylesheet" href="/jquery-ui-1.12.1/jquery-ui.min.css">

<!-- the script elements for the jQuery and jQuery UI libraries -->
<script src="http://code.jquery.com/jquery-3.1.1.min.js"></script>
<script src="/jquery-ui-1.12.1/jquery-ui.min.js"></script>

<!-- the script element for your external JavaScript file or your code -->
<script src="..."></script>
```

Description

- A jQuery UI download consists of a zip file that contains the CSS files, the images for the theme that has been selected, the jQuery UI files, and an HTML document that demonstrates the components in the download.

- The only folders and files that you have to include in your pages are the images folder and the min (compressed) versions of the first CSS file and the jQuery UI file.

- The external folder in a download includes the jQuery library file.

- The download also includes full and compressed versions of structure and theme CSS files, but you don't need them because the jquery-ui.css and jquery-ui.min.css files include the rule sets in both the structure and theme files.

- When you're building a download for a web page, you can keep the file sizes smaller by selecting just the widgets, interactions, and effects that the web page needs.

Figure 11-7   How to download jQuery UI and include it in your web pages

How to use any jQuery UI widget

The next four figures show how to use five of the widgets in their basic forms. That may be all the information that you need for using these widgets in your own web pages. All of these widgets, however, provide options, events, and methods that go beyond what these figures present. So, if you want to see how else these widgets can be used, you can review the jQuery UI documentation for the widgets, which is excellent.

For instance, figure 11-8 shows how to use the documentation for the Accordion widget. A good way to start is to click on the names of the examples in the right side bar to see how the widget can be used. Then, you can click on the View Source link to see the source code that makes the example work. After that, you can review the options, methods, and events for the widget by clicking on the API Documentation link. (These two links aren't shown here.)

After you're comfortable with the way a widget works, you're ready to implement it on a web page, which you do in three stages. First, you code the link and script elements for jQuery UI in the head element of the HTML as shown in the previous figure. Second, you code the required HTML for the widget. Third, you code the jQuery for running the widget.

Beyond that, though, you must make sure that the jQuery UI images folder and the jQuery CSS file have the relationship shown in this figure. Specifically, the images folder must be at the same level as the jQuery CSS file because that's where the CSS file looks to get the images that it requires.

In the jQuery example in this figure, you can see the general structure for the jQuery code that's required for a widget. This is similar to the code for using a plugin. First, the code for using the widget is within the ready() event handler. Second, a jQuery selector is used to select the HTML element that's used for the widget. Third, the method for running the widget is called. Fourth, any options for the widget are coded within the braces for the method.

The accordion documentation on the jQuery UI website

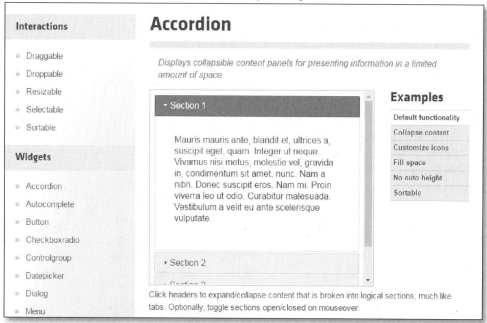

How to use the jQuery UI documentation

- In the left sidebar, click on a widget name to display its documentation.
- In the right sidebar, click on an example name to see a working example, then click on the View Source link to see the code for the example.
- Click the API Documentation link to display information about the widget's options, methods, and events.

The images folder and jquery-ui.min.css relationship that jQuery UI expects

The jQuery for using a widget

```
$(document).ready(function(){
    $("selector").widgetMethod({
        // option settings
    });
});
```

Description

- To use a jQuery UI *widget*, you code the HTML and jQuery for the widget. In the jQuery, you code a selector, the method to be used, and the options.
- For a widget that requires images, jQuery UI expects the CSS file and the images folder to be at the same level.

Figure 11-8 How to use any jQuery UI widget

How to use five of the most popular jQuery UI widgets

In the topics that follow, you'll learn how to use five of the most popular widgets that are currently supported by jQuery UI.

How to use the Accordion widget

Figure 11-9 shows how to use an Accordion widget, which consists of two or more headings and the contents for those headings. By default, an accordion starts with the panel for the first heading displayed, and only one panel can be open at a time. Then, when the user clicks on one of the other headings, the contents for that heading are displayed and the contents for the first heading are hidden.

As the HTML in this figure shows, an Accordion widget consists of a top-level div element that contains one h3 element and one div element for each item in the accordion.

In the jQuery for an accordion, you select the top-level div element of the accordion and call the accordion() method with or without options. Often, you'll use this method without options because its defaults work the way you want them to.

In the example in this figure, though, three options are coded. First, the event option changes the event that causes the contents of a heading to be displayed from the "click" to the "mouseover" (hover) event. Second, the heightStyle option is set to "content" so the height of the open panels is based on the height of the content. Third, the collapsible option is set to true, which means that all of the panels can be closed at the same time.

Although the basic formatting for an accordion is done by the CSS style sheet for jQuery UI, you can use your own style sheet to format the contents of a panel. In fact, you usually need to do that when the panel consists of several different types of HTML elements.

Because the jQuery code in this example is typical of the code for all widgets, this is a good time to take a close look at it. As you can see, this code uses parentheses, braces, commas, colons, and semi-colons in a way that can be bewildering to new programmers, and every punctuation mark is required for this code to work.

For that reason, it's usually easiest to copy a block of code like this into your script and modify it for whatever widget you're going to use. In general, you just change the selector for the widget, the method name, and the options. For the options, you code the name of the option before the colon and the value after it, with a comma after every option setting but the last one.

An Accordion widget

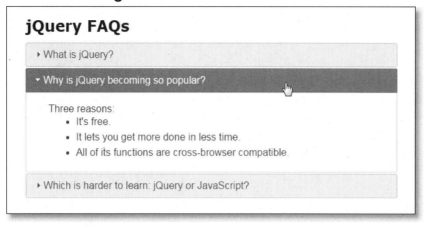

The HTML for the accordion

```
<div id="accordion">
    <h3>What is jQuery?</h3>
    <div><!-- the content for the panel --></div>

    <h3>Why is jQuery becoming so popular?</h3>
    <div><!-- the content for the panel --></div>

    <h3>Which is harder to learn: jQuery or JavaScript?</h3>
    <div><!-- the content for the panel --></div>
</div>
```

The jQuery for the accordion

```
$(document).ready(function(){
    $("#accordion").accordion({
        event: "mouseover",
        heightStyle: "content",
        collapsible: true
    });
});
```

Description

- The HTML consists of h3 elements that provide the headers for the panels, followed by div elements that contain the contents for the panels. These elements should be within an outer div element that represents the accordion.

- In the jQuery, the accordion() method is used to implement the accordion widget for the div element that represents the accordion.

- By default, a panel is opened when its header is clicked, one panel always has to be open, and all the panels open to the same size. But you can change that by setting options for the accordion() method.

- The basic formatting of the accordion is done by the CSS file for jQuery UI, but you can use your style sheet to format the contents within the panels, and you can modify the jQuery UI style sheet to change the appearance of the accordion.

Figure 11-9   How to use the Accordion widget

How to use the Tabs widget

Figure 11-10 shows how to use the Tabs widget. This widget has the same general function as an Accordion widget, but it displays the contents of a panel when the related tab is clicked.

As this figure shows, the HTML for a Tabs widget consists of a top-level div element that represents the widget. Then, this element contains an unordered list that contains the headings for the tabs, followed by one div element for each tab that contains the content of the tab. To relate the tab headings to their respective div elements, the href attributes of the <a> elements within the li elements are set to the ids of the div elements.

To activate a Tabs widget with jQuery, you just select the top-level div element and call the tabs() method. Usually, you don't need to set any options because the defaults work the way you want them to. However, you might want to use the event option to change the event for opening a tab from the click event to the mouseover event, which can work well with tabs.

Here again, the basic formatting for a Tabs widget is done by the CSS style sheet for jQuery UI. However, you can use your own style sheet to format the contents of a panel. In fact, you usually need to do that when the panel consists of several different types of HTML elements. You can also use your style sheet to override the UI formatting.

A Tabs widget

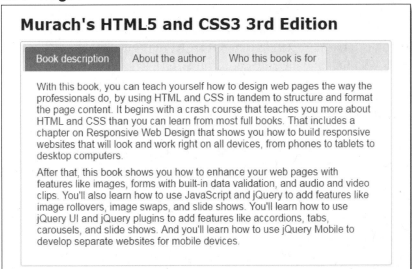

The HTML for the tabs

```
<div id="tabs">
    <ul>
        <li><a href="#tabs-1">Book description</a></li>
        <li><a href="#tabs-2">About the author</a></li>
        <li><a href="#tabs-3">Who this book is for</a></li>
    </ul>
    <div id="tabs-1"><!-- the content --></div>
    <div id="tabs-2"><!-- the content --></div>
    <div id="tabs-3"><!-- the content --></div>
</div>
```

The jQuery for the tabs

```
$(document).ready(function(){
    $("#tabs").tabs();
});
```

Description

- The HTML should consist of a div element that contains an unordered list that represents the tabs, followed by div elements that contain the contents for the tabs.

- The heading for each tab should be in an <a> element within an li element of the list. The href attribute for each tab should point to the id of the div element that contains the contents for the tab.

- In the jQuery, the tabs() method is used to implement the Tabs widget for the div element that represents the tabs. By default, a tab is switched to when its header is clicked.

- The basic formatting of the tabs is done by the CSS for jQuery UI, but you can use your own CSS to format the contents within the panels or override the UI formatting.

Figure 11-10   How to use the Tabs widget

How to use the Button and Dialog widgets

Figure 11-11 shows how the Button and Dialog widgets work. The HTML for a Button widget is often an input element of the "button" type, but this widget also works with the "submit", "reset", "radio", and "checkbox" types, and with <a> elements too.

When a Button widget is activated by the jQuery button() method, the HTML is converted into a button that uses the jQuery UI theme. Other than that, the button works its normal way. In the example in this figure, the Button widget is coded as an <a> element that contains an img element for a book, and jQuery UI changes its appearance. When the user clicks on it, the dialog box is opened.

The HTML for a Dialog widget consists of a div element that contains the contents for the dialog box. The title attribute of this element can be used to specify the heading for the dialog box. And the contents of this element can contain any HTML elements.

When the dialog box is displayed, it is both draggable and resizable. This means that you can drag the box by its title bar, and you can resize the box by dragging the resize handle in the lower right corner. You can also close the box by clicking on the "X" icon in the upper right corner.

To display a Dialog widget with jQuery, you use the dialog() method. If, for example, you want to display a dialog box right after a page is ready, you select the div element for the dialog box and call the dialog() method. If you want the user to have to close the dialog box before continuing, you can also set the modal option to true.

Usually, though, you want to open a dialog box when some event occurs, like clicking on a Button widget. Then, you use the jQuery code that's shown in this figure. First, the button() method is called to convert the HTML for the button to a Button widget. Then, an event handler for the click event of the button is set up. Within that event handler, the dialog() method of the dialog box is called to display the box. Here, the modal option is set to true so the user has to close the dialog box before proceeding. That's why the page behind the dialog box in this figure is dimmed.

You may also need to use some of the other options for a Dialog widget. If, for example, you want to change the height or width of the dialog box, you can set the height or width option. If you don't want the dialog box to be draggable and resizable, you can set those options to false. You can also use the title option to set the title for a dialog box if you don't want to use the title attribute for that purpose.

Incidentally, the Dialog widget is generally considered to be a nice improvement over the JavaScript technique for opening another window and using it as a dialog box. That's especially true because most browsers have built-in features for blocking popup windows.

A Button widget that activates a Dialog widget

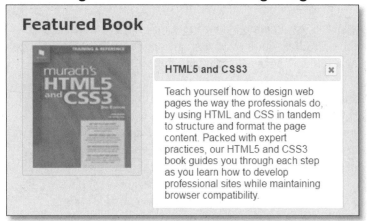

The HTML for the Button and Dialog widgets

```
<a id="book"><img src="images/3HTM.jpg" alt="HTML5 and CSS3 book"/></a>
<div id="dialog" title="HTML5 and CSS3" style="display:none;">
    <!-- the contents for the dialog box -->
</div>
```

The jQuery for the Button and Dialog widgets

```
$(document).ready(function(){
    $("#book").button();
    $("#book").click(function() {
        $("#dialog").dialog({
            modal: true
        });
    });
});
```

Description

- The HTML for a Button widget can be an input element with any of these type attributes: button, submit, reset, radio, or checkbox. It can also be an <a> element. When activated, jQuery UI styles a Button widget so it looks like a button.

- The HTML for a Dialog widget consists of a div element that contains the contents for the dialog box. The title attribute can be used to provide the heading for the dialog box.

- To prevent the Dialog widget from appearing when the page loads, set its display property to "none".

- In the jQuery, use the button() method to activate the Button widget. Then, in the click() event handler for the button, use the dialog() method to display the Dialog widget.

- jQuery UI provides many options for Dialog widgets. For instance, if the modal option is set to true, the box must be closed before the user can proceed. And the width option can be used to change the width of the box from its default of 300 pixels.

- By default, a dialog box is resizable and draggable, but you can change those options by setting them to false.

Figure 11-11   How to use the Button and Dialog widgets

How to use the Datepicker widget

Figure 11-12 shows how to use a Datepicker widget that is associated with a text box. Then, when the user clicks in the text box, a calendar is displayed. After the user selects a date, the calendar is hidden and the selected date appears in the text box.

To implement a Datepicker widget, you code a text box in the HTML. Then, you select that text box in the jQuery and call the datepicker() method. By default, the calendar looks like the one in this figure with the currently selected date displayed in mm/dd/yyyy format. But many options are available for customizing the date format, language, selectable date ranges, and more.

In the second jQuery example in this figure, three options are set. The first option sets the minimum date to the current date, which is done by assigning a new Date object to the option. The second option sets the maximum date that the widget will accept to 45 days after the current date. And the third option displays a panel beneath the calendar that contains Today and Done buttons. If the user clicks the Today button after moving to another month, the calendar returns to the month that contains the current date. If the user clicks the Done button, the calendar is closed.

A Datepicker widget with no options set

The HTML for the Datepicker widget

```
<label>Arrival date:</label>
<label><input type="text" id="datepicker"></label>
```

The jQuery for the Datepicker widget with no options

```
$(document).ready(function(){
    $("#datepicker").datepicker();
});
```

The jQuery for the Datepicker widget with three options

```
$(document).ready(function(){
    $("#datepicker").datepicker({
        minDate: new Date(),
        maxDate: +45,
        showButtonPanel: true
    });
});
```

Description

- The HTML for a Datepicker widget is a text box.
- The jQuery for a Datepicker widget is a call to the datepicker() method.
- By default, the Datepicker widget is displayed when the user moves the focus into the text box, and the current date is highlighted.
- jQuery UI provides many options for the Datepicker widget. For instance, minDate sets the minimum date that the user can select; maxDate sets the maximum date that the user can select; changeMonth and changeYear when set to true provide controls that let the user select the month and year that should be displayed; numberOfMonths sets the number of months that should be displayed; and showButtonPanel displays a bar at the bottom of the widget with Today and Done buttons.

Figure 11-12   How to use the Datepicker widget

Perspective

Now that you've completed this chapter, you should be able to use some of the popular jQuery plugins and jQuery UI widgets. That's an easy way to add features like tabs and accordions to your web pages. Later, if you want to create jQuery plugins of your own, section 3 and especially chapter 18 will provide the JavaScript skills that you need for doing that.

Terms

jQuery plugin
modal dialog box
jQuery UI (User Interface)
widget
theme

Summary

- If you need a common function for a web page, chances are that a *jQuery plugin* is already available for it. By using a plugin, you can often save hours of work and do the job even better than you would have done it on your own.

- To access a plugin, you code a script element for it in the head element of the HTML document. This script element must come after the script element for the jQuery library, because all jQuery plugins use that library.

- To use a plugin, you often need to use jQuery code to call its method within the ready() event handler for a page. Then, if the plugin requires options, you code the options as part of the method call. For some plugins, though, you just need to code the HTML and the required attributes correctly.

- *jQuery UI (User Interface)* is a JavaScript library that extends the jQuery library. Since the jQuery UI library uses the jQuery library, the script element for jQuery UI must come after the script element for jQuery.

- As you build a jQuery UI download, you can select the components for the features that you're going to use, including widgets, interactions, and effects. As you would expect, the fewer components you select, the smaller the jQuery UI file that has to be loaded into the user's browser.

- You can also select a *theme* to include with a jQuery UI download that will be used to style the jQuery UI components. You can also create a custom theme.

- The most widely-used jQuery UI components are the *widgets*. To use a widget, you code the prescribed HTML for it. Then, in the jQuery, you select the widget and run its primary method, often with one or more options.

Exercise 11-1   Experiment with the Cycle 2 plugin

In this exercise, you'll experiment with the Cycle 2 plugin and the slide show that's in figure 11-5. You'll also review the documentation for this plugin. This will give you a better idea of how you can use plugins.

Review the application

1. Use your text editor or IDE to open the HTML file in this folder:

    `javascript_jquery\exercises\ch11\cycle2\`

2. Note that the options for using the Cycle 2 plugin are coded as attributes in the HTML for the slide show. Then, run the application to see how it works.

Experiment with the options

3. Change the value of the data-cycle-fx option to "fadeout". Then, add a data-cycle-speed option with a value of "1000". Test the application to see how this changes the way it works.

4. Go to the website for the Cycle 2 plugin, which is at this URL:

    `http://jquery.malsup.com/cycle2/`

    Click on the Demos link on the Home page, then review any of the demos to see the information they present.

5. Go back to the Home page of the website, then click on the API link to learn more about the options you can use with this plugin.

6. If you're interested, try using one or more of these options.

Check out the download

7. Go back to the Home page one more time and click on the Download link. Then, click on the Download button for the production version of the plugin. In most browsers, this displays the JavaScript for the plugin. Although this isn't the way most downloads work, this is relatively common with plugins.

8. If the code for the plugin is displayed, download it by right-clicking in the code, selecting Save As from the menu that's displayed, and saving the file in a new folder named "js" in your website. Otherwise, use the standard technique to download the code.

9. Change the script element for the Cycle 2 plugin so it refers to the file you just downloaded. Then, make sure the application still works.

Exercise 11-2   Experiment with the Accordion widget

In this exercise, you'll review the jQuery UI demos and documentation for the Accordion widget. Then, you'll make some minor modifications to the application that uses this widget.

Review the demos and documentation for the widget

1. Go to the jQuery UI website at this URL:

    `http://jqueryui.com/`

    Then, click on the link for the Accordion widget in the left sidebar.

2. Use the accordion at the top of the page to see how it works. Then, click the View Source link below the accordion to display the code that implements it and review this code. In particular, notice that the accordion() method doesn't use any options.

3. Select one or more of the examples to the right of the accordion to see how they change the way the accordion works, and review the jQuery code to see what options are used.

4. Click the API Documentation link and review the options on the page that's displayed.

Review the application

5. Use your text editor or IDE to open the HTML file for the accordion application in this folder:

    `javascript_jquery\exercises\ch11\accordion\`

    Then, run the application to see how it works.

6. Modify the jQuery code for the accordion so the panels are displayed when the user double-clicks on them rather than when the mouse moves over them. Test this change.

7. Modify the jQuery code so all of the panels are closed when the application starts. To do that, use the active option. Then, test this change.

12

How to use Ajax, JSON, and Flickr

This chapter shows you how to use Ajax to update a web page with HTML, XML, or JSON data without loading a new web page into the browser. Since Ajax is commonly used to get data from popular websites, this chapter also shows how to use Ajax with the API for getting feeds from Flickr.

Introduction to Ajax

The four topics that follow introduce you to Ajax, the types of data that are commonly used with Ajax, and the XMLHttpRequest object that is the basis for Ajax.

How Ajax works

Ajax is the acronym for *Asynchronous JavaScript and XML*. As shown in figure 12-1, Google's Auto Suggest feature is a typical Ajax application. As you type the start of a search entry, Google uses Ajax to get the terms and links of items that match the characters that you have typed so far. Ajax does this without refreshing the page so the user doesn't experience any delays. This is sometimes called a "partial page refresh."

To make this work, all modern browsers provide an *XMLHttpRequest object* (or *XHR object*) that is used to send an Ajax request to the web server and to receive the returned data from the server. In addition, JavaScript is used in the browser to issue the request, parse the returned data, and modify the DOM so the page reflects the returned data. In many cases, a request will include data that tells the server what data to return.

On the web server, an application program or script that's written in a language like PHP or ASP.NET is commonly used to return the data that is requested. Often, these programs or scripts are written before the JavaScript developers use them so they know how their requests must be coded. Otherwise, the JavaScript developers and the server-side developers need to coordinate so the Ajax requests can be processed by the server scripts.

The two diagrams in this figure show how a normal HTTP request is made and processed as well as how an Ajax request is made and processed. The main difference is that the server returns an entire page for a normal HTTP request so the page has to be loaded into the browser. In contrast, an Ajax request sends an XMLHttpRequest object to get data and the server returns only the data. In addition, JavaScript is used to send the request, process the returned data, and script the DOM with the new data. As a result, the web page doesn't have to be reloaded.

Because this Ajax technology is so powerful, it is commonly used by websites like Facebook and Google Maps. When you post a comment to a friend's Facebook page, for example, the comment just appears. And when you drag within a Google Map, the map is automatically adjusted. In neither case is the page reloaded.

Beyond that, websites like YouTube, Twitter, and Flickr provide *Application Programming Interfaces (APIs)* that show how to use Ajax to get data from their sites. This means that you can get data from these sites to enhance your own web pages. Since this is a skill that every modern web developer should have, this chapter shows you how to use the API for Flickr.

Google's Auto Suggest is an Ajax application

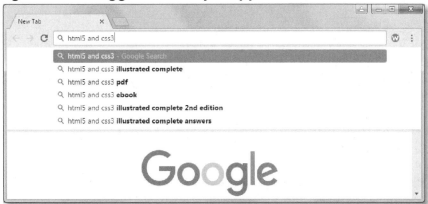

How a normal HTTP request is processed

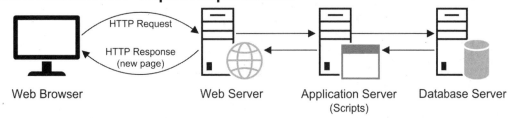

How an Ajax XMLHttpRequest is processed

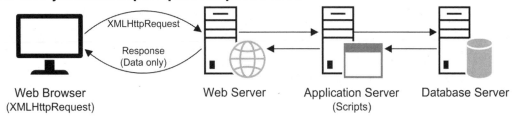

Description

- *Ajax* stands for *Asynchronous JavaScript and XML*. Unlike normal HTTP requests, Ajax lets you receive data from a web server without reloading the page. This is sometimes known as a "partial page refresh."

- As the Ajax name implies, JavaScript is essential to the use of Ajax because JavaScript not only sends the requests but also processes the responses and updates the DOM with the new data.

- To send an Ajax request, JavaScript uses a browser object known as an *XMLHttpRequest* (*XHR*) *object*. This object can include data that tells the application server what data is being requested.

- An XHR object is often processed by a program or script on the application server. Then, the JavaScript programmer must coordinate the Ajax requests with the application scripts.

- Today, websites like Google's Blogger, YouTube, Twitter, and Flickr provide *APIs* (*Application Programming Interfaces*) that let you use Ajax to get data from their sites.

Figure 12-1   How Ajax works

Common data formats for Ajax

Figure 12-2 presents the three common data formats for Ajax applications. The easiest one to use is HTML, which you're already familiar with. When you use Ajax to load HTML data into a web page, you don't have to parse the data because it already includes the HTML tags for the data. In contrast, you do have to parse the data when you work with XML or JSON data.

Ajax was originally designed to be used with *XML (eXtensible Markup Language)*, which is why XML is part of the Ajax name. XML is an open-standard, device-independent format for exchanging data across the Internet, and its syntax and document tree mimic that of HTML. The downside to XML is that it's relatively difficult to use JavaScript and jQuery to parse the data in XML files.

Today, *JSON (JavaScript Object Notation)* is the most popular format for working with Ajax. JSON, pronounced "Jason", is easy to understand, and most server-side languages already provide functions for JSON encoding. PHP for example, has the json_encode() function, and ASP.NET has the DataContractJsonSerializer class.

JSON is based on a subset of the JavaScript programming language, and it uses conventions that are familiar to programmers of C-style languages like C, C++, Java, and JavaScript. Since its structure is a hierarchy of name/value pairs that are returned as an object, it is relatively easy to parse the JSON data with JavaScript and jQuery.

Although HTML, XML, and JSON are the three most popular data formats for working with Ajax, they aren't the only ones that are supported. In fact, you can also use plain text, YAML, and CSV files with Ajax.

The common data formats for Ajax

Format	Description	File extension
HTML	Hypertext Markup Language	html
XML	eXtensible Markup Language	xml
JSON	JavaScript Object Notation	json is often used

XML data

```
<?xml version="1.0" encoding="utf-8"?>
<management>
    <teammember>
        <name>Agnes</name>
        <title>Vice President of Accounting</title>
        <bio>With over 14 years of public accounting ... </bio>
    </teammember>
    <teammember>
        <name>Wilbur</name>
        <title>Founder and CEO</title>
        <bio>While Wilbur is the founder and CEO ... </bio>
    </teammember>
</management>
```

JSON data

```
{"teammembers":[
    {
        "name":"Agnes",
        "title":"Vice President of Accounting",
        "bio":"With over 14 years of public accounting... "
    },
    {
        "name":"Wilbur",
        "title":"Founder and CEO",
        "bio":"While Wilbur is the founder and CEO ... "
    }
]}
```

Description

- The common data formats for working with Ajax are HTML, XML, and JSON.
- *XML* (*eXtensible Markup Language*) is an open-standard, device-independent format that must be parsed by JavaScript or jQuery in the browser.
- *JSON* (*JavaScript Object Notation*) is the most popular format for Ajax applications. In general, JSON files are smaller and faster than XML files. They are also easier to parse since JSON data is returned as JavaScript objects.
- Most server-side languages have methods that can be used to encode JSON data on the server. PHP 5.0 and later, for instance, has the json_encode() method, and ASP.NET 3.0 and later has the DataContractJsonSerializer class.
- For more information on JSON APIs that are built into your favorite programming language, you can visit www.json.org.

Figure 12-2   Common data formats for Ajax

The members of the XMLHttpRequest object

Figure 12-3 presents all of the *members* (methods, properties, and events) of the XMLHttpRequest object. This object is behind every Ajax request, no matter what type of data is being requested. You'll see how the members of this object are used in the application in the next figure.

The two methods that are used with every request are the open() and send() methods. The open() method is used to open a connection for a request. As you can see in the parameters for the open() method, this method specifies whether the request is a GET or POST request and it provides the URL for the request. In a production application, the URL is for the script or program on the application server that will process the request. When you're testing an application, though, the URL is typically for a file that contains test data.

After the open() method is issued, the send() method is used to send the request. If necessary, this method can include a data parameter that sends data to the server along with the request. This data is typically used to filter the data that's returned.

As you can see in the list of properties, the readyState property indicates the state of the request; the status and statusText properties provide the status code and status message that's returned by the server; and the responseText and responseXML properties provide the returned data in plain or XML format.

The last member in this figure is the onreadystatechange event that can be used for an event handler that processes the returned data. You'll see how this works in the next figure.

Incidentally, the GET and POST methods are the same ones that are used for an HTML form. When you use the GET method, the data is sent to the web server as part of the URL, but the total amount of data that can be sent is limited. When you use the POST method, the data that is sent is hidden and unlimited.

Members of the XMLHttpRequest object

Method	Description
`abort()`	Cancels the current request.
`getAllResponseHeaders()`	Returns a string that contains the names and values of all response headers.
`getResponseHeader(name)`	Returns the value of a specific response header.
`open(method,url[,async] [,user][,pass])`	Opens a connection for a request. The parameters let you set the method to GET or POST, set the URL for the request, set asynchronous mode to true or false, and supply a username and password if authentication is required. When asynchronous mode is used, the application continues while the request is being processed.
`send([data])`	Starts the request. This method can include data that gets sent with the request. This method must be called after a request connection has been opened.
`setRequestHeader(name,value)`	Specifies a name and value for a request header.

Property	Description
`readyState`	A numeric value that indicates the state of the current request: 0 is UNSENT, 1 is OPENED, 2 is HEADERS_RECEIVED, 3 is LOADING, and 4 is DONE.
`responseText`	The content that's returned from the server in plain text format.
`responseXml`	The content that's returned from the server in XML format.
`status`	The status code returned from the server in numeric format. Common values include 200 for success and 404 for not found.
`statusText`	The status message returned from the server in text format.

Event	Description
`onreadystatechange`	An event that occurs when the state of the request changes.

Description

- The table above shows the *members* (methods, properties, and events) that can be used with the XMLHttpRequest object.

Figure 12-3   The members of the XMLHttpRequest object

How to use the XMLHttpRequest object

Figure 12-4 shows how you can use the XMLHttpRequest object to get XML data from the web server without refreshing the web page. Here, the first example shows a portion of the XML file, but you can assume that this file includes all of the team members with full data in the bio fields. Then, the second example shows the div element that will receive the data returned by the XHR object.

The third example shows the JavaScript code for using an XHR object to send an Ajax request and receive the returned data. This is coded within the event handler for the ready event. The first statement in this JavaScript code uses the *new* keyword to create a new XHR object. This is followed by an event handler for the onreadystatechange event. The first statement in this handler is an if statement that tests whether the readyState property is 4 and the status property is 200, which means that the request has finished and was successful. If that's true, the if statement parses the returned data. Otherwise, it does nothing.

To parse the data, the first statement in the handler saves the responseXML property of the XHR object in a variable named xmlDoc. Then, the next statement uses the JavaScript getElementsByTagName() method to store the data for each team member in an array variable named team. Next, it sets a variable named html to an empty string. This is the variable that the for loop that follows will fill with the formatted data for the team members.

In the for loop, one statement is executed for each team member in the team array. This statement uses the getElementsByTagName() method to get the name, title, and bio data for each team member in the array. It also concatenates this data to the html variable along with br elements that provide the spacing between the data items. When the for loop finishes, the first statement after it uses the innerHTML property to save the data in the html variable as the HTML contents of the div element with "team" as its id. That will display the data as shown in the web page at the top of this figure.

At this point, though, the Ajax request hasn't been sent. The code has just set up the event handler for after it has been sent. To send the request, the open() method that follows the event handler opens the connection for the request. It sets the method for the request to GET, provides the URL for the XML data, and sets asynchronous to true. In this case, the URL parameter is a relative URL that shows that the team.xml file is in the same folder as the file that contains the JavaScript.

Then, the send() method sends the request. Once that's done, the onreadystatechange event will occur, and the event handler will parse the returned data if the request was successful.

With the exception of the ready() event method, this example uses JavaScript instead of jQuery. This should give you some idea of how the XHR object has been traditionally used. Please note, however, that jQuery could be used for this application. In fact, with the advent of jQuery, Ajax programming has become much easier. Just keep in mind that the XHR object is used with every Ajax request, whether or not jQuery is used to issue the request.

A web page that uses the XHR object and JavaScript to load XML data

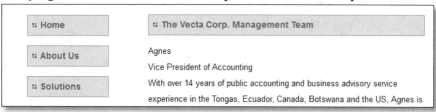

The XML file (team.xml)

```
<?xml version="1.0" encoding="utf-8"?>
<management>
    <teammember>
        <name>Agnes</name>
        <title>Vice President of Accounting</title>
        <bio>With over 14 years of public accounting ... </bio>
    </teammember>
    ...
</management>
```

The HTML div element that receives the data

```
<div id="team"></div>
```

The JavaScript for getting and parsing the data

```
$(document).ready(function() {
    var xhr = new XMLHttpRequest();
    xhr.onreadystatechange = function() {
        if (xhr.readyState == 4 && xhr.status == 200) {
            var xmlDoc = xhr.responseXML;
            var team = xmlDoc.getElementsByTagName("teammember");
            var html = "";
            for (i = 0; i < team.length; i++) {
                html +=
                    xmlDoc.getElementsByTagName("name")[i]
                        .childNodes[0].nodeValue + "<br>" +
                    xmlDoc.getElementsByTagName("title")[i]
                        .childNodes[0].nodeValue + "<br>" +
                    xmlDoc.getElementsByTagName("bio")[i]
                        .childNodes[0].nodeValue + "<br><br>";
            }
            document.getElementById("team").innerHTML = html;
        }
    };
    xhr.open("GET", "team.xml", true);
    xhr.send();
});
```

Description

- This application uses the XHR object to load all of the team members in the file named team.xml on the web server and display them in the div element with "team" as its id.

- The event handler for the onreadystatechange event parses the data returned by the method if the readyState property is 4 and the status property is 200.

Figure 12-4   How to use the XMLHttpRequest object

How to use the jQuery shorthand methods for Ajax

Now that you understand how Ajax works and how you use JavaScript with Ajax programming, you're ready to learn about the jQuery shorthand methods that make Ajax programming easier.

The jQuery shorthand methods for working with Ajax

Figure 12-5 summarizes the jQuery methods for working with Ajax. Here, the load() method is used to get HTML data. The $.get() and $.post() methods are commonly used to get XML data, which is the default data type for these methods. And the $.getJSON() method is used to get JSON data.

The examples show how these methods work. The first example uses the load() method to load the HTML from a file named solutions.html. The second example uses the $.get() method to load XML data. And the third example uses the $.getJSON() method to load JSON data.

In the second example, the $.get() method is coded with three parameters. The first parameter is the URL for a PHP script that will process the Ajax request. The second parameter passes data to the request in the form of a string. This data will be used by the PHP script to determine what data is returned. The third parameter names the function that will be called if the request is successful.

In the third example, the URL parameter for the $.getJSON() method is for a JSON file. This method doesn't have a data parameter, and its success parameter consists of an embedded function that will be called if the request is successful.

The $.each() method is also included in this figure. This method is commonly used for processing the data that's returned by an Ajax request. You'll see how this works in figure 12-8.

The shorthand methods for working with Ajax

Method	Description
load(*url*[,*data*][,*success*])	Load HTML data.
$.get(*url*[,*data*][,*success*[,*dataType*]])	Load data with a GET request.
$.post(*url*[,*data*][,*success*[,*dataType*]])	Load data with a POST request.
$.getJSON(*url*[,*data*][,*success*])	Load JSON data with a GET request.

The parameters for the shorthand methods

Parameter	Description
url	The string for the URL where the request is sent.
data	A map or string that is sent to the server with the request, usually to filter the data that is returned.
success	A callback function that is executed if the request is successful.
dataType	A string that specifies the type of data (html, xml, json, script, or text). The default is XML.

The $.each() method for processing the data that's returned

Method	Description
$.each(*collection*, *callback*)	The collection parameter is an object or array. The callback parameter is a function that's done for each item in the collection.

A load() method

```
$("#solution").load("solutions.html");
```

A $.get() method that includes data and calls a success function

```
$.get("getmanager.php", "name=agnes", showManager);
```

A $.getJSON() method with an embedded success function

```
$.getJSON("team.json", function(data){
    // the statements for the success function
}
```

Description

- jQuery includes several shorthand methods that let you request and receive HTML, XML, or JSON data.

- All of the shorthand methods let you include data that will be used by the web server to filter the results of the request so only the right results are returned. You can send this data as a query string (as in the second example above) or as a map (see figure 12-9).

- The only difference between the $.get() and $.post() methods is the method that is used for the request (GET or POST). These are the same methods that you specify when you set up an HTML form.

- The $.each() method is an expanded form of the each() method that can be used to process the items in the returned data (see figure 12-8).

Figure 12-5   The jQuery shorthand methods for working with Ajax

How to use the load() method to load HTML data

Figure 12-6 shows how to use the load() method to load HTML data with an Ajax request. For this example, three section elements are coded within a file named solutions.html. The ids for these elements are "vprospect", "vconvert", and "vretain", which refer to three products. Then, one of these section elements is loaded when the user clicks on the link for the product in the page shown here.

You can see how this works in the jQuery for this application. It consists of the event handlers for the click events of the three links. In the load() methods for these links, the URL not only consists of the name of the HTML file but also a reference to the section element for that link. For instance, #vconvert in the code that follows

```
$("#solution").load("solutions.html #vconvert");
```

gets the HTML for the section element with "vconvert" as its id.

The one benefit of using HTML data with Ajax requests is that the data is already within HTML elements that can be formatted by the CSS for the page. In other words, you don't have to parse the data that is returned by the request. In contrast, you do need to parse the XML or JSON data that is returned, as you will see in the next two figures.

By the way, you should know that to test the load() method with Chrome, IE, Edge, or Opera, the HTML files need to be on a web server. The load() method won't work if the HTML files are on a drive on your local computer or a file server such as a local network. However, this method will work from a local or network drive if you use the Firefox or Safari browsers. It will also work if you use an IDE like Aptana because Aptana provides its own internal web server.

A web page that loads HTML elements when one of the links is clicked

The HTML for the user interface

```
<p>Which Vecta Corp. solution are you interested in learning about?</p>
<a id="vprospect" href="#">vProspect 2.0</a> |
<a id="vconvert" href="#">vConvert 2.0</a> |
<a id="vretain" href="#">vRetain 1.0</a><br>
<div id="solution"></div>
```

The start of the second section element in the solutions.html file

```
<section id="vconvert">
    <p><strong>vConvert 2.0</strong></p>
    <p><img src="images/logo_vconvert.gif" width="63" height="36" >
        Create a highly user-friendly and easy-to-navigate information ...
    </p>
    <ul>
        <li>Build a visual and functional user front end that ... </li>
        <li>Cause the desired emotional response in a user to ...</li>
        ...
    </ul>
</section>
```

The jQuery that loads the data when a link is clicked

```
$(document).ready(function() {
    $("#vprospect").click(function() {
        $("#solution").load("solutions.html #vprospect");
    });
    $("#vconvert").click(function() {
        $("#solution").load("solutions.html #vconvert");
    });
    $("#vretain").click(function() {
        $("#solution").load("solutions.html #vretain");
    });
});
```

Description

- The load() function can only load content from files on the same server as the page making the call.

- During testing, you'll be able to load files from the file system in Firefox and Safari, but Chrome, IE, Edge, and Opera require all of the files to be on an actual web server.

Figure 12-6   How to use the load() method to load HTML data

How to use the $.get() or $.post() method to load XML data

The example in figure 12-7 shows how to use the $.get() method to load XML data from a web server. Remember, though, that the $.post() method works the same way, except the POST method is used to send the request.

The first parameter in the $.get() method in this example gives the URL for the XML file that will be loaded by the request. Here again, this URL is relative to the file that contains the jQuery code. Then, the second parameter is the function that will be used to process the returned data. The parameter for this function is the data that's returned by the request.

To process the returned data, this function issues the find() method for the data that's returned to find the children of the XML item named "management". Those children are the items named "teammember". Then, the each() method is chained to the children so it can be used to process each of the team members.

The first statement in the each() method sets a new variable named xmlDoc to the value of the *this* keyword, which is the team member that's being processed. Then, the next statement appends the data for that team member to the div element that will receive the processed data. Within the parameter for the append() method, three find() methods get the data for the "name", "title", and "bio" items in the returned data, and the text() method gets the text for those items.

To keep this application simple, the formatting for the data that's returned is limited. Specifically, the name field is parsed into an h3 element, and br elements are added after the title and bio fields to add spacing after these fields.

To test the use of the $.get() and $.post() methods, the files named in the URL have to be on a web server, not a file server. Specifically, the XML file must be in the same domain as the web page that's making the request. This is required because of the *cross-domain security policy* that is used by most browsers. Like the load() method, though, the $.get() and $.post() methods will work if you run them from Aptana because it provides its own internal web server.

A web page that loads XML data

The XML file (team.xml)

```xml
<management>
    <teammember>
        <name>Agnes</name>
        <title>Vice President of Accounting</title>
        <bio>With over 14 years of public accounting ... </bio>
    </teammember>
    ...
</management>
```

The HTML div element that receives the data

```html
<div id="team"></div>
```

The jQuery

```javascript
$(document).ready(function(){
    $.get("team.xml", function(data){
        $(data).find("management").children().each(function() {
            var xmlDoc = $(this);
            $("#team").append("<h3>" +
                xmlDoc.find("name").text() + "</h3>" +
                xmlDoc.find("title").text() + "<br>" +
                xmlDoc.find("bio").text() + "<br>");
        });
    });
});
```

Description

- The $.get() and $.post() methods work the same except for the method that's used to send the data in the XHR request.
- You can use the jQuery find() method to get the data in an XML file. Here, the first find() method starts a chain that gets the children (team members) of the management data that's returned, and the other three find() methods get the name, title, and bio fields for each team member.

Figure 12-7   How to use the $.get() or $.post() method to load XML data

How to use the $.getJSON() method to load JSON data

Figure 12-8 shows how to use the $.getJSON() and $.each() methods to load JSON data. In the $.getJSON() method, the first parameter provides the URL for the JSON file with json as its extension. Then, the second parameter is the function that processes the JSON data if the request is successful. Note that the parameter in this function, data, is an object that will receive the data for the request.

Within the success() function, the first $.each() method processes each collection of items in the returned object. In this case, the object contains a single collection of team members. The first parameter for this function is the object returned by the request. Then, the second parameter is a function that processes each item in the collection using another $.each() method. Here, each item is a team member.

The first parameter of the second $.each() method is the *this* keyword, which refers to the current team member. Then, because the data for each team member consists of key/value pairs, the function for the second parameter accepts a key and a value. Within this function, the name, title, and bio items are appended to the div element with "team" as its id.

To refer to the value of each data item in the inner loop, this example uses object notation like this:

`value.name`

This refers to the name item in the object for the current item in the inner loop. If, for example, this inner loop is being executed for the second team member, the data for value.name is Damon, and the data for value.title is Director of Development. This shows how much easier it is to parse JSON data than XML data.

In general, to test the use of the $.getJSON() method, the file named in the URL has to be on a web server, not a file server. It must also be in the same domain as the web page that's making the request. However, a simple application like this one where the URL points to a JSON file instead of a file for processing the request and returning JSON can be tested on your file server or computer.

A web page that loads JSON data

The JSON file (team.json)

```
{"teammembers":[
    {
        "name":"Agnes",
        "title":"Vice President of Accounting",
        "bio":"With over 14 years of public accounting... "
    },
    {
        "name":"Damon",
        "title":"Director of Development",
        "bio":"Damon is the Director of Development for ... "
    }
]}
```

The HTML div element that receives the data

```
<div id="team"></div>
```

The jQuery

```
$(document).ready(function(){
    $.getJSON("team.json", function(data){
        $.each(data, function() {
            $.each(this, function(key, value) {
                $("#team").append(
                    "Name: " + value.name + "<br>" +
                    "Title: " + value.title + "<br>" +
                    "Bio: " + value.bio + "<br><br>"
                );
            });
        });
    });
});
```

Description

- To process the returned JSON data, you can use nested $.each() methods. The function in the first method will process each collection in the returned data (in this case, a single collection of team members).

- The function in the second $.each() method will process each item (team member) in the collection. It will have two parameters that represent the key and value of each item. Then, you can use object notation to get the fields in the returned data.

Figure 12-8   How to use the $.getJSON() method to load JSON data

How to send data with an Ajax request

Figure 12-9 shows how to send data with an Ajax request. To do that, you use the data parameter of a shortcut method to supply either a string or a map that contains the data. In this figure, the first example uses a string to send one name/value pair that asks for a "name" data item that has a value of "wilbur". The second example uses a map that's coded within braces to send the same name/value pair.

The $.get() methods in both of these examples also include a third parameter that names the function that is called if the request is successful. Then, you code this function after the $.get() method. This function has one parameter that receives the data returned by the Ajax request. Of course, you can also code the function as a parameter the way it's done in the other examples in this chapter.

In some Ajax applications, forms are used to get the data that should be sent with a request. In that case, you can use the helper methods in this figure to package the data that's sent with the request. The serialize() method collects the entries for a form as a string. The serializeArray() method collects the entries for a form as an array of name/value pairs.

The next example in this figure shows how the serialize() method works with a request for data. Here, the first statement in the ready event handler uses the serialize() method to encode the form entries as a string and save that string in a variable named formData. This is followed by a $.get() method that uses the formData variable as its data parameter.

Whenever you send data with an Ajax request, you have to coordinate the data that you send with your request with the way the script on the server is written. For instance, you can tell from the first two examples that the PHP script in the file named getmanager.php accepts a data item named name. However, you can't tell if there are other data items that can be sent with a request.

Two ways to send data with an Ajax request

A $.get() method that uses a string for the data parameter

```
$(document).ready(function() {
    $.get("getmanager.php", "name=wilbur", showManager);
    function showManager(data) {
        // process data
    }
});
```

A $.get() method that uses a map for the data parameter

```
$(document).ready(function() {
    $.get("getmanager.php", {name:wilbur}, showManager);
    function showManager(data) {
        // process data
    }
});
```

The helper methods for working with Ajax

Function	Description
serialize()	Encode a set of form elements as a string that can be used for the data parameter of an Ajax request.
serializeArray()	Encode a set of form elements as an array of name/value pairs that can be used for the data parameter of an Ajax request.

The HTML for a form

```
<form id="contactForm">
    <!-- the controls for the form -->
</form>
```

jQuery that uses the serialize() method

```
$(document).ready(function() {
    var formData = $("#contactForm").serialize();
    $.get("processcontact.php", formData, processReturnedData);
    function processReturnedData(data) {
        // the statements for the success function
    }
});
```

Description

- When you send data with an Ajax request, the URL is for a server-side script such as a PHP file. Then, the script is responsible for returning the data in XML or JSON format.

- The data parameter in a jQuery shortcut method is a name/value pair that can be set either as a query string or a map.

- The jQuery helper functions for Ajax make it easy to package form data before sending it to the server.

Figure 12-9   How to send data with an Ajax request

How to use the $.ajax() method for working with Ajax

The syntax of the $.ajax() method

Figure 12-10 presents the syntax of the $.ajax() method, including some but not all of the options for this method. Besides a function that is executed when the request is successful, this method has options for functions that are done before the request is sent, when the request finishes, after the data is returned but before it is passed to the success() function, and when an error occurs. These functions give you more control over the way the method works.

Note in this summary that all four of these functions can have parameters. One of these parameters is jqXHR, which refers to the jQuery XHR object (or *jqXHR object*). This object is a superset of the standard XHR object that includes the properties of the XMLHttpRequest object. This means that you can use the properties in figure 12-3 with this object.

In the beforeSend() function, you can use the settings parameter to set properties in the jqXHR object before it is sent with the request. In the complete(), error(), and success() functions, the jqXHR object is passed to the function. The status parameter in these functions returns a string that represents the status of the request. And the error parameter in an error() function returns the text portion of the HTTP status.

The jsonp option is used to provide the name of a JSONP parameter that gets passed to the server. *JSONP*, or "JSON with padding", lets you request data from a server in a different domain, which is typically prohibited by web browsers due to their cross-domain security policies. JSONP is often used by the APIs for websites.

Other options for the $.ajax() method let you provide a password and username if they are needed for authentication. They also let you determine whether the returned data can be cached by the browser and how long a request can last before it times out as a failed request.

The syntax of the $.ajax() method

```
$.ajax({ options })
```

Some of the options for the $.ajax() method

Option	Description
`url`	The string for the URL where the request is sent.
`beforeSend(jqXHR, settings)`	A function that is executed before the request is sent. It can pass two parameters: the jqXHR object and a map of the settings for this object.
`cache`	A Boolean value that determines if the browser can cache the response.
`complete(jqXHR, status)`	A function that is executed when the request finishes. It can receive two parameters: the jqXHR object and a string that represents the status of the request.
`data`	A map or string that is sent to the server with the request, usually to filter the data that is returned.
`dataType`	A string that specifies the type of data (html, xml, json, script, or text).
`error(jqXHR, status, error)`	A function that is executed if the request fails. It can receive three parameters: the jqXHR object, a string that represents the type of error, and an exception object that receives the text portion of the HTTP status.
`jsonp`	A string containing the name of the JSONP parameter to be passed to the server. Defaults to "callback".
`password`	A string that contains a password that will be used to respond to an HTTP authentication challenge.
`success(data, status, jqXHR)`	A function that is executed if the request is successful. It can receive three parameters: the data that is returned, a string that describes the status, and the jqXHR object.
`timeout`	The number of milliseconds after which the request will time out in failure.
`type`	A string that specifies the GET or POST method.
`username`	A string that contains a user name that will be used to respond to an HTTP authentication challenge.

Description

- The $.ajax() method provides options that give you more control over the way the Ajax request works, such as providing a function for handling errors.

- The *jqXHR object* is jQuery's superset of the standard XMLHttpRequest object that provides the properties of that object.

- *JSONP*, or "JSON with padding", is a complement to JSON data that lets you request data from a server in a different domain, which is typically prohibited by web browsers due to their cross-domain security policies.

Figure 12-10   The syntax of the $.ajax() method

How to use the $.ajax() method to load data

When successful, the application in figure 12-11 is like the one in figure 12-7. However, the $.ajax() method sets the timeout option to 10000 milliseconds so it will time out with an error after 10 seconds. In addition, it provides two functions besides the function for successful completion.

In the beforeSend option, you can see the function that is executed before the Ajax request is sent. It just displays "Loading ..." in the div element that will receive the requested data, as shown in this figure. Of course, you could make this more interesting by displaying an animated gif like a progress indicator or a spinning wheel.

In the error option, you can see the function that is executed if an error occurs. This function is coded with three parameters: "xhr" for the jqXHR object, "status" for the string that describes the type of error that occurred, and "error" for the text portion of the HTTP status. Within the function, an alert() method is used to display the status of the request (xhr.status), a hyphen, and then the text portion of the HTTP status (error). If, for example, a 404 error occurs, an alert dialog box like the one in this figure will be displayed. This, of course, is a common error when the URL that's specified can't be found.

In the success option, you can see the function for processing the data that's returned. This function has a parameter named "data" that will receive the data returned by the request. Then, the code within this function is the same as the code in the function for the $.get() method in figure 12-7. The first statement uses the html() method to set the data in the div element with "team" as its id to an empty string. In this case, that replaces the "Loading..." message that was displayed while the request was being processed. The rest of the code uses the find() method to find the "management" data in the XML file, uses the children() method to get the children (team members) within the management data, and uses the each() method to process the data for each child.

A web page with a loading message and an alert dialog box for an error

The XML file

```
<management>
    <teammember>
        <name>Agnes</name>
        <title>Vice President of Accounting</title>
        <bio>With over 14 years of public accounting ... </bio>
    </teammember>
    ...
</management>
```

The HTML div element that receives the data

```
<div id="team"></div>
```

The jQuery

```
$(document).ready(function() {
    $.ajax({
        type: "get",
        url: "team.xml",
        beforeSend: function() {$("#team").html("Loading...");},
        timeout: 10000,
        error: function(xhr, status, error) {
            alert("Error: " + xhr.status + " - " + error);
        },
        dataType: "xml",
        success: function(data) {
            $("#team").html("");
            $(data).find("management").children().each(function() {
                var xmlDoc = $(this);
                $("#team").append("<h3>" +
                    xmlDoc.find("name").text() + "</h3>" +
                    xmlDoc.find("title").text() + "<br>" +
                    xmlDoc.find("bio").text() + "<br>");
            });
        }
    });
});
```

Description

- When successful, this application works like the one in figure 12-7. However, it also provides a timeout value and two functions besides the one for successful completion of the request.

Figure 12-11   How to use the $.ajax() method to load data

How to use Ajax with Flickr

Once you know how to use Ajax, you have the skills that you need for getting data from popular websites like YouTube, Twitter, and Flickr. In fact, you can get data from any website that provides an API for that.

To give you an idea of how this works, this chapter will now show you how to use Ajax with the API for Flickr. The goal here is not so much to show you how to use Flickr, but rather how to use the API for any website that lets you retrieve data using a URL.

How to use the feed API for Flickr

Flickr is a website that lets you store photos on it for free. This means that you can access your photos anywhere you are as long as you can connect to this website. Since you can also store a description for each photo that includes a thumbnail image and text within HTML tags, this site can also be used as a simple Content Management System (CMS).

The first table in figure 12-12 lists the feeds that Flickr provides. The feed you'll use most often is the public photos & video feed, and that's the one you'll learn about in the rest of this chapter. This feed allows unauthenticated, public access to any Flickr photos. To see the documentation for this feed, you can go to the URL at the top of this figure.

To retrieve data from the public photo feed, you start with the base URL shown in this figure. Then, you add one or more of the query parameters shown in the second table. To retrieve photos only for a specific user, for instance, you can include the id parameter as illustrated in the first example in this figure. To retrieve photos based on one or more tags that have been added to the photos, you can use the tags parameter. For instance, the first example retrieves all photos with the tag "vectacorp", and the second example retrieves all photos with the tags "waterfall" and "yosemite".

Note that both of these examples also include the jsoncallback parameter. This parameter is required when the format parameter is set to "json", as it is in the examples throughout this chapter. This will cause JSONP to be used as a complement to JSON. As you learned earlier in this chapter, this lets you request data from a server in a different domain, which is typically prohibited by web browsers due to their cross-domain security policies.

Incidentally, the default format for a Flickr feed is the Atom Syndication Format, which is an XML language and a W3 standard. Another common format that Flickr supports is RSS. In this chapter, though, JSON is used for all of the web feeds.

The URL for the Flickr public feed documentation

www.flickr.com/services/feeds/docs/photos_public/

Flickr feeds

Feed	Description
Public photos & video	Returns public content matching specified criteria.
Friends photostream	Returns public content from the contacts, friends, and family of a specified user.
Public favorites from a user	Returns public favorites for a specified user.
Group discussions	Returns recent discussions from a specified group.
Group pools	Returns items recently added to the pool of a specified group.
Forum discussions	Returns recent topics from the Flickr forum.
Recent activity	Returns recent activity for a specified user.
Recent comments	Returns recent comments by a specified user.

The base URL for retrieving a public photo stream

http://api.flickr.com/services/feeds/photos_public.gne

Common query parameters for the public photos feed

Parameter	Description
id	A user id.
ids	A comma-delimited list of user ids.
tags	A comma-delimited list of tags that identify the photos.
tagmode	Controls whether the returned items must match all of the tags specified or any of the tags specified. The default is all.
format	The format of the returned feed. Atom 1.0 is the default.
lang	The display language of the feed. The default is English.
jsoncallback	Optional unless the return format is set to JSON. Then, this parameter must be coded as jsoncallback=?

A URL that gets a JSON feed for a specific user id (in one line)

http://api.flickr.com/services/feeds/photos_public.gne?
id=82407828@N07&format=json&jsoncallback=?&tags=vectacorp

A URL that gets a JSON feed for all users (in one line)

http://api.flickr.com/services/feeds/photos_public.gne?
&format=json&jsoncallback=?&tags=waterfall,yosemite

Description

- Flickr is a website that lets you store your photos on it for free. That means you can access your photos wherever you are.

- Flickr provides a number of feeds that you can retrieve photos and related information from. In this chapter, you'll learn how to retrieve photos from the public photos & video feed. To do that, you use a URL with one or more query parameters as shown above.

Figure 12-12   How to use the feed API for Flickr

How to display Flickr data on a page

The table in figure 12-13 summarizes the Flickr data items that are returned from a photo feed. Here, the items data item represents the collection of returned items. You can use this item as the first parameter for the $.each() method to process each item. Then, within the callback function for the $.each() method, you can use the other data items in this table.

The example in this figure illustrates how this works. To start, the parameters of the URL are set so photos of waterfalls in Yosemite taken by all users will be returned in JSON format. Then, the $.getJSON() method is used to get the data from the public photo feed. Within the callback function for this method, the first statement declares a variable named html that will be used to store the HTML for the photos.

Next, the $.each() method is used to process each returned item. The callback function for this method formats the HTML for each item. This function receives two parameters. The first parameter is the index of the current item in the collection. The second parameter is the item itself.

In this case, the callback function includes the title of the photo as the content of an h2 element in the HTML. It also includes the URL for the photo (media.m) as the value of the src attribute of an img element. This is followed by an empty <p> element to add space between the items.

After all of the items are processed, the last statement in the callback function for the $.getJSON() method uses the html() method to set the HTML contents of an element with an id of "photos" to the value of the html variable. This causes the data for the photo feed to be displayed on the page.

Although it isn't used in this example, you should realize that the description data item is formatted as HTML in <p> elements. Because of that, you don't have to add the HTML like you do when you use the other data items. In addition, you should realize that the first <p> element contains the name of the user who posted the photo, along with a link to that user's page on Flickr. If the same user posted each photo, you'll probably want to remove this paragraph. You'll see how to do that in figure 12-15.

Data items returned by a photo feed

Data item	Description
items	The collection of returned items.
title	The title of the photo.
link	The URL for the Flickr page for the photo.
media.m	The URL for the photo.
date_taken	The date the photo was taken.
description	Descriptive text for a photo, plus a thumbnail image in an <a> element that links to the full photo on the Flickr site. This data is formatted with HTML tags so it's ready for display.
published	The date and time the photo was uploaded to Flickr.
author	The author's username and email.
author_id	The author's id.
tags	The filtering tags for a photo.

jQuery code that gets the titles and photos from a photo feed

```
var url = "http://api.flickr.com/services/feeds/photos_public.gne?" +
    "format=json&jsoncallback=?&tags=waterfall,yosemite";

$.getJSON(url, function(data){
    var html = "";
    $.each(data.items, function(i, item){
        html += "<h2>" + item.title + "</h2>";
        html += "<img src=" + item.media.m + ">";
        html += "<p></p>";
    });

    $("#photos").html(html);
});
```

Description

- You can use the $.getJSON() method that you learned about earlier in this chapter to get data from a Flickr feed. The data that's returned includes the items listed above.

- You can use the $.each() method with a callback function to process each item in the collection of items that's returned. The callback function receives two parameters: the index of the collection item and the item itself.

- The description data item consists of two or three <p> elements. The first <p> element contains a link to the user who posted the photo. If the same user posted each photo, you'll probably want to remove this paragraph. You can do that using JavaScript as shown in figure 12-15.

- The second <p> element in the description data item contains a thumbnail image within an <a> element that links to the image on the Flickr site.

- The third <p> element in the description data item is optional and can contain descriptive text.

Figure 12-13   How to display Flickr data on a page

How to review the feed from a website

In some cases, it may be helpful to see the JSON data that's returned from a website. That can help you identify the data items that you can use in your application in case they're not included in the documentation for the API or they're difficult to find in the documentation. That can also help you review the value of the data items so you can be sure that the correct data is displayed on a web page.

Figure 12-14 shows an easy way to display the data from a feed. Here, the URL for the Flickr feed that was shown in figure 12-13 has been copied and pasted into the address bar of a browser. Then, when the Enter key was pressed, the JSON data that will be returned to the application is displayed.

If you review this data, you can see that it's easy to tell what data items the feed contains. For instance, this example shows all of the data items for the first two items with the specified tags. Note that all of these items are contained within a data item named items. You saw how this item is used in the previous figure.

The Flickr feed for the URL in figure 12-13

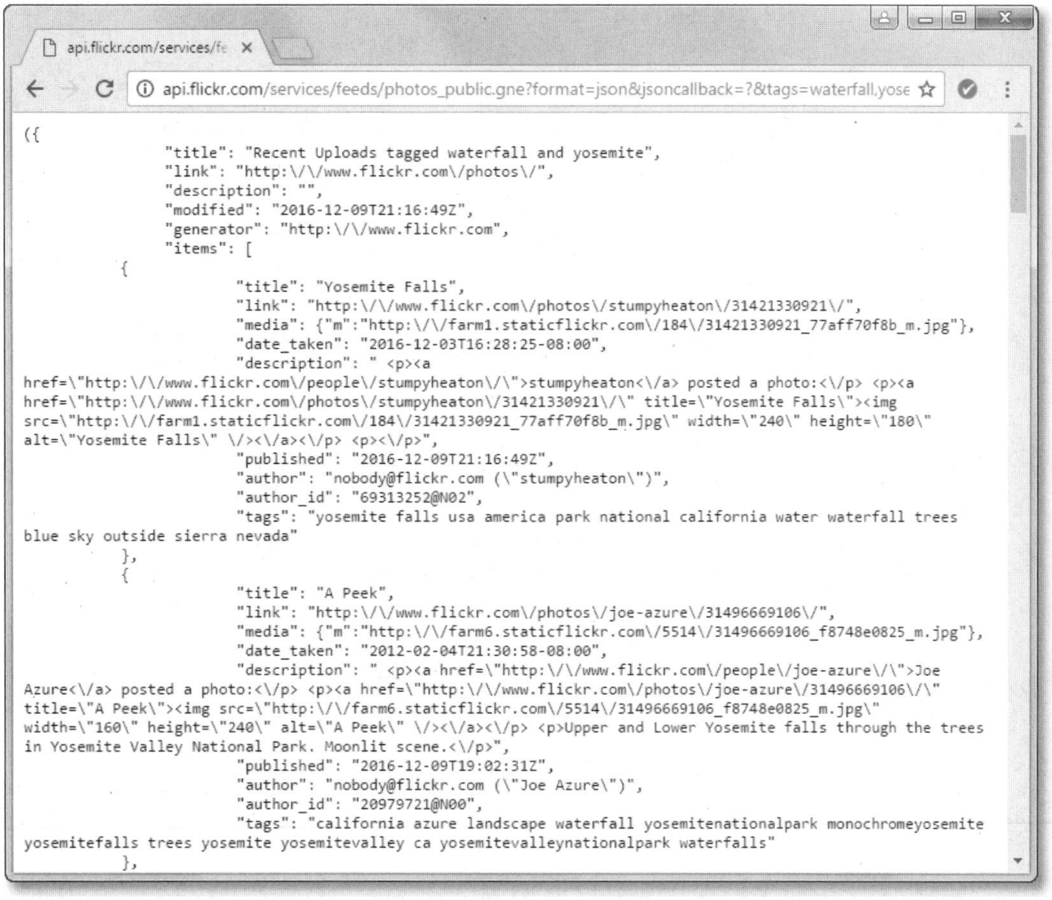


```
({
		"title": "Recent Uploads tagged waterfall and yosemite",
		"link": "http:\/\/www.flickr.com\/photos\/",
		"description": "",
		"modified": "2016-12-09T21:16:49Z",
		"generator": "http:\/\/www.flickr.com",
		"items": [
	   {
			"title": "Yosemite Falls",
			"link": "http:\/\/www.flickr.com\/photos\/stumpyheaton\/31421330921\/",
			"media": {"m":"http:\/\/farm1.staticflickr.com\/184\/31421330921_77aff70f8b_m.jpg"},
			"date_taken": "2016-12-03T16:28:25-08:00",
			"description": " <p><a
href=\"http:\/\/www.flickr.com\/people\/stumpyheaton\/\">stumpyheaton<\/a> posted a photo:<\/p> <p><a
href=\"http:\/\/www.flickr.com\/photos\/stumpyheaton\/31421330921\/\" title=\"Yosemite Falls\"><img
src=\"http:\/\/farm1.staticflickr.com\/184\/31421330921_77aff70f8b_m.jpg\" width=\"240\" height=\"180\"
alt=\"Yosemite Falls\" \/><\/a><\/p> <p><\/p>",
			"published": "2016-12-09T21:16:49Z",
			"author": "nobody@flickr.com (\"stumpyheaton\")",
			"author_id": "69313252@N02",
			"tags": "yosemite falls usa america park national california water waterfall trees
blue sky outside sierra nevada"
	   },
	   {
			"title": "A Peek",
			"link": "http:\/\/www.flickr.com\/photos\/joe-azure\/31496669106\/",
			"media": {"m":"http:\/\/farm6.staticflickr.com\/5514\/31496669106_f8748e0825_m.jpg"},
			"date_taken": "2012-02-04T21:30:58-08:00",
			"description": " <p><a href=\"http:\/\/www.flickr.com\/people\/joe-azure\/\">Joe
Azure<\/a> posted a photo:<\/p> <p><a href=\"http:\/\/www.flickr.com\/photos\/joe-azure\/31496669106\/\"
title=\"A Peek\"><img src=\"http:\/\/farm6.staticflickr.com\/5514\/31496669106_f8748e0825_m.jpg\"
width=\"160\" height=\"240\" alt=\"A Peek\" \/><\/a><\/p> <p>Upper and Lower Yosemite falls through the trees
in Yosemite Valley National Park. Moonlit scene.<\/p>",
			"published": "2016-12-09T19:02:31Z",
			"author": "nobody@flickr.com (\"Joe Azure\")",
			"author_id": "20979721@N00",
			"tags": "california azure landscape waterfall yosemitenationalpark monochromeyosemite
yosemitefalls trees yosemite yosemitevalley ca yosemitevalleynationalpark waterfalls"
	   },
```

Description

- To review a feed from the Flickr website, you can type or paste the URL for the feed into the address bar of your browser. Then, when you press the Enter key, you can see the contents of the JSON feed in the browser window.
- The JSON feed identifies the data items that you can use in your application. This is particularly important when you use Flickr because these items aren't identified in the documentation.
- You may also want to use this technique when the documentation for an API is difficult to understand. This can often save you time because you can tell exactly what data the application is going to get.

Figure 12-14 How to review the feed from a website

How to display descriptions for a Flickr photo feed

Figure 12-15 shows how to display the descriptions for the photos in a Flickr feed. In the example at the top of this figure, you can see the description for the first photo in the feed. Here, the description starts with a thumbnail image of the full image. This thumbnail is followed by text that describes the photo.

In the jQuery code for this application, you can see the parameters that are used for the URL. These parameters retrieve photos posted by a specific user that have a specific tag. The $.getJSON() and $.each() methods that follow are similar to the ones you saw in the previous figure. In this case, though, the description data item is used instead of the media.m data item.

Because the description data item is already formatted as HTML, it's just assigned to the html variable. To understand how this works, this figure presents the description for the first item in the JSON feed. As described in figure 12-13, the first paragraph includes a link to the user who posted the photo. Because this information isn't needed in this example, the last line of the jQuery code in the callback function for the $.each() method replaces this paragraph with an empty string. To do that, it uses the replace() method of a String object, which replaces the string in the first parameter with the string in the second parameter.

To get this replacement to work right, the first parameter in the replace() method must exactly match the data in the description. To make sure it does, you can paste the URL for the feed into the address bar of your browser and open the feed as described in the previous figure. Then, you can copy and paste the HTML that you want to replace. Note that this will only work if the HTML is the same for each item. In this case, this works because all of the photos were posted by the same user.

The next paragraph in the description contains an img element for a thumbnail image coded within an <a> element. The href attribute for this <a> element is set to the URL of the full image on the Flickr site. That way, if the user clicks on the thumbnail, the Flickr page for this photo will be displayed. Finally, the third paragraph contains the descriptive text for the photo.

A web page that displays titles and descriptions for a photo feed

The HMTL element that will receive the data from the feed

```
<div id="team"></div>
```

The jQuery that retrieves and displays the data

```
$(document).ready(function(){
    var url = "http://api.flickr.com/services/feeds/photos_public.gne?" +
              "id=82407828@N07&format=json&jsoncallback=?&tags=vectacorp";

    $.getJSON(url, function(data) {
        var html = "";
        $.each(data.items, function(i, item){
            html += "<h3>" + item.title + "</h3>";
            html += item.description;
            // Remove the first paragraph of the description
            html = html.replace(
                    "<p><a href=\"http://www.flickr.com/people/" +
                    "82407828@N07/\">zakruvalcaba<\/a>" +
                    " posted a photo:<\/p>", "");
        });
        $("#team").html(html);
    });
});
```

The description for the first item in the JSON feed

```
<p><a href="http://www.flickr.com/people/82407828@N07/">
    zakruvalcaba</a> posted a photo:</p>
<p><a href="http://www.flickr.com/photos/82407828@N07/7550727774/"
        title="Herbert"><img src="http://..." alt="Herbert" /></a></p>
<p>Herbert joined Vecta Corp. in October 1999 as Vecta Corp's ...</p>
```

Description

- This application uses the description data item to display the photo as well as the descriptive text. Because the description is formatted with HTML tags, it's not necessary to do that in the jQuery code.

- Because the thumbnail image in the description is within an <a> element, clicking on it goes to the full image on the Flickr site.

Figure 12-15   How to display descriptions for a Flickr photo feed

How to search for photos by tags

So far, you've seen examples that retrieve photos from Flickr that were posted by a specific user, that had specific tags, or that did both. Now, figure 12-16 shows how you can retrieve photos that have been posted by anyone and that have one or more tags entered by the user. Here, the results are shown after the user enters the tags "yacht" and "racing" and·clicks on the Search button.

The HTML for this web page includes two input elements. The first one is for the text box where the user enters the tags for the search. The second one is for the Search button that causes the photos to be retrieved. This HTML also includes a div element that will receive the data from the feed.

The jQuery for this application starts by defining a variable named searchTerm that will hold the tags entered by the user. Then, the click event handler for the Search button starts by setting this variable to an empty string. Next, it uses an if statement to determine if the user entered a value in the text box. If not, an alert() method is used to display a dialog box that tells the user that one or more tags must be entered. If so, the searchTerm variable is set to the value that was entered. Then, that variable is used as the value of the tags parameter in the URL for the query that will be sent to Flickr.

The rest of the code is similar to what you've seen in previous figures. It uses the $.getJSON() method to get the data from Flickr. Then, within the $.each() method, it gets the title, image, and tags for each photo and formats it as HTML. Finally, it sets the HTML for the div element so it contains that data.

A web page that searches for photos by tags

The HTML that gets the tags and receives the data from the feed

```
Search by tags: <input type="text" size="30" id="search">
<input type="button" value="Search" id="btnSearch">
<h1>Flickr Results</h1>
<div id="photos"></div>
```

The jQuery

```
$(document).ready(function(){
    var searchTerm;
    $("#btnSearch").click(function() {
        searchTerm = "";
        if ($("#search").val() == "") {
            alert("You must enter one or more tags!"); }
        else {
            searchTerm = $("#search").val();

            var url =
              "http://api.flickr.com/services/feeds/photos_public.gne?" +
              "format=json&jsoncallback=?&tags=" + searchTerm + "&tagmode=all";

            $.getJSON(url, function(data){
                var html = "";
                $.each(data.items, function(i, item){
                    html += "<h2>" + item.title + "</h2>";
                    html += "<img src=" + item.media.m + ">";
                    html += "<p><b>Tags: </b>" + item.tags + "</p>";
                });
                $("#photos").html(html);
            });
        }
    });
});
```

Figure 12-16   How to search for photos by tags

Perspective

Now that you've completed this chapter, you should be able to use jQuery to make Ajax requests that return HTML, XML, and JSON data from your server. You should also be able to use Ajax along with an API to get data from Flickr. These are powerful skills that are commonly used in modern websites.

Terms

Ajax (Asynchronous JavaScript and XML)
XMLHttpRequest (XHR) object
API (Application Programming Interface)
XML (eXtensible Markup Language)

JSON (JavaScript Object Notation)
member
cross-domain security policy
jqXHR object
JSONP

Summary

- *Ajax*, which stands for *Asynchronous JavaScript and XML*, lets you get data from a web server without refreshing the page. This means that a page can display new information based on the user's actions without the normal delays.

- To make an Ajax request possible, modern browsers provide an *XMLHttpRequest (XHR) object*. This object is used to make the request as well as receive the returned data. An enhanced version of this object called the *jqXHR object* is used with Ajax requests that are done with jQuery.

- When you use Ajax, you use JavaScript (or jQuery) to make the request, process the returned data, and update the DOM so the data is displayed on the web page.

- The three common data formats for Ajax are HTML, *XML* (*eXtensible Markup Language*), and *JSON* (*JavaScript Object Notation*). Because JSON makes it easier to parse the returned data, it has become the most popular format for working with Ajax.

- To make Ajax programming easier, jQuery provides shorthand methods like the $.get() and $.getJSON() methods, the $.ajax() method, the $.each() method, and two serialize methods for packaging form data so it can be used with an Ajax request.

- Many Ajax requests are processed on the web server by programs or scripts in languages like PHP or ASP.NET. Then, the web developers have to coordinate their Ajax requests with the programs or scripts that process the requests.

- *JSONP*, or "Jason with Padding", lets you get JSON data from a server in a different domain. This gets around the *cross-domain security policy* that most browsers have.

- Many popular websites such as Blogger, YouTube, Twitter, and Flickr provide *APIs* (*Application Programming Interfaces*) that let you use Ajax to get data from their sites.

Exercise 12-1   Enhance a Flickr application

In this exercise, you'll enhance a Flickr application so it includes additional information. When you're done, the web page should look like this:

Yosemite waterfalls

Spectacular Yosemite Sunset!

2016-12-12T08:25:09-08:00

<u>deepaksviewfinder</u> posted a photo:

Spectacular Sunset shot from Yosemite's Tunnel View. When we pulled in, nothing was really visible; heavy fog covered everything. Patience definitely paid off. We waiting along with about 3 dozen or more Photographers and the fog did eventually lift to give us a Spectacular Sunset. via 500px <u>ift.tt/2gEpHWI</u>

Will G Nagel OberonBlue

2016-09-15T14:31:59-08:00

<u>OberonBlue</u> posted a photo:

Dog Lake

Review the Flickr application

1. Use your text editor to open the HTML file in this folder:

    `javascript_jquery\exercises\ch12\flickr\`

2. Review the URL that's used to retrieve the data from Flickr, and notice that it includes two tags but no id.

3. Run the application to see that it displays the title and photo for each item that's returned. Point to any photo to see that it's not linked to the Flickr website.

Add additional information

4. Replace the last statement in the callback function for the $.each() method with a statement that adds the description data item to the html variable. Then, run the application to see that each photo is followed by a link to the author's Flickr page, a duplicate photo, and descriptive text (if there is any).

5. Click on any of the duplicate photos to see that it displays the photo on the Flickr website. Then, close the new tab or web page for the photo.

6. Use figure 12-14 as a guide to display the JSON feed that's returned to the application. Review this information for the first few items, paying particularly close attention to the HTML in the description data item.

7. Replace the statement in the jQuery code that adds an img element for the media.m data item to the html variable with a statement that adds a <p> element for the date_taken data item.

8. Improve the formatting for the data that's displayed. At the least, add some space below the paragraphs. Note, however, that you have no control over how the person who posted the photo entered the descriptive text.

Section 3

Advanced JavaScript skills

If you've read section 2, you know that you use jQuery for DOM scripting and you use JavaScript for everything else that an application has to do. That's why section 3 presents the other JavaScript skills that you're going to need as you build client-side applications.

In chapter 13, you'll learn more about working with numbers and strings, and you'll also learn how to work with dates. In chapter 14, you'll learn more about using control structures as well as how to handle exceptions and how to use regular expressions. In chapter 15, you'll learn how to work with the web browser, including how to use cookies and web storage. And in chapter 16, you'll learn more about working with arrays, including how to use associative arrays and arrays of arrays.

Then, the last two chapters in this book will take your JavaScript skills to a new level. In chapter 17, you'll learn how to create and use your own objects. In chapter 18, you'll learn how to use closures, modules, and immediately invoked function expressions (IIFEs). And at the end of that chapter, you'll learn how to create your own JavaScript plugins.

What's interesting about the chapters in this section is that all of the applications show how to apply the JavaScript skills that you learn as well as the jQuery skills that you learned in section 2. In other words, the applications are coded as they would be in the real world.

13

How to work with numbers, strings, and dates

In chapter 2, you learned some basic skills for working with numbers, strings, and dates. Now, you'll learn the other essential skills for working with data in your JavaScript applications.

How to work with numbers

In chapter 2, you learned how to declare numeric variables and perform common arithmetic operations. Then, in chapter 4, you learned how to round a decimal value to a fixed number of decimal places. Now, you'll build on those skills.

How to use the properties and methods of the Number object

Figure 13-1 starts with a table that summarizes five properties of the Number object that you can use to represent special values. For instance, Number.MAX_VALUE represents the largest positive value that can be represented by JavaScript. Curiously, each language has a maximum value that it can represent and JavaScript's is approximately 1798 followed by 305 zeros (an extremely large number). Similarly, MIN_VALUE is an extremely small number, POSITIVE_INFINITY is any number greater than the maximum value, and NEGATIVE_INFINITY is any number smaller than the minimum value.

The last property in this table stands for "not a number", which represents any non-numeric value. Because NaN can represent around 9 quadrillion different values, the equality test NaN == NaN will always return false. That's why you must use the isNaN() method to test whether a value is not a number.

When you code these properties, you always use Number as the object name as shown in the table. That's because these are *static properties*. However, you can also refer to the last three values in this table by using their shortcut names. For instance, the first example in this figure shows how to test a result for Infinity, -Infinity, or NaN and display an appropriate message.

When you divide 0 by 0 with JavaScript, the result is NaN. However, when you divide a non-zero number by zero, the result is either Infinity or -Infinity, depending on the sign of the non-zero number. This is different than the way most languages handle this. In other languages, division by zero usually results in a runtime error.

These examples are followed by a table that presents two methods of a Number object. Remember that a Number object is created when a numeric value is stored in a variable. Then, you can use the methods of the Number object to work with the values in these objects.

For instance, the first example after this table shows how to use the toFixed() method. Here, the third statement rounds the number 1.49925 to two decimal places, or 1.50. However, because the toFixed() method returns a string, this statement also uses the parseFloat() method to store the rounded value as a number in the tax variable, which converts it to 1.5. Then, the last statement in this example uses the toFixed() method again to ensure that any number that was rounded to 0 in the hundreds place is correctly displayed with two digits. As a result, 1.5 is converted to 1.50 before it is displayed by the alert() method.

Properties of the Number object

Property	Shortcut	Description
`Number.MAX_VALUE`		The largest positive value that can be represented.
`Number.MIN_VALUE`		The smallest positive value that can be represented.
`Number.POSITIVE_INFINITY`	`Infinity`	Represents positive infinity.
`Number.NEGATIVE_INFINITY`	`-Infinity`	Represents negative infinity.
`Number.NaN`	`NaN`	Represents a value that isn't a number.

Example 1: Testing for Infinity, -Infinity, and NaN

```
if ( result == Infinity ) {
    alert( "The result exceeds " + Number.MAX_VALUE ); }
else if ( result == -Infinity ) {
    alert( "The result is below " + Number.MIN_VALUE ); }
else if ( isNaN(result) ) {
    alert( "The result is not a number" );
else { alert( "The result is " + result ); }
```

Example 2: Division by zero

```
alert( 0 / 0 );                      // Displays NaN
alert( 10 / 0 );                     // Displays Infinity
```

Methods of a Number object

Method	Description
`toFixed(digits)`	Returns a string with the number rounded to the specified decimal digits.
`toString(base)`	Returns a string with the number in the given base. If base is omitted, 10 is used.

Example 3: Using the toFixed() method

```
var subtotal = 19.99, rate = 0.075;
var tax = subtotal * rate;           // tax is 1.49925
tax = parseFloat( tax.toFixed(2) );  // tax is 1.5
alert ( tax.toFixed(2) );            // displays 1.50
```

Example 4: Implicit use of the toString() method for base 10 conversions

```
var age = parseInt( prompt("Please enter your age.") );
alert( "Your age is " + age );
```

Description

- Any numerical operation that results in a number greater than Number.MAX_VALUE will return the value Infinity, and any operation that results in a number less than Number.MIN_VALUE will return the value -Infinity.

- Any numerical operation with a non-numeric operand will return NaN.

- You cannot test for equality with the value NaN. You must use the global method isNaN() to test if a value is NaN.

- Division of zero by zero results in NaN, but division of a non-zero number by zero results in either Infinity or -Infinity.

- The toString() method with no parameters is used implicitly whenever JavaScript needs to convert a number to a string.

Figure 13-1   How to use the properties and methods of the Number object

The last example in figure 13-1 shows how the toString() method is used implicitly by JavaScript. Here, the integer value in age is automatically converted to a string by the toString() method when age is concatenated with a string literal. This implicit conversion is done whenever a number is used in an expression that mixes string and number values. Occasionally, though, you may want to use the toString() method explicitly.

How to use the properties and methods of the Math object

Figure 13-2 shows how to use one of the properties and some of the common methods of the Math object. When you use them, Math is the object name because the property is a *static property* and the methods are *static methods*.

The first example shows you how to use the PI property, which returns the value of π. In this example, the PI property is used to calculate the area of a circle whose radius is 3.

The second example shows you how to use the abs(), or absolute value, method. When given a negative number, it returns that number as a positive value.

The third example shows you how to use the round() method. Note that in the third statement, -3.5 rounds up to -3. It does not round down to -4.

The fourth example shows you how to use the ceil() (ceiling) and floor() methods. The ceil() method always rounds a fractional value towards positive infinity. The floor() method always rounds a fractional value towards negative infinity.

The fifth example shows you how to use the pow() and sqrt() methods. The power parameter of the pow() method can be a fractional value. In the second statement, 125 is raised to the 1/3rd power. This is the equivalent of taking the cube root of 125.

The sixth example shows you how to use the min() and max() methods. These methods are not limited to two parameters, so you can supply as many parameters as needed. Then, these methods will find the minimum or maximum value in the list of parameters.

The last example shows how to use the exponentiation operator of ECMAScript 2015+ to raise a value to a specified power. This is an alternative to the pow() method of the Math object.

The Math object also provides many trigonometric and logarithmic methods. If you have the appropriate mathematical background, you should be able to use these methods with no problem. If you use them, though, one point to remember is that the trigonometric methods use radians to measure angles, not degrees.

One property of the Math object

Property	Description
`Math.PI`	Returns 3.141592653589793, which is the ratio of the circumference of a circle to its diameter

Example 1: The PI property

```
var area = Math.PI * 3 * 3;          // area is 28.274333882308138
```

Common methods of the Math object

Method	Description
`Math.abs(x)`	Returns the absolute value of x.
`Math.round(x)`	Returns the value of x rounded to the closest integer value. If the decimal part is .5, x is rounded up to the next higher integer value.
`Math.ceil(x)`	Returns the value of x rounded to the next higher integer value.
`Math.floor(x)`	Returns the value of x rounded to the next lower integer value.
`Math.pow(x, power)`	Returns the value of x raised to the power specified. The power may be a decimal number.
`Math.sqrt(x)`	Returns the square root of x.
`Math.max(x1, x2, ...)`	Returns the largest value from its parameters.
`Math.min(x1, x2, ...)`	Returns the smallest value from its parameters.

Example 2: The abs() method

```
var result_2a = Math.abs(-3.4);      // result_2a is 3.4
```

Example 3: The round() method

```
var result_3a = Math.round(12.5);    // result_3a is 13
var result_3b = Math.round(-3.4);    // result_3b is -3
var result_3c = Math.round(-3.5);    // result_3c is -3
var result_3d = Math.round(-3.51);   // result_3d is -4
```

Example 4: The floor() and ceil() methods

```
var result_4a = Math.floor(12.5);    // result_4a is 12
var result_4b = Math.ceil(12.5);     // result_4b is 13
var result_4c = Math.floor(-3.4);    // result_4c is -4
var result_4d = Math.ceil(-3.4);     // result_4d is -3
```

Example 5: The pow() and sqrt() methods

```
var result_5a = Math.pow(2,3);       // result_5a is 8 (the cube of 2)
var result_5b = Math.pow(125, 1/3);  // result_5b is 5 (cube root of 125)
var result_5c = Math.sqrt(16);       // result_5c is 4
```

Example 6: The min() and max() methods

```
var x = 12.5, y = -3.4;
var max = Math.max(x, y);            // max is 12.5
var min = Math.min(x, y);            // min is -3.4
```

The exponentiation operator of ECMAScript 2015+

```
var result_7a = Math.pow(2,3);       // result_7a is 8 (2³)
var result_7b = 2 ** 3;              // result_7b is 8 (2³)
```

Figure 13-2   How to use the properties and methods of the Math object

How to generate a random number

The random() method of the Math object generates a random number that is equal to or greater than zero but less than one. This is illustrated by the first example in figure 13-3. Often, though, you want a random number that is in a range other than from zero to one.

The second example presents a function that will generate a random number in a range between 1 and a specified maximum. The getRandomNumber() function takes a single parameter, which is the maximum value for the range of random numbers that the function should generate.

This function first declares a variable named random. This variable will hold the random number that's generated by the function. Next, the function validates the max parameter to ensure it is a number. If it fails the isNaN test, the function simply returns the random variable declared at the beginning of the function. This variable has not been assigned a value yet, so that means if the max parameter is not a number, the getRandomNumber() function returns undefined.

If the max parameter is a number, the function computes a whole number between 1 and max. To do this, the function gets a value from the random() method and multiplies it by the value of max. It then uses the floor() method to round the number down to the nearest integer and adds 1 to this result.

For example, if max is 6, then 6 times a random number between 0 and 1 returns a value from 0 to just less than 6. Then, using the floor() method rounds the number down to an integer that ranges from 0 to 5, and adding 1 to it returns a random number in the requested range.

The getRandomNumber() function in this figure is a simple one, but you could easily improve it by making it so you can pass in the minimum value for the range or have a range of decimals in addition to a range of whole numbers. There are many online examples of random number generation that you can use as examples.

The random() method of the Math object

Method	Description
`Math.random()`	Returns a random decimal number >= 0.0 but < 1.0.

Example 1: Generating a random number

```
var result = Math.random();
```

Example 2: A function that generates a random number

```
var getRandomNumber = function(max) {
    var random;

    if (!isNaN(max)) {
        // value >= 0.0 and < 1.0
        random = Math.random();

        // value is an integer between 0 and max - 1
        random = Math.floor(random * max);

        // value is an integer between 1 and max
        random = random + 1;
    }
    //if max is not a number, will return undefined
    return random;
};

// Returns an integer that ranges from 1 through 100
var randomNumber = getRandomNumber(100);
```

Description

- You can use the getRandomNumber() function in this figure to generate a random number between 1 and the specified maximum value.

- Random numbers can be used for testing and are often used in games or applications that provide animation.

- There are many ways to use the Math.random() function to create a random number generator. If you do an Internet search, you will find many examples, some with more extensive functionality than the simple generator shown here.

Figure 13-3 How to generate a random number

The PIG application

Figure 13-4 shows the user interface for a dice game called PIG. This application requires the use of just one die and illustrates the use of a random number generator.

When the application starts, the two bottom rows of the game are hidden. Then, the players enter their names into the Player 1 and Player 2 text boxes and click the New Game button to start the game. This displays the bottom two rows of the interface with the first player's name shown.

From that point on, the players take turns until one of them reaches 100 and wins. For each turn, a player can click the Roll button one or more times. If the player rolls a 2 or higher, that number is added to the player's points for that turn. Then, the player can click the Hold button to keep the points that have been earned during that turn. If the player rolls a 1 before clicking the Hold button, though, the turn ends and the player gets zero points for that turn.

The HTML

As this figure shows, the HTML for this application consists primarily of labels, text boxes, and buttons. Most important, of course, are the id attributes because these are the ones that are used in the JavaScript. That's why they're highlighted in this figure.

As you can see, the section at the bottom of the HTML has the id of "turn" and doesn't have a class attribute. This section is hidden when the application starts because the CSS sets its display property to "none". To display it, the JavaScript adds a class named "open" to this element, and the CSS for this class sets the display attribute to "block". If you want to see the CSS for this application, you can of course review it in the downloaded application.

Not shown in this figure are the script elements for the JavaScript files. Like all the applications in this section of the book, this one uses jQuery for DOM scripting, so the first script statement identifies the jQuery library. Then, the second script statement identifies the JavaScript file for this application.

The user interface for the PIG application

The HTML for the application

```html
<h1>Let's Play PIG!</h1>
<fieldset>
    <legend>Rules</legend>
    <ul>
        <li>First player to 100 wins.</li>
        <li>Players take turns rolling the die.</li>
        <li>Turn ends when player rolls a 1 or chooses to hold.</li>
        <li>If player rolls a 1, they lose all points earned ...</li>
        <li>If player holds, points earned during the turn ...</li>
    </ul>
</fieldset>
<label for="player1">Player 1</label>
    <input type="text" id="player1" >
<label for="score1">Score</label>
    <input type="text" id="score1" value="0" disabled><br>
<label for="player2">Player 2</label>
    <input type="text" id="player2">
<label for="score2">Score</label>
    <input type="text" id="score2" value="0" disabled>
<input type="button" id="new_game" value="New Game"><br>
<section id="turn">
    <p><span id="current"> </span>'s turn</p>
    <input type="button" id="roll" value="Roll">
    <input type="button" id="hold" value="Hold">
    <label for="die">Die</label>
        <input type="text" id="die" disabled>
    <label for="total">Total</label>
        <input type="text" id="total" disabled>
</section>
```

Figure 13-4   The HTML for the PIG application

The JavaScript

Figure 13-5 presents the JavaScript for this application. Like all of applications in this section of the book, this one starts with the jQuery ready() function. This ready() function contains two functions and three event handlers for the New Game, Roll, and Hold buttons.

The first function is the getRandomNumber() function that you reviewed in figure 13-3. The second is the changePlayer() function that's called when the turn for one player ends. The if statement in this function changes the name in the "current" span element to the name that's in the text box for the other player. Then, it sets the values of the "die" and "total" text boxes to zero and the focus to the Roll button.

The event handler for the click event of the New Game button starts by resetting the scores for the players to zero. Then, the if statement checks whether the name in the text box for either player is an empty space (blank). If either is, this function removes the "open" class from the "turn" section, which hides the last two rows in the user interface, and it displays a message that says the players must enter their names. Otherwise, the else clause of the if statement sets the class attribute for the section to "open", and calls the changePlayer() function.

The event handler for the click event of the Roll button starts by getting the total value for that turn from the "total" text box. Then, it calls the getRandomNumber() function to get the result of one roll of the die. If the result is 1, the total is reset to zero and the changePlayer() function is called. Otherwise, the result of the roll is added to the total value, and the die and total values are displayed in their text boxes so the player can roll again.

The event handler for the click event of the Hold button starts by declaring a variable named score and getting the total value from the "total" text box. Next, an if statement tests whether the current player is player 1. If so, the code gets the score1 Textbox object and stores it in the score variable. Otherwise, it gets the score2 Textbox object, and stores it in the score variable. Then, it sets the new value of the score Textbox object to the value of the score Textbox object plus the total value. Finally, if the score value is greater than or equal to 100, an alert dialog box is displayed that declares the winner and the newGame() function is called. Otherwise, the changePlayer() function is called.

The JavaScript for the application

```javascript
$( document ).ready(function() {
    var getRandomNumber = function(max) {
        var rand;
        if (!isNaN(max)) {
            random = Math.random();
            random = Math.floor(random * max);
            random = random + 1;
        }
        return rand;
    };
    var changePlayer = function() {
        if ( $("#current").text() == $("#player1").val() ) {
            $("#current").text( $("#player2").val() );
        } else {
            $("#current").text( $("#player1").val() );
        }
        $("#die").val("0");
        $("#total").val("0");
        $("#roll").focus();
    };
    $("#new_game").click( function() {
        $("#score1").val("0");
        $("#score2").val("0");
        if ( $("#player1").val() == "" || $("#player2").val() == "" ) {
            $("#turn").removeClass("open");
            alert("Please enter two player names.");
        } else {
            $("#turn").addClass("open");
            changePlayer();
        }
    });
    $("#roll").click( function() {
        var total = parseInt( $("#total").val() );
        var die = getRandomNumber(6);
        if (die == 1) {
            total = 0;
            changePlayer();
        } else { total = total + die; }
        $("#die").val(die);
        $("#total").val(total);
    });
    $("#hold").click( function() {
        var score;
        var total = parseInt( $("#total").val() );
        if ( $("#current").text() == $("#player1").val() ) {
            score = $("#score1");
        } else { score = $("#score2"); }

        score.val( parseInt( score.val() ) + total );
        if (score.val() >= 100) {
            alert( $("#current").text() + " WINS!" );
            newGame();
        } else { changePlayer(); }
    });
});
```

Figure 13-5   The JavaScript for the PIG application

How to work with strings

In chapter 2, you learned how to create and work with simple strings. Then, in chapter 4, you learned one property and a few of the methods of the String object. Now, you'll review this property and these methods and you'll learn about some other methods.

How to use the properties and methods of the String object

Figure 13-6 describes one property and several methods of String objects. The length property lets you find out how many characters are in a string. This is illustrated by the first example. Because the positions in a string are numbered from zero, not 1, the last character in a string is at the position identified by the length minus 1.

Example 2 in this figure shows you how to use the charAt() method. Here, the J in JavaScript is the character at position 0, and the character at position 4 is S.

Example 3 shows you how to use the concat() method. If you specify more than one parameter, the strings are concatenated in order. This is the same operation performed by the + operator when one of the two operands is a string. Although there was a performance difference between using + and the concat() method in earlier implementations of JavaScript, there is little difference today. As a result, you can usually use whichever coding method you prefer. You'll see the use of both methods in this book.

Example 4 shows the use of the indexOf() method. If you omit the position parameter, the search is performed from the start of the string. If the search string isn't found, the method returns -1.

Example 5 shows the use of the substr() and substring() methods. Note that the character specified in the end parameter for the substring() method is *not* included in the result. If start is greater than end, the two values are swapped. If either value is less than 0, it is replaced with 0. If either value is greater than the length of the string, it is replaced with the length of the string.

Example 6 shows you how to use the toUpperCase() and toLowerCase() methods. These methods have no parameters, but don't forget to include the empty set of parentheses after the method name.

One property of a String object

Property	Description
length	The number of characters in the string.

Example 1: Displaying the length of a string

```
var message_1 = "JavaScript";
var result_1 = message_1.length;            // result_1 is 10
```

Methods of a String object

Method	Description
charAt(*position*)	Returns the character at the specified position in the string.
concat(*string1*, *string2*, ...)	Returns a new string that is the concatenation of this string with each of the strings specified in the parameter list.
indexOf(*search*, *start*)	Searches the string for the first occurrence of the search string starting at the position specified or the beginning if the position is omitted. If the search string is found, it returns the position in the string. If not found, it returns -1.
substr(*start*, *length*)	Returns the substring from start position through the number of characters specified by the length parameter.
substring(*start*)	Returns the substring from the start position to the end of the string.
substring(*start*, *end*)	Returns the substring from the start position to, but not including, the end position.
toLowerCase()	Returns the string with uppercase letters converted to lowercase.
toUpperCase()	Returns the string with lowercase letters converted to uppercase.

Example 2: The charAt() method

```
var message_2 = "JavaScript";
var letter = message_2.charAt(4);           // letter is "S"
```

Example 3: The concat() method

```
var message_3 = "Java";
var result_3 = message_3.concat("Script"); // result_3 is "JavaScript"
```

Example 4: The indexOf() method

```
var result_4a = message_2.indexOf("a");     // result_4a is 1
var result_4b = message_2.indexOf("a", 2); // result_4b is 3
var result_4c = message_2.indexOf("s");     // result_4c is -1
```

Example 5: The substr() and substring() methods

```
var result_5a = message_2.substr(4, 5);     // result_5a is "Scrip"
var result_5b = message_2.substring(4);     // result_5b is "Script"
var result_5c = message_2.substring(0,4);   // result_5c is "Java"
```

Example 6: The toLowerCase() and toUpperCase() methods

```
var result_6a = message_2.toLowerCase();    // result_6a is "javascript"
var result_6b = message_2.toUpperCase();    // result_6b is "JAVASCRIPT"
```

Figure 13-6   How to use the properties and methods of the String object

Examples of working with strings

In the previous figure, you saw simple examples that used the string methods. Now, figure 13-7 shows you how to perform more complex manipulations by using combinations of string methods and loops. This should give you some ideas for how you can apply these methods in your own applications.

Example 1 shows how to trim the spaces off the beginning of a string by using a function named ltrim() that takes the string to be trimmed as its only parameter. This function first initializes the start variable to 0. Then, a while loop tests the character at the start position. As long as it is a space, the start position is moved forward one character and the loop continues. The loop exits when it finds a non-space character, and the function returns the substring from the current value of the start position to the end.

Example 2 shows you how to use a function named rtrim() to trim spaces off the end of a string. This is like the ltrim() function, but the end variable is set to the last position in the string (length - 1). Then, the while loop tests the character at the end position. As long as it is a space, the end position is moved backward one character. The loop exits when it finds a non-space character, and the function then returns the substring from the beginning to the current value of the end position + 1. Here, end + 1 is used because the substring() method doesn't return the character specified by the end position.

Example 3 shows you how to trim spaces off both ends of a string by combining the ltrim() and rtrim() functions. This type of trimming is often done when working with user entries.

Example 4 shows how to perform a case insensitive test for equality between two strings. This is useful because the == operator is case sensitive when used with strings. This example just uses the toLowerCase() function to convert each string to lowercase before doing the comparison.

Example 5 shows you how to use a function named equalIgnoreCase() to perform a case insensitive test for equality between two strings. Like example 4, this function tests the equality of the two parameters that are passed to it after it converts them both to lowercase.

Example 1: How to trim spaces off the beginning of a string

```
var ltrim = function( text ) {
    var start = 0;
    while ( text.charAt(start) == " " ) {
        start++;
    }
    return text.substring(start);
};
var result = ltrim("  JavaScript");      // result is "JavaScript"
```

Example 2: How to trim spaces off the end of a string

```
var rtrim = function( text ) {
    var end = text.length - 1;
    while ( text.charAt(end) == " " ) {
        end--;
    }
    return text.substring(0, end + 1);
};
var result = rtrim("JavaScript    ");    // result is "JavaScript"
```

Example 3: How to combine ltrim and rtrim to trim all spaces

```
var trim = function( text ) {
    return ltrim( rtrim(text) );
};
var result = trim("  JavaScript    ");    // result is "JavaScript"
```

Example 4: How to compare two strings ignoring case

```
var text1 = "JavaScript";
var text2 = "javascript";
if ( text1.toLowerCase() == text2.toLowerCase() ) {
    alert("The strings are the same.");
}
```

Example 5: A function for comparing two strings while ignoring case

```
var equalIgnoreCase = function( text1, text2 ) {
    return text1.toLowerCase() == text2.toLowerCase();
};

if ( equalIgnoreCase("JavaScript", "javascript") ) {
    alert("The strings are the same.");
}
```

Figure 13-7   Examples of working with strings

How to work with dates and times

In chapter 4, you learned how to create Date objects and how to use four methods for working with them. In this topic, you'll learn more about creating Date objects and using the methods of those objects.

In JavaScript, dates are represented by the number of milliseconds since midnight, January 1, 1970. Positive values come after this date while negative values come before. Internally, the dates are stored in universal time, or Greenwich Mean Time (GMT). However, JavaScript has access to the time zone on the client's computer and adjusts the dates to the local time.

How to create Date objects

Figure 13-8 presents four ways to create Date objects with JavaScript. The first example shows how to create a Date object that represents the local time on the user's computer. This is done by specifying the Date constructor with no parameters. This is the method that you learned in chapter 4.

The second example shows how to create a Date object by specifying a date and time in a string parameter. In this case, the year must be four digits, and the hours must be specified in 24-hour (or military) time. For example, 3:15pm is 15:15 on a 24-hour clock. If you omit the time, midnight is used.

The third example shows how to create a Date object by specifying the parts of the date. Here, year and month are required. Then, if day is omitted, 1 is used. And if any of the remaining date parts are omitted, 0 is used.

When you use this method, remember that the months are numbered from 0 through 11 where 0 is January and 11 is December. As a result, 3 is April and 10 is November. This makes it easier to use the month numbers with arrays, which are also numbered starting with 0.

The fourth example shows you how to create a Date object by copying another Date object. This lets you manipulate the copy without affecting the original. You'll learn more about that in the next two figures.

The last example shows you some unexpected results you might get if you use a string parameter with dashes or with a 2-digit year. Not all browsers produce these results, but some do, so you should keep this in mind when working with the Date object. If, for example, you're accepting dates from users, you'll want to validate them to make sure they're in a correct format before passing them as an argument to the Date object.

How to create a Date object that represents the current date and time

```
var now = new Date();
```

How to create a Date object by specifying a date string

```
var electionDay = new Date("11/6/2018");
var grandOpening = new Date("2/16/2017 8:00");
var departureTime = new Date("4/6/2017 18:30:00");
```

How to create a Date object by specifying date parts

Syntax of the constructor

```
new Date( year, month, day, hours, minutes, seconds, milliseconds )
```

Examples

```
var electionDay = new Date(2018, 10, 6);            // 10 is November
var grandOpening = new Date(2017, 1, 16, 8);        // 1 is February
var departureTime = new Date(2017, 3, 6, 18, 30);   // 3 is April
```

How to create a Date object by copying another Date object

```
var invoiceDate = new Date("8/8/2017");
var dueDate = new Date( invoiceDate );
// You can then add a number of days to due_date. See figure 13-10.
```

Some unexpected results when specifying a date string

```
var electionDay = new Date("11-6-2018");            // Invalid Date
var electionDay = new Date("11/6/18");              // 11/8/1916
```

How the constructor for the Date object works

- If you call the Date constructor with no parameters, it creates a new Date object and sets it to the current date and time.

- If you call the Date constructor with a string as the parameter, the constructor parses the string as a date or a date and time and uses it to create a new Date object. However, you may get unexpected results if you don't use slashes and a 4-digit year in the parameter.

- If you call the Date constructor with two or more numbers as parameters, the numbers are used in the order shown above to create a new Date object. In this case, year and month are required, but the remaining parameters are optional.

- If you call the Date constructor with another Date object as the parameter, it creates a new Date object that is a copy of the other Date object.

- If you call the Date constructor with parameters that aren't a valid date, it creates a new Date object that contains "Invalid Date".

Description

- In JavaScript, dates are represented by the number of milliseconds since midnight, January 1, 1970.

- When you create a Date object, the date and times are specified as local time. Local time is in the time zone specified on the computer that's running the user's web browser.

- Month numbers start with 0, so January is 0 and December is 11. This allows these values to be used with arrays.

Figure 13-8   How to create Date objects

The methods of the Date object

Figure 13-9 describes several methods that are provided by the Date object. The first group of methods creates a formatted string from a date. However, as the examples show, you can't control the format used by these methods. In the next figure, though, you'll learn how to create your own formats for date and time strings.

The methods in the second group are used to extract the parts from a Date object. Here, all of the methods except the getTime() method return the date part from the local time. In contrast, the getTime() method uses universal time. There is also a getYear() method that returns a two-digit year, but its use is not recommended.

The methods in the third group are used to set new values for the parts in a Date object. These methods let you use values that are outside the allowed range. Then, any value over or under the allowed range will cause the next most significant date part to roll over.

For example, if you set the hours of a date to 25, the time will be set to 1 and one day will be added to the day of the month. Or, if you set the day of the month to 0, the month will be rolled back one and the day will be set to the last day of that month. By letting you use values that are out of the normal range, JavaScript provides a mechanism to perform date math using any of the parts of the date or time. You'll see examples of this in the next figure.

The formatting methods of a Date object

Method	Description
`toString()`	Returns a string containing the date and time in local time using the client's time zone.
`toDateString()`	Returns a string representing just the date in local time.
`toTimeString()`	Returns a string representing just the time in local time.

Examples of the formatting methods
```
var birthday = new Date( 2017, 0, 7, 8, 25);     // Jan 7, 2017 8:25am
alert( birthday.toString() );         // "Sat Jan 07 2017 08:25:00 GMT-0500"
alert( birthday.toDateString() );     // "Sat Jan 07 2017"
alert( birthday.toTimeString() );     // "08:25:00 GMT-0500"
```

The get methods of a Date object

Method	Description
`getTime()`	Returns the number of milliseconds since midnight, January 1, 1970 in universal time (GMT).
`getFullYear()`	Returns the four-digit year in local time.
`getMonth()`	Returns the month in local time, starting with 0 for January.
`getDate()`	Returns the day of the month in local time.
`getDay()`	Returns the day of the week (1=Sunday, 2=Monday, and so on).
`getHours()`	Returns the hour in 24-hour format in local time.
`getMinutes()`	Returns the minutes in local time.
`getSeconds()`	Returns the seconds in local time.
`getMilliseconds()`	Returns the milliseconds in local time.

The set methods of a Date object

Method	Description
`setFullYear(year)`	Sets the four-digit year in local time.
`setMonth(month)`	Sets the month in local time.
`setDate(day)`	Sets the day of the month in local time.
`setHours(hour)`	Sets the hour in 24-hour format in local time.
`setMinutes(minute)`	Sets the minutes in local time.
`setSeconds(second)`	Sets the seconds in local time.
`setMilliseconds(ms)`	Sets the milliseconds in local time.

Description

- Except for the getTime() method, the get and set methods use the time zone specified on the user's computer to work with local time.

- There are complementary get and set methods that start with getUTC and setUTC that work with the Date object in universal time (GMT). For example, the getUTCHours() method returns the hour in 24-hour format in universal time.

Figure 13-9   The methods of the Date object

Examples of working with dates

Figure 13-10 shows how you can apply the methods of the last figure. The first example shows you how to format a date. The last three examples show you how to perform calculations with dates. This should give you some ideas for how you can use Date objects in your own applications.

Example 1 shows you how to format a date. To do that, the JavaScript code first creates a new Date object that contains a date and time. Next, it extracts the year, month, and date parts, and it adds 1 to the month number. Then, it builds a text string using these values. As the string is built, the month and date numbers are padded with a leading zero if they are less than ten.

Example 2 shows you how to calculate the number of days from the current date until the New Year. First, the current date is retrieved in a Date object and a copy of this object is made. Then, the month and day in the copy are set to January 1st, and 1 is added to the year. At this point, the now variable contains the current date and the newYear variable contains the January 1st date.

Next, the number of milliseconds between the two dates is calculated by subtracting the dates that are extracted by the getTime() method. Then, the number of days is calculated by dividing the number of milliseconds by the number of milliseconds in one day (86,400,000) and rounding that value up using the ceil() method. Last, a message is displayed that indicates the number of days remaining. To do that, an if-else statement is used to alter the message when there is only one day left.

Example 3 shows you how to calculate a due date. Here, the invoiceDate variable contains a Date object with the current date. Then, a dueDate variable is created that contains a Date object with the same date as the one in the invoiceDate variable. Last, 21 is added to the date in the dueDate object so the due date is 21 days after the invoice date.

Example 4 shows you how to determine the last day of the current month. Here, the endOfMonth variable starts at today's date. Then, 1 is added to the month, and the day is set to zero. This rolls the date back one day, which causes 1 to be subtracted from the month and the day of the month to be set to the last day of the month. If, for example, the current date is December 2, adding 1 to the month number rolls it over to month 0, or January. Then, when the date is set to zero, the date and month roll back to December 31.

Example 1: How to display the date in your own format

```
var departTime = new Date(2017, 3, 6, 18, 30);        // Apr. 6, 2017 6:30pm
var year = departTime.getFullYear();
var month = departTime.getMonth() + 1;     // add 1 since months start at 0
var day = departTime.getDate();

var dateText = year + "-";
if (month < 10) {
    month = "0" + month; // pad month
}
dateText += month + "-";
if (day < 10) {
    day = "0" + day;        // pad day
}
dateText += day;
// final dateText is "2017-04-06"
```

Example 2: How to calculate the days until the New Year

```
var now = new Date();              // get the current date and time
var newYear = new Date(now);       // copy the current date and time
newYear.setMonth(0);               // set the month to January
newYear.setDate(1);                // set the day to the 1st
newYear.setFullYear( newYear.getFullYear() + 1 );    // add 1 to the year

var timeLeft = newYear.getTime() - now.getTime();    // time in milliseconds
var daysLeft = Math.ceil( timeLeft / 86400000 );     // convert ms to days

var message = "There ";
if (daysLeft == 1) {
    message += "is one day";
}
else {
    message += "are " + daysLeft + " days";
}
message += " left until the New Year.";

// If today is April 6, 2017, message is
// "There are 271 days left until the New Year."
```

Example 3: How to calculate a due date

```
var invoiceDate = new Date();
var dueDate = new Date( invoiceDate );
dueDate.setDate( dueDate.getDate() + 21 );   // due date is 3 weeks later
```

Example 4: How to find the end of the month

```
var endOfMonth = new Date();

// Set the month to next month
endOfMonth.setMonth( endOfMonth.getMonth() + 1 );

// Set the date to one day before the start of the month
endOfMonth.setDate( 0 );
```

Figure 13-10   Examples of working with dates

The Count Down application

To illustrate the use of strings and dates, the next two figures present a Count Down application. This web application accepts an event name and event date from a user and calculates the number of days until that event. To do that, this application uses a Date object for the calculation and a String object to create the message that's displayed.

The HTML and CSS

In figure 13-11, you can see the HTML and CSS for this application. In the head element of the HTML, you can see the two script elements for the JavaScript files. The first one identifies the jQuery library. The second one identifies the JavaScript file that's shown in the next figure.

The HTML in the main element consists of two text boxes and a button. When the user enters data into the text boxes and clicks the Countdown! button, the number of days until the event is displayed in the <p> element below the button.

As before, the id attributes for these elements are the ones that are used in the JavaScript. That's why they're highlighted in this figure.

In the CSS in this figure, you can see the rule set for the <p> element that has "message" as its id attribute. This sets the font color to red and the font weight to bold.

The user interface for the Count Down application

Countdown To...

Event Name: Tax Day

Event Date: 4/17/2017

[Countdown!]

67 day(s) until tax day! (Mon Apr 17 2017)

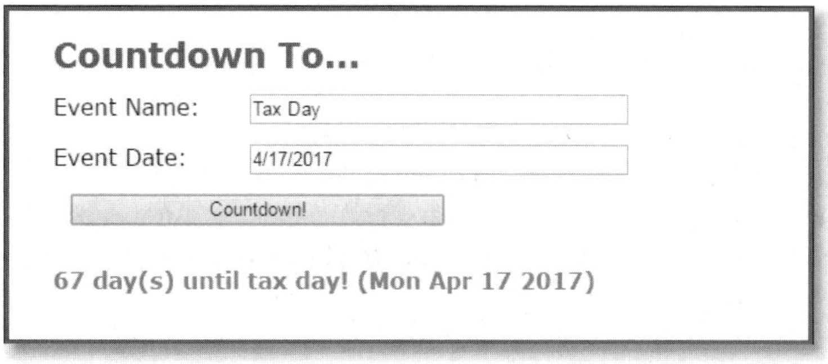

The HTML for the application

```html
<!DOCTYPE html>
<html>
<head>
    <title>Countdown To...</title>
    <link rel="stylesheet" href="countdown.css">
    <script src="https://code.jquery.com/jquery-3.1.1.min.js"></script>
    <script src="countdown.js"></script>
</head>
<body>
    <main>
        <h1>Countdown To...</h1>

        <label for="event">Event Name:</label>
        <input type="text" name="event" id="event"><br>

        <label for="date">Event Date:</label>
        <input type="text" name="date" id="date"><br>

        <input type="button" name="countdown" id="countdown"
            value="Countdown!">

        <p id="message"> </p>
    </main>
</body>
</html>
```

The CSS rule set for the <p> element

```css
#message {
    font-weight: bold;
    color: red;
}
```

Figure 13-11   The HTML and CSS for the Count Down application

The JavaScript

As before, the JavaScript in figure 13-12 starts with the jQuery ready() function. This ready() function contains just one event handler. It is for the click event of the Countdown button.

This event handler starts by getting the event name and date that the user entered. Then, it retrieves the <p> element with "message" as its id and stores it in a variable named message. It's important to note that the first two lines just get the value of an element, while the last one gets the element itself. This element is the one that displays messages to the user, and you'll see how it's used by the code shortly.

Next, the code starts a series of data validation checks using if statements. First, it uses the length property of the String object to make sure that the user entered something for the event and the event date. Second, it uses the indexOf() method of the String object to make sure the date has been entered with slashes. Third, it uses the substring() method of the String object to get the last four characters of the date string, and then uses the isNaN() method to make sure those characters are a number. Fourth, it uses the date string entered by the user to create a new Date object, and then checks to see if the object contains "Invalid Date".

If any of these data validation checks fail, they use the text() method of the of the <p> element in the message variable to display an appropriate error message and then return. This means that as soon as a check fails, the message is displayed and the function stops running.

If all the data validation checks pass, the code calculates the number of days until the event. To do that, it creates a new Date object with the current date and stores it in the today variable. It calculates the number of milliseconds in a day and stores it in the oneDay variable. It uses the getTime() method of the Date object to subtract the today value from the event date value, which are both in milliseconds, and divides the result by the oneDay value, which is in milliseconds. The result of this calculation is then rounded up using the Math.ceil() method and stored in the days variable, which now represents the number of days until the event.

Next, this function checks to see if the date entered by the user is in the future, in the past, or is today's date. If the number of days is zero, the date entered by the user is today. If the number of days is less than zero, the date is in the past. And if the number of days is greater than zero, the date is in the future. For each result, this function constructs a different message and uses the text() method of the <p> element to display that message.

To build these messages, the concat() method of the String object is used. Notice that you can call this method whether you are working with a string variable like event or days.toString() or with a string literal like "Hooray! Today is ". Depending on the message, the event name is either made all lower case by using the toLowerCase() method or capitalized by using the substring and toUpperCase() methods. And in each message, the date entered by the user is displayed using the toDateString() method of the Date object.

The JavaScript for the Countdown application

```javascript
$( document ).ready(function() {

    $("#countdown").click( function() {
        var event = $("#event").val();
        var dt = $("#date").val();
        var message = $("#message");

        // make sure task and due date are entered
        if (event.length == 0 || dt.length == 0) {
            message.text( "Please enter both a name and a date." );
            return;
        }
        // make sure due date string has slashes and a 4-digit year
        if (dt.indexOf("/") == -1) {
            message.text( "Please enter the date in MM/DD/YYYY format." );
            return;
        }
        var year = dt.substring(dt.length - 4);
        if (isNaN(year)) {
            message.text( "Please enter the date in MM/DD/YYYY format." );
            return;
        }
        // convert due date string to Date object and check for validity
        var date = new Date(dt);
        if (date == "Invalid Date") {
            message.text( "Please enter the date in MM/DD/YYYY format." );
            return;
        }

        // calculate days
        var today = new Date();
        var oneDay = 24*60*60*1000; // hrs * mins * secs * milliseconds
        var days = ( date.getTime() - today.getTime() ) / oneDay;
        days = Math.ceil(days);

        // create and display message
        if (days == 0) {
            message.text( "Hooray! Today is ".concat(event.toLowerCase(),
                "!\n(", date.toDateString(), ")") );
        }
        if (days < 0) {
            //capitalize event
            event = event.substring(0,1).toUpperCase() + event.substring(1);
            message.text( event.concat(" happened ", Math.abs(days),
                " day(s) ago. \n (", date.toDateString(), ")") );
        }
        if (days > 0) {
            message.text( days.toString().concat(" day(s) until ",
                event.toLowerCase(), "!\n(", date.toDateString(), ")") );
        }
    });

    $("#event").focus();
});
```

Figure 13-12   The JavaScript for the Count Down application

Perspective

This chapter has presented the essential skills for working with numbers, strings, and dates. To add to this skillset, you can read chapter 16, which shows how to use the string methods for working with arrays.

Terms

static property
static method

Summary

- To work with numeric data, you can use the *static properties* and *static methods* of the Number and Math objects. This includes the random() method of the Math object, which generates a random number from 0 to 1.

- The length property of a String object returns the number of characters in the string, and the methods of a String object let you work with the characters in the string.

- In JavaScript, dates are stored in Date objects, and they are represented by the number of milliseconds since midnight, January 1, 1970.

- The constructors of the Date object let you create a Date object in four different ways. Then you can use the methods of the Date object to work with the date in the object.

Exercise 13-1 Enhance the Future Value application

In this exercise, you'll enhance a Future Value application that looks like the one that follows. Along the way, you'll work with large numbers, use a random number generator, work with dates, and work with strings.

Future Value Calculator

Total Investment:	22471
Annual Interest Rate:	5
Number of Years:	36
Future Value:	$130,147.90
	Calculate

Today is 12/14/2016 at 12:16.

Open, review, and test the application

1. Use your text editor or IDE to open the index.html and future_value.js files for the Future Value application, which can be found in this folder:

   `javascript_jquery\exercises\ch13\future_value\`

   Then, test this application with valid values to see how it works.

2. Review the JavaScript code for this application. There you can see that the getRandomNumber() function of figure 13-3 has been copied into the file so you can use it later on.

Work with large numbers

3. Test this application with these values: 10000 for investment amount, 15 for interest rate, and 1000 for number of years. Notice that this returns the future value with e notation and as many significant digits as JavaScript provides for.

4. Change the entry for the number of years to 10000 and test the application again. This time, it returns Infinity for the future value amount. Runaway loops like this are a common error that causes an application to produce values of Infinity and -Infinity.

5. Modify the JavaScript by adding an if statement to the for loop that calculates the future value. This if statement should test whether future value is equal to infinity. If it is, the if statement should use the alert() method to display a message like this, where i is the counter for the loop:

   ```
   Future value = Infinity
   i = 4995
   ```

   This if statement should also set the value of i to the value of years so the loop will end.

6. Add an alert() method that displays the maximum value of a JavaScript number after the for loop finishes since this has nothing to do with the calculation. Then, test the application to see the alert messages that are displayed.

Use a random number generator

7. Comment out the three statements that get investment, rate, and years from the text boxes. Then, use the getRandomNumber() function to get random values for investment, rate, and years. The maximum values for these variables should be 50000, 15, and 50. The application should get these random values each time the user clicks the Calculate button, these values should be displayed in the first three text boxes, and future value should be calculated using these values.

8. Comment out the alert() method that you added in step 6. Then, test this application by clicking on the Calculate button several times to see how the values are varied. This illustrates how a random number generator can be used to quickly test an application with a wide range of values.

Format the future value with a dollar sign and commas

9. Create a new function named formatFV() that gets the future value after it has been calculated and returns a formatted version of that value like the one shown above.

   To do this, you need to use the indexOf() method to get the location of the decimal point and the substring() method to extract the cents, hundreds, thousands, and millions digits from the future value. Then, you can concatenate the parts with a dollar sign, commas, and decimal point. The trick is that some future values won't have millions digits, so you need to provide for that with if statements.

10. Modify the click event handler for the Calculate button so it calls this method to format the future value after it has been calculated and then displays it in the future value text box.

Add the current date to the <p> element below the button

11. Start by creating a new function named getDate() that gets the current date and formats it like this:

    `Today is 04/15/2017 at 14:29.`

    To do that, you need to get a Date object that contains the current date. Then, you need to use the Date methods to extract the appropriate date and time parts so you can format them as shown above. Note that 24-hour format is used.

12. Modify the ready event handler so it calls the getDate() method to get the formatted date and then displays it in the <p> element below the button in the HTML.

14

How to work with control structures, exceptions, and regular expressions

In chapter 3, you were introduced to conditional expressions and the if, while, do-while, and for statements. Now, you'll learn more about coding these expressions and statements, including how to use the conditional operator and the switch, break, and continue statements.

After that, you'll learn how to handle any exceptions that might be thrown by an application, and how to use regular expressions. Both of these skills are useful when validating user input.

What else you need to know about control structures

In chapter 3, you learned how to code conditional expressions and how to use them in if, for, and while statements. Now, you'll learn more about using these structures.

How to use the equality and identity operators

In chapter 3, you learned how to use the *equality operators* that are shown at the top of figure 14-1. For simple comparisons, these operators work fine. But when the tests are more complex, unexpected results may occur, for two reasons.

First, the equality operators perform *type coercion*. This means that if different types of data are being compared, the values will be converted to the same data type before the comparison takes place. For example, in the test 3 == "3", the string "3" is converted to the number 3 and then the comparison is done.

Second, the type conversion that's done for type coercion is different from the type conversion that's done by the parseInt() and ParseFloat() methods. For instance, an empty string is converted to 0 during type coercion, but the parseFloat() method converts an empty string to NaN.

These problems can be avoided by using the *identity operators* presented in the second table in this figure. That's because the identity operators don't perform type coercion. Then, if two values of different types are compared, the result will always be false. For this reason, some IDEs consider the use of the identity operators a best practice, and warn you when you use equality operators.

How to use the break and continue statements

The break and continue statements give you additional control over how loops work. The *break statement* skips to the end of the current loop. The *continue statement* skips to the start of the next iteration of the loop.

The first example in figure 14-1 shows how the break statement can be used in a while statement that will loop forever because its condition is set to true. However, this loop will only run until the user enters a valid number in the prompt dialog box. Then, a break statement ends the loop so the entry can be processed.

The second example shows how the continue statement can be used in a while loop. Here, the loop runs while a number ranges from 1 to 40. Then, within the loop, the number is divided by 5 and the remainder is tested to see whether it is zero. If so, the continue statement skips to the start of the loop. If not, the number is added to the sum variable. When the loop ends, that sum is displayed in an alert dialog box. Although you could easily code this example so it doesn't require a continue statement, this illustrates how this statement can be used.

The equality operators

Operator	Description	Example
`==`	Equal	`lastName == "Hopper"`
`!=`	Not equal	`months != 0`

The identity operators

Operator	Description	Example
`===`	Equal	`lastName === "Hopper"`
`!==`	Not equal	`months !== 0`

Example 1: The break statement in a while loop

```
var number;
while (true) {
    number = parseInt( prompt("Enter a number from 1 to 10.") );
    if ( isNaN(number) || number < 1 || number > 10 ) {
        alert("Invalid entry. Try again."); }
    else {
        break;
    }
}
alert(number);
```

Example 2: The continue statement in a while loop

```
var sum = 0;
var number = 0;
while ( number <= 40 ) {
    number++;
    if ( number % 5 !== 0 ) {
        continue; }                    // if number isn't divisible by 5
    sum += number;
}
alert(sum);          // displays sum of 5, 10, 15, 20, 25, 30, 35, 40
```

Description

- The *equality operators* perform *type coercion* whenever that's necessary. That means they convert data from one type to another. For example, they often convert strings to numbers before the comparisons.

- However, the type conversion that's done by the equality operators is different from that done by the parseInt() or parseFloat() methods.

- The *identity operators* do not perform type coercion. If the two operands are of different types, the result will always be false.

- The *break statement* ends a loop. In other words, it jumps out of the loop.

- The *continue statement* ends the current iteration of a loop, but allows the next iteration to proceed. In other words, it jumps to the start of the loop.

- When you're working with nested loops, the break and continue statements apply only to the loop that they're in.

Figure 14-1   The equality and identity operators and the break and continue statements

How to use the switch statement

A *switch statement* is a convenient way to express a certain form of if statement. Specifically, it can be used in place of an if statement with multiple else if clauses in which one expression is tested for equality with several values. This is illustrated by the statements in figure 14-2.

The switch statement starts with the keyword *switch* followed by a *switch expression* inside of parentheses. This expression is not a conditional expression. It is an expression that returns a single value that will be used to determine which *case* to execute. The expression is often as simple as a single variable as shown in the examples in this figure.

When the switch statement is executed, it checks each of the values in the *case labels*. If it finds one that's equal to the result of the expression, it executes the code that follows that case label. It continues executing until it reaches either a *break statement* or the end of the switch statement.

If no case labels match the value in the switch expression, the switch statement starts executing the code that follows the default label. But this default case is optional. If it is omitted and no case labels match the expression, the switch statement won't execute any code.

In the first example in this figure, the expression is just a variable named letterGrade that should contain a letter. Then, each case label is checked against the value of this variable. If, for example, letterGrade is "B", the switch statement starts executing the code after the label for that case and sets the message variable to "above average". It then encounters a break statement and no further code is executed by the switch statement. If letterGrade had been "Z", however, the code after the default label would have been executed and the message would have been set to "invalid grade".

In the second example, the case labels are coded in a way that provides *fall through*. This occurs when code starts executing at one case label but doesn't encounter a break statement, so it passes another case label and keeps executing. Although this is often discouraged because it can be confusing, this example shows one case where fall through is useful.

In this example, the same code should be executed when letterGrade is "A" or "B". Instead of repeating the code, two case labels are placed before the code. Then, if letterGrade is "A", the switch statement will fall through and execute the code after the case for "B". Likewise, if letterGrade is "D", the switch statement will fall through and execute the code after the case for "F". Except for cases like this, though, you should avoid using fall through in your switch statements because that can lead to unexpected errors and be hard to debug.

When you use a switch statement, you can nest if statements within the cases. You can also nest switch statements within the cases of another switch statement. As always, you need to use caution with nesting since it can make your code confusing and hard to maintain.

A switch statement with a default case

```
switch ( letterGrade ) {
    case "A":
        message = "well above average";
        break;
    case "B":
        message = "above average";
        break;
    case "C":
        message = "average";
        break;
    case "D":
        message = "below average";
        break;
    case "F":
        message = "failing";
        break;
    default:
        message = "invalid grade";
        break;
}
```

A switch statement with fall through

```
switch ( letterGrade ) {
    case "A":
    case "B":
        message = "Scholarship approved.";
        break;
    case "C":
        message = "Application requires review.";
        break;
    case "D":
    case "F":
        message = "Scholarship not approved.";
        break;
}
```

Description

- The *switch statement* starts by evaluating the *switch expression* in the parentheses.

- After evaluating the expression, the switch statement transfers control to the *case label* that has the value that matches the value of the expression. Then, it executes the statements for that *case*. It stops executing when it reaches a *break statement* or the end of the switch statement.

- The default case is optional and may be omitted. If included, you can only have one default case. It is usually the last case in the switch statement, but it can be anywhere.

- If a case doesn't contain a break statement, execution will *fall through* to the next label.

- You can nest if statements or other switch statements within the cases of a switch statement.

Figure 14-2   How to use the switch statement

How to use the conditional operator

Figure 14-3 shows how to use JavaScript's *conditional operator*. This is JavaScript's only *ternary operator*, which means it has three operands. In contrast, a *unary operator*, such as **++**, has one operand and a *binary operator*, such as *****, has two operands.

Since the conditional operator has three operands, it needs two symbols to separate them. As the syntax at the top of this figure shows, the question mark and colon are used as the separators.

When executed, the conditional operator first evaluates the conditional expression to get a true or false result. Then, if the conditional expression is true, the result of the expression in the middle operand is used as the result of the conditional operator. If the conditional expression is false, the result of the expression in the last operand is used as the result of the conditional operator.

The first example in this figure shows how to use the conditional operator to set a variable to one of two values based on the comparison. If the age is 18 or more, message will contain "Can vote". If the age is less than 18, message will contain "Cannot vote".

The second example shows how to use an expression in one of the operands. If hours is over 40, overtime will contain 1.5 times the pay rate for the hours over 40. If hours is not over 40, overtime will be zero.

The third example shows how to select between a singular or plural ending for use in a message to the user. If errorCount is 1, the ending will be empty. Otherwise, "s" will be used for the ending.

The fourth example shows how to add one to a value or set it back to 1 depending on whether the value is at its maximum. For example, if maxValue is 10 and value is 6, the test will be false and value will become the value plus 1. However, when value reaches 10, it will be set to 1 rather than value.

If you need to perform this kind of rollover of a variable but the starting value is 0 instead of 1, you don't have to use the conditional operator. Instead, you can use the % operator. For example, if you execute this statement repeatedly with a starting value of 9

```
value = (value + 1) % 10
```

the values will range from 0 to 9 and then back to 0.

The fifth example shows how to combine the conditional operator with the return keyword so the result is returned by a function. Here, if number is greater than highest, highest is returned. Otherwise, the number is returned.

For clarity, it is often better to use if statements than conditional operators. This is illustrated by the last two examples in this figure. Nevertheless, many JavaScript programmers like to use conditional operators because it means less coding.

Syntax of the conditional operator

```
( conditional_expression ) ? value_if_true : value_if_false
```

Examples of using the conditional operator

Example 1: Setting a string based on a comparison

```
var message = ( age >= 18 ) ? "Can vote" : "Cannot vote";
```

Example 2: Calculating overtime pay

```
var overtime = ( hours > 40 ) ? ( hours - 40 ) * rate * 1.5 : 0;
```

Example 3: Selecting a singular or plural ending based on a value

```
var ending = ( errorCount == 1 ) ? "" : "s";
var message = "Found " + errorCount + " error" + ending + ".";
```

Example 4: Setting a value to 1 if it's at a maximum value when adding 1

```
var value = ( value == maxValue ) ? 1 : value + 1;
```

Example 5: Returning one of two values based on a comparison

```
return ( number > highest ) ? highest : number;
```

How conditional operators can be rewritten with if statements

Example 1 rewritten with an if statement

```
var message;
if ( age >= 18 ) {
    message = "Can vote";
} else {
    message = "Cannot vote";
}
```

Example 4 rewritten with an if statement

```
if ( value == maxValue ) {
    value = 1;
}
else {
    value = value + 1;
}
```

Description

- The conditional operator first evaluates the conditional expression. Then, if the expression is true, the value that results from the middle operand is returned. But if the expression is false, the value that results from the third operand is returned.

- Although the use of the conditional operator can lead to cryptic code, JavaScript programmers commonly use this operator. For clarity, though, conditional operators can be rewritten with if statements.

Figure 14-3   How to use the conditional operator

How to use the AND and OR operators for selections

In chapter 3, you learned how to use the logical operators AND and OR in compound conditional expressions. In that case, because each conditional expression returned a Boolean value, the entire expression returned a Boolean value. However, you can also use the AND and OR operators with other types of expressions.

Remember too that AND and OR are *short-circuit operators*, so the evaluation doesn't continue if one of the operands determines whether the entire expression is true or false. Because of that, these operators return the value of the last operand that's evaluated. As a result, you can use the AND and OR operators in *selections* that assign values to variables, as shown in figure 14-4.

In the first example, both operands use identity operators to return a Boolean value. This means that the OR operator will return a Boolean value. If, for example, the state variable is equal to "CA", the entire expression is going to be true, the evaluation stops, and true is stored in the selected variable. But if the state variable isn't equal to "CA", the evaluation continues and either true or false is returned based on the evaluation of the next operand.

In contrast, the second example could return several different data types, depending on the values of the operands. If the first operand is null or undefined, it's evaluated as false and the AND operator short-circuits. This means that the second operand isn't evaluated, and the AND operator returns the value of the first operand, which is null or undefined. Otherwise, the second operand is evaluated, and the result of calling the toString() method is returned. If the toString() method doesn't exist, the result of calling it is undefined. If it does exist, it returns a string.

The third example could also return several data types depending on the values of its operands, but it won't return null or undefined. If the first operand isn't null or undefined, it's evaluated as true and the OR operator short-circuits. This means the second operand isn't evaluated, and the OR operator returns whatever value the first operand contains. Otherwise, the second operand is evaluated, and it returns a string.

The fourth example shows how to use the OR operator to provide a default value. It assigns either the value of the dt variable or a new Date object to the selected variable. Specifically, if the value of the dt variable isn't null or undefined, its value is assigned to the selected variable. But if it is null or undefined, it evaluates as false and the second operand is evaluated. As a result, a new Date object is assigned to the selected variable.

Keep in mind that all of these examples can be rewritten by using if statements. That is illustrated by the rewrites of the four examples. If you study these, you'll get a better idea of what the selections are doing.

This also means that you may never have to use selections in your own coding. Nevertheless, it's good to know how they work because you'll often see them in the coding that's done by professional programmers. After you get used to seeing them, you may also find that they're useful in your own code.

Examples of selections

Example 1: An OR selection that returns a Boolean value of true or false

```
var selected = (state === "CA" || state === "NC");
```

Example 2: An AND selection that returns a null, undefined, or String value

```
var selected = state && state.toString();
```

Example 3: An OR selection that won't return null or undefined values

```
var selected = state || "CA";                    // state value or "CA"
```

Example 4: An OR selection that sets a default value

```
var selected = dt || new Date();
```

How these selection examples could be rewritten

Example 1

```
var selected = false;
if (state === "CA || state === "NC") {
    selected = true;
}
```

Example 2

```
var selected;
if ( state ) {
    selected = state.toString();
}
```

Example 3

```
var selected = "CA";
if (state) {
    selected = state;
}
```

Example 4

```
var selected = dt;
if ( !selected ) {
    selected = new Date();
}
```

Description

- The AND and OR operators return the value of the last operand they evaluate. Because of that, you can use them in *selections* and store the value they return in a variable.

- This works due to the *short-circuit evaluation* of the logical operators. This means that the AND and OR operators only evaluate the second expression if necessary.

- Although you can rewrite selections with if statements, professional programmers often use selections in their code.

Figure 14-4   How to use the AND and OR operators for selections

The Invoice application

The two figures that follow show a web application that calculates a discount amount and total for an invoice. This application uses some of the conditional expressions and selection structures described in this chapter to determine the discount percent.

Figure 14-5 shows the user interface for the Invoice application. It consists of a drop-down list, four text boxes, and a button. The drop-down list is used to select the type of customer: Regular, Loyalty Program, or Honored Citizen. The first text box accepts an invoice subtotal amount from the user. And the next three text boxes are used to display the results of the calculation.

The HTML

In the HTML, you can see that a select element is used for the drop-down list, and the values that it returns are "reg" for Regular, "loyal" for Loyalty Program, and "honored" for Honored Citizen. You'll see these values used by the JavaScript code in the next figure.

Otherwise, this code is similar to what you've been seeing. Of interest are the id attributes because they're used by the JavaScript code. Also, note that the last three text boxes have their disabled attributes turned on. This means that the user can't enter data into them and their backgrounds are shaded.

The user interface of the Invoice application

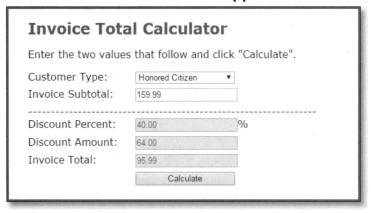

Some of the HTML for the application

```
<main>
    <h1>Invoice Total Calculator</h1>
    <p>Enter the two values that follow and click "Calculate".</p>

    <label for="type">Customer Type:</label>
    <select id="type">
        <option value="reg">Regular</option>
        <option value="loyal">Loyalty Program</option>
        <option value="honored">Honored Citizen</option>
    </select><br>

    <label for="subtotal">Invoice Subtotal:</label>
    <input type="text" id="subtotal"><br>
    -----------------------------------------------------------------<br><br>
    <label for="percent">Discount Percent:</label>
    <input type="text" id="percent" disabled>%<br>
    <label for="discount">Discount Amount:</label>
    <input type="text" id="discount" disabled><br>
    <label for="total">Invoice Total:</label>
    <input type="text" id="total" disabled><br>

    <label> </label>
    <input type="button" id="calculate" value="Calculate">
</main>
```

Description

- The Invoice application calculates a discount amount and a total for an invoice.
- It uses conditional expressions to calculate different discount amounts for different kinds of customers.

Figure 14-5   The HTML for the Invoice application

The JavaScript

The JavaScript code in figure 14-6 starts with the jQuery ready() event handler. After that, it declares the calculateDiscount() function, which receives the value of the customer type and the amount of the invoice subtotal. Then it uses a switch statement to check the customer type. A switch statement is used here because the code is evaluating a single expression, which is the value of the customer parameter.

The code after the first case label is executed if the customer type is Regular. This code has an if-else statement that checks the value of the subtotal parameter and returns a discount amount of zero for a subtotal under 100, 10% for a subtotal between 100 and 250, 25% for a subtotal between 250 and 500, and 30% for a subtotal greater than or equal to 500.

There are two things to note about the code in this first case label. First, it shows that you can nest an if statement within a switch statement. Second, it demonstrates when you'd use an if statement rather than a switch statement. You might think you could use a switch statement here because you're checking one thing, the value of the subtotal parameter. However, it's difficult (though not impossible) to use conditions like less than or greater than in a case label. Because of that, most programmers use if-else statements in this kind of scenario.

The code after the second case label is executed if the customer type is Loyalty Program. This code simply returns a discount rate of 30%. The code after the third case label is executed if the customer type is Honored Citizen. Here, the code uses the conditional operator to return a discount amount of 40% if the subtotal amount is less than 500, or 50% otherwise. Finally, the switch statement has a default label that returns a discount of zero in all other cases.

The event handler for the click event of the Calculate button starts by declaring three variables that will be used by the function as it does its processing. It then uses jQuery to get the values that the user entered for customer type and invoice subtotal. Note that it sets a default value of zero for the subtotal if the user left it blank. It also calls the parseFloat() method to convert the subtotal amount to a decimal.

Then, the code calls the calculateDiscount() function and passes it the customer type and subtotal values. The code then uses the discountPercent value returned by that function to calculate the discount amount and total amount of the invoice.

After that, the code reloads the subtotal text box so the subtotal entry will be displayed with two decimal digits. Then, the code uses jQuery to display the discount percent, discount amount, and invoice total in the related text boxes.

The event handler ends by setting the focus on the Customer drop-down list so the user can perform another calculation. The last line of the ready() function also sets the focus on the type drop-down list.

The JavaScript for the Invoice application

```javascript
$( document ).ready(function() {
    var calculateDiscount = function(customer, subtotal) {
        switch( customer ) {
            case "reg":
                if (subtotal < 100) {
                    return 0;
                } else if (subtotal >= 100 && subtotal < 250) {
                    return .1;
                } else if (subtotal >= 250 && subtotal < 500) {
                    return .25;
                } else if (subtotal >= 500) {
                    return .3;
                }
                break;
            case "loyal":
                return .3;
                break;
            case "honored":
                return (subtotal < 500) ? .4 : .5;
                break;
            default:
                return 0;
                break;
        }
    };

    $( "#calculate" ).click(function() {
        var discountAmount, invoiceTotal, discountPercent;

        var customerType = $("#type").val();
        var subtotal = $("#subtotal").val() || 0;  // default value of zero
        subtotal = parseFloat(subtotal);

        discountPercent = calculateDiscount(customerType, subtotal);
        discountAmount = subtotal * discountPercent;
        invoiceTotal = subtotal - discountAmount;

        $("#subtotal").val( subtotal.toFixed(2) );
        $("#percent").val( (discountPercent * 100).toFixed(2) );
        $("#discount").val( discountAmount.toFixed(2) );
        $("#total").val(  invoiceTotal.toFixed(2) );

        // set focus on type drop-down when done
        $("#type").focus();
    );

    // set focus on type drop-down on initial load
    $("#type").focus();
});
```

Figure 14-6   The JavaScript for the Invoice application

How to handle exceptions

Runtime errors can also be referred to as *exceptions.* Because exceptions shouldn't occur in real-world applications, most programming languages provide a way to handle the exceptions that are *thrown* by an application so the applications don't crash. This programming process is referred to as *exception handling.* In this topic, you'll learn how to handle exceptions in your JavaScript applications.

How to use try-catch statements

To handle exceptions in JavaScript, you use a *try-catch statement* as shown in figure 14-7. First, you code a *try block* around the statement or statements that may throw an exception. Then, you code a *catch block* that contains the statements that will be executed if an exception is thrown by any statement in the try block. If necessary, you can also code a *finally block* that is executed whether or not an exception is thrown, but that block is optional.

The first example in this figure shows how you can use a try-catch statement to catch any exceptions that are thrown in the try block. Then, if an exception is thrown by one of the statements in that block, the execution of the program jumps to the first statement in the catch block. In this example, the catch block contains just one alert() method that displays an error message.

When an exception is thrown, an Error object is created that contains information about the exception. To access the Error object, you code a variable name in the parentheses after the catch keyword. Then, you can use the name and message properties of the Error object in that variable to display the error information. This is illustrated by the catch block in the first example. Here, the variable name for the Error object is error, but it could be any valid name.

Of course, you don't have to use the Error object in the catch block. This is illustrated by the catch block in the second example in this figure. In this case, a custom message is displayed by the alert() method. Keep in mind, though, that you have to code a name for the Error object in the parentheses after the catch keyword even if you don't use it.

You should also know that if an exception is thrown in a function like the one in this figure and it isn't caught by a try-catch statement, the exception is passed to the calling function. This passing of the exception continues until the exception is caught or the application ends with a runtime error.

An interesting feature of JavaScript is that it throws fewer exceptions than other languages. For example, JavaScript has an Infinity value so it doesn't throw an error when an arithmetic expression divides by zero. JavaScript also has a NaN value so it doesn't throw an error when you pass a string to the parseInt() function. As a result, you need to do less exception handling when you use JavaScript than you do with other languages.

The syntax for a try-catch statement

```
try { statements }
catch(errorName) { statements }
[ finally { statements } ]        // the finally block is optional
```

Two properties of Error objects

Property	Description
name	The type of error
message	The message that describes the error

A try-catch statement for a calculateFV() function

```
var calculateFV = function(investment,rate,years) {
    try {
        var futureValue = investment;
        for (var i = 1; i <= years; i++ ) {
            futureValue += futureValue * rate / 100;
        }
        futureValue = futureValue.toFixed(2);
        return futureValue;
    }
    catch(error) {
        alert (error.name + ": " + error.message)
    }
};
```

A catch block that displays a custom message

```
catch(error) {
    alert("The calculateFV function has thrown an error." );
};
```

Description

- You can use a *try-catch statement* to process any errors that are thrown by an application. These errors are referred to as *exceptions*, and this process is known as *exception handling*.

- In a try-catch statement, you code a *try block* that contains the statements that may throw exceptions. Then, you code a *catch block* that contains the statements that are executed when an exception is thrown in the try block.

- The optional *finally block* is executed whether or not the statements in the catch block are executed.

- The *errorName* variable in the catch block gives you access to the Error object. This object has two properties that you can use to display the error type and message.

Figure 14-7   How to use try-catch statements to handle exceptions

How to create and throw Error objects

In some cases, you will want to *throw* your own exceptions. If, for example, you're creating a utility library that will be used by other programmers, you can throw exceptions to alert those using your library that something is wrong.

To throw an exception, you first create a new Error object. Then, you use the *throw statement* to throw it. This is illustrated by figure 14-8.

To create a new Error object, you call the Error constructor and pass one parameter to it that contains a message. This message is then stored in the Error object's message property. In general, it's best to make your message as specific as possible about what the error is and where it occurred.

After you create an Error object, you can use the throw statement to throw it. This is illustrated by the first example in this figure. Here, a function that calculates future value throws an exception if one of the values it receives is invalid. When the exception is thrown, the function ends and control is passed to the function that called it.

Then, the function that receives it can catch the exception and display its message property. Or, the programmer who is using the function can fix the code so appropriate values are passed to the function. In this example, the exception is caught by a try-catch statement in the function that called it. This example also illustrates the use of a finally block that sets the focus on the text box for the investment entry.

This use of try-catch statements makes sense when you're calling functions that somebody else has written and you're not sure what the arguments should be. Then, if the called functions throw exceptions with clear error messages, you can find out what you're doing wrong and debug your code. Once that's done, you can usually remove the try-catch statements because they shouldn't be necessary.

As the table in this figure shows, JavaScript also provides a hierarchy of Error objects that it throws. For instance, a RangeError object is thrown when a numeric value has exceeded an allowable range. A ReferenceError object is thrown when the JavaScript code refers to a variable that hasn't been defined. And a SyntaxError object is thrown when the syntax of a statement is invalid.

As the example below this table shows, you can also create and throw any of these object types. Then, that object type is displayed by the name property of the Error object. If, for example, you create and throw a RangeError object, its name property is set to "RangeError".

The syntax for creating a new Error object

```
new Error(message)
```

The syntax for the throw statement

```
throw errorObject;
```

A calculateFV() method that throws a new Error object

```
var calculateFV = function( investment, rate, years ) {
    if ( isNaN(investment) || investment <= 0 ) {
        throw new Error(
            "calculateFV requires an investment amount greater than 0." ); }
    if ( isNaN(rate) || rate <= 0 ) {
        throw new Error(
            "calculateFV requires an annual rate greater than 0." ); }
    var futureValue = investment;
    for (var i = 1; i <= years; i++ ) {
        futureValue += futureValue * rate / 100; }
    return futureValue.toFixed(2);
};
```

A try-catch statement that catches the Error object that has been thrown

```
try {
    $("future_value").text = calculateFV(investment,rate,years); }
catch(error) {
    alert (error.name + ": " + error.message); }
finally {
    $("investment".focus(); }
```

Some of the error types in the Error hierarchy

Type	Thrown when
RangeError	A numeric value has exceeded the allowable range
ReferenceError	A variable is read that hasn't been defined
SyntaxError	A runtime syntax error is encountered
TypeError	The type of a value is different from what was expected

A statement that throws a RangeError object

```
throw new RangeError("Annual rate is invalid.");    // throws RangeError
```

Two reasons for using throw statements

- To test the operation of a try-catch statement
- To throw an error from a function that lets the calling code know that one or more of the arguments that were passed are invalid

Description

- To create a new Error object, you use its constructor with a string as the parameter. If the parameter isn't a string, it is converted to one.
- To trigger a runtime error, you use the *throw statement*. It can throw a new or existing Error object.

Figure 14-8   How to create and throw Error objects

How to use regular expressions

Regular expressions are coded patterns that can be used to search for matching patterns in strings. These expressions are commonly used to validate the data that is entered by users. In the topics that follow, you'll learn the most important skills for using regular expressions for this purpose.

How to create and use regular expressions

Figure 14-9 shows how regular expressions work. To start, you create a *regular expression object* that contains the *pattern* that will be used. To do that, you can use either syntax that's shown at the top of this figure.

With the first technique, you use the new keyword with the RegExp() constructor, and you code the pattern in quotation marks as the parameter. With the second technique, you code a *regular expression literal*, which consists of the pattern between slashes. In either case, you create a new RegExp object that contains the pattern. In the two statements in the first example, that pattern is simply "Babbage".

Once you've created a regular expression object, you can use it to find pattern matches in a string. To do that, you can use the test() method of the regular expression object. This is illustrated by the two statements in the second example that use this method.

In the first statement, the test() method searches for the pattern "Babbage" in the variable named inventor. Since that variable contains "Charles Babbage", the pattern is found and the method returns true. In the second statement, the variable named programmer contains "Ada Lovelace", so the pattern isn't found and the method returns false.

In addition to the pattern that you code when you create a regular expression object, you can code one or more *flags* to set one or more properties of the object to true. To do that when you use the RegExp() constructor, you code a string for the second parameter that includes the flags you want to use. To do that when you code a regular expression literal, you code the flags after the slash that follows the expression.

The third example illustrates how this works. Here, both statements create a regular expression object with the pattern "lovelace". Both statements also include the *i* flag, which sets the ignoreCase property of the object to true. That changes the test that's done from the default of case-sensitive to case-insensitive. Because of that, the test in the fourth example will return a value of true when the programmer variable, which contains the string "Lovelace", is checked for the pattern.

Two ways to create a regular expression object

By using the RegExp() constructor

```
var variableName = new RegExp("expression"[, "flags"]);
```

By coding a regular expression literal

```
var variableName = /expression/[flags];
```

One method of a regular expression

Method	Description
test(*string*)	Searches for the regular expression in the string. It returns true if the pattern is found and false if it's not found.

Two statements that create a regular expression that will find "Babbage"

```
var pattern = new RegExp("Babbage");
var pattern = /Babbage/;
```

How to use the test() method of a regular expression

Two strings to test

```
var inventor = "Charles Babbage";
var programmer = "Ada Lovelace";
```

How to use the test() method to search for the pattern

```
alert ( pattern.test(inventor) );      // displays true
alert ( pattern.test(programmer) );    // displays false
```

Two statements that create a case-insensitive regular expression

```
var pattern = new RegExp("lovelace", "i");
var pattern = /lovelace/i;
```

How to use a case-insensitive regular expression

```
alert ( pattern.test(programmer) );    // displays true
```

Description

- A *regular expression* defines a *pattern* that can be searched for in a string. This pattern is stored in a *regular expression object*.

- To create a regular expression object, you can use the RegExp() constructor. Then, the pattern is coded within quotation marks as the first parameter.

- Another way to create a regular expression object is to code a *regular expression literal*. To do that, you code a pattern within two forward slashes.

- You can use the test() method of a regular expression object to search for the pattern in the string parameter.

- You can use *flags* to set one or more properties of a regular expression object to true. You can code flags within quotation marks as the second parameter of the RegExp() constructor or on a regular expression literal following the second slash.

- You can use the i flag to change the ignoreCase property to true so the regular expression pattern is case-insensitive rather than case-sensitive.

Figure 14-9   How to create and use regular expressions

How to match special characters and types of characters

The trick to using regular expressions is coding the patterns, and that can get complicated. That's why the next two figures move from the simple to the complex as they show you how to create patterns. To start, though, remember that all letters and numbers represent themselves in a pattern.

The first table in figure 14-10 shows you how to include special characters in a pattern. To do that, you start with the *escape character*, which is the backslash. For instance, \\ is equivalent to one backslash; \/ is equivalent to one forward slash; and \xA9 is equivalent to \u00A9, which is equivalent to the copyright symbol.

Note, however, that this table doesn't include all of the special characters that you need to precede with backslashes. For instance, the second table points out that you need to use \. to represent a period, and the first table on the next page points out that you need to use \$ to match a dollar sign.

The examples after the first table show how these special characters can be used in regular expression patterns. Here, the second and third statements use a regular expression literal followed by .test to call the test() method for that expression object. The second statement looks for one slash in the variable named string and finds it. The third statement looks for the copyright symbol and finds it.

Then, the fourth statement uses the first technique in figure 14-9 to create a RegExp object. But when you use the RegExp() constructor to create a regular expression object, you have to code two backslashes in the pattern for every one that you use in a regular expression literal. That's because the RegExp() constructor takes a string parameter, and the backslash is also the escape character for strings. For this reason, it's easier to use regular expression literals. In this example, the pattern is equivalent to one backslash, but the fifth statement doesn't find it because the string variable contains the escape sequence for a new line (\n), not a backslash.

The second table shows how to match types of characters instead of specific characters. If, for example, the literal is /MB\d/, the pattern will match the letters MB followed by any digit. Or, if the literal is /MB.../, the pattern will match MB followed by any three characters.

The examples after this table show how this works. Here, the second statement looks for MB followed by any character and finds it. The third statement looks for MB followed by either T or F and finds it. And the fourth statement looks for MBT- followed by any character that's not a letter, number or the underscore. It doesn't find a match, though, because the string contains MBT-3.

How to match special characters

Pattern	Matches
\\	Backslash character
\/	Forward slash
\t	Tab
\n	Newline
\r	Carriage return
\f	Form feed
\v	Vertical tab ·
[\b]	Backspace (the only special character that must be inside brackets)
\udddd	The Unicode character whose value is the four hexadecimal digits.
\xdd	The Latin-1 character whose value is the two hexadecimal digits. Equivalent to \u00dd.

Examples

```
var string = "©2017 MMA Inc.\nAll rights reserved (5/2017).";
alert( /\//.test(string) );          // matches / and displays true
alert( /\xA9/.test(string) );        // matches © and displays true
var pattern = new RegExp("\\\\");    // same as /\\/
alert( pattern.test(string) );       // displays false since there's no \
```

How to match types of characters

Pattern	Matches
.	Any character except a newline (use \. to match a period)
[ ]	Any character in the brackets (use \[or \] to match a bracket)
[^]	Any character not in the brackets
[a-z]	Any character in the range of characters when used inside brackets
\w	Any letter, number, or the underscore
\W	Any character that's not a letter, number, or the underscore
\d	Any digit
\D	Any character that's not a digit
\s	Any whitespace character (space, tab, newline, carriage return, form feed, or vertical tab)
\S	Any character that's not whitespace

Examples

```
var string = "The product code is MBT-3461.";
alert( /MB./.test(string) );         // displays true
alert( /MB[TF]/.test(string) );      // displays true
alert( /MBT-\W/.test(string) );      // displays false
```

Description

- The backslash is used as the *escape character* in regular expressions.
- When you use the RegExp() constructor, any backslash in your pattern must be preceded by another backslash. That's because the backslash is also the escape character in strings.

Figure 14-10   How to match special characters and types of characters

How to match string positions, subpatterns, and repeating patterns

Figure 14-11 presents some additional skills for creating regular expressions. The first table in this figure shows how to match characters at specific positions in a string. For instance, the pattern `/^com/` will find the letters "com" at the start of a string. And the pattern `/com$/` will find the letters "com" at the end of a string. This is illustrated by the examples after this table.

Here, the last example displays false because "Ad" is followed by another word character. To say that another way, "Ad" is found at the beginning of a word but not at the end of a word (the first word in the string is "Ada"). One use of the \b pattern is to find whole words.

The second table shows how to group and match a *subpattern* that is coded in parentheses. This is illustrated by the examples after this table. Here, the second statement will match a subpattern of either "Rob" or "Bob".

If you code more than one subpattern in a pattern, the patterns are numbered from left to right. Then, if you want to repeat the subpattern in the pattern, you can specify the number of the pattern that you want to repeat. This is illustrated by the third statement after the table. Here, the `\1` indicates that the first pattern, which matches any three letters, numbers, or underscores, should be used again. This returns true because that pattern is repeated. It would also return true if the pattern were `/(Rob) \1/` because "Rob" is repeated.

The third table shows how to use a *quantifier* that's coded in braces to match a repeating pattern. For instance, `/\d{3}/` will match any three digits in succession, and `/\${1,3}/` will match from one to three occurrences of a dollar sign. Here again, this is illustrated by the examples that follow the table. The third statement matches three digits at the start of a string, a hyphen, three more digits, another hyphen, and four digits at the end of the string. And the fourth statement matches a left parenthesis at the start of the string, three digits, a right parenthesis, zero or one space (as indicated by the question mark quantifier after the space), three more digits followed by a hyphen, and four digits at the end of the string. Both of these patterns can be used to validate phone numbers.

Then, the pattern in the fifth statement combines the patterns of the third and fourth statements so a phone number can start with either three digits in parentheses or three digits followed by a hyphen. Here again, the question mark after the space means that zero or one space can be used after an area code in parentheses, so this pattern will find telephone numbers like 559-555-1234, (559)555-1234, and (559) 555-1234.

These tables and examples should get you started coding patterns of your own. And you'll get more proficient with them as you study the examples in the rest of this chapter. Before you take on a complex pattern, though, you might want to do an Internet search for "regular expressions" or "regular expression library" first. You'll probably find that someone else has already written the pattern you need.

How to match string positions

Pattern	Matches
^	The beginning of the string (use \^ to match a caret)
$	The end of the string (use \$ to match a dollar sign)
\b	Word characters that aren't followed or preceded by a word character
\B	Word characters that are followed or preceded by a word character

Examples

```
var inventor = "Charles Babbage";
alert( /^Charles/.test(inventor) );          // displays true
alert( /Babbage$/.test(inventor) );          // displays true
alert( /^Babbage/.test(inventor) );          // displays false

var programmer = "Ada Lovelace";
alert( /Ad/.test(programmer) );              // displays true
alert( /Ad\b/.test(programmer) );            // displays false
```

How to group and match subpatterns

Pattern	Matches
(subpattern)	Creates a subpattern (use \(and \) to match a parenthesis)
|	Matches either the left or right subpattern (use \\| to match a vertical bar)
\n	Matches the subpattern in the specified position

Examples

```
var name = "Rob Robertson";
alert( /^(Rob)|(Bob)\b/.test(name) );        // displays true
alert( /^(\w\w\w) \1/.test(name) );          // displays true
```

How to match a repeating pattern

Pattern	Matches
{n}	Pattern must repeat exactly *n* times (use \{ and \} to match a brace)
{n,}	Pattern must repeat *n* or more times
{n,m}	Subpattern must repeat from *n* to *m* times
?	Zero or one of the previous subpattern (same as {0,1})
+	One or more of the previous subpattern (same as {1,})
*	Zero or more of the previous subpattern (same as {0,})

Examples

```
var phone = "559-555-6627";
var fax   = "(559) 555-6635";
alert( /^\d{3}-\d{3}-\d{4}$/.test(phone) );          // displays true
alert( /^\(\d{3}\) ?\d{3}-\d{4}$/.test(fax) );       // displays true

var phonePattern = /^(\d{3}-)|(\(\d{3}\) ?)\d{3}-\d{4}$/;
alert( phonePattern.test(phone) );                   // displays true
alert( phonePattern.test(fax) );                     // displays true
```

Figure 14-11   How to match string positions, subpatterns, and repeating patterns

Regular expressions for data validation

Figure 14-12 starts with some patterns that are commonly used for data validation. For instance, the first pattern is for phone numbers, so it matches 3 digits at the start of the string, a hyphen, 3 more digits, another hyphen, and 4 digits at the end of the string. Similarly, the second one is for credit card numbers, so it matches four groups of 4 digits separated by hyphens.

The third pattern is for 5- or 9-digit zip codes. It requires 5 digits at the start of the string. Then, it uses the ? quantifier with a subpattern that contains a hyphen followed by four digits. As a result, this subpattern is optional.

The fourth pattern is for email addresses. It makes sure there's an @ sign and a period, allows letters, numbers, underscores, dashes, and periods before and after the @ sign, but only allows letters after the period. It uses the + quantifier to ensure at least one character before and after the @ sign and after the period.

The fifth pattern is for dates in the mm/dd/yyyy format, but it also accepts a date in the m/dd/yyyy format. To start, this pattern uses the ? quantifier to show that the string can start with zero or one occurrences of 0 or 1. This means that the month in the date can be coded like 03/19/1940 or 3/19/1940. But if two digits are used for the month, the first digit has to be either 0 or 1.

Then, the pattern calls for one digit, a slash, either 0, 1, 2, or 3, another digit, another slash, and four more digits. As a result, this pattern doesn't match a string if its first month digit is greater than 1 or if its first day digit is greater than 3. But this will still match invalid dates like 19/21/2016 or 9/39/2017, so additional data validation is required. You'll see the additional validation later.

The examples that follow these patterns show how they can be used in your code. The first example uses the phone number pattern with the test() method and displays an error message if a match isn't found. The second example works the same way, but it uses the date pattern. Remember, though, that this pattern will match some invalid date formats.

This figure ends by presenting a function named isEmail() that is based on the SMTP specification for how an email address may be formed. This function is a more complete validation of an email address than just a regular expression.

In brief, this isEmail() function splits the address into the parts before and after the @ symbol and returns false if there aren't two parts or if either part has too many characters. Next, this function builds a regular expression pattern named localPart by combining two subpatterns with the | character, which means that the string can match either subpattern. Then, it searches for the pattern in the part of the address before the @ symbol. If it doesn't find the pattern, it returns false.

Similarly, the last part of this function builds a regular expression pattern named domainPart by combining two subpatterns. Then, it searches for the pattern in the part of the address after the @ symbol. If it doesn't find the pattern, it returns false. Otherwise, it returns true because the email address is valid.

Of course, it is the patterns in this function that are the most difficult to understand. The good news is that you don't need to understand this pattern to use it. In fact, many programmers find complex patterns like this online and use them without completely understanding them.

Regular expressions for testing validity

A pattern for testing phone numbers in this format: 999-999-9999

```
/^\d{3}-\d{3}-\d{4}$/
```

A pattern for testing credit card numbers in this format: 9999-9999-9999-9999

```
/^\d{4}-\d{4}-\d{4}-\d{4}$/
```

A pattern for testing zip codes in either of these formats: 99999 or 99999-9999

```
/^\d{5}(-\d{4})?$/
```

A pattern for testing emails in this format: username@mailserver.domain

```
/^[\w\.\-]+@[\w\.\-]+\.[a-zA-Z]+$/
```

A pattern for testing dates in this format: mm/dd/yyyy

```
/^[01]?\d\/[0-3]\d\/\d{4}$/
```

Examples that use these expressions

Testing a phone number for validity

```
var phone = "559-555-6624";                 // valid phone number
var phonePattern = /^\d{3}-\d{3}-\d{4}$/;
if ( !phonePattern.test(phone) ) {
    alert("Invalid phone number");          // not displayed
}
```

Testing a date for a valid format, but not for a valid month, day, and year

```
var startDate = "8/10/217";                 // invalid date
var datePattern = /^[01]?\d\/[0-3]\d\/\d{4}$/;
// this pattern will match dates like 19/21/2016 and 9/39/2017
if ( !datePattern.test(startDate) ) {
    alert("Invalid start date");            // displays error message
}
```

A function that does more complete validation of an email address

```
var isEmail = function(email) {
    if (email.length === 0) { return false; }
    var parts = email.split("@");
    if (parts.length !== 2) { return false; }
    if (parts[0].length > 64) { return false; }
    if (parts[1].length > 255) { return false; }

    var address =
        "(^[\\w!#$%&'*+/=?^`{|}~-]+(\\.[\\w!#$%&'*+/=?^`{|}~-]+)*$)";
    var quotedText = "(^\"(([^\\\\\"])|(\\\\[\\\\\"]))+\"$)";
    var localPart = new RegExp( address + "|" + quotedText );
    if ( !localPart.test(parts[0]) ) { return false; }

    var hostnames =
        "((([a-zA-Z0-9]\\.)|([a-zA-Z0-9][-a-zA-Z0-9]{0,62}[a-zA-Z0-9]\\.))+";
    var tld = "[a-zA-Z0-9]{2,6}";
    var domainPart = new RegExp("^" + hostnames + tld + "$");
    if ( !domainPart.test(parts[1]) ) { return false; }

    return true;
};
alert (isEmail("grace@yahoo.com"));          // displays true
alert (isEmail("grace@yahoocom"));           // displays false
```

Figure 14-12   Regular expressions for data validation

The Account Profile application

Now, to show you how you can use regular expressions for data validation, this chapter presents an Account Profile application. This application represents a simplified version of a web page that stores the data the users enter when they register.

Figure 14-13 presents the user interface for this application. After the user enters data and clicks the Save button, the JavaScript code checks the data for validity. Then, if the data isn't valid, the application displays error messages to the right of input text boxes.

The HTML and CSS

In the HTML, you can see the script elements in the head section. They show that this application uses the core jQuery library and its own JavaScript file.

You can also see that the main element consists of an h1 element and several input elements. After each of these input elements is a span element in which the error message for that entry will be displayed. But note that these span elements don't have id attributes. That's because this application uses jQuery to access these span elements.

The last input element for this page is a button with an id of "save". It is used to start the validation of the data that's been entered.

After the HTML, you can see one of the CSS style rules for this application. It just applies the color red to the span elements.

The Account Profile application with error messages

The HTML

```
<html>
<head>
    <title>My Account Profile</title>
    <link rel="stylesheet" href="profile.css">
    <script src="https://code.jquery.com/jquery-3.1.1.min.js"></script>
    <script src="profile.js"></script>
</head>

<body>
<main>
    <h1>My Account Profile</h1>
    <label for="email">E-Mail:</label>
        <input type="text" name="email" id="email">
        <span> </span><br>
    <label for="phone">Mobile phone:</label>
        <input type="text" name="phone" id="phone">
        <span> </span><br>
    <label for="zip">ZIP Code:</label>
        <input type="text" name="zip" id="zip">
        <span> </span><br>
    <label for="dob">Date of Birth:</label>
        <input type="text" name="dob" id="dob">
        <span> </span><br>

    <input type="button" id="save" value="Save">
</main>
</html>
```

Some of the CSS

```
span { color: red; }
```

Description

- The Account Profile application lets a user change profile information. It uses regular expressions and conditional expressions to validate the data the user enters.

- In real life, an application like this would then save the information to the server, most likely using jQuery and Ajax.

Figure 14-13   The HTML and CSS for the Account Profile application

The JavaScript

Figure 14-14 presents the JavaScript code for this application. It starts with a function named isDate(). This function uses a regular expression to determine whether the value passed to it is a valid date. The reason this code is in a function is because, as you saw in figure 14-12, a regular expression by itself can't fully validate a date.

As a result, this function first tests the value that it receives to see if it passes the regular expression check. If it doesn't, the isDate() function returns false. But if it does, the function gets the month and day parts of the date and makes sure the month is between 1 and 12 and the day isn't greater than 31. In real life, of course, you would refine this code to handle months that have fewer than 31 days and to handle leap years. But this gives you an idea of what you can do.

This function is followed by the click() event handler for the Save button. It starts by using jQuery to set the text of all the span elements in the page to an empty string. This clears any error messages that might have been displayed previously. Then, this code declares a Boolean variable named isValid and sets its default value to true. This variable will be used to keep track of whether the data entered by the user is valid.

Next, the code uses jQuery to retrieve the values entered by the user for email address, mobile phone, zip code, and date of birth. After that, the code issues a series of if statements to check those values.

The first three if statements check the email, phone, and zip code values. First, they check to see if the user entered values. Then, they use the test() method of a regular expression to see if the value is valid. If either of these checks fails, the isValid variable is set to false and an error message is displayed. Note that this code uses the jQuery next() method to find the span element that's the sibling of the text box and set its text.

The last if statement checks the date of birth value. It starts by checking if the user entered a date of birth. After that, it passes the date of birth to the isDate() function to check if it's valid. If either of these checks fails, the isValid variable is set to false and an error message is displayed.

The last if statement checks the value of the isValid variable. If it's still true, all of the data entered by the user is valid. Then, the jQuery code (not shown) saves the profile information to the server.

This event handler ends by setting the focus on the Email text box. This makes it easier for the user to either enter new profile information or correct any invalid entries. The last line of the ready() event handler also sets the focus on the Email text box.

The JavaScript for the Account Profile application

```javascript
$(document).ready(function(){

    var isDate = function(date) {
        if ( ! /^[01]?\d\/[0-3]\d\/\d{4}$/.test(date) ) { return false; }

        var index1 = date.indexOf( "/" );
        var index2 = date.indexOf( "/", index1 + 1 );
        var month = parseInt( date.substring( 0, index1 ) );
        var day = parseInt( date.substring( index1 + 1, index2 ) );

        if ( month < 1 || month > 12 ) { return false; }
        if ( day > 31 ) { return false; }
        return true;
    };

    $( "#save" ).click(function() {
        $("span").text("");    // clear any previous error messages
        var isValid = true;    // initialize isValid flag

        var email = $("#email").val();
        var phone = $("#phone").val();
        var zip = $("#zip").val();
        var dob = $("#dob").val();

        if ( email === "" ||
                ! /^[\w\.\-]+@[\w\.\-]+\.[a-zA-Z]+$/.test(email) )
        {
            isValid = false;
            $( "#email" ).next().text("Please enter a valid email.");
        }
        if ( phone === "" || ! /^\d{3}-\d{3}-\d{4}$/.test(phone) ) {
            isValid = false;
            $( "#phone" ).next().text(
                "Please enter a phone number in NNN-NNN-NNNN format.");
        }
        if ( zip === "" || ! /^\d{5}(-\d{4})?$/.test(zip) ) {
            isValid = false;
            $( "#zip" ).next().text("Please enter a valid zip code.");
        }
        if ( dob === "" || !isDate(dob) ) {
            isValid = false;
            $( "#dob" ).next().text(
                "Please enter a valid date in MM/DD/YYYY format.");
        }

        if ( isValid ) {
            // code that saves profile info goes here
        }

        $("#email").focus();
    });

    // set focus on initial load
    $("#email").focus();
});
```

Figure 14-14   The JavaScript for the Account Profile application

Perspective

Now that you've finished this chapter, you should know how to use the identity operators, the break and continue statements, the switch statement, and the conditional operator, as well as how to use AND and OR operators in selections. You should also know when and how to handle exceptions and how to create and use regular expressions for data validation.

Terms

equality operator	try-catch statement
type coercion	try block
identity operator	catch block
break statement	finally block
continue statement	throw statement
switch statement	regular expression
case label	regular expression object
conditional operator	pattern
short-circuit evaluation	regular expression literal
selection	escape character
exception	subpattern
throw an exception	quantifier
exception handling	flag

Summary

- Unlike the *equality operators*, the *identity operators* don't use *type coercion* in their comparisons. If an identity operator is used to compare two variables that aren't of the same type, the result is always false.

- The *break statement* jumps out of a loop and ends the loop. The *continue statement* jumps to the start of the loop but lets the loop continue.

- The *switch statement* lets you code the statements for *cases* that are based on the value of a single expression.

- The *conditional operator* returns one value if a condition is true and another if it is false. This is an alternative to a simple if-else statement.

- When the AND and OR operators are used in expressions that are assigned to variables, the expression is called a *selection*. In a selection, the value of the last operand that is evaluated is stored in the variable, and this depends on the *short-circuit evaluation* that is done by JavaScript.

- An *exception* is a runtime error that is *thrown* when an error condition occurs. To catch an exception, you use a *try-catch statement*, which consists of a *try block*, a *catch block*, and an optional *finally block*.

- You can also create and throw your own exceptions in the form of Error objects. This can be useful when you're writing functions that are going to be used by others.

- A *regular expression* defines a *pattern* that can be searched for in a string. This pattern is stored in a *regular expression object*.

- The test() method of a regular expression object is commonly used to test the validity of user entries.

Exercise 14-1   Enhance the Prime Number application

This exercise will give you a chance to practice some of the skills that you learned for working with control structures. In its initial form, this application determines whether the number that's entered is a prime number, which is one that can only be divided by one and itself.

Find Prime Numbers

Enter Number: `17`

Calculate

17 is a prime number.

Test the application and review the code

1. Use your text editor or IDE to open the JavaScript file in this folder:
    ```
    javascript_jquery\exercises\ch14\prime\
    ```

2. Run the application and test it with a prime number like 11 and a non-prime number like 10.

3. Review the JavaScript file, noting how the isPrimeNumber() function uses the conditional operator and the break statement.

Change the code to display all the prime numbers up to the one entered

Now you'll enhance the application so it will display all the prime numbers up to and including the one that's entered. When you're done, the application will look like this:

Find Prime Numbers

Enter Number: `31`

Calculate

2 3 5 7 11 13 17 19 23 29 31

4. In the click event handler, comment out the code that calls the isPrimeNumber() function and the code that displays the message about whether the number is prime.

5. Still in the handler, add code that clears any previous text from the message label. Then, code a loop that iterates through the numbers from 1 to the number entered by the user. Within the loop, the isPrimeNumber() function should be called for each number. Then, if the number is prime, it should be added to the text that will be displayed in the message label. If it isn't prime, the code should continue with the next iteration of the loop.

Exercise 14-2   Add exception handling to the Future Value application

In this exercise, you'll add exception handling to a Future Value application. Here's what the application looks like when an error message is displayed.

Future Value Application

Investment amount: [   ]

Interest rate: [   ]

Years: [   ]

Future Value:

[Calculate   ] [Clear   ]

RangeError: All entries must be numbers greater than zero

1. Open and review the HTML and JavaScript files in this folder:
   `javascript_jquery\exercises\ch14\future_value\`

2. Test the application with valid entries. Then, try to make the application throw an exception by clicking the Calculate button with no entries in the text boxes or with string entries like "one" or "two". Either way, the application displays a future value of zero without throwing an exception. This shows how difficult it is to make a JavaScript application throw an exception.

3. In the JavaScript file, add exception handling to the click event handler for the Calculate button. Put all of the statements in this handler except the last two in the try block, and display an error message like the one shown above in the catch block. The message should include both the name and message properties of the Error object.

4. To have the application throw a runtime error, change the name of one of the parameters in the calculateFutureValue() function. Then, test this to see the message that's displayed. This is a programming error, though, not the type of runtime error that requires exception handling. Now, fix the error.

5. Add a throw statement after the if statement in the calculateFutureValue() function. It should throw a RangeError object with the message shown above. A throw statement like this can be used to test the exception handling of an application. Now, test this change.

6. To see how this might work in a real application, move the throw statement into the if statement above it. Then, test the application to see that the message above is displayed when any of the arguments are invalid. This type of coding is often included in a function that's used by other programs. It forces the user to pass valid arguments to the function.

Exercise 14-3   Enhance the Account Profile application

This exercise asks you to enhance the Account Profile application for this chapter by adding validation for two new fields:

My Account Profile

E-Mail:	grace@yahoo.com	
Mobile phone:	555-123-4567	
ZIP Code:	12345	
Date of Birth:	5/18/80	Please enter a valid date in MM/DD/YYYY format.
Credit Card #:	1111222233334444	Please enter a credit card in NNNN-NNNN-NNNN-NNNN format.
Expire date:	11/20	Please enter a valid date in MM/YYYY format.
Save		

Open and test the application

1. Open the HTML and JavaScript files in this folder:

   `javascript_jquery\exercises\ch14\profile\`

2. Test the application and notice that two fields have been added for a credit card number and an expiration date. Because no validation is provided for these fields, though, you can enter any values in them.

Validate the credit card field

3. In the JavaScript file, find the click() event handler for the Save button and add a line of code that gets the value entered for the credit card.

4. Add an if statement that checks whether the user entered something for the credit card. If there's an entry, use a regular expression to make sure the credit card number is in the correct format.

5. If either of these checks fails, display an error message in the span element after the input element for the credit card number. Then, test the application.

Validate the expiration date field

6. Modify the isDate() function so it accepts a second parameter that will indicate the type of date that's passed to it. The two types are a full date in the MM/DD/YYYY format and a credit card date in the MM/YYYY format. Then, modify the code that validates the date of birth so it uses this type.

7. Add code to the isDate() function that validates a credit card date using the code that validates a full date as a guide.

8. Add an if statement to the click() event handler for the Save button that checks whether the user entered something for the expiration date. If so, call the isDate() function to make sure the date is in the correct format.

9. If either of these checks fails, the application should display an error message. Test the application one more time.

15

How to work with browser objects, cookies, and web storage

In this chapter, you'll learn how to use browser objects to navigate browser pages and to get information about the browser. You'll also learn how to use JavaScript to put cookies on a user's web browser and how to read and use those cookies. Last, you'll learn how to use web storage, which is another way to store information in the user's browser.

How to script browser objects

In this topic, you'll learn how to use the location and history objects of the browser. As you'll see, the location object lets you work with the URL for a web page. It also lets you control the reloading of the current web page and the loading of new web pages. The history object lets you work with the pages that are stored in your browser's history.

You should know, however, that with the rise of JavaScript frameworks that handle these types of processing, you're less likely to use the location and history objects in your own applications. For instance, many of the frameworks for single page applications (SPAs) handle page navigation and history for you. Still, it's good to have a basic understanding of how these objects work.

How to use the location object

The location object has properties and methods that parse the URL that's in the address bar of the browser. This is illustrated in figure 15-1, which starts with a URL that contains the six parts that can be parsed. This URL includes the parameters that are sent to the server along with the HTTP request. These parameters are taken from the fields within an HTML form.

In the URL, these parameters start after the question mark that follows the URL address. These parameters consist of *name/value pairs* that are connected by equals signs. If more than one parameter is passed to the server, they are separated by ampersands. In this example, two parameters named first and last are sent to the server.

After the parameters, this URL contains a placeholder name that starts with the pound sign (#). It represents a placeholder on the page that has been created by an <a> tag. Then, when the page is loaded, it is scrolled to the placeholder.

With that as background, you can better understand what the eight location properties in the table in this figure represent. For example, the href property stores the entire URL. The host property stores a combination of the hostname and port properties. And the other six properties store parts of the URL.

Next, this figure summarizes two methods of the location object. The first method lets you reload the current page either from cache memory or from the server if the force parameter is set to true. The second method lets you load a new page while replacing the current page in the browser history.

The first example in this figure shows two ways to use the location object to load a new page in the browser. The second example shows you how to use the reload() method to reload pages. And the third example shows how to use the replace() method to load a new page.

When the replace() method is used to load a new page, the current page in the URL history is overwritten. To illustrate, suppose the user first visits page1.html and then visits page2.html so page1 and page2 are in the browser's history list. Then, if page2 uses the replace() method to load page3.html, page3 will replace page2 in the history list. At that point, if the user clicks the browser's Back button, the user will go to page1.html instead of page2.html.

A URL with search parameters

```
http://www.murach.com:8181/javascript/location.html?first=G&last=Hopper#result
```

Properties of the location object

Property	Description	Value in the URL above
href	The complete URL of the web page	Complete URL
protocol	The protocol portion of the URL including the colon	http:
hostname	The host name portion of the URL	www.murach.com
port	The port number of the web server	8181
host	The host name and port number	www.murach.com:8181
path	The path to the web page	/javascript/location.html
search	The query string from the URL	?first=G&last=Hopper
hash	The anchor name from the URL	#result

Methods of the location object

Method	Description
reload(*force*)	Reloads the current web page. If the parameter is set to true, the browser loads the page from the server rather than from cache memory.
replace(*url*)	Loads a new page in the browser and overwrites the current page in the history list.

How to load a new web page

```
location.href = "http://www.murach.com";
location = "http://www.murach.com";
```

How to reload a web page

```
location.reload();        // reloads the current page from the cache
location.reload(true);    // reloads the current page from the server
```

How to load a new page and overwrite the current history page

```
location.replace("http://www.murach.com");
```

Description

- The properties of the location object let you examine different parts of the current URL.
- The methods of the location object give you greater control over how the current page is reloaded and how a new page is loaded into the browser.

Figure 15-1   How to use the location object

This is useful when a page checks to see whether a feature like cookies or Java is enabled and loads different pages depending on the result. To illustrate, suppose the index.html page uses the replace() method to load main_cookies.html if cookies are enabled and main_nocookies.html if they aren't. Without the replace() method, if the user clicks the Back button, the index.html page will be loaded again, and the user will end up back at one of the main pages. With the replace() method, though, the index.html page won't be in the history list.

How to use the history object

The history object represents the user's history list of viewed web pages. However, because of privacy concerns, the amount of information you can get from the history object is limited. As a result, the properties and methods of the history object are limited as shown by figure 15-2.

For instance, the length property tells how many URLs there are in the history list. However, there's no way to find out at which position the current page is in the history list. As a result, you can't tell whether the current page is first, last, or somewhere in the middle of the history list.

Similarly, the methods shown in this figure are limited. Here, the back() method is equivalent to clicking the Back button in the browser. The forward() method is equivalent to clicking the Forward button. The go() method with a numeric parameter lets you simulate multiple clicks of the Forward or Back button. And the go() method with a substring parameter goes to the last URL in the history list that contains that substring.

You should also know that HTML5 introduced two more methods to the history object: the pushState() and replaceState() methods. These methods are generally used with Ajax calls to mimic the way that the history object works with traditional round trips to the server.

One property of the history object

Property	Description
`length`	The number of URLs in the history object

Methods of the history object

Method	Description
`back()`	Goes back one step in the URL history
`forward()`	Goes forward one step in the URL history
`go(position)`	Goes forward or back the specified number of steps in the URL history
`go(substring)`	Goes to the most recent URL in the history that contains the substring

How to use the back() method

```
history.back();
```

How to use the forward() method

```
history.forward();
```

How to use the go() method

Go forward two URLs

```
history.go(2);
```

Go back three URLs

```
history.go(-3);
```

Go to the most recent URL that contains "google"

```
history.go("google");
```

Description

- The history object is an array that holds a history of the pages that have been loaded.

- There is no way to determine what the URLs in the history object are. You can only get the URL of the current page from the location object.

- Since there is no way to determine the position of the current URL in the history object, you can't find out if there are pages to go back or forward to.

- HTML5 introduced two more methods to the history object: pushState() and replaceState(). These methods let you add specific information to the history stack when you make Ajax calls.

Figure 15-2   How to use the history object

The Tutorial application

Figure 15-3 presents the user interface for a Tutorial application that controls what gets put into the history object. That in turn determines what pages are displayed when the user clicks the browser's Back button. In this case, the tutorial pages aren't added to the history object.

In the starting page for this application, the Enter and Tutorial buttons give the users a choice of going right to the main page (not shown) or taking a tutorial before going to the main page. If the users click the Tutorial button, they navigate through three tutorial pages before going to the main page. To make that navigation work, the first tutorial page has a Next button, the second tutorial page has a Prev and Next button, and the third tutorial page has a Prev and Finish button.

After the users navigate through the tutorial pages, they are on the main page of the application, not the starting page. Then, if the users click the browser's Back button, they are taken back to the starting page. This is true whether they clicked the Enter button to go to the main page or navigated through the tutorial before getting to the main page. That's because the JavaScript for the tutorial pages doesn't let the tutorial pages get stored in the browser's history, and that illustrates one use of the history object.

The HTML

Figure 15-3 presents some of the HTML used by the files in the Tutorial application. Not shown here are the CSS file that the application uses, or the link to the jQuery CDN that each page of the application has in its head element. Also, for simplicity, this application doesn't have a separate JavaScript file. Instead, each file in the application has script tags in its head element with embedded JavaScript.

The HTML shown here is in the main element for each page, and it consists of h1, <p>, and input elements for buttons. Each button has an id attribute that's used by the embedded JavaScript to provide the navigation.

Notice that in the tutorial3.html file, the id of the second button is "next", even though the text for that button is "Finish". This is just to keep the code consistent. However, you could change the id of that button to "finish" if you thought that would make the code clearer.

The Tutorial application and the pages of the tutorial in the browser

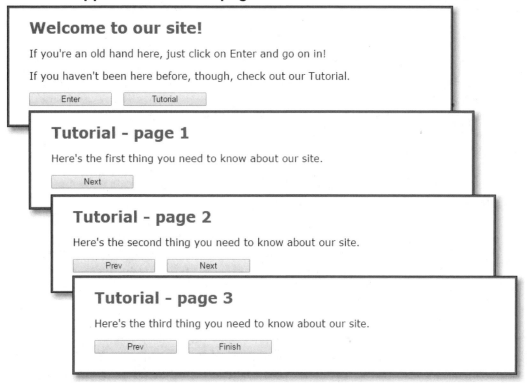

The HTML in the main element of the index.html file

```
<h1>Welcome to our site!</h1>
<p>If you're an old hand here, just click on Enter and go on in!</p>
<p>If you haven't been here before, though, check out our Tutorial.</p>
<input type="button" id="enter" value="Enter">
<input type="button" id="tutorial" value="Tutorial">
```

The HTML in the main element of the tutorial files

tutorial1.html

```
<h1>Tutorial - page 1</h1>
<p>Here's the first thing you need to know about our site.</p>
<input type="button" id="next" value="Next">
```

tutorial2.html

```
<h1>Tutorial - page 2</h1>
<p>Here's the second thing you need to know about our site.</p>
<input type="button" id="prev" value="Prev">
<input type="button" id="next" value="Next">
```

tutorial3.html

```
<h1>Tutorial - page 3</h1>
<p>Here's the third thing you need to know about our site.</p>
<input type="button" id="prev" value="Prev">
<input type="button" id="next" value="Finish">
```

Figure 15-3   The user interface and HTML for the Tutorial application

The JavaScript

Figure 15-4 presents the JavaScript for the four pages you saw in the previous figure. For each page, this JavaScript is in the jQuery ready() event handler that you learned about in chapter 8.

The index.html page has event handlers for the Enter and Tutorial buttons. Each of these sets the value of the location object to navigate either to the main page of the application or the first page of the tutorial. Since this code sets the value of the location object, the index.html page will appear in the browser's history.

The tutorial1.html page has an event handler for the Next button. This event handler uses the replace() method of the location object to navigate to the second page of the tutorial. Because it uses the replace() method, the tutorial1.html page won't be in the browser's history.

The tutorial2.html page has event handlers for the Prev and Next buttons. Each of these uses the replace() method of the location object to navigate either back to the first page of the tutorial or forward to the third page of the tutorial. As before, because it uses the replace() method, the tutorial2.html page won't be in the browser's history.

The tutorial3.html page has event handlers for the Prev and Finish buttons. Each of these uses the replace() method of the location object to navigate either back to the second page of the tutorial or forward to the main page of the application. Like the two examples you've already seen, the tutorial3.html page won't be in the browser's history.

With this code, a user can navigate back and forth among the tutorial pages, and those tutorial pages will never be stored in the browser's history. This means a user can navigate through a one-time tutorial without accidentally navigating back to its pages later in the application.

The JavaScript in the document.ready event of each file

index.html

```
$( "#enter" ).click(function() {
    location = "main.html";
});

$( "#tutorial" ).click(function() {
    location = "tutorial1.html";
});
```

tutorial1.html

```
$( "#next" ).click(function() {
    location.replace("tutorial2.html");
});
```

tutorial2.html

```
$( "#prev" ).click(function() {
    location.replace("tutorial1.html");
});

$( "#next" ).click(function() {
    location.replace("tutorial3.html");
});
```

tutorial3.html

```
$( "#prev" ).click(function() {
    location.replace("tutorial2.html");
});

$( "#next" ).click(function() {
    location.replace("main.html");
});
```

Description

- The JavaScript on the index.html page sets the value of the location object to navigate to another page. This means that the index.html page will be in the browser's history.

- The three tutorial html pages use the replace() method of the location object to navigate to another page. This means that the tutorial pages won't be in the browser's history.

Figure 15-4   The JavaScript for the Tutorial application

How to use cookies

Cookies let a web server or web page store information in a user's browser and retrieve it when the user requests a new page. This concerns some web users because they've heard rumors that cookies can transmit viruses, steal passwords, and copy files from their hard drive. Although those rumors aren't true, it is true that the use of cookies is often abused.

One of the common abuses is done by advertisers who use cookies to track the websites you have visited. These cookies are called *third-party cookies* because they are sent from the advertisers, not the websites you visit. To combat this abuse, modern web browsers let you block third-party cookies by changing browser options.

In this topic, you'll learn how to use cookies in a way that makes a web application work better for the user. In particular, you'll learn how to use cookies to save user data so the users won't have to re-enter that data the next time they use the application.

An introduction to cookies

A *cookie* is a short text string that is stored by the browser as a *name/value pair*. When you request a web page, the server can return a cookie as part of the HTTP response. If it does and the browser has cookies enabled, the web browser will store the cookie. Then, when you load another page from the server, the browser sends the cookie back to the server as part of the HTTP request. This process is illustrated in figure 15-5.

At the least, a cookie must start with a name/value pair that's connected by an equals sign. For instance, the first example in this figure pairs the cookie name email with the value grace@yahoo.com. This pair can then be followed by any of the attributes that are listed in the table. Note that these name/value pairs must be separated by semicolons and spaces.

If a cookie doesn't include a max-age attribute, it's called a *session cookie*. This type of cookie is deleted when the browser window is closed. But if a cookie includes a max-age attribute with a positive value, the cookie is a *persistent cookie* that will be stored by the web browser on the user's hard drive until the number of seconds in this attribute elapses. This is illustrated by the second example in this figure, which sets the max-age attribute to 21 days (21 * 24 * 60 * 60 = 1,814,400 seconds).

Typically, the path attribute for a cookie is set to the root folder of the website as shown in both examples. That way, every page in the website will have access to the cookie.

Next, you're going to see how JavaScript can be used to create, read, and delete cookies. As far as the web browser is concerned, cookies created in JavaScript are treated the same as cookies received from the web server.

A browser usually gets a cookie as part of an HTTP response

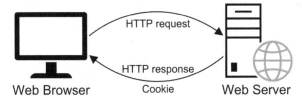

A browser sends the cookie back to the server with each HTTP request

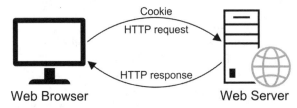

Attributes of a cookie

Attribute	Description
`max-age`	The lifetime of the cookie in seconds
`path`	The path on the web server that can see the cookie
`domain`	The domain names that can see the cookie
`secure`	If present, the cookie must be encrypted when it is transmitted, and it can only be transmitted when the browser and server are connected by HTTPS or another secure protocol.

Cookie examples

```
email=grace@yahoo.com; path=/
username=ghopper; max-age=1814400; path=/
```

Description

- A *cookie* is a small text string that is stored by a web browser. A cookie consists of name/value pairs, and it must start with a name/value pair that names the cookie and provides a value for the cookie.

- The browser usually gets a cookie from a web server as part of an HTTP response. Then, the browser sends the cookie back to the server as part of each HTTP request.

- A *session cookie* is deleted when the web browser is closed.

- A *persistent cookie* is saved by the web browser after the browser is closed. This type of cookie has an expiration date that is after the current date.

- JavaScript can also be used to create, read, and delete cookies.

Figure 15-5   An introduction to cookies

How to create cookies

To work with cookies, JavaScript provides a special object called the document.cookie object. To create a cookie, you first create a text string that represents the cookie. Then, you set the document.cookie object equal to the cookie's text string. This causes the browser to create and store the cookie.

This is illustrated by the examples in figure 15-6. To create a session cookie, the first example stores the name of the cookie (tasks) and an equals sign in a variable named cookie. Then, it appends the value for the name/value pair to the cookie variable.

Note, however, that cookie values can't include semicolons, commas, or white space, but this value does. As a result, the encodeURIComponent() function is used to encode the illegal characters so they can be used. For instance, each white space in this value will be converted to %20. Later, when the cookie is retrieved, the decodeURIComponent() function will be used to convert the data back to its original form.

The next statement in this example appends a path to the cookie string. Then, the cookie string is assigned to the document.cookie object, which stores the cookie on the browser. Because this is a session cookie, it will be deleted when the browser is closed.

The second example in this figure creates a persistent cookie. This works like the first example, but it adds a max-age attribute to the cookie. This time, the cookie will be stored on the user's hard drive after the browser is closed, but it will be deleted after 21 days.

When you add a cookie to the document.cookie object, you should realize that the text string for the new cookie doesn't replace the current text string in the object. Instead, the text string for the new cookie is added to the end of the existing text string. That way, you can store more than one cookie in the browser.

This is illustrated by the third example in this figure. Here, the first statement adds a cookie named email to the browser, and the second statement adds a cookie named username. Then, the third statement replaces the value in the email cookie since that cookie already exists. You can see the resulting cookies following these statements.

The last example in this figure shows a function that creates either a session or a persistent cookie. It accepts three parameters called name, value, and days. Inside the function, it first concatenates the cookie name with an equals sign and the encoded version of the cookie value. Then, it checks whether the days parameter has a value. If it does, the function appends a max-age attribute to the cookie, using the days value to calculate the number of seconds. Finally, it appends the root path to the cookie and assigns the cookie to document.cookie.

By the way, you would probably want to add some data validation to this function in a production application. For instance, you might want to make sure that the days parameter contains a numeric value and that the name parameter doesn't contain any illegal characters. But this should give you an idea of what you can do.

Two functions for working with cookies

Function	Description
`encodeURIComponent(value)`	Encodes values that contain semicolons, commas, or whitespace
`decodeURIComponent(value)`	Decodes values that have been encoded

How to create a session cookie

```
var cookie = "tasks" + "=";                    // create the cookie name
cookie +=                                       // encode and add the data
    encodeURIComponent("Feed dog\nWater plants");
cookie += "; path=/";                           // add the path
document.cookie = cookie;                       // store the cookie
```

How to create a persistent cookie

```
var cookie = "tasks" + "=";                    // create the cookie name
cookie +=                                       // encode and add the data
    encodeURIComponent("Feed dog\nWater plants");
cookie += "; max-age=" + 21 * 24 * 60 * 60; // add the max-age attribute
cookie += "; path=/";                           // add the path
document.cookie = cookie;                       // store the cookie
```

How to add multiple cookies to the document.cookie object

```
document.cookie = "email=john@doe.com; path=/"
document.cookie = "username=ghopper; max-age=1814400; path=/"
document.cookie = "email=grace@yahoo.com; path=/"
```

The cookies that are added to the document.cookie object

```
email=grace@yahoo.com; username=ghopper
```

A setCookie() function that creates a session or persistent cookie

```
var setCookie = function( name, value, days ) {
    // concatenate cookie name and encoded value
    var cookie = name + "=" + encodeURIComponent(value);

    // if there's a value for days, add max-age to cookie
    if (days !== undefined) {
        cookie += "; max-age=" + days * 24 * 60 * 60;
    }
    // add the path and then store the cookie
    cookie += "; path=/";
    document.cookie = cookie;
};
```

How to use the setCookie() function to create a persistent cookie

```
setCookie("tasks", "Water plants", 21);
```

Description

- Although cookie values can't include semicolons, commas, or whitespace, you can use the encodeURIComponent() function to encode those values. Then, you must use the decodeURIComponent() function to decode the values when the cookies are retrieved.

- To add multiple cookies to the cookie object, you assign multiple name/value pairs. Unlike other JavaScript objects, each assignment doesn't overwrite the previous one.

Figure 15-6   How to create cookies

How to read cookies

Figure 15-7 shows how to read the cookies that have been stored on a browser. Remember that more than one cookie can be stored in a browser, and these cookies are stored in a single document.cookie object. Then, the name/value pairs are separated by semicolons and spaces.

The easiest way to retrieve cookies is to store the value of document.cookie in a variable. When you do that, the value in the variable is a string. Then, you can use the methods of the String object to retrieve the data you want.

This figure presents a function named getCookieByName() that allows you to retrieve a specified cookie from the document.cookie object. To start, this function gets the string value from the document.cookie object and stores it in a variable named cookies. Then, it uses the indexOf() method of this string to locate the starting index of the name of the cookie.

Note here that the code that calls the indexOf() method appends an equals sign to the name it's looking for. This increases the chances that the indexOf() method will return the correct index. For instance, suppose the cookie string contains both email=grace@yahoo.com and tasks=send%20email. If you pass "email" to the indexOf() function, you might get the index of the word "email" in the tasks cookie. But if you pass "email=", you'll get the index of the name of the email cookie.

Next, the code checks the start variable to see what value the indexOf() method returned. If the value is -1, there's no cookie with that name in the cookie string. In that case, the function returns an empty string and is done.

However, if the value in the start variable isn't -1, the code continues processing the cookie string. First, it adjusts the start variable to make sure that the cookie name and the equals sign aren't included in the string that the function returns. It does this by incrementing the start variable by the length of the cookie name, plus 1 for the equals sign.

Then, the code calls the indexOf() method of the cookie string again to get the index of the semi-colon at the end of the cookie. Note that it passes the start variable as the second parameter of the indexOf() method. This ensures that the indexOf() method will start looking for the semi-colon at the start of the specified cookie value, rather than at the beginning of the cookie string.

If the indexOf() method returns -1 this time, that means that the cookie is the last one in the string. That's because the last cookie in the string doesn't have an ending semicolon. In this case, the end position of the cookie is the same as the end positon of the cookie string. Then, the end variable is set to the value of the length of the cookie string.

At this point, the code has the starting index and the ending index of the cookie value to be retrieved. Then, it uses the substring() method of the cookie string to retrieve the value of the cookie. Finally, it calls the decodeURIComponent() function and returns the decoded value of the cookie.

The last example in this figure shows how to use the getCookieByName() function. Here, the tasks cookie from the cookie string at the top of the page is retrieved and stored in a variable named tasks.

Three cookies in the document.cookie object

```
username=ghopper; status=active; tasks=Water%20plants
```

A getCookieByName() function that gets a cookie by name

```javascript
var getCookieByName = function(name) {
    var cookies = document.cookie;

    // get the starting index of the cookie name followed by an equals sign
    var start = cookies.indexOf(name + "=");

    if (start === -1) { return ""; } // no cookie with that name
    else {
        // adjust so the name and equals sign aren't included in the result
        start = start + (name.length + 1);

        // get the index of the semi-colon at the end of the cookie value,
        // or the length of the string in the case of the last cookie
        var end = cookies.indexOf(";", start);
        if (end === -1) { end = cookies.length; }

        // use the start and end indexes to get the cookie value
        var cookieValue = cookies.substring(start, end);

        // return the decoded cookie value
        return decodeURIComponent(cookieValue);
    }
};
```

How to use the getCookieByName() function to read a cookie

```javascript
var tasks = getCookieByName("tasks");          // tasks = "Water plants"
```

Description

- When you assign the document.cookie object to a variable, its value is stored as a String object. Then you can use the methods of the String object to locate the cookie value you want. You learned how to use many of these methods in chapter 13.

- One method of the String object that's often used with cookies is the split() method, which lets you break up the cookie string into an array of cookies. You'll learn how to use the split() method in chapter 16.

- This manipulation of the cookie string is possible because the cookie string follows such a predictable pattern.

Figure 15-7   How to read cookies

How to delete cookies

To delete a cookie, you store the cookie a second time, but with no value and with a max-age attribute that has a value of zero. The other parts of the cookie such as the path and domain must be set to the same values as when the cookie was first created, though. If you try to change the path or domain of the cookie, your attempt to delete the cookie will be ignored.

Figure 15-8 shows how to delete a cookie. Here, the first example is the cookie to be deleted, and the second example is the code for deleting it. If you study the code for deleting a cookie, you'll see that the code is similar to the code for creating a persistent cookie, but with two differences. First, no value is supplied for the cookie. Second, the max-age attribute is set to zero. Then, when the updated cookie is stored in the document.cookie object, the cookie will be deleted.

The third example in this figure shows a deleteCookie() function that deletes a cookie. It uses the name parameter to create a cookie with no value and a max-age value of 0. This causes the cookie to be deleted. After this function, you can see a statement that calls it to delete the cookie named tasks.

The cookie to delete

```
tasks=Feed dog; max-age=1814400; path=/
```

How to delete a cookie

```
var cookie = "tasks=";                  // set the name and data
cookie += "; max-age=" + 0;             // set max-age to 0
cookie += "; path=/";                   // set the path
document.cookie = cookie;               // delete the cookie
```

A deleteCookie()function that deletes a cookie

```
var deleteCookie = function(name) {
    document.cookie = name + "=''; max-age=0; path=/";
};
```

How to use the deleteCookie() function to delete a cookie

```
deleteCookie("tasks");
```

Description

- To delete a cookie, you set its max-age attribute to 0.

- When you delete a cookie, the data must be empty, but the equals sign is still required. Also, the path and domain must match the path and domain that were used when the cookie was created.

- There's no way to use JavaScript to determine the path and domain for a cookie once it has been created. However, as you'll see in a moment, you can use the Applications panel of the Chrome browser to get this information.

Figure 15-8   How to delete cookies

The Task List application

To show you how you can use cookies to make an application more useful, this chapter presents a Task List application. This application saves the items in the task list in a persistent cookie. That way, the task list will be available to the user each time the user accesses the page, at least until the cookie expires. Note, however, that because the task list is stored in the user's current browser, it won't be available if the user switches to a different browser.

Another thing you should know is that if you run this application by double-clicking on the index.html file, it won't work in Chrome. That's because Chrome disables cookies in websites that are run from the file system (that is, websites with a URL that begins with file:///).

There are two ways to fix this problem. First, you can use the Firefox browser, which supports cookies for file URLs. Second, you can run the application in Chrome from within an IDE. See figure 1-21 for information on how to do this in Aptana.

The HTML and CSS

Figure 15-9 presents the user interface for this application. The text box and two buttons let the user add and delete tasks, and the task list is displayed in the textarea element to the right of the text box and buttons. In the head element in the HTML, you can see that this application uses one CSS file and one JavaScript file in addition to the jQuery library.

In the main element of the HTML, the section element contains the textarea element that will display the list of tasks. Then, the id of the section element, which is "tasks", is used by the CSS file to float the section element to the right of the text box and buttons. Also, note that the id of the text area is "task_list" and the ids of the Add Task and Clear Tasks button are "add_task" and "clear_task". These of course are the ids that will be used by the JavaScript.

The Task List application in the browser

Task List

Task

Task List
```
Finish current project
Meet with Mike
Get specs for new project
```

Add Task

Clear Tasks

The HTML file

```html
<!DOCTYPE html>
<html>
<head>
    <title>Task List</title>
    <link rel="stylesheet" href="task_list.css">
    <script src="https://code.jquery.com/jquery-3.1.1.min.js"></script>
    <script src="task_list.js"></script>
</head>
<body>
  <main>
    <h1>Task List</h1>
    <section id="tasks">
        <label for="task_list">Task List</label><br>
        <textarea id="task_list" rows="6" cols="50"></textarea>
    </section>

    <label for="task">Task</label><br>
    <input type="text" name="task" id="task"><br>

    <input type="button" name="add_task" id="add_task" value="Add Task"><br>
    <input type="button" name="clear_tasks" id="clear_tasks"
        value="Clear Tasks">
  </main>
</body>
</html>
```

The CSS for the div element with "tasks" as its id

```css
#tasks {
    margin-top: 0;
    float: right;
}
```

Description

- The Task List application lets the user build a list of tasks to be done and displays the tasks in the textarea element.
- The user can add new tasks to the list or clear all of the tasks.
- The tasks are stored in a persistent cookie on the user's browser.

Figure 15-9   The HTML and CSS for the Task List application with cookies

The JavaScript

Figure 15-10 presents the JavaScript file for this application. It starts with the jQuery ready() event handler. Within this event handler are three functions that the application uses to work with cookies.

The setCookie(), getCookieByName(), and deleteCookie() functions are the same as the functions you saw earlier in this chapter. To review, the setCookie() function accepts a name, a value, and an optional number of days, and it creates either a session or persistent cookie. The getCookieByName() function accepts a name and returns either an empty string or the value of the cookie with that name. And the deleteCookie() function accepts a name and deletes the cookie with that name.

These functions are followed by the event handler for the click event of the Add Task button. This handler starts by getting the task input element and storing it in a variable named textbox. Then, it uses the jQuery val() method to retrieve the text the user has entered in the textbox. After that, it checks if the text is equal to an empty string. If it is, the code displays an error message and sets the focus on the task input element so the user can make another entry.

If the user has entered a task, this handler uses the getCookieByName() function to retrieve a cookie named tasks. Remember that this function returns a string, even if there's no such cookie in the browser. Because of that, this code can use the concat() method of the tasks string to append the task entered by the user. It also appends a new line character, so the tasks can be displayed with one task per line in the textarea element.

Next, this handler calls the setCookie() function to create a cookie named tasks whose value is the value in the tasks variable. Since this code passes a value of 21 for the days parameter, the cookie that's set is a persistent one that will expire in 21 days. Note here that if the tasks cookie doesn't exist yet, the setCookie() function will create it. But if it does exist, the setCookie() function will update its value.

After the cookie is updated and stored, the event handler clears the tasks input element. Then, it re-displays the tasks by calling the getCookieByName() function and passing the value it returns to the val() method of the textarea element. Finally, it sets the focus back on the task input element, so the application is ready for the user to enter another task.

The next event handler is for the Clear Tasks button. This code uses the deleteCookie() function to delete the cookie named tasks. After that, it clears all the tasks displayed in the textarea element, and it sets the focus on the task input element, so the application is ready for the user to enter another task.

The ready() event handler ends by calling the getCookieByName() function and passing the value it returns to the val() method of the textarea element. This way, any tasks that are already stored in the persistent cookie on the user's browser will be displayed when the application first loads. Last, this handler sets the focus on the task input element.

The JavaScript

```javascript
$(document).ready(function(){

    var setCookie = function(name, value, days) {
        var cookie = name + "=" + encodeURIComponent(value);
        if (days !== undefined) {
            cookie += "; max-age=" + days * 24 * 60 * 60;
        }
        cookie += "; path=/";
        document.cookie = cookie;
    };
    var getCookieByName = function(name) {
        var cookies = document.cookie;
        var start = cookies.indexOf(name + "=");

        if (start === -1) { return ""; } // no cookie with that name
        else {
            start = start + (name.length + 1);

            var end = cookies.indexOf(";", start);
            if (end === -1) { end = cookies.length; }

            var cookieValue = cookies.substring(start, end);
            return decodeURIComponent(cookieValue);
        }
    };
    var deleteCookie = function(name) {
        document.cookie = name + "=''; max-age=0; path=/";
    };

    $("#add_task").click(function() {
        var textbox = $("#task");
        var task = textbox.val();
        if (task === "") {
            alert("Please enter a task.");
            textbox.focus();
        } else {
            var tasks = getCookieByName("tasks");
            tasks = tasks.concat( task, "\n" );
            setCookie( "tasks", tasks, 21 ); // 21 day persistent cookie

            textbox.val( "" );
            $("#task_list").val( getCookieByName("tasks") );
            textbox.focus();
        }
    });
    $("#clear_tasks").click(function() {
        deleteCookie( "tasks" );
        $("#task_list").val( "" );
        $("#task").focus();
    });

    // display tasks on initial load
    $("#task_list").val( getCookieByName("tasks") );
    $("#task").focus();
});
```

Figure 15-10   The JavaScript for the Task List application

How to use web storage

In the past, cookies were the only option for storing data on the user's system. But cookies have some downsides. They are passed to the server with every HTTP request. And the storage in a cookie is limited to about 4,000 bytes.

Fortunately, modern browsers now offer *web storage* that can be processed by JavaScript on the browser. Then, the data isn't passed to the server with every HTTP request. In addition, web storage can be used to store approximately 5MB of data.

Web storage includes both *local storage* and *session storage*. The difference is that items in local storage persist between browser sessions, like a persistent cookie. But items in session storage are removed when the browser session ends, like a session cookie. Another advantage of web storage over cookies is that they're much easier to work with, as you'll see next.

How to use local and session storage

Figure 15-11 shows how to work with local and session storage. To do that, you use the localStorage and sessionStorage objects, which store their items in *key/value pairs*. Then, you use the setItem(), getItem(), removeItem(), and clear() methods of the objects to work with the items.

For instance, the setItem() method requires two parameters that provide the key for an item and the value for the item. So you can use code like this to add items with the keys "email" and "phone" that store the email address and phone number for a user:

```
localStorage.setItem("email", "grace@yahoo.com");
localStorage.setItem("phone", "555-555-1212");
```

Then, you can use the getItem() method with the item key as the parameter to retrieve the data for the phone item with a statement like this:

```
var phone = localStorage.getItem("phone");
```

To simplify, you can use the shortcut syntax shown in this figure. For instance, you can use this code to save the email and phone items:

```
localStorage.email = "grace@yahoo.com";
localStorage.phone = "555-555-1212";
```

And this code to retrieve the items:

```
var phone = localStorage.phone;
```

The shortcut syntax is used in the example in this figure. Here, if statements test to see whether the "hits" items in local storage and session storage exist. If so, it converts the value in that key/value pair to a number and adds 1 to it. If not, it saves a new item named "hits" with a value of 1 in it. After that, the alert() method is used to display the value of the "hits" item in both local and session storage. The message box shown here assumes that the user closed the browser after the first 8 page hits and then reopened the page for two more hits.

The syntax for working with local or session storage

```
localStorage.setItem("itemname", "value")    // saves the data in the item
localStorage.getItem("itemname")             // gets the data in the item
localStorage.removeItem("itemname")          // removes the item
localStorage.clear()                         // removes all items

sessionStorage.setItem("itemname", "value")  // saves the data in the item
sessionStorage.getItem("itemname")           // gets the data in the item
sessionStorage.removeItem("itemname")        // removes the item
sessionStorage.clear()                       // removes all items
```

The shortcut syntax for getting or saving an item

```
localStorage.itemname                        // saves or gets the data in the item
sessionStorage.itemname                      // saves or gets the data in the item
```

JavaScript that uses local and session storage for hit counters

```
$(document).ready(function() {
    if (localStorage.hits) {
        localStorage.hits = parseInt(localStorage.hits) + 1;
    } else { localStorage.hits = 1; }

    if (sessionStorage.hits) {
        sessionStorage.hits = parseInt(sessionStorage.hits) + 1;
    } else { sessionStorage.hits = 1; }

    alert("Number of hits this browser: " + localStorage.hits + "\n\n" +
          "Number of hits this session: " + sessionStorage.hits);
});
```

A message box that shows the current value of both hits fields

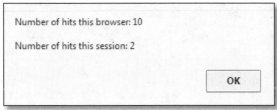

Description

- *Web storage* lets the web page use JavaScript to store data in *key/value pairs*. This feature is currently supported by every modern browser.

- One type of web storage is *local storage*, which is retained indefinitely. Another type of web storage is *session storage*, which is lost when the user ends the session by closing the browser or tab for the page.

- Unlike cookies, web storage is meant to be accessed by JavaScript, not server-side code. This means that web storage isn't passed to the server along with each HTTP request.

- You can also store more data in web storage than you can in cookies. In fact, the HTML5 specification recommends a storage limit of 5MB.

- To refer to web storage, you use the localStorage or sessionStorage objects.

Figure 15-11   How to use web storage

The Task List application with web storage

Figure 15-12 presents the JavaScript for a version of the Task List application that's been updated to use local storage instead of a persistent cookie. As you can see, this code is much simpler because it no longer needs specialized functions to create, retrieve, and delete cookies. Instead, it just uses the methods of the localStorage object.

In addition to being simpler, this version of the Task List application also stores the task list in the browser indefinitely instead of just for 21 days. That's because local storage doesn't have an expiration date. Of course, sometimes you may want to remove something from local storage after a set amount of time has elapsed. In those cases, you can set another key/value pair with an expiration date for the item, and then use that date to trigger the deletion of the item.

There are two more things to note in the code presented here. First, the code uses both full method names and the shortcut syntax. Usually, it's just a matter of personal preference which one you use.

Second, the statement that retrieves the tasks from local storage uses the OR operator (| |) to set a default value of an empty string if no tasks are retrieved. This way, the value of tasks is always a String object. Without this default value, the call to the concat() method in the next statement would throw an error when there are no tasks in local storage.

The Task List application in the browser

Task List

Task

[   ]

[Add Task   ]

[Clear Tasks   ]

Task List
```
Finish current project
Meet with Mike
Get specs for new project
```

The JavaScript

```javascript
$(document).ready(function(){

    $("#add_task").click(function() {
        var textbox = $("#task");
        var task = textbox.val();
        if (task === "") {
            alert("Please enter a task.");
            textbox.focus();
        } else {
            var tasks = localStorage.tasks || "";   // default value of ""
            localStorage.tasks = tasks.concat( task, "\n" );

            textbox.val( "" );
            $("#task_list").val( localStorage.tasks );
            textbox.focus();
        }
    });

    $("#clear_tasks").click(function() {
        localStorage.removeItem( "tasks" );
        $("#task_list").val( "" );
        $("#task").focus();
    });

    // display tasks on initial load
    $("#task_list").val( localStorage.tasks );
    $("#task").focus();

});
```

Description

- This version of the Task List application stores tasks in local storage on the user's browser rather than in a cookie.
- The HTML for this application is the same as it is in figure 15-9.

Figure 15-12   The Task List application with web storage

How to use Chrome to work with items in the browser

Sometimes as you test an application that uses cookies or web storage, it can be helpful to see what values are currently stored. So now, you'll learn how to use the Application panel of the Chrome browser to do just that.

This can be useful not only for testing your own applications, but for seeing what items other websites are storing in your browser. For example, you can navigate to google.com and then open the Application panel to see what Google is storing on your computer, which can be an interesting exercise. The Application panel will also show you what's in the browser-based databases that most modern browsers support.

In addition to letting you see what a website has stored on your computer, the Application panel lets you delete and edit items. This can be useful when testing and debugging your own applications. But you'll want to be careful about doing this for other websites, since you might delete something that affects the way the website works for you.

How to view and delete cookies

You can use the technique described in figure 15-13 to see the cookies that your application has stored in the browser. For each cookie, the Application panel displays information like its name, value, path, and expiration date.

You can also use the Application panel to delete cookies. This can be handy during the development of an application. Unlike web storage items, though, you can't edit the value of a cookie in the Application panel.

How to view, edit, and delete items in web storage

You can use the technique described in figure 15-13 to see the web storage items that your application has stored in the browser. For these items, the Application panel displays the key and value fields for the items that are stored in local or session storage.

As with cookies, you can use the Application panel to delete items in web storage. Unlike cookies, you can also use the Application panel to edit items in web storage. This can be useful when you're developing an application.

The cookies for an application in the Application panel

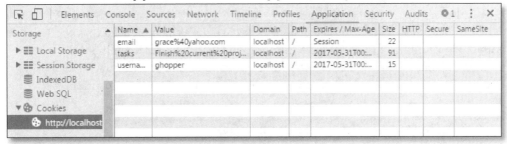

The local storage items for an application in the Application panel

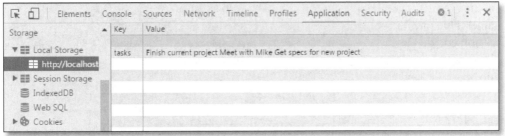

How to use the Application panel in Chrome to work with stored items

- Press F12 to open the developer tools.
- Click on the Application tab at the top of the tools window, and then look for the Storage section in the pane on the left-hand side.
- To work with cookies, click the arrow beside Cookies to expand that section, and then click on the website URL. That will display the cookies in the grid.
- To work with web storage, click the arrow beside Local Storage or Session Storage to expand that section, and then click on the website URL. That will display the key/value pairs for that type of storage in the grid.

How to delete a cookie or web storage item

- Right-click the item you want to delete and then click on "Delete".
- You'll need to refresh the page to see the result of this action in the application.

How to edit a web storage item

- Right-click the value you want to edit and then click on "Edit Value".
- Edit the text in the value field and then click out of that field when you're done. You'll need to refresh the page to see the result of this action in the application.

Description

- You can use the Application panel in Chrome's developer tools to work with cookies and items in local and session storage.
- You can delete both cookies and web storage items, but only web storage allows editing.

Figure 15-13   How to use Chrome to work with items in the browser

Perspective

Now that you've finished this chapter, you have the skills you need to work with the location and history objects, cookies, and web storage. Keep in mind, though, that because you can view the values of cookies and web storage, they aren't secure. So you shouldn't store personal information or passwords in them.

Terms

cookie	web storage
name/value pair	session storage
session cookie	local storage
persistent cookie	key/value pair
third-party cookie	

Summary

- The properties of the location object let you examine different parts of the current URL, and the methods give you greater control over how a new page is loaded into the browser.

- The history object holds a history of the pages that a user has visited. You can use its methods to control what's stored in the history object and how the navigation between pages works.

- A *cookie* is a small text string that is stored on a user's web browser. A cookie consists of a *name/value pair*, and can be a *session cookie* or a *persistent cookie*. A session cookie is removed when the browser closes, but a persistent cookie is removed after a set amount of time has elapsed.

- Cookies are passed between the browser and the server on each HTTP request and response. They can be created, read, and deleted with JavaScript.

- *Web storage* provides another way to store data on a user's browser. Web storage items are stored in *key/value pairs*, but these items aren't passed between the browser and the server like cookies are.

- Web storage comes in two types. *Local storage* remains indefinitely, while *session storage* is lost when the browser session ends.

- You can use Chrome's developer tools to view and delete cookies and items in local and session storage. You can also use these tools to edit items in local and session storage.

Exercise 15-1   Test the Tutorial application

In this exercise, you'll test the Tutorial application that was presented in this chapter. Then you'll make a few changes to better illustrate how it uses the location and history objects.

Open and test the Tutorial application

1. Use your text editor or IDE to open the HTML files in this folder:

   `c:\javascript_jquery\exercises\ch15\tutorial\`

2. Review the main.html file. Notice that there is a script element at the bottom of the page that use the document.write() method to display the value in the length property of the history object.

3. Review and run the index.html file. First, click on the Enter button to go directly to the main page. Then, look at the bottom of the page and see that there are two pages in history.

4. Use the Back button on the page or the browser's back button to go back to the initial page, which is the index.html page.

5. Click on the Tutorial button and click through all the pages of the tutorial. When you get to the main page, note that there are still only two pages in history. This shows that none of the tutorial pages were stored in the history object.

6. Use the Back button on the page or the browser's back button to go back to the initial page. Once again, because the tutorial pages aren't in history, this takes you back to the index.html page.

Adjust the application so the pages of the tutorial are stored in history

7. Change the JavaScript code in the script element of the tutorial1.html file so it sets the value of the location object rather than calling the replace() method. Do the same for tutorial2.html and tutorial3.html.

8. Save your changes, run the application, and repeat steps 3 through 6 to see how the application works now. This time, when you get to the main page after clicking through the tutorial pages, it says that there are 5 pages in history. And when you click the back button, you go back to the last page of the tutorial, not to the initial page of the application. This shows that the tutorial pages are now stored in the history object.

Exercise 15-2   Enhance the Task List application

In this exercise, you'll adjust the Task List application that uses web storage so the tasks in local storage have an expiration date. That way, they'll behave more like a persistent cookie rather than staying in local storage indefinitely.

Open and test the Task List application

1. Use your text editor or IDE to open the HTML and JavaScript files in this folder:

    ```
    c:\javascript_jquery\exercises\ch15\task_list\
    ```

2. Run the application in Chrome and enter a task or two. Then click on the F12 button to open the developer tools, and navigate to the Application panel. In the Storage pane, expand the Local Storage node and then select the URL for the website to view the tasks storage item that you just added.

3. Click on the Clear Tasks button to clear the tasks, and then close the browser.

Enhance the task storage to include an expiration date

4. Display the task_list.js file. Then, find the line of code in the event handler for the click event of the Add Task button that adds the updated tasks to local storage.

5. After that code, create a new Date object for today's date and add 21days to that date. Then, call the toDateString() method of the Date object and store the resulting value in local storage in a property named expiration.

6. Repeat step 2. Notice that this time there's a tasks storage item and an expiration storage item.

7. In the event handler for the click event of the Clear Tasks button, add code that removes the expiration item from local storage.

8. In the displayTasks() function, comment out the line of code that sets the value of the task_list textarea element. Then, write code that retrieves the expiration value from local storage and converts it to a Date object. After that, create a Date object for today's date.

9. Code an if statement that checks whether the expiration date is in the past. To do that, compare the values returned by the getTime() method of each Date object. Then, if the expiration date is in the past, remove both the tasks and expiration items from local storage. If not, retrieve the tasks from local storage and display them as before.

10. Run the application and enter a task or two if none are already there. Next, open the Application panel and edit the expiration date so it's in the past. Then, refresh the application. Notice that the tasks are cleared from both the application display and from local storage.

16

How to work with arrays

In chapter 3, you were introduced to arrays. Now, in this chapter, you'll learn more about working with arrays, which are an important part of many JavaScript applications. For example, you can use an array to hold a list of tasks that you can update and display.

How to create and use an array

To start, you'll review the skills you learned in chapter 3 and learn the other skills for creating and using arrays.

How to create an array

An *array* is an object that contains one or more items called *elements*. Each of these elements can be a primitive data type or an object. For instance, you can store numbers, strings, and Date objects in the same array.

The *length* of an array indicates the number of elements that it contains. Because JavaScript arrays are dynamic, you can change the length of an array by adding or removing elements from the array.

Figure 16-1 shows two ways to create an array. When you use the first method, you use the new keyword with the Array() constructor to create an array with the number of elements that is indicated by the length parameter. This length must be a whole number that is greater than or equal to zero. If you don't specify the length, the array will be empty.

When you use the second method, you just code a set of brackets. This gives you the same result that you get with the first method and no parameter, an empty array.

Next, this figure shows you how to create a new array and assign values to its elements in a single statement. In this case, you code the values in a list that's separated by commas. For instance, the first group of examples shows a statement that creates an array named rates that contains four numeric values and a statement that creates an array named names that contains three strings.

Note, however, that when you create an array with the new keyword, the array list must not be a single number. Otherwise, it will be treated as the length of the array, not a value in the array.

To refer to the elements in an array, you use an *index* that ranges from zero to one less than the number of elements in an array. In an array with 12 elements, for example, the index values range from 0 to 11. This is the reason the getMonth() method of a Date object numbers the months from 0 to 11 instead of 1 to 12. Then, the return value of the getMonth() method can be used as an index for an array of month names.

To use an index, you code it within brackets after the name of the array. In this figure, all of the examples use literal values for the indexes, but an index can also be a variable that contains an index value. If you try to access an element that hasn't been assigned a value, the value of undefined will be returned.

The last group of examples in this figure shows how to assign values to an empty array. To do that, you refer to the elements by using indexes, and you assign values to those elements.

The syntax for creating an array

Using the new keyword with the Array object name

```
var arrayName = new Array(length);
```

Using an array literal

```
var arrayName = [];
```

The syntax for creating an array and assigning values in one statement

Using the new keyword with the Array object name

```
var arrayName = new Array(arrayList);
```

Using an array literal

```
var arrayName = [arrayList];
```

How to create an array and assign values in one statement

```
var rates = new Array(14.95, 12.95, 11.95, 9.95);
var names = ["Grace", "Charles", "Ada"];
```

The syntax for referring to an element of an array

```
arrayName[index]
```

Code that refers to the elements in an array

```
rates[2]        // Refers to the third element in the rates array
names[1]        // Refers to the second element in the names array
```

How to assign values to an array by accessing each element

How to assign numbers to an array that starts with four undefined elements

```
var rates = new Array(4);
rates[0] = 14.95;
rates[1] = 12.95;
rates[2] = 11.95;
rates[3] = 9.95;
```

How to assign strings to an array that starts with no elements

```
var names = [];
names[0] = "Grace";
names[1] = "Charles";
names[2] = "Ada";
```

Description

- An *array* can store one or more *elements*. The *length* of an array is the number of elements in the array.

- If you create an array without specifying the length, the array doesn't contain any elements.

- When you create an array of one or more elements without assigning values to them, each element is set to undefined.

- To refer to the elements in an array, you use an *index* where 0 is the first element, 1 is the second element, and so on.

Figure 16-1   How to create an array

How to add and delete array elements

There is one property and one operator that can help you modify arrays. They are described in figure 16-2.

To add an element to the end of an array, you can use the length property of the array as the index of the new element. This is illustrated by the first example in this figure. Since this property will always be 1 more than the highest index used in the array, this adds the new element at the end of the array.

To add an element at a specific index, you use its index to refer to the element and assign a value to it. This is illustrated by the second example. If you use an index that's greater than the length of the array, the elements that you skipped over will be created and assigned the value of undefined.

To delete an element from an array, you can use the delete operator. This is illustrated by the third example. When you do this, the deleted element is left in the array with an undefined value. In other words, the elements that are above the element that you deleted are not shifted down to fill in this gap. Later in this chapter, though, you'll learn how to use the splice() method of an array to delete elements without leaving a gap in the array.

To remove all the elements in an array, you set the length property of the array to zero. This is illustrated by the fourth example. Note that this is different than using the delete operator, because the elements are not left in the array with an undefined value. Rather, the elements are completely removed, leaving the array with no elements.

In JavaScript, a *sparse array* is an array with a large number of elements but few assigned elements. This is illustrated by the fifth example in this figure. Here, the array has 1001 elements, but only two of these elements have assigned values. With some programming languages, space would be reserved for all 1001 elements in the computer's memory. With JavaScript, though, space is only reserved for the elements that have assigned values.

One property and one operator for an array

Property	Description
`length`	The number of elements in an array.

Operator	Description
`delete`	Deletes the contents of an element and sets the element to undefined, but doesn't remove the element from the array.

How to add an element to the end of an array

```
var numbers = [1, 2, 3, 4];       // array is 1, 2, 3, 4
numbers[numbers.length] = 5;      // array is 1, 2, 3, 4, 5
```

How to add an element at a specific index

```
var numbers = [1, 2, 3, 4];       // array is 1, 2, 3, 4
numbers[6] = 7;                   // array is 1, 2, 3, 4, undefined, undefined, 7
```

How to delete an element at a specific index

```
var numbers = [1, 2, 3, 4];       // array is 1, 2, 3, 4
delete numbers[2];                // array is 1, 2, undefined, 4
```

How to remove all elements

```
var numbers = [1, 2, 3, 4];       // array contains four elements
numbers.length = 0;               // removes all elements from array
```

A sparse array that contains 999 undefined elements

```
var numbers = [1];                // array is 1
numbers[1000] = 1001;             // array contains 1 and 1001 with 999
                                  // undefined elements in between
```

Description

- One way to add an element to the end of an array is to use the length property as the index.

- If you add an element at a specific index that isn't the next one in sequence, undefined elements are added to the array between the new element and the end of the original array.

- When you use the delete operator, the element's value is deleted but the element stays in the array with an undefined value.

- To remove all the elements from an array, you can set the array's length property to zero. Unlike the delete operator, this removes all the elements, not just the elements' values.

- A *sparse array* is a large array with few defined elements. For efficiency, though, JavaScript only reserves space for the elements that are assigned values.

- You can also add items to an array by using the methods of an Array object as shown in figure 16-5.

Figure 16-2   How to add and delete array elements

How to use for loops to work with arrays

For loops are commonly used to process one array element at a time by incrementing an index variable. Figure 16-3 shows how this works.

The first example in this figure shows how to create an array and fill it with the numbers 1 through 10. First, the code creates an empty array named numbers. Then, an index variable named i is used to loop through the first ten elements of the array by using values that range from 0 to 9. In the body of this loop, one is added to the value in i and the result is stored in the element. As a result, the element at index 0 stores a 1, the element at index 1 stores a 2, and so on.

Next, this example displays the values in the array. First, it creates an empty string named numbersString. Then, it uses a for loop to access the elements in the array. In the for loop, the length property of the array is used to control how many times the loop executes. This allows the same code to work with arrays of different lengths. Inside the for loop, the value in the element and a space are concatenated to the end of numbersString. Finally, numbersString is displayed, which shows the ten numbers that were stored in the array.

The second example in this figure shows how you can calculate the sum and average of an array of totals. First, the code creates an array named totals that stores four total values. Then, it creates a variable named sum that is initialized to zero. Next, it uses a for loop to access each of the elements in the totals array and add it to the sum. Finally, it calculates the average by dividing the sum by the length of the array.

Next, this example displays the totals, the sum, and the average. First, it creates an empty string named totalsString. Then, it uses a for loop to concatenate the value of each element and a new line character to totalsString. Finally, it displays a message containing totalsString, the sum, and the average.

Code that puts the numbers 1 through 10 into an array

```
var numbers = [];
for (var i = 0; i < 10; i++) {
    numbers[i] = i + 1;
}
```

Code that displays the numbers array

```
var numbersString = "";
for (var i = 0; i < numbers.length; i++) {
    numbersString += numbers[i] + " ";
}
alert( numbersString );
```

The message that's displayed

Code that computes the sum and average of an array of totals

```
var totals = [141.95, 212.95, 411, 10.95];
var sum = 0;
for (var i = 0; i < totals.length; i++) {
    sum += totals[i];
}
var average = sum / totals.length;
```

Code that displays the totals array, the sum, and the average

```
var totalsString = "";
for (var i = 0; i < totals.length; i++) {
    totalsString += totals[i] + "\n";
}
alert( "The totals are:\n" + totalsString + "\n" +
       "Sum: " + sum.toFixed(2) + "\n" + "Average: " + average.toFixed(2) );
```

The message that's displayed

Description

- When you use a *for loop* to work with an array, you can use the counter for the loop as the index for the array.

Figure 16-3   How to use for loops to work with arrays

How to use for-in loops to work with arrays

In contrast to a for loop, a *for-in loop* makes it easier to work with an array. Figure 16-4 shows how this type of loop works.

As the syntax at the top of this figure shows, the for-in loop doesn't require separate expressions that initialize, test, and increment an index counter like a for loop does. Instead, you declare a variable that will be used to refer to the index of each element in the array. Then, within the loop, you can use this variable to access each element in the array.

The first example in this figure stores the numbers 1 through 10 in an array and creates an empty string named numbersString. Then, it uses a for-in loop to concatenate each of the numbers in the array and a space to the string. Last, it displays the numbers in a message box.

The second example shows the differences in the ways that for loops and for-in loops handle the undefined elements in an array. In short, a for loop processes the undefined elements, but a for-in loop skips over them. You can see these differences in the messages that are displayed for each of the loops in this example.

You should know, though, that an array can contain two types of undefined elements. The first type is an element that doesn't have a value assigned to it so it is undefined. The second type is an element that has a value of "undefined" assigned to it. Although the for-in loop skips the first type of undefined element, it processes the second type of undefined element.

To illustrate, the fourth line in the second example in this figure

```
delete names[1]
```

creates the first type of undefined element. But the fifth line

```
names[names.length] = undefined
```

creates the second type of undefined element. As you can see in this figure, the for-in loop processes the undefined value created in the fifth line and displays "undefined" as the last value in the array. The message for the for loop, by contrast, shows both types of undefined values.

The syntax of a for-in loop

```
for (var elementIndex in arrayName) {
    // statements that access the elements
}
```

A for-in loop that displays the numbers array in a message box

```
var numbers = [1, 2, 3, 4, 5, 6, 7, 8, 9, 10];
var numbersString = "";
for (var index in numbers) {          // The start of the for-in loop
    numbersString += numbers[index] + " ";
}
alert( numbersString );
```

The message that's displayed

Code that shows the difference between for and for-in loops

```
var names = ["Grace", "Charles", "Ada"];
names[4] = "Alan";                  // Grace, Charles, Ada, undefined, Alan
names[names.length] = "Linus";      // Linus is added to the end of the array
delete names[1];                    // Charles is deleted from the array
names[names.length] = undefined;    // value of "undefined" added to the array

var namesString1 = "The elements displayed by the for loop:\n\n";
for (var i = 0; i < names.length; i++) {    // The start of the for loop
    namesString1 += names[i] + "\n"; }      // Includes undefined elements

var namesString2 = "The elements displayed by the for-in loop:\n\n";
for (var i in names) {                       // The start of the for-in loop
    namesString2 += names[i] + "\n"; }       // Omits undefined elements

alert( namesString1 );
alert( namesString2 );
```

The messages that are created by the for and the for-in loops

Description

- You can use a *for-in statement* to create a *for-in loop* that accesses only those elements in an array that are specifically assigned values. This includes undefined values if the undefined value was specifically assigned.

Figure 16-4   How to use for-in loops to work with arrays

How to use the methods of an Array object

In this topic, you'll learn some of the methods that JavaScript provides to help you work with arrays. Although a few of these methods are part of the ECMAScript 5 (ES5) specification, all modern browsers support ES5. In addition, the ES5 methods are in the ES5 shim.js file described in figure 1-17. So you should be able to use any of these methods in your applications.

Methods that accept simple parameters

Figure 16-5 summarizes methods for working with arrays that accept either no parameters or simple parameters like strings or numbers. The first seven methods listed here modify the original array. The last eight, by contrast, leave the original array unmodified and return a new value based on that array.

The first two methods, push() and pop(), are used to add elements to and remove elements from the end of an array. This lets you use an array as a stack in which the last element added to it is the first element removed (last-in, first-out). In this case, the oldest element is at the start of the array.

The next two methods, unshift() and shift(), are used to add elements to and remove elements from the start of an array. These methods also let you use an array as a stack in which the last element added to it is the first element removed. In this case, though, the oldest element is at the end of the array.

The reverse() method lets you change the order of the elements in an array, while the splice() method lets you remove, replace, and add elements in an array. To remove elements, you call the splice() method with the index of the first element to remove and the number of elements to remove. To replace elements, you call the splice() method with the index of the first element to replace, the number of elements to be replaced, and a list of the replacement values. To add elements, you call the splice() method with the index of the element just after the insertion point in the array, a zero, and a list of the values to add.

The slice() and concat() methods let you create a new array from part or all of an array, and the original array isn't modified. If you want the original array to be replaced by the new array, you can set the old array equal to the new array.

The join(), toString(), and toLocaleString() methods let you create a single string that contains the elements in the array. They differ mainly in how they handle the separator string. These methods use an empty string for any undefined elements.

The isArray() method accepts an object and returns a Boolean value. As you might guess, it returns true if the object it's passed is an array, and false if it isn't.

The last two methods are similar to the String methods of the same name. But instead of returning the position of a character in a string, they return the index of an element in an array. Also, like the String methods, they return -1 if the element isn't found. The indexOf() method starts its search from the beginning of the array, while the lastIndexOf() method starts its search from the end. Both have an optional start parameter, so you can specify the index to start searching from.

Methods of an Array object that accept simple parameters

Method	Description
push(*element_list*)	Adds one or more elements to the end of the array, and returns the new length of the array.
pop()	Removes the last element in the array, decrements the length, and returns the element that it removed.
unshift(*element_list*)	Adds one or more elements to the beginning of the array, and returns the new length of the array.
shift()	Removes the first element in the array, decrements the array length, and returns the element that it removed.
reverse()	Reverses the order of the elements in the array.
splice(*start, number*)	Removes the number of elements given by the second parameter starting with the index given by the first parameter. It returns the elements that were removed.
splice(*start, number, element_list*)	Removes the number of elements given by the second parameter starting with the index given by the first parameter, and replaces those elements with the ones given by the third parameter. It returns the elements that were removed.
slice(*start, number*)	Returns a new array that starts with the index given by the first parameter and continuing for the number of elements given by the second parameter.
concat(*array_list*)	Returns a new array that consists of the original array concatenated with the arrays in the array list.
join([*separator*])	When no parameter is passed, this method converts all the elements of the array to strings and concatenates them separated by commas. To change the separator, you can pass this method a string literal.
toString()	Same as the join() method without any parameter passed to it.
toLocaleString()	Same as the toString() method but using a locale-specific separator.
isArray(*object*)	Checks whether the object passed to it is an array. Returns true if it is, false if it isn't.
indexOf(*value, start*)	Returns the first index at which the first parameter is found, or -1 if the value isn't found. The second parameter specifies the index to start searching from and is optional.
lastIndexOf(*value, start*)	Returns the last index at which the first parameter is found, or -1 if the value isn't found. The second parameter specifies the index to start searching from and is optional.

Description

- The first seven methods shown above modify the original array.
- The last eight methods shown above produce a new array, string, Boolean, or integer value, and leave the original array unmodified.
- The last three methods shown above are part of the ES5 specification.

Figure 16-5   The methods of an Array object that accept simple parameters

Methods that accept functions as parameters

The methods you saw in the last figure accepted simple parameters. By contrast, the methods summarized in figure 16-6 accept a function definition as a parameter. A function definition that's passed to another function like this is a *callback function*, and it's used by the function that receives it to complete its task.

The first method shown here lets you change the sort order of the elements in an array. By default, the sort() method treats all of the elements as strings. This means that the numbers 5, 10, 101, and 250 are sorted as 10, 101, 250, and 5. If you need to sort the array in numeric order, though, you can pass a function to the sort() method with the syntax presented in the first summary below the table. This function compares two values at a time and returns a positive value, a negative value, or zero. Then, the sort() method uses this return value to determine where an element should go in relation to the other elements.

The next five methods accept a function whose syntax is presented in the second summary below the table. The first parameter of this function is the value of the current element being processed, and it's required. The next parameter is the index of the current element, and the third is the array itself. These methods execute this function once for each element in the array.

The forEach() method returns a value of undefined. The every() and some() methods, by contrast, return a Boolean value based on whether the elements in the array meet a condition tested by the function. As their names suggest, the every() method returns true if all the array elements pass the test, and the some() method returns true if some pass.

The map() and filter() methods both return new arrays. The map() method returns an array that contains the result of calling the function on each element. The filter() method, on the other hand, returns an array that contains only those elements of the original array that meet the specified condition of the function.

The last two methods, reduce() and reduceRight(), return all the elements in the array reduced to a single value. The functions that are passed to these methods use the syntax presented in the third summary below the table. The first parameter of this function is the value returned by the last function call. This is how these methods keep track of the single value that the array elements will be reduced to. The rest of the parameters of this function work the same as the parameters in the second summary. The only difference between reduce() and reduceRight() is the order in which the elements are processed.

When you call the sort() method on an array with undefined elements, the undefined elements are moved to the end of the array. For the rest of the methods described here, the function won't execute when the element is undefined.

The last seven methods presented in this table accept an optional second parameter. For the forEach(), every(), some(), map(), and filter() methods, this parameter lets you set the value of its function's *this* keyword. For the reduce() and reduceRight() functions, this parameter is an initial value for the previous value parameter used by its function.

Methods of an Array object that accept functions as parameters

Method	Description
sort([*comparison_function*])	Accepts an optional function to change the default sort order. If no function is passed, sorts the elements into ascending alphanumeric sequence, converting numeric elements to strings if necessary. The optional function should have the syntax shown below and should return a positive value if x is greater than y, zero if x and y are equal, and a negative value if x is less than y.
forEach(*function, this*)	Accepts a function that is executed once for each element. Returns a value of undefined.
every(*function, this*)	Accepts a function that tests each element in the array to see if it meets a specified condition. Returns true if all elements in the array pass the test, false otherwise.
some(*function, this*)	Accepts a function that tests each element in the array to see if it meets a specified condition. Returns true if at least one element in the array passes the test, false otherwise.
map(*function, this*)	Accepts a function that is executed once for each element, and returns a new array containing the results of each function call.
filter(*function, this*)	Accepts a function that is executed once for each element, and returns a new array containing the elements that meet the specified condition of the function.
reduce(*function, init*)	Accepts a function that returns all the elements reduced to one value, processed in ascending order.
reduceRight(*function, init*)	Accepts a function that returns all the elements reduced to one value, processed in descending order.

The syntax of the function for the sort() method

```
function(x, y);
```

The syntax of the function for the forEach(), every(), some(), map(), and filter() methods

```
function(currentValue, currentIndex, array);
```

The syntax of the function for the reduce() and reduceRight() methods

```
function(previousValue, currentValue, currentIndex, array);
```

Description

- The sort() method moves undefined elements to the end of the array. For the other methods shown here, the functions they receive won't be called for undefined elements.

- The forEach(), every(), some(), map(), and filter() methods accept an optional second parameter. This parameter is the value of the *this* keyword.

- The reduce() and reduceRight() methods also accept an optional second parameter. This parameter is an initial value for the previousValue parameter in the function the method accepts.

- All of these methods, with the exception of sort(), are part of the ES5 specification.

Figure 16-6   The methods of an Array object that accept functions as parameters

Examples of the Array methods

Figure 16-7 shows you how to use some of the methods you learned in the last two figures. If you study those figures along with these examples and the comments in the code, you shouldn't have much trouble understanding how these methods work.

First, the push() and pop() methods are used to add and remove elements. As you can see in this example, these methods modify the array. Because of that, it contains different elements after these methods are called.

Second, the slice() and concat() methods are used to create new arrays. Here, the slice() method is used to create a new array that consists of two elements taken from an array named names. Then, the concat() method is used to combine the two arrays in another new array. When all of the statements are finished, there are three arrays named names, namesSlice, and namesConcat. And, unlike the first example, in this case the original array, names, hasn't changed.

Third, the join() and toString() methods are used to create a string that lists the array's elements. The difference between them is that the join() method, which uses a comma by default, lets you specify the separator for the elements.

Fourth, the sort() method is used without and with a parameter. Without a parameter, the elements are sorted as strings. This means that alphabetic elements are sorted in alphabetic order, but numbers aren't sorted in numeric order.

If you want to sort the elements in an array numerically, you can pass a function to the sort() method. As you learned, this function should receive two parameters, and it should return a positive, zero, or negative value based on a comparison of the two parameter values. The returned value should be positive if the first parameter is greater than the second, zero if they're equal, and negative if the first parameter is less than the second.

In this example, this function is named comparison(), and it returns x - y. This causes the numbers to be sorted in ascending sequence. Then, this function definition is passed to the method.

Fifth, the map() method is used to create a new array that contains the results of executing the function on each item of the original array. As before, the example starts by creating an array to work with. Then, it calls the map() method, passes it a function that multiplies the value by itself, and stores the result in a variable called squared. In this example, the function parameter is declared at the same time it is passed, which is a common coding pattern.

Next, the map() method is called again, but this time it's passed the sqrt() method of the Math object to get the square roots of the numbers in the array. Since the original array isn't affected by calls to the map() method, the numbers array is unchanged after these two method calls.

Finally, the filter() method is used to retrieve certain elements from an array. Like the map() method, the filter() method creates a new array. However, instead of returning the result of executing the function on every element in the array, filter() only returns an element if the function call returns true. Here, for example, the checkPrime() function is passed to the filter() method so that only the prime numbers in an array of numbers are returned.

How to use the push() and pop() methods to add and remove elements

```
var names = ["Grace", "Charles", "Ada"];
names.push("Alan", "Linus");      // names is Grace, Charles, Ada, Alan, Linus
var removedName = names.pop();    // removedName is Linus
console.log( names.join() );      // Grace,Charles,Ada,Alan
```

How to use the slice() and concat() methods

```
var names = ["Grace", "Charles", "Ada", "Alan"];
var namesSlice = names.slice(0, 2);   // namesSlice is Grace, Charles
console.log( names.join(", ") );      // Grace, Charles, Ada, Alan

var namesConcat = names.concat(namesSlice);
console.log( namesConcat.join() );    // Grace,Charles,Ada,Alan,Grace,Charles
```

How to use the join() and toString() methods

```
var names = ["Grace", "Charles", "Ada", "Linus"];
console.log( names.join() );          // Grace,Charles,Ada,Linus
console.log( names.join(", ") );      // Grace, Charles, Ada, Linus
console.log( names.toString() );      // Grace,Charles,Ada,Linus
```

How to use the sort() method

For alphanumeric sorting

```
var names = ["Grace", "Charles", "Ada", "Alan", "Linus"];
names.sort();                     // names is Ada, Alan, Charles, Grace, Linus
```

For numeric sorting in ascending sequence

```
// The function used for the parameter of the sort method
var comparison = function(x, y) {
    return x - y;
};
var numbers = [520, 33, 9, 199];
numbers.sort(comparison);         // numbers is 9, 33, 199, 520
```

How to use the map() method

```
var numbers = [1,4,9,16];
// define and pass the function argument in one step
var squared = numbers.map(function( value ) {
    return value * value;
});                                       // squared is 1,16,81,256
// pass an object's method as the function argument
var root = numbers.map( Math.sqrt );      // root is 1,2,3,4
```

How to use the filter() method

```
var numbers = [1,2,3,4,5,6,7,8,9,10,11,12,13,14,15,16,17,18,19,20];
var checkPrime = function( value ){
    var isPrime = true;
    for ( var i = 2; i < value; i++ ) {
        if ( value % i === 0 ) {
            isPrime = false;
            break;
        }
    }
    return isPrime;
};
var prime = numbers.filter( checkPrime );    // prime is 1,2,3,5,7,11,13,17,19
```

Figure 16-7   Examples of the methods of the Array object

The Task List application

To show you how some of the skills you've just learned can be used in an application, the next two figures present the Task List application you saw in the last chapter, updated to use arrays.

The user interface

Like before, this application displays the tasks that the user adds to the task list in a text area on the right side of the page. Now, though, the tasks will be sorted in ascending alphabetical order. To add a task, the user enters the task in the first text box and clicks on the Add Task button. To clear all the tasks, the user clicks on the Clear Tasks button.

Unlike before, this version doesn't store the tasks in a cookie or local storage. That's so you can focus on how the application uses arrays. Later, though, you'll see a version of this application that does store the tasks in local storage. Then, you'll see how the methods for working with arrays make this easier.

The JavaScript

Figure 16-8 presents the JavaScript for this application. As usual, it starts with the jQuery ready() event handler. Then, the JavaScript creates an array object to hold tasks entered by the user, a function that displays those tasks, and event handlers for the Add Task and Clear Tasks buttons. The ready() event handler ends by setting the focus on the Task textbox.

The displayTaskList() function starts by calling the sort() method of the tasks array to sort the tasks in ascending alphabetical order. After that, it calls the join() method of the array to convert the array elements to a single string. It passes the resulting string to the val() method of the textarea element.

As you can see, the call to the join() method here passes the newline character. This means the string that's set as the value of the textarea element will have a separator of the newline character. Finally, the function sets the focus on the task text box.

The event handler for the click event of the Add Task button starts by retrieving the text box element containing the new task. Then, it retrieves the value of the text box and checks it to make sure the user entered something. If not, it notifies the user.

If the user did enter a task, the code calls the push() method of the tasks array to add the new task to the end of the task items. Finally, it clears the Task text box and calls the displayTaskList() function to update the textarea with the new task data.

The event handler for the click event of the Clear Tasks button starts by assigning a new array object to the tasks variable. This overwrites the previous array object, replacing any items it may have contained with a new array that has no items. After that, it clears the textarea element that displays the tasks, and it sets the focus on the Task text box.

The Task List application

The JavaScript for the application

```javascript
$(document).ready(function(){
    var tasks = [];   // array that will hold the tasks

    var displayTaskList = function() {
        tasks.sort();

        $("#task_list").val( tasks.join( "\n" ) );
        $("#task").focus();
    };

    $("#add_task").click(function() {
        var textbox = $("#task");
        var task = textbox.val();
        if (task === "") {
            alert("Please enter a task.");
            textbox.focus();
        } else {
            tasks.push( task );
            textbox.val( "" );
            displayTaskList();
        }
    });

    $("#clear_tasks").click(function() {
        tasks = [];
        $("#task_list").val( "" );
        $("#task").focus();
    });

    // set focus on initial load
    $("#task").focus();
});
```

Description

- This application uses an array to store the tasks added by the user.
- To display the tasks, the application uses the array's sort() and join() methods.
- To add a new task to the end of the array, the application uses the array's push() method.
- To clear the tasks, the application assigns a new array to the tasks variable. This overwrites the array that the tasks variable previously held.

Figure 16-8   The JavaScript for the Task List application

Other skills for working with arrays

Now that you've learned the basic skills for creating and working with arrays, you're ready to learn some other skills for working with arrays. Keep an eye out, too, for some of the skills from the last figures in the examples coming up.

How to use a String method to create an array

Figure 16-9 presents the split() method of a String object. This method can be used to divide a string into multiple substrings based on a separator character that's coded as the first parameter. It then creates a new array with each of the substrings as elements. If you code a second parameter, it is used to limit the number of elements that can be included in the new array.

The first example in this figure shows how to split a string that's separated by spaces into an array named nameParts. Next, it displays the length of the new array and the elements in the array. Then, it moves the element at the last index in the array (length - 1) into a variable named lastName and displays the contents of that variable.

Note in this example that the second alert() method doesn't need to call the toString() method to display the elements in the array. That's because the alert() method expects a string, and it automatically calls the toString() method for any parameter that isn't a string. In this case, because the parameter is an array, the toString() method concatenates the elements in the array and separates them with commas.

Similarly, the second example shows how to split a string that's separated by hyphens into an array. Then, the third example shows how to split a string into individual characters. This happens when you call the split() method with an empty string as its parameter.

Note the ways that the examples so far use the join() and toString() methods of the array. The second example calls the join() method and specifies the string literal "/" as the separator, which produces the string "1/2/2017". The third example, by contrast, doesn't specify a separator when it calls join(), so the default separator of a comma is used. And the first example calls the toString() method, which works the same way as the third example's call of the join() method.

The fourth example shows what happens if the separator character isn't in the string. Here, a date string is created that has hyphens, but the split() method is called with a slash as the separator. In this case, the resulting array only has one element and it is a copy of the original date string.

The fifth example shows how to limit the number of substrings copied into the new array. Here, the split() method uses a space as the separator, but it limits the number of substrings to one. The result is an array that contains just the first name in one element.

A String method that creates an array

Method	Description
`split(separator, limit)`	Splits a string into an array based on the value of the separator parameter and returns the array. The optional limit parameter specifies the maximum number of elements in the new array.

How to split a string that's separated by spaces into an array

```
var fullName = "Grace M Hopper";
var nameParts = fullName.split(" ");      // creates an array
alert( nameParts.length );                // displays 3
alert( nameParts );                       // displays Grace,M,Hopper
var lastName = nameParts[nameParts.length - 1];
alert( lastName );                        // displays Hopper
```

How to split a string that's separated by hyphens into an array

```
var date = "1-2-2017";
var dateParts = date.split("-");          // creates an array
alert( dateParts.length );                // displays 3
alert( dateParts.join("/") );             // displays 1/2/2017
```

How to split a string into an array of characters

```
var fullName = "Grace Hopper";
var nameCharacters = fullName.split("");
alert( nameCharacters.length );           // displays 12
alert( nameCharacters.join() );           // displays G,r,a,c,e, ,H,o,p,p,e,r
```

How it works if the string doesn't contain the separator

```
var date = "1-2-2017";
var dateParts2 = date.split("/");
alert( dateParts2.length );               // displays 1
alert( dateParts2.join() );               // displays 1-2-2017
```

How to get just one element from a string

```
var fullName = "Grace M Hopper";
var firstName = fullName.split(" ", 1);
alert( firstName.length );                // displays 1
alert( firstName );                       // displays Grace
```

Description

- The split() method of a String object is used to convert the components of a string into the elements of an array.

- If a string doesn't include the separator that's specified in the parameter of the split() method, the entire string is returned as the first element in a one-element array.

- If the separator that's specified by the parameter is an empty string, each character in the string becomes an element in the array that's returned by the method.

Figure 16-9   How to use a String method to create an array

How to create and use an associative array

So far, the arrays you've worked with have used whole numbers as the indexes. In contrast, an *associative array* is an array that uses strings as the indexes. In figure 16-10, you can learn how to create and work with associative arrays.

The first example in this figure creates an associative array with four elements. First, it creates an empty array. Then, it stores four values in the array using strings for the indexes. Finally, it displays the length of the associative array. However, because the length property of an array only counts elements with numeric indexes, the length is zero.

Luckily, you can use the keys() method of the Object object to return an array that contains the names of the associative array's string indexes. Then, you can use that array's length property to get the length of the associative array. The last statement in this example shows how that works.

The second example adds an element to the array with another string index. The new value is the result of a calculation that uses two existing elements of the array, and the toFixed() method is used to round the result.

The third example displays a formatted string that's built from the elements in the array. In the dialog box that follows, you can see that the array now contains five elements.

The fourth example shows how to use the for-in loop with an associative array. This for-in loop builds a formatted string that contains the element indexes and values. The comments after the last statement show the string that would be displayed by the alert statement.

Although you can mix numeric and string indexes within a single array, you usually should avoid doing that because mixed arrays present some unnecessary complications. If you do mix them, the length property indicates only the number of elements with numeric indexes. If you process a mixed array with a for loop, the associative elements aren't included in the processing. And if you process a mixed array with a for-in loop, all of the elements are processed.

Finally, you should know that when you add elements with string indexes like this, what you're really doing is adding properties to the Array object. That's why the Object.keys() method works to get the number of elements. You'll learn more about objects in chapter 17.

How to create an associative array with four elements

```
var item = [];
item["itemCode"] = 123;
item["itemName"] = "HTML5";
item["itemCost"] = 54.5;
item["itemQuantity"] = 5;
alert( item.length );                    // Displays 0
alert( Object.keys(item).length );       // Displays 4
```

How to add an element to the associative array

```
item["lineCost"] = (item["itemCost"] * item["itemQuantity"]).toFixed(2);
```

How to retrieve and display the elements in the associative array

```
alert( "Item elements:\n\nCode = " + item["itemCode"] +
       "\nName = " + item["itemName"] +
       "\nCost = " + item["itemCost"] +
       "\nQuantity = " + item["itemQuantity"] +
       "\nLine Cost = " + item["lineCost"] );
```

The message displayed by the alert() method

```
Item elements:

Code = 123
Name = HTML5
Cost = 54.5
Quantity = 5
Line Cost = 272.50


                              OK
```

How to use a for-in loop with the associative array

```
var result = "";
for ( var i in item ) {
    result += i + " = " + item[i] + "\n";
}
alert( result );
// "itemCode = 123\nitemName = HTML5\nitemCost = 54.5\n" +
// "itemQuantity = 5\nlineCost = 272.50"
```

Description

- When you create an *associative array*, you use strings as the indexes instead of numbers.
- If you mix numeric and string indexes in an array, the length will indicate only the number of elements with numeric indexes, a for loop will only process the elements with numeric indexes, and a for-in loop will process all the elements.
- When you add string indexes like this, what you're actually doing is adding properties to the array object (see chapter 17). Because of this, some of the array properties and methods don't work as expected. For instance, the length property returns 0 and the pop() method returns undefined.
- The Object.keys() method shown above is part of the ES5 specification. Because it's in the ES5 shim.js file described in figure 1-17, though, you should be able to use it in applications that run in older browsers.

Figure 16-10   How to create and use an associative array

How to create and use an array of arrays

Although JavaScript doesn't let you create multi-dimensional arrays, you can get the same effect by creating an *array of arrays*. To do that, you store arrays in each element of another array. These arrays don't have to be the same length, and you will often see an associative array nested inside a numerically indexed array. In figure 16-11, you can learn how to create and use an array of arrays.

The first example in this figure shows how to create and use an array of arrays. First, it creates an empty array called testScores. Then, it stores arrays of test scores in the first four elements of the outer testScores array.

The next two statements in the first example shows how to access the elements in this array. Here, the first statement displays the value in the element at index 1 of the array that's in the element at index 0 of the testScores array. The second statement displays the value in the element at index 3 of the array that's in the element at index 2 of the testScores array.

The second example in this figure shows how to nest associative arrays in a numerically indexed array. Here, the first statement creates an array named invoice that will be numerically indexed.

The second group of statements stores an empty array as the first element in the invoice array. After that, it adds four elements to the empty array, using strings as indexes. This creates an associative array nested within a numeric array.

The third group of statements illustrates another way to add an associative array as an element of a numeric array. In this case, a new array called item is created, and four elements with string indexes are added to it. Then, the item array is passed to the push() method of the invoice array. This adds the item array to the end of the invoice array.

Note that if you're going to add arrays this way, you can't re-use the item array for the next array you want to add. That's because the push() method puts a reference to the item array, rather than a copy of it, in the element of the invoice array. So you'll need to declare a separate array variable for each array you want to add. You'll learn more about references in chapter 17.

The fourth group of statements accesses the elements of the nested arrays. Here, the first statement displays the value of the itemCode element that's in the first element (index 0) of the invoice array. This displays 123. Then, the second statement displays the value of the itemName element that's in the second element (index 1) of the invoice array. This displays jQuery.

How to create and use an array of arrays

Code that creates an array of arrays

```
var testScores = [];
testScores[0] = [80, 82, 90, 87, 85];
testScores[1] = [79, 80, 74];
testScores[2] = [93, 95, 89, 100];
testScores[3] = [60, 72, 65, 71];
```

Code that refers to elements in the array of arrays

```
alert( testScores[0][1] );        // displays 82
alert( testScores[2][3] );        // displays 100
```

How to create and use an array of associative arrays

Code that creates an array

```
var invoice = [];                 // create an empty invoice array
```

Code that adds an associative array to the invoice array directly

```
invoice[0] = [];
invoice[0]["itemCode"] = 123;
invoice[0]["itemName"] = "HTML5";
invoice[0]["itemCost"] = 54.5;
invoice[0]["itemQuantity"] = 5;
```

Code that creates an associative array and then adds it to the invoice array

```
var item = [];
item["itemCode"] = 456;
item["itemName"] = "jQuery";
item["itemCost"] = 52.5;
item["itemQuantity"] = 2;
invoice.push(item);   // add the item array to the end of the invoice array
```

Code that refers to the elements in the array of associative arrays

```
alert( invoice[0]["itemCode"] );   // displays 123
alert( invoice[1]["itemName"] );   // displays jQuery
```

Description

- Although JavaScript doesn't provide for multi-dimensional arrays, you can get the same effect by creating an *array of arrays*. In an array of arrays, each element in the first array is another array.

- The arrays within an array can be regular arrays or associative arrays.

- To refer to the elements in an array of arrays, you use two index values for each element. The first value is for an element in the primary array. The second value is for an element in the array that's in the element of the primary array.

- If necessary, you can nest arrays beyond the two dimensions that are illustrated here. In other words, you can create an array of arrays of arrays. As usual, be careful with this as your code can become hard to read and maintain if it's too complex.

Figure 16-11   How to create and use an array of arrays

The Task List 2.0 application

To show you how some of the skills you've just learned can be used in an application, the next two figures present the Task List 2.0 application. It is like the application that you saw earlier in this chapter, but it uses an array of arrays for the task list and it stores the task list in local web storage.

Like before, this application displays the user's tasks in a textarea element on the right side of the page. Now, though, the tasks include a due date, and are sorted by this date in ascending order. Additionally, the application uses the jQuery UI DatePicker widget for the Due Date text box. As you'll see in the next figure, three options have been coded for this widget so the user can select a month and year from drop-down lists and so a date can't be selected if it's before the current date. Using this widget makes it easier for the user to select a date, and also easier to ensure that only dates are entered for this value.

In this application, the task list is saved when the user closes the browser tab or window. It is also restored when the user re-opens the page.

The HTML

The HTML and CSS for this application are mostly the same as what you saw earlier in this chapter, so only the changes are presented in figure 16-12. First, the head element contains script and link elements for jQuery UI, as well as for the core jQuery library. Note that the jQuery UI element comes after the jQuery element.

Second, the main element now includes an input element for the due date as well as for the task text. Note that you don't have to do anything special to this input element for it to work with the DatePicker widget.

This figure also shows the format for the tasks that are stored in a single name/value pair in local storage. Here, the tasks are separated by pipes, and the due date and text of each task are separated by tildes. You'll see how the application works with this format next, when you look at the JavaScript code.

The Task List application

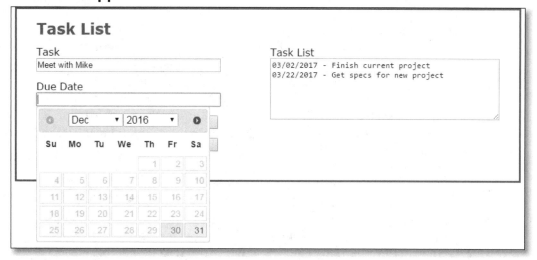

The HTML for the application

The head element

```
<title>Task Manager</title>
<link rel="stylesheet"
    href="//code.jquery.com/ui/1.12.1/themes/base/jquery-ui.css">
<link rel="stylesheet" href="task_list.css">
<script src="https://code.jquery.com/jquery-3.1.1.min.js"></script>
<script src="https://code.jquery.com/ui/1.12.1/jquery-ui.js"></script>
<script src="task_list.js"></script>
```

The main element

```
<h1>Task Manager</h1>
...
<label for="task">Task</label><br>
<input type="text" name="task" id="task"><br>

<label for="due_date">Due Date</label><br>
<input type="text" name="due_date" id="due_date"><br>
...
```

The string that's stored in local storage

```
Get specs for new project~~03/22/2017|Finish current project~~03/02/2017|
```

Description

- This updated Task List application lets the user add a due date to a task. It uses the jQuery UI DatePicker widget, and it stores the task and due date in an array of arrays.

- The tasks are stored in local storage in a single string. The text and due date of a task entry are separated by tildes (~~), while the tasks themselves are separated by pipes (|).

Figure 16-12   The HTML for the Task List 2.0 application

The JavaScript

Figure 16-13 presents the JavaScript that's coded in the jQuery ready() function. To fit this on the page, though, the ready() function isn't shown.

The first function within the ready() function is the displayTaskList() function. It starts by retrieving the string of tasks from local storage. Then, it checks to see if that string is empty. If not, the code creates a new array named tasks, and uses the split() method of the string to split it on the pipe separator. It stores the array that's returned by the split() method in a variable named interim.

This function then loops through the interim array and calls the split() method again on each item in that array. This time, though, it splits the string on the tilde separator. Finally, it uses the push() method of the tasks array to add each array returned by the split() method to the end of the tasks array. When this code finishes, the tasks variable is an array of arrays, with each array in the array representing the text and due date of a task.

Next, this function sorts the array of arrays by due date. It does this by passing a callback function to the sort() method of the tasks array. This callback function compares two array elements. Since this is an array of arrays, that means the two elements being compared are arrays. So, the callback function gets the due date value from each array and converts it to a Date object. Then, it returns -1, 1, or 0, depending on whether the first date is less than, greater than, or equal to the second date. This sorts the dates in ascending order.

When the sort finishes, this function uses the reduce() method of the tasks array to create a single string for display. Remember that the callback function for the reduce() method accepts the previous value returned by the callback, plus the current element in the array. Since this is an array of arrays, that means the current element is an array. So, the callback function concatenates the two values in the array, separated by a dash and ending with the newline character. The call to the reduce() method also sets the initial value of the prev parameter to an empty string so the concatenation works properly.

Finally, this function sets the value of the textarea element to the value of the taskString variable, which is either an empty string or the result of the reduce() method. Then, it sets the focus on the Task text box.

The next function is the event handler for the click event of the Add Task button. It gets the task and due date entered by the user. If the entries are valid, it retrieves the task string from local storage and creates an array called newTask with the task and due date values. Then, it calls that array's join() method to create a new task string and adds it to the string in local storage. Note that it adds a pipe character at the end to separate this task from any task that's added later.

This is followed by the event handler for the click event of the Clear Tasks button. This event handler just clears local storage, clears the text area, and sets the focus on the text box for a task entry.

Next, the ready() function associates the Date Picker widget with the Due Date text box. So when a user clicks in that text box, the DatePicker will appear.

Last, the ready() function calls the displayTaskList() function. As you've seen, that function starts the application by getting the task list from web storage and displaying it.

The JavaScript in the document.ready() function

```javascript
var displayTaskList = function() {
    var taskString = localStorage.tasks || "";
    if (taskString.length > 0) {
        var tasks = [];

        var interim = taskString.split( "|" );
        for (var i = 0; i < interim.length - 1; i++) {
            tasks.push( interim[i].split( "~~" ));
        }

        tasks.sort(function(arr1, arr2) {
            var a = new Date(arr1[1]); // 2nd element of first array
            var b = new Date(arr2[1]); // 2nd element of second array
            if ( a < b ) { return -1; }
            else if ( a > b ) { return 1; }
            else { return 0; }
        });

        taskString = tasks.reduce( function( prev, current ) {
            return prev + current[1] + " - " + current[0] + "\n";
        }, ""); // pass initial value for prev parameter
    }

    $("#task_list").val( taskString );
    $("#task").focus();
};
$( "#add_task" ).click(function() {
    var task = $("#task").val();
    var dueDate = $("#due_date").val();

    if (task === "" || dueDate === "") {
        alert("Please enter a task and due date.");
        $("#task").focus();
    } else {
        var taskString = localStorage.tasks || "";
        var newTask = [task, dueDate];
        localStorage.tasks = taskString + newTask.join( "~~" ) + "|";

        $("#task").val("");
        $("#due_date").val("");
        displayTaskList();
    }
});
$( "#clear_tasks" ).click(function() {
    localStorage.removeItem("tasks");
    $("#task_list").val("");
    $("#task").focus();
});
$( "#due_date" ).datepicker({
    changeMonth: true,
    changeYear: true,
    minDate: 0
});

// display tasks on initial load
displayTaskList();
```

Figure 16-13   The JavaScript for the Task List 2.0 application

Perspective

Arrays are an important part of many JavaScript applications, and JavaScript provides some excellent methods for working with arrays. In the chapters that follow, you'll see other uses of arrays and other ways to work with them.

Terms

array	for loop
element	for-in loop
length	callback function
index	associative array
sparse array	array of arrays

Summary

- An *array* can store one or more *elements*. The *length* of an array is the number of elements in the array. To refer to the elements in an array, you use an *index* where 0 is the index of the first element in the array.

- Both *for loops* and *for-in loops* can be used to work with the elements in an array. In contrast to a for loop, though, a for-in loop only accesses the elements in the array that have values specifically assigned to them.

- JavaScript provides many methods for working with Array objects, including a set of methods that became available with ECMAScript 5.

- You can use the split() method of a String object to create an array from substrings within a string.

- An *associative array* uses strings for the indexes instead of numbers.

- In an *array of arrays*, each element in one array contains another array.

Exercise 16-1   Enhance the Task List application

This exercise will give you a chance to work with arrays as you enhance the first version of the Task List application in this chapter. The enhanced version has a new Delete Task button, and looks like this:

Task List

Task

Add Task

Delete Task

Clear Tasks

Task List

Finish current project
Get specs for next project
Meet with Mike

Open, test, and review this application

1. Use your text editor or IDE to open the HTML and JavaScript files in this folder:

   `javascript_jquery\exercises\ch16\task_list\`

2. Test this application in Chrome by using the Add Task button to add tasks to the list and the Clear Tasks button to clear the list. Then, add a new task and click on the Delete button to see that it doesn't do anything yet.

3. Review the JavaScript file for this application to see that the ready() event handler contains an event handler for the click event of the Delete button.

Code the Delete Task event handler

4. Code the event handler for the Delete button so it uses the prompt() method to ask the user for the index number of the task to delete, starting with zero for the first task. Next, sort the tasks to make sure their order matches the order of the displayed tasks.

5. Still in the handler, use the splice() method of the tasks array to delete the element at the specified index. Then, call the displayTaskList() function to re-display the tasks.

6. Run the application and test the Delete Task button. Notice that if you enter an index value that isn't in the array or a value that isn't a number, nothing happens.

7. Add data validation to the Delete Task event handler so the user's entry has to be a number and has to be an index value that's in the array. You can use the length property of the task array for this, but remember that array indexes are zero based, so you'll need to subtract 1 from the length value for this to work.

8. Display a message to the user if either data validation check fails. Then, test this change.

Exercise 16-2   Enhance the Task List 2.0 application

This exercise will give you a chance to work with an array of arrays as you enhance the second version of the Task List application in this chapter. The enhanced version has a new Filter button that lets you filter tasks by a search term. In the example that follows, only the first and third tasks will be displayed when the user clicks the OK button in the dialog box:

Open, test, and review this application

1. Use your text editor or IDE to open the HTML and JavaScript files in this folder:

   ```
   javascript_jquery\exercises\ch16\task_list_web\
   ```

2. Test this application in Chrome by using the Add Task button to add a few tasks to the list. Then, click on the Filter button to see that it doesn't do anything yet.

3. Review the JavaScript file for this application. Note here that the ready() event handler contains an empty event handler for the click event of the Filter button.

4. Also note that this code is different from the code in the book application. Here, the functionality of the displayTaskList() function has been divided into two functions: getSortedTasksArray() and displayTaskList(). Note too that the displayTaskList() function now accepts a parameter containing the array of tasks to display, and it calls the getSortedTasksArray() function if it doesn't receive anything.

Code the Filter event handler

5. In the event handler for the Filter button, use the prompt() method to ask the user for the text to search for. This prompt should inform the user that all tasks will be displayed if nothing is entered, as shown above. The value returned by the prompt() method should be stored in a variable named searchTerm.

6. Code an if-else statement that tests whether the value of the searchTerm variable is an empty string. If it is, the code should call the displayTaskList() function with no parameter to retrieve and display all the tasks in local storage.

7. If the value of the searchTerm variable isn't an empty string, the else clause should (1) call the getSortedTasksArray() function to get the tasks from local storage as a sorted array of arrays, and (2) use the toLowerCase() method to set the value of the searchTerm variable to all lowercase characters.

8. Still in the else clause, the code should call the filter() method of the tasks array (see figures 16-6 and 16-7) to filter the tasks based on the searchTerm variable. This method returns an array of the items that have been filtered, and that array should be stored in an array named filtered. The trick to using the filter method is coding the function that is passed to the filter method as its argument. This function should return true if the element should be included in the filtered array or false if it shouldn't be.

   But remember that you're filtering an array of arrays. This means that the parameter for the function that you pass to the filter() method is a task array with two elements. The first element is the text string for the task, and the second element is the date string. When you code this function, you want to include any task arrays for which the search term is found in either the date or the text element. And you should do the comparisons with lowercase text values so capitalization won't affect the comparisons.

   The last statement of the else clause should call the displayTaskList() function and pass it the filtered array variable so only the filtered tasks will be displayed.

9. Test the application by clicking the Filter button and entering a search term. Then, click the Filter button again and leave the text box blank to make those items that were filtered out re-appear.

17

How to create and use your own objects

In chapter 4, you learned how to use native JavaScript object types like Number, String, and Date, and you've been using JavaScript objects ever since. Now, in this chapter, you'll learn how to create and use your own objects. As you will see, this is a way to group related data and functions, and that makes it easier to maintain and reuse the code that you create.

Basic skills for working with objects

This topic presents the basic skills for creating and using objects. That includes how to create and use libraries that store your objects.

How to create and use the native object types

In contrast to other languages, JavaScript has the flat hierarchy of *native object types* that's shown by the chart in figure 17-1. At the top level is the Object object type. At the next level are the other native object types like the String, Number, Boolean, Date, and Array object types that you've already learned about. In addition, you can see that Function is a native object type.

This hierarchy means that all of the object types at the second level *inherit* the properties and methods of the Object type. This also means that every object type can use the properties and methods of the Object type. For instance, the Object type has a toString method that converts an object to a string.

After the hierarchy chart, this figure shows the syntax for creating a new *instance* of an object type with the *new* keyword. This figure then shows an example of creating a new Date object.

However, you can also create a new instance of a native object type by declaring a variable with a literal value. When you do that, JavaScript automatically converts the value to the corresponding native object. You can see this in the examples, where instances of String, Number, Boolean, Array, Function, and Object object types are created by storing literal values in a variable.

In fact, it's a best practice to use literal values like this to create native objects rather than using the new keyword. However, since JavaScript doesn't have a literal date value, you need to use the new keyword to create Date objects.

Last, this figure shows how to access the *properties* and *methods* of an object. The common way to do that is to code the object name, the dot operator, and the property or method name.

However, as the comments after these examples show, you can also access a property or method by coding the object name followed by the property or method name within brackets. When you use brackets, though, the property or method name must be in quotes. Otherwise, JavaScript will interpret the identifier as a variable name rather than a property name.

The JavaScript hierarchy of some of the native object types

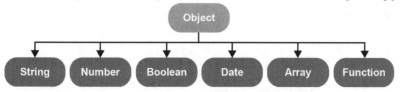

The syntax for creating a new object of a native type

```
var variableName = new ObjectType(arguments);
```

How to create a new object of the Date type

```
var today = new Date();
```

How to create a new object of a native type with literal values

How to create a new object of the String type

```
var lastName = "Hopper";              // Same as new String("Hopper");
```

How to create a new object of the Number type

```
var taxRate = .0875;                  // Same as new Number(.0875);
```

How to create a new object of the Boolean type

```
var validFlag = true;                 // Same as new Boolean(true);
```

How to create a new object of the Array type

```
var tasks = [];                       // Same as new Array();
```

How to create a new object of the Function type

```
var isValue = function() {...};       // Same as new Function('...');
```

How to create a new object of the Object type

```
var invoice = {};                     // Same as new Object();
```

How to use the properties and methods of the native object types

How to use the length property of a String object

```
length = lastName.length;             // Same as lastName["length"];
```

How to use the toFixed method of a Number object

```
formattedRate = taxRate.toFixed(4);   // Same as taxRate["toFixed"](4);
```

Description

- JavaScript provides a two-level hierarchy of *object types*. The top-level consists of the Object object type. The next level consists of types like String, Number, Date, and Array.

- All object types at the second level *inherit* the *properties* and *methods* of the Object object type. They also provide their own properties and methods.

- When you create a variable with a literal value, JavaScript converts it to the corresponding native object type. It's a best practice to create native objects this way, rather than with the new keyword. However, JavaScript doesn't have a literal date value, so you need to use the new keyword with Date objects.

- To access a property or method, you can use the dot operator or brackets. For instance, the associative arrays you saw in figure 16-11 use brackets.

Figure 17-1   How to create and use the native object types

How to create your own objects with object literals

The simplest way to create your own object is by storing an *object literal* in a variable. To do that, you declare a variable that's equal to a pair of braces. Then, within the braces, you can code the properties and methods for the object, as shown in figure 17-2. When you create an object in this way, you are actually creating an instance of the Object object type.

In example 1 in this figure, an object named invoice is initialized with one property named taxRate that has a value of 0.0875. As you can see, the property name and value must be separated by a colon.

In example 2, the invoice object is initialized with one method named getTotal(). Here, the method name is followed by a colon and a function expression that does the task of the method. What's happening here is that a function is stored as a property of the object. A property that stores a function definition like this is called a *method* of the object.

In example 3, the invoice object is initialized with a property and two methods. Here, the property and methods must be separated by commas. Note also that the two methods of the object use the *this* keyword to get the value of the taxRate property or to call another method. That's because the *this* keyword in the method of an object usually refers to the object itself.

After you create the properties and methods for an object, you can use them just as you use the properties and methods of native objects. That means you can use either the dot operator or brackets to refer to the properties and methods. In practice, though, the dot operator is commonly used because it's easier to code and easier to understand. This is illustrated by the next set of examples.

The last set of examples in this figure shows that you can also *nest* one object within another. In this case, a terms object is nested within an invoice object. To do that, the invoice object is initialized with one property named terms, and the terms property is itself an object that is initialized with two properties named taxRate and dueDays.

How to initialize a new object with properties and methods

Example 1: How to initialize a new object with one property

```
var invoice = { taxRate: 0.0875 };
```

Example 2: How to initialize a new object with one method

```
var invoice = {
    getTotal: function( subtotal, salesTax ) {
        return subtotal + salesTax;
    }
};
```

Example 3: How to initialize a new object with properties and methods

```
var invoice = {
    taxRate: 0.0875,
    getSalesTax: function( subtotal ) {
        return ( subtotal * this.taxRate );
    },
    getTotal: function( subtotal ) {
        return subtotal + this.getSalesTax( subtotal );
    }
};
```

How to refer to the properties and methods of an object

```
alert( invoice.taxRate );                   // Displays 0.0875
var salesTax = invoice.getSalesTax(100)     // salesTax = 8.75
var invoiceTotal = invoice.getTotal(100)    // invoiceTotal = 108.75
```

How to nest objects and refer to the nested properties and methods

How to nest one object within another

```
var invoice = {
    terms: {
        taxRate: 0.0875,
        dueDays: 30
    }
};
```

How to refer to the properties and methods of a nested object

```
alert( invoice.terms.taxRate );             // Displays 0.0875
```

Description

- When you create an object with a literal value (known as an *object literal*), you can add properties by coding pairs of property names and values that are separated by colons.

- When a property name is paired with a function, it's called a method. In strict mode, you can't have duplicate property or method names.

- Inside a method, the value of the *this* keyword is usually the object itself. You'll learn more about the this keyword later in this chapter.

- If necessary, you can *nest* one object inside another by making the inner object a property of the outer object.

Figure 17-2   How to create your own objects with object literals

How to extend or modify an object

After you create an object, you can extend the object by adding new properties and methods to it. This is illustrated by the first set of examples in figure 17-3. To add a property, you assign a new property to an object and give it a value. To add a method, you assign a new property and code a function expression as its value.

Once a property has been created, you can modify it by assigning a new value to it. This is illustrated by the second example in this figure. You can also change a method by assigning a new function expression to it.

To remove a property from an object, you can use the *delete operator* as shown in the third example. Here, the delete operator is used to remove the taxRate property from the invoice object. Once deleted, the property has a value of undefined, just as though it had never been created.

When you create an object and store it in a variable, you need to realize that JavaScript actually stores a *reference* to the object in the variable. This is illustrated by the diagram in this figure. In this case, both the today and now variables refer to the same Date object.

This means that if you change the Date object that the today variable refers to, the change will also be seen through the now variable. If, for example, you use the setFullYear() method of the today variable to set the year to 2018, the getFullYear() method of the now variable will get 2018. This is the same mechanism that is used when you pass an argument by reference.

How to add properties and methods to an object

```
var invoice = {};                          // Creates a new object literal
invoice.taxRate = 0.0875;                  // Adds the taxRate property
invoice.getSalesTax = function(subtotal) { // Adds the getSalesTax method
    return ( subtotal * this.taxRate );
};
```

How to modify the value of a property

```
invoice.taxRate = 0.095;
```

How to remove a property from an object

```
delete invoice.taxRate;
alert( invoice.taxRate );                  // Displays undefined
```

Two variables that refer to the same object

```
today = new Date();
now = today;
```

A diagram that illustrates these references

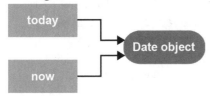

Description

- Once an object is created, you can add new properties and methods to it. You can also change the value of an existing property by assigning a new value to it, and you can change a method by assigning a new function expression to it.

- To remove a property or method from an object, you can use the *delete operator*.

- A variable or property holds a *reference* to an object, not the object itself. When you pass an object to a function as an argument, you are passing a reference to the object.

Figure 17-3   How to extend or modify an object

How to create and use JavaScript libraries

A *library* is a file that contains a group of related functions, objects, or both. Often, you'll write your own libraries, but you can also use third-party libraries like jQuery and jQuery UI. Some of the benefits of organizing your code in libraries are listed in figure 17-4.

One of the main benefits of libraries is code re-use. This is because you can write a function or object once and then use it from several different places in your code.

Another benefit of libraries is that they help you keep your JavaScript files smaller, which makes them easier to understand and easier to re-use. For example, you can write a library that provides functionality for working with web storage. Since that's all it does, it will be small. Then, you can include that file with any applications that need to use web storage.

Finally, organizing your JavaScript code in libraries encourages you to group code that has similar functionality. This, in turn, encourages *separation of concerns*. For example, one library might focus on web storage, while another focuses on data validation, while another focuses on working with dates and times. When you group your code in libraries like this, your application is easier to maintain and the code is easier to re-use in other applications.

The first example in this figure shows a simple library file named library_mpg.js. As its name suggests, it contains an object named mpg with properties and methods for calculating miles per gallon.

Next is an example that shows how to include this JavaScript library in an application and use it. Since a JavaScript library is just a JavaScript file, you use a script element to include a library just as you've been doing throughout this book. The first script element in the index.html file in this figure refers to the jQuery library, and the next one refers to the mpg library. The last script element is for the main JavaScript file that uses both these libraries.

When you include library files in this way, the JavaScript works as if all of the code were in the same file. However, you do need to think about the order in which you include the files. Specifically, if one file depends on the functionality in another file, you need to include the files in the proper order. For example, the jQuery UI library uses the functionality in the jQuery library. So when you use jQuery UI, you not only need to make sure that you include jQuery, but also that the script element for jQuery UI comes after the script element for jQuery. The same goes for working with your own libraries.

For instance, in the example shown here, the main JavaScript file depends on both the mpg library and the jQuery library. Therefore, its script element needs to be coded after the script elements for both of those libraries. However, the mpg library doesn't depend on any other file, so its script element could be coded either before or after the jQuery library.

The benefits of JavaScript libraries

- They let you group similar functionality in a single file.
- They make your code easier to understand, maintain, and reuse.
- They encourage the separation of concerns.

An example of a simple library file (library_mpg.js)

```
var mpg = {
    miles: 0,
    gallons: 0,
    calculate: function() {
        return this.miles / this.gallons;
    }
};
```

How to include and use JavaScript libraries in your application

In the index.html file

```
<head>
    <title>Calculate MPG</title>
    <link rel="stylesheet" href="mpg.css">
    <script src="https://code.jquery.com/jquery-3.1.1.min.js"></script>
    <script src="library_mpg.js"></script>
    <script src="main.js"></script>
</head>
```

In the main.js file

```
$( document ).ready(function() {
    $("#calculate").click( function() {
        mpg.miles = parseFloat( $("#miles").val() );
        mpg.gallons = parseFloat( $("#gallons").val() );
        $("#mpg").val( mpg.calculate().toFixed(1) );
    });
});
```

Description

- A JavaScript *library* is an external file that contains related functions, objects, or both.
- JavaScript libraries range from simple collections of functions and objects that you write yourself to extensive third-party libraries like jQuery.
- A JavaScript library is normal JavaScript, so you create a library by grouping related functions and objects in a single file. You should also name your JavaScript libraries so it's clear what they do.
- You include JavaScript libraries in your applications by using script elements. If a JavaScript file depends on a library, you must make sure that the script element for the needed library precedes the one for the file that uses it.

Figure 17-4   How to create and use JavaScript libraries

The Miles Per Gallon application

The Miles Per Gallon application in figure 17-5 is another version of the application you saw back in section one of this book. The difference is that this version uses an object and a library file to organize its code. This makes it easier to understand the code that works with miles per gallon, and easier to reuse it on other pages or in another application.

The HTML

The first two script elements in the head section identify the two JavaScript libraries that are used by this application: the jQuery library and the mpg library. The last script element is for the main JavaScript file that uses both of these libraries.

The HTML in the main element contains two text box elements for the user to enter the number of miles driven and the number of gallons used. Then, there's a text box element to display the calculated miles per gallon. Note that this last text box includes the disabled attribute, so it can display data but the data can't be changed by the user. Finally, there are two buttons, one that calculates the miles per gallon and one that clears all the text boxes.

The HTML shown here is similar to what you've seen in other applications in this book. The most important thing to note about it is the id attributes that the JavaScript code (or, more accurately, the jQuery code) will use to work with the HTML elements.

The Miles Per Gallon application

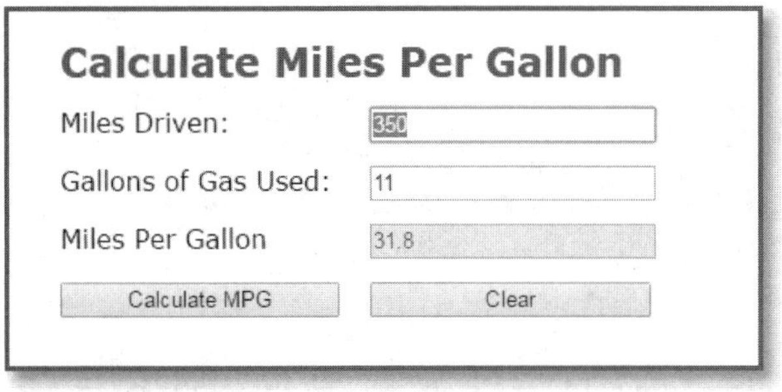

The HTML

```html
<head>
    <title>Calculate MPG</title>
    <link rel="stylesheet" href="mpg.css">
    <script src="https://code.jquery.com/jquery-3.1.1.min.js"></script>
    <script src="library_mpg.js"></script>
    <script src="main.js"></script>
</head>
<body>
    <main>
        <h1>Calculate Miles Per Gallon</h1>
        <label for="miles">Miles Driven:</label>
            <input type="text" id="miles"><br>
        <label for="gallons">Gallons of Gas Used:</label>
            <input type="text" id="gallons"><br>
        <label for="mpg">Miles Per Gallon</label>
            <input type="text" id="mpg" disabled><br>

        <input type="button" id="calculate" value="Calculate MPG">
        <input type="button" id="clear" value="Clear">
    </main>
</body>
```

Description

- This application is an updated version of the application you saw in chapter 4. It accepts number of miles driven and number of gallons used from the user, and it calculates the miles per gallon.

- This application links to the jQuery library and to a library file that contains an object with properties and methods for calculating miles per gallon. Then, it has a main JavaScript file that uses these libraries.

- Since the main JavaScript file depends on both the jQuery library and the mpg library, its script element is coded after the script elements for those libraries.

Figure 17-5   The user interface and HTML for the Miles Per Gallon application

The JavaScript

Figure 17-6 presents two files. The library_mpg.js file is a library file for working with miles per gallon. It contains an object literal named mpg with two properties and two methods. The miles and gallons properties have initial values of zero. The isValid() method checks that the values in the miles and gallons properties are valid, and the calculate() method uses the two properties to calculate the miles per gallon. Note that both of these methods use the *this* keyword to access the properties.

The second file is the main.js file. This is the main JavaScript file, and it contains the jQuery ready() function. The ready() function starts by attaching an event handler to the click event of the Calculate MPG button. This handler first sets the miles and gallons properties of the mpg object to the values entered by the user. Then, it calls the isValid() method of the mpg object to check if the user entered valid data. If not, the code alerts the user.

If the user did enter valid data, the event handler calls the calculate() method of the mpg object and sets the value that the method returns as the value of the Miles Per Gallon text box. Note that the value returned by the calculate() method is a Number object. Because of that, the code can call its toFixed() method to limit the display to one decimal point.

Next, this event handler calls the select() method of the Miles Driven text box. This method works like the focus() method except that in addition to moving the focus to the text box, it also selects the text in the text box as shown in the previous figure. That makes it easier to enter another value.

After that, the ready() function attaches an event handler to the click event of the Clear button. This event handler sets the values of all the text boxes to empty strings and sets the focus on the Miles Driven text box. Finally, the ready() function sets the focus on the Miles Driven text box when the application first loads.

An important thing to note about this code is that the main JavaScript file is able to use the mpg object without doing anything special. That's because the script element for the library file comes before the script element for the main file in the index.html file. Therefore, the main file can use the mpg object in the library file just as if it were coded at the start of the main file.

Often, object literals like this are all you need for what you want to do. Sometimes, though, you need to create more than one instance of an object. Then, you can use constructor functions to create the instances that you need, and you'll learn about that next.

The library_mpg.js file

```javascript
var mpg = {
    miles: 0,
    gallons: 0,
    isValid: function() {
        if ( isNaN(this.miles) || isNaN(this.gallons) ) {
            return false;
        } else if ( this.miles <= 0 || this.gallons <= 0 ) {
            return false;
        } else {
            return true;
        }
    },
    calculate: function() {
        return this.miles / this.gallons;
    }
};
```

The main.js file

```javascript
$( document ).ready(function() {
    $("#calculate").click( function() {
        mpg.miles = parseFloat( $("#miles").val() );
        mpg.gallons = parseFloat( $("#gallons").val() );
        if ( !mpg.isValid() ) {
            alert("Both entries must be numeric and greater than zero");
        } else {
            $("#mpg").val( mpg.calculate().toFixed(1) );
            $("#miles").select();
        }
    });

    $("#clear").click( function() {
        $("#miles").val( "" );
        $("#gallons").val( "" );
        $("#mpg").val( "" );

        $("#miles").focus();
    });

    $("#miles").focus();
});
```

Description

- The mpg library file contains an object literal named mpg. This object has two properties, miles and gallons, and two methods, isValid() and calculate().

- The isValid() method checks that the data in the miles and gallons properties is valid, while the calculate() method uses the miles and gallons properties to calculate miles per gallon. These methods use the *this* keyword to refer to the miles and gallons properties.

- The main JavaScript file uses the properties and methods of the mpg object to calculate and display the miles per gallon based on the data entered by the user.

Figure 17-6   The JavaScript for the Miles Per Gallon application

How to create and call constructors

A *constructor function* (or just *constructor*) is a special kind of function that creates an *object type*. Then, you can call the constructor to create multiple *instances* of that object type, each of which inherits the methods of that type.

How to create your own object types with constructor functions

Figure 17-7 shows how to code constructors that can be used to create multiple instances of an object type. Here, the first group of examples shows how to code constructors that create instances of Invoice objects. Within the body of each constructor, the *this* keyword is used to refer to the new object that the constructor will create. By convention, the names of constructor functions start with a capital letter, which is partly to remind programmers to use the new keyword when calling a constructor.

The first constructor in this group is named Invoice. It accepts no parameters, and it creates two properties named subtotal and taxRate. In this case, both properties are undefined.

Often, though, you'll want to set the initial values for an object's properties. To do that, you code the constructor with one or more parameters that it will use to set the initial values of the properties for each object that it creates. This is illustrated by the next constructor. It accepts two parameters that it uses to set the initial values of the subtotal and taxRate properties. Incidentally, the parameter and property names don't have to be the same, but that's a common coding practice.

After you code a constructor, you can add methods to it. To do that, you add each method to the constructor's *prototype object*. This is illustrated by the next set of examples. For each method, you code the name of the constructor function, a dot, the word *prototype*, another dot, and the name of the method that you're adding. Then, you set that equal to the function that will become the method. This method will be available to all instances of the Invoice object type that are created by the constructor.

The third group of examples shows how to use object types. To create an instance of an object type, you call its constructor with the new keyword. This returns a new instance of the object type. Here, two Invoice objects are created from the constructor, each with its own subtotal and tax rate values, and the instances (or *objects*) assigned to variables named invoice1 and invoice2.

After the objects have been created, you can refer to their properties and methods just as you refer to the properties and methods of any other object. This is illustrated by the next examples. Here, the subtotal property of the invoice1 object and the taxRate property of the invoice2 object are retrieved and displayed. Then, the getInvoiceTotal() method of the invoice1 object and the getTaxAmount() method of the invoice2 object are called.

How to use a constructor function to create an Invoice object type

How to code a constructor with no parameters

```
var Invoice = function() {
    this.subtotal;
    this.taxRate;
};
```

How to code a constructor with two parameters

```
var Invoice = function(subtotal,taxRate) {
    this.subtotal = subtotal;
    this.taxRate = taxRate;
};
```

How to add methods to the Invoice object type

```
// The getTaxAmount method is added to the Invoice prototype
Invoice.prototype.getTaxAmount = function() {
    return ( subtotal * this.taxRate );
};
```

```
// The getInvoiceTotal method is added to the Invoice prototype
Invoice.prototype.getInvoiceTotal = function() {
    return subtotal + this.getTaxAmount( this.subtotal );
};
```

How to create instances of the Invoice object type with two parameters

```
var invoice1 = new Invoice(1000.00, 0.075);
var invoice2 = new Invoice(100.00, 0.0875);
```

How to access a new object's properties

```
alert (invoice1.subtotal);      // displays 1000.00
alert (invoice2.taxRate);       // displays 0.0875
```

How to use a new object's methods

```
invoice1.getInvoiceTotal();     // returns 1075.00
invoice2.getTaxAmount();        // returns 8.75
```

Description

- If you want to be able to create multiple *instances* of your own object types, you can code a *constructor function* (or just *constructor*) for the objects to be created. Then, to create an *instance* of the object type, you call the constructor with the *new* keyword.

- If the constructor function has parameters, you pass the data for the object that's going to be created to the constructor.

- You code the methods for a constructor on the *prototype object* of the object type. That way, all the instances of the object type that are created by the constructor function share the same methods. This keeps duplicate definitions of the method out of memory, and also allows any changes to the method to be available to all instances of the object type.

- By convention, constructor names start with an uppercase letter. That helps programmers remember that they need to use the new keyword when they call the constructor. If you forget the new keyword, the object is still created, but it may behave strangely.

Figure 17-7   How to create your own object types with constructor functions

What else you should know about prototypes

If you've worked in other programming languages, you're probably familiar with classes. A *class* is a description of the properties and methods of an object, but it isn't an object itself. Languages that use classes to define and create objects are called *class-based* or *classical languages*. In contrast, JavaScript uses prototypes to create objects so it can be referred to as a *prototypal language*. Unlike a class, a *prototype* is an object, and it's *cloned* to create a new object.

A new object that's created by cloning a prototype object has references to the methods of that prototype, rather than actual copies of those methods. For example, an object literal has a reference to the toString() method on the prototype of the Object object. Thus, all object literals refer to the same toString() method of the Object object. This keeps duplicate copies of the toString() method out of memory.

You can see how this works in the first example in figure 17-8. Here, two instances of the Date object type are created, each with a different date string. Thus, they hold different data. However, each object also has access to the toDateString() method, as the alert statements show. That's because the toDateString() method is on the prototype object of the Date object type.

This works even if a method is added to the prototype object after you've created an instance of an object type. This is illustrated by the second example. Here, a method named toNumericDateString() is added to the prototype object of the Date object type. As the alert statements show, this method is then available to the two instances of the Date object type that were created before.

This example shows that it's possible to add methods to the prototype objects of the native data types. But please note that this isn't a recommended practice. It's shown here just to illustrate the concept.

The third example shows that this works differently when you add a property or method to an instance of an object type. In that case, a new property or method is added to memory for that instance only. In this example, a property named hasExtension is added to the taxDay instance of the Date object. But as the alert statements show, this property is only available to that instance, not to the xmas instance.

A property like this is called a *direct* or *own property*, and it can be used to *override* a prototype property, as shown by the fourth example. Here, a method named toDateString() is added to the xmas instance of the Date object type. This adds a new method to memory for that instance. Since it has the same name as a method on the prototype, it overrides (replaces) that method. But as the alert statements show, it only overrides it for this instance of the Date object type.

These examples should give you better perspective on how object types, prototype objects, and the instances of an object type work. The application that follows should enhance that perspective by showing how all of these concepts can be applied.

Code that creates two instances of the Date object type

```
var taxDay = new Date("4/17/2017");
var xmas = new Date("12/25/2017");

alert( taxDay.toDateString() );          // Displays Mon Apr 17 2017
alert( xmas.toDateString() );            // Displays Mon Dec 25 2017
```

Code that adds a method to the prototype object of the Date object type

```
Date.prototype.toNumericDateString = function() {
    var m = this.getMonth() + 1; // month is zero based
    var d = this.getDate();
    var y = this.getFullYear();
    return m + "/" + d + "/" + y;
};

alert( taxDay.toNumericDateString() );   // Displays 4/17/2017
alert( xmas.toNumericDateString() );     // Displays 12/25/2017
```

Code that adds an own property to one instance of the Date object type

```
taxDay.hasExtension = true;

alert( taxDay.hasExtension );            // Displays true
alert( xmas.hasExtension );              // Displays undefined
```

Code that uses an own property to override a prototype property

```
xmas.toDateString = function() {
    return "It's Christmas Day";
};

alert( taxDay.toDateString() );          // Displays Mon Apr 17 2017
alert( xmas.toDateString() );            // Displays It's Christmas Day
```

Description

- Many programming languages use *classes* to create objects. JavaScript, by contrast, uses *prototype objects* that are cloned to create new objects. This kind of language is called *classless* or *prototypal*.

- When you create a new object, it's *cloned* from the prototype object of its object type and it inherits all of the methods of that prototype. For example, an object literal is cloned from the prototype of the Object object type, and a string literal is cloned from the prototype of the String object type.

- When you add a method to the prototype object of an object type, it's available to all instances of that object type. Those instances have a reference to the method, not a copy of the method. This keeps duplicate function definitions out of memory.

- When you add a property or method to an instance of an object type, it's created directly on the instance, not on the prototype. Because of that, it's only available to that instance. This kind of property is called a *direct* or *own property*.

- You can use own properties to *override* the methods on a prototype object, but the method will only be overridden for that instance of the object.

Figure 17-8   What else you should know about prototypes

The Trips application

The Trips application in figure 17-9 logs the destination, miles driven, and miles per gallon for several trips rather than calculating a single miles per gallon value. Because of that, a separate Trip object will be needed for each trip. This application uses a constructor function to create the Trip objects, and it stores these objects in an array.

The HTML

Like the Miles Per Gallon application, the script elements in the head section of this application identify the jQuery library, a custom library, and the main JavaScript file that uses these libraries. Since the main JavaScript file depends on both the jQuery library and the trips library, it's coded last.

As before, the HTML in the main element contains text boxes for user input about a trip. It also contains a button that calculates miles per gallon and adds that trip to the display. The HTML also contains a div element with an id attribute of "trips" that contains a textarea element. This is where the trip information is displayed.

The CSS snippet below the HTML in this figure shows the style rule for the "trips" element. Here, you can see that this style rule floats the trips div to the right.

The Trips application

Trips Log

Destination:	Seaside
Miles Driven:	75
Gallons of Gas Used:	3.2
	Add Trip

```
Seattle: Miles - 350; MPG - 31.8
San Francisco: Miles - 650; MPG - 32.5
Seaside: Miles - 75; MPG - 23.4

Cumulative MPG:29.3
```

The HTML

```html
<head>
    <title>Trips Log</title>
    <link rel="stylesheet" href="trips.css">
    <script src="https://code.jquery.com/jquery-3.1.1.min.js"></script>
    <script src="library_trip.js"></script>
    <script src="main.js"></script>
</head>
<body>
    <main>
        <h1>Trips Log</h1>
        <div id="trips">
            <textarea id="trip_list" rows="8" cols="42"></textarea>
        </div>
        <label for="destination">Destination:</label>
            <input type="text" id="destination"><br>
        <label for="miles">Miles Driven:</label>
            <input type="text" id="miles"><br>
        <label for="gallons">Gallons of Gas Used:</label>
            <input type="text" id="gallons"><br>

        <label> </label>
        <input type="button" id="add_trip" value="Add Trip">
    </main>
</body>
```

Some of the CSS for the application

```css
#trips {
    float: right;
}
```

Description

- This application calculates and stores the miles per gallon for one or more trips.
- It uses a constructor function to create a Trip object type. This object type contains the methods needed to validate a trip, calculate the miles per gallon, and display information about the trip. The code for the Trip constructor is in a separate library file.
- This application stores instances of Trip objects in an array.

Figure 17-9   The user interface and HTML for the Trips application

The JavaScript

Figure 17-10 presents two files. The library_trip.js file is for working with the data a user enters for a trip. It contains a constructor function that creates a Trip object type. This constructor accepts three parameters that it uses to set the initial values of the destination, miles, and gallons properties. Within the body of the constructor, the *this* keyword refers to the new object that the function will create.

The code that follows the constructor adds three methods to the prototype of the Trip object type. Since these methods are added to the prototype, each instance of the Trip object type that this constructor creates will hold a reference to these methods.

The first two methods are like the ones in the Miles Per Gallon application. The isValid() method checks that the user has entered valid data, while the calculateMpg() method uses the data from the user to calculate miles per gallon.

Then, the toString() method creates a string that displays information about the trip. This demonstrates what you learned in figure 17-8 about using an own property to override a prototype property. Here, the toString() method replaces the toString() method that was inherited from the Object object type.

The second file for this application is the main.js file. It contains the jQuery ready() function that drives the application. This function starts by creating an empty array to hold Trip objects. Then, it creates a function named display-Trips() that displays all the trips in that array.

The displayTrips() function starts by initializing a string variable named displayString and a numeric variable named mpgTotal. Then, it loops through the Trip objects in the array. For each Trip object, it calls the toString() method and adds that value to the displayString variable. It also calls the calculateMpg() method and adds that value to the mpgTotal variable. Note too that the for loop adds a newline character at the end of the data for each trip so the data will be displayed on its own line.

When the loop completes, the function calculates the cumulative miles per gallon for all the trips by dividing the value in the mpgTotal variable by the number of trips. Then, it adds this cumulative mpg to the display string. Finally, it sets the display string as the value of the textarea element, and it sets the focus back on the Destination text box.

Next is an event handler for the click event of the Add Trip button. This handler creates a new instance of a Trip object, passing it the values entered by the user. Then, it calls the isValid() method of the Trip object to check if the user entered valid data. If not, the code alerts the user. Otherwise, it adds the Trip object to the array and calls the displayTrips() function.

The ready() function ends by putting the focus on the text box for the destination entry. That makes it easy for the user to start entering data.

The library_trip.js file

```javascript
var Trip = function( destination, miles, gallons ) {
    this.destination = destination;
    this.miles = parseFloat( miles );
    this.gallons = parseFloat( gallons );
};
Trip.prototype.isValid = function() {
    if (this.destination == "" || isNaN(this.miles) || isNaN(this.gallons)){
        return false;
    } else if (this.miles <= 0 || this.gallons <= 0){
        return false;
    } else {
        return true;
    }
};
Trip.prototype.calculateMpg = function() {
    return this.miles / this.gallons;
};
Trip.prototype.toString = function() {
    var mpg = this.calculateMpg().toFixed(1);
    return this.destination + ": Miles - " + this.miles + "; MPG - " +  mpg;
};
```

The main.js file

```javascript
$( document ).ready(function() {
    var trips = [];

    var displayTrips = function() {
        var displayString = "", mpgTotal = 0;

        for (var i in trips) {
            displayString += trips[i].toString() + "\n";
            mpgTotal += trips[i].calculateMpg();
        }
        var cumulativeMpg = mpgTotal / trips.length;
        displayString += "\nCumulative MPG:" + cumulativeMpg.toFixed(1);

        $("#trip_list").val( displayString );
        $("#destination").select();
    };

    $("#add_trip").click( function() {
        var trip = new Trip(
          $("#destination").val(), $("#miles").val(), $("#gallons").val() );
        if ( !trip.isValid() ) {
            alert("Please complete all fields. Miles and gallons "
                + " must be numeric and greater than zero.");
        } else {
            trips.push( trip );
            displayTrips();
        }
    });

    $("#destination").focus();
});
```

Figure 17-10   The JavaScript for the Trips application

How to create a factory function

As you just learned, you can use constructor functions to create multiple instances of an object that refer to the same prototype object. However, there's another way to do this that some programmers prefer.

How to use the create() method of the Object object

Constructor functions in JavaScript let you create an object type and customize its prototype. They also provide a familiar syntax to programmers who are used to working with classical languages. However, JavaScript isn't a classical language, and some programmers wanted another way to create new objects that would make the prototypal nature of JavaScript more obvious. To address this, ECMAScript 5 added a create() method to the Object object type.

The table at the top of figure 17-11 shows the syntax of this create() method. The first parameter is the prototype object that you want to use for the new object. The second parameter is an optional object that describes the properties the new object should have. Because this parameter may not work correctly in ES3, it won't be used in this chapter.

The first example in this figure shows how to use the create method. Here, the prototype of the Object object is used as the prototype for the new object. This is the same as creating a new object with an object literal.

Usually, though, you'll use the create() method with a custom prototype object. This is illustrated by the second group of examples. Here, a custom prototype object is created with a single method named getTotal(). Then, this custom prototype is used with the create() method to create an invoice object. After that, subtotal and taxRate properties are added to the invoice object.

Just like when you use a constructor, the getTotal() method shown here is only created once on the prototype object. Then, the objects that are returned by the calls to the create() method refer to that method. Unlike when you use a constructor, though, the create() method doesn't create a new object type. Instead, each object created by the create() method is of the Object object type.

The last example in this figure shows how to use the create() method in a *factory function*. Factory functions are functions that create, initialize, and return objects. They are similar to constructor functions in that you can add properties to the object and initialize those properties with the values passed to the function. But you don't need to use the new keyword with a factory function. Because of that, the name of a factory function shouldn't start with a capital letter. Also, a factory function must specifically return the object that the function creates.

The code that follows the factory function shows how it can be used. Note that this code doesn't use the *new* keyword to create an object. Note too that you call the methods of an object created by a factory function in the same way that you call the methods of an object created by a constructor function.

The create() method of the Object object type

Method	Description
create(*prototype, properties*)	Creates a new object. The first parameter is the prototype that the new object inherits. The optional second parameter sets the new object's properties.

How to use the create() method to create a new object

```
var obj = Object.create( Object.prototype );    // the same as = {};
```

A custom prototype object with one method

```
var invoicePrototype = {
    getTotal: function() {
        return this.subtotal + (this.subtotal * this.taxRate);
    }
};
```

Code that uses the custom prototype object with the create() method

```
var invoice = Object.create( invoicePrototype );
invoice.subtotal = 100;
invoice.taxRate = 0.075;
alert( invoices.getTotal() );                   // displays 107.50
```

A factory function that uses the create() method to create an object

```
var getInvoice = function( subtotal, taxRate ) {
    var invoicePrototype = {
        getTotal: function() {
            return this.subtotal + (this.subtotal * this.taxRate);
        }
    };
    var invoice = Object.create( invoicePrototype );
    invoice.subtotal = subtotal;
    invoice.taxRate = taxRate;
    return invoice;
};
```

Code that uses the factory function

```
var invoice = getInvoice( 100, 0.075 );
alert( invoices.getTotal() );                   // displays 107.50
```

Description

- Another way to create new objects is to use the create() method of the Object object. After you create a new object with the create() method and a custom prototype, you add any properties that the prototype object needs.

- A *factory function* uses the create() method to create new objects. Because this method doesn't create a new object type, you don't call the factory function with the *new* keyword.

- Some programmers prefer to use factory functions because they don't require the use of the *new* keyword and they make the prototypal nature of JavaScript clear.

- The create() method is in the sham.js file for ES5 described in figure 1-17. That's because the optional second parameter may not work correctly in ES3.

Figure 17-11   How to use the create() method of the Object object

The Trips application with a factory function

Figure 17-12 presents the trip library file and the main JavaScript file of the Trips application that you saw earlier in this chapter. Here, though, they're rewritten to use a factory function instead of a constructor function.

The trip library file contains a getTrip() function, which is the factory function. Like the earlier constructor function, this function accepts three parameters that it uses to set the initial values of the destination, miles, and gallons properties.

Unlike the earlier constructor function, however, this function doesn't use the *this* keyword to refer to the new object that the function will create. Rather, a new object named tripPrototype is created with the methods that the objects returned by the function will use. Then, this prototype object is passed to the Object.create() method, and the resulting object is stored in a variable named trip. Finally, the destination, miles, and gallons properties are added to the trip object, and the trip object is returned.

The main JavaScript file shown here isn't much different from the one you saw in figure 17-10. It still starts with an empty array to hold trip objects, and it still uses the toString() and calculateMpg() methods of those trip objects.

The only real difference is in the event handler for the Add Trip button. It creates a new trip object by calling the getTrip() factory function instead of the Trip() constructor function, and it doesn't use the *new* keyword. The rest of the code is the same.

As you can see, there isn't much difference between using a constructor function and using a factory function. Which one you choose is mostly a matter of personal preference.

The library_trip.js file

```javascript
var getTrip = function( destination, miles, gallons ) {
    var tripPrototype = {
        isValid: function() {
            if ( this.destination === "" || isNaN(this.miles)
                    || isNaN(this.gallons) ) {
                return false;
            } else if ( this.miles <= 0 || this.gallons <= 0 ) {
                return false;
            } else {
                return true;
            }
        },
        calculateMpg: function() {
            return this.miles / this.gallons;
        },
        toString: function() {
            var mpg = this.calculateMpg().toFixed(1);
            return this.destination + ": Miles - "
                + this.miles + "; MPG - " + mpg;
        }
    };
    var trip = Object.create( tripPrototype );
    trip.destination = destination;
    trip.miles = parseFloat( miles );
    trip.gallons = parseFloat( gallons );
    return trip;
};
```

The main.js file

```javascript
$( document ).ready(function() {
    var trips = [];

    var displayTrips = function() {
        var displayString = "", mpgTotal = 0;

        for (var i in trips) {
            displayString += trips[i].toString() + "\n";
            mpgTotal += trips[i].calculateMpg();
        }
        ...
    };

    $("#add_trip").click( function() {
        var trip = getTrip (
          $("#destination").val(), $("#miles").val(), $("#gallons").val() );
        if ( !trip.isValid() ) {
            alert("Please complete all fields. Miles and gallons "
                + " must be numeric and greater than zero.");
        } else {
            trips.push( trip );
            displayTrips();
        }
    });
    ...
});
```

Figure 17-12   The Trips application with a factory function

Advanced skills for working with objects

Now, you'll learn some advanced skills for working with objects. Although you won't use these skills in every application, you should at least be aware of them so you can use them when they're appropriate.

How to use the arguments property of a Function object

When you call a function in JavaScript, the arguments are stored in the parameter list of the function. This is similar to other programming languages. What sets JavaScript apart is that the parameters are also stored in the arguments property of that Function object.

This arguments property is similar to an array. Within this property, each of the arguments that are passed to the function is stored in an element starting with index 0. Then, you can access these elements by using their indexes.

Note, however, that the arguments property isn't a true array object, so you can't use the properties and methods of an array that you learned about in the last chapter. The good news is that there's a way around this, which you'll learn in figure 17-16.

The first example in figure 17-13 shows how to use the arguments property to access an argument that's passed to a function. Here, the element at index 0 in the arguments property is used in an expression that returns true if the argument is divisible by 2 with no remainder.

The second example shows how to use the length property of the arguments property to determine the number of arguments passed to a function. Here, the countArgs function just displays the number of arguments that are passed to it.

The third example shows how to use the arguments property to create a function that can receive a variable number of arguments. Here, the Invoice constructor has one parameter in its parameter list, which it uses to set the initial value of the taxRate property. After that, the constructor loops through the arguments property, and adds any other argument values to the items array. In this case, the constructor assumes that the additional parameters are item codes. This way, a new instance of an Invoice object can be initialized with just a tax rate, or with a tax rate and one or more item codes.

The fourth example shows how to use the arguments property to create a function with optional parameters. Here, a method is added to the Invoice object type that uses the join() method of the items array to create a list of all the item codes. This method starts by checking the arguments property to see if a parameter was passed to the function. If it was, the method passes this parameter to the join() method as the separator. Otherwise, the method uses a default value of a comma and a space for the separator. This makes the separator parameter optional.

The fifth example shows you how the third and fourth examples work. Here, a new Invoice instance is initialized with a tax rate of 0.07 and three item codes. Then, the listItems() method is called without a parameter, and the default separator is used. Finally, the listItems() method is called again, this time with a value for the separator parameter, and that value is used rather than the default.

A function that uses the arguments property to get an argument

```
var isEven = function() {
    return arguments[0] % 2 === 0;
};

isEven( 6 )                              // returns true
```

How to determine the number of arguments that have been passed

```
var countArgs = function() {
    alert( "Number of arguments: " + arguments.length );
};

countArgs( 1, "Text", true );        // Displays "Number of arguments: 3"
```

An Invoice constructor that accepts a variable number of arguments

```
var Invoice = function(taxRate) {
    this.items = [];
    this.taxRate = taxRate;
    if ( arguments.length > 1 ) {
        for (var i = 1; i < arguments.length; i++) { // skip first argument
            this.items.push( arguments[i] );
        }
    }
};
```

An Invoice method that provides a default value for an argument

```
Invoice.prototype.listItems = function(separator) {
    var sep = ( arguments.length === 0 ) ? ", " : separator;
    return this.items.join( sep );
};
```

An instance of Invoice with a tax rate and 3 item codes

```
var invoice = new Invoice(0.07, "ABC1", "ABC2", "ABC3");
alert( invoice.listItems() );                // Displays ABC1, ABC2, ABC3
alert( invoice.listItems(" | ") );           // Displays ABC1 | ABC2 | ABC3
```

Description

- In JavaScript, all functions are objects, and all of the arguments passed to a function are stored in the arguments property of the Function object.

- The arguments property is similar to an array, so you can use an index to access its elements. But it isn't a true array, so you can't use the array methods of chapter 16 with it. In figure 17-16, though, you'll learn how to "borrow" those array methods to work with the arguments property.

- If a function uses the arguments property to get the arguments that are passed to it, the calling statement can pass more or fewer arguments than the parameter list specifies.

Figure 17-13   How to use the arguments property of a Function object

How to create cascading methods

A *cascading method* is a method of an object that can be chained with other methods. To do that, the method must return a reference to the original object by using the *this* keyword. This is illustrated by figure 17-14.

The first example presents a tasklist object with two methods. Since neither of these methods returns a reference to the tasklist object, they can't be chained. If you try to chain the methods, a runtime error will occur. Thus, these methods must be called one at a time.

The second example presents these same methods, but now they each end with this statement:

```
return this;
```

This returns a reference to the tasklist object so the methods can be chained.

Since chaining is commonly used with method calls, it's a good practice to provide for chaining by returning the object at the end of a method. Of course, if you're returning something else, like a Boolean value or a string, then you can't return the object too. But whenever you can return the object, you should.

By the way, code that uses cascading methods is sometimes called *fluent*. That's because a line of code like

```
tasklist.load().display( $("tasks") );
```

reads like a sentence.

Two methods that modify an object but don't return the object

The load and display methods of the tasklist object

```
var tasklist = {
    load: function() {
        // load code goes here
    },
    display: function(div) {
        // display code goes here
    }
};
```

Chaining these method calls won't work

```
tasklist.load().display( $("tasks") );          // TypeError
```

The methods must be called one at a time

```
tasklist.load();
tasklist.display( $("tasks") );
```

Two methods that modify an object and then return the object

The load and display methods of the tasklist object

```
var tasklist = {
    load: function() {
        // load code goes here
        return this;
    },
    display: function(div) {
        // display code goes here
        return this;
    }
};
```

Chaining these method calls does work

```
tasklist.load().display( $("tasks") );
```

Description

- A *cascading method* is a method of an object that can be chained with other methods. This style of coding is sometimes called *fluent* because of the way it reads.

- A method must return the object represented by the *this* keyword if it's going to be chained with other methods.

Figure 17-14   How to create cascading methods

How to inherit methods from another object

When you create objects, you can *inherit* methods from other objects. This lets you create a base object with common methods and then extend it with more specialized methods. As figure 17-15 shows, you use an object's prototype to inherit its methods, and you can do that by using constructors or the Object.create() method.

The first set of examples shows how to inherit methods with constructors. First, the code creates a constructor named Percent with a property named rate. Then, it adds a single method named getPercent() to the prototype. This method accepts a subtotal parameter and returns the result of multiplying the subtotal amount by the rate property.

Next, the code creates another constructor named Commission with properties named rate and isSplit. It then sets the prototype object of the Commission object type to a new instance of the Percent object type. As a result, the Commission object type inherits the methods of the Percent object type.

Then, the code adds a calculateCommission() method to the prototype. This method calculates a commission by using the getPercent() method it inherited and its own isSplit property.

Note that the rate property has to be defined again in the Commission constructor, even though it's defined in the Percent constructor. That's because it isn't defined on the Percent prototype object, so it isn't inherited.

The last example in the first set shows how to use the Commission constructor. Here, the Commission constructor is used to create a new object named commission. Then, its rate and isSplit properties are set, and its getPercent() and calculateCommission() methods are called.

The second set of examples shows how to inherit methods with the Object.create() method. First, the code creates a prototype object named percentPrototype that contains a single method named getPercent(). As before, this method accepts a subtotal parameter and returns the result of multiplying the subtotal amount by the rate property.

Next, the code creates a prototype object named commissionPrototype. It passes the percentPrototype object to the create() method that creates this object. As a result, the commissionPrototype object inherits the getPercent() method.

Then, as before, the code adds a calculateCommission() method to the prototype. This method calculates a commission by using the getPercent() method it inherited and its own isSplit property.

The last example shows how to use this object. Here, the commissionPrototype object is used to create a new object named commission. Then, its rate and isSplit properties are set, and its getPercent() and calculateCommission() methods are called.

How to inherit methods using constructors

A constructor function that creates a Percent object

```
var Percent = function() {
    this.rate;
};
Percent.prototype.getPercent = function(subtotal) {
    return subtotal * this.rate;
};
```

A constructor for a Commission object that inherits the Percent object

```
var Commission = function() {
    this.rate;
    this.isSplit;
};
Commission.prototype = new Percent();                          // inherit
Commission.prototype.calculateCommission = function(subtotal) {
    var percent = this.getPercent(subtotal);
    return (this.isSplit) ? percent / 2 : percent;
};
```

An instance of the Commission object type

```
var commission = new Commission();
commission.rate = 0.085;
commission.isSplit = true;
alert( commission.getPercent(140) );                  // Displays 11.9
alert( commission.calculateCommission(140) );         // Displays 5.95
```

How to inherit methods using the Object.create() method

A percentPrototype object

```
var percentPrototype = {
    getPercent: function(subtotal) { return subtotal * this.rate; }
};
```

A commissionPrototype object that inherits the percentPrototype object

```
var commissionPrototype = Object.create(percentPrototype);   // inherit
commissionPrototype.calculateCommission = function(subtotal) {
    var percent = this.getPercent(subtotal);
    return (this.isSplit) ? percent / 2 : percent;
};
```

An instance of a commission object

```
var commission = Object.create(commissionPrototype);
commission.rate = 0.07;
commission.isSplit = false;
alert( commission.getPercent(100) );                  // Displays 9.8
alert( commission.calculateCommission(100) );         // Displays 9.8
```

Description

- *Inheritance* lets you share base functionality among several objects.

- To inherit the methods of an object created by a constructor, set the prototype object of the child object to an instance of the parent object.

- To inherit methods with the Object.create() method, pass the parent object as the prototype.

Figure 17-15   How to inherit methods from another object

How to use the *this* keyword

To this point, you've been using the *this* keyword within the methods of an object to refer to that object. You should know, however, that the value of *this* depends on how a function is invoked, as summarized by the first table in figure 17-16.

In addition, every function has three methods that you can use to specify the value of *this* for that function. When you use one of these methods, you specify the value of *this* in the first argument that you pass to the function, as indicated by the syntax for these methods in the second table in this figure. These methods also let you pass any other arguments that the function might need. With the call() and bind() methods, you pass these other arguments in a comma separated list. With the apply() method, though, you pass these arguments in an array.

The call() and apply() methods of a function let you specify the value of *this* at the time that function is invoked. One common use of these methods is to "borrow" functionality from other objects. For example, these methods let you use the properties and methods of the Array object to work with the arguments property of a function, which isn't a true array. You can see how this works in the first two examples.

The first example shows how to use the call() method to borrow the join() method of the Array object. Here, the displayArguments() function is used to join and display the arguments that are passed to it. To do that, it starts by invoking the call() method on the join() method of the Array object type's prototype object. The first argument that's passed to the call() method is the arguments property, which sets the arguments property as the value of *this* for the join() method. Then, the second argument is the separator that the join() method will use to join the arguments. The last statement in this example shows the result of calling the displayArguments() function with three arguments.

The second example illustrates how you can accomplish the same thing using the apply() method. Here, the second argument is coded as an array with a single element that contains the separator that will be used by the join() method.

In contrast to the call() and apply() methods, the bind() method of a function lets you specify the value of *this* at the time that function is coded or assigned. Then, the value of *this* can't be changed for that function, no matter how that function is invoked later on.

As you'll see in the next chapter, the bind() method is commonly used when working with closures. Another use of this method is to override the default behavior of an event handler. This is illustrated by the third example. Here, an object literal named salesTax has a property named taxRate and a method named calculate() that uses the *this* keyword to refer to the taxRate property.

Next, the calculate() method is assigned as the event handler for the click event of a button. Because the bind() method of the calculate() method is called with the salesTax object as it's argument, *this* is set to the salesTax object. Then, the calculate() method can use *this* to refer to the taxRate property of the salesTax object. If the bind() method wasn't used, *this* would refer to the button that raised the click event. Then, since that button doesn't have a taxRate property, the calculate() method wouldn't work correctly.

The value of the this keyword depends on how the function is invoked

How function is invoked	Value of the *this* keyword
Normal function call	Undefined in strict mode; the Window object in non-strict mode.
As a method of an object	The object that contains the function.
As an event handler	The object that raised the event (e.g, the button that was clicked).

Methods of a function for specifying the value of this

Method	Description
`call(thisArg[, arg1]...)`	Lets you specify the value of *this* at the time you invoke a function. Parameters other than *this* are coded individually.
`apply(thisArg, argArray)`	Lets you specify the value of *this* at the time you invoke a function. Parameters other than *this* are coded as an array.
`bind(thisArg[, arg1]...)`	Lets you specify the value of *this* at the time you code or assign a function. Parameters other than *this* are coded individually.

How to use the call() method to borrow a method from the Array object

```
var displayArguments = function() {
    var display = Array.prototype.join.call(arguments, " ");
    alert( display );
};
displayArguments("Michael", "R", "Murach");    // Displays Michael R Murach
```

An apply() method that produces the same results

```
var display = Array.prototype.join.apply(arguments, [" "]);
```

How to use the bind() method to override *this* in an event handler

```
$(document).ready(function(){
    // an object literal for a salesTax object
    var salesTax = {
        taxRate: 0.08,
        calculate: function() {
            var amount = parseFloat( $("#amount").val() );
            alert( "Sales tax = $" + amount * this.taxRate );
        }
    };

    // the bind method makes sure that 'this' is the salesTax object
    $("#sales_tax").click(
        salesTax.calculate.bind( salesTax );
    );
});
```

Description

- All functions have a *this* keyword whose value depends on how the function is invoked. All functions also have three methods that allow you to specify the value of *this*.
- The call() and apply() methods can be used to "borrow" methods from another object such as the Array object.
- The bind() method can be used to assign a method of an object as an event handler. Then, the value of *this* can't be changed when the event is raised.

Figure 17-16   How to use the *this* keyword

The Task List application

The Task List application in figure 17-17 is another version of the application you've seen in earlier chapters. This version has a due date as well as a task name, uses a div element to display the tasks, adds links to delete individual tasks, and uses objects and object libraries. This application will illustrate many of the skills that you've just learned.

The HTML and CSS

The script elements in the head section identify the libraries that are used by this application: jQuery, jQuery UI, a task library, a storage library, and a task list library. The last script element is for the main JavaScript file that uses these libraries. The script elements are in this order because the storage library depends on the task library, the task list library depends on both the storage and task libraries, and the main JavaScript file depends on the task list and task libraries, as well as on jQuery and jQuery UI.

The HTML in the main element contains a div element with an id attribute of "tasks". The individual tasks, as well as the links the user can use to delete them, are added directly to this div element by the JavaScript code, as you'll see in a minute. There's also a second div element with no id attribute but a class attribute of "clear".

The CSS snippet below the HTML shows the style rules for the div element with the "tasks" id and the "clear" class. Here, you can see that the tasks style rule floats the tasks div to the right. It also sets the div's width, margins, and padding, and it puts a border around it. Finally, it sets a minimum height so that when there are no tasks in local storage, the bordered area will be roughly the same height as the text box and buttons.

This is followed by the CSS style rule for the <a> elements within the tasks div. It contains only one declaration, which adds some space to the right of the <a> elements.

Last, the style rule for the div with the "clear" class sets the CSS clear property to "both". This clears the floating of the elements that precede it. If you omit this style rule, the border of the tasks div element won't expand as tasks are added to the task list.

The Task List application

The HTML

```html
<head>
    <title>Task List</title>
    <link rel="stylesheet"
        href="//code.jquery.com/ui/1.12.1/themes/base/jquery-ui.css">
    <link rel="stylesheet" href="task_list.css">
    <script src="https://code.jquery.com/jquery-3.1.1.min.js"></script>
    <script src="https://code.jquery.com/ui/1.12.1/jquery-ui.js"></script>
    <script src="library_task.js"></script>
    <script src="library_storage.js"></script>
    <script src="library_tasklist.js"></script>
    <script src="task_list.js"></script>
</head>
<body>
    <main>
        <h1>Task List</h1>
        <div id="tasks"></div>
        <label for="task">Task:</label><br>
            <input type="text" name="task" id="task"><br>
        <label for="due_date">Due Date:</label><br>
            <input type="text" name="due_date" id="due_date"><br>
        <input type="button" id="add_task" value="Add Task"><br>
        <input type="button" id="clear_tasks" value="Clear Tasks">
        <div class="clear"></div>
    </main>
</body>
```

Some of the CSS for the application

```css
#tasks {
    float: right;
    width: 25em;
    margin: 0 0 .5em;
    padding: 1em;
    border: 2px solid black;
    min-height: 5em;
}
#tasks a { margin-right: 0.5em; }
.clear { clear: both; }
```

Description

- This application uses the jQuery and jQuery UI libraries and some custom library files.

Figure 17-17   The user interface, HTML, and CSS for the Task List application

The task and storage libraries

Figure 17-18 presents two library files. The library_task.js file is the library for working with individual tasks. It contains a constructor function named Task that accepts parameters named task and dueDate. Within the constructor, a property named text is created and assigned the value in the task parameter.

The constructor then uses its arguments property to see if it's received a dueDate parameter. If it has, it converts the value in that parameter to a Date object and assigns it to a property named dueDate. If it hasn't, it assigns a new Date object with a default value of one month from the current date to the dueDate property. Because of that, the dueDate parameter is optional.

Next, the code adds two methods to the prototype object of the Task object type. The isValid() method makes sure that the user has entered a value for the text property and that the dueDate property is a date in the future. The toString() method returns a string that displays the values of the text and dueDate properties.

The second file is the library_storage.js file. This is the library that gets the tasks in and out of storage. It contains two factory functions. The getLocalStorage() function contains general methods named get(), set(), and clear() that add strings to and retrieve strings from local storage. All three methods use the object's key property to indicate which item in local storage to work with. This is a general-purpose factory function that could be used in other applications.

In contrast, the getTaskStorage() factory function inherits the methods of the getLocalStorage factory function. Then, it uses that base functionality to create two specific methods, retrieveTasks() and storeTasks(), that convert the strings from local storage to arrays and then to Task objects, and vice versa. This shows how the base functionality of a more general object can be inherited and extended by a more specific object.

It should be noted that you could easily use a factory function in the task library or constructor functions in the storage library. As stated before, either will work, and which you use is a matter of personal preference.

The library_task.js file

```javascript
var Task = function(task, dueDate) {
    this.text = task;
    if (arguments.length === 1) {
        this.dueDate = new Date();
        this.dueDate.setMonth( this.dueDate.getMonth() + 1 );
    } else { this.dueDate = new Date( dueDate ); }
};
Task.prototype.isValid = function() {
    if (this.text === "") { return false; }
    var dt = new Date();
    if (this.dueDate.getTime() <= dt.getTime() ) { return false; }
    return true;
};
Task.prototype.toString = function() {
    return this.text + "<br>Due Date: " + this.dueDate.toDateString();
};
```

The library_storage.js file

```javascript
var getLocalStorage = function(key) {
    var prototype = {
        get: function() { return localStorage.getItem(this.key) || ""; },
        set: function(str) { localStorage.setItem(this.key, str); },
        clear: function() { localStorage.setItem(this.key, ""); }
    };
    var storage = Object.create( prototype );
    storage.key = key;
    return storage;
};

var getTaskStorage = function(key) {
    var prototype = getLocalStorage(key);
    prototype.retrieveTasks = function() {
        var str = this.get();
        if (str.length === 0) { return []; }
        else {  // convert each interim string to a Task object
            var interim = str.split( "|" );
            return interim.map( function( current ) {
                var t = current.split( "~~" );
                return new Task( t[0], t[1] );
            });
        }
    };
    prototype.storeTasks = function(tasks) {
        if (!Array.isArray(tasks)) { this.set( "" ); }
        else {  // convert each Task object to an interim string
            var interim = tasks.map( function( current ) {
                return current.text + "~~" + current.dueDate.toDateString();
            });
            this.set( interim.join( "|" ) );
        }
    };
    var storage = Object.create(prototype);
    storage.key = key;
    return storage;
};
```

Figure 17-18   The task and storage libraries for the Task List application

The task list library

Figure 17-19 shows the library for working with the task list. It contains an object named tasklist that holds, edits, and displays tasks. Because only one instance of this object is needed, it's coded as an object literal that has two properties and seven methods. Also, each of the methods returns the *this* keyword, so they're chainable.

The tasks property contains an array that holds instances of Task objects. The storage property contains an instance of the storage object that it gets by calling the getTaskStorage() factory function in the storage library.

The load() method calls the retrieveTasks() method of the storage object to retrieve the tasks from local storage as an array of Task objects. The save() method calls the storeTasks() method of the storage object to convert the Tasks objects in the array to a string that's stored in local storage.

The sort() method calls the sort() method of the tasks array. It passes that method a function that sorts the Task objects in the array by due date. The add() method accepts an instance of the Task object. It uses the push() method of the tasks array to add the task to the array.

The delete() method accepts an index parameter. It starts by calling the sort() method to sort the tasks. It does this to make sure the tasks are in the same sort order as those displayed in the browser. Then, it removes the task at the specified index in the tasks array using the splice() method of that array.

The clear() method calls the clear() method of the storage object to remove the string in local storage. This method is one of the ones that the storage object inherited.

The last method is the display() method, which accepts a div element as a parameter. It starts by calling the sort() method to sort the tasks. Then, it loops through the tasks and constructs an HTML string.

This HTML string has a Delete link for each task, and the href attribute of each Delete <a> element has a placeholder value of "#". Then, the title attribute is given the value of the index of the task item in the array. This is how the application knows the index of the task to delete. After creating the HTML string, the method displays the tasks by passing the HTML string to the jQuery html() method of the div object.

Next, the method adds event handlers to the <a> elements that it just added to the div element. To do this, it chains the jQuery find() and each() methods, which finds each <a> element and then loops through them. Then, within the each() method, it uses the on() event method to add a click event handler to the <a> element, which is represented by $(this).

The event handler for each <a> element uses the methods of the tasklist object to load the tasks, delete the task whose index is in the title attribute, save the updated tasks to local storage, and display the tasks in the div. As you can see, these four method calls are chained, so they all appear on one line. That's because the methods of the tasklist object all return the *this* keyword. Finally, this event handler prevents the default action of the link and sets the focus on the first input element on the page.

The library_tasklist.js file

```javascript
var tasklist = {
    tasks: [],
    storage: getTaskStorage("tasks"),
    load: function() {
        this.tasks = this.storage.retrieveTasks();
        return this;
    },
    save: function() {
        this.storage.storeTasks(this.tasks);
        return this;
    },
    sort: function() {
        this.tasks.sort( function(task1, task2) {
            if ( task1.dueDate < task2.dueDate ) { return -1; }
            else if ( task1.dueDate > task2.dueDate ) { return 1; }
            else { return 0; }
        });
        return this;
    },
    add: function(task) {
        this.tasks.push(task);
        return this;
    },
    delete: function(i) {
        this.sort();
        this.tasks.splice(i, 1);
        return this;
    },
    clear: function() {
        this.storage.clear();
        return this;
    },
    display: function(div) {
        this.sort();

        var html = "";
        for (var i in this.tasks) {
            html = html.concat("<p>");
            html = html.concat("<a href='#' title='", i, "'>Delete</a>");
            html = html.concat(this.tasks[i].toString());
            html = html.concat("</p>");
        }
        div.html(html);

        // add onclick event handler to each <a> element just added to div
        div.find("a").each(function() {
            $(this).on("click", function(evt){
                tasklist.load().delete(this.title).save().display(div);
                evt.preventDefault();
                $("input:first").focus();
            });
        });
        return this;
    }
};
```

Figure 17-19   The task list library for the Task List application

Note that because this function is an event handler, the value of *this* is the Delete link that was clicked. That's why the title property of *this* contains the index of the task to delete.

The main JavaScript file

Figure 17-20 shows the main JavaScript file for this application. It starts with the jQuery ready() function, which then attaches event handlers for the click events of the Add Task and Clear Tasks buttons, activates the jQuery UI datepicker widget for the Due Date text box, loads and displays the task list, and sets the focus on the Task textbox.

The ready() function and the event handlers call methods of the tasklist object. This is possible because the tasklist object is coded as an object literal, so it's available as soon as its file is loaded. In contrast, the Task object type is created by a constructor function. When one of these functions needs a Task object, then, it has to create an instance of one with the new keyword.

The event handler for the Add Task button starts by checking if the user has entered a due date. If so, the Task constructor is called and passed this due date as well as the task description. If there's no due date, only the task description is passed to the Task constructor. Remember from figure 17-18, though, that if a date isn't passed, the constructor creates a default due date of one month from the current date.

Next, the event handler calls the Task object's isValid() method to make sure the user entered a valid task. If so, the code calls four methods of the tasklist object to load the tasks from local storage, add the new task, save the updated tasks array back to local storage, and display the new task list. Once again, these methods are chained because they all return the *this* keyword. After that, the function clears the Task text box.

However, if the task isn't valid, this event handler notifies the user. And valid or not, the function ends by setting the focus on the Task text box.

The event handler for the Clear Tasks button starts by calling the clear() method of the tasklist object. Then, it clears the div element that displays the tasks, as well as the Task and Due Date text boxes. Finally, it sets the focus on the Task text box.

After the functions are defined, chaining is used to call the load() and display() methods of the tasklist object. This retrieves and displays any tasks that are in local storage when the page loads. The ready() function ends by setting the focus on the Task text box.

The main JavaScript file for the Task Manager application

```javascript
$( document ).ready(function() {
    $("#add_task").click( function() {
        if ( $("#due_date").val() === "" ) {
            var newTask = new Task( $("#task").val() );
        } else {
            var newTask = new Task( $("#task").val(), $("#due_date").val() );
        }

        if ( newTask.isValid() ) {
            tasklist.load().add(newTask).save().display( $("#tasks") );
            $("#task").val("");
        } else {
            alert("Please enter a task and a future due date.");
        }
        $("#task").focus();
    });

    $("#clear_tasks").click( function() {
        tasklist.clear();
        $("#tasks").html("");
        $("#task").val("");
        $("#due_date").val("");
        $("#task").focus();
    });

    $("#due_date").datepicker({
        changeMonth: true,
        changeYear: true
    });

    tasklist.load().display( $("#tasks") );
    $("#task").focus();
});
```

Description

- The ready function adds click event handlers for the Add Task and Clear Tasks buttons, and applies a jQuery UI datepicker widget to the Due Date text box. After that, it chains two methods of the tasklist object. These methods retrieve any tasks in storage when the application loads and display them in the "tasks" div element.

- The click event handler for the Add Task button creates a new Task object with data entered by the user, and then calls that object's isValid() method to make sure the user data is valid. If so, the code chains several methods of the tasklist object. These methods retrieve the tasks in storage, add the new task, save the tasks back to storage, and display the updated tasks in the "tasks" div element.

Figure 17-20   The main JavaScript file for the Task List application

Perspective

Now that you've finished this chapter, you should be able to develop applications that are built around your own objects. That in turn should make your applications easier to maintain and your code easier to reuse. That's especially true for applications that are large or complex.

Terms

native object type	prototype object
object type	class
instance of an object type	classical language
inheritance	prototype
property	prototypal language
method	classless
object literal	cloning a prototype
delete operator	direct property
reference	own property
library	override
separation of concerns	factory function
constructor function	cascading method
constructor	fluent

Summary

- JavaScript provides a two-level hierarchy of *native object types*. All object types at the second level *inherit* the properties and methods of the Object object type.

- You can create an object by coding an *object literal* with properties and methods. Within a method, the *this* keyword usually refers to the object itself.

- Once an object is created, you can add new properties and methods to it, change the value of existing properties and methods, and delete properties and methods.

- A variable holds a *reference* to an object, not the object itself.

- You can use a *constructor* to create your own object type, and you can add methods to the object type's *prototype object*. When a constructor is called with the new keyword, an *instance* of that object type is created so you can create multiple instances of the same object type.

- You can use the create() method of the Object object to create a new object that's based on a custom prototype object. You can do this within a *factory function* to create instances of the prototype object without using constructors.

- In JavaScript, all functions are objects, and all of the arguments passed to a function are stored in the arguments property of the function object.

- *Cascading methods* are created by returning the *this* keyword. This creates methods that can be chained. This way of coding is sometimes called *fluent*.

- You can *inherit* the methods of another object by passing its prototype object to the Object.create() method. You can also use constructors to inherit the methods of another object by setting a constructor's prototype object to a new instance of the object to be inherited.

- All functions have a *this* keyword, but its value depends on how the function is invoked. By default, the *this* keyword in a constructor refers to the object created by the constructor.

- You can use the bind() method of a function to set the value of *this* when a function is coded or assigned. This means that the value of its *this* keyword can't be changed.

- You can use the call() and apply() methods of a function to set the value of *this* when a function is invoked. These methods can be used to "borrow" methods from another object.

Exercise 17-1   Enhance the Task List application so it uses objects

This exercise asks you to enhance the Task List application by updating the code so it uses cascading methods.

Open, test, and review the application

1. Use your text editor or IDE to open the JavaScript files in this folder:
    `\javascript_jquery\exercises\ch17\task_list\`

2. Test this application in Chrome by adding three tasks and deleting one. Then, review the code in the JavaScript files for this application.

Change the tasklist object so it uses cascading methods

3. In the main JavaScript file (task_list.js), find the code at the end of the ready() event handler that loads and displays the tasks in storage. Then, chain the calls to the load and display methods of the tasklist object.

4. Run the application and note that your tasks don't display. Open the Console panel of the developer tools and review the error messages there.

5. In the task list library (library_tasklist.js), update all the methods so they return the value in the *this* keyword.

6. Run the application again. This time, everything should work correctly.

Update the application to chain the method calls

7. In the main JavaScript file, find the event handler for the click event of the Add Task button and chain the method calls to the tasklist object it contains. Then, run the application and test it by adding a task.

8. In the task list library, find the display method and chain the method calls to the tasklist object it contains. Then, run the application and test it by deleting a task.

Exercise 17-2 Enhance the Countdown application to use objects and libraries

This exercise asks you to enhance the Countdown application from chapter 13 so it uses objects and libraries.

Open, test, and review the application

1. Use your text editor or IDE to open the JavaScript file in this folder:

   `\javascript_jquery\exercises\ch17\countdown\`

2. Run the application in Chrome, add an event name and event date, and click the Countdown button to see how it works. Then, review the code in the event handler for the click event of the Countdown button. Note that the code is relatively difficult to read and understand.

Add three JavaScript library files

3. Add three JavaScript files to the application. Name them library_event, library_validation, and library_messages.

4. Add script elements to the head element of the index.html file to include these new files. For now, don't worry about the order of the files.

Use a constructor to create an Event object type in the event library file

5. In the event library file, code a constructor function named Event that accepts two parameters named name and dateString. Store the values of these parameters in properties of the same name.

6. Add another property named date. Set this property's value to a new Date object, passing it the value of the dateString parameter.

7. Back in the event handler for the click event of the Countdown button, find the code that loads the data entered by the user into variables named event and date. Replace this code with a new instance of the Event object. Be sure to pass the values entered by the user to the constructor.

8. Replace all the code in the event handler that uses the event or date variables with code that uses the name, dateString, or date property of the instance of the Event object. Then, test the application to make sure it still works correctly.

9. Add another property named days to the Event constructor.

10. Add a method named calculateDays() to the prototype of the Event object type. Then, move the code that calculates the number of days to this method. Instead of returning the number of days, though, store this value in the days property.

11. Replace the code in the event handler that calculates the number of days with code that calls the calculateDays() method. Then, replace all the code that uses the days variable with code that uses the new days property. Now, test the application to make sure these changes work correctly.

Move the validation code to the validation library file

12. In the validation library file, code an object literal named validation with four methods named isEmpty(), hasNoSlashes(), isInvalidYear(), and isInvalidDate(). Each method should accept one parameter named val.

13. Code the isEmpty() method so it returns true if the string argument it receives is empty, or false if it isn't. You can use the conditional operator here, or a traditional if-else statement.

14. Find the code in the event handler that checks the length of the event name and date, and replace that code with calls to the isEmpty() method. Now, test the application to make sure it still works correctly after this change.

15. Find the code that checks for slashes, a 4-digit year, and an invalid date and move it into the related methods in the validation library file.

Move the messages code to the messages library file

16. In the messages library file, code an object literal named message with five methods named required(), invalidDate(), past(), future(), and today(). The first two should accept no parameters, and the last three should accept an Event object as a parameter.

17. Since the messages library now depends on the event library, make sure that the script elements for these libraries are in the proper order in the index.html file.

18. Find the code in the event handler that displays notification strings to the user. Move these strings so they are returned by the appropriate method in the messages library.

19. Replace the code that you moved with calls to the new messages methods, and test your changes.

Review your changes

20. Review the code in the event handler for the click event of the Countdown button. Note how it's now more concise and easier to follow.

21. **Bonus:** Make the code even more concise by moving the validation code to inputMissing() and invalidDate() methods on the prototype of the Event object type. Since this makes the event library depend on the validation library, make sure your script elements are in the proper order.

18

How to create and use closures, IIFEs, the module pattern, and plugins

In this chapter, you'll learn some advanced techniques that will raise your skills to the expert level. Then, you'll learn how you can use these techniques to create your own plugins that can be used by others. Because the examples in this chapter use objects, you'll want to be sure to read chapter 17 first.

How to use closures

Closures are a powerful feature of the JavaScript language, but they can also be hard to understand. In the figures that follow, you'll learn what closures are and how to use them.

How closures work

In chapter 4, you learned about *scope*, which refers to the visibility of JavaScript objects. In brief, a variable or function that's created outside a function has *global scope*, so it can be seen and used by any other JavaScript object. In contrast, a variable or function that's created inside a function has *local scope*, so it can only be seen and used inside the function that it's in.

To understand closures, you need to understand two more things about scope. First, an object has access to its own scope as well as to the scope of the object that contains it. This is called the *scope chain*.

Second, if an object in the scope chain has something referring to it, it will stay in scope even if the object that contains it is *out of scope*. The most common way to create such a reference is for an outer function to return an inner function that refers to something in the outer function's scope. This is what a *closure* is.

You can see how this works in the example in figure 18-1. Here, a function named createClickCounter() contains a variable named count that is set to zero. It also contains an inner function named clickCounter() that increments the outer count variable by one. This inner function then logs the id of the element that was clicked and the current value of the count variable. Finally, the outer createClickCounter() function returns the inner clickCounter() function.

The critical thing to note about this code is that the count variable is in the outer function, not the inner function. This means that when the definition of the inner function is returned by the outer function, the count variable will stay "alive", because the inner function has a reference to it.

Next, event handlers are assigned to the click events for two buttons. These event handlers look different than what you're used to, though. Specifically, instead of including an anonymous function to handle the events, the createClickCounter() function is invoked by including parentheses after it.

When the createClickCounter() function is invoked, its count variable is created and set to zero and its inner clickCounter() function definition is returned and used as the button's event handler. At that point, the createClickCounter() function finishes and goes out of scope. Remember, though, that the inner function refers to the outer function's count variable, and the button refers to the inner function. These references mean that the count variable is still in scope, even though the createClickCounter() function that contains it is out of scope.

This also means that each button has a separate version of the count variable in its scope chain. That's because the createClickCounter() function is invoked twice, once for each button. So, each button has access to a different internal count variable that will keep track of how many times it's been clicked.

An example that illustrates a closure

```
$( document ).ready(function() {
    var createClickCounter = function() {
        var count = 0;      // outer function's local variable

        // inner function that refers to the outer function's local variable
        var clickCounter = function() {
            count++;
            // the value of 'this' is the clicked element
            console.log(this.id + " count is " + count);
        };

        // returning the inner function creates a closure
        // that keeps the variables it refers to "alive"
        // even after the outer function is out of scope.
        return clickCounter;
    };

    // each call to createClickCounter assigns the inner function
    // as the button's event handler.
    // each closure refers to a separate count variable.
    $("#first_button").click( createClickCounter() );
    $("#second_button").click( createClickCounter() );
});
```

The Console panel after clicking the two buttons several times

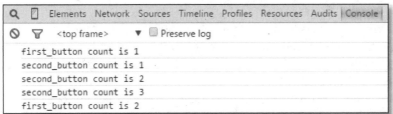

Description

- The *scope chain* in JavaScript refers to what is *in scope*, or what can be seen and used by an object.

- An object that is created within another object has access to its own scope as well as the scope of the object that contains it.

- An object in the scope chain will be available, or "alive", as long as something is referring to it. This is true even if the object that contains it has finished executing and is *out of scope*.

- A *closure* is created when an inner function refers to one or more objects in the scope of the outer function that contains it.

Figure 18-1   How closures work

Finally, this means that each count variable is available in the scope chain of the button it's attached to, but nowhere else. If you try to access it directly, you'll get an exception. This protects each internal count variable from being changed or deleted by other code.

The example in figure 18-1 is followed by a screen that shows Chrome's console panel after the two buttons named first_button and second_button have been clicked a few times each. Notice that clicking either button doesn't affect the click count of the other button.

How to use closures to create private state

In chapter 7, you saw a slide show application with all of its code in the onload() event handler. In the real world, of course, you would move code like that to a library file. In that case, though, if you use standard functions or objects in the file, they will be global and could be called and even overwritten or deleted by other code. One way to get around that problem is to use closures to create *private state* to protect these objects.

To illustrate, the example in figure 18-2 presents a function called getSlideshow that contains several variables and functions and returns an object with three methods. For now, the code in the functions and methods isn't shown. What's important is where the variables, functions, and methods are placed in the code.

First, this function declares several variables that hold values that the slideshow needs. After that, this code creates two functions that perform actions that the slideshow needs. Because these variables and functions are coded inside the outer function, they have local scope. This means that they are available to the other objects within the outer function, but they can't be called by code outside that outer function. Therefore, they are private.

Finally, this code creates and returns an object that contains three methods. These methods are inner functions that refer to the variables and functions of the outer function. Thus, they create closures. Returning an object with methods like this is a common way to return more than one inner function from an outer function.

Next is an example that calls the getSlideshow() function and stores the object it returns in a variable named slideshow. Then, it calls the loadImages() method and passes it an array of slides. Note that as long as the slideshow variable is "alive", the variables and functions in the getSlideShow() function are "alive" too, even though the getSlideShow() function has completed and is out of scope. Also note that there's no way to access the private objects of this function directly. You can only call the public methods, which then access the private objects.

A function that creates a closure with private state

```
var getSlideshow = function() {
    // private variables
    var timer, play = true, speed = 2000;
    var nodes = { image: null, caption: null };
    var img = { cache: [], counter: 0 };

    // private functions
    var stopSlideShow = function() { ... };
    var displayNextImage = function() { ... };

    //public methods that have access to private variables and functions
    return {
        loadImages: function(slides) { ... },
        startSlideShow: function() { ... },
        togglePlay: function(e) { ... }
    };
};
```

Code that creates and uses the slideshow object returned by the function

```
var slideshow = getSlideshow();        // create the slideshow object
slideshow.loadImages(slides);          // pass an array of slides to the
                                       // loadImages() method
```

Description

- All variables and functions in global scope are publically available. Similarly, all the properties and methods of a JavaScript object that's in global scope are publically available. That means that critical objects can be overwritten or deleted.

- To protect the objects that an application needs to function properly, you can use closures to create *private state*.

- As you saw in the last figure, you create a closure by returning an inner function that refers to objects in the outer function that contains it. However, if you want to return multiple inner functions, you can code them as methods of an object, as shown above.

Figure 18-2   How to use closures to create private state in objects

How to work with the this keyword in closures

As you've seen, an inner function has access to the scope of the outer function that contains it. However, this doesn't apply to the value of an outer function's *this* keyword. That's because the outer function and the inner function each has its own *this* keyword.

For instance, the tax object in the examples in figure 18-3 has a method named displayFullPrice() that returns an anonymous function. In this scenario, displayFullPrice() is the outer function, and the value of *this* for that outer function is the tax object.

The anonymous function, meanwhile, is the inner function. As you learned in chapter 17, the value of *this* for a function depends on how the function is invoked. If it's invoked normally, *this* is undefined in strict mode and it refers to the Window object in non-strict mode. If it's assigned as an event handler, *this* is the element that raised the event. In either case, though, *this* isn't the tax object and therefore doesn't have a calc() method.

Fortunately, you can use the bind() method to set the value of *this* for the inner function to the tax object. This is illustrated by the first example in this figure. Here, after the closing brace of the inner function, the outer function calls the bind() method of the inner function and passes the value of its own *this* keyword, which is the tax object. This sets the tax object as the value of *this* for the inner function, no matter how it's later invoked. Because of that, the inner function will always work correctly.

Most of the time, using the bind() method in this way is all you need to do when an inner function needs access to the *this* keyword of an outer function. Sometimes, though, you need to access the value of *this* for both the outer function and the inner function. If, for example, the inner function is attached as a button's event handler, the value of *this* is the button that was clicked. In that case, you might want to use some of the properties of that button in your code.

To do that, you can store the value of the outer function's *this* keyword in a variable. Then, because the inner function has access to the outer function's scope, it will have access to both the variable containing the outer *this* keyword and its own *this* keyword.

This is illustrated by the second example. Here, the value of *this* for the outer function is stored in a variable named "that". This adheres to a programming convention that says that when you store the value of *this* in a variable, the name of the variable should be "that", "self", or "me". Be aware, though, that the Window object also has a global property named self, so it's better to use "that" or "me".

You should also know that the arguments property of a function works similarly. That is, each function has its own arguments property, so you can't access the outer function's arguments property from within the inner function. However, you can store the outer function's arguments property in a variable if the inner function needs to use it.

How to use the bind() method to set the value
of an inner function's *this* keyword

```
var tax = {
    rate: 0.075,
    calc: function(sub) { return (sub + (sub * this.rate)).toFixed(2); },
    displayFullPrice: function(subtotal) {
        // call bind() method on inner function so that value of 'this' is
        // always the tax object, no matter how inner function is invoked
        return function() {
            alert( "Full price = $" + this.calc(subtotal) );
        }.bind(this);
    }
};
```

Attach the inner function as an event handler for a button

```
$("#camera").click( tax.displayFullPrice(125) );
// Displays "Full price = $134.38" when button is clicked
```

How to use a variable to store the value
of an outer function's *this* keyword

```
var tax = {
    rate: 0.075,
    calc: function(sub) { return (sub + (sub * this.rate)).toFixed(2); },
    displayFullPrice: function(subtotal) {
        // store value of outer function 'this' keyword so inner function
        // has access to it as well as to its own 'this' keyword. If inner
        // function is used as an event handler, 'this' is clicked element.
        var that = this;
        return function() {
            alert( "Full price for " + this.id + " = $"
                + that.calc(subtotal) );
        };
    }
};
```

Attach the inner function as an event handler for a button

```
$("#camera").click( tax.displayFullPrice(125) );
// Displays "Full price for camera = $134.38" when button is clicked
```

Description

- Although an inner function has access to the variables in the outer function that contains it, each function has its own *this* keyword.

- If an inner function needs access to the outer function's this keyword, the outer function can pass it using the bind() method of the inner function. As you learned in figure 17-16, this sets the value of the inner function's *this* keyword.

- Sometimes, an inner function needs access to both the outer function's *this* keyword and its own *this* keyword. In this case, the outer function can store the value of *this* in a variable. Then, the inner function has access to that variable. By convention, such a variable is named "that", "self", or "me".

- Each function also has its own arguments property. So, if an inner function needs access to the outer function's arguments property, the outer function can store it in a variable.

Figure 18-3   How to work with the this keyword in closures

The Slide Show application

Now that you know how closures work, you'll see the Slide Show application of chapter 7 rewritten so it uses closures. This will protect the variables and functions the application needs for its internal operations.

The HTML

Figure 18-4 shows the HTML for the rewritten Slide Show application. In the head element, you can see that this version requires a slide show library and the main JavaScript file.

In the main element, this version of the application provides an img element whose id is image and a span element whose id is "caption". These elements will display the image and text for the current slide. Unlike the application in chapter 7, though, this one doesn't code the images of the slide show in <a> elements within an unordered list. Rather, this application uses JavaScript to load information about the images in the slide show. You'll see how this works in a minute.

Another difference between the HTML shown here and the HTML in chapter 7 is that this application includes a button element whose id is "play_pause". As its name suggests, this button allows a user to pause a slide show that's running, and play a slide show that's stopped.

The Slide Show application in the browser

The head element in the HTML file

```html
<head>
    <title>Fishing Slide Show</title>
    <link rel="stylesheet" href="slideshow.css"/>
    <script src="https://code.jquery.com/jquery-3.1.1.min.js"></script>
    <script src="library_slideshow.js"></script>
    <script src="main.js"></script>
</head>
```

The main element in the HTML file

```html
<main>
    <h1>Fishing Slide Show</h1>
    <p><input type="button" id="play_pause" value="Pause"></p>
    <p><img src="images/release.jpg" id="image" alt=""></p>
    <p><span id="caption">Catch and Release</span></p>
</main>
```

Description

- This Slide Show application is an updated version of the one you saw in chapter 7.
- One difference is that this application has a Pause button that allows the user to stop the slide show on the image currently in the browser. Then, the button's text changes from "Pause" to "Resume", and the user can click on the Resume button to start the slide show again.
- Another difference is that the slide show library has been rewritten to use closures. This protects its internal variables and functions from being overwritten by outside code.

Figure 18-4   The HTML for the Slide Show application

The slide show library

Figure 18-5 shows the JavaScript code in the slide show library. First, this code starts with a function called createSlideshow(). This function declares a timer variable, a Boolean play variable, a numeric speed variable, a nodes variable that's an object literal, and an img variable that's an object literal. Because these variables are inside the outer createSlideshow() function, they have local scope. That means they can't be accessed by code outside the function, so they can't be changed or deleted by outside code.

After that, the stopSlideShow() and displayNextImage() functions contain code similar to what you saw in chapter 7. Like the variables above them, these functions are inside the createSlideshow() function. Therefore, they have local scope and can't be accessed by outside code. Also, because these functions are inside another function, they have access to the outer function's scope, so they can use all the private variables.

After creating the private variables and functions the slide show needs for its internal operations, the outer function creates and returns an object literal that has three methods: loadImages(), startSlideShow(), and createToggleHandler(). Each of these methods refers to the private variables and functions defined earlier, so those variables and functions will stay alive as long as the object returned by the createSlideshow() function stays alive. The first two methods also return the *this* keyword so they can be chained.

The loadImages() method has code that is similar to code you saw in chapter 7. However, this version gets information about the images in the slide show from the slides parameter rather than from a ul element in the page. The startSlideShow() method starts by checking if any arguments were sent to it. If so, the method stores information from those arguments in its private variables. As you'll see, this is how the slide show gets information about the img and span elements it will display the slides in. After that, startSlideShow() passes the displayNextImage() function and the speed variable to the setInterval() function to start the slide show, and it stores the timer object in the timer variable.

The createToggleHandler() method is a method that returns a function. That's because it's meant to attach an event handler to the Pause/Resume toggle button. It starts by storing a reference to its *this* keyword in a variable named me. This value refers to the object literal that contains the createToggleHandler() method.

Then, the inner function checks the private play variable. If it's true, it calls the private stopSlideShow() function to stop the slide show. If it's false, it calls the startSlideShow() method to start the slide show. However, because startSlideShow() is a method of the object literal, not a private function, the code uses the me variable that contains a reference to the object literal to call it.

Next, the inner function sets the value of the button that was clicked based on the value of the private play variable. It can do that because the inner function will be an event handler for a button, so the value of *this* will be that button.

Finally, the inner function toggles the value of the private play variable. It does this by setting it to the opposite of its current value.

The library_slideshow.js file

```javascript
var createSlideshow = function() {
    // private variables and functions
    var timer, play = true, speed = 2000;
    var nodes = { image: null, caption: null };
    var img = { cache: [], counter: 0 };

    var stopSlideShow = function() { clearInterval( timer ); };
    var displayNextImage = function() {
        img.counter = ++img.counter % img.cache.length;
        var image = img.cache[img.counter];
        nodes.image.attr("src", image.src);
        nodes.caption.text( image.title );
    };

    // public methods that have access to private variables and functions
    return {
        loadImages: function(slides) {
            var image;
            for ( var i = 0; i < slides.length; i++ ) {
                image = new Image();
                image.src = "images/" + slides[i].href;
                image.title = slides[i].title;
                img.cache.push( image );
            }
            return this;
        },
        startSlideShow: function() {
            if (arguments.length === 2) {
                nodes.image = arguments[0];
                nodes.caption = arguments[1];
            }
            timer = setInterval(displayNextImage, speed);
            return this;
        },
        createToggleHandler: function() {
            var me = this;          // store 'this', which is the object literal
            return function() {
                // 'this' is the clicked button; 'me' is the object literal
                if ( play ) { stopSlideShow(); } else { me.startSlideShow(); }
                this.value = (play) ? "Resume" : "Pause";
                play = ! play;    // toggle play flag
            };
        }
    };
};
```

Description

- This library consists of an outer function named createSlideshow(). It contains several variables and functions that are available to every function inside the outer function, but not to outside code. In other words, these variables and functions are private.

- The createSlideshow() function returns an object literal with three methods. These three methods are inner functions that refer to the private state of the outer function.

Figure 18-5   The slide show library for the Slide Show application

The main JavaScript file

Figure 18-6 shows the main JavaScript file for this version of the Slide Show application. The ready() function starts by calling the global createSlideshow() function of the last figure to create the slideshow object. As you'll recall, this function returns an object with three methods that are needed for running the slide show.

Next, the ready() function creates an array of slide objects with information about the images that will be in the slideshow. After that, it calls the createToggleHandler() method of the slideshow object to get the function that it will use as the event handler for the click event of the Play/Pause button.

Finally, the ready() function chains two of the slideshow object's methods. First, it calls the loadImages() method and passes it the array of slide objects. Then, it calls the startSlideShow() method and passes it the image and span elements that will be used to display the slide show.

Below the code in this figure, you can see the slideshow object in the Watch Expressions pane of the Sources panel in Chrome's developer tools. Note that only the three public methods, plus the object's prototype object, are visible. This shows that outside code can't access variables like speed or nodes, or functions like stopSlideShow() or displayNextImage(). This means that the users of the slide show library can't overwrite or delete the private variables and functions that the slideshow object needs to function properly.

The main JavaScript file

```
$( document ).ready(function() {
    // create the slideshow object
    var slideshow = createSlideshow();

    var slides = [
        {href:"release.jpg", title:"Catch and Release"},
        {href:"deer.jpg", title:"Deer at Play"},
        {href:"hero.jpg", title:"The Big One!"},
        {href:"bison.jpg", title:"Roaming Bison"}
    ];

    $("#play_pause").click( slideshow.createToggleHandler() );

    slideshow.loadImages(slides).startSlideShow($("#image"), $("#caption"));
});
```

The slideshow object in the Watch Expressions pane

```
▼ Watch Expressions                          + C
▼ slideshow: Object
  ▶ createToggleHandler: function () {
  ▶ loadImages: function (slides) {
  ▶ startSlideShow: function () {
  ▶ __proto__: Object
```

Description

- This code calls the createSlideshow() function and stores the object it returns in a variable named slideshow. Then, it uses the methods of that object to attach an event handler for the play_pause button, set up the slide show, and start the slide show.

- You can examine the slideshow object in Chrome's developer tools to see that only the three methods returned by the createSlideshow() function are available to outside code. As a result, there's no way to overwrite any of the slideshow object's private state.

Figure 18-6   The main JavaScript file for the Slide Show application

How to use immediately invoked function expressions

Immediately invoked function expressions (IIFEs) are frequently used in JavaScript applications. In the topics that follow, you'll see how they work and how they are integral to the module pattern. In conversation, an IIFE is commonly referred to as an "iffy."

How to code an IIFE

Normally, you first define a function and then invoke it, as in the first example in figure 18-7. However, when you use an IIFE, you define and invoke a function expression in one step. This is illustrated by the second example. Here, the function definition is inside parentheses, and the function is invoked by adding parentheses at the end.

You can code the parentheses of an IIFE in one of two ways, as shown in the third set of examples. You'll see both coding styles in books and online examples. Although some programmers have strong opinions about which one is best, both styles work, so you can choose whichever one is easiest for you to understand and use. This book uses the first style.

You should also know that if an IIFE comes after the start of a line of code, the JavaScript engine doesn't require the outside parentheses. Nevertheless, you should still use them, since it's a programming convention that helps other programmers recognize that you're using an IIFE.

IIFEs can be used to keep variables and functions out of global scope and to keep variables and functions from conflicting with other variables and functions of the same name. For instance, in the last example in this figure, a variable named today is used to store both a String object and a Date object. Since the today variable that holds the Date object is within an IIFE, it doesn't conflict with the other today variable. IIFEs can also be used to correct a problem with closures in loops, as you'll see in the next figure.

Like any other function, you can code a parameter list for a function that will be immediately invoked. Then, you pass those arguments within the parentheses that invoke the IIFE. You'll see examples of this in the next figure as well as in other figures in this chapter.

A function expression that is defined and then invoked

```
var sayHello = function() {     // define function
    console.log("Hello");
};
sayHello();                     // invoke function
```

An immediately invoked function expression (IIFE)

```
(function() {                   // define and invoke function
    console.log("Hello");
})();
```

Two ways to code the parentheses of an IIFE

```
(function() { console.log ("Hello"); } ) ();
(function() { console.log ("Hello"); } () );
```

Some benefits of using an IIFE

- Helps you keep variables and functions out of global scope.

- Helps keep variables and functions from conflicting with other variables and functions that have the same name.

- Can be used to create private state.

An IIFE that keeps a variable from conflicting with another variable of the same name

```
// a variable named 'today' that holds a String object
var today = "Today is the first day of the rest of your life.";

// an IIFE that contains a variable named 'today' that holds a Date object.
today = today + (function() {
    var today = new Date();
    if (today.getDay() === 0 || today.getDay() === 6) {
        return " Plus, it's the weekend!";
    } else { return ""; }
})(); // Invoke the IIFE

alert(today);  // Displays the String object
```

Description

- An *immediately invoked function expression (IIFE)* is a function that is defined and invoked all at once.

- An IIFE should be always coded within parentheses, so the JavaScript engine as well as other programmers will interpret it as an IIFE.

- Like a regular function call, an IIFE ends with opening and closing parentheses that can include arguments. In the next figure, you'll see how to send arguments to an IIFE.

- If no reference to the IIFE remains when it's done running, its scope is destroyed, even if the function or file that contains it is still in scope.

Figure 18-7   How to code an immediately invoked function expression (IIFE)

How to use an IIFE to solve the closure loop problem

If you're working with closures in a loop, you can have a problem if you don't understand the two points at the start of figure 18-8. First, an inner function has access to the values in its scope chain by reference. This means that if the value of an outer variable changes, then its value will change inside the inner function as well. Second, the values of the variables in a function are determined when the function is invoked, not when the function is defined.

The first example in this figure illustrates the loop problem. Here, an onload event handler starts by creating an array of website names and storing them in an array variable named topSites. Then, it uses the find() method to get the three <a> elements that are in a div element named top_sites. It stores the resulting array in a variable named links.

Next, the code loops through the topSites array. Within the loop, it uses the value of the i variable to get the <a> element with the corresponding index from the links array. Then, it uses the value of the current element in the topSites array to set the element's text attribute to the current site name. Last, it attaches an event handler to the element's onclick event. This event handler should display a message indicating which link the user clicked on.

The screen that follows shows how the <a> elements look in the page, and the result of clicking on the middle link. As expected, the three elements display the names of the three sites in the topSites array. But unexpectedly, they all say "You clicked on Twitter" when clicked.

Why is this? The event handler for the click event of the <a> elements is coded within the ready() event handler, which means it's a function within a function. That's why it has access to the i variable and the topSites array that are defined in the outer ready() function. But, it has access to them by reference. That means that each time through the loop, the value of i changes, both in the outer ready() function and in the inner click() function. So, when the link is clicked in the page, the click() function takes the current value of i, which is the last index in the array, and uses it to retrieve and display the site name.

One way to fix this is to rewrite the code so it uses a function that returns a function. The next example shows how this is done. First, it shows a function called createHandler() that accepts a name parameter and returns a function. Then, in the loop, the createHandler() function is called, and it's passed the current value of the topSites array. Because the createHandler() function is being invoked, the value of name is set to the current site name. Then, the function that the createHandler() function returns is set as the <a> element's event handler.

Another way to fix this is to rewrite the code so it uses an IIFE, as in the last example. Since an IIFE is a regular function, you can pass arguments to it in the parentheses that invoke the function. In this case, the current value of the topSites array is passed to the IIFE, so it will be used as the name parameter in the function.

What else you need to know about closures

- An inner function has access to the values in its scope chain by reference. This means that if an outer variable changes, it will change for the inner function, too.

- The values of the variables in a function are set when the function is invoked, not when it's defined.

How this affects closures in a loop

Assigning click event handlers in a loop

```
$(document).ready(function() {
    var topSites = ["Google", "Facebook", "Twitter"];
    var links = $("top_sites").find("a");
    for (var i in topSites) {
        $(links[i]).text(topSites[i]);
        // This is a closure so value of i is by reference and can change.
        // When the function is invoked, value of i will be its last value.
        $(links[i]).click( function() {
            alert("You clicked on " + topSites[i]);
        });
    }
});
```

Result of loop – all links display the last value

How to fix the loop problem by calling a function that returns a function

```
$(document).ready(function() {
    /* topSites and links variables go here */
    var createHandler = function(name) {
        return function() { alert("You clicked on " + name); };
    };
    for (var i in topSites) {
        $(links[i]).text(topSites[i]);
        $(links[i]).click( createHandler(topSites[i]) );
    }

});
```

How to fix the loop problem by using an IIFE

```
$(document).ready(function() {
    /* topSites and links variables go here */
    for (var i in topSites) {
        $(links[i]).text(topSites[i]);
        $(links[i]).click(
            (function(name) {
                return function() {
                    alert("You clicked on " + name);
                };
            })(topSites[i]) // value for 'name' parameter passed to the IIFE
        );
    }
});
```

Figure 18-8   How to use an IIFE to solve the closure loop problem

How to work with the module pattern

Many developers and third-party libraries use the *module pattern*, which uses an IIFE to create a single instance of an object that has private state. In the topics that follow, you'll learn how to use this pattern in your own code.

What the module pattern is

A *singleton* is a pattern in which you can have only one instance of an object. The easiest way to create a singleton in JavaScript is with an object literal. For example, the tasklist object you saw in figure 17-19 is a single object that's in charge of all the operations of working with tasks in the Task List application. It's created when the file that contains it loads, and there's no way to create a second one. The problem with object literals, though, is that they can't have private state.

You can overcome this problem by using a function to create a closure with private state. However, that means you can create multiple instances of the object by making multiple calls to the function that produces it.

Sometimes, having more than one instance of the object is what you want. That's the case with the createClickCounter() function in figure 18-1. But other times, this causes problems. For example, if you had two slideshow objects that held references to different images or you had play variables that were out of sync, the Slide Show application might not work correctly.

The *module pattern* allows you to combine the benefits of object literals and closures. It uses an IIFE to create a single instance of the object that's returned by the function that creates the closure, which can be referred to as a *module*. That way, you get a single instance of an object, but that object has private state.

The first example in figure 18-9 shows how this works. Here, the slideshow library is rewritten to use an IIFE. This IIFE has private state, and it returns an object that refers to that private state. Since it's immediately invoked, it doesn't need to be called to create the object. Instead, the global slideshow variable will contain the object returned by the IIFE as soon as the library file loads and the IIFE runs. Like an object literal, you can overwrite it, but you can't create a second instance of it.

As the second example in this figure shows, the module pattern is often used in conjunction with namespaces. A *namespace* lets you keep your objects out of the global namespace, which helps you avoid *name collisions* with other libraries. To create a namespace, you assign an object literal to a variable. Then, you add the IIFE to the object.

Note that the second statement assigns the namespace if it already exists or an object literal if it doesn't. That prevents you from overwriting an existing namespace.

The module pattern is also easy to augment, so you can split the code for an object into multiple files. This is helpful when you have a large code base or multiple programmers. You'll learn how to augment a module in the next figure.

The pros and cons of object literals vs closures

Type	Pros and cons
Object literal	Pros: There's only one, and it doesn't need to be created in code before it can be used.
	Cons: All properties and methods are public.
Closure	Pros: Creates private state that protects the object's inner operations.
	Cons: Must be created before it can be used, and it can create more than one instance.

A module pattern that creates a single slideshow object with private state

```javascript
var slideshow = (function() {
    // private variables and functions
    var timer, play = true;
    var nodes = { image: null, caption: null };
    var img = { cache: [], counter: 0 };

    var stopSlideShow = function() { ... }
    var displayNextImage = function(){ ... }

    // public properties and methods
    return {
        speed: 2000,
        loadImages: function(slides) { ... },
        startSlideShow: function(){ ... },
        createToggleHandler: function(){ ... }
    }
})(); // Invoke the IIFE to create the object
```

How to create a namespace

An object literal that's used as a namespace

```javascript
var myapp = {};
```

How to ensure you don't overwrite an existing namespace

```javascript
var myapp = myapp || {};
```

A single slideshow object added to the myapp namespace

```javascript
myapp.slideshow = (function() {
    ...
})(); // Invoke the IIFE to create the object
```

Description

- The *module pattern* uses an immediately invoked function expression (IIFE) to create a single instance of the object, or *module*, that's returned by the function. That way, you get the benefits of an object literal while still having the private state of a closure.

- Since the module pattern makes it easy to augment an object, you can split an object among multiple files. This is helpful when you have a large code base or multiple programmers.

- The module pattern is often used in conjunction with *namespaces*.

- Several third-party libraries use the module pattern, including jQuery.

Figure 18-9   What the module pattern is

How to augment a module and use accessor properties

Figure 18-10 shows you how to *augment* a module. The first example in this figure *imports* the myapp.slideshow module that was created in the last figure by passing it as an argument to the IIFE. That way, the mod parameter of the IIFE contains the myapp.slideshow object.

To augment the module, this IIFE adds a method named changeSpeed to the myapp.slideshow object in the mod parameter. The changeSpeed method accepts a parameter named speed, creates a private variable named newSpeed, and calls the parseInt function to convert the value in the speed parameter to an integer. Then, it sets the object's speed property to either the newSpeed value or a default value. Finally, it returns the value of the *this* keyword so the changeSpeed method can be chained.

As in the example in the last figure, this pattern allows you to create methods with private state. Also, the new methods are added to the module as soon as the file loads and the IIFE runs. This means that files that augment an existing module should be loaded after the file that creates the module, but before any other files that might use the new methods.

Once a method has been added to a module, it can be used like any other method. This is illustrated by the second example in this figure. Here, the changeSpeed method is chained with the startSlideShow method.

One drawback of distributing the code for a module across several files is that you have to make private state public if you want to be able to work with it. For example, the slideshow object in the last figure made its speed property public so it could be changed by the code in this figure. This leads to situations where internal operations can be overwritten or changed.

One way to address this drawback is to use accessor properties. Unlike a standard property, an *accessor property* is not the actual location of the property's value. Rather, it contains *getter* and *setter* functions that read and write the property's data. An accessor property with only a getter is a *read-only property*, while an accessor property with only a setter is a *write-only property*.

You can use the second parameter of the create() method you learned about in figure 17-11 to create accessor properties. This second parameter expects a single object that contains one or more objects that contain the name of the property and the getter and setter functions that the property will use.

The last example in this figure shows how to add an accessor property named interval to the slideshow object. Here, the IIFE that creates the slideshow object is coded with a private speed variable and a prototype object that will contain the public methods for the object. Then, a new properties object is coded with an object that contains the getter and setter methods for the interval property. The getter returns the value of the private speed variable, while the setter sets the value of the speed variable only if the data is acceptable. This provides limited access to the private state of the slideshow object, while protecting that private state.

An example that uses an IIFE to augment the slideshow object

```
(function(mod) {
    mod.changeSpeed = function(speed) {
        // private state
        var newSpeed = parseInt(speed);

        // set slideshow speed - use default speed if number not OK
        this.speed = (isNaN(newSpeed) || newSpeed < 500) ? 2000 : newSpeed;

        // return 'this' so method can be chained
        return this;
    };
})(myapp.slideshow); // invoke IIFE; import the module to be augmented
```

An example that uses the slideshow object's new method

```
$("#change_speed").click(function() {
    var ms = prompt("Enter slideshow speed in milliseconds.", "2000");
    myapp.slideshow.changeSpeed(ms).startSlideShow();
});
```

How to use an accessor property to provide limited access to a private variable

```
myapp.slideshow = (function() {
    var speed = 2000, ...
    var prototype = {...};

    var properties = {
        interval: {
            get: function() { return speed; },
            set: function( s ) {
                speed = ( isNaN(s) || s < 500 ) ? 2000 : s;
            }
        }
    };

    // create and return the slideshow object
    return Object.create( prototype, properties );

})(); // Invoke the IIFE
```

Description

- To *augment* a module, you use an IIFE, and you *import* the module to be augmented by passing it as an argument when you invoke the IIFE.

- One drawback of the first example shown above is that the slideshow object had to make the private speed variable public for it to be changed. To address this drawback, you can use the second parameter of the create() method to create accessor properties.

- An *accessor property* uses getter and setter functions to retrieve and set the value of a private variable. That way, you can include code in these functions that limit what outside code can do with the private variable, while still providing access to that variable.

- This second parameter of the create() method doesn't work correctly in older browsers, even with the shim and sham files described in figure 1-17.

Figure 18-10   How to augment a module and use accessor properties

The Slide Show application
with the module pattern

This topic adds two updates to the Slide Show application you saw earlier in this chapter. First, it uses the module pattern to create the slideshow object. This way, only one instance of the object is allowed, which makes the application more stable. But the slideshow object can still use private state to protect its internal operations.

Second, it uses accessor properties for the slide show's speed and for the array that holds the slide show's images. This way, the speed of the slide show and the list of images can be accessed when the module is augmented, but those private variables themselves remain protected.

Figure 18-11 shows the user interface of the updated Slide Show application. As you can see, this version of the application adds two more buttons. The first one allows a user to change the speed of the slide show. When it's clicked, a prompt showing the current interval between slides, in milliseconds, is shown, and the user is asked to enter a new interval. The second one allows a user to see a list of the images in the slide show. When it's clicked, an alert displays a comma separated list of all the image names.

The HTML

In the head section of the HTML for this application, you can see three script elements in addition to the script element for the jQuery CDN. First, the library_slideshow.js file contains the code that creates the namespace for this application as well as the module object itself, so it's loaded first. Second, the library_slideshow_enhancements.js file contains code that augments the slide show module, so it's loaded second. Third, since the main JavaScript file uses the module that's created in the first file and augmented in the second, it's loaded last.

The body of the HTML is almost identical to the HTML you saw earlier. The only difference is that this version has two new buttons with the ids "change_speed" and "view_slides". These are the buttons that are described above.

The Slide Show application after the Change Speed button is clicked

The HTML

```html
<head>
    <title>Image Slide Show</title>
    <link rel="stylesheet" href="slideshow.css"/>
    <script src="https://code.jquery.com/jquery-3.1.1.min.js"></script>
    <script src="library_slideshow.js"></script>
    <script src="library_slideshow_enhancements.js"></script>
    <script src="main.js"></script>
</head>
<body>
    <main>
        <h1>Fishing Slide Show</h1>
        <p><input type="button" id="play_pause" value="Pause">
           <input type="button" id="change_speed" value="Change Speed">
           <input type="button" id="view_slides" value="View Slides"></p>
        <p><img src="images/release.jpg" id="image" alt=""></p>
        <p><span id="caption">Catch and Release</span></p>
    </main>
</body>
```

Description

- This Slide Show application adds a button that changes the slide show's speed and a button that displays a list of the images in the slide show.

- The application uses the module pattern for the slideshow object. This lets the application use a single object with private state, and it allows the code to be split among multiple files.

- The application uses accessor properties to access the slide show's private state. This provides access to outside code while protecting the application's internal operations.

Figure 18-11   The HTML for the Slide Show application with the module pattern

The slide show library

Figure 18-12 shows the slide show library file. This is the file that loads first, and it contains the code for the myapp namespace and the code that creates the slideshow object. It starts with a line of code that creates the namespace. This is followed by an IIFE that adds a slideshow object to that namespace.

Most of the code in the IIFE is the same as the code shown earlier, so to save space it isn't shown here. Like the slideshow application you saw earlier in this chapter, the private state in this IIFE is available to the object that is returned by the IIFE. Also like the earlier application, the private state in this IIFE isn't available to outside code.

An important difference between this code and the code shown earlier is that the function in this code is invoked as soon as the file loads. That way, a single instance of the slideshow object is created. What's more, it isn't possible to create a second instance of the object. Instead, loading this file again would just recreate the object, not create a new one. And coding a new value for myapp. slideshow would overwrite that object, not create a new one.

Another important difference is that this code adds two accessor properties named interval and images. This allows outside code to work with the speed and img.cache variables, even though they are both protected in private state.

The interval property has both a getter function and a setter function. The getter function simply returns the value of the private speed variable. The setter function, by contrast, has code that does two things. First, it checks that the parameter it receives is numeric and more than 500 milliseconds. If it is, it assigns this value to the speed variable. But if it isn't, it assigns a default value of 2000 milliseconds to the speed variable. This protects the internal workings of the slideshow if the user enters unexpected data.

Second, the setter function calls the private stopSlideShow() function. That's because, as you learned in chapter 7, you need to stop an interval timer and restart it if you want to change the interval.

The images property has only a getter function. Because of that, it is read-only. However, unlike the interval property, the images property doesn't return the img.cache variable itself. That's because if it did, the images in the slide show could be deleted or replaced, which would affect the slide show's operations. Instead, the slice() method is used to return a new array. That way, any outside code has access to a copy of the array rather than the array itself.

As you can see, then, accessor properties give you a lot of flexibility. They allow you to provide some public access to private state, all while protecting that state and performing any other tasks the slide show needs to function properly.

The library_slideshow.js file

```javascript
// create the namespace used by the application
var myapp = myapp || {};

// create the slideshow object and add it to the namespace
myapp.slideshow = (function() {
    // private variables and functions
    var timer, play = true , speed = 2000;   // speed is private
    var nodes = { image: null, caption: null };
    var img = { cache: [], counter: 0 };

    var stopSlideShow = function() { clearInterval( timer ); }
    var displayNextImage = function() { ... }
    var setPlayText = function(btn) { ... }

    // prototype object for public methods
    var prototype = {
        loadImages: function(slides) { ... },
        startSlideShow: function() { ... },
        createToggleHandler: function(){ ... }
    };

    // property descriptor object(s)
    var properties = {
        interval: {
            get: function() { return speed; },
            set: function( s ) {
                speed = ( isNaN(s) || s < 500 ) ? 2000: s;
                stopSlideShow();
            }
        },
        images: { // read-only property because only has a getter
            get: function() {
                return img.cache.slice(0); // returns a copy of the array
            }
        }
    };

    // create and return the slideshow object
    return Object.create( prototype, properties );

})(); // Invoke the IIFE
```

Description

- The slide show library creates the myapp namespace, and then adds the slideshow object to it using an IIFE and the module pattern. The private variables and functions in the IIFE are available to the methods of the object that it returns, but not to outside code.

- The IIFE is invoked as soon as the file loads. That way, a single instance of the slideshow object is created.

- The private speed and img.cache variables are accessible only through the accessor properties created by the object that's passed as the second parameter of the create() method. This protects the internal functioning of the slideshow object while still allowing some public access to these private variables.

Figure 18-12   The slide show library for the Slide Show application

The slide show enhancements library

Figure 18-13 shows the slide show enhancements library. This is the library that loads second, and it contains the code that augments the slideshow object.

The enhancements library consists of an IIFE. The first line of the IIFE includes a parameter named mod. This parameter receives the myapp.slideshow object when the function is invoked.

The IIFE augments the slideshow object it receives by adding two methods to it. The first method, changeSpeed(), uses the interval property of the slideshow object to set the slide show speed to the value it receives. First, though, it calls the parseInt() function to convert that value to a whole number. Since the interval property uses a default value if it receives unacceptable data, this method doesn't need to do any further data validation. Finally, it returns the value of *this* so the method can be chained.

The second method, displaySlides(), uses the images property of the slideshow object to get a list of the images in the slide show. Since the images property is an array of Image objects, this method uses the map() method of that array to convert each Image object to a string. It does this by passing a function that splits the src property of each Image object on the "/" separator so each element of the array that's returned contains one portion of the file path or name. Then, it returns the last element of the resulting array, which will be a file name like "release.jpg". Finally, the method returns the string produced by calling the join() method on the array of strings returned by the map() method.

The last line of the enhancements library invokes the IIFE and passes the myapp.slideshow object as an argument. But notice that it doesn't need to create the myapp.slideshow object before it uses it. That's because this object will be created by the IIFE in the last figure when that file is loaded. Also, because the slide show module is augmented within an IIFE, these new methods are available as soon as this file loads and the IIFE runs.

The main JavaScript file

Figure 18-13 shows the main JavaScript file. It starts with the jQuery ready() function, which then starts by creating an *alias* for the myapp.slideshow object. This is because namespaces can make object names quite long, especially if you have nested namespaces. If you store an object with a long name in a variable with a shorter name, then, your code is easier to type, read, and understand. However, make sure to use a local variable as an alias, not a global variable.

Next, the code sets up the slides array and attaches the event handlers for the buttons. Notice that the event handler for the click event of the Change Speed button uses the interval property of the slideshow object to tell the user the current speed of the slide show. Then, after it gets a new speed from the user, it passes it to the changeSpeed() method and chains the startSlideShow() method.

After that, the click event handler for the View Slides button calls the displaySlides() method of the slideshow object. Finally, the ready() function loads the slides and starts the slide show.

The library_slideshow_enhancements.js file

```javascript
(function(mod) {
    mod.changeSpeed = function(speed) {
        this.interval = parseInt(speed);
        return this; // return 'this' so method can be chained
    };
    mod.displaySlides = function() {
        var slides = this.images.map( function( current ) {
            var pieces = current.src.split("/");
            return pieces[pieces.length - 1]; // return last array element
        });
        return slides.join(", ");
    };
})(myapp.slideshow); // invoke IIFE; import the object to be augmented
```

The main JavaScript file

```javascript
$( document ).ready(function() {
    var slideshow = myapp.slideshow; // use an alias to make code shorter

    var slides = [
        {href:"release.jpg", title:"Catch and Release"},
        {href:"deer.jpg", title:"Deer at Play"},
        {href:"hero.jpg", title:"The Big One!"},
        {href:"bison.jpg", title:"Roaming Bison"}
    ];
    $("#play_pause").click( slideshow.createToggleHandler() );
    $("#change_speed").click( function() {
        var ms = prompt( "Current speed is "
            + slideshow.interval + " milliseconds.\n"
            + "Please enter a new speed in milliseconds."
        , 2000 );
        slideshow.changeSpeed(ms).startSlideShow();
    });
    $("#view_slides").click( function() {
        alert( slideshow.displaySlides() );
    });
    slideshow.loadImages(slides).startSlideShow($("#image"), $("#caption"));
});
```

Description

- The slide show enhancements library adds two new methods to the existing slideshow object. It does this by using an IIFE and importing the slideshow object.

- The changeSpeed() method changes the speed of the slide show. It can do that because the interval property allows limited access to the private speed variable. Also, because the interval property uses a default value if it receives bad data, the changeSpeed() method doesn't need to do any data validation.

- The displaySlides() method displays a comma-separated list of the image files in the slide show. It can do that because the viewSlides property provides an array of Image objects.

- The main file uses an alias to work with the slideshow object in the myapp namespace.

- The event handler for the click event of the "change_speed" button gets the new speed from the user and then chains the changeSpeed() method and startSlideShow() methods.

Figure 18-13   The slide show enhancements library and main JavaScript file

How to use the module pattern to create jQuery plugins

One of the features of jQuery is that it provides an *API* (*Application Programming Interface*) that lets you create your own plugins. Sometimes, for example, you can't find a plugin that does what you want, or you don't trust its source, or it does far more than you need. In those cases, it makes sense to build your own plugin. And now that you have the JavaScript skills that you've learned in this book, you have all the skills for creating your own jQuery plugins.

The structure of a plugin

Since the jQuery library uses the module pattern that you just learned about, the jQuery object is available in your web pages without needing to be called or created. That's why the script element for the core jQuery library must be included before anything that depends on it.

That also means that you can use an IIFE to create plugins that augment the jQuery object. The examples in figure 18-14 show how this works.

The first example shows how to use an IIFE to import the jQuery object so it can be modified. Here, the jQuery library is imported within parentheses at the end of the IIFE and assigned to the $ sign parameter of the function. Not only is this the standard way to work with the module pattern, it also has the benefit of preventing conflicts with other libraries and plugins that use the $ sign.

Within the IIFE, $.fn refers to the jQuery object's prototype object. This prototype object is where you add your methods when you create a plugin. It's also a good practice to add only one method to the $.fn object for each plugin.

The second example shows how to make your plugin chainable. It does this by returning the *this* keyword. The third example shows how to make your plugin able to iterate through all the selected elements by putting its code inside the jQuery each() method. If, for example, the jQuery selector selects all <a> elements in the page, a plugin whose code is inside an each() method will apply its code to each selected <a> element. Plugins that use this technique support *implicit iteration*.

The fourth example shows how to combine the coding practices in the second and third examples to write plugins that support chaining and implicit iteration. This works because the each() method also returns *this*, so returning the result of the each() method is the same as ending your plugin code with "return this". This is the way most professionals code plugins.

This figure also shows the naming conventions for plugin files as well as the API standards for plugins. As you've learned, you use the each() method within the plugin function to support implicit iteration, and you return the *this* keyword to preserve chaining. Beyond that, you should be sure to end all method definitions with a semicolon, and you should provide reasonable defaults if your plugin offers options. Above all, your plugin should be well documented if it's going to be used by others.

The module pattern of a jQuery plugin

An IIFE that imports the jQuery object and adds a method to its prototype

```
(function($){
    $.fn.pluginName = function() {
        // the code for the plugin
    };
})(jQuery);
```

A method that returns the *this* keyword so it can be chained

```
(function($){
    $.fn.pluginName = function() {
        // the code for the plugin
        return this;
    };
})(jQuery);
```

A method that uses the each() method so it iterates all selected elements

```
(function($){
    $.fn.pluginName = function() {
        this.each(function() {
            // the code for the plugin
        });
        return this;
    };
})(jQuery);
```

The way most professionals code a plugin

```
(function($){
    $.fn.pluginName = function() {
        return this.each(function() {
            // the code for the plugin
        });
    };
})(jQuery);
```

Naming conventions for plugin files

```
jquery.pluginName.js
```

The API standards for plugins

- The plugin should support *implicit iteration*.
- The plugin should preserve chaining by returning the selected object.
- The plugin definitions should end with a semicolon.
- The plugin options should provide reasonable defaults.
- The plugin should be well documented.

Description

- jQuery uses the module pattern, so a jQuery plugin augments the jQuery object.
- For many plugins, most of the code will be in the function of the each() method.
- When the plugin finishes, the value of *this* should be returned to the calling application.

Figure 18-14   The structure of a plugin

How to code a plugin that highlights the items in a menu

Now that you know the structure of a plugin, figure 18-15 shows how to create a simple plugin. This plugin highlights a menu item when the mouse enters that item, and it returns the item to its original state when the mouse leaves it.

This figure shows the HTML for the nav element that will be affected by the plugin and the CSS style rules for the nav element. Notice the mouseover class in the CSS. This is what will be added and removed to create the highlight effect.

The code for this plugin uses the coding practices you learned in the previous figure. First, it imports the jQuery object. Then, it adds the plugin method to the $.fn prototype object, puts its code inside the each() method, and returns the value of the each() method.

Within the each() method, the first statement uses the find() method to get the <a> elements that are children of the element the plugin is applied to, and it stores them in a variable named items. Then, the code provides functions for the mouseover and mouseout events of those <a> elements. The function for the mouseover event uses the jQuery addClass() method to add the mouseover class to the <a> element. This changes the element's color and background color when the mouse is over it. The function for the mouseout event uses the jQuery removeClass() method to remove the mouseover class from the <a> element. This restores the element to its previous color and background color when the mouse leaves the element.

Because the plugin is stored in a file named jquery.highlightmenu.js, the script element for the plugin reflects this. Then, the jQuery to activate the plugin selects the nav element by type and calls the highlightMenu method of the plugin.

A menu that is highlighted by the highlightMenu plugin

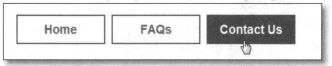

The HTML for the menu

```html
<nav>
    <ul>
        <li><a href="index.html">Home</a></li>
        <li><a href="faq.html">FAQs</a></li>
        <li><a href="contact.html">Contact Us</a></li>
    </ul>
</nav>
```

The CSS for the menu

```css
nav ul {
    list-style-type: none; }
nav ul li {
    border: blue solid 2px;
    float: left;
    margin-right: 10px; }
nav ul li a {
    text-decoration: none;
    text-align: center;
    display: block;
    width: 120px;
    padding: .5em;
    color: green;
    font-weight: bold;
    font-size: 120%; }
.mouseover {
    background-color: blue;
    color: white; }
```

The highlightMenu plugin in a file named jquery.highlightmenu.js

```javascript
(function($){
    $.fn.highlightMenu = function() {
        return this.each(function() {
            var items = $(this).find("a");
            items.mouseover(function() {
                $(this).addClass("mouseover");
            });
            items.mouseout(function() {
                $(this).removeClass("mouseover");
            });
        });
    };
})(jQuery);
```

jQuery that uses the highlightMenu plugin

```javascript
$(document).ready(function() {
    $("nav").highlightMenu();
});
```

Figure 18-15   The Highlight Menu plugin

How to add options to a plugin

To make a plugin more useful, you usually provide some options for it. To do that, you can use the coding technique that is illustrated in figure 18-16.

To start, you code an options parameter in the function for the plugin method. This is highlighted in this figure. This parameter will receive all of the options that are set by the user as properties in an object literal.

As the API standards for plugins in figure 18-14 point out, a plugin should always provide defaults for the options. That way, the users don't have to set the options if they don't want to. To provide defaults, you can use the $.extend() method as shown in this example. Here, a variable named o stores the object that's created by the $.extend() method.

The first parameter of the $.extend() method consists of an object literal that provides the default properties for the options object. The second parameter is the parameter that's passed to the plugin, which is the object literal set by the user. Then, when this method is executed, the user options in the second parameter are merged with the default options in the first parameter, and the user options replace any default options with the same name. The result is that the o variable contains one property for each option, and that property contains either the default value or the value that the user set to override the default value.

Then, the o variable is used in the mouseover() and mouseout() event handlers. For example, the code in the mouseover() function passes the value of o.mouseoverClass to the addClass() method. That way, if the user has passed in a different CSS class to use, the plugin will use it. Otherwise, the plugin will use the default class named mouseover.

This version of the highlight menu plugin also lets the user specify whether a mouseout class should be applied when the mouse leaves the link, and what that mouseout class should do. This allows for effects like making links that have been hovered over a different color than those that have not. The default behavior of the plugin is to apply the mouseout class and to use the default class named mouseout.

To show how to use the plugin with options, the last example in this figure sends in one option. In this case, the useMouseout property is changed to false from its default value of true. This means that the plugin will simply remove the default mouseover class on mouseout rather than applying the mouseout class.

The highlightMenu plugin with options

```
(function($){
    $.fn.highlightMenu = function(options) {
        var o = $.extend({
            "mouseoverClass"  : "mouseover",
            "mouseoutClass"   : "mouseout",
            "useMouseout"     : true
        }, options);

        return this.each(function() {
            var items = $(this).find("a");
            items.mouseover(function() {
                $(this).addClass(o.mouseoverClass);
                if (o.useMouseout) {
                    $(this).removeClass(o.mouseoutClass);
                }
            });
            items.mouseout(function() {
                $(this).removeClass(o.mouseoverClass);
                if (o.useMouseout) {
                    $(this).addClass(o.mouseoutClass);
                }
            });
        });
    };
})(jQuery);
```

jQuery that uses the highlightMenu plugin and sets one of its options

```
$(document).ready(function() {
    $("nav").highlightMenu({
        useMouseout: false
    });
});
```

Description

- To provide options for a plugin, you code a parameter for the plugin that will receive the options that the user sets. In the example above, this parameter is named "options".

- To set the default options, you use the $.extend() method, which merges the properties in its first parameter, an object literal, with the properties in its second parameter, which is the object literal that is passed to the plugin by the calling statement. This object literal is the one that contains the user's options.

Figure 18-16   The Highlight Menu plugin with options

A Blackjack application that uses a blackjack plugin

To show you a more realistic example of a jQuery plugin, this section presents an application for a Blackjack (or 21) card game. Its user interface is shown in figure 18-17, and it uses a jQuery plugin named blackjack to provide the game functionality.

As you will see, the code for this plugin illustrates many of the skills that you've learned in this chapter as well as in the last chapter. For instance, it uses object literals, constructor functions, and objects that have private state. And since it's based on a jQuery plugin, it uses an IIFE and the module pattern. Although it will take some effort, you'll learn a lot by studying this code until you understand it.

The HTML and the main JavaScript file

In the head section of the HTML for this application, you can see three script elements. This first one is for the jQuery CDN, and the second is for a minified version of the blackjack plugin file. The last script element is for the main JavaScript file. They're coded in this order because the main JavaScript file depends on the plugin file, and the plugin file depends on jQuery.

Also in the head section are two link elements for the CSS files this application needs. The first one is for the CSS file for the blackjack plugin. Though not shown here, it provides style rules for the layout of the HTML that the plugin provides. The second one is for the main CSS file for the application. It's best to code the link elements in this order so you can override the CSS styles for the plugin if you want to.

The body of the HTML contains a main element, which then contains an h1 element and a div element with an id attribute of "blackjack". This is all the HTML that this blackjack application needs to work with the blackjack plugin.

The main JavaScript file for the Blackjack application starts with the jQuery ready() function. Then, the jQuery to activate the plugin selects the blackjack div by id and calls the blackjack() method of the plugin, passing in an option that sets the name of the player.

In the next few figures, you'll see that the code for the plugin is spread across several files to make it easier to work with. Then, the last figure shows how you can use minifier software to combine the code in several files into the single file that's used for the plugin.

A Blackjack application that uses a blackjack plugin

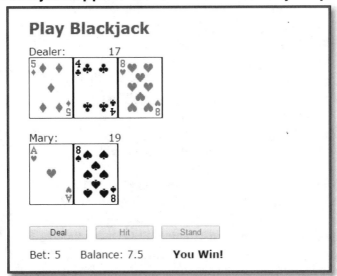

The HTML

```
<head>
    <title>Play Blackjack</title>
    <link href="jquery.blackjack.css" rel="stylesheet" />
    <link rel="stylesheet" href="main.css">
    <script src="https://code.jquery.com/jquery-3.1.1.min.js"></script>
    <script src="jquery.blackjack.min.js"></script>
    <script src="main.js"></script>
</head>
<body>
    <main>
        <h1>Play Blackjack</h1>
        <div id="blackjack"></div>
    </main>
</body>
```

The main JavaScript file

```
$( document ).ready(function() {
    $("#blackjack").blackjack({
        playerName: "Mary"
    });
});
```

Description

- The Blackjack application uses a custom jQuery plugin to add the functionality of the blackjack game.

- The HTML file for the application links to the CSS and JavaScript files the plugin needs, and it includes a div element with an id attribute of "blackjack". The main JavaScript file then attaches the plugin to that div element and passes some options to the plugin.

Figure 18-17   The HTML and main JavaScript file for the Blackjack application

The deck and hand files of the blackjack plugin

Figure 18-18 shows the library file for the deck of cards. Because it has some private state to protect, it's coded as an IIFE. That way, as soon as this file loads, an object named deck with one property and three methods is created. The private state consists of a function named resetCards(). This function uses a nested loop to create an array of strings with elements like "1-c" and "2-h" that represent cards like the ace of clubs and the two of hearts.

The single property of the deck object is an array of strings named cards. Its initial value is set by calling the private resetCards() function when the IIFE is invoked.

The three methods of the deck object are needsShuffling(), shuffle(), and deal(). The needsShuffling() method returns true if the number of cards remaining in the cards array is less than 10. The shuffle() method shuffles the cards by calling the resetCards() function and restoring the cards array to hold all 52 cards. It also alerts the player that the deck is being shuffled.

The deal() method of the deck object uses the Math.random() and Math.floor() methods to randomly select an index from the cards array. It then uses that index value to get the card string at that index. Next, it uses the splice() method of the cards array to remove the selected card from the cards array, and it returns the selected card.

This figure also shows the library file for an individual blackjack hand. Because the application needs more than one blackjack hand (both the dealer and the player will have one), this library uses a constructor function to create instances of a Hand object type.

The constructor starts by initializing a cards property to an empty array, and a total property to zero. Then, it adds five methods to the prototype object of the Hand object type.

The hasAce() method uses the some() method of the cards array, which accepts a function that uses the split() method to get the numeric portion of the card string. If the number of the card is "1", then that card is an ace and the function returns true. Otherwise, it returns false. Finally this method returns the result of the some() method, which is true if any of its elements returned true.

The add() method starts by adding the string value it receives to the cards array. Then, it uses the reduce() method of the cards array, which accepts a function that gets the numeric portion of each card, converts it to an integer, and adds it to the previous total, making sure that face cards only add 10. After that, it checks to see if any aces in the hand should count for 1 or 11, and it sets the total property to this new total.

The hasBlackJack(), busted(), and mustHit() methods return Boolean values. The first two indicate whether the hand is a blackjack or over 21. The last one indicates whether the hand is under 17 or is equal to 17 with an ace that counts as 11 (a soft 17), in which case another card must be taken. Otherwise, if the hand is equal to 17 but doesn't include an ace (a hard 17), no more cards are taken.

The jquery.blackjack.deck.js file

```
var deck = (function() {
    var resetCards = function() {  // protected private function
        var cards = [], suits = ["c","d","h","s"];
        for (var s in suits) {
            for (var i=1; i<=13; i++) { cards.push(i + "-" + suits[s]); }
        }
        return cards;
    };
    return {
        cards: resetCards(),
        needsShuffling: function() {
            return (this.cards.length < 10) ? true : false;
        },
        shuffle: function() {
            this.cards = resetCards();
            alert("Shuffling...");
        },
        deal: function() {
            var i = Math.floor(Math.random() * this.cards.length);
            var card = this.cards[i];
            this.cards.splice(i, 1); // remove card from deck
            return card;
        }
    };
})(); //IIFE
```

The jquery.blackjack.hand.js file

```
var Hand = function() {
    this.cards = [];
    this.total = 0;
};
Hand.prototype.hasAce = function() {
    return this.cards.some( function(curr) {
        return (curr.split("-")[0] === "1") ? true : false;
    });
};
Hand.prototype.add = function(card) {
    this.cards.push(card);
    var total = this.cards.reduce( function(prev, curr) {
        var num = parseInt(curr.split("-")[0]);
        if (num > 10) { return prev + 10; }
        else { return prev + num; }
    }, 0); // set initial value of prev parameter to zero

    if ( total <= 11 && this.hasAce() ) { total = total + 10; }
    this.total = total;
};
Hand.prototype.hasBlackJack = function() {
    if (this.cards.length === 2 && this.total === 21 ) { return true; } };
Hand.prototype.busted = function() {
    return (this.total > 21) ? true : false; };
Hand.prototype.mustHit = function() { // only applies to dealer
    if (this.total < 17) { return true; }
    else if (this.total === 17 && this.hasAce() ) { return true; }
    else { return false; } };
```

Figure 18-18   The deck and hand libraries of the blackjack plugin

Incidentally, since the mustHit() method only applies to the dealer, this library could be coded as a Hand object type with just the first four methods. Then, you could code a Dealer object type that inherits the Hand object type and adds the mustHit() method.

The game file of the blackjack plugin

Figure 18-19 shows the library file for a blackjack game. Since only one game object is needed and it doesn't need to protect any private state, it's coded as an object literal.

The game object has three properties: dealer, player, and balance. The dealer and player properties contain instances of Hand objects, while the balance property is a numeric value that keeps track of the player's current balance.

The game object has five methods: deal(), hit(), playerWins(), dealerWins(), and updateBalance(). The deal() method starts by calling the shuffle() method of the deck object if the deck needs shuffling. Then, it stores new instances of Hand objects in the dealer and player properties. This replaces any previous instances of the Hand object that those properties might hold. Finally, it calls the deal() method of the deck object four times to deal two cards each to the dealer and player. It does this by calling the add() method of the dealer and player properties, starting with the player and going in alternating order.

The hit() method accepts a parameter named hand whose value indicates if the player or the dealer gets another card. If the value of the hand parameter is "dealer", the method uses the add() method of the dealer property and the deal() method of the deck object to add one card to the dealer's hand. Otherwise, it uses the add() method of the player property and the deal() method of the deck object to add one card to the player's hand.

The playerWins() and dealerWins() methods work similarly to each other. Each uses the busted() method and the total property of the Hand object to determine whether the dealer or the player has won the current hand.

The updateBalance() method accepts a parameter named amount and adds it to the balance property. First, though, it checks to see if the player has a blackjack. If so, it adjusts the value of the amount parameter to reflect a 3:2 payout before adding it to the balance.

The jquery.blackjack.game.js file

```javascript
var game = {
    dealer: new Hand(),
    player: new Hand(),
    balance: 0,
    deal: function() {
        if ( deck.needsShuffling() ) { deck.shuffle(); }
        this.dealer = new Hand();
        this.player = new Hand();
        this.player.add( deck.deal() );
        this.dealer.add( deck.deal() );
        this.player.add( deck.deal() );
        this.dealer.add( deck.deal() );
    },
    hit: function(hand) {
        if ( hand.toLowerCase() === "dealer" ) {
            this.dealer.add( deck.deal() );
        }
        else { this.player.add( deck.deal() ); }
    },
    playerWins: function() {
        if (this.dealer.busted() || (!this.player.busted()
                && this.dealer.total < this.player.total) ) {
            return true;
        }
        else { return false; }
    },
    dealerWins: function() {
        if (this.player.busted() || (!this.dealer.busted()
                && this.player.total < this.dealer.total) ) {
            return true;
        }
        else { return false; }
    },
    updateBalance: function(amount) {
        if ( this.player.hasBlackJack() ) {
            amount = amount + (amount * 0.50);
        }
        this.balance = this.balance + amount;
    }
};
```

Figure 18-19   The game library file of the blackjack plugin

The main file of the blackjack plugin

Figure 18-20 shows the main file for the blackjack plugin. This file is quite long, so the basic jQuery code for things like setting the text of labels and preloading card images has been removed for brevity. However, you can review all of this code in the download for this chapter.

As you can see, the blackjack plugin uses an IIFE, the module pattern, and the API standards you learned about in figure 18-14. The code within the IIFE starts by adding a method named blackjack to the prototype object of the jQuery object. The blackjack method accepts an options parameter and provides default values for these options, which are the name of the dealer, the name of the player, and the amount of the bet.

After that, it puts the code for the plugin inside the each() method and returns the result of the each() method. The code in the each() method starts by generating the HTML that the plugin uses. Again, most of this has been removed to save space, but you can review it in the accompanying download. Once the HTML has been generated, it's added to the page using the html() method of the element that the blackjack method is attached to. In the Blackjack application, that's the div element whose id attribute is "blackjack".

Next, the plugin creates a private function named showResults(). This function displays all the cards, including the dealer's hole card, displays the total value of both hands, and disables the Hit and Stand buttons. Then, it uses the methods of the game object to determine who won the hand, and it notifies the user and updates the player's balance accordingly.

Finally, the plugin attaches event handlers for the click events of the Deal, Hit, and Stand buttons. The Deal event handler starts by calling the deal() method of the game object. Then, it uses the dealer and player properties of the game object to see if either has a blackjack. If so, the handler calls the showResults() function. Otherwise, the handler shows the cards of each hand (minus the dealer's hole card) and the total of the player's hand.

The Hit event handler calls the hit() method of the game object for the player. Then, it uses the player property of the game object to see if the player busted. If so, the handler calls the showResults() function. Otherwise, the handler shows the new cards and total for the player's hand.

The Stand event handler shows all the cards and totals for both hands and starts an interval timer. The function that's passed to the setInterval() function uses the dealer property of the game object to see if the dealer must hit. If so, the function calls the hit() method of the game object for the dealer. Otherwise, the function clears the timer and calls the showResults() function.

The function that's passed to the timer will be called repeatedly until the dealer no longer needs to hit. Then, the results of the hand will be displayed. The reason a timer is used here is to simulate a dealer dealing cards one at a time. Without a timer, the dealer's cards would all appear at once when the player clicks the Stand button, which wouldn't be as realistic.

The jquery.blackjack.js file

```
(function($){
    $.fn.blackjack = function(options) {
        var o = $.extend({
            "dealerName": "Dealer",
            "playerName": "Player",
            "bet": 5
        }, options);

        /* preload card images */

        return this.each(function() {
            // create and load HTML for plugin
            var html = "<label>" + o.dealerName + ":</label>";
            html = html + "<span> </span>";
            html = html + "<div id='dealer'> </div>";
            ...
            $(this).html(html);

            var showResults = function() {
                /* show all cards and totals, disable Hit and Stand */
                if ( game.playerWins() ) {
                    $("#outcome").text( "You Win!" );
                    game.updateBalance( o.bet );
                } else if ( game.dealerWins() ) {
                    $("#outcome").text( "You Lose :(" );
                    game.updateBalance( - o.bet );
                } else { $("#outcome").text( "PUSH" ); }
                $("#balance").text( "Balance: " + game.balance );
            };
            $("#deal").click( function() {
                game.deal();
                if (game.dealer.hasBlackJack()||game.player.hasBlackJack())
                    { showResults(); }
                else { /* show cards (hide hole card) & player total */ }
            });
            $("#hit").click( function() {
                game.hit("player");
                if ( game.player.busted() ) { showResults(); }
                else { /* show player cards and total */ }
            });
            $("#stand").click( function() {
                /* show dealer cards and total and disable Hit and Stand */
                var timer = setInterval( function() {
                    if ( game.dealer.mustHit() ) {
                        game.hit("dealer");
                        /* show dealer cards and total */
                    } else {
                        clearInterval(timer);
                        showResults();
                    }
                },
                1000);
            });
        });
    };
})(jQuery);
```

Figure 18-20   The main file of the blackjack plugin

How to compress and combine the files for a plugin

In the last several figures, you've seen that the code for the blackjack plugin is kept in four different JavaScript files. As you've learned, it's easier to develop and maintain code like this, and it also encourages code reuse. For example, the deck object could be reused in a poker or solitaire plugin.

However, it's easier to use a jQuery plugin when its code is in just one file. Additionally, the comments and whitespace that make a JavaScript file easier for a developer to read and understand can increase the file size and download times of a file.

To address these issues, you can use a *minification* tool to remove white space, comments, and line breaks from your JavaScript code to decrease the file size. Most of these tools also change the names of local variables to single characters, and they allow you to combine several files into one.

The table at the top of figure 18-21 lists some of the most popular tools for minifying your JavaScript. The ones on the left are online tools, while the ones on the right can be downloaded and installed on your computer.

This figure also shows the user interface for the minification tool at jscompress.com. This is the tool that was used to compress the four JavaScript files of the last few figures into the single jquery.blackjack.min.js file that the script element of figure 18-17 links to. Finally, this figure shows some of the JavaScript in this file so you can see how the code was compressed.

Some popular JavaScript minification tools

Online tools
javascript-minifier.com
jscompress.com
Grunt (http://gruntjs.com/)

Download tools
JSMin (http://crockford.com/javascript/jsmin)
YUI Compressor (http://yui.github.io/yuicompressor/)
Grunt (http://gruntjs.com/)

The jscompress.com website with the four plugin files uploaded

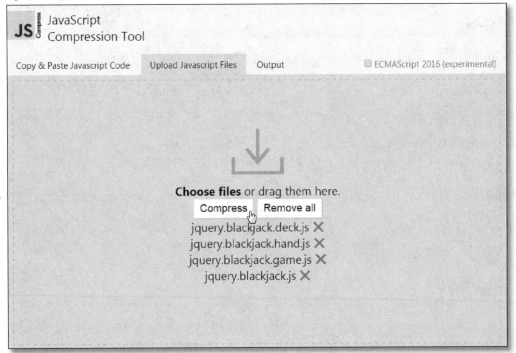

Some of the JavaScript code in the resulting jquery.blackjack.min.js file

```
"use strict";var deck=function(){var a=function(){var a=[],b=["c","d","h","s
"];for(var c in b)for(var d=1;d<=13;d++)a.push(d+"-"+b[c]);return a};return{
cards:a(),needsShuffling:function(){return
...
b=setInterval(function(){game.dealer.mustHit()?(game.hit("dealer"),
a("#dealer").html(e(game.dealer.cards)),a("#dealer").prev().text(game.deal-
er.total)):(clearInterval(b),f())},1e3)}),a("#deal").focus()}}}}(jQuery);
```

Description

- It's easier to develop and maintain code that's kept in separate libraries. However, it's easier to download and use a plugin that's kept in one file. Also, the whitespace and comments in a JavaScript file can increase its size and download time.

- *Minification* tools allow you to compress and combine multiple files into a single file.

Figure 18-21   How to compress and combine the files for a plugin

Perspective

This chapter has presented some concepts and skills that are difficult by any programming measures and many of them are unique to JavaScript programming. Now, if you can apply these concepts and skills to your own applications and plugins, you're well prepared for JavaScript programming in the real world.

Terms

closure	alias
scope chain	augment a module
in scope	import a module
out of scope	accessor property
private state	getter function
immediately invoked function expression (IIFE)	setter function
	read-only property
module pattern	write-only property
module	Application Programming Interface (API)
singleton	
namespace	implicit iteration
name collision	minification

Summary

- The *scope chain* refers to what can be seen and used by an object. An object has access to its own scope and the scope of every object that contains it.

- A *closure* is created when an inner function refers to one or more objects in the scope of the outer function. As long as a reference to the inner function is alive, the outer function's variables stay *in scope*.

- Closures can be used to create *private state* that protects an object's internal functions from outside code.

- Every function has its own *this* keyword. An inner function can have access to an outer function's *this* keyword by using the bind() method or storing the value of *this* for the outer function in a variable.

- *Immediately invoked function expressions (IIFEs)* create and invoke a function all at once.

- A *namespace* is a grouping of certain, usually related, objects. In JavaScript, you create a namespace by adding objects to an empty object literal. Then, you can use *aliases* in your code to shorten long names.

- The *module pattern* lets you create a single instance of an object, or *singleton*, that has private state. It combines the benefits of object literals and closures. To create or *augment* a *module*, you use an IIFE.

- An *accessor property* uses functions to read and write the property value. A *getter function* reads the value, and a *setter function* writes the value.

- The jQuery library uses the module pattern, so you use IIFEs to create plugins that augment that library.

- jQuery provides an *API* (*Application Programming Interface*) for creating plugins.

- You can use *minification* tools to remove whitespace and comments from JavaScript code and to combine multiple files into one.

Exercise 18-1   Create a Reveal plugin

In this exercise, you'll create a plugin named Reveal. This plugin will do the work of the FAQs application. That is, it will open or close a panel on alternative clicks of a heading.

1. Use your text editor or IDE to open the HTML and JavaScript files for the FAQs application in this folder:

    `c:\javascript_jquery\exercises\ch18\reveal\`

2. In the jquery.reveal.js file, you can see the standard plugin structure with the method name set to reveal. In the faqs.js file, you can see the jQuery for the FAQs application.

3. Test this application and see that it works because it's using the faqs.js file. But for this exercise, the use of that file should be replaced by the use of the Reveal plugin.

4. Copy the code for the click event handler of the faqs h2 elements into the each method of the reveal file. Then, change the selector for the faqs h2 elements to the *this* keyword so this plugin will work with any elements.

5. In the HTML file, delete the script element that adds the faqs.js file. Also, note that this HTML file already contains a script element for the Reveal plugin.

6. Add a statement to the ready() event handler in the last script element that calls the Reveal plugin. Then, test this application. It should show and hide the answers of the FAQs application.

7. Add another statement to the ready() event handler that sets the focus to the first <a> element of this application.

8. Note that this Reveal plugin can be used for any application that works like this. The user just has to change the selection that's used.

Exercise 18-2   Update the Task List application to use the module pattern

Break the Task List application

1. Use your text editor or IDE to open the HTML and JavaScript files for the Task List application in this folder:

   `c:\javascript_jquery\exercises\ch18\task_list`

2. Run the application and add a few tasks. Then, close the browser.

3. At the start of the ready() function in the task_list.js file, add this line of code:

   `tasklist.storage = null;`

4. Test this change in Chrome, and note that the tasks you entered in step 2 don't display when the page loads. Then, press the F12 key to bring up Chrome's developer tools, and click on Console to view the error messages. The application has been broken.

5. Delete the statement that you added in step 3, and test the application to make sure it's working correctly again.

Update the Task List application to use the module pattern

6. In the library_tasklist.js file, change the code so the tasklist variable is assigned the object that's returned by an IIFE rather than an object literal. The easiest way to do this might be to code an empty IIFE and then copy and paste the current object literal so it's returned by the IIFE.

7. In the body of the IIFE, before the return statement, code a tasks variable that holds an empty array. Then, delete the tasks property and adjust the code in the methods so they refer to "tasks" and not "this.tasks".

8. After the tasks variable but still before the return statement, code a storage variable that holds the result of calling the getTaskStorage() function. Use "tasks_18" as the name of the item in storage so it doesn't conflict with any tasks you may have added for other chapters. Then, delete the storage property and adjust the code in the methods so they refer to "storage" and not "this.storage".

9. Test the application to make sure it still works correctly.

Try to break the Task List application again

10. Once again, at the start of the ready() function in the task_list.js file, add this line of code:

    `tasklist.storage = null;`

11. Test this change in Chrome, and note that the application still works correctly. That's because you've just added a new, unused property to the tasklist object. The storage variable is no longer available to outside code, so this change didn't affect it.

Appendix A

How to set up your computer for this book

This appendix shows how to install the software that we recommend for editing and testing the web pages and applications for this book. That includes Aptana Studio 3 as the text editor for both Windows and Mac OS users, plus the Chrome and Firefox browsers for both Windows and Mac OS users. This appendix also shows you how to download and install the source code for this book.

As you read these descriptions, please remember that most websites are continually upgraded. As a result, some of the procedures in this appendix may have changed since this book was published. Nevertheless, these procedures should still be good guides to installing the software.

How to install Chrome and Firefox

When you develop JavaScript applications, you need to test them on all of the browsers that the users of the application are likely to use. For a commercial application, that usually includes Chrome, Internet Explorer, Edge, Firefox, Safari, and Opera. Then, if an application doesn't work on one of those browsers, you need to debug it.

As you do the exercises and work with the applications in this book, though, you can test your applications on just two browsers. Windows users should use Internet Explorer or Edge plus Chrome, and Mac OS users should use Safari and Chrome. Then, if you need to debug an application, you can use Chrome's developer tools as described in chapter 5.

The first procedure in figure A-1 is for downloading and installing Chrome. As part of this procedure, we recommend that you make Chrome your default browser. Then, you can follow the second procedure in this figure to download and install Firefox so you can use it for any additional testing you want to do. If you want to install Opera or Safari, you can use a similar procedure.

Note that if you're going to use Aptana Studio 3 to edit your web pages and applications, you should install any of the browsers you're going to use before you install Aptana. That way, Aptana will automatically provide for running an application in those browsers.

The website address for downloading Chrome

`https://www.google.com/intl/en-US/chrome/browser/`

How to install Chrome

1. Go to the website address above.
2. Click on the Download Chrome button.
3. Review the Google Chrome Terms of Service that are displayed. Then, indicate if you want to automatically send usage statistics and crash reports to Google.
4. Click the Accept and Install button.
5. When you're asked what you want to do with ChromeSetup.exe, click the Save button. The executable file is downloaded to your computer.
6. When the file finishes downloading, click the Run button to start the installation.
7. If you're asked if you want to allow the program to make changes to your computer, click the Yes button.
8. When Chrome is started and the Welcome page is displayed, you can play the video for information on options like making Chrome your default browser. You can also use the SET UP menu to customize Chrome.
9. To start using Chrome, click the New Tab to display the Google home page.

The website address for downloading Firefox

`http://www.mozilla.com`

How to install Firefox

1. Go to the website address above.
2. Click on the Free Download button.
3. Save the exe file to your C drive.
4. Run the exe file and respond to the resulting dialog boxes.

Description

- Because Chrome is the most popular browser today, we suggest that you test all of the exercises that you do for this book in this browser.
- If you have a Windows system, Internet Explorer or Edge will already be on it and you should test with it as well.
- If you have a Mac, Safari will already be on it and you should test with it too. You won't be able to install Internet Explorer or Edge because they don't run on Macs.
- Because Firefox, Safari, and Opera are also popular browsers, you may want to install them too. To install Safari and Opera, you can use a procedure similar to the one above for installing Firefox.

Figure A-1   How to install Chrome and Firefox

How to install Aptana Studio 3

If you're already comfortable with a text editor that works for editing HTML, CSS, and JavaScript, you can continue using it. But otherwise, we recommend that you use Aptana Studio 3. It is a free editor that offers many features, it runs on both Windows and Mac OS systems, and chapter 1 presents a quick tutorial on it that will get you started right. Before you install Aptana Studio 3, be sure to install any browsers you want to use as described in figure A-1.

On a Windows system

Figure A-2 shows how to download and install Aptana Studio 3 on a Windows system. Note here that before you can install Aptana Studio 3 on a Windows 10 system, you must install a JavaScript-based framework called Node.js.

On a Mac OS system

Figure A-2 also shows how to download and install Aptana Studio 3 on a Mac OS system.

The website address for downloading Aptana Studio 3

http://www.aptana.com/products/studio3/download

How to install Aptana Studio 3 on a Windows system

1. Go to the website address above.

2. Click on the Download Aptana Studio 3 button near the bottom of the page.

3. If a dialog box is displayed asking if you want to run or save the exe file, click on the Save button.

4. If a Save As dialog box is displayed, identify the location where you want the exe file saved.

5. When the Download finishes, use Windows Explorer to find the exe file, and double-click on it to start it.

6. As you step through the wizard that follows, you can accept all of the default settings that are offered.

7. After Aptana Studio 3 is installed, start it. Then, if you don't have a Git application installed on your system, Aptana will ask you if you want it to install a Portable Git application. Accept that option because Aptana won't run without it.

How to install Aptana Studio 3 on a Mac OS X system

1. Go to the website address above.

2. Click on the Customize Your Download button, and select Mac OS X.

3. Click on the Download Aptana Studio 3 button, and click on the Save File button in the resulting dialog box.

4. When the Download finishes, double-click on the dmg file in the Downloads folder to display the Aptana Studio 3 window.

5. Double-click the Aptana Studio 3 Installer folder to start the installation.

6. When the installation is complete, start Aptana Studio 3. Then, if you don't have a Git application installed on your system, Aptana will ask you if you want it to install a Portable Git application. Accept that option because Aptana won't run without it.

Description

- Aptana runs on Windows, Mac, and Linux systems.

- Git is a source code management tool that Aptana requires. If necessary, Aptana will install it for you when you start Aptana for the first time.

- Chapter 1 of this book presents a tutorial that will get you off to a fast start with Aptana.

Note for Windows 10 installation

- Before you install Aptana Studio 3 on a Windows 10 system, you must install Node.js. To do that, go to this website address to automatically download an installer file named node-v0.10.13-x86.msi:

  http://titanium-studio.s3.amazonaws.com/nodejs/node-V0.10.13-x86.msi

  Then, run this file to install Node.js.

Figure A-2   How to install Aptana Studio 3 as your text editor

How to install and use the source code for this book

The next two figures show how to install and use the source code for this book. One figure is for Windows users, the other for Mac OS users.

For Windows users

Figure A-3 shows how to install the source code for this book on a Windows system. This includes the source code for the applications in this book, the starting files for the exercises, and the solutions for the exercises.

When you finish this procedure, the book applications, exercises, and solutions will be in the three folders that are in the first group in this figure, but the exercises will also be in the next folder that's shown. So, when you do the exercises, you use the subfolders and files in this folder:

`\javascript_jquery\exercises`

but you have backup copies of these subfolders and files in this folder:

`\murach\javascript_jquery\exercises`

That way, you can restore the files for an exercise to their original state by copying the files from the second folder to the first.

As you do the exercises, you may want to copy code from a book application into a file that you're working with. That's easy to do because the applications are in this folder:

`\murach\javascript_jquery\book_apps`

When you finish an exercise, you may want to compare your solution to ours, which you'll find in this folder:

`\murach\javascript_jquery\solutions`

You may also want to look at a solution when you're having trouble with an exercise. That will help you get past the problem you're having so you can continue to make progress. Either way, the solutions are an important part of the learning process.

The Murach website

`www.murach.com`

The Windows folders for the applications, exercises, and solutions

`\murach\javascript_jquery\book_apps`
`\murach\javascript_jquery\exercises`
`\murach\javascript_jquery\solutions`

The Windows folder for doing the exercises

`\javascript_jquery\exercises`

How to download and install the source code on a Windows system

1. Go to www.murach.com, and go to the page for *Murach's JavaScript and jQuery (3rd Edition)*.

2. Scroll down the page until you see the "FREE downloads" tab and then click on it. Then, click on the DOWNLOAD NOW button for the exe file for Windows. This will download a setup file named jqu3_allfiles.exe onto your hard drive.

3. Use Windows Explorer to find the exe file on your hard drive. Then, double-click this file. This installs the source code for the book applications, exercises, and solutions into the folders shown above. After it does this install, the exe file copies the exercises folder to \javascript_jquery so you have two copies of the exercises.

How to restore an exercise file

- Copy it from its subfolder in

  `\murach\javascript_jquery\exercises`

  to the corresponding subfolder in

  `\javascript_jquery\exercises`

Description

- The exe file that you download stores the exercises in two different folders. That way, you can do the exercises using the files that are stored in one folder, but you have a backup copy in case you want to restore the starting files for an exercise.

- As you do the exercises that are at the ends of the chapters, you may want to copy code from a book application into the file you're working on. That's easy to do because all of the applications are available in the book_apps folder.

- In the solutions folder, you can view the solutions for the exercises.

Figure A-3   How to install the source code for this book on a Windows system

For Mac OS users

Figure A-4 shows how to install the source code for this book on a Mac OS system. This includes the source code for the applications in this book, the starting files for the exercises, and the solutions for the exercises.

When you finish this procedure, the book applications, exercises, and solutions will be in the three folders that are listed in this figure. Then, before you start the exercises, you should copy the exercises folder from

`documents\murach\javascript_jquery`

to

`documents\javascript_jquery`

That way, you can restore the files for an exercise to their original state by copying the files from the first folder to the second.

As you do the exercises, you may want to copy code from a book application into a file that you're working with. That's easy to do because the applications are in this folder:

`documents\murach\javascript_jquery\book_apps`

When you finish an exercise, you may want to compare your solution to ours, which you'll find in this folder:

`documents\murach\javascript_jquery\solutions`

You may also want to look at a solution when you're having trouble with an exercise. That will help you get past the problem you're having so you can continue to make progress. Either way, the solutions are an important part of the learning process.

The Murach website

www.murach.com

The Mac OS folders for the book applications and exercises

```
documents\murach\javascript_jquery\book_apps
documents\murach\javascript_jquery\exercises
documents\murach\javascript_jquery\solutions
```

The Mac OS folder for doing the exercises

```
documents\javascript_jquery\exercises
```

How to download and install the source code on a Mac OS system

1. Go to www.murach.com, and go to the page for *Murach's JavaScript and jQuery (3rd Edition)*.

2. Scroll down the page until you see the "FREE downloads" tab and then click on it. Then, click on the DOWNLOAD NOW button for the zip file for any system. This will download a setup file named jqu3_allfiles.zip onto your hard drive.

3. Move this file into the Documents folder of your home folder.

4. Use Finder to go to your Documents folder.

5. Double-click the jqu3_allfiles.zip file to extract the folders for the book applications, exercises, and solutions. This will create a folder named murach\javascript_jquery in your documents folder that will contain the book_apps, exercises, and solutions folders.

6. Create two copies of the exercises folder by copying the exercises folder from

   ```
   documents\murach\javascript_jquery
   ```

   to

   ```
   documents\javascript_jquery
   ```

How to restore an exercise file

* Copy it from its subfolder in

  ```
  documents\murach\javascript_jquery\exercises
  ```

  to the corresponding subfolder in

  ```
  documents\javascript_jquery\exercises
  ```

Description

* This procedure stores the exercises in two different folders. That way, you do the exercises using the files that are in one folder, but you also have a backup copy.

* If you want to copy code from a book application into an exercise file that you're working on, you can find all of the applications in the book_apps folder.

* In the solutions folder, you can view the solutions for the exercises at the end of each chapter.

Figure A-4   How to install the source code for this book on a Mac OS system

Index

X

100% Guarantee

When you order directly from us, you must be satisfied. Our books must work better than any other programming books you've ever used...both for training and reference...or you can send them back within 60 days for a prompt refund. No questions asked!

Mike Murach, Publisher

Ben Murach, President

Have you mastered HTML and CSS?

The best web developers master HTML and CSS along with JavaScript and jQuery. That's why *Murach's HTML5 and CSS3* is the perfect companion to this book. Get it today and see for yourself!

Web development books

Murach's HTML5 and CSS3 (4th Ed.)	$57.50
Murach's JavaScript (2nd Ed.)	54.50
Murach's JavaScript and jQuery (3rd Ed.)	57.50
Murach's PHP and MySQL (3rd Ed.)	$57.50
Murach's Java Servlets and JSP (3rd Ed.)	57.50
Murach's ASP.NET 4.6 Web Programming with C# 2015	59.50

Core programming language books

Murach's Python Programming	$57.50
Murach's Beginning Java with NetBeans	57.50
Murach's Beginning Java with Eclipse	57.50
Murach's Java Programming (5th Ed.)	59.50
Murach's C# 2015	57.50
Murach's Visual Basic 2015	57.50

Database/SQL books

Murach's MySQL (2nd Ed.)	$54.50
Murach's Oracle SQL and PL/SQL for Developers (2nd Ed.)	54.50
Murach's SQL Server 2016 for Developers	57.50

Prices and availability are subject to change. Please visit our website or call for current information.

We want to hear from you

Do you have any comments, questions, or compliments to pass on to us? It would be great to hear from you! Please share your feedback in whatever way works best.

 www.murach.com

 twitter.com/MurachBooks

 1-800-221-5528
(Weekdays, 8 am to 4 pm Pacific Time)

 facebook.com/murachbooks

 murachbooks@murach.com

 linkedin.com/company/
mike-murach-&-associates

What software you need for this book

- To enter and edit JavaScript, HTML, and CSS, you can use any text editor, but we recommend Aptana Studio 3 for both Windows and Mac OS users. It is a free editor with many excellent features.

- To help you get started with Aptana Studio 3, chapter 1 provides a short tutorial.

- To test the JavaScript and jQuery applications that you develop on a Windows system, we recommend that you use Chrome and Internet Explorer or Edge. On a Mac OS system, we recommend that you use Chrome and Safari. Then, to debug your applications, you can use Chrome's developer tools. All of these browsers are free.

- To help you install these products, appendix A provides the website addresses and procedures that you'll need.

The downloadable applications and files for this book

- All of the applications that are presented in this book.

- The starting files for the exercises in this book.

- The solutions for the exercises.

How to download the applications and files

- Go to www.murach.com, and go to the page for *Murach's JavaScript and jQuery (3rd Edition)*.

- Scroll down the page until you see the "FREE downloads" tab and then click on it.

- If you're using a Windows system, click the DOWNLOAD NOW button for the exe file to download a file named jqu3_allfiles.exe. Then, find this file in Windows Explorer and double-click on it. That will install the files for this book in this directory: c:\murach\javascript_jquery.

- If you're using a Mac, click the DOWNLOAD NOW button for the zip file to download a file named jqu3_allfiles.zip onto your hard drive. Then, move this file into the Documents folder of your home folder, use Finder to go to your Documents folder, and double-click on the zip file. That will create a folder named javascript_jquery that contains all the files for this book.

- For more information, please see appendix A.

www.murach.com